ADDITIONAL COOKBOOKS AND DVD SETS AVAILABLE FROM THE PUBLISHERS OF *COOK'S COUNTRY* INCLUDE:

The *America's Test Kitchen* Library Series

The How Can It Be Gluten-Free Cookbook

The How Can It Be Gluten-Free Cookbook: Volume 2

The *America's Test Kitchen* Complete Vegetarian Cookbook

The Best Mexican Recipes

The Make-Ahead Cook

The *America's Test Kitchen* Do-It-Yourself Cookbook

Slow Cooker Revolution

The Best Simple Recipes

Slow Cooker Revolution Volume 2: The Easy-Prep Edition

Healthy Slow Cooker Revolution

Comfort Food Makeovers

From Our Grandmothers' Kitchens

Cook's Country Annual Editions
from each year of publication (2005–2015)

From the Editors of *Cook's Illustrated*

The *Cook's Illustrated* Meat Book

The *Cook's Illustrated* Baking Book

The Science of Good Cooking

Cook's Illustrated Cookbook

The Best One-Dish Suppers

Soups, Stews & Chilis

The New Best Recipe

The Best Skillet Recipes

The Best Slow & Easy Recipes

The Best Chicken Recipes

The Best International Recipe

The Best Make-Ahead Recipe

The Best 30-Minute Recipe

The Best Light Recipe

The *Cook's Illustrated* Guide to
Grilling and Barbecue

Best American Side Dishes

Cover & Bake

Steaks, Chops, Roasts, and Ribs

Baking Illustrated

Perfect Vegetables

Italian Classics

The Best American Classics

1993–2015 *Cook's Illustrated* Master Index

Cook's Illustrated Annual Editions
from each year of publication (1993–2015)

America's Test Kitchen

100 Recipes: The Absolute Best Way to Make the True Essentials

Cook's Country Eats Local

Kitchen Hacks: How Clever Cooks Get Things Done

The *America's Test Kitchen* New Family Cookbook

The Complete Cooking for Two Cookbook

The *America's Test Kitchen* Cooking School Cookbook

Pressure Cooker Perfection

The Best of *America's Test Kitchen* (2007–2016 Editions)

Cooking for Two (2009–2013 Editions)

The *America's Test Kitchen* Family Baking Book

The *America's Test Kitchen* Family Cookbook

The *America's Test Kitchen* Healthy Family Cookbook

The *America's Test Kitchen* Quick Family Cookbook

The *America's Test Kitchen* Series Companion Cookbooks

America's Test Kitchen: The TV Companion Cookbook
(2011–2015 Editions)

The Complete *America's Test Kitchen* TV Show Cookbook
(2010–2016 Editions)

America's Test Kitchen: The TV Companion Cookbook (2009)

Behind the Scenes with *America's Test Kitchen* (2008)

Test Kitchen Favorites (2007)

Cooking at Home with *America's Test Kitchen* (2006)

America's Test Kitchen Live! (2005)

Inside *America's Test Kitchen* (2004)

Here in *America's Test Kitchen* (2003)

The *America's Test Kitchen* Cookbook (2002)

The *America's Test Kitchen* Series DVD Sets
(featuring each season's episodes from our hit
public television series)

The *America's Test Kitchen* 4-DVD Set (2002–2015 Seasons)

The *America's Test Kitchen* 2-DVD Set (2001 Season)

The *Cook's Country* TV Series Cookbooks and DVD Sets
(featuring each season's episodes from our hit
public television series)

The Complete *Cook's Country* TV Show Cookbook

The *Cook's Country* 2-DVD Set (Seasons 1–8)

Visit our online bookstore at CooksCountry.com to order any of our cookbooks and DVDs listed above. You can also order subscriptions, gift subscriptions, and any of our cookbooks and DVDs by calling 800-611-0759 inside the U.S., or 515-246-6911 if calling from outside the U.S.

$35.00

Published by America's Test Kitchen, 17 Station Street, Brookline, MA 02445
ISBN-13: 978-1-940352-40-4   ISSN: 1552-1990

To get home delivery of *Cook's Country*, call 800-526-8447 inside the U.S., or 515-247-7571 if calling from outside the U.S.,
or subscribe online at CooksCountry.com.

2015 Recipe Index

Cook's Country

FEBRUARY/MARCH 2015

CooksCountry.com
$5.95 U.S./$6.95 CANADA

Adding the rich, smoky flavor of bacon to classic meatloaf seemed like a winner. And it was—after we spent several days in the test kitchen developing a technique that yields crisp bacon on top and real bacon flavor throughout. PAGE 4

7 25274 05251 6

03>

Cook's Country

Dear Country Cook,

Marie Briggs, our Vermont town baker, made the world's best nutmeg doughnuts. I know since I pretty much grew up on them. Years later, I made her recipe for coffee hour at the Methodist church, consuming two hot-out-of-the-oil specimens in the kitchen beforehand. A friend of mine, Nate, runs Saratoga Orchards and has a Rube Goldberg–style cider doughnut contraption. I buy a half-dozen in a small white paper bag and they are gone before I get back to the farm.

Our country store, Sherman's, sells doughnuts, as does the more touristy country store to the north. Even well-heeled New Yorkers show up in fancy cars early on Saturday mornings to grab their fill before the inventory runs out. (These are folks who are probably gluten-free the rest of the week.)

Last November, on the first day of deer season, I dropped my four-pointer off at the local butcher shop. The owner offered me a free doughnut and I, of course, picked the cake doughnut, the style that reminded me most of Marie.

Some things are constants in country life. Weather. Parades. Church suppers. Hunting season. And doughnuts. The sweetest constant of them all.

Cordially,

Christopher Kimball
Founder and Editor, Cook's Country

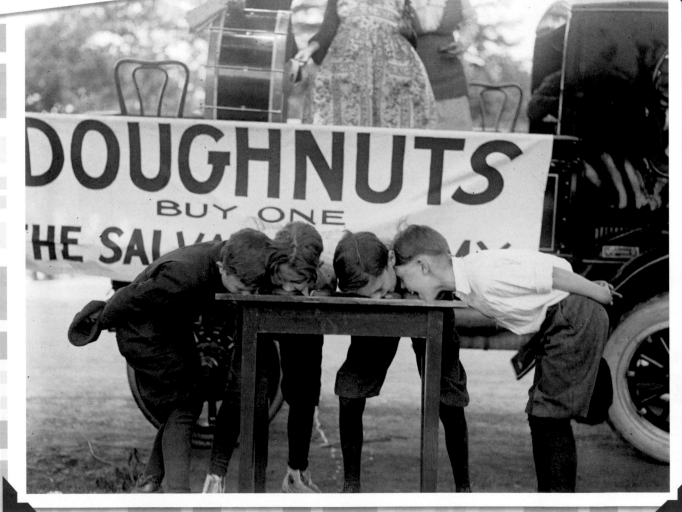

Cook'sCountry

Founder and Editor Christopher Kimball
Editorial Director Jack Bishop
Editorial Director, Magazines John Willoughby
Executive Editor Tucker Shaw
Managing Editor Scott Kathan
Executive Food Editor Bryan Roof
Senior Editors Hannah Crowley, Lisa McManus, Diane Unger
Test Kitchen Director Erin McMurrer
Associate Editors Shannon Friedmann Hatch, Christie Morrison
Test Cooks Morgan Bolling, Aaron Furmanek, Cecelia Jenkins, Ashley Moore, Cristin Walsh
Assistant Editors Lauren Savoie, Kate Shannon
Senior Copy Editor Megan Ginsberg
Copy Editor Krista Magnuson
Executive Assistant Christine Gordon
Test Kitchen Manager Leah Rovner
Senior Kitchen Assistants Michelle Blodget, Alexxa Grattan
Kitchen Assistants Maria Elena Delgado, Ena Gudiel
Executive Producer Melissa Baldino
Co-Executive Producer Stephanie Stender
Associate Producer Kaitlin Hammond

Contributing Editors Erika Bruce, Eva Katz, Jeremy Sauer
Consulting Editors Anne Mendelson, Meg Ragland
Science Editor Guy Crosby, PhD
Executive Food Editor, TV, Radio & Media Bridget Lancaster

Managing Editor, Web Christine Liu
Senior Editor, Cooking School Mari Levine
Associate Editors, Web Jill Fisher, Roger Metcalf
Assistant Editor, Web Charlotte Wilder
Senior Video Editor Nick Dakoulas

Design Director Amy Klee
Photography Director Julie Cote
Art Director Susan Levin
Associate Art Director Lindsey Timko
Art Director, Marketing Jennifer Cox
Staff Photographer Daniel J. van Ackere
Color Food Photography Keller + Keller
Styling Catrine Kelty, Marie Piraino
Deputy Art Director, Marketing Melanie Gryboski
Associate Art Director, Marketing Janet Taylor
Designer, Marketing Stephanie Cook
Associate Art Director, Photography Steve Klise

VP, Marketing David Mack
Circulation Director Doug Wicinski
Circulation & Fulfillment Manager Carrie Fethe
Partnership Marketing Manager Pamela Putprush
Marketing Assistant Marina Tomao

Director, Business Systems Alice Carpenter
Project Manager Britt Dresser
Development Manager Mike Serio

Chief Operating Officer Rob Ristagno
VP, Digital Products Fran Middleton
VP, New Product Development Michael Burton
Production Director Guy Rochford
Senior Color & Imaging Specialist Lauren Robbins
Production & Imaging Specialists Heather Dube, Dennis Noble
Client Services Manager Kate Zebrowski
Sponsorship Sales Associate Morgan Mannino
Senior Controller Theresa Peterson
Customer Loyalty & Support Manager Amy Bootier
Customer Loyalty & Support Reps Rebecca Kowalski, Andrew Straaberg Finfrock, Juliet Tierney

Director, Retail Book Program Beth Ineson
Retail Sales & Marketing Manager Emily Logan
Human Resources Manager Adele Shapiro
Publicity Deborah Broide

ON THE COVER: Bacon-Wrapped Meatloaf, Keller + Keller, Catrine Kelty
ILLUSTRATION: Greg Stevenson

Follow us on **Pinterest**
pinterest.com/TestKitchen

Follow us on **Twitter**
twitter.com/TestKitchen

Find us on **Facebook**
facebook.com/CooksCountry

Cook's Country magazine (ISSN 1552-1990), number 61, is published bimonthly by Boston Common Press Limited Partnership, 17 Station St., Brookline, MA 02445. Copyright 2015 Boston Common Press Limited Partnership. Periodicals postage paid at Boston, MA, and additional mailing offices, USPS #023453. Publications Mail Agreement No. 40020778. Return undeliverable Canadian addresses to P.O. Box 875, Station A, Windsor, ON N9A 6P2. POSTMASTER: Send address changes to Cook's Country, PO Box 6018, Harlan, IA 51593-1518. For subscription and gift subscription orders, subscription inquiries, or change of address notices, visit AmericasTestKitchen.com/support, call 800-526-8447 in the U.S. or 515-248-7684 from outside the U.S., or write to us at Cook's Country, P.O. Box 6018, Harlan, IA 51593-1518. PRINTED IN THE USA.

Contents

CHICKPEA SALADS, 29

PUB-STYLE BURGERS 24

CHOCOLATE CHESS PIE, 22

Features

Departments

America's Test Kitchen is a very real 2,500-square-foot kitchen located just outside Boston. It is the home of Cook's Country and Cook's Illustrated magazines and the workday destination of more than three dozen test cooks, editors, and cookware specialists. Our mission is to test recipes until we understand how and why they work and arrive at the best version. We also test kitchen equipment and supermarket ingredients in search of products that offer the best value and performance. You can watch us work by tuning in to Cook's Country from America's Test Kitchen (CooksCountry.com) and America's Test Kitchen (AmericasTestKitchen.com) on public television.

Ask Cook's Country

BY CHRISTIE MORRISON

I'm never exactly sure how small I should cut my vegetables. What's the difference between "chopped" and "chopped fine" in your recipes?
Cat Herrington, Charlottesville, Va.

Cutting ingredients to the correct size is important to the success of a recipe. Uniformity of size is the top concern, since ingredients cut to different sizes will have different cooking times: Some of your vegetables might burn, for instance, while the bigger chunks continue to cook. In the test kitchen, a ruler is a necessary tool for all our test cooks to ensure that ingredients are cut to specifications and cook for the same amount of time, every time. Keep these conversions in mind the next time you prep.

CHOPPED COARSE (½ to ¾ inch)

CHOPPED (¼ to ½ inch)

CHOPPED FINE (⅛ to ¼ inch)

MINCED (1⁄16 inch)

I've heard some red wines described as "tannic." Can white wines be tannic, too?
Barbara Nestor, Ashland, Pa.

Wines that are characterized as tannic are high in tannins, polyphenols—or a group of chemical compounds—that occur naturally in wood, plant leaves, and the skins, stems, and seeds of fruits like grapes, plums, pomegranates, and cranberries. Tannins have a bitter flavor and astringent quality that has a drying effect on your tongue. One of the challenges of wine making is striking a favorable balance between tannins and sweetness, and wines are manipulated to enhance or suppress either characteristic depending on the varietal. Intense, full-bodied red wines like Malbec or Cabernet Sauvignon are often high in tannins, since the pressed grape juice spends a good deal of time in contact with the grape skins, stems, and seeds before being aged in wood barrels (another source of tannins).

White wines are seldom described as tannic in the same way. They tend to be significantly lower in tannins than red wines since the juice spends so little time exposed to the grape skins. Any tannic characteristics they do exhibit are more likely the effect of oak aging.
THE BOTTOM LINE: Call them crisp, call them fruity, but don't call white wines tannic. While white wines may contain tannins, their levels are too low to produce the bitterness and astringency that we would characterize as tannic.

Why does a double scoop of ice cream make me thirsty?
Andrew Fuga, Philadelphia, Pa.

We asked around the office to see if this was a common affliction, and about half the people said that yes, ice cream does leave a parched mouth. (Most also said they had thought that they were alone in their thirstiness.)

When in doubt, we often look to our science editor for explanation. He told us that sweet foods (like ice cream) behave much like salty foods when eaten in quantity. As ice cream is digested and sugar is rapidly absorbed into the blood, the concentration of sugar in the blood becomes higher than the concentration of sugar in the body's other cells. Since nature abhors an imbalance, osmosis kicks in, forcing water out of the cells, through membranes, and into the blood to equalize the relative concentrations of sugar. The brain senses that the cells are losing moisture, and the craving for a glass of water kicks in.
THE BOTTOM LINE: You're not imagining that post–ice cream thirst. Go ahead and treat yourself to a tall drink of water.

How are Marcona almonds different from regular almonds?
Christopher Stillman, Natick, Mass.

Most almonds consumed in the United States are produced in California; the United States is the largest producer of almonds in the world. Just behind the United States in production is Spain, home to the Marcona variety of almonds.

Marcona almonds are easy to distinguish from California almonds. They are shorter and rounder than our domestic almonds. Plus, their texture sets them apart: Marconas are softer and more tender to the bite than California almonds, which have a firm crunch. Tasters also noticed a pronounced sweetness in Marcona almonds, as well as a slight greasiness to the touch due to their higher fat content.

Like other almonds, Marconas are sold roasted or blanched and are used in salads, cheese plates, and desserts. They are also sold fried in oil and tossed with sea salt and herbs (a common preparation in Spain). However, the

If I have to let my roasted chicken rest for 15 to 20 minutes after it comes out of the oven, won't it be too cold to serve?
Treesa Weaver-Rich, Hillsdale, Mich.

It's helpful to think of resting as part of the cooking process. When you remove a roast from the oven, it continues to cook because of the heat trapped inside. This "carryover cooking" continues in proportion to the density and size of the meat and the temperature at which you were cooking it. So, for example, a whole chicken roasted at 400 degrees will carryover cook for longer than either a whole chicken roasted at 350 degrees or chicken parts roasted at 400 degrees. As the meat rests, the juices inside redistribute as well. During cooking, the muscle fibers contract and squeeze liquid out of their cells. Resting gives the fibers a chance to relax and draw moisture back inside. Slicing into a roast before it has sufficiently rested will result in that liquid escaping onto your cutting board rather than being reabsorbed into the meat.

The resting time recommended in your recipe takes these factors into consideration. And since heat moves from the hotter exterior to the cooler interior of the meat, we often suggest lightly tenting the roast with foil to keep the exterior warm without trapping too much moisture inside the tent. Since even light tenting can cause crisp skin to become soggy, we don't usually recommend tenting for chicken and turkey.

But won't the roast cool down too much to serve warm? To find out, we roasted a chicken according to one of our favorite recipes and checked the temperature when we removed it from the oven: 160 degrees in the breast and 175 degrees in the thigh. Then we took the temperature after 20 minutes of (untented) rest on a carving board. The chicken was still over 140 degrees—and almost too hot to carve. Since most meat tastes best when it's above 100 degrees, the chicken was still comfortably within the serving zone.

We recommend resting all large cuts of meat, though resting times vary. However, thinner cuts like steaks, pork chops, and chicken parts cool more quickly. In these cases, we usually recommend only about 5 minutes' resting time to ensure that the proteins are still ideal for serving.
THE BOTTOM LINE: Large cuts of meat hold on to heat far longer than you would expect, so don't rush the rest.

	Temperature	Rest Time	Tent?
ROAST CHICKEN	175 degrees (thigh)	20 minutes	No
ROAST TURKEY	175 degrees (thigh)	30 to 40 minutes	No
BEEF ROAST, MEDIUM RARE	125 degrees (center)	30 minutes	Loosely
PORK ROAST	140 degrees (center)	10 to 20 minutes	Loosely if unglazed

biggest difference between the almond varieties is price: Marcona almonds cost about twice as much as California almonds.
THE BOTTOM LINE: Marcona almonds have a sweeter flavor and softer texture than California almonds. You can use them in much the same way that you use domestic almonds, but at double the price, they are probably best enjoyed as a treat rather than as a pantry staple.

To ask us a cooking question, visit **CooksCountry.com/ask**. Or write to Ask *Cook's Country*, P.O. Box 470739, Brookline, MA 02447. Just try to stump us!

MARCONA ALMONDS

CALIFORNIA ALMONDS

Kitchen Shortcuts

COMPILED BY SHANNON FRIEDMANN HATCH

DOUBLE DUTY
Dressing on the Go
Stan Sack, Key West, Fla.

I've found another use for my surplus of squirt-tip bicycle water bottles: as vessels for transporting homemade salad dressing to potlucks and parties. The plastic containers have a wide mouth for adding ingredients, seal tightly, are easy to grip, and won't shatter en route. I usually unscrew the cap to serve, but you could even squeeze the dressing out through the top.

NEAT TRICK
Break It in the Box
Patrick Starnes, Nashville, Tenn.

When I need to break long-strand dried pasta, like spaghetti, before cooking, I do it in the box: Just grip each end of the closed box, center it on the edge of the counter, and gently bend until the pasta inside breaks. This method contains any stray noodles that would otherwise scatter across the kitchen when the pasta snaps.

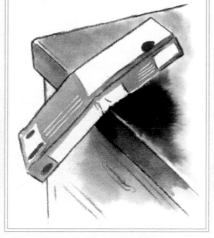

TIDY TIP
High Five Dry
Karen Tirabassi, West Henrietta, N.Y.

I used to lay my dishwashing gloves over the edge of the sink between cleanups, but they never fully dried. I've discovered that if I thread a pair of open tongs through the rungs of a dish rack, ends pointed up, I can put a glove on each end. Held upright, they dry much more thoroughly.

COOL TIP
Better Tortilla Storage
Gayle Keaney, Cincinnati, Ohio

I use only a few tortillas at once, so I freeze the rest of the package. The problem is that the tortillas stick together and tear when I try to remove one or two for my next meal. Now, I put a square of parchment paper in between the tortillas before freezing. It takes a minute, but it saves a ton of hassle in the long run. And I reuse the squares of parchment paper every time.

CLEVER TIP
Cooking with Kids
Mary McArthur, Rodmond, Wash.

Accurately reading a recipe is the key to success in the kitchen. To help my daughters as they learn, I print out the recipe and place it inside a clear sheet protector. As they use each ingredient and complete each step, they cross it off with a dry-erase marker.

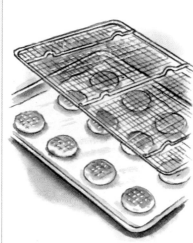

DOUBLE DUTY
Easier Cookie Press
Carlyn Fischer, Cambria, Wis.

I've always made a crisscross pattern with a fork on the top of my peanut butter cookie dough. Recently, I've realized that my cooling rack makes a fine design, and I have to press only once for a whole batch.

COOL TIP
Streamlining Frozen Meals
Helene Schachter, Great Neck, N.Y.

Whenever I freeze food that will need additional preparation (not just defrosting), I wrap the dish, place a copy of the recipe on top, wrap it again, and freeze it. That way, I know how to finish the dish without having to dig up the recipe again.

Submit a tip online at CooksCountry.com/kitchenshortcuts or send a letter to Kitchen Shortcuts, Cook's Country, P.O. Box 470739, Brookline, MA 02447. Include your name, address, and phone number. If we publish your tip, you will receive a free one-year subscription to Cook's Country. Letters may be edited for clarity and length.

The Ultimate Bacon-Wrapped Meatloaf

Bacon-wrapped meatloaf? Sounds like a winner. But it takes a bit more than just slapping on some bacon to make it work. BY CRISTIN WALSH

I
T'S HARD TO imagine that meatloaf could be improved upon, but I recently came across a cookbook recipe for bacon-wrapped meatloaf. The way the author described it, this dish had all the makings of something extraordinary: meatloaf draped in crisp, smoky bacon and brushed with a sweet barbecue glaze. I found a handful of other recipes for this meatloaf and got busy cooking in the test kitchen. The smell of six bacon-wrapped meatloaves cooking had my tasters champing at the bit to try them.

But my tasters' anticipation turned to disappointment once they started putting fork to loaf. The big problems were bland, greasy meatloaves; saccharine glazes; and lots and lots of flabby, chewy, unrendered bacon. These failed recipes made me determined to crack the code of bacon-wrapped meatloaf.

I knew what I wanted: a flavorful, moist, tender meatloaf with plenty of smoky, crisp bacon wrapped around its exterior. Luckily for me, the test kitchen has been around the block with meatloaf before, so I had plenty of knowledge to get me started. I began by making a meatloaf using equal parts ground beef and pork, which I dressed with onion and garlic, bound with a panade of saltines and milk, and bolstered with eggs. I shaped the loaf free-form (to bake on a rack where the fat can drain away); draped bacon over the top, tucking the ends under as best I could; brushed the exterior with bottled barbecue sauce; and baked it. The loaf was moist and the bacon did crisp in places, but the bacon also shrank dramatically, leaving gaping spaces on the loaf. The meatloaf itself was good, but you didn't get any bacon flavor unless you got a bite with the bacon on top—I wanted bacon flavor throughout. Plus, the barbecue sauce didn't add much.

If some bacon is good, I thought, more bacon would be better. To infuse the bacon flavor deep into the meatloaf, I tried ditching the ground pork and adding chopped bacon to the ground beef mixture. After a few tests, I found it easiest to buzz a medium onion with four slices of bacon in a food processor before sautéing them together and incorporating them into the meat.

As for the bacon on the exterior, I had a plan to use a loaf pan not for baking but to help me shape the loaf

What's even better than a bacon-wrapped meatloaf? A bacon-wrapped meatloaf that has chopped bacon added to the ground beef inside.

with bacon on top. To start, I shingled bacon slices on plastic wrap laid inside a loaf pan and then formed the meatloaf on top of the bacon. Using the sides of the plastic, I pressed the bacon into the formed loaf and used the plastic to invert the meatloaf onto a thin foil sling placed on a rack. This meatloaf certainly had a stronger bacon presence, and the exterior slices now covered the loaf evenly.

The bottled barbecue sauce brushed on top was the weak link, even when we used our favorite brand. I tried another batch with added liquid smoke, but that gave the glaze too much smoke flavor and not enough nuance. Rather than giving up on the bottled sauce, I doctored it with cider vinegar, Worcestershire sauce, and spicy mustard to cut the sweetness. This time the glaze imparted a subtle, complex smoky flavor that

tasters loved. So much, in fact, that they suggested adding it to the interior of the meatloaf for increased depth and all-around smoky flavor. This worked great, as did adding an extra layer of glaze between the bacon and the meat. A finishing pass under the broiler ensured that the bacon was impeccably browned and crisp and that the spicy-sweet glaze caramelized to perfection. It was the ideal finish to a meatloaf less ordinary.

BACON-WRAPPED MEATLOAF

Serves 6 to 8

Bulls-Eye Original is our favorite barbecue sauce. Do not use thick-cut bacon for this recipe, as the package will yield fewer strips for wrapping the meatloaf. Oscar Mayer Naturally Hardwood Smoked Bacon is our winning thin-sliced bacon.

- ¼ cup bottled barbecue sauce, plus extra for serving
- 1 tablespoon cider vinegar
- 1 tablespoon Worcestershire sauce
- 1 tablespoon spicy brown mustard
- 17 square or 19 round saltines, crushed (⅔ cup)
- 4 slices coarsely chopped bacon, plus 8 whole slices
- 1 onion, chopped coarse
- 3 garlic cloves, minced
- ⅓ cup whole milk
- 2 large eggs plus 1 large yolk
- ⅓ cup minced fresh parsley
- ¾ teaspoon salt
- ½ teaspoon pepper
- 1½ pounds 90 percent lean ground beef

1. Adjust oven rack to upper-middle position and heat oven to 375 degrees. Line rimmed baking sheet with aluminum foil and set wire rack in sheet. Whisk barbecue sauce, vinegar, Worcestershire, and mustard together in bowl; set aside glaze.

2. Process saltines in food processor until finely ground, about 30 seconds; transfer to large bowl. Pulse chopped bacon and onion in now-empty processor until coarsely ground, about 10 pulses. Transfer bacon mixture to 10-inch non-stick skillet and cook over medium heat until onion is soft and translucent, about 5 minutes. Add garlic and cook until fragrant, about 30 seconds. Set aside off heat.

3. Add milk, eggs and yolk, parsley, salt, pepper, and 2 tablespoons glaze to saltines and mash with fork until chunky paste forms. Stir in bacon mixture until combined. Add beef and knead with your hands until combined.

4. Lightly spray 8½ by 4½-inch loaf pan with vegetable oil spray. Line pan with large sheet of plastic wrap, with extra plastic hanging over edges of pan. Push plastic into corners and up sides of pan. Line pan crosswise with remaining 8 bacon slices, overlapping them slightly and letting excess hang over edges of pan (you should have at least ½ inch of overhanging bacon). Brush bacon with 3 tablespoons glaze. Transfer meatloaf mixture to bacon-lined pan and press mixture firmly into pan. Fold bacon slices over mixture.

5. Using metal skewer or tip of paring knife, poke 15 holes in one 14 by 3-inch piece of foil. Center foil rectangle on top of meatloaf. Carefully flip meatloaf onto wire rack so foil is on bottom and bacon is on top. Gripping plastic, gently lift and remove pan from meatloaf. Discard plastic. Gently press meatloaf into 9 by 5-inch rectangle.

6. Bake until bacon is browned and meatloaf registers 150 degrees, about 1 hour. Remove from oven and heat broiler. Brush top and sides of meatloaf with remaining 2 tablespoons glaze. Broil meatloaf until glaze begins to char and meatloaf registers 160 degrees, 3 to 5 minutes. Using foil as sling, transfer meatloaf to carving board and let rest for 15 minutes. Slice and serve, passing extra barbecue sauce.

TEST KITCHEN TECHNIQUE
That's a Wrap
We found that using a loaf pan to wrap our meatloaf in bacon gave us the most consistent results with the least amount of work.

1. After spraying the pan with vegetable oil, line it with plastic wrap and eight slices of bacon. Brush the bacon with glaze.

2. Next, we press the meatloaf mixture into the pan, fold the bacon ends over the loaf, and top it with perforated foil.

3. Finally, invert the foil-topped loaf, bacon and all, onto a wire rack set in a baking sheet, remove the plastic, press the meatloaf into shape, and bake.

Green Goddess Salad

This classic San Francisco dressing shows best over a salad of crunchy romaine, savory bacon, and velvety avocado. BY AARON FURMANEK

YOU CAN'T GO wrong with a salad of crunchy romaine with bacon and avocado. But such salads are too often overwhelmed by heavy dressings. I wanted to find a dressing that complemented these ingredients with bright, invigorating flavor.

Green goddess dressing is an ideal solution. Its fresh flavor is strong enough to lend a light, tangy contrast to the bacon and creamy avocado.

While modern versions of green goddess dressing often contain avocado, the original version, credited to chef Philip Roemer of the Palace Hotel in San Francisco during the 1920s, does not. Since we were already putting avocado in the salad, we decided to follow Roemer's lead and skip the avocado in the dressing.

A combination of fresh and dried herbs proved to be the best here: Fresh parsley and chives added brightness, while dried tarragon lent subtle licorice flavor. A single anchovy fillet disappeared into the dressing and added depth and nuance.

Three kinds of herbs lend brightness to this classic dressing.

ROMAINE SALAD WITH GREEN GODDESS DRESSING

Serves 4

Reduced-fat mayonnaise works well in this dressing.

- 1 tablespoon lemon juice
- 1 tablespoon water
- 2 teaspoons dried tarragon
- ¾ cup mayonnaise
- ¼ cup sour cream
- ¼ cup chopped fresh parsley
- 1 garlic clove, chopped
- 1 anchovy fillet, rinsed
- ¼ cup minced fresh chives
  Salt and pepper
- 4 slices bacon
- 2 romaine lettuce hearts (12 ounces), quartered lengthwise
- 1 avocado, halved, pitted, and cut into ½-inch pieces
- 1 small shallot, sliced into thin rings

1. Combine lemon juice, water, and tarragon in bowl and let sit for 15 minutes.

2. Process mayonnaise, sour cream, parsley, garlic, anchovy, and tarragon mixture in blender until smooth, about 30 seconds, scraping down sides of blender jar as needed. Transfer dressing to bowl and stir in chives. Season with salt and pepper to taste. Refrigerate for 1 hour to let flavors blend.

3. Meanwhile, cook bacon in 12-inch skillet over medium heat until crispy, 7 to 9 minutes. Transfer to paper towel–lined plate and let cool. Crumble bacon into bite-size pieces.

4. Place romaine hearts on platter, cut sides up, and drizzle liberally with dressing. Top with avocado, shallot, and bacon. Season with pepper to taste, and serve.

Don't Fear the Fish
The single anchovy fillet we call for in this recipe may seem superfluous, but it adds savory depth to the dressing (without tasting like fish). Try adding a minced anchovy to your next batch of beef stew or tomato sauce—it will boost the flavor considerably. Anchovies are sold jarred or canned. Extra jarred anchovies can be refrigerated right in the jar according to package directions. But extra canned anchovies should be transferred to a nonreactive airtight container, covered with oil, and refrigerated for up to two weeks.

New Orleans Grillades

Many recipes for this Louisiana braise call for slicing pork shoulder into superthin steaks.
But there's an easier way. BY MORGAN BOLLING

THE SHORT LIST of iconic New Orleans foods includes gumbo, beignets, jambalaya, and po' boys. But there's one more Louisiana dish that deserves attention: grillades.

Despite what your French translation dictionary may claim, grillades (pronounced "GREE-ahds") are not grilled. Rather, they're thinly sliced cuts of meat (usually pork, veal, or beef, and sometimes even fillets of trout) that are browned and then slowly stewed in a roux-thickened, tomato-based gravy with a Louisiana spice mix and the New Orleans trinity of green bell peppers, celery, and onions. The dish is simmered until the meat is fork-tender and full of the peppery flavors of its thick stewing liquid. It's traditionally served over a bed of rice (sometimes grits) that thirstily absorbs the flavorful sauce.

I wanted to see if I could create my own version. I gathered a diverse sample of existing recipes and cooked five of them. The results were disappointing. The meat was tough, and most of the gravy sauces were dull, pasty, and bland. Bland? Not a goal of most Louisiana cooking. I clearly needed to bump up the spices.

▶ Visit **CooksCountry. com/whiterice** to find our foolproof recipe for perfect white rice.

Although some fancy restaurants serve grillades made with veal and some recipes call for beef, I made up my mind to use less expensive (and in my opinion, more flavorful) pork. Tests showed that rib chops, loin chops, and tenderloin all dried out during the long stewing time, but cuts of meat with more connective tissue, such as pork shoulder and country-style ribs, held up better.

Pork shoulder, though, generated a problem: irregularly shaped steaks. I could pound the steaks to get more consistent pieces, but what a pain. A colleague suggested pork blade chops, cut from the end of the pork shoulder, which have more fat and connective tissue than standard rib or loin chops. I cut the bones off eight of them and started in on searing, four pieces at a time, in my Dutch oven. I was pleased to see that the meat didn't dry out or toughen up, and it was more evenly cooked since all pieces were a consistent size and thickness. Plus, buying presliced chops saved me a ton of time and effort.

A potent, supersavory tomato-based gravy is the defining element of grillades.

With that settled, I was on to the sauce. As the defining element of the dish, it needed a strong, sharp personality.

First, I'd focus on structure. Most recipes call for starting the braising liquid with a sauce-thickening roux, which requires cooking flour with fat. It can add 20 to 30 minutes to the cooking time, but I pulled from past test kitchen knowledge and achieved a similar result in less time by toasting the flour in a skillet in advance. This 3-minute jump start meant I could achieve a deep brown roux in the Dutch oven in just 2 minutes more. Seasoned with a mix of powerful spices, the gravy distributed complex and evocative flavors throughout the dish.

But spice isn't the same as heat, and I wanted some punch—enough to proudly announce itself but not send tasters running for cold water or beers. I increased the cayenne in my spice mix, but its flavor was still a little flat. One of my initial recipes called for serving the grillades with Tabasco sauce, a time-honored and ubiquitous Louisiana ingredient; I tried stirring some into the sauce to finish it. Just right. The vinegar in the Tabasco added a sharp hit of acidity, making my sauce much more complex and layered.

Backstory
Cooks' Treat

Where do grillades come from? Culinary historian Randolph Cheramie of the Folse Culinary Institute in Thibodaux, Louisiana, points to the bayou, where "boucherie" parties, all-in community pig roasts, can go all night. The cooks wake up before dawn to start the pig and inevitably get hungry before it's ready (which can take 16 hours or more). They'll slice some pork off the rotisserie and stew it in a cast-iron pot with bacon, tomatoes, and aromatics to make a preparty meal. When the zydeco band fires up and the crowds gather, the cooks are fueled up and ready to go.

Like many Louisiana towns, St. Martinville hosts an annual boucherie.

PORK GRILLADES Serves 6 to 8

We prefer pork blade chops because they hold up to stewing better than loin chops. Blade chops aren't typically available boneless; ask your butcher to bone them for you. Use our Louisiana Seasoning (recipe follows) or your favorite store-bought variety.

- 1 cup all-purpose flour
- 8 (6- to 8-ounce) bone-in pork blade-cut chops, ½ inch thick, bones discarded, trimmed
- 2 tablespoons Louisiana seasoning
  Salt and pepper
- ½ cup vegetable oil
- 1 onion, chopped
- 1 green bell pepper, stemmed, seeded, and chopped
- 1 celery rib, chopped
- 2 garlic cloves, minced
- 2 cups chicken broth
- 1 (14.5-ounce) can whole peeled tomatoes, crushed by hand with juice
- 2 slices bacon
- 1 tablespoon Worcestershire sauce
- 1 bay leaf
- 1 teaspoon Tabasco sauce, plus extra for serving
- 4 cups cooked rice
- 2 scallions, sliced thin

1. Adjust oven rack to lower-middle position and heat oven to 350 degrees. Toast ¼ cup flour in small skillet over medium heat, stirring constantly, until just beginning to brown, about 3 minutes; set aside.

2. Season chops with 1½ teaspoons Louisiana seasoning, salt, and pepper. Whisk remaining ¾ cup flour and remaining 1½ tablespoons Louisiana seasoning together in shallow dish. Working with 1 chop at a time, dredge in seasoned flour, shaking off excess; transfer chops to plate.

3. Heat oil in Dutch oven over medium heat until shimmering. Add 4 chops and cook until browned, 3 to 5 minutes per side; transfer to plate. Repeat with remaining 4 chops.

4. Remove all but ¼ cup oil from Dutch oven and return to medium heat. Add toasted flour to pot and cook, whisking constantly, until deep brown, about 2 minutes. Add onion, bell pepper, celery, and 1 teaspoon salt and cook, stirring often, until vegetables are just softened, about 3 minutes. Add garlic and cook until fragrant, about 30 seconds.

5. Stir in broth, tomatoes and their juice, bacon, Worcestershire, and bay leaf, scraping up any browned bits. Nestle chops into liquid and add any accumulated pork juices from plate. Bring to simmer, cover, and transfer to oven. Cook until fork slips easily in and out of pork, about 1 hour.

6. Remove grillades from oven. Discard bacon and bay leaf; stir in Tabasco. Season with salt and pepper to taste. Serve over rice, sprinkled with scallions and passing extra Tabasco.

LOUISIANA SEASONING
Makes about ¾ cup

You'll need just 2 tablespoons of this Cajun seasoning for our Pork Grillades recipe; try the leftover seasoning on scrambled eggs, boiled potatoes, or roast chicken.

- 5 tablespoons paprika
- 2 tablespoons garlic powder
- 1 tablespoon dried thyme
- 1 tablespoon cayenne pepper
- 1 tablespoon celery salt
- 1 tablespoon salt
- 1 tablespoon pepper

Combine all ingredients in bowl.

TASTING LOUISIANA SEASONING

Whether called Cajun or Creole, most Louisiana spice blends contain a mix of paprika, garlic, thyme, salt, pepper, and cayenne—ingredients typically found in the region's signature dishes. We had 22 cooks and editors sample five seasonings labeled Creole or Cajun on white rice and in pork grillades.

Our tasters preferred saltier and spicier blends. We liked the "pungent" kick from products that list black pepper, cayenne, or chili powder high on their ingredient lists, and tasters also thought that products with more sodium had "more complex" flavors: Our favorite product contains 350 milligrams of sodium per ¼-teaspoon serving. Seasonings with less than 130 milligrams of sodium were "flat" and "bland," and one salt-free product was "completely boring."

When we tested the products against our homemade recipe for Louisiana seasoning in pork grillades, the homemade blend won out for its "balanced" complexity, so we think it's worth the extra time and effort. But if you're in a pinch, reach for Tony Chachere's Original Creole Seasoning, a local Louisiana favorite. An added bonus: At $0.28 per ounce, it's the cheapest seasoning of the bunch. Visit **CooksCountry.com/mar15** for the full tasting story and chart. –LAUREN SAVOIE

RECOMMENDED

TASTERS' NOTES

TONY CHACHERE'S Original Creole Seasoning
Price: $2.25 for 8 oz ($0.28 per oz)
Ingredients: Salt, red pepper, black pepper, chili powder (chili pepper, spices, salt, garlic powder), garlic, silicon dioxide (to prevent caking)
Sodium: 350 mg per ¼ teaspoon

"Vibrant" and "zesty," this "grainy" spice mix had strong notes of garlic and red pepper, with a "punch of heat" and a "slightly sweet" aftertaste. In grillades, it lent a "lively," "bright" flavor, though it was "slightly saltier" than our house mix.

McCORMICK Perfect Pinch Cajun Seasoning
Price: $3.00 for 3.18 oz ($0.94 per oz)
Ingredients: Salt, spices (including red pepper, black pepper, thyme, and celery seed), paprika, garlic, and onion
Sodium: 80 mg per ¼ teaspoon

This "rustic," "woodsy" seasoning had a "mild but present" mix of "warm spice" and "vegetable" flavors with a "pungent," "pleasant heat." "This is the real deal," said one taster, though a few found its texture "a bit dusty."

RECOMMENDED WITH RESERVATIONS

ZATARAIN'S Creole Seasoning
Price: $4.97 for 8 oz ($0.62 per oz)
Ingredients: Salt, dextrose, spices (including red pepper, paprika), garlic, sugar, onion, disodium inosinate and guanylate (flavor enhancers), extractives of paprika, and natural flavor
Sodium: 340 mg per ¼ teaspoon

This "punchy" spice mix was "bold from the get-go," with "lots of garlic," "slight sweetness," and "lingering spiciness." However, some tasters found it too "salt-centric," possibly from the addition of other flavor enhancers like disodium inosinate and guanylate.

SPICE ISLANDS Louisiana Style Cajun Seasoning
Price: $10.85 for 2.3 oz ($4.72 per oz)
Ingredients: Dehydrated garlic, salt, spices, paprika (as color), dehydrated onion, red pepper
Sodium: 40 mg per ¼ teaspoon

While "rustic" and "peppery," with a "mild" spiciness, this product had "herbal," "oregano-heavy" notes and a "chunky" texture that drew some unfavorable comparisons with "Italian seasoning."

NOT RECOMMENDED

FRONTIER Organic Cajun Seasoning
Price: $4.38 for 2.08 oz ($2.11 per oz)
Ingredients: Organic paprika, organic onion, organic garlic, organic marjoram, organic thyme, organic fennel seed, organic cumin, organic cayenne
Sodium: 0 mg per ¼ teaspoon

This salt-free product's overwhelming "anise" notes and "dusty" texture seemed misplaced to tasters. "I wouldn't have guessed that this is Cajun seasoning," said one. In grillades, this product was the "blandest" of the bunch.

BLADE CHOP
Best for slow braising.

The Right Chop

The problem with buying pork chops is that markets call chops by different names. Since grillades are braised, it's important that you don't buy a lean chop, which would be better quickly grilled or sautéed. Flavorful blade chops may not look pretty, but their fat and connective tissue softens and melts out with braising.

Rediscovering Baked Steak

Put away your steak knives: Baked (or "smothered") steaks are fork-tender and supremely beefy.

BY CHRISTIE MORRISON

BAKED STEAK, ALSO called smothered steak, is a mostly hands-off dinner that makes the most of inexpensive steaks. The majority of recipes for this dish are from midcentury cookbooks, when only cheap cuts were available to most households. These cuts have more connective tissue than tender cuts, so they are best when gently braised, which is what "baked" steaks really are.

Most recipes for baked steak follow a similar route: Four (or so) steaks from the chuck, blade, or round are seasoned, sometimes dredged in flour, and browned; sliced onions and mushrooms are placed, sautéed or raw, in the pan with the steaks along with broth and very simple seasoning.

Preparing and tasting these recipes helped me make some initial decisions. Chuck steaks were out because their rendered fat made everything greasy. Round steaks had a dry texture. I settled on 1-inch-thick blade steaks cut from the shoulder muscle. These flavorful steaks are often bypassed (in spite of their attractive price tag) because of the line of gristle that bisects each steak. I hoped that the longer cooking time here would melt out the gristle.

Some recipes call for simply nestling the raw steaks into a bed of onions and mushrooms and setting the pan in the oven; this seemed like a missed opportunity. By dredging the steaks in flour and quickly browning them, I built fond in the pan and added starch that would help thicken the sauce. Plus, the finished steaks now had some textural contrast and flavorful browning.

Since I was already taking time to brown the steaks in a skillet, I hated to spend more time on the stovetop before baking. For now, I would add the sliced onions and mushrooms to the skillet after I scraped up the flavorful fond left by the steaks. Then I placed the steaks on top of the mound of vegetables and added a cup of beef broth and a tablespoon of soy sauce (to enhance the beefy flavor). I covered the skillet and popped it into a 350-degree oven.

After 2 hours of baking, the steaks were swimming in a pool of liquid. The vegetables had cooked down significantly, releasing their juices into the broth and effectively stewing the meat. The blade steaks were pretty tender (and the connective tissue had softened con-siderably) but needed a little more time to be just right. Also, the intense steam in the pan had softened the seared crust. So I returned the steaks to the oven, uncovered, for another half-hour. The surfaces of the steaks emerged nicely crusty and browned and the sauce had reduced a bit—but not quite enough.

I tested the dish with decreasing amounts of broth before realizing that the onions and mushrooms were releasing enough liquid to braise the meat on their own. I had just enough sauce now, but its texture was a bit thin. Needing a stronger thickener, I switched from dredging the steaks in flour to dredging them in cornstarch; this made the sauce thick enough to cling lightly to the meat and vegetables. Fine-tuning the flavors, we found that a tablespoon of tomato paste added sweetness, depth, and an appealing color to the sauce. A few cloves of garlic and a little chopped rosemary gave the sauce extra intensity.

My humble dish was met with smiles from tasters. "I didn't think I'd like it so much," one taster admitted. Exactly.

Blade steaks are the best choice here: They are deeply flavorful and tender when braised—and they're cheap, too.

BAKED STEAK WITH ONIONS AND MUSHROOMS Serves 6

You can use white button mushrooms in place of the cremini.

- 6 (6- to 8-ounce) beef blade steaks, 1 inch thick, trimmed
  Salt and pepper
- ⅓ cup cornstarch
- ¼ cup vegetable oil
- 1 tablespoon water
- 1 tablespoon soy sauce
- 1 tablespoon tomato paste
- 2 onions, halved and sliced thin
- 8 ounces cremini mushrooms, trimmed and sliced thin
- 2 garlic cloves, minced
- 1 teaspoon chopped fresh rosemary
- 2 tablespoons chopped fresh parsley

1. Adjust oven rack to middle position and heat oven to 300 degrees. Pat steaks dry with paper towels and season with salt and pepper. Spread cornstarch in shallow dish. Working with 1 steak at a time, dredge steaks in cornstarch, shaking off excess, and transfer to plate.

2. Heat 2 tablespoons oil in 12-inch skillet over medium-high heat until just smoking. Add 3 steaks at a time and cook until browned, about 3 minutes per side, then return to plate. Repeat with remaining 2 tablespoons oil and remaining 3 steaks.

3. Remove skillet from heat and discard oil. Combine water, soy sauce, and tomato paste in now-empty skillet, scraping up any browned bits. Stir in onions, mushrooms, garlic, rosemary, and ¼ teaspoon salt. Place steaks in single layer on top of onion mixture and add any accumulated steak juices.

4. Cover skillet, transfer to oven, and bake for 2 hours. Uncover and continue to bake until steaks are browned and fork tender, about 30 minutes longer. Transfer steaks to platter, tent loosely with aluminum foil, and let rest for 5 minutes. Season onion mixture with salt and pepper to taste and spoon over steaks. Sprinkle with parsley. Serve.

Crowded Pleaser

With two sliced onions, 8 ounces of sliced mushrooms, and six steaks, the skillet is very crowded. The tight fit encourages flavor transfer between meat and vegetables.

Spinach and Potato Gratin

Adding spinach freshens up an old favorite—but then you have to solve the soggy problems it creates.

BY CHRISTIE MORRISON

A POTATO GRATIN, FOR some, is a done deal—potatoes, cream, and cheese all bubbly and brown. But it's also a starting point, a foundation to be built on. To combat winter's gray days, I wanted to introduce verdant spinach and savory ham to give the dish a fresh appeal.

Unfortunately, spinach and potatoes have very different cooking times. How would I preserve the bright color and flavor of the spinach, which cooks fairly quickly, until the longer-cooking potatoes became tender? The recipes I found for spinach-potato gratin mostly called for insulating the spinach by placing it between layers of potato slices. But this approach didn't fly with my tasters, as the layer of spinach (I tried both sautéed fresh spinach and thawed and drained frozen spinach) steamed between the potato layers and gave the gratin a soggy, watered-down flavor. There was one more-promising recipe, though, that called for placing the spinach on top of the potatoes and liquid; the spinach stayed fairly moist and didn't taste steamed, but it did overcook and turn an ugly army-green color by the time the potatoes cooked through. I had some work to do to figure out how to keep the spinach from overcooking.

While we often prefer the good flavor and convenience of frozen spinach in cooked applications, my tasters voiced a preference for fresh spinach in the gratin. Since I'd need to sauté the spinach before assembling the gratin, I wanted to keep the rest of the recipe simple and straightforward. That meant forgoing a cooked white sauce for a dump-and-stir sauce of liquid dairy (milk, half-and-half, heavy cream, or some combination) mixed with grated Parmesan, salt, pepper, and a touch of nutmeg. After several head-to-head tests, I wasn't surprised that my tasters preferred heavy cream.

I quickly learned that starchy russet potatoes were the only way to go, as Yukon Golds and waxy red potatoes didn't provide the starch necessary to help thicken the no-cook sauce. Most of our gratin recipes call for 3 pounds of potatoes (sliced ⅛ inch thick), but I knew that such a thick layer of sliced spuds would take a while to cook through—and by that time the spinach would be overcooked. What if I used fewer potatoes? That way, the potatoes

The starch from thinly sliced russet potatoes helps thicken the creamy sauce.

would cook through before the spinach was spent. I reduced the amount of potatoes in my recipe to 2 pounds, which was still sufficient for four to six people. My thinner gratin—I could now simply place the sliced potatoes in the bottom of the buttered dish without having to shingle them—baked through in about half the time, leaving the spinach in great shape.

I still had a problem, however. The heavy cream that tasters preferred left the gratin too rich and covered up the earthy flavor of the spinach (and the potatoes, for that matter). Cutting the cream with chicken broth helped lighten the gratin and, with less fat to get in the way, allowed the other flavors to shine. The gratin as a whole, though, was still a

little flat. Increasing the amount of seasoning helped the situation, but it was a one-note answer. One taster suggested including bacon or pancetta to add salty complexity, but both options required cooking—an extra step I was hoping to avoid. Instead, I tried adding chopped Black Forest ham for a similar salty, meaty element. The ham complemented the cooked spinach, enhancing but not overwhelming the flavor. Almost there.

By definition, a gratin needs to have a crust of some kind. Toasted bread crumbs and panko both made for a dusty texture that covered up the spinach, but a sprinkling of grated Parmesan browned beautifully and complemented the greens. A dish this rich and delicious shouldn't be this easy.

POTATO, HAM, AND SPINACH GRATIN Serves 8

Do not prepare the potatoes ahead of time or store them in water; the potato starch is essential for thickening the sauce. A mandoline makes quick work of slicing the potatoes.

- 1½ cups heavy cream
- 1 cup chicken broth
- 1½ ounces Parmesan cheese, grated (¾ cup)
- 1 teaspoon salt
- 1 teaspoon pepper
- ⅛ teaspoon ground nutmeg
- 1 tablespoon unsalted butter
- 8 ounces (8 cups) baby spinach
- 3 garlic cloves, minced
- 4 ounces thinly sliced Black Forest ham, chopped fine
- 2 pounds russet potatoes, peeled and sliced ⅛ inch thick

1. Adjust oven rack to middle position and heat oven to 400 degrees. Grease 13 by 9-inch baking dish. Whisk cream, broth, ½ cup Parmesan, salt, pepper, and nutmeg together in bowl; set aside.

2. Melt butter in 12-inch nonstick skillet over medium-high heat. Add spinach and garlic and cook until spinach is wilted, about 3 minutes, stirring often. Off heat, stir in ham. Transfer spinach mixture to paper towel–lined plate to drain.

3. Arrange potatoes in even layer in prepared dish. Distribute spinach mixture evenly over potatoes. Pour cream mixture over spinach mixture and sprinkle with remaining ¼ cup Parmesan. Bake until potatoes are tender and cheese is spotty brown, 35 to 40 minutes. Let cool for 15 minutes. Serve.

Two-Tiered Solution

Spinach adds moisture to the mix, so to minimize sogginess, we lay it in a single layer atop the potatoes rather than nestling it in.

Flank Steak Peperonata

Peperonata—sweet peppers slowly stewed in olive oil—can take ages to prepare. We wanted a quick version to serve with steak for a weeknight supper. BY DIANE UNGER

PEPERONATA IS AN Italian condiment of sweet peppers stewed in olive oil with onion, tomato, wine or vinegar, and garlic until the peppers are soft and the flavors have melded—think roasted red peppers without the char. Its sweet, earthy flavor and smooth texture make it good hot, cold, or at room temperature. You'll find it on Italian American tables alongside meats, fish, and eggs; on salads and sandwiches; or as part of an antipasti platter. I wanted to make peperonata part of a sensational-yet-easy weeknight dinner, and my first thought was to pair it with quick-cooking flank steak.

I decided to tackle the peperonata first and then figure out a way to unite it with the steak. I started by gathering a bunch of recipes to try and was surprised at how different they were. While nearly all called for a mix of red and yellow bell peppers (for a nice presentation), some recipes called for roasting the peppers first, some required cutting the peppers in large chunks nearly 2 inches wide, and others called for thinly slicing the peppers. One recipe even called for peeling raw peppers with a vegetable peeler.

After tasting such a wide range of peperonatas, my tasters and I had some opinions. Since I wanted this to be a weeknight dish, roasting and peeling the peppers were both off the table—as were long-cooked versions, which did not fit my Tuesday-night timetable. I cobbled together a working recipe based on what I had learned from these initial tests: I wanted the peppers cut small so the skin wasn't noticeable and so they'd cook to tenderness relatively quickly, and I wanted a good amount of acid to cut through the richness of the olive oil.

I started by cutting two red and two yellow bell peppers into ¼-inch-wide strips, trying first lengthwise and then crosswise. My tasters thought that the shorter crosswise strips were easier to eat, so I cut the onion into slices of a similar size. After testing varying amounts of olive oil to cook the peperonata, I settled on ⅓ cup, which was enough to coat the peppers well without feeling greasy. In testing garlic amounts, I found that six cloves of garlic, crushed, added just the right amount of nutty

How about a supereasy chocolate cake for dessert? Visit CooksCountry.com/wackycake for our Wacky Cake recipe.

Tangy, sweet *peperonata* makes the perfect condiment for tender slices of spice-rubbed flank steak.

bite to the mix. I cooked everything covered until the peppers were just tender. Then I uncovered the skillet and added a can of diced tomatoes along with their juice, some capers and their brine (which tasters preferred to vinegar or wine), and red pepper flakes for a little heat. Finished with chopped basil for freshness, the flavorful peperonata was ready to be introduced to the flank steak.

My first test proved that simply searing the flank steak, slicing it, and serving it with the peperonata made for an easy but uninspired dish. For more punch, I rubbed the steak with a mixture of salt and dried oregano and let it sit while I made the peperonata; this gave the salt a chance to work its way into the meat for deep seasoning, while the oregano strengthened the Italian flavor profile. For even faster, more thorough seasoning, I cut the 2-pound flank steak lengthwise into three long strips before rubbing it with the salt-oregano mixture; this increased the surface area for the salt to be absorbed.

I wiped out the nonstick skillet and cooked the three strips of steak to a nice medium-rare, which took about 6 minutes per side over medium-high heat. I let the steak strips rest for about 10 minutes and then cut them into thin slices (against the grain of the meat for maximum tenderness). I drizzled the slices with olive oil and seasoned them with salt and pepper. Just right—the flank steak and peperonata finally tasted like they belonged together.

FLANK STEAK PEPERONATA
Serves 4 to 6

Look for a flank steak of even thickness. The *peperonata* can be made up to two days in advance.

- 1 (2-pound) flank steak, trimmed
- 2 teaspoons dried oregano
  Kosher salt and pepper
- ⅓ cup plus 1 tablespoon extra-virgin olive oil, plus extra for serving
- 2 red bell peppers, stemmed, seeded, quartered, and cut crosswise into ¼-inch-wide strips
- 2 yellow bell peppers, stemmed, seeded, quartered, and cut crosswise into ¼-inch-wide strips
- 1 onion, quartered through root end and sliced crosswise into ¼-inch-wide strips
- 6 garlic cloves, crushed and peeled
- 1 (14.5-ounce) can diced tomatoes
- 2 tablespoons capers plus 4 teaspoons caper brine
- ⅛ teaspoon red pepper flakes
- ½ cup chopped fresh basil

1. Cut steak lengthwise with grain into 3 equal pieces. Combine oregano and 2 teaspoons salt in bowl. Season steaks all over with salt mixture, wrap in plastic wrap, and refrigerate for at least 30 minutes or up to 24 hours.

2. Heat ⅓ cup oil in 12-inch nonstick skillet over medium-high heat until just smoking. Add red and yellow bell peppers, onion, garlic, and 1¼ teaspoons salt. Cover and cook, stirring occasionally, until vegetables are soft, about 10 minutes.

3. Stir in tomatoes and their juice, capers and brine, and pepper flakes. Continue to cook, uncovered, until slightly thickened, about 5 minutes. Season with salt and pepper to taste. Transfer peperonata to bowl, cover, and keep warm.

4. Wipe out skillet with paper towels. Pat steaks dry with paper towels and season with pepper. Heat remaining 1 tablespoon oil in now-empty skillet over medium-high heat until just smoking. Cook steaks until well browned and each registers 125 degrees (for medium-rare), 5 to 7 minutes per side. Transfer steaks to carving board, tent with aluminum foil, and let rest for 10 minutes.

5. Stir basil into peperonata. Slice steaks thin on bias against grain. Season steak slices with salt and pepper and drizzle with extra oil. Serve steak with peperonata.

Southern-Style Green Beans

Boiling fresh beans for an hour? It sounds old-fashioned, but the velvety beans and flavor-packed broth are worth the time. BY MORGAN BOLLING

S OME COOKS I KNOW preach the gospel of crisp-tender vegetables and will ardently caution against the sin of overcooking them. But I think that vegetables are just as often undercooked and can sometimes benefit from more thorough cooking. One dish that illustrates this point well is Southern-style green beans, in which the beans are boiled with potatoes and pork for upwards of an hour until they are silky-soft and infused with deliciously salty, meaty, full flavor. As a bonus, you get to drink the rich cooking liquid known as pot liquor (or pot likker).

I gathered a bunch of recipes for this dish and found that many of them suffered from the same problem: a lack of specifics. In particular, several simply called for water without giving an amount; others listed "potatoes" without saying what kind or how they should be prepped. As for the pork, recipes called for bacon, ham hock, salt pork, or country-ham trimmings. Some recipes included sugar or lemon, while others went virtually unseasoned. I selected a sample of recipes that represented these variables and got busy cooking.

The results were disappointing. Too sweet, underseasoned, and too salty were my tasters' big complaints— as were potatoes that either fell apart or were too hard. As for the pot liquor, some versions had none; others had pot liquor that was lacking in flavor.

Starting with 1½ pounds of beans, I ran a few tests and determined that 4 cups of water was the right amount. I tested different types of potatoes and landed on a pound of red potatoes cut into 1-inch pieces, which I added after the beans had simmered for about 20 minutes and then let cook for another half-hour, until everything was perfectly tender. As for the pork products, I tried them all (save for the country-ham trimmings, which are hard to find in much of the country) and settled on meaty-tasting ham hocks, which I started with the beans and then removed at the end so I could pick the meat and return it to the pot. For other seasonings, my tasters rejected sugar and lemon but liked the simple additions of sautéed onion, garlic, and a little vinegar.

These ultratender, superflavorful, long-cooked green beans are definitely not al dente—and in this case, that's a good thing.

These ultratender green beans are deeply infused with rich pork flavor.

SOUTHERN-STYLE GREEN BEANS AND POTATOES Serves 6 to 8

Do not drain off the cooking liquid before serving: This flavorful, savory pot liquor should be sipped with the meal. Leftover pot liquor can be used as a soup base.

- 1 tablespoon vegetable oil
- 1 onion, halved and sliced thin
- 4 cups water
- 1½ pounds green beans, trimmed and cut into 1½-inch lengths
- 2 (12-ounce) smoked ham hocks
- 3 garlic cloves, crushed and peeled
  Salt and pepper
- 1 pound red potatoes, unpeeled, cut into 1-inch pieces
- 1 teaspoon cider vinegar (optional)

1. Heat oil in Dutch oven over medium-high heat until shimmering. Add onion and cook until translucent, about 4 minutes.

2. Add water, green beans, ham hocks, garlic, and 2¼ teaspoons salt and bring to boil. Reduce heat to low, cover, and simmer for 20 minutes. Stir in potatoes, cover, and continue to simmer until potatoes are tender, about 30 minutes longer, stirring halfway through cooking.

3. Off heat, remove ham hocks and let cool for 5 minutes. Chop meat and return to pot; discard skin and bones. Gently stir in vinegar, if using, to avoid breaking up potatoes. Season with salt and pepper to taste. Serve.

Carolina Chicken Bog

This simple, savory one-pot dish isn't hard to put together—as long as you get the timing just right.

BY NICK IVERSON

WHAT'S IN A NAME? Not much, if the name is Carolina chicken bog, an unpromising label that woefully undersells this wonderful dish. A staple in the Lowcountry and northern coastal kitchens of South Carolina, bog combines inexpensive ingredients—chicken, smoky sausage, and rice—into an easy one-pot meal that works for big weekend gatherings or simple weeknight suppers.

I tested several recipes for chicken bog; they ranged from spicy to bland and from complicated to simple. Some called for a whole chicken, others called for seasoned rice. Some were served stew-style, with a healthy portion of broth; others aimed for a drier, sticky rice studded with chicken and sausage.

After a visit to Loris, South Carolina, to watch bog masters at work (see "On the Road"), I decided I wanted the less-soupy style of bog, with a final dish that's more like a pilaf than a stew, but with sticky, not separate, grains of rice. To get there, I knew that timing would be everything; I needed the rice to absorb just the right amount of liquid in just the right amount of time.

About that liquid: I wanted a deeply flavorful broth to make certain that the entire pot was infused with chicken flavor. Rather than cutting up a whole bird and risking overcooking the white meat, I opted for more forgiving chicken thighs—skin-on and bone-in for maximum flavor. The first step was to brown six thighs in a Dutch oven to render the fat (and flavor) from the skin. I next transferred them to a plate, reserving a tablespoon of chicken fat in the pot and discarding the spent skin.

Using this rendered fat to cook down the onions and brown the sausage (we chose kielbasa) ensured strong chicken flavor throughout the dish. A few cloves of minced garlic added depth; all were stirred together with the broth.

So far so good. But here came the tricky part: The chicken was not yet fully cooked through, and I hadn't even touched the rice. So I decided to return the chicken to the pot and add the rice at the same time, hoping to have everything finish together.

I cut the chicken from the bones (not easy, given that the insides were still raw) and stirred it into the broth with the rice. I covered the pot, turned down the heat, and let it simmer. Twenty

Don't get bogged down by the name: This is a straightforward, satisfying dish of rice, chicken, and sausage cooked in broth.

minutes later, when the rice was cooked, I gave it a taste. Alas, the chicken was still not cooked through, and the rice wasn't as flavorful as it should have been. Back to the kitchen.

This time, after stirring the broth into the pot, I added the now-skinless chicken thighs for 30 minutes to thoroughly cook through. I fished them out, set them aside on a carving board, and

stirred the rice into the cooking liquid, now bolstered by even more chicken flavor thanks to the chicken's half-hour simmer. Once the pot returned to a boil, I reduced the heat and covered it. After 20 minutes, the rice had absorbed the perfect amount of liquid and was slightly sticky with just a hint of starch on the outside of each grain.

While the rice cooked, I used my

hands to remove the chicken meat from the bones (much easier now that the thighs were cooked through and slightly cooled) and tear it into shreds. As I stirred these pieces of chicken into the now-cooked rice, the rice clumped onto my fork with a pleasant, sticky, dare I say boggy texture. My tasters and I could now take great big, chewy bites of this delicious one-dish dinner.

CAROLINA CHICKEN BOG

Serves 6 to 8

Wellshire Farms Smoked Polska Kielbasa is the test kitchen's preferred kielbasa.

- 6 (5- to 7-ounce) bone-in chicken thighs, trimmed
  Salt and pepper
- 1 tablespoon vegetable oil
- 8 ounces smoked kielbasa sausage, cut into ½-inch-thick rounds
- 1 onion, chopped fine
- 3 garlic cloves, minced
- 4 cups chicken broth
- 2 cups long-grain white rice

1. Pat chicken dry with paper towels and season with salt and pepper. Heat oil in Dutch oven over medium heat until just smoking. Cook chicken, skin side down, until well browned, 6 to 8 minutes; transfer chicken to plate. Discard skin.

2. Pour off all but 1 tablespoon fat from pot and return to medium heat. Add sausage and onion and cook until onion is translucent and sausage begins to brown, 3 to 5 minutes. Add garlic and cook until fragrant, about 30 seconds. Add broth, chicken, 1 teaspoon salt, and 1 teaspoon pepper and bring to boil. Reduce heat to low, cover, and simmer until chicken is tender, about 30 minutes.

3. Remove chicken from pot and set aside. Stir rice into pot, cover, and continue to cook over low heat until rice is tender, about 20 minutes.

4. Shred chicken into bite-size pieces; discard bones. Gently fold shredded chicken into rice mixture. Remove from heat and let sit, covered, for 10 minutes. Serve.

On the Road
Championship Bogs

We traveled to Loris, South Carolina, where the annual Loris Bog-Off Festival is a hotly contested affair. Entrants cook up bogs in large cast-iron Dutch ovens, carefully stirring with wooden "bogging spoons" worn down from years of pot stirring. Recipes are guarded jealously, but the basics—chicken, sausage, and rice—are shared by all.

Pimento Cheese

There are as many paths to pimento cheese as there are back roads in the South. We wanted to find the most direct route. BY CHRISTIE MORRISON

AS SOUTHERN COMFORT foods go, pimento cheese is right up there with fried green tomatoes and ham biscuits. Except it's not really Southern at all, according to food historian Robert Moss. Pimento cheese, he says, has roots in New York. In the late 19th century, cream cheese (produced in New York state) and pimentos (imported from Spain) were new to the American marketplace. Before long, consumers were combining them to spread on sandwiches. In 1908, the first published recipe for pimento cheese appeared in *Good Housekeeping*. By 1910, prepared pimento cheese was on store shelves.

So why is pimento cheese so closely associated with the South? "I've never been fully able to answer this," Moss told us. "A lot of it has to do with the Southern tradition of bringing dips and spreads to community gatherings. People would compete with each other to have the best."

Devotees have strongly held beliefs about what belongs in pimento cheese, but most will agree on cheddar cheese, mayonnaise, drained and diced pimentos, and cayenne or a splash of hot sauce. Other often-used components include cream cheese, pickles, olive juice, and grated onion.

Today, the most iconic version of pimento cheese may be the one served at the Augusta National Golf Club in Georgia. I mail-ordered a tub from the local WifeSaver restaurant that used to supply it to the golf club and whipped up a few more recipes claiming to be "the best pimento cheese ever" for a five-way taste test. (The WifeSaver version was passable but not great.)

The more popular versions had a chunky, homespun quality, so I quickly determined that the food processor, which many recipes employ, wasn't the way to go—the processed ingredients had the consistency of whipped cream cheese. Instead, I'd mix by hand to get the pebbly spread I was looking for.

After settling on the type of cheese to pair with the cream cheese (combinations of Colby and Monterey Jack paled in comparison with 100 percent sharp yellow cheddar), I found that ⅔ cup mayonnaise to 1 pound grated cheese was a balanced ratio for flavor and the best spreadable texture.

To round out the flavor, I added

Crackers provide an easy, direct delivery system for this iconic spread. Make sure to also try it with crudités or on a ham sandwich.

just a teaspoon each of lemon juice and Worcestershire sauce and ¼ teaspoon of cayenne for some gentle heat. I spread some on a cracker for a final test . . . and experienced a sudden rise in popularity in the test kitchen. If the true test of pimento cheese is how it brings people together, then I think I have a winner on my hands.

PIMENTO CHEESE Makes about 3 cups

You will need one 4-ounce jar of pimentos for this recipe. Yellow cheddar cheese is traditional, but you can substitute white cheddar cheese. Use the pimento cheese as a sandwich spread or serve it with crackers or crudités.

- ⅔ cup mayonnaise
- 2 tablespoons cream cheese, softened
- 1 teaspoon lemon juice
- 1 teaspoon Worcestershire sauce
- ¼ teaspoon cayenne pepper
- 1 pound yellow sharp cheddar cheese
- ⅓ cup pimentos, patted dry and minced

1. Whisk mayonnaise, cream cheese, lemon juice, Worcestershire, and cayenne together in large bowl.

2. Shred 8 ounces cheddar on large holes of box grater. Shred remaining 8 ounces cheddar on small holes of box grater. Stir pimentos and all cheddar into mayonnaise mixture until thoroughly combined. Serve. (Pimento cheese will keep refrigerated for at least 1 week.)

SMOKED PIMENTO CHEESE

Substitute 8 ounces smoked cheddar cheese, shredded on small holes of box grater, for finely shredded sharp cheddar.

Pasta with Mushroom Sauce

We found the trick to coaxing deep, earthy flavors from supermarket mushrooms.

BY AARON FURMANEK

MOST SUPERMARKET mushrooms don't look like much in the produce case. The little buttons or shiitakes seem spongy and sad, destined for a supporting role at best. But I had a feeling I could coax satisfying earthy and meaty flavors from supermarket mushrooms for an easy weeknight pasta supper.

I tried several recipes, most of which called for cutting the fresh mushrooms into 1-inch pieces, browning them in butter or oil, and adding onion, shallot, or garlic. Then they direct you to hit the pan with a bit of white wine and scrape up the flavorful browned bits the mushrooms leave behind before tossing the lot with pasta and finishing with a sprinkle of cheese and parsley.

If only it were that simple. My experiments, so promising in theory, lacked anything more than shallow mushroom flavor. I had work to do.

I tried slowing things down to encourage the mushrooms to give up more flavor. I cooked them covered for 5 minutes to help them release their liquid. Then I cooked them uncovered for an additional 10 minutes to drive off the excess water. While this technique consolidated the flavors, I wasn't developing much fond, those flavorful browned bits left on the bottom of the pan. I found that if I coarsely chopped half the mushrooms (leaving the rest quartered for visual impact later), the smaller pieces left behind more fond. I then tossed the sauce with cooked pasta and served it to my tasters. The sauce was delicious, but it was just sitting on, rather than connecting to, the pasta.

Drawing on earlier test kitchen experiments with one-pot pasta dishes, I wondered if I could create a cohesive mushroom sauce in a Dutch oven and then add water and pasta directly to the pot to boil until the pasta was done.

Fingers crossed, I gave the technique a swing, using 4 cups of water and campanelle pasta (I'd settled on this short shape for its mushroom-cradling capabilities). Almost there; the pasta was nicely cooked, but even though I was finishing the sauce with plenty of Pecorino Romano and butter, the sauce was thin and lacked body.

I was about to set aside this technique when a colleague suggested a solution: elbow grease. I gave the process another try, but after adding the final ingredients

Fresh shiitake and button mushrooms, plus dried porcini, give this one-pot pasta deliciously deep mushroom flavor.

of Pecorino, lemon juice, and butter, plus a bit of water to loosen things up, I vigorously stirred the pasta for 1 minute, which drew as much starch from the pasta as possible. The minute of exertion was well worth it. The starch added body and structure to the sauce, which now clung greedily to the pasta. I had an inexpensive but elegant dish with deep mushroom flavor in every bite.

KEY DISCOVERY Doubling Down for Big Impact

Chopping half the mushrooms creates more fond for a flavorful sauce; quartering the rest gives big, meaty mushroom texture.

COARSELY CHOPPED   QUARTERED

PASTA WITH MUSHROOM SAUCE
Serves 4

If you can't find shiitake mushrooms, cremini mushrooms can be substituted or white mushrooms can be used exclusively, but don't omit the dried porcini. Parmesan cheese can be substituted for the Pecorino Romano.

- 12 ounces shiitake mushrooms, stemmed
- 12 ounces white mushrooms, trimmed
- 4 tablespoons unsalted butter
  Salt and pepper
- 2 shallots, minced
- 2 tablespoons minced fresh sage
- 4 garlic cloves, minced
- ¼ ounce dried porcini mushrooms, rinsed and chopped fine
- ½ cup dry white wine
- 4 cups water plus ¼ cup hot water
- 12 ounces (3¾ cups) campanelle, penne, or fusilli
- 2 ounces Pecorino Romano cheese, grated (1 cup), plus extra for serving
- 1 tablespoon lemon juice
- 2 tablespoons minced fresh chives

1. Coarsely chop half of shiitake mushrooms and white mushrooms; then quarter remaining shiitake mushrooms and white mushrooms. Melt 2 tablespoons butter in Dutch oven over medium-high heat. Add all shiitake mushrooms and white mushrooms (both chopped and quartered) and ¾ teaspoon salt. Cover and cook until mushrooms release their liquid, about 5 minutes. Uncover and continue to cook, stirring occasionally, until all liquid has evaporated and mushrooms begin to brown, about 10 minutes.

2. Add shallots, sage, garlic, and porcini mushrooms and cook until fragrant, about 1 minute. Add wine and cook until evaporated, about 2 minutes. Stir in 4 cups water, pasta, and 1¼ teaspoons salt and bring to boil. Reduce heat to medium, cover, and cook, stirring occasionally, until pasta is tender, 12 to 15 minutes.

3. Off heat, stir in Pecorino, ¼ cup hot water, lemon juice, remaining 2 tablespoons butter, and ½ teaspoon pepper. Stir vigorously for 1 minute, until sauce is thickened. Season with salt and pepper to taste. Transfer to serving dish and sprinkle with chives. Serve, passing extra Pecorino separately.

Little Italy Zeppoles

To make these light, crisp confections, which are like a cross between doughnuts and fried dough, you need a little know-how—and two leaveners. BY MORGAN BOLLING

GO TO AN Italian American festival, such as the annual Feast of San Gennaro in New York's Little Italy, and you'll likely pass multiple booths selling fresh zeppoles. These deep-fried Italian confections are golden brown and crispy on the outside and soft and airy inside, with a light sprinkle of powdered sugar on top. They usually aren't eccentric or fancy in their flavorings, nor are they meant to be; their charm is their simplicity.

I was reminded of this on my fifth day of testing as I pulled the 18th batch out of the frying oil and sampled a disappointing, stodgy zeppole, overworked and overthought—so far from the simple fried dough ball I'd set out to create.

I'd started my testing according to our usual methods in the test kitchen: frying a variety of zeppoles from existing recipes using the two standard options of yeasted and *choux* batters. Unfortunately, none matched what I had devoured at street fairs.

I quickly ditched the choux batter. Choux is a simple batter of flour, eggs, butter, and water that's used for cream puffs and éclairs. Without a leavening agent like yeast or soda, choux relies on its moisture for leavening: When heated, the water inside the batter turns to steam, creating pockets of air and puffing the pastry. In my testing I'd found the choux-dough zeppoles lacking in flavor

Our light, tender zeppoles are best served warm.

and the dough itself fussy to work with.

Instead, I focused on yeasted dough, which proved both easier and more flavorful in those early tests. Stirring together flour, sugar, water, and yeast and letting it rest for 15 minutes before dropping spoonfuls into the hot oil gave me flavorful little nuggets, but not the light, fluffy zeppoles I was aiming for. Taking a cue from earlier test kitchen experimentation, I decided to double up on leavening and use both yeast and baking powder. Though usually used independently, putting both to work can make a lighter, fluffier end product—and did just that in this case. My zeppoles were noticeably lighter and still maintained a mild, yeasted flavor.

I loved these simple zeppoles—they

were so easy to make, beautiful and delicious and satisfying—but despite warnings about inquisitive cats, I couldn't help being curious: Could I improve on them even more?

I continued experimenting, adjusting the amounts of vanilla, sugar, and salt. I went further into untraditional territory, adding ingredients from milk to ricotta to see if they improved the texture or added appealing flavors. I even diverted from the traditional coating of confectioners' sugar, trying sprinkles of cocoa, cinnamon, and salt. But as I continued to test these tweaks against my straightforward two-leavener zeppoles tossed with powdery confectioners' sugar, none matched up.

When I ran out of detours to take,

I traced my steps back to that simple 15-minute recipe. I tinkered just a bit, adjusting proportions to make the perfect amount for a small group to share. I fried off that final batch, and when my tasters quickly devoured them, I realized, as with many things in life, sometimes the simplest path is the best.

ZEPPOLES Makes 15 to 18 zeppoles

This dough is very wet and sticky. If you own a 4-cup liquid measuring cup, you can combine the batter in it to make it easier to tell when it has doubled in volume in step 1. Zeppoles are best served warm.

- 1⅓ cups (6⅔ ounces) all-purpose flour
- 1 tablespoon granulated sugar
- 2 teaspoons instant or rapid-rise yeast
- 1 teaspoon baking powder
- ½ teaspoon salt
- 1 cup warm water (110 degrees)
- ½ teaspoon vanilla extract
- 2 quarts peanut or vegetable oil
  Confectioners' sugar

1. Combine flour, granulated sugar, yeast, baking powder, and salt in large bowl. Whisk water and vanilla into flour mixture until fully combined. Cover tightly with plastic wrap and let rise at room temperature until doubled in size, 15 to 25 minutes.

2. Set wire rack in rimmed baking sheet and line rack with triple layer of paper towels. Adjust oven rack to middle position and heat oven to 200 degrees. Add oil to large Dutch oven until it measures about 1½ inches deep and heat over medium-high heat to 350 degrees.

3. Using greased tablespoon measure, add 6 heaping tablespoonfuls of batter to oil. (Use dinner spoon to help scrape batter from tablespoon if necessary.) Fry until golden brown and toothpick inserted in center of zeppole comes out clean, 2 to 3 minutes, flipping once halfway through frying. Adjust burner, if necessary, to maintain oil temperature between 325 and 350 degrees.

4. Using slotted spoon, transfer zeppoles to prepared wire rack; roll briefly so paper towels absorb grease. Transfer sheet to oven to keep warm. Return oil to 350 degrees and repeat twice more with remaining batter. Dust zeppoles with confectioners' sugar and serve.

Snapshot: 1966

A street vendor in New York City's Little Italy neighborhood fries zeppoles for a hungry crowd.

Getting to Know Thickeners

Achieving the right consistency in a sauce, custard, pie, or jam takes a little knowledge . . . and some help from these common thickeners. BY CHRISTIE MORRISON

All-Purpose Flour
SLURRIED, ROUX-ED, OR PASTED

Flour can thicken a substance alone, as part of a slurry, or in conjunction with a fat. In a roux, a mixture of flour and fat is cooked to eliminate the raw flour flavor before introducing liquid. In a beurre manié, a paste of flour and softened butter is added to a soup or sauce to finish it. In either case, combine them with liquid gradually and whisk them in well before the mixture boils, when the flour's starches cause the mixture to thicken.

Cornstarch
STIR-FRY STRENGTHENER

Because cornstarch is a pure starch, it is a more effective thickener than flour (which is only 75 percent starch). But cornstarch-thickened sauces break down more quickly than flour-thickened ones, so be sure to follow the cooking times for recipes thickened with cornstarch and to reduce the heat once the dish has thickened. Cornstarch is the go-to thickener for stir-fries; first mix it with cold liquid to form a slurry before adding the thickener to hot liquids to prevent clumping.

Heavy Cream
RICH REDUCTION

Just a few tablespoons of heavy cream, which is 38 percent fat, can add distinct richness to sauces. Reducing heavy cream by boiling increases the concentration of fat globules to create the texture of a starch-thickened sauce. Cream was the only thickener we needed in our recipe for Creamed Kale with Chestnuts: **CooksCountry.com/ creamedkale**.

Butter
SMOOTH FINISHER

The ultimate sauce finisher, butter contributes a glossy sheen, richness, flavor, and thickening to pan sauces (and to custards like lemon curd). But in order to achieve the right body, it's important to add butter off the heat. Because butter is an emulsion that can be broken by high temperatures, at around 160 degrees your nicely thickened sauce will lose its body.

Egg Yolks
CURD, NOT CURDLED

Rich custards like crème anglaise and lemon curd rely on egg yolks to achieve a creamy texture. Temperature is key to their thickening ability: If the yolks get too hot, their proteins coagulate and lose water, leaving you with a curdled, watery sauce. The takeaway? Don't boil custards thickened with egg yolks; you'll know that your custard has thickened when a spatula leaves a clear trail in the pan.

Pectin
SURE JELLED

Commercial pectin begins with apple or citrus extract and is chemically processed to produce a dry, powdered substance. Unlike gelatin, regular pectin requires the presence of sugar and acid in order to gel (that's why there's special pectin for low-sugar jams and preserves). We use pectin to achieve strength without rubberiness in our Raspberry Chiffon Pie: **CooksCountry.com/raspberrychiffonpie**.

Potato Starch
QUICKER TO THICKEN

Potato starch begins to thicken liquid before it reaches a simmer, while other starches must simmer for several minutes first. But the large starch granules can cause finished sauces to appear grainy, and it tends to thin out after prolonged cooking. For best results, add potato starch later in the cooking process, and take your sauce or soup off the heat as soon as it thickens.

Tapioca
SLOW-COOKER HERO

Tapioca starch comes from the tropical root vegetable cassava, also called manioc or yuca. This neutral-tasting thickener can be an asset in some fruit pies and in the slow cooker. For our Slow-Cooker Hearty Beef Stew (**CooksCountry. com/slowcookerbeefstew**), Minute tapioca—our favorite brand—was able to maintain its power over long hours in the slow cooker (unlike flour and cornstarch).

Gelatin
GOOD FORM

We use this pure protein in a variety of ways in the test kitchen: to thicken soups and braises, to stabilize whipped cream, and to shore up fruit pies like our Icebox Strawberry Pie (**CooksCountry.com/ iceboxstrawberrypie**). Gelatin is sold in thin sheets and powdered. Both forms must be hydrated in cold water before being melted and incorporated. Basically, gelatin is used to turn liquids into solids (think your grandmother's green Jell-O fruit salad).

Arrowroot
CLEAR GEL

Arrowroot has almost twice the thickening power of flour. Unlike flour and cornstarch, it doesn't become cloudy as it thickens, so it leaves pie fillings and sauces clear. We've found arrowroot to have a slimy quality in recipes with dairy, so we don't recommend its use in puddings and custards. Arrowroot is almost as powerful as cornstarch; use 1½ teaspoons of arrowroot for every 1 teaspoon of cornstarch.

Okra
GUMBO ESSENTIAL

Okra has a long growing season in the southern United States. Elsewhere you're likely to find it frozen (we couldn't tell the difference between fresh and frozen when cooked). The long, green, tapered pods have a mild vegetable flavor that gets lost in spicy dishes; they're used for their sticky, mucilaginous insides. Once okra is sliced and its liquid is released, it becomes a thickener in Louisiana dishes like gumbo and étouffée.

Agar-Agar
SEAWEED STABILIZER

This complex carbohydrate is made from red algae, a form of seaweed. Available in flakes or powdered form, agar-agar has a thickening power similar to gelatin and is often used as a vegan alternative. The thickening strength can vary from brand to brand, but we generally found ¾ teaspoon of agar-agar flakes comparable to 1 teaspoon of gelatin when used to thicken 1 cup of liquid. Unlike gelatin, however, the agar-agar flakes need to soak in water for 10 minutes before the mixture is boiled for 10 minutes longer.

**PORK CHOPS WITH CHERRY TOMATOES
AND BALSAMIC REDUCTION**

STRIP STEAKS WITH HERB-HORSERADISH BUTTER

CUBAN QUESADILLAS

QUICK TURKEY CHILI

STRIP STEAKS WITH HERB-HORSERADISH BUTTER Serves 4

✔ **WHY THIS RECIPE WORKS:** Compound butters, like this one, are a quick and easy way to dress up any cut of meat or fish.

- 3 tablespoons unsalted butter, softened
- 2 tablespoons minced fresh chives
- 1 teaspoon prepared horseradish
- 1 teaspoon grated lemon zest plus 1 tablespoon juice
  Salt and pepper
  Pinch cayenne pepper
- 2 (1-pound) boneless strip or rib-eye steaks, about 1 inch thick, trimmed and halved crosswise
- 1 tablespoon vegetable oil

1. Combine butter, chives, horseradish, lemon zest and juice, ¼ teaspoon salt, ¼ teaspoon pepper, and cayenne in bowl; set aside.

2. Pat steaks dry with paper towels and season with salt and pepper. Heat oil in 12-inch skillet over medium-high heat until just smoking. Cook steaks until well browned and meat registers 125 degrees (for medium-rare), 3 to 5 minutes per side. Transfer to plate, tent loosely with foil, and let rest for 10 minutes. Divide butter among steaks and serve.

TEST KITCHEN NOTE: The test kitchen's preferred horseradish is Boar's Head Pure Horseradish.

PORK CHOPS WITH CHERRY TOMATOES AND BALSAMIC REDUCTION Serves 4

✔ **WHY THIS RECIPE WORKS:** After softening the cherry tomatoes in the skillet, we add balsamic vinegar and reduce the mixture to a potent glaze before finally enriching it with butter.

- 4 (8- to 10-ounce) bone-in pork rib chops, ½ inch thick, trimmed
  Salt and pepper
- 2 tablespoons vegetable oil
- 1 shallot, sliced thin
- 12 ounces cherry tomatoes, halved
- 2 garlic cloves, minced
- ⅓ cup balsamic vinegar
- 2 tablespoons unsalted butter
- 2 ounces blue cheese, crumbled (½ cup)
- ¼ cup chopped fresh basil

1. Pat pork dry with paper towels and season with salt and pepper. Heat oil in 12-inch skillet over medium-high heat until just smoking. Add pork and cook until well browned and cooked through, about 4 minutes per side; transfer to platter and tent loosely with foil.

2. Add shallot to now-empty skillet and cook until just softened, about 1 minute. Add tomatoes and cook until just softened, about 1 minute. Stir in garlic and cook until fragrant, about 30 seconds. Add vinegar, scraping up any browned bits, and cook until thickened and becoming syrupy, about 2 minutes.

3. Pour any accumulated meat juices from platter into skillet. Off heat, whisk in butter and season with salt and pepper to taste. Pour sauce over pork, top with blue cheese and basil, and serve.

QUICK TURKEY CHILI Serves 4

✔ **WHY THIS RECIPE WORKS:** Pureeing half the beans in broth helps thicken the chili and gives it a silky texture. We add the raw turkey straight to the chili so it stays in large chunks.

- 2 (15-ounce) cans pinto beans, rinsed
- 1½ cups chicken broth
- 2 tablespoons vegetable oil
- 1 onion, chopped fine
- 2 tablespoons chili powder
- 1 tablespoon ground cumin
- 3 garlic cloves, minced
- 1 teaspoon sugar
- 1 (4-ounce) can chopped green chiles
- 12 ounces ground turkey

1. Process 1 can of beans and ½ cup broth in food processor to coarse paste, about 10 seconds; set aside. Heat oil in Dutch oven over medium-high heat until just smoking. Add onion and cook until softened, about 5 minutes. Stir in chili powder, cumin, garlic, and sugar and cook until fragrant, about 1 minute. Stir in chiles, pureed bean-broth mixture, remaining can of beans, and remaining 1 cup broth.

2. Add turkey and stir to break up meat into large chunks. Bring to boil, reduce heat to medium-low, and simmer until chili is slightly thickened, 15 to 20 minutes. Serve.

TEST KITCHEN NOTE: Ground chicken is a fine substitute for turkey in this chili.

CUBAN QUESADILLAS Serves 4

✔ **WHY THIS RECIPE WORKS:** We decided to put a new twist on Cuban sandwiches and turn them into quesadillas. We combined sliced deli meats, Swiss cheese, and a quick pickle relish in flour tortillas. After giving them just a few minutes in the skillet, we had a tasty alternative to those well-known pressed sandwiches.

- ½ cup dill pickle chips, patted dry and chopped fine
- ¼ cup pickled banana pepper rings, patted dry and chopped fine
- 3 tablespoons yellow mustard
- 2 tablespoons mayonnaise
- ¼ teaspoon pepper
- 4 (10-inch) flour tortillas
- 8 ounces thinly sliced deli ham
- 8 ounces thinly sliced deli turkey
- 4 ounces sliced Swiss cheese
- 2 tablespoons vegetable oil

1. Combine pickles, banana peppers, mustard, mayonnaise, and pepper in bowl; set aside 2 tablespoons relish. Spread remaining relish over half of each tortilla (about 1½ tablespoons each), leaving ½-inch border around edge. Top relish side of each tortilla with one-quarter of ham, turkey, and Swiss cheese and fold tortilla over filling, pressing firmly to seal.

2. Heat 1 tablespoon oil in 12-inch nonstick skillet over medium-high heat until shimmering. Cook 2 quesadillas until golden brown and crispy, 1 to 2 minutes per side. Transfer to cutting board. Repeat with remaining 1 tablespoon oil and remaining 2 quesadillas. Cut into wedges and serve, passing reserved relish.

TEST KITCHEN NOTE: Patting the pickles and banana peppers dry helps keep these quesadillas crisp.

GNOCCHI WITH CREAMY TOMATO SAUCE

SPICY SHRIMP LETTUCE WRAPS WITH MANGO SALSA

LEMONY CHICKEN WITH WILTED SPINACH AND POTATOES

CARIBBEAN-STYLE CHICKEN WITH COCONUT MILK AND CILANTRO

SPICY SHRIMP LETTUCE WRAPS WITH MANGO SALSA
Serves 4

✓ **WHY THIS RECIPE WORKS:** For flavorful and tender shrimp, we toss them in a mixture of salt, pepper, and chili powder and cook them quickly in a hot skillet.

- ½ ripe mango, peeled and cut into ¼-inch pieces
- ½ red onion, chopped fine
- ¼ cup chopped fresh cilantro
- 1 jalapeño chile, stemmed, seeded, and minced
- 3 tablespoons olive oil
- 2 tablespoons lime juice
  Salt and pepper
- 1 pound extra-large shrimp (21 to 25 per pound), peeled, deveined, and tails removed, cut into ½-inch pieces
- 2 teaspoons chili powder
- 1 head Bibb lettuce (8 ounces), leaves separated

1. Combine mango, onion, cilantro, jalapeño, 1 tablespoon oil, lime juice, ½ teaspoon salt, and ¼ teaspoon pepper in bowl; set aside.

2. Pat shrimp dry with paper towels, season with salt and pepper, and sprinkle with chili powder. Heat remaining 2 tablespoons oil in 12-inch nonstick skillet over medium-high heat until just smoking. Add shrimp to skillet and cook until spotty brown and cooked through, about 4 minutes. Spoon shrimp into lettuce leaves and top with mango salsa. Serve.

TEST KITCHEN NOTE: If you cannot find Bibb lettuce, substitute 1 head green leaf lettuce.

GNOCCHI WITH CREAMY TOMATO SAUCE Serves 4

✓ **WHY THIS RECIPE WORKS:** We build deep flavor by cooking the browned gnocchi in a quick tomato sauce enriched with cream.

- ¼ cup extra-virgin olive oil
- 1 pound vacuum-packed gnocchi
- 1 onion, chopped fine
- 4 garlic cloves, minced
- 1 (28-ounce) can crushed tomatoes
- ½ cup water
  Salt and pepper
- ½ cup heavy cream
- 2 ounces Parmesan cheese, grated (1 cup)
- ½ cup chopped fresh basil

1. Adjust oven rack to upper-middle position and heat oven to 475 degrees. Heat 2 tablespoons oil in 12-inch nonstick skillet over medium-high heat until shimmering. Add gnocchi and cook until lightly browned, about 4 minutes; transfer to plate.

2. Add remaining 2 tablespoons oil and onion to now-empty skillet and cook until onion is softened, about 3 minutes. Stir in garlic and cook until fragrant, about 30 seconds. Stir in tomatoes, water, ½ teaspoon salt, and ½ teaspoon pepper and cook until slightly thickened, about 5 minutes.

3. Add cream and browned gnocchi to pan. Reduce heat to low and simmer, stirring occasionally, until gnocchi are tender, 5 to 7 minutes; transfer to 2-quart casserole dish. Sprinkle with Parmesan and bake until cheese is well browned, about 8 minutes. Sprinkle with basil and serve.

TEST KITCHEN NOTE: The partially cooked, vacuum-packed gnocchi found in the pasta aisle work best here, but refrigerated or frozen gnocchi can also be used.

CARIBBEAN-STYLE CHICKEN WITH COCONUT MILK AND CILANTRO Serves 4

✓ **WHY THIS RECIPE WORKS:** A potent mixture of coconut milk, jerk seasoning, and cayenne both seasons the chicken and acts as the base for the sauce.

- 6 (5- to 7-ounce) bone-in chicken thighs, trimmed
- 2 tablespoons jerk seasoning
  Pinch cayenne pepper
- 1 tablespoon vegetable oil
- 4 garlic cloves, sliced thin
- 1 (20-ounce) can pineapple chunks, drained
- 1 (13.5-ounce) can coconut milk
- ½ cup chopped fresh cilantro
  Salt and pepper
- ¼ cup cashews, toasted and crushed

1. Adjust oven rack to middle position and heat oven to 450 degrees. Pat chicken dry with paper towels and season with jerk seasoning and cayenne. Heat oil in 12-inch skillet over medium-high heat until shimmering. Add chicken, skin side down, and cook until well browned, about 5 minutes. (Do not flip.)

2. Transfer skillet to oven and roast until chicken registers 175 degrees, about 15 minutes. Transfer chicken to platter, skin side up, and tent loosely with foil. Pour off all but 2 tablespoons fat from skillet.

3. Return skillet to medium-high heat (handle will be very hot), add garlic, and cook until fragrant, about 30 seconds. Stir in pineapple and coconut milk, scraping up any browned bits. Bring to simmer and cook until slightly thickened, about 5 minutes. Stir in ¼ cup cilantro and season with salt and pepper to taste. Pour sauce over chicken. Sprinkle with cashews and remaining ¼ cup cilantro. Serve.

LEMONY CHICKEN WITH WILTED SPINACH AND POTATOES
Serves 4

✓ **WHY THIS RECIPE WORKS:** Browning the potatoes in the chicken drippings boosts their flavor.

- 1 pound fingerling potatoes, unpeeled, halved lengthwise
- 3 tablespoons extra-virgin olive oil
  Salt and pepper
- 4 (6- to 8-ounce) boneless, skinless chicken breasts, trimmed
- 3 tablespoons lemon juice
- 1 tablespoon unsalted butter
- 3 garlic cloves, minced
- 1 teaspoon minced fresh thyme
- 3 ounces (3 cups) baby spinach
- 2 ounces goat cheese, crumbled (½ cup)

1. Combine potatoes, 1 tablespoon oil, and ¼ teaspoon salt in bowl. Microwave, covered, until tender, about 7 minutes. Pat chicken dry with paper towels and season with salt and pepper. Heat 1 tablespoon oil in 12-inch nonstick skillet over medium-high heat until just smoking. Cook until chicken is browned and registers 160 degrees, about 6 minutes per side. Transfer to plate and tent loosely with foil.

2. Add potatoes to now-empty skillet, cut side down, and cook until golden brown, about 3 minutes. Stir in 2 tablespoons lemon juice, butter, garlic, thyme, and ¼ teaspoon pepper and cook until fragrant, about 30 seconds. Stir in spinach and cook until just wilted, about 30 seconds. Transfer potato mixture to platter, top with chicken, and drizzle with remaining 1 tablespoon lemon juice and remaining 1 tablespoon oil. Top with goat cheese and serve.

TEST KITCHEN NOTE: Jump-starting the potatoes in the microwave helps cut down on their skillet time.

French Toast Casserole

French toast casserole sounds like an ideal family breakfast, but only if the dish looks and tastes like breakfast, not dessert. BY ASHLEY MOORE

MAKING FRENCH TOAST is no sweat if it's just for a few people, but it can quickly turn laborious and time-consuming when you need to cook breakfast for a crowd. French toast casserole, a one-dish breakfast for six to eight people, solves that problem. No more standing at the stove flipping slice after slice, dripping egg wash on the counter, serving one person at a time.

The basic process for French toast casserole is straightforward and familiar. It goes something like this: Stack two layers of sliced bread in a casserole dish with plenty of brown sugar and cinnamon; pour an egg-and-milk mixture over the top and let it soak in; then slide the casserole into the oven for a half-hour or so. When it's done, you slice and serve it, dousing each stack of bread with maple syrup, and/or dusting it with confectioners' sugar. Couldn't be simpler.

Want some bacon the side? Read r taste test of permarket bacon CooksCountry.com/ permarketbacon.

But my initial tests of existing cookbook recipes quickly revealed the problem with this sunny scenario: All five versions that I tried looked and tasted a lot like bread pudding—soft and squishy and nothing like conventional crisp-crusted French toast. And though some did deliver decent flavor, all were too sweet, even before we poured on the syrup. I wanted this to look and taste like breakfast, not dessert.

The first decision I had to make was what kind of bread to use. White bread just disintegrated in the custard. Challah, while great for traditional skillet French toast, was too delicate for this oven version (because of the extra weight from stacking). A colleague suggested trying potato bread. I was skeptical, but the sturdy slices were just big enough to fit six per layer in the dish. But would they hold up to the custard? Yes: Potato bread soaked up the egg mixture and baked into a tidy casserole that was easily divided into two-slice portions.

But two layers of French toast in the casserole dish looked a little shallow and sad, and who wants a sad breakfast? I wondered if a triple-decker French toast casserole would work just as well.

I started with a dusting of brown sugar, cinnamon, and nutmeg in the bottom of a buttered dish to create a sweet base and help anchor my slices. Next came a layer of bread, followed by a sprinkle of the sugar mixture. I repeated with two more layers and then poured the egg mixture over everything. I slipped the dish into the oven (uncovered, so that the top would get a little bit browned) and crossed my fingers.

Success. The three-layer casserole worked just fine and looked and felt abundant and exciting when it came out of the oven. Individual portions served from the dish looked just like "real" French toast.

I'm not one to gild lilies, but this dish needed one last flourish: a sprinkle of toasted sliced almonds, a touch that produced a satisfying crunch.

Many recipes for French toast casserole call for soaking the bread in the custard overnight, which is a great idea if you'd like to do the work the night before and reap the benefits in the morning. We tested this technique with our recipe and it worked just fine. In fact, tasters noticed only a very slight texture difference in a side-by-side test between an overnight soak and no presoak at all. Good news for both planners and procrastinators.

FRENCH TOAST CASSEROLE
Serves 6 to 8

We developed this recipe using Martin's Potato Bread, which has 16 slices per loaf, so you'll need to buy two loaves. With other brands, it may also be necessary to trim the slices to fit six in a single layer.

- 1 tablespoon unsalted butter, softened, plus 6 tablespoons unsalted butter, melted
- ¾ cup packed (5¼ ounces) brown sugar
- 1 tablespoon ground cinnamon
- ½ teaspoon ground nutmeg
- ⅛ teaspoon salt
- 18 slices potato sandwich bread
- 2½ cups whole milk
- 6 large eggs
- ¼ cup sliced almonds, toasted Confectioners' sugar

1. Adjust oven rack to middle position and heat oven to 350 degrees. Grease 13 by 9-inch baking dish with softened butter. Mix brown sugar, cinnamon, nutmeg, and salt together in bowl.

2. Sprinkle 3 tablespoons brown sugar mixture evenly over bottom of prepared dish. Place 6 bread slices (use bread heels here) in even layer in bottom of dish. Brush bread with 1½ tablespoons melted butter and sprinkle with 3 tablespoons sugar mixture.

3. Place 6 bread slices in single layer over first layer, brush with 1½ tablespoons melted butter, then sprinkle with 3 tablespoons sugar mixture. Place remaining 6 bread slices over previous layer and brush with 1½ tablespoons melted butter.

4. In separate bowl, whisk milk and eggs together until well combined. Pour milk mixture over bread and press lightly to submerge. Sprinkle with almonds and remaining heaping 3 tablespoons sugar mixture.

5. Bake until casserole is slightly puffed and golden brown and bubbling around edges, about 30 minutes. Transfer casserole to wire rack, brush with remaining 1½ tablespoons melted butter, and let cool for 15 minutes. Sprinkle with confectioners' sugar and serve.

TO MAKE AHEAD

The assembled casserole, minus almonds and remaining heaping 3 tablespoons sugar mixture, can be covered and refrigerated for up to 12 hours. When ready to cook, sprinkle with almonds and sugar mixture and bake as directed in step 5.

This crowd-pleasing casserole can be baked right away or assembled the night before and baked in the morning.

New York Bialys

They're not well known outside New York City, but these savory rolls should be.

BY CRISTIN WALSH

KISSING COUSIN TO the bagel, the bialy was first brought to the United States by Jewish immigrants from Poland (specifically the city of Bialystok, in the northeast of the country) who settled in the lower part of Manhattan in the early 20th century (see "Bialys' Birthplace"). Downtown bakeries producing the golden, chewy, onion-and-poppy-seed-filled rolls eventually became so prevalent that the Lower East Side was once referred to as Bialy-town.

I searched our cookbook library for recipes, finding plenty that claimed to produce authentic New York bialys. But once I had mixed, kneaded, filled, and baked a few versions, I was left scratching my head. How could such disparate rolls all be "authentic"? I'd produced dense and chewy bialys, light and tender bialys, and a few in-betweens. And the onion fillings ran the gamut from dark to golden, from sweet to savory. With so many recipes leading me down such different paths, I decided a little legwork was in order to find out just what an authentic New York bialy should be.

Kossar's, the oldest bialy bakery in the United States, opened for business on the Lower East Side in 1934, and the bialys made there are considered the best and most authentic in the city. I got my hands on a batch and tried them for myself. The edges were puffed and lightly brown, with a generous dimple in the middle to hold the sweet onion filling. I was taken by the salty flavor and soft but chewy texture of the roll.

Back in the kitchen, the onion filling proved to be the easy part. Simply sautéing the finely chopped onions in olive oil with kosher salt until they were golden and sweet and then stirring in the poppy seeds created a perfect onion filling. I could turn my attention to the more complicated conundrum: the roll.

I started with a simple dough of bread flour, water, yeast, and salt. I allowed it to double in size and then shaped it into flat rounds, dimpled the rounds, and filled them with cooked onions before baking. The rolls were denser and chewier than those I had found in New York and lacked the distinctive salty flavor. So I upped the salt amount to a generous 2 tablespoons of kosher salt, and to address the discrepancy in the texture, I tried all-purpose flour rather than bread flour, thinking that its lower

Bialys are best eaten warm out of the oven, but they'll keep well (in an airtight container) for a few days on the kitchen counter.

gluten content would help tenderize the dough. The end product was two steps closer to my goal, but the rolls were still too tough.

The recipe I was using required an initial proof before portioning and shaping the rolls, but once shaped and filled, the rolls were immediately baked. Previous baking experience suggested that letting the dough rest after portioning it might give the gluten a chance to relax

and the yeast an opportunity to create bigger air pockets within the dough, ultimately producing more-tender bialys.

This time, after the initial rise, I shaped the dough into 12 equal-size balls and allowed them to rest at room temperature for an additional 30 minutes. After this second rise, I shaped the rested balls into 5-inch flat disks and gave them one more chance to rest before filling and baking. The texture

was improved, but the bialys were pale. I wanted a crusty exterior with golden-brown spots, so I turned to an obvious but often overlooked browning agent: sugar. The addition of just 1 tablespoon of sugar to the entire batch did wonders to improve the browning on the crust.

Finally, I had bialys that were golden brown, were tender yet chewy, and held just enough sweet onion filling to balance the salty flavor of the roll.

After dividing the dough and letting it rest, use this method to create the iconic shape.

MAKE A WELL
Use a greased and floured dry measuring cup to create a well in the center of the risen bialy dough.

ADD ONION MIXTURE
Fill the wells with about a tablespoon of our rich onion filling, and bake.

BIALYS Makes 12 bialys

If you substitute table salt for kosher, cut the salt amounts in half.

DOUGH

- 2 **cups warm water (110 degrees)**
- 1 **tablespoon sugar**
- 2 **teaspoons instant or rapid-rise yeast**
- 4¾ **cups (23¾ ounces) all-purpose flour**
- 2 **tablespoons kosher salt**

FILLING

- 3 **tablespoons olive oil**
- 3 **onions, chopped fine**
- 1 **teaspoon kosher salt**
- 1 **tablespoon poppy seeds**

1. FOR THE DOUGH: In bowl of stand mixer, combine warm water, sugar, and yeast and let sit until foamy, about 3 minutes. Add flour and salt to yeast mixture. Fit stand mixer with dough hook and knead on low speed until dough comes together, about 3 minutes.

2. Turn out dough onto lightly floured counter and knead by hand until smooth, about 1 minute. Transfer dough to greased bowl and cover tightly with plastic wrap. Let dough rise at room temperature until almost doubled in size, about 1 hour.

3. Line 2 rimmed baking sheets with parchment paper and lightly flour parchment. Gently press center of dough to deflate. Transfer dough to lightly floured counter and divide into 12 equal pieces. Form each piece into rough ball by pulling dough edges underneath so top is smooth. Arrange 6 balls on each prepared sheet and cover loosely with plastic. Let dough rise at room temperature for 30 minutes.

4. FOR THE FILLING: Heat oil in 12-inch nonstick skillet over medium heat until shimmering. Add onions and salt and cook until golden brown, about 10 minutes. Off heat, stir in poppy seeds.

5. Adjust oven racks to upper-middle and lower-middle positions and heat oven to 475 degrees. On lightly floured counter, use your hands to gently press each dough ball into 5-inch round.

Return to sheets and cover loosely with plastic. Let dough rise at room temperature until puffy, 15 to 20 minutes.

6. Grease and flour bottom of round 1-cup dry measuring cup (or 3-inch-diameter drinking glass). Press cup firmly into center of each dough round until cup touches sheet to make indentation for filling. (Reflour cup as needed to prevent sticking.)

7. Divide filling evenly among bialys (about 1 heaping tablespoon each) and smooth with back of spoon. Bake until spotty golden brown, 15 to 20 minutes, rotating and switching sheets halfway through baking. Transfer bialys to wire rack and let cool for 10 minutes. Serve.

Back Story
Bialys' Birthplace

When food writer Mimi Sheraton set out in 1992 to discover the origins of the bialy, she went straight to the widely acknowledged source: Bialystok, Poland. But the trail was cold; no bakeries in Bialystok sold bialys. After interviewing far-flung former Bialystokers from New York to Argentina, Sheraton learned that while the bialy (*bialystoker kuchen*) was known in Bialystok in the early 1900s, the story of its origin had been lost. In her 2000 book *The Bialy Eaters*, Sheraton wrote: "It is doubtful that anyone will ever know unequivocally who first formed a bialystoker kuchen and when. My guess is that it originated by accident as a variation on the more ubiquitous *pletzl* . . . Given the random fickleness of fate, I conjecture that one day an unbaked pletzl fell onto a bakery floor and was stepped on with the heel of a shoe. Not wanting to waste anything, the frugal baker topped it with onions and poppy seeds, baked it, tasted it, and proclaimed it a eureka moment in bread history."

TESTING INEXPENSIVE ELECTRIC CITRUS JUICERS

One lemon for a vinaigrette is easy enough to juice by hand, but for larger extraction projects we use an electric citrus juicer. A good one should extract maximum juice with minimal effort and be easy to clean and store. Our favorite electric citrus juicer, the Breville Stainless Steel Juicer, is all those things, but at $200, it's an investment. Could we find a good citrus juicer for less than $100?

We compared seven models priced from $20 to $82; all have a spinning reamer that you hand-push a halved citrus fruit into to force out the juice. We juiced 10 limes, 10 oranges, and 10 grapefruits with each and measured how much juice they pressed from the fruit, and how quickly. We also considered how challenging they were to use, clean, and store, and how quietly they operated.

Except for the motorized bases, all the juicer parts are top-rack dishwasher-safe. Only one was annoying to clean: It has six detachable parts, and some were hard to snap together. We docked points accordingly.

Two juicers trap the juice in attached carafes; five just dispense their juice from a spout, it's up to you to capture the juice. We preferred attached carafes.

Testers found that a good juicer can extract 30 percent more juice than a bad one. The difference? Their reamers. If the ridges were too sharp, they cut into the fruit, sectioning it and spinning it around instead of pushing into the pulp; too dull and they left good juice behind. The best juicers came with two medium-ridged reamers that could accommodate fruit of different sizes.

The Dash Go Dual Citrus Juicer was the ultimate victor; while it's not as sturdy, powerful, or easy to use as the $200 Breville, it's quiet and smooth, and it plowed through the fruit with ease. The second-place model, the Black & Decker Citrus Juicer, is our previous Best Buy; it was redesigned since we last tested. It worked well, but its motor is louder, and while it never stopped working, testers did note a burning smell toward the end of big jobs. Visit **CooksCountry.com/mar15** for the full testing story and results chart. –HANNAH CROWLEY

TOO DULL
Poor reamers leave too much juice in the fruit.

JUST RIGHT
The best reamers leave little behind.

KEY **Good** ★★★ **Fair** ★★ **Poor** ★

HIGHLY RECOMMENDED	CRITERIA		TESTERS' NOTES
DASH Go Dual Citrus Juicer **Price:** $19.99 **Model:** JB065	Juice Extraction Cleanup Ease of Use	★★★ ★★★ ★★★	This juicer expertly and securely extracted juice with two sizes of medium-ridged reamers. An attached carafe saved us from spills and detached easily for table use. It's cheap, light, and easy to clean, with a screen for adjusting pulp levels and a quiet motor that won't wake late sleepers.
RECOMMENDED			
BLACK & DECKER Citrus Juicer **Price:** $19.99 **Model:** CJ625	Juice Extraction Cleanup Ease of Use	★★★ ★★★ ★★½	This juicer has both large and small reamers with sharp ridges that efficiently juiced citrus of all sizes. It has an adjustable pulp screen and was light, cheap, and easy to clean. It has a sturdy attached carafe and a nice pouring spout so it can be used at the table, but its louder motor is less preferable for quiet mornings.
RECOMMENDED WITH RESERVATIONS			
JUICEMAN Citrus Juicer **Price:** $29.99 **Model:** JCJ4000S	Juice Extraction Cleanup Ease of Use	★★★ ★★★ ★★	This juicer's large and small reamers have deep ridges that scoured the last drop of juice from citrus of all sizes. It spun the fastest, so it juiced quickly and efficiently, but it doesn't have an attached carafe and it stuttered occasionally, which didn't impede juicing but made us suspicious of its motor.
NOT RECOMMENDED			
DASH Citrus Bar **Price:** $49.99 **Model:** DCJ001SIL	Juice Extraction Cleanup Ease of Use	★ ★ ★	This is the only machine that juices two fruit halves at once, but it wasn't any faster. Its reamer's ridges were too sharp and cut into the fruit instead of pressing out the juice. Oranges were OK, but limes proved too small and grapefruits too large. Cleanup was a pain, too, with lots of individual pieces that were fussy to snap together.

Poppy Seed Chicken Casserole

This Southern staple often starts with canned soup. We aimed for a fresher take.

BY ASHLEY MOORE

PAY A VISIT to the Blue Willow Inn restaurant in Social Circle, Georgia, for a buffet lunch and you may encounter the poppy seed chicken casserole, a rich, creamy, savory chicken dish with a crunchy cracker topping that was once widespread in the American South.

I found existing recipes in regional and historic cookbooks and cooked up five versions for a tasting in the test kitchen. These first attempts resulted in heavy, creamy, gelatinous messes with bland, artificial flavor. Comments ranged from the generous "not awful" to the more precise "gross." "Only one way to go from here—up!" said one optimistic taster.

Down but not out, I quizzed a colleague from the South who remembered this casserole from her childhood and encouraged me to persevere. And so, determined, I took a red pen to my ingredient list. Out went the cans of soup; in came fresh mushrooms and chicken broth. Out went the three sticks of butter; in came white wine and fresh thyme. (Don't worry, I kept some heavy cream in the mix. This isn't a spa dish, after all.)

Drawing on established test kitchen knowledge, I knew that simply stirring together mushrooms, onions, chicken broth, and cream would net a loose, crumbly casserole. To get a creamy dish, I needed to thicken the sauce. A béchamel base (flour cooked with butter and then milk, the same sauce used to bind traditional macaroni and cheese) seemed too laborious, and a test using a cornstarch slurry introduced an off-putting flavor. Simply sprinkling flour over the mushrooms and onions as they cooked created a strong base for the broth and cream to build on. For an even more velvety texture, I stirred in ½ cup of cream cheese.

The casserole needs cooked chicken, but rather than baking or poaching chicken as part of my prep, I decided to save myself some time by using meat torn from a store-bought rotisserie chicken. A tablespoon of poppy seeds stirred into the mix gave the dish its traditional signature look (and a very faint pop of texture).

At this point, I had this casserole's

> What brand of chicken broth should you buy? Go to CooksCountry.com/chickenbrothtasting to read our taste test of supermarket broths.

base down pat. But what about the crunchy topping? Existing recipes called for crushed Town House crackers or Ritz Crackers. Why leave this element to chance? I prepared two casseroles, one with a Ritz-based topping, the other with Town House. The crushed Ritz, stirred with melted butter and a few additional poppy seeds, baked up just a bit more brown, crunchy, and flavorful. The toughest part now was waiting around for this savory Southern dish to cool down enough to eat.

POPPY SEED CHICKEN CASSEROLE

Serves 6

To crush the Ritz Crackers, seal them in a large zipper-lock bag and smack them with a rolling pin or heavy saucepan.

- 4 tablespoons unsalted butter
- 1 pound white mushrooms, trimmed and sliced thin
- 1 onion, halved and sliced thin
- 1 teaspoon minced fresh thyme
  Salt and pepper
- ½ cup dry white wine
- ¼ cup all-purpose flour
- 1¾ cups chicken broth
- 1 cup heavy cream
- 4 ounces cream cheese
- 1 (2½-pound) rotisserie chicken, skin and bones discarded, meat shredded into bite-size pieces (3 cups)
- 2 tablespoons poppy seeds
- 15 Ritz Crackers, crushed coarse

1. Adjust oven rack to middle position and heat oven to 350 degrees. Melt 2 tablespoons butter in Dutch oven over medium-high heat. Add mushrooms, onion, thyme, 1 teaspoon salt, and 1 teaspoon pepper and cook, stirring occasionally, until liquid has evaporated and mushrooms begin to brown, 5 to 7 minutes. Add wine and cook until evaporated, about 3 minutes.

2. Stir in flour until vegetables are well coated and cook for 1 minute. Stir in broth and cream, scraping up any browned bits, and cook until slightly thickened, about 3 minutes. Stir in cream cheese and cook until melted, about 2 minutes. Stir in chicken and 1 tablespoon poppy seeds. Remove from heat and season with salt and pepper to taste. Transfer chicken mixture to 8-inch square baking dish.

3. Microwave remaining 2 tablespoons

Fresh mushrooms and dry white wine help us reinvent this buffet favorite.

butter in medium bowl until melted, about 20 seconds. Add crackers and remaining 1 tablespoon poppy seeds and toss to combine. Sprinkle cracker mixture evenly over chicken mixture. Bake casserole until topping is golden brown and filling is bubbling around edges, about 15 minutes. Let cool for 15 minutes before serving.

TO MAKE AHEAD

The casserole can be prepared through step 2, covered, and refrigerated for up to 24 hours. When ready to cook, microwave chicken mixture in baking dish, uncovered, until hot in center, about 5 minutes, stirring halfway through cooking. Sprinkle cracker mixture over top and bake casserole as directed in step 3.

KEY INGREDIENT Poppy Seeds

Poppy seeds are harvested from the dried pods of the *Papaver somniferum* plant, which also contains the raw material used to make opium. The seeds have no narcotic effects, but they can go rancid, so freeze them in an airtight container for up to six months.

SAFE SEEDS These won't make you sleepy.

Winter Vegetable Hash

Who says hash needs meat? The right mixture of vegetables, browned and cooked to tenderness, does the trick just fine. BY CHRISTIE MORRISON

HASH IS OFTEN a raid-the-refrigerator kind of dish, traditionally made with pieces of last night's meat plus potatoes and any other vegetables you have on hand. Mash it together, fry it up until crisp, and you're good to go. But you don't need meat to make a great hash. I set out to build a hearty vegetable hash that would work equally well at breakfast, lunch, or dinner.

I started by choosing vegetables that are available year-round so that I could enjoy this recipe even in the wintertime: Brussels sprouts, carrots, and potatoes, plus onion and garlic. But hashing together vegetables of very different densities presented a challenge: cooking times. The dense potatoes and carrots would take longer to soften than the leafy Brussels sprouts. Normally, we'd get around this by precooking the spuds and roots, but the last thing I wanted to do was haul out another pot. Cutting the potatoes and carrots into ½-inch pieces and starting them together in the microwave with a little oil solved the problem, coaxing them toward tender in only 6 minutes. While that was going on, I could prep the Brussels sprouts.

Brussels sprouts are typically shredded, sliced, halved, or cut into wedges when cooked into dishes like hash. I tried each preparation in the skillet but found that the first two tended to steam rather than brown—and good browning is what really elevates this vegetable to something special (steamed Brussels sprouts can have an unpleasant, sulfury taste). Halving or cutting the sprouts into wedges, on the other hand, provided nice flat surfaces that picked up flavorful browning. But the lack of moisture in the pan prevented the sprouts from cooking through, leaving me with halves or wedges that, while beautifully browned, were still undercooked and tough.

I looked at my bowl of microwaved potatoes and carrots. In addition to the tablespoon of oil I'd added to help steam the vegetables, there was now extra moisture from the cooked vegetables. If I added this liquid to the skillet along with the vegetables, would I have enough liquid to soften the browned sprouts?

Only one way to find out. I added the lot, covered the skillet, and cooked the vegetables for about 5 minutes,

giving them a stir halfway through. Sure enough, the sprouts softened right up and the precooked potatoes and carrots browned nicely.

I added some fresh thyme for savory depth and a tablespoon of butter for richness and shine, plus a few sliced scallions (both the white and green parts) for a fresh kick, and my hash was ready for the table—breakfast, lunch, or dinner.

BRUSSELS SPROUT AND POTATO HASH
Serves 4

Red potatoes are best here because their sturdy nature means they won't break apart in the hash. Look for small Brussels sprouts, no bigger than a golf ball, as they're likely to be sweeter and more tender than large sprouts. If you can find only large sprouts, halve them and cut each half into thirds.

- 1 pound red potatoes, unpeeled, cut into ½-inch chunks
- 2 carrots, peeled and cut into ½-inch chunks
- 3 tablespoons olive oil
  Salt and pepper
- 1 pound Brussels sprouts, trimmed and quartered lengthwise
- 1 onion, chopped fine
- 2 tablespoons water
- 1 tablespoon minced fresh thyme
- 1 garlic clove, minced
- 1 tablespoon unsalted butter
- 2 scallions, sliced thin

1. Toss potatoes, carrots, 1 tablespoon oil, ½ teaspoon salt, and ¼ teaspoon pepper together in large bowl. Cover and microwave until tender, 5 to 7 minutes, stirring halfway through cooking.

2. Meanwhile, heat 1 tablespoon oil in 12-inch nonstick skillet over medium-high heat until shimmering. Add Brussels sprouts and cook until browned, 6 to 8 minutes, stirring occasionally. Add onion, water, thyme, garlic, microwaved vegetables, remaining 1 tablespoon oil, ¾ teaspoon salt, and ¼ teaspoon pepper. Reduce heat to medium, cover, and cook until Brussels sprouts are tender, 5 to 7 minutes longer, stirring halfway through cooking.

3. Off heat, stir in butter and season with salt and pepper to taste. Sprinkle with scallions and serve.

This hearty vegetable hash is equally great as a side dish to roasted meats or for breakfast with an egg on top.

TEST KITCHEN TECHNIQUE **Cooking Brussels Sprouts Properly**
Brussels sprouts are dense, meaning that it's easy to achieve deep browning before they're cooked through. Here's how we make sure they're brown *and* tender.

1. QUARTER
Trim the sprouts, then quarter them through the stem; this helps them hold together.

2. BROWN
Sear the sprouts in oil to create flavorful browning.

3. ADD WATER
Just a little water creates enough steam to cook the Brussels sprouts through.

Chocolate Chess Pie

We knew that introducing smooth, silky chocolate to this simple Southern pie would instantly elevate the dish, if only we could make it work. (We did.) BY AARON FURMANEK

WHAT'S THE POINT of chess pie? Simplicity, of course, coupled with plenty of sweetness. Chess pies—creamy custards baked in pie shells—are country-kitchen staples, delivering a soothing dose of comfort with accessible ingredients and a minimum of effort. They are everyday pies, easy to make, easy to love, charming, and, dare I say, humble—in the very best sense of the word.

The test kitchen has visited this territory before with recipes for lemon chess pie and buttermilk pie. But we wanted to take chess pie in a more luxurious direction with chocolate. I found several existing recipes for chocolate chess pie in my initial research, but none agreed on exactly what this pie should be: Some described the pie as "rich" and "fudgy," while others claimed to produce pies that were "buttery" or "creamy." I knew I wanted something sweet, soft, soothing, and with big chocolate flavor that was nowhere near bitter. It was time to get to work.

Per our usual process, I started by preparing and tasting pies made using the recipes I'd found. They mostly followed the same procedure: Stir together melted butter and chocolate (either cocoa powder or melted baking chocolate) with granulated sugar; beat in a few eggs; add vanilla and sometimes cream, milk, buttermilk, or evaporated milk; and bake in a partially baked pie shell. A few of the pies also called for a bit of cornmeal—a typical ingredient in chess pie—to help create the textural contrast of the thin top layer.

My panel of tasters and I were surprised at how varied these first pies were. Some were dense and fudgy, while others were light, thin, and almost runny. I decided I'd aim for a pie that was big on chocolate flavor, but light on texture—a soft custard with a delicate, sugary crust on top.

I took various elements from these recipes to create a rough working recipe. We preferred the richness of pies made with melted unsweetened chocolate to those made with cocoa. We favored a little cream over tangy buttermilk or cloying evaporated milk. And after two or three tries, I settled on four eggs, plus two additional yolks, for the silkiest, creamiest texture. Three tablespoons of flour helped everything

A sprinkle of sugar just before baking helps form the crackly top layer of the pie.

cohere enough to slice neatly.

The biggest bugaboo in my testing proved to be the baking temperature: Custards are notoriously fussy in the oven. Most of my initial recipes called for pies to be cooked at anywhere from 325 degrees to 375 degrees. After testing several pies, I found that baking at 350 degrees and higher caused the eggs to puff too much, cooking the outside of the filling faster than the inside and

resulting in a collapsed, sunken pie. I found that a 325-degree oven and a 35- to 40-minute baking time gave me the most consistent pie, with a softly textured but fully cooked custard, a satisfying chocolate flavor, and a golden-brown shell.

Now for the final touch: The delicate crackly crust atop the custard. My tasters weren't fond of cornmeal's flavor in this chocolate pie. Instead, I sprinkled an

even coat of granulated sugar over the pie just as I was putting it in the oven. The resulting crisp, delicate sugar crust provided that extra textural contrast I wanted.

It took many experiments—and plenty of failed pies—to get there, but finally I had a handsome chocolate chess pie that was simple to prepare, as promised, but thanks to the chocolate, full of complex luxury, too.

CHOCOLATE CHESS PIE

Serves 8 to 12

Our preferred unsweetened chocolate is Hershey's Unsweetened Baking Bar. Take care when melting the chocolate in the microwave, using only 50 percent power and stopping to stir every 30 seconds or so. This pie needs to sit for 4 hours after baking to set up. Serve with our Tangy Whipped Cream, if desired.

1	(9-inch) store-bought pie dough round
12	tablespoons unsalted butter, cut into 12 pieces
3	ounces unsweetened chocolate, chopped
1½	cups (10½ ounces) plus 1 teaspoon sugar
3	tablespoons all-purpose flour
½	teaspoon salt
4	large eggs plus 2 large yolks
¼	cup heavy cream
1½	teaspoons vanilla extract

> ● Find the recipe for our **Lemon Chess Pie** at CooksCountry.com/lemonchesspie. Checkmate.

TANGY WHIPPED CREAM

Makes 1½ cups

Be sure that the heavy cream and sour cream are cold before whipping.

1	cup heavy cream, chilled
¼	cup sour cream, chilled
¼	cup packed (1¾ ounces) light brown sugar
⅛	teaspoon vanilla extract

Using stand mixer fitted with whisk, whip all ingredients together on medium-low speed until foamy, about 1 minute. Increase speed to high and whip until soft peaks form, 1 to 3 minutes.

1. Adjust oven rack to middle position and heat oven to 375 degrees. Roll dough into 12-inch circle on lightly floured counter. Loosely roll dough around rolling pin and gently unroll it onto greased 9-inch pie plate, letting excess dough hang over edge. Ease dough into plate by gently lifting edge of dough with your hand while pressing into plate bottom with your other hand.

2. Trim overhang to ½ inch beyond lip of plate. Tuck overhang under itself; folded edge should be flush with edge of plate. Crimp dough evenly around edge of pie using your fingers. Wrap dough-lined plate loosely in plastic and freeze until dough is firm, about 15 minutes.

3. Line chilled pie shell with 2 (12-inch) squares of parchment paper, letting parchment lie over edges of dough, and fill with pie weights. Bake until lightly golden around edges, 18 to 25 minutes. Carefully remove parchment and weights, rotate crust, and continue to bake until center begins to look opaque and slightly drier, 3 to 6 minutes. Remove from oven and let cool completely. Reduce oven temperature to 325 degrees.

4. Microwave butter and chocolate in bowl at 50 percent power, stirring occasionally, until melted, about 2 minutes.

In separate bowl, whisk 1½ cups sugar, flour, and salt together until combined. Whisk eggs and yolks, cream, and vanilla into sugar mixture until combined. Whisk chocolate mixture into sugar-egg mixture until fully incorporated and no streaks remain.

5. Pour filling into cooled pie shell. Sprinkle top of pie with remaining 1 teaspoon sugar. Bake until center of pie is just set and registers 180 degrees, 35 to 40 minutes. (Slight crust will form on top.) Transfer to wire rack and let cool completely, about 4 hours. Serve. (Pie can be refrigerated for up to 4 days. Bring to room temperature before serving.)

WHAT CAN GO WRONG Common Pitfalls for Custard Pies

SLUMPED CRUST
Our method calls for filling a chilled pie shell filled with pie weights (set on parchment paper in the shell) before prebaking. If you don't use pie weights when prebaking, your crust may shrink and pull away from the edges of the pie plate, and its compromised structure may leave your pie with a soggy bottom.

RUNNY SLICES
It's not easy to wait for dessert, but it's important to allow custard pies to cool and set up for at least 4 hours for clean, even slices. Slicing and serving the pie before it's completely cooled and set will result in pudding on a plate. Still delicious, but not exactly the look you want.

The American Table
What's in a Name? Or the Case of the Missing "E"

Chess pie is really a catchall term for a whole category of one-crust custard pies, from lemon to chocolate. Though now best known as a Southern dessert, chess pies were common fare across North America at least as far back as the early 19th century, and likely even before that—some culinary historians believe that English settlers brought the pie over to the New World as early as the 17th century.

But where did its curious name come from?

While Mary Randolph's 1825 cookbook *The Virginia House-wife* contained a recipe for "Transparent Pudding," which is essentially a chess pie with a different name, the earliest published recipe we could find for a pie called "chess" was in the October 1866 edition of *American Agriculturalist*. A reader named Mrs. Samuel P. May, from Grimes County, Texas, submitted the recipe for the simple custard pie, which she called "the best pie we ever ate," to the periodical; editors loved and printed the recipe.

One derivation theory suggests that "chess" pie is a merely a clipped version of "chest" pie, meaning it could be stored in a nonrefrigerated pie chest. Another theory points to a colloquialism along the lines of, "it's no big deal, it's jes' (chess) pie."

But the most likely etymology ties chess pie to an archaic English spelling of "cheese," which was often spelled with just one "e" in the middle: chese. According to culinary historian and Southern food expert Damon Lee Fowler, the word "cheese," or "chese," was often used to signify the types of curds and custards commonly used in single-crust pies. Linguistic license, which early Americans were fond of exercising, allowed cheese pie, or chese pie, to become chess pie.

Cooking Class Pub-Style Burgers

Getting a flawless, juicy pub-style skillet burger starts at the butcher counter.

BY BRYAN ROOF

PUB-STYLE BURGERS
Serves 4

Sirloin steak tips are also sold as flap meat. You will need to freeze the meat for 35 minutes before processing it. Be gentle when shaping the patties, taking care not to overwork the meat so the burgers won't become dense. Serve with your favorite toppings.

- 2 pounds sirloin steak tips, trimmed of excess fat and cut into ½-inch chunks
- 4 tablespoons unsalted butter, melted and cooled slightly
  Salt and pepper
- 1 teaspoon vegetable oil
- 4 hamburger buns, toasted and buttered

1. Place steak on baking sheet in single layer. Freeze steak until very firm and starting to harden around edges but still pliable, about 35 minutes.

2. Place one-quarter of steak in food processor and pulse until finely ground into ¹⁄₁₆-inch pieces, about 35 pulses, stopping to redistribute around bowl as necessary to ensure meat is evenly ground. Transfer meat to second baking sheet. Repeat with remaining 3 batches of steak. Spread meat over sheet and inspect carefully, discarding any long strands of gristle or large chunks of hard meat or fat.

3. Adjust oven rack to middle position and heat oven to 300 degrees.

Drizzle butter over ground meat and add 1 teaspoon pepper. Gently toss with fork to combine. Divide meat into 4 lightly packed balls. Gently flatten into patties ¾ inch thick and about 4½ inches in diameter. (Patties can be refrigerated, covered, for up to 1 day.)

4. Season 1 side of patties liberally with salt and pepper. Using spatula, flip patties and season other side. Heat oil in 12-inch skillet over high heat until just smoking. Using spatula, transfer burgers to skillet and cook without moving them for 2 minutes. Using spatula, flip burgers and cook for 2 minutes longer. Transfer patties to rimmed baking sheet. Bake until burgers register 125 degrees for medium-rare or 130 degrees for medium, 3 to 6 minutes.

5. Transfer burgers to plate and let rest for 5 minutes. Transfer to buns and serve.

PUB-STYLE BURGER SAUCE
Makes about 1 cup

- ¾ cup mayonnaise
- 2 tablespoons soy sauce
- 1 tablespoon packed dark brown sugar
- 1 tablespoon Worcestershire sauce
- 1 tablespoon minced fresh chives
- 1 garlic clove, minced
- ¾ teaspoon pepper

Whisk all ingredients together in bowl.

STEP-BY-STEP **Ten Steps to Juicy Pub-Style Burgers**

1. FREEZE
Freeze ½-inch chunks of steak on a baking sheet just until very firm and starting to harden around the edges.
WHY? Firm, slightly frozen meat is chopped more efficiently in the food processor; meat straight from the fridge smears and tears.

2. GRIND
Pulse the meat until finely ground into ¹⁄₁₆-inch pieces.
WHY? A coarse grind stays loosely packed, ensuring a tender burger.

3. INSPECT
Spread the meat over a baking sheet and inspect carefully, discarding any long strands of gristle or large chunks of hard meat or fat.
WHY? Gristle and fat get in the way of the delicate texture of the freshly ground meat.

4. ADD BUTTER
Drizzle butter over ground meat and add 1 teaspoon of pepper.
WHY? Gently working melted butter into the ground meat not only ensures that the burgers cook up juicy but also encourages flavorful browning.

5. USE FORK
Resist the urge to mix the meat with your hands and use a fork instead.
WHY? A fork will help distribute the butter more evenly and keep the meat grind loose.

Core Techniques

Add Fat

Leaner cuts make the best burgers, because fattier cuts come with baggage—more gristle and sinew that can make them hard to chew even after grinding. Incorporating extra fat (in this case, butter) into lean ground meat before cooking does more than just add flavor; it also dials up the juiciness on the inside of the burger and encourages browning in the pan for faintly crisp edges. This works well in any burger recipe, particularly ones that call for leaner meats like chicken, turkey, or fish. Starting with a lean cut and adding in your own fat also allows you to control how much fat ultimately ends up in your burger.

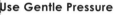

Use Gentle Pressure

Whenever working with ground meat, shape the patties with a gentle hand. The meat will adhere as it cooks to create a cohesive burger. If you pack the patties too tightly, the meat will bind too tightly, and you'll end up with tough, dry, chewy burgers. Our favorite technique is to start with a loosely packed ball of meat and then gently pat it down to a ¾-inch-thick disk.

Cook Twice

The key to thick skillet burgers with a crisp, seared exterior and a juicy medium-rare interior is a two-step process: first a hot sear on the stovetop to create a nice brown crust and then a visit to a relatively low, 300-degree oven to bring the interior of the burger to medium-rare or medium without leaving the exterior leathery or burnt. (For beef, 125 degrees is the goal for medium-rare; 130 degrees for medium.)

Ground Meat Primer

Why Grind at Home?

Meat ground at home has much better texture and flavor than supermarket ground beef. What's more, by purchasing intact cuts of meat and grinding the meat yourself, you know exactly what's in your burger. No pink slime here, and you can safely cook to medium-rare without worry. We've found that a food processor is an excellent tool for grinding meat at home, producing a coarse grind that's perfect for burgers. But the food processor doesn't grind the meat as finely as a commercial meat grinder, so stray pieces of gristle are more obvious. To avoid these pockets of chewy gristle, purchase a cut of meat that has little sinew, like sirloin steak tips (aka flap meat), and inspect the meat closely after it's ground. Low-sinew burgers are also lower in fat, but don't worry about the lower fat content producing dry or tough burgers—that's why we add butter to the mix.

Best Cuts to Grind for Burgers

We recommend grinding sirloin steak tips for these burgers, but short ribs and well-trimmed chuck roast also have the right texture and fat content (you still should add the butter). Avoid the round, which has a tendency to have liver-like flavors.

DON'T MAKE THIS MISTAKE Eating in Haste

To make sure our thick burgers are cooked correctly, we sear them in a skillet (for a flavorful brown crust) and finish cooking them in the oven. But that's not the end of the story; it is imperative that you let the cooked burgers sit undisturbed for 5 minutes before tucking into them. Why? Heat forces the meat's juices to the center of the burger, and if you cut (or bite) into a burger straight out of the oven, those collected juices will spurt out. A short rest allows the juices to redistribute evenly back into the meat so that the burger is moist and juicy.

UNRESTED BURGER
If you don't let your burgers rest for 5 minutes after you take them out of the oven, you run the risk of losing all their juices.

6. FORM
Divide the meat into four lightly packed balls and then gently flatten into ¾-inch-thick patties, about 4½ inches in diameter.
WHY? Forming the patties gently helps prevent overworking the meat, which can make for tough burgers.

7. SALT NOW
Sprinkle the patties with salt and pepper.
WHY? Salting is essential for a well-seasoned burger, but salt also removes water from the meat—not a path to a tender burger, so don't salt too early.

8. SEAR
Cook the burgers briefly on each side over high heat until well browned.
WHY? This will caramelize the exterior of the meat and form a flavorful crust.

9. BAKE
Transfer the burgers to a baking sheet and bake in a low, 300-degree oven until they reach the desired temperature.
WHY? Searing on the stove and finishing in a low-heat oven ensures a well-browned crust and juicy center.

10. LET REST
Transfer the burgers to a plate and let rest for 5 minutes.
WHY? Resting allows the juices to redistribute evenly throughout the patty.

Slow Cooker Hungarian Goulash

This beef stew should be rich, beefy, and full of sweet pepper flavor. Sounds like a job for the slow cooker. BY DIANE UNGER

BEEF, SLOWLY SIMMERED to tenderness with onion, carrot, garlic, sweet paprika, tomato paste, sweet peppers, and broth and then enriched with a stir of sour cream and spooned over egg noodles: There is a lot to like about Hungarian goulash. I hoped that making this dish in the slow cooker would save effort while still producing a complex, richly flavored stew.

Many goulash recipes call for starting on the stovetop, browning cubes of stew beef in batches and removing it from the pan, sautéing aromatics and spices in the drippings, stirring in flour and broth, and then transferring the mixture to the oven to slowly and evenly cook until the meat is tender. But I wanted to see if I could make slow-cooker goulash without having to brown the meat.

I turned to the test kitchen's great recipe for this stew that skips the stovetop browning, instead leaving the stew uncovered in the oven to let the meat above the surface of the liquid brown in the dry heat. I was pretty sure it wouldn't work in a covered slow cooker (slow cookers don't get hot enough if you keep the cover off), but I tried it anyway; sure enough, it failed. The stew turned out watery, with muted flavors. I needed to figure out the best way to adapt this recipe to the moist environment of the slow cooker.

Big Paprika Punch

We use a full ⅓ cup of sweet paprika—about twice the amount used in some other recipes—as the key seasoning in our Slow-Cooker Hungarian Goulash. To extract the most flavor from this mild spice, we combine it with roasted red peppers, tomato paste, and vinegar. But we don't stop there. We then sauté this mixture to "bloom" the flavors before adding it to the slow cooker with the beef. The result? Incredible depth of flavor.

OUR FAVORITE
Earthy, fruity paprika from **The Spice House.**

A puree of roasted red peppers, lots of paprika, tomato paste, and vinegar forms the backbone of the sauce.

I rebooted and started over with the same test kitchen version, knowing I'd make some changes along the way. I salted the cubed beef chuck-eye roast (our preferred cut for braising) to start the seasoning process. I cooked 6 cups of diced onion and 4 carrots (cut into 1-inch pieces) until the vegetables had softened. To that, I added a pureed mixture of drained, jarred roasted red peppers, a full ⅓ cup of sweet Hungarian paprika, a bit of tomato paste to deepen the flavor, and vinegar for balance.

When developing this recipe, we found that the key to bringing out the full sweet, peppery flavor of the paprika was to cook the mixture until it had reduced, concentrated, and turned a deep rust color. Instead of deglazing the pot with 1 cup of beef broth as the recipe called for, I scaled back the liquid to just 5 tablespoons so the stew wouldn't be watery.

I did a side-by-side test and found that when I used only 5 tablespoons of liquid, tasters couldn't tell the difference between a goulash made with beef broth and one made with water, so I went

with the latter. I stirred the mixture into the cubed beef in the slow cooker, put the cover on, and felt my hopes rise as I turned it on.

After the slow cooker ran for about 7 hours on high heat, I lifted off the cover and took a step back. How could the goulash still be so watery? On further consideration, I knew that the liquid had to have come from the beef as the stew cooked. To tighten it up, this stew needed a stiff shot of . . . something.

In my next round of tests, I added flour to the sautéed vegetables in increasing increments until I settled on 3 tablespoons, which was just the right amount to thicken the sauce enough to cling to and coat the egg noodles that were waiting in the wings. For a traditional finishing touch (and after removing any surface fat from the goulash), I stirred in sour cream—after tempering it with some of the hot gravy so the shock of the heat wouldn't cause the sour cream to break.

Finally, I had a hearty bowl of meaty, thick, Hungarian goulash without even opening the oven door.

SLOW-COOKER HUNGARIAN GOULASH
Serves 6

Do not substitute hot or smoked Spanish paprika for the sweet paprika. Since paprika is vital to this recipe, it is best to use a fresh container. Our favorite paprika is The Spice House Hungarian Sweet Paprika. Serve this rich stew over egg noodles or spaetzle.

- 1 (4-pound) boneless beef chuck-eye roast, trimmed and cut into 1½-inch pieces
  Salt and pepper
- 1 (12-ounce) jar roasted red peppers, rinsed
- ⅓ cup sweet paprika
- 2 tablespoons tomato paste
- 1 tablespoon distilled white vinegar
- 2 tablespoons vegetable oil
- 4 pounds onions, chopped (6 cups)
- 4 carrots, peeled and cut into 1-inch chunks
- 3 tablespoons all-purpose flour
- 1 bay leaf
- 5 tablespoons water
- ½ cup sour cream
- 2 tablespoons minced fresh parsley

1. Pat beef dry with paper towels and season with 1 teaspoon salt; transfer to slow cooker. Process red peppers, paprika, tomato paste, and vinegar in food processor until smooth, about 2 minutes, scraping down sides of bowl as needed; set aside.

2. Heat oil in Dutch oven over medium heat until shimmering. Add onions, carrots, and 1 teaspoon salt and cook, covered, until onions are softened, 8 to 10 minutes, stirring occasionally. Stir in flour, bay leaf, and red pepper mixture and cook until mixture begins to brown and stick to bottom of pot, about 2 minutes. Stir in water, scraping up any browned bits.

3. Stir onion mixture into slow cooker until beef is evenly coated. Cover and cook until meat is tender, 6 to 7 hours on high, or 7 to 8 hours on low.

4. Turn off slow cooker, let stew settle for 5 minutes, then skim fat from surface with large spoon. Discard bay leaf. Combine sour cream and ½ cup hot stew liquid in bowl (to temper sour cream), then stir mixture into stew. Season with salt and pepper to taste. Serve, sprinkled with parsley.

Cooking for Two French Onion Soup

A soup built on slow-caramelized onions in less than an hour? We cracked the code.

BY CHRISTIE MORRISON

CLASSIC FRENCH ONION soup is an exercise in patience—it involves building a rich beef stock and then slowly caramelizing onions until they're meltingly soft and sweet. A traditional toasted crouton blanketed in melted Gruyère cheese adds an irresistible finish.

Unfortunately, in many streamlined recipes the cheesy crouton provides tasty camouflage for a bowl full of ersatz broth and barely tender, flavorless onions. To make a worthwhile French onion soup for two, we'd need to come up with a streamlined way to get deeply caramelized onions and richly flavored stock while keeping the cooking time to a minimum.

I started by looking at the test kitchen's standard caramelized onion technique. We've found that a large, low-sided skillet usually works best for caramelizing onions since it allows moisture to evaporate, hastening the caramelizing process. That's fine, of course, when you don't mind firing up the stove twice and using two heavy pans—first to cook the onions and then to simmer the soup—but for a weeknight dish for two, it was a nonstarter. Since the first step in caramelizing onions is cooking them until they've softened and released their moisture, I turned to the microwave. After just 10 minutes of unattended cooking (plus ½ teaspoon of salt to help the onions release their moisture), I had fully softened onions. After draining the onions of their liquid, I was ready to caramelize.

I melted some butter in a large saucepan (fine for caramelization here, because the onions had already expelled their excess moisture in the microwave) over medium-high heat. We traditionally use lower heat to caramelize onions so they cook before they burn, but since I was starting with already-cooked onions, I thought I could be a little more aggressive (and hopefully save some time) by using a higher flame. After about 10 minutes, the onions began to develop some color. But even though I was making sure to stir them frequently, I noticed that the onions were browning unevenly. To even things out, I deglazed the pot with 2 tablespoons of water. Besides reducing hot spots, this technique loosened the browned bits from the bottom of the pot and

kept them from burning. I repeated the process a second time until the onions were uniformly golden-brown and glazy in just 18 minutes—saving me nearly an hour of cooking time.

Now I could address the soup base. While recipes in our archive have used beef and chicken broth—alone or in combination—for French onion soup, I found that chicken broth was sufficient to add savory depth to this quicker soup without cloaking the onions' earthy sweetness. I did find that a few tablespoons of dry sherry—which we preferred to red or white wine's acidic finish—added warm complexity. To round out the flavors, I tossed a few sprigs of thyme and a bay leaf into the mixture to steep as the soup simmered.

The last step was the cheesy crouton. Traditionally, the soup is ladled into ovensafe bowls, topped with a toasted crouton and cheese, and broiled until the cheese is bubbling and browned. But since the last 15 minutes of the soup's cooking time were hands-off, I decided to make better use of my time: While the soup simmered, I broiled the croutons twice (once to toast the bread and again to melt the cheese) and then added them to the finished soup. *Et voilà!* I had a meal of rich, cheesy French onion soup in 45 minutes.

FRENCH ONION SOUP FOR TWO

Look for small or demi-baguettes in the bakery section of your supermarket. Three onions weigh about 1½ pounds.

- 3 **onions, halved and sliced thin**
  Salt and pepper
- 2 **tablespoons unsalted butter**
- ½ **teaspoon brown sugar**
- 4 **tablespoons water**
- 3 **tablespoons dry sherry**
- 3 **cups chicken broth**
- 2 **sprigs fresh thyme**
- 1 **bay leaf**
- 4 **(½-inch-thick) slices baguette**
- 2 **ounces Gruyère cheese, shredded**
  (½ cup)

1. Combine onions and ½ teaspoon salt in bowl and microwave, covered, until fully softened, about 10 minutes; drain. Melt butter in large saucepan over medium-high heat. Add onions, sugar,

We simplify the process (and eliminate the need for special crocks) by broiling the cheesy croutons on a baking sheet.

and ¼ teaspoon pepper and cook until onions are golden brown, stirring occasionally, about 12 minutes.

2. Add 2 tablespoons water and cook until nearly evaporated, scraping up any browned bits, about 3 minutes. Add remaining 2 tablespoons water and cook until onions are brown, scraping up any browned bits, about 3 minutes. Stir in sherry and cook until evaporated, about 2 minutes.

3. Stir in broth, thyme sprigs, and bay leaf. Increase heat to high and bring to boil. Reduce heat to medium-low, cover, and simmer for 15 minutes. Discard thyme sprigs and bay leaf and season with salt and pepper to taste.

4. Meanwhile, adjust oven rack 6 inches from broiler element and heat broiler. Arrange baguette slices on parchment paper–lined baking sheet and broil until deep golden brown, 1 to 2 minutes per side. Remove bread from oven and divide cheese evenly among slices; broil until melted and bubbly, 2 to 4 minutes.

5. Ladle soup into bowls and place 2 baguette slices in each bowl. Serve.

TEST KITCHEN TECHNIQUE
Faster Caramelized Onions

Classic French onion soup can take all afternoon to make—just caramelizing the onions can easily eat up an hour. For a two-person guest list, we needed to speed things up.

Our two-step process for faster caramelized onions starts the salted sliced onions in the microwave where they cook, covered, until soft, which takes about 10 minutes. Then we drain off the exuded liquid and sauté the onions not slowly, but quickly—don't forget to stir—until brown, about 12 minutes. Then we deglaze twice to extract every ounce of flavor before adding the broth.

COOK TWICE; SAVE TIME
Microwave and then sauté.

Surprise: We like this lower-fat version of baked stuffed shrimp even more than the original. BY CRISTIN WALSH

SHRIMP IS FULL of good stuff for your body: protein, omega-3 fatty acids, and minerals. And it's relatively low in fat and calories. But classic baked stuffed shrimp packs a whopping 670 calories and 39 grams of fat per serving of five shrimp. So how does a seaside classic become so bad for you? Bread, butter, and full-fat mayo. I was determined to cut the calorie count in half and the fat content by far more than that, without sacrificing satisfaction.

Full-fat recipes often call for using bread crumbs or crushed buttery crackers that are then drenched in up to a stick of melted butter. Celery, garlic, lemon, and wine or herbs are added—and fatty mayonnaise, too—before the mixture is packed into jumbo shrimp that have been flattened for stuffing. They taste great but come with a cost.

My first target: calorie-heavy bread. As I investigated options for alternatives, I discovered some eye-opening numbers. Prepackaged bread crumbs had 110 calories per ounce, while buttery crackers boasted 140 calories; both were too much for me. Easy homemade white bread crumbs, with 80 calories per ounce, were a move in the right direction.

Next I went after the butter. Butter acts as not only a flavoring in the stuffing but also as a binder for the bread. But thanks to earlier test kitchen experiments with shrimp burgers, I knew I had another ingredient at hand to accomplish both of those tasks just as

well: shrimp. Four shrimp processed into a paste and mixed in gave me a substantive stuffing. But it was crumbly; losing the butter meant sacrificing moisture and smoothness. Hello, low-fat mayo. A half-cup was just enough to keep the stuffing moist while holding the fat count in check.

With the stuffing base under control, I decided to pump up the flavor. A bit of diced celery sautéed with garlic in a very spare amount of butter gave a little crunch and just a suggestion of indulgence. Lemon zest and juice and a bit of white wine added brightness and acidity. Parsley rounded out the lineup with an herby note.

Rather than sabotaging shrimp's healthy reputation with mounds of bread and butter, this baked stuffed shrimp recipe keeps the calories and fat in check—and to our surprise, we even preferred it to the original.

The Numbers

Nutritional information is for one serving of five shrimp.

Traditional Baked Stuffed Shrimp
CALORIES 670
FAT 39 g • SATURATED FAT 19 g

***Cook's Country* Reduced-Fat Baked Stuffed Shrimp**
CALORIES 330
FAT 9 g • SATURATED FAT 3 g

By replacing some of the butter and crumbs in the stuffing with ground shrimp, we amplify the flavor and cut fat and calories at the same time.

TEST KITCHEN TECHNIQUE How to Stuff Shrimp

Shrimp don't have a natural cavity to fill; in this case, "stuffing" means creating a flat surface for the filling.

BUTTERFLY AND CUT
Use a paring knife to slice about halfway into the convex side of each shrimp. Remove vein if necessary. Cut a 1-inch slit through the center of each shrimp.

"STUFF"
Place the shrimp, sliced side down, on the prepared baking sheet and spoon on the stuffing, pressing to make sure it adheres.

REDUCED-FAT BAKED STUFFED SHRIMP
Serves 4

Look for shrimp labeled "U15," which indicates that the number of shrimp per pound is under 15. Our favorite low-fat mayonnaise is Hellmann's Light.

- 4   slices hearty white sandwich bread
- 24 extra-jumbo shrimp (U15), peeled and deveined
- 1   tablespoon unsalted butter
- 2   celery ribs, chopped fine
- 2   garlic cloves, minced
- ½   cup low-fat mayonnaise
- 2   tablespoons minced fresh parsley
- 1   tablespoon dry white wine
- 2   teaspoons grated lemon zest plus 1 tablespoon juice
- ¼   teaspoon salt
- ⅛   teaspoon pepper

1. Adjust oven rack to upper-middle position and heat oven to 375 degrees. Pulse bread in food processor to coarse crumbs, about 10 pulses. Transfer to rimmed baking sheet and bake until golden and dry, about 8 minutes, stirring halfway through baking. Transfer crumbs to large bowl to cool.

2. Line rimmed baking sheet with foil and spray with vegetable oil spray. Discard tails from 4 shrimp, then pulse shrimp in food processor until coarsely chopped, about 5 pulses; transfer to bowl with cooled bread crumbs.

3. Melt butter in 10-inch nonstick skillet over medium heat. Add celery and cook until softened, about 5 minutes. Add garlic and cook until fragrant, about 30 seconds. Transfer to bowl with processed shrimp. Stir in mayonnaise, parsley, wine, lemon zest and juice, salt, and pepper until well combined.

4. Pat remaining 20 shrimp dry with paper towels. Using paring knife and holding shrimp with curve facing upward toward you, butterfly shrimp. Cut 1-inch slit through center of each shrimp so they lie flat.

5. Lay shrimp butterflied side down on prepared sheet. Divide filling among exposed sides of shrimp near head, about 1 heaping tablespoon per shrimp, pressing to adhere. Allow tails to curl up over stuffing. Bake until shrimp are opaque, 12 to 15 minutes, rotating sheet halfway through baking.

6. Remove shrimp from oven and heat broiler. Broil shrimp until crumbs are deep golden brown and crisp, 1 to 3 minutes. Serve.

With a few extra ingredients and a simple technique, you can transform a humble
can of chickpeas into a bright and lively salad. BY ASHLEY MOORE

HEALTHFUL, INEXPENSIVE, EASY. Canned chickpeas are a slam-dunk convenience food in most regards—except flavor: On their own, they don't offer much. But these nutty little nuggets, round and firm, make a solid foundation for easy—and flavorful—side salads or light lunches.

I started my experiments by tossing a few cans of chickpeas with a simple vinaigrette and assorted add-ins. And the results were just fine: By adding flavorful ingredients like briny olives, sweet carrots, and peppery arugula, I'd created an array of dishes that my colleagues enjoyed well enough. But I wasn't satisfied. A salad should be more than the sum of its parts, and while the parts in these salads were tasty, each salad, as a whole, didn't sing. The dressing and its flavors didn't infuse the chickpeas, instead leaving a pool of vinaigrette at the bottom of the bowl. Fine for mopping up with a heel of bread, but I wanted the dressing to impart more than just surface flavor to the chickpeas.

A coworker wondered whether heating up the chickpeas would help the dressing adhere. Suspicious, but eager to try something that didn't involve a skillet or a saucepan, I dropped the strained chickpeas into a bowl and gave the microwave a whirl. Just a minute and a half on high power and the warmed chickpeas seemed to soak up more dressing, adding a more cohesive flavor to the salad. But why?

I reached out to our science editor for an explanation. He told me that the seed coats that cover chickpeas (and protect them from bugs and fungi) are rich in pectin. Because pectin is sensitive to heat and moisture, blasting the chickpeas in the microwave breaks it down, which in turn weakens the protective seed coating and creates a more porous inner surface. The dressing can then easily penetrate the seed coat and cling to the chickpeas, delivering a satisfying punch of flavor with each bite.

With that discovery, I was off and running. Besides the savory olive and arugula salad, I developed a sweet-sour version with carrots and golden raisins, one with pungent arugula and licorice-y fennel, a version with orange slices and red onion, and a summery salad with roasted red peppers and feta.

CHICKPEA SALAD WITH CARROTS, ARUGULA, AND OLIVES
Serves 4
The test kitchen prefers Pastene Chick Peas. Shred the carrots on the large holes of a box grater or use a food processor fitted with the shredding disk.

- 2 (15-ounce) cans chickpeas, rinsed
- ¼ cup extra-virgin olive oil
- 2 tablespoons lemon juice
  Salt and pepper
  Pinch cayenne pepper
- 3 carrots, peeled and shredded
- 1 ounce (1 cup) baby arugula, chopped coarse
- ½ cup pitted kalamata olives, chopped coarse

1. Microwave chickpeas in medium bowl until hot, about 1 minute 30 seconds. Stir in oil, lemon juice, ¾ teaspoon salt, ½ teaspoon pepper, and cayenne and let sit for 30 minutes.
2. Add carrots, arugula, and olives and toss to combine. Season with salt and pepper to taste. Serve.

CHICKPEA SALAD WITH CARROTS, RAISINS, AND ALMONDS
Substitute lime juice for lemon juice and ½ cup golden raisins, ¼ cup chopped fresh mint, and ¼ cup toasted sliced almonds for arugula and olives.

CHICKPEA SALAD WITH FENNEL AND ARUGULA
Substitute 1 fennel bulb, stalks discarded, bulb halved, cored, and cut into ¼-inch pieces, for carrots and olives.

CHICKPEA SALAD WITH ORANGE, RED ONION, AND CHIPOTLE
Substitute 3 oranges, segmented; ½ cup thinly sliced red onion; ½ cup fresh cilantro leaves; and 2 teaspoons minced canned chipotle chile in adobo sauce for carrots, arugula, and olives.

CHICKPEA SALAD WITH ROASTED RED PEPPERS AND FETA
Substitute ½ cup chopped jarred roasted red peppers, ½ cup crumbled feta cheese, and ¼ cup chopped fresh parsley for carrots, arugula, and olives.

Heating the chickpeas before dressing them helps them absorb more flavor.

New sprays promise performance without the chemicals—
can any take the heat? BY LAUREN SAVOIE

A SPRITZ FROM a can is far faster than greasing by hand, and cooking sprays help limit the amount of oil for lower-fat cooking. But many consumers have questions about the health effects and environmental safety of added chemicals in cooking sprays. Manufacturers have responded by launching innovative new sprays that allow them to avoid the standard chemicals. How do they perform compared with traditional aerosols?

To find out, we tried four top-selling traditional aerosol sprays and three innovative sprays. We chose each brand's canola oil product or "original" oil blend. Throughout the testing we compared each product's performance with that of plain canola oil sprayed from our winning refillable oil mister, the Orka Flavor and Oil Mister with Filter.

Most cooking sprays are aerosols; "aerosol" simply means small particles dispersed in air or gas. The particles in traditional aerosol cooking sprays are oil, an emulsifier called lecithin (found naturally in soybeans, eggs, and milk), and an antifoaming agent (usually dimethyl silicone). The gas is usually a liquid propellant such as propane. Two innovative products, PAM Organic Canola Oil and Spectrum Naturals Canola Spray Oil, make a "cleaner" aerosol by eliminating the antifoaming agent and switching the propellant to a naturally occurring gas like carbon dioxide. The third product,

Winona Pure 100% Canola Oil, uses a nonaerosol "bag-on-valve" system in which the gas and oil never mix in the can. When Winona's trigger is pushed, compressed air squeezes an oil-filled bag inside, forcing out the oil.

We set to work oiling Bundt pans and muffin tins; coating waffle irons; and spraying stainless-steel skillets for fried eggs, omelets, and chicken stir-fries. All the products were adept at preventing sticking—until we got to the fried eggs. While both traditional and innovative aerosols easily released eggs from skillets, eggs made with plain canola oil or Winona's nonaerosol spray stuck to pans. The reason? Unlike the other products, the Winona spray and plain canola oil don't contain lecithin, which helps the oil adhere evenly to the pan's entire surface, leaving no bare spots. Products with lecithin released foods more readily than plain oil.

But lecithin has a dark side. It can cause oil to darken at a lower temperature and impart off-flavors to food. Our instructions for chicken stir-fry call for heating oil in a skillet until smoking, but while plain canola oil is still clear at its smoke point, five of the six sprays with lecithin turned almost black before they started smoking, giving "burnt popcorn" or "spoiled margarine" flavors to food.

Dimethyl silicone, the antifoaming chemical, clearly helped some products spray more consistently in even mists; products without dimethyl silicone pooled and dripped. It also helped prevent browning.

In the end, we weren't convinced that innovative aerosols are better than traditional aerosols; however, we found one nonaerosol spray that doesn't contain chemicals and won't cause unwanted darkening: Winona Pure 100% Canola Oil. But because it doesn't contain lecithin, it is slightly less effective at preventing sticking.

For stickier tasks, we preferred PAM Original No-Stick Spray (it costs $0.50 per ounce, compared with about $0.17 per ounce for plain canola oil). This spray perfectly released foods, misted evenly, and browned 20 degrees after its smoke point. (Why? PAM Original's oil blend includes palm oil, a highly saturated oil that, along with dimethyl silicone, helps discourage browning.) For an all-around great spray, we're sticking with PAM.

Lecithin: Love It or Loathe It?

Lecithin helps oil sprays adhere to the pan and create a nonstick surface. But lecithin can also cause some oils to darken and give a burnt or spoiled flavor to food. Our winner, PAM Original Cooking Spray, has a fix in the mix: Its blend includes palm oil, a highly saturated oil that inhibits browning.

DARK AND FUNKY
Lecithin can cause some oils to darken at lower temperatures.

KEY **Good ★★★** Fair ★★ Poor ★

RECOMMENDED	CRITERIA		TESTERS' NOTES
PAM Original No-Stick Spray **Price:** $2.99 for 6 oz ($0.50 per oz) **Ingredients:** Canola oil, palm oil, coconut oil, lecithin from soybeans (nonstick agent), dimethyl silicone (for antifoaming), rosemary extract (preservative), propellant	Taste Spraying Nonstick Browning	★★½ ★★★ ★★★ ★★	This best-selling brand corners the market on cooking spray and for good reason: This product sprayed in a fine, broad mist without pooling or foaming and effortlessly released eggs, chicken, waffles, and cakes. In addition to canola oil, PAM Original also contains palm oil—a highly saturated oil—which makes this spray less prone to unwanted browning and funky flavors.
WINONA Pure 100% Canola Oil **Price:** $4.65 for 5 oz ($0.93 per oz) **Ingredients:** Canola oil	Taste Spraying Nonstick Browning	★★★ ★½ ★★ ★★★	This innovative product combines the purity of an oil mister with the convenience of a supermarket spray. It performed identically to plain canola oil, maintaining its clear color and neutral flavor well past 400 degrees. The absence of lecithin makes this spray slightly less effective.
CRISCO Original No-Stick Cooking Spray **Price:** $3.53 for 6 oz ($0.59 per oz) **Ingredients:** Canola oil, soy lecithin, dimethyl silicone (for antifoaming), propellant	Taste Spraying Nonstick Browning	★★ ★★ ★★★ ★½	This spray breezed through all our tests, and its broad mist adhered well to the crevices of waffle irons and Bundt pans. Our one gripe: its low browning point, which changed its normally "neutral" taste from "slightly buttery" to "burnt popcorn" when cooking at temperatures higher than 400 degrees.
SMART BALANCE Non-Stick Cooking Spray, Original **Price:** $3.19 for 6 oz ($0.53 per oz) **Ingredients:** Vegetable oil blend (canola, soy, and olive oils), soy lecithin, grain alcohol (preservative), dimethyl-polysiloxane, and propellant	Taste Spraying Nonstick Browning	★★ ★½ ★★★ ★½	This product was perfectly adept at preventing sticking but sprayed quickly and directly, making it hard to control the amount of oil on the pan. It does contain an antifoaming agent, so this is likely the result of a bad nozzle. When sampled plain, this spray tasted "neutral," but it took on a "spoiled margarine" flavor when heated until smoking.
MAZOLA Original Cooking Spray **Price:** $4.41 for 5 oz ($0.88 per oz) **Ingredients:** Canola oil, soy lecithin, dimethylpolysiloxane, propellant	Taste Spraying Nonstick Browning	★★ ★½ ★★★ ★½	While this product had a superfine mist that evenly coated pans and efficiently released sticky foods, it required constant shaking to form a steady stream and stopped spraying with plenty of oil left in the can. Still, it didn't bog down food with grease, and tasters liked its "clean" flavor.
NOT RECOMMENDED			
PAM Organic Canola Oil **Price:** $4.39 for 5 oz ($0.88 per oz) **Ingredients:** Organic canola oil, organic grain alcohol (added for clarity), organic lecithin from soybeans (prevents sticking), propellant	Taste Spraying Nonstick Browning	★ ★ ★★★ ★	This spray was less appealing than its nonorganic counterpart, taking on an unappetizing dark brown color 100 degrees before its smoke point (because it lacks an antifoaming agent) and making waffles and cakes greasy from excessive oil pooling. Tasters didn't like the flavor either, calling it "chemical" and "sour."
SPECTRUM NATURALS Canola Spray Oil **Price:** $8.09 for 16 oz ($0.51 per oz) **Ingredients:** Mechanically (expeller) pressed canola oil, soy lecithin, propellant	Taste Spraying Nonstick Browning	★ ★ ★★★ ★	With no antifoaming agent, this spray coated the pan in thick, unappealing froth and turned black when heated to 400 degrees. While perfectly adept at preventing sticking, this product had a "fishy" flavor and charred color when heated that were intolerable to most testers.

Trust what's in the bag, not on it. BY HANNAH CROWLEY

BROWN RICE IS shedding its hippie image. It's whole-grain, gluten-free, cheap, and healthy—and according to Nielsen, national sales of brown rice increased 58 percent from 2006 to 2011. Brown rice is booming.

We like brown rice plain as a side dish or in pilafs and salads. To find the best product, we surveyed supermarkets and chose seven national best sellers. We focused on long-grain rice, as it's what we use most for its fluffy and discrete kernels. We first selected four top-selling dried products, and then because brown rice can take 45 minutes to an hour to cook, we added three prepared products to our lineup. All three are fully cooked and reheated at home in the microwave for 1 to 4½ minutes, depending on the product; two are shelf-stable and one is frozen. We passed over the boxes of traditional dried instant rice; their grains are usually steamed and dried at the factory to make them cook faster, and we've always found them spongy.

We tried the rice three ways, including both styles—dry and microwaveable—in each tasting. First we baked the four dried products according to our Foolproof Oven-Baked Brown Rice recipe, and for the second we simmered them on the stovetop, following package instructions. We microwaved the three quick products per their directions, comparing them with the baked and then with the simmered dry rice. Finally, we tried all seven products in a room-temperature rice salad; we boiled the four dried products according to the recipe and microwaved the three quick products, adding them to the recipe when it called for cooked, cooled rice.

We soon noticed our first pattern: Tasters always preferred good old-fashioned dry rice (when prepared right). It's firmer, with a pleasant nutty bite. And convenience products, for the most part, aren't worth it. "Did you accidentally cook the box?" asked one taster eating Uncle Ben's Ready Rice, a shelf-stable product. We looked into it and found that the rice is parboiled, just like the company's dry instant rice; its grains were clumpy and mealy. Another flop was Birds Eye Steamfresh, the frozen rice. According to our science editor, the harsh process of cooking, freezing, and reheating causes some of the starches to form crystals that trap water, drying out parts of the grains. It also releases starch molecules called amylose, which makes the rice mushy when reheated.

One quick product, though, did turn out consistently decent; Minute Ready to Serve Brown Rice isn't perfect, but it's a good fast alternative. Its grains were firmer than those of regular brown rice, earning comparisons to wheat berries and barley. But it's also more expensive: $1.20 per 1-cup serving versus $0.25 for our winner. It comes salted and oiled, which tasters didn't mind, but you do sacrifice control.

As for the dry rice, when cooked according to our own recipes, all performed admirably. Testers ranked them nearly identically in both the basic baked brown rice recipe and when boiled and cooled for the room-temperature salad. All four products had similar scores for flavor and texture, so we turned to each product's package instructions. While we've perfected brown rice in our recipes, we know that sometimes people use the package for prep, too.

Talk about mixed results: When we cooked each product according to its instructions, one was great, one was decent, and two were utter mush. Wondering if we'd done something wrong, we cooked the latter two again, getting the same results: "gelatinous" "oatmeal," "like baby food." But these very same products were excellent in our own recipes. What gives?

All the stovetop package instructions use the absorption method, meaning you add a set amount of water and a set amount of rice and cook the two together until the water is absorbed. We looked at the water ratios called for on each package and found that the best rice called for a ratio of 1¾ cups water to 1 cup rice; the product that was pretty good calls for 2 cups water to 1 cup rice; and the two mushy products call for 2½ cups water to 1 cup rice. The mushy products don't sell bad rice; they're just telling you to add too much water. As an experiment, we cooked the two mushy products with the water ratio called for in our best rice, 1¾ cups per cup of rice, and they vastly improved.

Our winning rice, Lundberg Organic Brown Long Grain Rice, covered all the bases. It works great with a range of cooking methods and has its own smart instructions. Lundberg is the only company in our tasting that grows its own rice, and that level of control, coupled with smart directions, turns out consistently superior, firm, nutty grains.

RECOMMENDED

LUNDBERG Organic Brown Long Grain Rice
Price: $3.79 for 32 oz ($0.25 per cup cooked)
Style: Dry
Fat: 2 g per cup cooked
Sodium: 0 mg per cup cooked

TASTERS' NOTES

This dry rice has the best instructions and works with a range of other cooking methods. Tasters said its kernels were "plump" and "almost springy," as well as "distinct and pleasantly chewy." They were the most flavorful, too: "buttery," "nutty," and "earthy."

RICELAND Extra Long Grain Natural Brown Rice
Price: $1.88 for 32 oz ($0.11 per cup cooked)
Style: Dry
Fat: 1.3 g per cup cooked
Sodium: 0 mg per cup cooked

This rice's directions were slightly more successful because they called for less water, but the rice was still a bit "soft." Cooked with alternative instructions, it was very good, with "firm, intact grains" that were "chewy, yet distinct," "nutty," "rich," and "toasted."

CAROLINA Whole Grain Brown Rice (sold as Carolina in the Northeast, Mahatma everywhere else)
Price: $4.19 for 32 oz ($0.25 per cup cooked)
Style: Dry
Fat: 1.3 g per cup cooked
Sodium: 0 mg per cup cooked

This rice is good—if you ignore its package instructions. Prepared correctly, it can be "pleasantly chewy," with "distinct individual grains." Neutral in flavor and softer than other products we tried, some tasters compared it with white rice.

GOYA Brown Rice
Price: $2 for 16 oz ($0.25 per cup cooked)
Style: Dry
Fat: 0 g per cup cooked
Sodium: 0 mg per cup cooked

This rice turned to mush when prepared according to its package instructions. But adjust the cooking method and you get "nicely chewy," "tender yet toothsome" kernels. It was milder in flavor, "kind of white rice-y."

MINUTE Ready to Serve Brown Rice
Price: $2.39 for 8.8 oz ($1.20 per cup cooked)
Style: Shelf-stable microwavable
Fat: 3.5 g per cup cooked
Sodium: 150 mg per cup cooked

This fully cooked microwavable rice isn't perfect, but it consistently turned out decent rice in 60 seconds. The grains were "bouncy," "almost like wheat berries." They also come lightly oiled and salted, which tasters thought added nice flavor but which does limit control.

BEST QUICK

NOT RECOMMENDED

BIRDS EYE Steamfresh Whole Grain Brown Rice
Price: $2.59 for 10 oz ($1.30 per cup cooked)
Style: Frozen
Fat: 1 g per cup cooked
Sodium: 5 mg per cup cooked

The sole frozen product was OK dressed with vinaigrette in a salad, but otherwise tasters found it "dry" and "mushy." The process of cooking, freezing, and reheating the rice is harsh on the grains and leaves them dry on the inside and "pasty" outside. It was also bland, with notes of "dust" and "metal."

UNCLE BEN'S Ready Rice Whole Grain Brown
Price: $2.39 for 8.8 oz ($1.20 per cup cooked)
Style: Shelf-stable microwavable
Fat: 3 g per cup cooked
Sodium: 15 mg per cup cooked

"Arid like the Sahara!" declared one taster of this "dry," "crumbly" parboiled rice, with intermittently "chewy," "hard," straw-like kernels. At best it was bland and underseasoned; at worst, tasters said it was "oddly fragrant," and "floral," like "chemicals" or "wet newspaper."

Heirloom Recipe

We're looking for recipes that you treasure—the ones that have been handed down in your family for a generation or more; that always come out for the holidays; that have earned a place at your table and in your heart, through many years of meals. Send us the recipes that spell home to you. Visit CooksCountry.com/heirloomrecipes (or write to Heirloom Recipes, *Cook's Country*, P.O. Box 470739, Brookline, MA 02447) and tell us a little about the recipe. Include your name and mailing address. **If we print your recipe, you'll receive a free one-year subscription to *Cook's Country*.**

MOTHER'S MINCEMEAT COOKIES

"When I was young, we had these at holidays. But as I got older, they seemed to appear more often throughout the year."

Alice Jacobs, Troy, N.Y.

Makes 20 cookies

You will need a 3-inch cookie cutter for this recipe.

- 2 tablespoons all-purpose flour
- 2 tablespoons sugar
- ¾ cup jarred mincemeat
- 3 tablespoons brandy
- ½ cup walnuts, toasted and chopped fine
- 4 (9-inch) store-bought pie dough rounds

1. Whisk ¼ cup water, flour, and sugar together in medium saucepan until smooth. Stir in mincemeat and brandy. Bring to simmer over medium heat and cook, stirring constantly, until mixture has thickened, 2 to 4 minutes. Transfer to bowl, stir in walnuts, and let cool completely.

2. Adjust oven racks to upper-middle and lower-middle positions and heat oven to 375 degrees. Line 2 rimmed baking sheets with parchment paper. Working with 2 pie dough rounds at a time, roll into 12-inch rounds on lightly floured counter. Using 3-inch cookie cutter, cut 10 circles from each dough round.

3. Working with 1 circle at a time, moisten edge with water and place 2 teaspoons mincemeat filling in center. Top with second circle and press edges to seal. Crimp cookie edge with your fingers. Cut small vent hole in center of cookie. Repeat with remaining circles and filling. Place 10 cookies on each prepared sheet, 1½ inches apart.

4. Bake until light golden brown around edges, 16 to 18 minutes, switching and rotating sheets halfway through baking. Let cookies cool on sheets for 5 minutes, then transfer to wire rack and let cool completely. Serve.

COMING NEXT ISSUE

We get a jump on warmer weather with **Cracker-Crusted Fried Chicken**, **Lemon-Herb Potato Salad**, and **Toffee Squares**. We'll give you the keys to easy weeknight dinners like **One-Pan Pork Chops and Vegetables**, **Pasta with Cherry Tomatoes**, and **Reduced-Fat Chicken Enchiladas**. You'll want two of our **Beef on Weck Sandwiches**. And we'll show you the tricks to **Slow-Cooker Chicken Stock** and a perfect **Italian Meat Sauce**. Don't miss our new recipes.

FIND THE ROOSTER!

A tiny version of this rooster has been hidden in the pages of this issue. Write to us with its location and we'll enter you in a random drawing. The first correct entry drawn will win our winning inexpensive electric citrus juicer, and each of the next five will receive a free one-year subscription to *Cook's Country*. To enter, visit CooksCountry.com/rooster by March 31, 2015, or write to Rooster FM15, *Cook's Country*, P.O. Box 470739, Brookline, MA 02447. Include your name and address. Marlene Rice of Cheshire, Massachusetts, found the rooster on page 14 of our October/November 2014 issue and won our favorite slow cooker.

WEB EXTRAS

Free for 4 months online at CooksCountry.com

Chicken Broth Tasting
Creamed Kale with Chestnuts
Icebox Strawberry Pie
Inexpensive Electric Citrus Juicers Testing (full story)
Lemon Chess Pie
Louisiana Seasoning Tasting (full story)
Raspberry Chiffon Pie
Single Pie Crust
Slow-Cooker Hearty Beef Stew
Supermarket Bacon Tasting
Wacky Cake
White Rice

READ US ON iPAD

Download the *Cook's Country* app for iPad and start a free trial subscription or purchase a single issue of the magazine. All issues are enhanced with full-color Cooking Mode slide shows that provide step-by-step instructions for completing recipes, plus expanded reviews and ratings. Go to CooksCountry.com/iPad to download our app through iTunes.

Follow us on **Pinterest**
pinterest.com/TestKitchen

Follow us on **Twitter**
twitter.com/TestKitchen

Find us on **Facebook**
facebook.com/CooksCountry

RC = Recipe Card

King Cake

The colors of Mardi Gras—not to mention a delicious cinnamon-pecan swirl—
make this tasty cake festive enough for any party.

To make this cake, you will need:

- 1 **cup plus scant 3 tablespoons whole milk**
- 3 **large eggs**
- 8 **tablespoons unsalted butter, melted**
- 4½ **cups (22½ ounces) all-purpose flour**
- ½ **cup (3½ ounces) granulated sugar**
- 2¼ **teaspoons instant or rapid-rise yeast**
- 1 **teaspoon salt**
- 1¼ **cups pecans, toasted and ground fine**
- ¾ **cup packed (5¼ ounces) light brown sugar**
- 2 **teaspoons ground cinnamon**
- 1 **miniature porcelain toy baby (optional)**
- 2 **cups (8 ounces) confectioners' sugar**
- 1 **tablespoon each yellow, green, and purple colored decorating sugars**

FOR THE CAKE: Whisk 1 cup milk, eggs, and melted butter together in bowl of stand mixer. Stir in flour, granulated sugar, yeast, and salt until just combined. Attach bowl to stand mixer and fit with dough hook. Mix on medium-low speed for 10 minutes. Transfer dough to greased bowl, cover tightly with plastic wrap, and let rise at room temperature until doubled in size, 1½ to 2 hours.

Grease 12-cup nonstick Bundt pan. Combine pecans, brown sugar, and cinnamon in bowl. Roll out dough into 18 by 14-inch rectangle on lightly floured counter, with long side parallel to counter edge. Spray lightly with water and sprinkle evenly with nut mixture. Place baby, if using, along bottom edge of dough. Roll dough away from you into log and pinch along seam to seal. Form into ring and seal ends together. Place seam side up into

prepared pan, cover loosely with plastic, and let rise at room temperature until doubled in size, about 1 hour. Adjust oven rack to middle position and heat oven to 350 degrees.

Bake until deep golden brown and cake registers 190 degrees, 30 to 35 minutes, rotating halfway through baking. Let cool in pan for 10 minutes. Remove cake from pan, transfer to wire rack seam side down, and let cool completely, about 2 hours.

FOR THE ICING: Whisk confectioners' sugar and remaining scant 3 tablespoons milk together in bowl until smooth. Pour over cooled cake. Sprinkle ⅙ of top with half of yellow sugar, then repeat on opposite side. Repeat with green and purple sugars to form alternating bands of color. Serve.

Inside This Issue

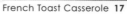

Cook's Country

These soft, buttery rolls—also known as "Yankee rolls" for their Northeast origin—are easier to make than they look. But it still took a few weeks in the test kitchen to get them delicately tender with crisp edges. PAGE 20

CooksCountry.com
$5.95 U.S./$6.95 CANADA

Dear Home Cook,

Ten years ago, I visited a haberdashery (OK, a hat store) in Cincinnati. The Greek owner was an opera fan, as am I, and quite sociable, so we got to talking. Meanwhile, two teenagers walked by outside the plate-glass window, eating sandwiches on the run. He looked at them, turned to me, and said, "Even dogs don't eat and walk at the same time!"

So what's wrong with the photo below? Well, besides the choice of food, this young man is both standing up while eating and eating alone. Researchers in Denmark have determined that families that sit down and share food are more likely to produce nicer kids. Sharing food draws family and friends together. Sociologists call this "pro-social" behavior—I call it good manners.

Most cultures sit down and share food. Maybe that's a good place to start if we want to change the world, one plate at a time.

Cordially,

Christopher Kimball
Founder and Editor, Cook's Country

Cook's Country

Founder and Editor Christopher Kimball
Editorial Director Jack Bishop
Editorial Director, Magazines John Willoughby
Executive Editor Tucker Shaw
Managing Editor Scott Kathan
Executive Food Editor Bryan Roof
Senior Editors Hannah Crowley,
Lisa McManus, Diane Unger
Test Kitchen Director Erin McMurrer
Associate Editors Shannon Friedmann Hatch,
Christie Morrison
Test Cooks Morgan Bolling, Aaron Furmanek,
Ashley Moore, Cristin Walsh
Assitant Test Cook Cecelia Jenkins
Assistant Editors Lauren Savoie, Kate Shannon
Senior Copy Editor Megan Ginsberg
Copy Editor Krista Magnuson
Executive Assistant Christine Gordon
Assistant Test Kitchen Director Leah Rovner
Senior Kitchen Assistants Michelle Blodget,
Alexxa Grattan
Kitchen Assistants Maria Elena Delgado,
Ena Gudiel, Jason Roman
Executive Producer Melissa Baldino
Co-Executive Producer Stephanie Stender
Associate Producer Kaitlin Hammond

Consulting Creative Director Amy Klee
Contributing Editors Erika Bruce, Eva Katz, Jeremy Sauer
Consulting Editors Anne Mendelson, Meg Ragland
Science Editor Guy Crosby, PhD
Executive Food Editor, TV, Radio & Media
Bridget Lancaster

Managing Editor, Web Christine Liu
Senior Editor, Cooking School Mari Levine
Associate Editors, Web Jill Fisher, Roger Metcalf
Senior Video Editor Nick Dakoulas

Design Director, Print Greg Galvan
Photography Director Julie Cote
Art Director Susan Levin
Associate Art Director Lindsey Timko
Art Director, Marketing Jennifer Cox
Staff Photographer Daniel J. van Ackere
Color Food Photography Keller + Keller
Styling Catrine Kelty, Marie Piraino
Deputy Art Director, Marketing Melanie Gryboski
Associate Art Director, Marketing Janet Taylor
Designer, Marketing Stephanie Cook
Associate Art Director, Photography Steve Klise

VP, Print and Direct Marketing David Mack
Circulation Director Doug Wicinski
Circulation & Fulfillment Manager Carrie Fethe
Partnership Marketing Manager Pamela Putprush
Marketing Assistant Marina Tomao

Director, Business Systems Alice Carpenter
Manager, Business & Content Systems Dustin Brandt
Project Manager Britt Dresser
Development Manager Mike Serio

Chief Operating Officer Rob Ristagno
VP, Digital Products Fran Middleton
VP, New Product Development Michael Burton
Production Director Guy Rochford
Senior Color & Imaging Specialist Lauren Robbins
Production & Imaging Specialists Heather Dube,
Dennis Noble
Director, Marketing & Sales Operations Deborah Fagone
Client Services Manager Kate Zebrowski
Sponsorship Sales Associate Morgan Mannino
Senior Controller Theresa Peterson
Customer Loyalty & Support Manager Amy Bootier
Customer Loyalty & Support Reps Rebecca Kowalski,
Andrew Straaberg Finfrock, Juliet Tierney

Director, Retail Book Program Beth Ineson
Retail Sales & Marketing Manager Emily Logan
Human Resources Manager Adele Shapiro
Publicity Deborah Broide

IN THE COVER: *Butter Fan Rolls,* Keller + Keller, Catrine Kelty
ILLUSTRATION: Greg Stevenson

Follow us on **Pinterest**
pinterest.com/TestKitchen

Follow us on **Twitter**
twitter.com/TestKitchen

Find us on **Facebook**
facebook.com/CooksCountry

Cook's Country magazine (ISSN 1552-1990), number 62, is published bimonthly by Boston Common Press Limited Partnership, 17 Station St., Brookline, MA 02445. Copyright 2015 Boston Common Press Limited Partnership. Periodicals postage paid at Boston, MA, and additional mailing offices, USPS #023453. Publications Mail Agreement No. 40020778. Return undeliverable Canadian addresses to P.O. Box 875, Station A, Windsor, ON N9A 6P2. POSTMASTER: Send address changes to Cook's Country, P.O. Box 6018, Harlan, IA 51593-1518. For subscription and gift subscription orders, subscription inquiries, or change of address notices, visit americasTestKitchen.com/support, call 800-526-8447 in the U.S., or 515-248-7684 from outside the U.S., or write to us at Cook's Country, P.O. Box 6018, Harlan, IA 51593-1518. PRINTED IN THE USA.

Contents

APRIL/MAY 2015

ONE-PAN PORK CHOP DINNER, 14

BRAISED SPRING VEGETABLES, 13

NORTH CAROLINA LEMON PIE, 22

Features

Departments

AMERICA'S TEST KITCHEN
RECIPES THAT WORK

America's Test Kitchen is a very real 2,500-square-foot kitchen located just outside Boston. It is the home of *Cook's Country* and *Cook's Illustrated* magazines and the workday destination of more than three dozen test cooks, editors, and cookware specialists. Our mission is to test recipes until we understand how and why they work and arrive at the best version. We also test kitchen equipment and supermarket ingredients in search of products that offer the best value and performance. You can watch us work by tuning in to *Cook's Country from America's Test Kitchen* (CooksCountry.com) and *America's Test Kitchen* (AmericasTestKitchen.com) on public television.

Ask Cook's Country

BY MORGAN BOLLING

What is the best way to toast whole almonds, and how do you know when they're fully toasted?
Val Sullivan, Aurora, Colo.

Toasting almonds—or any nuts—helps release their essential oils and makes them more flavorful. If you're toasting less than 1 cup of nuts, place them in a dry skillet set over medium heat and stir frequently until they're fragrant and have darkened slightly, 3 to 5 minutes. If you're toasting more than a cup, put the nuts on a rimmed baking sheet and toast them in a preheated 350-degree oven for about 7 minutes, shaking the sheet frequently to prevent scorching.

Properly toasted whole nuts are not just browned on the outside, but all the way through the nut flesh—cut one in half to check for light browning.

BOTTOM LINE: Toast small amounts of nuts on the stovetop and larger amounts in the oven. A nut is properly toasted when it is brown throughout.

MORE THAN SKIN DEEP
Toasting nuts develops flavor inside, too.

I keep seeing coconut water in the grocery store. Is it similar to the canned stuff I cook with?
Sally Lamoretti, Erie, Pa.

Coconut water, also referred to as coconut juice, is the thin liquid found in the center of a coconut. It has become increasingly trendy lately, in part because of its purported hydrating qualities.

Coconut water is very different from coconut milk. While coconut water is naturally occurring, coconut milk is made by steeping coconut flesh in water and then straining out the solids. Coconut water has a much lower fat content than coconut milk (less than 1 gram per cup as opposed to about 50 grams per cup). It therefore tastes thinner and less rich. It also tastes sweeter, which makes sense given that it typically contains more than three times the sugar of coconut milk.

Tasters thought that coconut water had more of a floral flavor and weaker coconut notes than coconut milk. Because it is so vastly different, coconut water is not suitable for cooking.

BOTTOM LINE: Coconut water has a significantly thinner consistency and is bland in flavor compared with coconut milk, so it is suitable only for drinking, not cooking.

I recently had grilled avocado at a restaurant and loved the look of it. But when I cooked avocado at home, it was bitter. What gives?
Ben Randow, Middletown, Conn.

Many people caution against cooking avocados, saying that exposure to heat can turn the otherwise softly sweet avocado bitter and unpleasant. After grilling a few avocado halves and finding a range of flavor results, from pleasant to inedible, we consulted our science editor to find out whether heat was the culprit. He explained that the unpleasant flavor in cooked avocado comes from avocado's specific chemical makeup—when it reaches a certain level of heat and is held there for a certain amount of time, chemi-

cal changes occur, resulting in off-flavors.

To test the theory, we tried microwaving, grilling, and baking avocados. We also made a large batch of avocado soup and cooked it to a variety of temperatures for different lengths of time. We found that avocados need to reach 140 degrees and stay there longer than 20 minutes (or 190 degrees for 1½ minutes) in order to trigger the chemical release and produce unpleasantly bitter flavors. This explains why grilled and fried avocados, which have added visual appeal and texture but are not extensively heated, don't taste bitter.

BOTTOM LINE: Avocados can handle short bursts of heat—just long enough for grill marks—but extensive cooking of this fruit will create off-putting flavors.

QUICK COOKING IS OK
But too much cooking makes avocado bitter.

I know that nothing beats homemade, but sometimes I like to take a shortcut and purchase frosting from my grocery store. Do you have a suggestion for how much frosting I would need for a standard cake?
Christy Hunter, Ames, Iowa

While we do not suggest that you use canned frosting from the baking aisle from a flavor standpoint, we recognize its value in a pinch. In order to answer your question, we measured the amount of frosting sold in a standard can and created a conversion. A typical 1-pound container from the baking aisle contains just over 1½ cups of frosting.

Manufacturers claim that each can should be able to frost one 9-inch layer cake. But by our measurements, these cans contain much less than what's needed.

Be aware that our measurements allow for a layer of frosting between ¼ inch and ½ inch thick, so if you have a heavy hand when frosting, budget for more.

We did find that you can stretch canned frosting by chilling it in the refrigerator for 1 hour and then whipping it with a whisk attachment for 5 minutes. Doing so, we were able to expand a typical can's 1½ cups of frosting to just under 2½ cups. This

WELL-FROSTED
Plenty of good stuff.

SKIMPY
Frosted according to the can.

frosting was lighter in texture but was able to cover a lot more of our 9-inch cake (though we still needed two cans to get the job done).

BOTTOM LINE: We recommend homemade frosting, but in a pinch, you can follow our chart to determine how many cans of frosting you'll need for standard cake sizes.

Cake Size	Amount of Frosting Needed	Canned Frosting
9-inch two-layer cake	4 cups	3 cans
9-inch three-layer cake	5½ cups	4 cans
13 by 9-inch one-layer sheet cake	4 cups	3 cans
24 cupcakes	3 cups (2 tablespoons/cupcake)	2 cans
Add a decorative edge	+ 1 cup	+ 1 can
Add writing on top of a cake	+ 4 tablespoons	+ 4 tablespoons

I love cooking with bacon fat, but my girlfriend is a vegetarian. Is there a meatless substitute that tastes similar?
Louis Timmons, Los Alamos, N.M.

In a bid to build a substitute that would mimic bacon fat's savory, smoky, sweet, and fatty qualities, we tested a variety of fats (coconut oil, vegetable oil, olive oil, Crisco, and butter) flavored with a range of ingredients in various proportions, including soy sauce, smoked paprika, chiles in adobo, miso paste, porcini mushrooms, liquid smoke, maple syrup, maple extract, apple cider vinegar, and more.

After all this testing, the closest substitute was a combination of ¼ cup of refined coconut oil, 2 teaspoons of miso paste, 1 teaspoon of maple syrup, and ¼ teaspoon of liquid smoke. We heated all the ingredients in a 10-inch skillet over low heat for 5 minutes. Then we strained the mixture through a fine-mesh strainer.

The concoction was satisfactory as a cooking medium, but tasters found that, ultimately, it lacked the unmistakable porky qualities of bacon. And with so many ingredients, it was ridiculously complicated to create.

Because bacon fat's smoke point is close to those of olive oil and canola oil, either will work as a direct substitute for cooking. They just will not yield the same flavor results.

BOTTOM LINE: While our formula for faux bacon fat may get you close, nothing truly captures the savory, smoky, sweet flavors of bacon fat—except bacon fat.

▶ To ask us a cooking question, visit **CooksCountry.com/ask**. Or write to Ask *Cook's Country*, P.O. Box 470739, Brookline, MA 02447. Just try to stump us!

Kitchen Shortcuts

COMPILED BY SHANNON FRIEDMANN HATCH

NEAT TRICK
For Good Measure
Ann Musgrove, Eugene, Ore.

It was always a hassle to find my set of measuring spoons in the drawer. And since mine were held together with a ring, I grew tired of cleaning the whole set when I used just one. My solution was to individually place the ones I use most often in a decorative toothbrush holder on my counter. It looks nice and they're always at hand.

TIDY TIP
Egg Protection
Sanna King, Winchester, Mo.

When I take deviled eggs to a gathering, I line muffin tins with cupcake liners and place an egg in each cup. This way they don't slide around, and the liners make serving easy.

CLEVER TIP Preserving Bacon Flavor
Bill Schlag, Chardon, Ohio

I like to save bacon fat and use it in place of butter or oil in savory dishes that benefit from a bit of pork flavor. After letting it cool for 20 minutes, I pour the fat into an ice cube tray and freeze it. Once they are frozen, I put the cubes (approximately 2 tablespoons each) into a zipper-lock bag for storage.

Submit a tip online at CooksCountry.com/kitchenshortcuts or send a letter to Kitchen Shortcuts, Cook's Country, P.O. Box 470739, Brookline, MA 02447. Include your name, address, and phone number. If we publish your tip, you will receive a free one-year subscription to Cook's Country. Letters may be edited for clarity and length.

NEAT TRICK
Pitching a New (Plastic Wrap) Tent
Anne Holub, Chicago, Ill.

Plain toothpicks will tent plastic wrap over cakes just fine, but for warm-weather get-togethers, I like to use cocktail umbrellas. They don't poke through the plastic, and they add a festive touch.

CLEVER TIP
Pastry Bag Prop
Virginia Perkins, Laredo, Texas

I didn't think I had a container tall enough to hold my large pastry bag upright—that is, until I tried my blender jar. It supports the bag so that I have both hands free to fill it.

SMART TIP
Portable Spice Rack
Paulette Phillips, Westfield, Wis.

We love to travel in our little camper, but storage space is at a premium. Rather than carry full-size spice bottles, I place what we need in a compact seven-day pill box. I use painter's tape to label the spices. Each snap-shut compartment holds about 2 tablespoons, plenty for our trip.

DOUBLE DUTY
Safety Blade
Dawn Provencher, La Luz, N.M.

Whenever I have kids help me in the kitchen, I'm careful to keep sharp knives out of their reach. I've found that many items—dough, some fruits and vegetables, and cheese, for example—can be cut easily and safely by kids using a bench scraper. Not only is its edge blunt, but its wide handle allows for a good grip.

Herb-Stuffed Pork Roast

To transform dry, disappointing pork loin into a flavorful centerpiece, you have to go deep.

BY MORGAN BOLLING

PORK LOIN CAN be disappointing. Lean and mild, it's too often overcooked, leading to sad suppers of dry, flavorless meat that no amount of marinade, sauce, crust, or stuffing can save. I set out to make a moist, flavorful pork loin roast that would restore my faith in this readily available cut and serve as a resplendent centerpiece for a happy gathering.

The test kitchen has been down the pork loin route before, so I had a few guidelines to help me get started. We like to pull the meat from the oven when it reaches 135 degrees, as carryover cooking will take the internal temperature to 140 degrees, at which point the pork is perfectly cooked. I made the decision to go with a boneless roast here, as they are easier to find and to work with than the bone-in variety. But to make it remarkable, I knew I'd have to add flavor.

I started with two beautiful boneless loin roasts. I'd need a way to deeply season them: I tested brining the pork versus rubbing it with a salt mixture and letting it sit, refrigerated, for several hours. After a few tests it became clear that salting the meat was much easier, as I didn't have to wrestle a big brine bucket in and out of the refrigerator.

Cooking the pork to the proper temperature was relatively easy; a handful of tests showed that searing the roast in a skillet on the stovetop before roasting it in a low, 275-degree oven was the surest path to perfectly cooked pork. The sear added a little of the depth of flavor that this cut so sorely needs. And the low oven temperature cooked the lean meat gently while minimizing the chance of overcooking. For an even better sear, I added a little sugar to the salt rub.

As for pairing the pork with flavorful ingredients, I started by testing different sauces to serve with the roast. After a few days of sampling sauces, my tasters whittled down the options for this springtime roast to two Italian favorites: pesto (made with olive oil, garlic, Parmesan, and basil) and *salsa verde* (consisting of parsley, anchovies, capers, and lemon). I took a little culinary liberty and combined the two into a serious but lively sauce: briny, herby, bright, and complex.

My tasters liked the sauce so much,

With garlic, Parmesan, parsley, basil, capers, anchovies, and lemon, the green swirl inside this roast is much more than just decorative.

in fact, that they wanted more of it. Could I stuff the roast with more of this bright green elixir? I tried cutting a pocket into the roast, stuffing it, and tying it up with twine; this worked OK, but the pocket didn't hold much stuffing. A better option was opening the roast like a book, pounding it to an even thickness, and smearing on a good coating of the sauce. Then I rolled up the roast, tied it to hold its shape,

seared it, and put it in the oven.

Wow. Now the bright sauce seasoned the roast inside and out, imparting a wide range of flavors to every bite. Backtracking slightly, I found that butterflying the roast before rubbing on the salt/sugar mixture allowed even more of the seasoning to infuse the meat. What's more, I could do this ahead of time; the rub needs at least an hour to work its magic, but you can

rub and refrigerate the roast up to a day before you cook it. I was almost done.

While waiting for my next pork loin to rest, I threw together a quick pan sauce, taking advantage of the flavorful pork drippings by cooking them down with garlic, shallot, chicken broth, and wine. I sliced into the roast and knew I was finally in business: a mahogany crust, juicy meat, a bright herby stuffing, and an easy, tasty sauce for serving.

HERB-STUFFED PORK LOIN Serves 8

Plan ahead: The roast must be seasoned at least 1 hour or up to 24 hours in advance. You will need an ovensafe nonstick skillet for this recipe.

- 1 (3- to 3½-pound) boneless center-cut pork loin roast
- 1 tablespoon packed brown sugar
  Kosher salt and pepper
- 6 tablespoons extra-virgin olive oil
- 8 garlic cloves (3 sliced thin, 5 unpeeled)
- 2 ounces Parmesan cheese, grated (1 cup)
- ¾ cup minced fresh parsley
- ½ cup chopped fresh basil
- ¼ cup capers, minced
- 3 anchovy fillets, rinsed and minced
- 1 teaspoon grated lemon zest plus 2 teaspoons juice
- 1 shallot, peeled and halved
- 2 sprigs fresh rosemary
- 1½ tablespoons all-purpose flour
- ¼ cup dry white wine
- 2 cups chicken broth
- ¼ cup heavy cream

1. Position roast fat side up on cutting board. Insert knife two-thirds of way up from bottom of roast along 1 long side and cut horizontally, stopping ½ inch before edge to create flap. Open up flap. At hinge, cut down into thicker portion of roast, stopping ½ inch from bottom. Pivot knife parallel to cutting board and cut horizontally in opposite direction, stopping ½ inch before edge, to create second flap. Open up this flap and lay meat flat. If meat is of uneven thickness, cover roast with plastic wrap and pound to even thickness with meat pounder.

2. Combine sugar and 1 tablespoon salt in bowl. Sprinkle roast all over with sugar-salt mixture. Transfer roast to gallon-size zipper-lock bag, seal, and refrigerate for at least 1 hour or up to 24 hours.

3. Adjust oven rack to middle position and heat oven to 275 degrees. Heat ¼ cup oil and sliced garlic cloves in ovensafe 12-inch nonstick skillet over medium-high heat until garlic begins to brown slightly, about 3 minutes. Transfer garlic and oil to bowl and let cool for 5 minutes. Stir Parmesan, parsley, basil, capers, anchovies, lemon zest, and ½ teaspoon pepper into garlic oil.

4. Place roast on cutting board, cut side up. Spread herb mixture evenly over surface of roast, leaving ½-inch border on all sides. Starting from short side farthest from exterior fat cap, roll tightly, then tie with kitchen twine at 1-inch intervals. Season roast with pepper.

5. Heat remaining 2 tablespoons oil in now-empty skillet over medium-high heat until just smoking. Brown roast on all sides, about 10 minutes. Flip roast seam side down in skillet. Add shallot, rosemary sprigs, and unpeeled garlic cloves to skillet and transfer to oven. Cook until thickest part of roast registers 135 degrees, 65 to 70 minutes. Transfer roast to carving board, tent loosely with aluminum foil, and let rest for 30 minutes. Do not clean skillet.

6. Meanwhile, use spoon to smash garlic in skillet (skillet handle will be hot). Place skillet over medium-high heat and cook until shallot and garlic are sizzling. Stir in flour and cook, stirring, for 1 minute. Add wine and cook until nearly evaporated, about 2 minutes. Add broth and cream and bring to boil. Reduce heat to medium-low and simmer until sauce is reduced to about 1 cup and thickened, 10 to 12 minutes. Strain through fine-mesh strainer set over small saucepan; discard solids. Stir in lemon juice. Season with salt and pepper to taste. Cover and keep warm.

7. Discard twine and slice roast ½ inch thick. Serve, passing sauce separately.

TEST KITCHEN TECHNIQUE Butterflying and Stuffing a Pork Loin

OPEN AND SEASON With fat side up, cut into the loin two-thirds up from the bottom, stopping ½ inch from the edge. Peel back the top flap and cut down, stopping ½ inch from the bottom. Now cut back into the thicker mass, again stopping ½ inch from the edge. Open up loin, flatten, season, and refrigerate for 1 to 24 hours.

FILL AND ROLL Spread the filling evenly over the interior side, leaving a ½-inch border on all sides. Carefully roll the roast leaving the fat side up. Tie at 1-inch intervals.

Apples Fried with Bacon

Not all historical dishes merit reviving, but after tinkering, this one was ready for a comeback.

BY ASHLEY MOORE

ONCE A POPULAR country-style dish, apples fried with bacon also has White House connections: Presidents Ulysses S. Grant and Jimmy Carter would request the dish for breakfast before tackling the pressing issues of the day. I embarked on a journey to learn more about this unexpected pairing.

After diving a little deeper (as far back as 1878, in Marion Harland's cookbook *The Dinner Year Book*), I learned that, for many years, this sweet and salty combination was enjoyed as a side dish at dinnertime, too. I collected various recipes—some old, some new—and headed into the test kitchen.

The basic method—sautéing sliced apples in bacon fat—was the same across all the recipes I uncovered; what few disparities existed were mostly about the variety of apple to use and how exactly the apples were cut. I found it easy to pick a lane on the shape of the apples: Coarsely chopped apples cooked much too quickly and turned to mush, while rings were unwieldy. I settled on thick wedges—four per apple—which looked great on the plate and provided plenty of surface area for caramelization. I also decided to keep the peels on to help the apple quarters hold their shape.

Tasters preferred sweeter apples (Fuji, Gala, or Braeburn) to tart Granny Smiths. But I was frustrated by the structure and texture of the apples—one batch was too mushy, the next too firm. I wanted apple slices that were tender and nicely browned but still held their shape. I put the microwave to use here, zapping the apples for 5 minutes to soften them. After draining them and patting them dry with paper towels, I sautéed the partially cooked apples in the rendered bacon fat (about 3 to 4 minutes per side) to caramelize the exteriors. Just right.

Bacon, lemon, and sage give this dish formidable flavor.

I added a spritz of lemon juice for a pop of brightness, a bit of salt and pepper for balance, and a toss of fresh chopped sage for depth.

APPLES FRIED WITH BACON
Serves 4 to 6

Be sure to thoroughly dry the apples after draining them in step 1 so they caramelize. Depending on how your apples are cut, it may be necessary to prop them up against one another as they cook.

- 3 Fuji, Gala, or Braeburn apples, cored and quartered
- 1 tablespoon sugar
  Salt and pepper
- 3 slices bacon, cut into ½-inch pieces
- 1 tablespoon chopped fresh sage
- 2 teaspoons lemon juice

1. Microwave apples in covered bowl until softened, about 5 minutes. Drain apples in colander, then pat dry with paper towels. Toss apples, sugar, ½ teaspoon salt, and ¼ teaspoon pepper together in bowl until apples are evenly coated.

2. Meanwhile, cook bacon in 12-inch nonstick skillet over medium heat until crisp, 5 to 7 minutes. Using slotted spoon, transfer bacon to paper towel–lined plate, leaving fat in skillet.

3. Arrange apples in skillet, with 1 cut side down, and increase heat to medium-high. Cook until well browned, 3 to 4 minutes. Flip apples to second cut side and continue to cook until well browned on second side, about 3 minutes longer. Off heat, stir in sage, lemon juice, and bacon until combined. Season with salt and pepper to taste. Serve.

Beef on Weck

To do justice to Buffalo's signature sandwich, we worked our way from the outside in. BY MORGAN BOLLING

RESIDENTS OF BUFFALO, New York, put beef on weck sandwiches right up there with Buffalo wings as their most beloved local dish. The sandwich is a relatively simple affair—a salty roll called a *kummelweck* is piled high with thinly sliced roast beef, jus, and horseradish sauce. But as with many seemingly simple recipes, getting it just right isn't so easy. Especially in a home kitchen.

While most sandwiches are all about the filling, the kummelweck rolls are at least as important as the beef in this case. These rolls are similar to kaiser rolls but are accented with caraway seeds and a hefty dose of kosher salt. Making the rolls from scratch was more work than I wanted to do, so I tried several methods for adding salt and caraway seeds to plain store-bought kaiser rolls. In the end, the most effective trick was to microwave a slurry of cornstarch and water to create a "glue" to brush on top of the rolls, which I then sprinkled with salt and caraway seeds before lightly toasting them in the oven. The rolls were nicely seasoned with a soft interior and crusty, salty exterior.

▶ Need more Buffalo? Find our recipe for Boneless Buffalo Chicken at CooksCountry.com/ bonelessbuffalochicken.

If I was going through the effort of roasting beef for sandwiches, I wanted to make enough to feed a crowd (about eight sandwiches), so I'd need a sizable cut. Chuck roast was too chewy. Top round came in inconsistent shapes and was difficult to cook evenly. Tenderloin was too expensive. Eye round, a lean, inexpensive cut from the steer's hind-quarters, proved to be just right.

We usually cook eye round at a low temperature to gently break down its connective tissue and make what can be a tough cut more tender. But at 275 degrees, it took well over an hour for the meat to get to medium-rare—not including the resting time required before slicing it. I wanted to speed things up. The answer was simple: Just by dividing the roast into two long strips, I was able to cook the meat in half the time.

Beef on weck aficionados (and they are plentiful, believe me) will tell you that the meat must be sliced very thin, which is not easy with a warm, soft, medium-rare roast (unless you own a

Two keys to tender beef: Cook it past medium-rare to medium, and slice it as thinly as you can.

meat slicer). I tried a few tricks to make this task easier, including letting the meat rest longer and even freezing the meat after cooking. Nothing worked.

I was at my wit's end when a colleague suggested something radical: Cook the roasts to medium instead of medium-rare. Skeptical (and reluctant), I let my next roasts reach 130 degrees. After they had a half-hour rest, I was delighted to find that the roasts were

much easier to slice thin because the meat was firmer. And even my most discerning tasters deemed the medium beef flavorful and tender.

To complete my sandwich, I quickly threw together a jus based on the pan drippings and created an easy dump-and-stir horseradish sauce. But even with all the components put together, the sandwiches still lacked cohesion. At some restaurants in Buffalo where beef on

weck is served, the roll is dipped quickly in jus before the sandwich is assembled. My tasters didn't love how this made the roll slightly soggy, but tossing the roast beef slices with some of the jus and horseradish before piling it on the rolls brought everything together.

I finally had meaty, salty, satisfying beef on weck sandwiches that were good enough to stand up to the genuine article.

BEEF ON WECK SANDWICHES

Makes 8 sandwiches

Buy refrigerated prepared horseradish, not the shelf-stable kind. Note that the cooked beef must rest for 30 to 60 minutes before slicing.

HORSERADISH SAUCE

- ½ cup prepared horseradish, drained
- 1 tablespoon sour cream
- 1 tablespoon mayonnaise

BEEF

- 1 (2- to 2½-pound) boneless eye-round roast, trimmed
- 5 teaspoons vegetable oil
  Kosher salt and pepper
- 2 teaspoons minced fresh thyme
- ¼ cup prepared horseradish, drained

JUS

- 1 onion, chopped fine
- 1 teaspoon vegetable oil
- 1 teaspoon cornstarch
- 2½ cups beef broth
- 1 sprig fresh thyme

WECK

- 8 kaiser rolls, split
- 2 teaspoons caraway seeds
- 1½ teaspoons kosher salt
- 2 tablespoons water
- ½ teaspoon cornstarch

1. FOR THE HORSERADISH SAUCE: Combine horseradish, sour cream, and mayonnaise in bowl; set aside.

2. FOR THE BEEF: Adjust oven rack to middle position and heat oven to 275 degrees. Cut roast in half lengthwise to make 2 even-size roasts. Rub each roast with 1 teaspoon oil and season each with 1 teaspoon salt, 1 teaspoon pepper, and 1 teaspoon thyme. Tie roasts with kitchen twine at 1-inch intervals.

3. Heat remaining 1 tablespoon oil in 12-inch ovensafe skillet over medium-high heat until just smoking. Add both roasts and cook until browned on all sides, 6 to 8 minutes. Transfer skillet to oven and cook until roasts register 130 degrees, 28 to 32 minutes. Transfer roasts to carving board, tent loosely with aluminum foil, and let rest for at least 30 minutes or up to 1 hour. Reserve skillet and any meat drippings. Increase oven temperature to 400 degrees.

4. FOR THE JUS: Return skillet with meat drippings to medium-high heat (skillet handle will be hot) and add onion and oil. Cook until onion is just softened, about 3 minutes, scraping up any browned bits. Whisk cornstarch into broth. Add broth mixture and thyme sprig to skillet and bring to boil. Reduce heat to medium-low and simmer until reduced by half and slightly thickened, about 7 minutes. Strain jus through fine-mesh strainer set over small saucepan; discard solids. Cover and keep warm.

5. FOR THE WECK: Place rolls on rimmed baking sheet. Combine caraway seeds and salt in bowl. Whisk water and cornstarch together in separate bowl. Microwave cornstarch mixture until consistency of glue, about 30 seconds. Brush cornstarch mixture on roll tops, then sprinkle with caraway mixture. Bake until caraway mixture is set and rolls are crusty, about 7 minutes.

6. Slice roasts against grain as thin as possible. Toss sliced meat, ⅓ cup jus, and horseradish together in bowl and season with salt and pepper to taste. Sandwich meat mixture in rolls (about ½ cup per roll). Serve with horseradish sauce and individual portions of jus for dipping.

AND ON THE SIDE: THE BEST DILL PICKLE SPEARS

With chefs and home cooks pickling everything in sight these days, we wondered if the quality of supermarket pickles had improved in recent years. Most supermarket pickles are what the industry calls "fresh packed," meaning they're made by soaking fresh cucumbers in vinegar and salt. The pickles are then either pasteurized, making them shelf-stable, or immediately packed in jars and refrigerated.

We tried three shelf-stable and two refrigerated products, all marketed as "kosher dill." Kosher, in this case, has nothing to do with Jewish dietary restrictions but denotes the presence of garlic, a common seasoning in Jewish deli pickles. We served all the spears, lightly chilled, to 21 America's Test Kitchen staffers.

Tasters could easily identify the shelf-stable spears, which were "atomic green," thanks to food coloring. They're gently cooked before packaging and thus have a "wilted" texture. The two refrigerated products took home top honors for their "fresher" taste and "more crisp" texture. Refrigerated pickles have a shorter shelf life, so they don't sit in their liquid as long and are much crunchier than the oversaturated shelf-stable pickles. Tasters also thought that most of the shelf-stable pickles had "off," "chemical" aftertastes.

Garlic was also important—these are kosher pickles, after all—and many bottom-ranked products use garlic powder instead of fresh garlic. Our winning product is one of only two to use real chopped garlic, and it was praised for its "peppery" spiciness and "bold" garlic flavor. (The other product with fresh garlic uses whole cloves, which didn't saturate the pickling liquid enough to be detected by tasters.)

Tasters deemed our winning product, extra-garlicky Boar's Head Kosher Dill Pickle Spears, the crispest and freshest spears of the bunch. Found in the refrigerated section of the supermarket, these "crunchy," "tart" spears are minimally processed and our top pick. –LAUREN SAVOIE

RECOMMENDED

	TASTERS' NOTES
BOAR'S HEAD Kosher Dill Pickle Spears Price: $3.99 for 26 oz ($0.15 per oz) Refrigerated: Yes Pasteurized: No	Tasters thought that this refrigerated product was "pleasantly crisp," with "great snap" and a "clean," bright green color. These pickles were "slightly spicy," "very garlicky," and had the "homemade pickle flavor" that tasters loved.
CLAUSSEN Pickles, Kosher Dill Spears Price: $3 for 24 oz ($0.13 per oz) Refrigerated: Yes Pasteurized: No	"Sweet," "salty," and "a little spicy," this refrigerated product had the "familiar," "classic" pickle profile. Tasters thought that these slender spears had "perfect crunch," "crispy skin, and "clean," "fresh" flavor.
MT. OLIVE Kosher Dill Spears Price: $2.79 for 24 oz ($0.12 per oz) Refrigerated: No Pasteurized: Yes	These thick wedges were "sweet and sour," with a "slight kick of pepper" and "supersalty" flavor. Though a few tasters thought that these shelf-stable, "juicy" spears were "mushy," most enjoyed their "crispy" skin and "smooth," "soft" core.

RECOMMENDED WITH RESERVATIONS

FARMER'S GARDEN BY VLASIC Kosher Dill Spears Price: $3.99 for 26 oz ($0.15 per oz) Refrigerated: No Pasteurized: Yes	While accents of carrots, red peppers, and whole garlic cloves lent this shelf-stable pickle an attractive appearance, tasters thought that the pickles were "too seedy," "wilted," and "slightly mushy." "Feels like these cucumbers have been sitting around too long."

NOT RECOMMENDED

VLASIC Kosher Dill Spears Price: $3.29 for 24 oz ($0.14 per oz) Refrigerated: No Pasteurized: Yes	This shelf-stable pickle was the "least fresh of the bunch," with an "atomic green" color and "slimy," "oversaturated" interior. Most tasters also noted a "chemical," "soapy" aftertaste and a "cloyingly sweet" flavor.

Cracker-Crusted Fried Chicken

Crunchy cracker crumbs can make a great fried chicken coating. But it took three weeks in the test kitchen and 60 pounds of chicken to get the texture just right. BY DIANE UNGER

FEW KITCHEN TASKS are as satisfying as frying chicken. I'm fascinated by the way the oil sounds (like a light spring rain), and I love the way the skin crackles and the juices burst out when you take your first bite. I've developed many fried chicken recipes in the test kitchen, so when I read about a style of fried chicken coated in cracker crumbs, my curiosity was aroused. But I had a feeling that perfecting this recipe wasn't going to be a walk in the park.

I gathered a handful of recipes, placed an initial order for 30 pounds of chicken parts, and began brining, coating, and frying. My tasters and I learned a lot from this first sampling of recipes: Most produced dull, underseasoned chicken. And the crumb coatings were problematic. Those that called for straight-up saltine crumbs yielded unpleasantly hard shells covering the chicken, while crumbs that were tossed with butter made for greasy and soggy fried chicken. But one recipe, which called for a combination of crushed saltines and flour, produced a crust that was crisp and golden. The meat wasn't very flavorful, but at least I had a starting point.

I decided to work on the cracker-crumb coating first and then deal with the flavor-challenged chicken itself. Instead of finely grinding the crackers in a food processor, which basically created a powder, I put the crackers in a plastic bag and crushed them with a rolling pin to create slightly coarser crumbs that I hoped would highlight the subtle flavor of the crackers. To make the coating even crispier, I replaced some of the all-purpose flour with cornstarch and added a teaspoon of baking powder for a lighter, cracklier crunch. A hefty 2 teaspoons of ground black pepper ensured that the coating had a nice little kick.

Now for the chicken. The test kitchen often turns to brining (submerging the chicken in a saltwater solution for at least 1 hour or up to 4 hours) to keep chicken moist during frying. I wanted this chicken to be highly seasoned, so I added soy sauce, Worcestershire sauce, cayenne pepper, and some granulated garlic to the brine. After the chicken parts had spent a few hours in the brine, I thoroughly dried them, coated them in my cracker-crumb mixture, let them sit for about a half-hour to allow the crackers to adhere, and then fried up a batch.

Irregularly shaped saltine crumbs help create an extra-crunchy coating.

Anticipation mounted as I lowered five pieces of chicken into my pot of hot oil and waited patiently for them to cook through to golden brown (which took about 14 minutes). While the first batch cooled, I fried the last five pieces and then called my eager tasters.

Success. The chicken skin was rendered, the coating was crisp, and the meat was juicy and seasoned down to the bone.

Lemon and Herb Potato Salad

CRACKER-CRUSTED FRIED CHICKEN Serves 4

Use a Dutch oven that holds 6 quarts or more. This recipe requires brining the chicken for at least 1 hour before coating.

Salt and pepper
2 tablespoons Worcestershire sauce
2 tablespoons soy sauce
2 teaspoons cayenne pepper
2 teaspoons granulated garlic
3 pounds bone-in chicken pieces (split breasts cut in half crosswise, drumsticks, thighs, and/or wings), trimmed
36 square saltines (1 sleeve)
½ cup all-purpose flour
½ cup cornstarch
1 teaspoon baking powder
3 quarts peanut or vegetable oil

1. Whisk 1½ quarts cold water, 2 tablespoons salt, Worcestershire, soy sauce, cayenne, and granulated garlic together in large container until salt dissolves. Add chicken, cover, and refrigerate for at least 1 hour or up to 4 hours.

2. Place saltines in 1-gallon zipper-lock bag, seal, and crush to medium-fine crumbs with rolling pin (you should have about 1 cup). Transfer crumbs to large bowl and whisk in flour, cornstarch, baking powder, 2 teaspoons pepper, and ½ teaspoon salt until combined.

3. Set wire rack in rimmed baking sheet. Set second wire rack in second rimmed baking sheet and line half of rack with triple layer of paper towels. Working with 1 piece at a time, remove chicken from brine and transfer to saltine mixture, pressing firmly so coating adheres to chicken. Transfer coated chicken to prepared rack (without paper towels). Refrigerate for at least 30 minutes or up to 2 hours.

4. Add oil to large Dutch oven until it measures about 2 inches deep and heat over medium-high heat to 350 degrees. Add half of chicken to hot oil and fry until breasts register 160 degrees and drumsticks/thighs/wings register 175 degrees, 13 to 16 minutes. Adjust burner, if necessary, to maintain oil temperature between 300 and 325 degrees. Transfer chicken to paper towel–lined side of second wire rack to drain on each side for 30 seconds, then move to unlined side of rack. Return oil to 350 degrees and repeat with remaining chicken. Serve.

Forget the mayonnaise. An herbed vinaigrette makes it light and fresh.

BY CHRISTIE MORRISON

MOST RECIPES FOR potato salad call for little more than cooked potatoes and mayonnaise (with some hard-cooked eggs, chopped celery, or pickles sometimes thrown in). I'm a fan of this creamy and satisfying combination, but sometimes you want a lighter, fresher approach. Cooked potatoes tossed with vinaigrette (common in French or Austrian potato salads) have an added springtime bonus: With no eggy mayo that could spoil in the sun, they're well suited to picnics and warm-weather events.

I wanted firm but tender chunks of potato that would retain their shape once dressed and not clump up in a starchy blob. Waxy red potatoes are lower in starch than fluffy russets and, unpeeled, cut a more colorful figure than Yukon Golds. But even the red potatoes began to break down as they neared the end of cooking, giving off the starch I was trying to avoid. How could I get tender potatoes without all the starch?

In a word, science. During testing for prior recipes, the test kitchen has learned that when pectin in potatoes begins to dissolve during cooking, it causes the cell walls to break down and release starch. Adding acid to the cooking water slows down this process, resulting in slightly firmer potatoes and less starch. After a few tests, I found that 2 tablespoons of vinegar added to the potato cooking water was just enough to minimize the starch without prolonging the cooking time. My potatoes were tender but held their shape when tossed with vinaigrette.

About that vinaigrette: I didn't want the supersharp variety that leaves the insides of your cheeks aching or a sweet one that covered up the subtle, earthy potato flavors. Lemon juice, instead of vinegar, sharpened the dressing just enough without being harsh and, along with a bit of lemon zest, added citrus pop. Extra-virgin olive oil provided nice richness. To make sure that the dressing penetrated the potatoes, I tossed 2 tablespoons of the vinaigrette with the drained but still hot potatoes before spreading the cooked spuds onto a baking sheet to cool. Once the potatoes came to room temperature, I added the rest of the vinaigrette and some chopped onion for bite, and I tossed it all with fragrant herbs: tarragon, parsley, and chives (added last to preserve their fresh flavors). Two tablespoons of capers added a briny note.

You can mix up the herbs in this salad if you like: Try it with basil, cilantro, and mint.

LEMON AND HERB RED POTATO SALAD Serves 8

To rinse the onion, place it in a fine-mesh strainer and run it under cold water. This removes some of the onion's harshness. Drain, but do not rinse, the capers here.

3 pounds red potatoes, unpeeled, cut into 1-inch chunks
2 tablespoons distilled white vinegar
Salt and pepper
2 teaspoons grated lemon zest plus 3 tablespoons juice
⅓ cup extra-virgin olive oil
½ cup finely chopped onion, rinsed
3 tablespoons minced fresh tarragon
3 tablespoons minced fresh parsley
3 tablespoons minced fresh chives
2 tablespoons capers, minced

1. Combine potatoes, 8 cups water, vinegar, and 2 tablespoons salt in Dutch oven and bring to boil over high heat. Reduce heat to medium and cook at strong simmer until potatoes are just tender, 10 to 15 minutes.

2. Meanwhile, whisk lemon zest and juice, 1 teaspoon salt, and ½ teaspoon pepper together in large bowl. Slowly whisk in oil until emulsified; set aside.

3. Drain potatoes thoroughly, then transfer to rimmed baking sheet. Drizzle 2 tablespoons dressing over hot potatoes and toss gently until evenly coated. Let potatoes cool, about 30 minutes, stirring once halfway through cooling.

4. Whisk dressing to recombine and stir in onion, tarragon, parsley, chives, and capers. Add cooled potatoes to dressing and stir gently to combine. Season with salt and pepper to taste. Serve warm or at room temperature.

Bierock Casserole

Bierocks—handheld buns filled with beef, cabbage, and cheese—are definitely tasty, but they take a long time to make. We wanted the same great flavors in casserole form. BY ASHLEY MOORE

BEEF-FILLED BIEROCKS, ALSO known as runsas, are common in the high plains country of Nebraska, Kansas, and eastern Colorado, where descendants of Eastern European immigrants settled in the late 19th century to ranch and farm. The handheld buns are made from a soft, sweet, yeasted dough stuffed with a meaty, gooey filling of ground beef, onions, cabbage, and cheese.

Our June/July 2012 recipe for Bierocks is a popular one in the test kitchen—the last time I made the buns, I had a line of fellow cooks eager to grab one for lunch. But mixing and kneading dough, letting it rise for an hour, splitting it into individual buns and stuffing each one, and then letting them rise for yet another hour before baking was too much for a weeknight supper. Was there an easier route?

I found several existing recipes for bierock casserole, which seemed like a great idea. But after making a few versions, I identified a significant problem: the dough itself. While some had the subtle sweetness that characterizes individual bierocks, none had the tender texture that I wanted. What's more, none were quick enough. A colleague recommended using the dough from our Quicker Cinnamon Buns (October/November 2013) since it has a soft texture and faint sweetness and needs only 30 minutes to rise—just the right amount of time to prepare the filling. It worked perfectly.

The filling required only some minor tweaks. I increased the amount of beef and shredded green cabbage from our original recipe. After cooking the beef, cabbage, and onions together in a Dutch oven, I drained off the extra liquid with a colander. After a few tests using different types of cheeses (including Colby Jack, Monterey Jack, and cheddar), I settled on American cheese for its flavor and meltability. A bit of yellow mustard added a sharp note.

I allowed the filling to cool in the casserole dish for 10 minutes before draping the rolled dough over the top and crimping the edges. For ventilation, and to prevent any unwanted overflows, I made three rows of three slits. After brushing the top with egg for a shiny finish, I slid the casserole into the oven. Just 20 minutes later, I had another line of tasters with forks at the ready.

BIEROCK CASSEROLE Serves 6 to 8

We prefer whole milk here, but reduced-fat milk will also work in the dough.

DOUGH

- 1 cup whole milk
- 1 tablespoon instant or rapid-rise yeast
- 2 tablespoons sugar
- 2 cups (10 ounces) all-purpose flour
- 1¾ teaspoons baking powder
- ½ teaspoon salt
- 2 tablespoons unsalted butter, melted

FILLING

- 1 tablespoon vegetable oil
- 3 pounds 85 percent lean ground beef
- 1 small head green cabbage, cored and chopped fine (8 cups)
- 2 onions, chopped fine
  Salt and pepper
- 1 tablespoon all-purpose flour
- 6 ounces American cheese, chopped
- 2 tablespoons yellow mustard

- 1 large egg beaten with 1 tablespoon water

1. FOR THE DOUGH: Microwave ¼ cup milk in small bowl until it registers 110 degrees, 15 to 20 seconds. Stir in yeast and 1 teaspoon sugar and let sit until mixture is bubbly, about 5 minutes.

2. Whisk flour, baking powder, salt, and remaining 5 teaspoons sugar together in large bowl. Stir in melted butter, yeast mixture, and remaining ¾ cup milk until dough forms (dough will be sticky). Transfer dough to well-floured counter and knead until smooth ball forms, about 2 minutes. Transfer dough to greased large bowl, cover tightly with plastic wrap, and let rise for 30 minutes.

3. FOR THE FILLING: Meanwhile, adjust oven rack to middle position and heat oven to 375 degrees. Heat oil in Dutch oven over medium-high heat until just smoking. Add beef, cabbage, onions, 2½ teaspoons salt, and 2½ teaspoons pepper; cover and cook for 5 minutes. Uncover and continue to cook, breaking up beef with spoon, until beef is no longer pink and cabbage is wilted, 10 to 15 minutes. Stir in flour until fully incorporated and cook for 1 minute. Let beef mixture drain in colander set in sink for 5 minutes.

4. Return beef mixture to now-empty pot and stir in cheese and mustard. Season with salt and pepper to taste.

The sweet dough and savory beef are balanced by a couple of tablespoons of tangy yellow mustard in the filling.

Transfer filling to 13 by 9-inch baking dish and let cool for 10 minutes.

5. Roll dough into 18 by 12-inch rectangle. Brush rim and interior lip of dish with egg wash (reserve remainder). Loosely roll dough around rolling pin and unroll it over dish. Trim overhanging dough to ½ inch beyond lip of dish. Fold overhanging dough inward so folded edge is flush with inner edge of dish. Crimp dough evenly around edge of dish with your fingers.

6. Brush top of casserole liberally with remaining egg wash. Using paring knife, cut nine 1-inch vent holes in dough. Bake until crust is golden brown and filling is bubbling, about 20 minutes. Transfer casserole to wire rack and let cool for 20 minutes. Serve.

Handheld Origins

Our inspiration for this casserole comes from traditional bierocks, also called runsas. These single-serving buns are individually stuffed with meat filling.

LITTLE PACKAGES
Sweet on the outside, savory within.

Garden State Health Salad

This sweet-and-sour salad became popular at the Claremont Diner in Verona, New Jersey. The diner is gone, but we wanted the salad to live on. BY DIANE UNGER

HEALTH SALAD, ALSO known as Claremont Salad, is a deli side dish that's been ubiquitous at storefront delis and roadside diners in New Jersey and other parts of the Northeast for decades. The mayo-less cabbage and vegetable slaw tossed in a sweet-and-sour dressing benefits from aging in the refrigerator to tenderize the sturdy vegetables and marry the flavors. You'll find variations of this salad using many vegetable combinations, but the common denominators are green cabbage, green bell pepper, carrot, and onion. The sour component of the salad comes from white or cider vinegar. The sweet? Sugar.

After trying a few existing recipes, I was left wondering, why is this called "health" salad? The examples I produced were hardly what I would deem healthy. Some were sickeningly sweet (calling for upwards of ½ cup of sugar) and some surprisingly oily (with anywhere from ½ to 1 cup of vegetable oil). This salad had potential, but I needed to figure out how to get the right balance of sweet, sour, and salty.

I cobbled together a recipe using the components we liked from a handful of recipes in my initial test. First I chopped the cabbage coarsely (tasters didn't care for the shredded coleslaw cut that's sometimes used); then I added thinly sliced onion, carrot, green bell pepper, and a cucumber, which tasters preferred peeled, halved, and sliced thin.

Moving on to the dressing, I tried different combinations and proportions of cider vinegar and distilled white vinegar before settling on distilled white vinegar diluted with water (¾ cup vinegar to ¼ cup water) to mellow its acidity. To that, I added ¼ cup of sugar to balance the sourness. Some garlic, salt, pepper, and red pepper flakes, plus 2 tablespoons of olive oil, completed the dressing. Heating the dressing before pouring it over the vegetables ensured that the sugar was fully dissolved and that the dressing soaked into the vegetables.

A hallmark of health salad preparation is letting it sit in its dressing to soften up the vegetables and even out the flavors. I tested letting the dressed salad sit in the fridge for a range of times, from 1 hour up to six days (which several recipes advised in order to "tenderize" the vegetables). I found that 2 hours was the minimum for tender vegetables, and the salad was just fine for up to three days before the texture of the vegetables started to deteriorate.

The keys to this deli-style salad—which can be made three days ahead—are a properly balanced dressing and a nice rest.

HEALTH SALAD Makes 8 cups

This salad needs to be refrigerated for at least 2 hours before serving.

- ½ head green cabbage, halved, cored, and chopped coarse (5 cups)
- 1 green bell pepper, stemmed, seeded, quartered, and sliced thin crosswise
- 1 onion, halved and sliced thin
- 1 cucumber, peeled, halved lengthwise, and sliced thin
- 1 carrot, peeled and sliced thin
- ¾ cup distilled white vinegar
- ¼ cup water
- ¼ cup sugar
- 2 tablespoons olive oil
- 2 garlic cloves, smashed and peeled
  Salt and pepper
- ¼ teaspoon red pepper flakes

1. Combine cabbage, bell pepper, onion, cucumber, and carrot in large bowl. Bring vinegar, water, sugar, oil, garlic, 2 teaspoons salt, and pepper flakes to simmer in medium saucepan over medium-high heat, stirring to dissolve sugar.

2. Once simmering, pour vinegar mixture over vegetables and stir to combine. Cover with plastic wrap and refrigerate for at least 2 hours, stirring occasionally. Season with salt and pepper to taste. Serve. (Health salad will keep, refrigerated, for up to 3 days.)

Chicken California

James Beard championed this turn-of-the-century dish from California's San Joaquin Valley, but his recipe left some mysteries to solve. BY MORGAN BOLLING

IN THE TEST kitchen, when we have a sauce that needs thickening, we summon the usual suspects: cornstarch, roux, flour. So when I recently discovered a recipe in which the final sauce was thickened with cornmeal, I was skeptical. But given that the recipe was from the illustrious James Beard, one of the giants of American cooking, I knew that I needed to try it.

In his landmark 1972 cookbook *American Cookery*, Beard describes the recipe, Chicken California, as "an excellent example of California ranch cookery at the beginning of the century." It calls for coating chicken pieces in cornmeal and braising them in a flavorful sauce made with chili powder, a few warm spices like cumin and coriander, and red wine. Beard then uses a cornmeal slurry (a mixture of water and cornmeal) to thicken the sauce before finishing the dish with chopped green olives, toasted almonds, and fresh cilantro. The eclectic list of ingredients evokes California's deep and diverse agricultural history, but could cornmeal really bring them all together?

Preparing the recipe the first time produced a deeply flavorful dish with disparate tastes and textures that, while enticing, called for some refinement. Though intimidating to consider rethinking a recipe from an American culinary pioneer (and a man who helped develop the culinary techniques I learned at school), my tasters and I had a few ideas for how to update the dish.

I started with the part that initially made me do a double take: the cornmeal thickener, which felt gritty in the final sauce. Since there was no exact measurement for how much should be added (Beard's list just calls for "cornmeal for thickening"), I overdid it with ½ cup and my sauce felt both gritty and sludgy. I cut back the amount of cornmeal by half and tried soaking it in water for 20 minutes to soften the grains. This helped, but I was hoping to avoid the 20-minute wait.

One of my tasters suggested that I add the cornmeal slurry early on in the cooking process so that it could soften while the chicken braised. When I tried this, it cut back the grittiness of the sauce considerably. But it also muted the corn flavor. I decided to try skipping the slurry and adding the cornmeal early on, as I built the braising liquid, toasting

One ingredient you can't see—cornmeal—adds subtle sweetness and helps thicken the sauce of this unusual braise.

it alongside the chili powder. After a few side-by-side tests I found that 2 tablespoons of cornmeal was the perfect amount to properly thicken—and flavor—the sauce with no residual grit.

With the cornmeal thickener figured out, I wanted to focus on flavors, of which Beard's original recipe has many. His hefty dose of chili powder with cumin seed, coriander, and nutmeg was invigorating but threatened to

overpower the dish. I wanted to balance the flavors to allow the unexpected almonds and olives to come through more clearly. Because most chili powders contain a mix of spices (not just dried chiles), I ditched Beard's original additions of cumin, coriander, and nutmeg. Tasters unanimously agreed that they liked this edited version, which still produced a complex, multilayered dish.

A tablespoon of brown sugar (which

we preferred to white sugar) added a very subtle balancing note of sweetness, and a generous sprinkle of cilantro introduced a welcome brightness. All the elements came together for a final dish that was greater than the sum of its seemingly disparate parts.

One thing I knew I couldn't improve on was Beard's recommendation at the end of his recipe: "Beer goes well with this menu."

CHICKEN CALIFORNIA

Serves 4 to 6
Serve over rice or mashed potatoes.

- 3 pounds bone-in chicken pieces (split breasts cut in half crosswise, drumsticks, and/or thighs), trimmed
  Salt and pepper
- ½ cup plus 2 tablespoons cornmeal
- 5 tablespoons olive oil
- 1 onion, chopped fine
- 3 garlic cloves, minced
- 1 tablespoon chili powder
- 1 cup dry red wine
- 1¼ cups chicken broth
- 1 tablespoon packed brown sugar
- ⅓ cup sliced almonds, toasted
- ⅓ cup pitted green olives, chopped coarse
- ⅓ cup chopped fresh cilantro

1. Pat chicken dry with paper towels and season with salt and pepper. Place ½ cup cornmeal in shallow dish. Dredge chicken in cornmeal, shaking off excess; transfer to plate. Heat 2 tablespoons oil in Dutch oven over medium heat until shimmering. Add half of chicken and cook until evenly browned, about 3 minutes per side; transfer to plate. Wipe out pot with paper towels and repeat with 2 tablespoons oil and remaining chicken. Wipe out pot.

2. Return now-empty pot to medium heat, add remaining 1 tablespoon oil and onion, and cook until soft, about 3 minutes. Add garlic, chili powder, and remaining 2 tablespoons cornmeal and cook until fragrant, about 30 seconds. Stir in wine and cook until reduced by half, about 3 minutes.

3. Add broth, sugar, ½ teaspoon salt, ½ teaspoon pepper, and chicken and bring to boil. Cover, reduce heat to low, and simmer for 10 minutes. Flip chicken and continue to simmer, covered, until breasts register 160 degrees and thighs/drumsticks register 175 degrees, 8 to 10 minutes longer.

4. Off heat, transfer chicken to shallow casserole dish. Season sauce with salt and pepper to taste. Pour sauce over chicken and sprinkle with almonds, olives, and cilantro. Serve.

The American Table
Shaking That (Almond) Tree

After the Gold Rush of 1849, it became clear that California's real pay dirt wasn't in the Sierra mountains, but in the rich soil of California's Central Valley—San Joaquin Valley to the south, Sacramento Valley to the north. Immigrants from Russia, Italy, Armenia, Germany, Japan, Mexico, China, and many other parts of the world streamed into the area and began to plant. In the floodplains around Stockton, nut-tree groves—walnuts first, then almonds—took shape.

The nut harvest was modest for decades, mostly because of the manpower needed to get the things off the trees. Early farmers employed schoolkids to climb, pick, and toss; later, rubber mallets were used to whack the trees and knock out seeds.

But in the 1940s a war-induced labor shortage inspired Robert Paul Barton of Escalon to develop the first mechanical harvester, the Barton Cable Shaker. The contraption drove up to a tree, grasped the trunk, and vigorously shook it until the nuts fell in a shower onto a net spread on the ground. Within a decade, versions of the Shaker had transformed the process across the valley, making almonds easier to pick. Production skyrocketed and prices fell.

KEY INGREDIENTS **West Coast in the Kitchen**
The disparate ingredients in chicken California reflect the astonishing variety of crops grown in the Central Valley. To make the most of each component, we add them in various stages during the recipe—chili powder and red wine go in early, so their earthy flavors meld throughout the dish, while olives, almonds, and cilantro go in later to finish things off with fresher textures and flavors.

ECLECTIC MIX
Careful timing ensures that these flavors cooperate.

Braised Spring Vegetables

It's an unlikely scenario—early season vegetables cooked at a low simmer to amplify their fresh flavors—but it works.

BY AARON FURMANEK

The tender, tasty braised radishes in this dish are a revelation.

IN A BID to make the most of their freshness, seasonal spring vegetables like asparagus and peas are often barely cooked. Others, like radishes, are usually served raw. But as many chefs know, cooking spring vegetables low and slow can actually produce a lively, warm side dish that brings out the distinct flavors of each individual vegetable while offering a bit of warmth on a still-cool spring evening.

To start, I trimmed some radishes and dropped them into a Dutch oven with just over a cup of water. After a 5-minute simmer, they transformed from assertive and peppery to soft and sweet. Next into the pot went 2-inch lengths of asparagus, some sliced leeks and fennel, and then, about 5 minutes later, some frozen peas. (We love frozen peas in the test kitchen; of the vegetables available in the frozen foods section, they're among the most successful.) Adding the vegetables in intervals helped ensure that none would overcook.

After a few minutes, the broth was rich and the vegetables were lovely to look at. But the combination of flavors confounded my tasters' tastebuds. The leeks were too pungent and stringy, and the fennel seemed bulky and intrusive. There were too many things in the pot. A few rounds of refinement left us with the true stars of the dish: asparagus, peas, and radishes.

I established a subtle savory base by sautéing some sliced shallot along with a bit of garlic, thyme sprigs, and red pepper flakes. In went the radishes and water, this time with some citrus zest for freshness, a bay leaf for depth, and some salt for seasoning. Next, some asparagus and, finally, the peas, which just needed to be brought to temperature. The vegetables were radiant, and the broth was invigorating and complex. A toss of chopped fresh tarragon was a final nod to spring.

BRAISED SPRING VEGETABLES
Serves 4
You can use ¼ teaspoon of dried thyme in place of the fresh sprigs.

- ¼ cup extra-virgin olive oil
- 1 shallot, sliced into thin rings
- 2 garlic cloves, sliced thin
- 3 fresh thyme sprigs
  Pinch red pepper flakes
- 10 radishes, trimmed and quartered lengthwise
- 1¼ cups water
- 2 teaspoons grated lemon zest
- 2 teaspoons grated orange zest
- 1 bay leaf
  Salt and pepper
- 1 pound asparagus, trimmed and cut into 2-inch lengths
- 2 cups frozen peas
- 4 teaspoons chopped fresh tarragon

1. Heat oil, shallot, garlic, thyme sprigs, and pepper flakes in Dutch oven over medium heat until shallot is just softened, about 2 minutes.

2. Stir in radishes, water, lemon zest, orange zest, bay leaf, and 1 teaspoon salt. Cover and cook until radishes can be easily pierced with tip of paring knife, 3 to 5 minutes. Stir in asparagus and continue to cook, covered, until tender, 3 to 5 minutes.

3. Off heat, stir in peas and let sit, covered, until peas are heated through, about 5 minutes. Discard thyme sprigs and bay leaf. Stir in tarragon and season with salt and pepper to taste. Transfer to shallow platter and serve.

One-Pan Pork Chop Dinner

Pork chops and roasted vegetables pair well on the plate, but could we get them to cook together on the same baking sheet? BY CHRISTIE MORRISON

W E ARE ALWAYS looking for ways to streamline recipes to make life easier for the home cook. So a one-pan meal of pork chops with roasted potatoes and carrots sounded great: simple, tasty, and easy to clean up. But once I lined up all the ingredients in the test kitchen, it quickly became clear that I'd have a few problems to solve.

The most obvious issue was cooking time: Thin pork chops cook in as little as 5 minutes, but even large, 1-inch-thick, center-cut, bone-in chops cook in only 10 to 15 minutes. Roasting vegetables to a soft, tender stage would require at least twice that time.

My other problem was flavor: I knew before starting that browning the chops on the stovetop—which we often do to build flavor—didn't make sense here. I'd have to sear them first in an ovensafe skillet and then transfer them along with the vegetables to the oven. But four big pork chops and 2 pounds of vegetables (enough to feed four) wouldn't fit comfortably even in a large skillet. I'd have to come up with another way to add flavor.

But for now, I'd focus on the cooking time. My plan was to partially roast the vegetables in the oven on a rimmed baking sheet (which promotes fast cooking and browning) and then add the large chops on top of the vegetables after about 30 minutes—and not use a skillet at all.

I tossed sliced Yukon Gold potatoes, coarsely cut carrots and fennel bulb, and a big handful of peeled garlic cloves with a tablespoon of extra-virgin olive oil and some minced fresh rosemary. Then I dumped the mixture onto the baking sheet and slid it into the oven. After a few tests, I found that roasting at 450 degrees on the upper-middle rack allowed the vegetables to brown at such a pace that I didn't need to open the oven to stir them during cooking—a definite plus.

While the vegetables were roasting, I focused my attention on adding flavor to the main ingredient, the chops. Since stovetop searing was off the table, I tried rubbing the chops with sugar to see if that would help them brown in the oven, but it still took too long: The chops were basically jerky by the time they picked up significant color. I decided instead to use a potent spice

A little paprika in the spice rub helps these chops develop nice color in the oven.

rub. I tried several combinations, and my tasters voted in favor of a fragrant blend of sweet paprika, coriander, salt, and pepper. This mix added a subtle but energetic pop of flavor to the pork and gave it an attractive color (thanks to the paprika). Now that the meat had some real flavor, I could work out the timing.

After about 25 minutes in the oven, the vegetables were almost—but not quite—tender. Working quickly, I balanced the raw, spice-rubbed chops on top of the vegetables and returned the pan to the oven. Elevating the chops on top of the vegetables allowed air to circulate under the meat, which sped up the cooking. What's more, as the pork juices and seasonings dripped down onto the vegetables, they took

on beautiful meaty flavors. The hot vegetables, in turn, helped speed up the cooking time of the chops; after just 10 to 15 minutes, the chops hit a perfect 140 degrees and the vegetables were nicely tender.

The chops and vegetables were well seasoned, but I wanted a jolt of freshness to tie the meat and vegetables together. I turned to common pantry ingredients—red wine vinegar, a bit of minced shallot, some extra-virgin olive oil, and a little sugar for balance—and then whisked in a couple of tablespoons of fresh parsley and drizzled the bright green sauce over the finished dish.

This dish was delicious and easy, and done in 40 minutes of roasting—just right for an easy weeknight supper.

ONE-PAN PORK CHOPS AND ROASTED VEGETABLES
Serves 4

This recipe was developed using Diamond Crystal kosher salt. If you substitute table salt, reduce the amount of salt in each part of the recipe by half. Columela Extra Virgin Olive Oil won our taste-test of supermarket extra-virgin oils.

- 4 (10-ounce) bone-in center-cut pork chops, 1 to 1¼ inches thick, trimmed
- ⅓ cup extra-virgin olive oil Kosher salt and pepper
- 1 teaspoon paprika
- 1 teaspoon ground coriander
- 1 pound Yukon Gold potatoes, unpeeled, halved lengthwise and cut crosswise into ½-inch-thick slices
- 1 pound carrots, peeled and cut into 3-inch lengths, thick ends quartered lengthwise
- 1 fennel bulb, stalks discarded, bulb halved, cored, and cut into ½-inch-thick wedges
- 10 garlic cloves, peeled
- 2 teaspoons minced fresh rosemary
- 2 tablespoons minced fresh parsley
- 1 small shallot, minced
- 4 teaspoons red wine vinegar
- ⅛ teaspoon sugar

1. Adjust oven rack to upper-middle position and heat oven to 450 degrees. Pat pork dry with paper towels and rub with 1 teaspoon oil. Combine 2 teaspoons salt, 1 teaspoon pepper, paprika, and coriander in small bowl. Season pork chops all over with spice mixture; set aside.

2. Toss potatoes, carrots, fennel, garlic, rosemary, 1 tablespoon oil, 1½ teaspoons salt, and ¼ teaspoon pepper together in large bowl. Spread vegetables in single layer on rimmed baking sheet. Roast vegetables until just tender, about 25 minutes.

3. Carefully place pork chops on top of vegetables and return to oven. Roast until chops register 140 degrees and vegetables are fully tender, 10 to 15 minutes longer, rotating sheet halfway through roasting.

4. Meanwhile, combine parsley, shallot, vinegar, sugar, ½ teaspoon salt, ¼ teaspoon pepper, and remaining ¼ cup oil in bowl. Transfer vegetables and pork to platter and drizzle with vinaigrette. Serve.

Pasta with Roasted Tomatoes

Slow-roasting tomatoes can take hours. We wanted the same deep flavors in a fraction of the time. BY AARON FURMANEK

I LIKE PASTA TOSSED with regular tomato sauce as much as the next guy, but I get really excited at the thought of pasta with roasted tomatoes. Slow-roasting tomatoes gives them a beautiful dimpled, caramelized look while also mellowing their sharp flavors into a soft, savory sweetness. But the usual method (roasting at a low temperature for an hour or two and then tossing with pasta) doesn't cut it for an easy weeknight pasta dinner. So I set out to create a recipe that produced rich, slow-roasted tomato flavor, without the time commitment.

Regarding the main ingredient, I figured that cherry tomatoes would be a great choice since their small size means they cook quickly. Most recipes I found for roasted cherry tomatoes call for halving them and then cooking them at around 350 degrees for 40 to 50 minutes. Unfortunately, the tomatoes were inconsistently browned and sometimes overcooked with this method. I wanted to eliminate the guesswork and have sufficiently blistered tomatoes with deep flavor while keeping the oven time under 30 minutes.

For my next test, I tossed halved cherry tomatoes with several good glugs of extra-virgin olive oil plus minced garlic, red pepper flakes, a little sugar, tomato paste (which is already concentrated and, thus, would help mimic long-cooked flavor), salt, and pepper and roasted them at 425 degrees for 20 minutes, thinking that the higher temperature would help the tomatoes achieve that trademark blistered skin. Instead, what I found was barely shriveled skin with only mild blistering and a soggy texture rather than concentrated sweetness.

My next thought was to preheat the baking sheet so that the tomatoes would start cooking immediately. This produced only slightly more blistering on the tomatoes, and nearly all their natural juices seeped out and evaporated—meaning I was losing lots of great flavor. These results didn't justify preheating the baking sheet, so I looked for other solutions.

I tried increasing the oven temperature in 25-degree increments to 450, 475, and 500 degrees. Blistering and browning improved at higher temperatures, but the tomatoes were drying out too much. Up to this point, I had been halving the tomatoes, but for the next test, I left them whole and repeated the test at the different oven temperatures. Not only did the recipe get easier— I no longer had to halve 3 pints of tomatoes—but the whole tomatoes blistered better than the halved tomatoes in my previous tests. And since the tomatoes held on to their juices longer, their flavorful liquid didn't evaporate, which made the finished dish taste even better.

But in finding a solution to the tomatoes, I created a problem with the garlic. Roasting tomatoes in a hotter-than-normal oven worked well for the tomatoes, but the garlic burned around the edges of the pan. So to ensure that the garlic wouldn't burn, I centered the tomatoes on the baking sheet and then placed the garlic in the middle of the tomatoes. This insulated the garlic enough so that it cooked, but didn't burn, during roasting.

Tossed with pasta, Parmesan, and some fresh basil, my roasted cherry tomatoes made for a fast, easy, delicious weeknight dinner that tasted like it took twice as long to prepare.

PASTA WITH ROASTED CHERRY TOMATOES
Serves 4

You will need 3 pints of cherry tomatoes for this recipe; you can use an equal amount of grape tomatoes. Linguine or capellini can be substituted for the spaghetti.

- 3 tablespoons extra-virgin olive oil
- 5 garlic cloves, sliced thin
- 2 teaspoons tomato paste
  Salt and pepper
- 1 teaspoon sugar
- ⅛ teaspoon red pepper flakes
- 1¾ pounds cherry tomatoes
- 1 pound spaghetti
- ½ cup coarsely chopped fresh basil
- 1 ounce Parmesan cheese, grated (½ cup), plus extra for serving

1. Adjust oven rack to middle position and heat oven to 500 degrees. Line rimmed baking sheet with parchment paper. Whisk 2 tablespoons oil, garlic, tomato paste, 1½ teaspoons salt, sugar, ¼ teaspoon pepper, and pepper flakes together in large bowl. Add tomatoes and toss to combine.

2. Transfer tomato mixture to prepared sheet and push tomatoes toward center of sheet. Scrape any remaining garlic and tomato paste from bowl into center of tomatoes. Bake until tomatoes are blistered and browned, about 20 minutes.

3. Bring 4 quarts water to boil in large pot. Add pasta and 1 tablespoon salt and cook, stirring often, until al dente. Reserve 1 cup cooking water, then drain pasta and return it to pot.

4. Add basil, roasted tomato mixture, ½ cup reserved cooking water, and remaining 1 tablespoon oil to pasta and toss to combine. Adjust consistency with remaining reserved cooking water as needed and season with salt and pepper to taste. Transfer to serving dish and sprinkle with Parmesan. Serve, passing extra Parmesan separately.

For potent tomato flavor, we toss whole cherry tomatoes with a mixture that includes oil, garlic, tomato paste, and sugar before roasting them.

TEST KITCHEN TECHNIQUE
An Orderly Arrangement

To prevent scorching, center the tomatoes on the sheet. Nestle the garlic slices in the tomato cluster.

Getting to Know Fruit Condiments

Can you tell a compote from a chutney? A jam from a preserve? It's easy to get confused since grocery store labels are often inexact. Here's the real deal when it comes to preserved fruit. BY CHRISTIE MORRISON

Preserves
BIG FRUIT

Fruit preserves are whole pieces or large chunks of fruit suspended in jelly or very thick syrup. Preserves tend to be less sweet than jams and jellies since they traditionally are made with equal parts fruit and sugar. The sugar plays an important role in helping the preserves set, though pectin is often used, too.

Jam
THICK AND CHUNKY

Jam is made from crushed or finely chopped fruit, which is cooked with pectin and sugar until thickened (jams traditionally contain more sugar than fruit by weight). We use jam as a filling for pastries and other desserts like our Peanut Butter and Jam Cake (**CooksCountry. com/peanutbutterandjamcake**).

Jelly
CRYSTAL CLEAR

Unlike preserves and jam, jelly contains no fruit bits; it almost always requires additional pectin to set up properly. The final ingredient is sugar, and like jams, jellies contain more sugar than fruit or fruit juice. We melted strawberry jelly and used it as a glaze in our recipe for Easy Fresh Fruit Tart (**CooksCountry.com/easyfruittart**).

Marmalade
RENDERED RIND

Marmalade almost always contains pieces of rind, which gives it a unique texture and also a faint bitterness. While marmalade was historically made with quinces, today it is usually made with sour Seville oranges; find our recipe at **CooksCountry.com/orangemarmalade**.

Fruit Curd
RICH SPREAD

Lemon curd gets all the glory, but curds—citrusy chilled custards—are also made with lime, orange, and grapefruit. It's important to cook the curd until it reaches 170 degrees; the egg yolks will thicken and cling to a spoon at that point (boiling will break the custard). The curd will continue to thicken as it cools.

Compote
SLOW POACHED

Usually served as part of a dessert, a compote is fresh or dried fruit slowly simmered in heavy sugar syrup with various spices and (sometimes) liqueur. Compotes made with the concentrated flavor of dried fruit can benefit from the addition of hearty herbs like rosemary and thyme.

Conserve
A LITTLE NUTTY

Similar to marmalade, a conserve is a thick, chunky, cooked condiment that often contains fruit rind. Due to the rind's high pectin content, conserves don't usually require added pectin. Conserves differ from marmalades, however, in that they usually contain nuts and dried fruits like raisins or currants.

Chutney
SHARP NOTE

Besides fruit, vinegar is the key ingredient in fruit chutneys. Spices and a touch of heat (chutneys vary in spiciness) add complexity. Though chutneys are usually cooked on the stovetop, we've also used the microwave to speed things up; check out our five easy fruit chutneys (**CooksCountry.com/5easychutneys**).

Fruit Butter
NOT TOO SWEET

Deeply flavored fruit butters require long cooking times to achieve their heavy consistency. Apples and pears make popular fruit butters; their sweetness is complemented by spices and sometimes apple cider or brandy. Try our apple butter (**CooksCountry.com/applebutter**) spread on toast or with cheese.

Relish
CHOPPED APPEAL

Unlike most of these other condiments, a fruit relish isn't necessarily cooked. Relishes can be sweet or savory and made of cooked, pickled, or raw ingredients. We process cranberries, a whole orange, and an apple with sugar and spices for our Cranberry-Apple-Orange Relish (**CooksCountry.com/CAOrelish**).

Mostarda
POTENT CONCOCTION

This sweet-savory Italian condiment features candied fruits preserved in a mustardy syrup: Mustard powder, seed, and oil can all be used. Try our homemade Peach Mostarda (**CooksCountry. com/peachmostarda**) alongside roasted meats, spooned over seared fish, or even added to a pan sauce.

Fruit Paste
STIFF STUFF

Fruit paste is most commonly made with pectin-rich quince or guava. Spanish *membrillo* and Portuguese *marmelada* are quince pastes that are cooked with sugar until dark and thick and then cooled until firm and sliceable. Fruit paste will keep in the refrigerator for up to six months.

ORECCHIETTE WITH PEAS, PINE NUTS, AND RICOTTA

CHICKEN-AVOCADO SALAD SANDWICHES

STRIP STEAKS WITH SAUTÉED ONION AND MUSHROOMS

CRISP PARMESAN PORK CUTLETS WITH TOMATO SAUCE

CHICKEN-AVOCADO SALAD SANDWICHES

Serves 4

✓ **WHY THIS RECIPE WORKS:** For a twist on chicken salad, we combine tangy buttermilk, mashed avocado, and a lime vinaigrette to act as the "mayonnaise."

- ¼ cup buttermilk
- 2 tablespoons lime juice
- 1 tablespoon extra-virgin olive oil
- 1 teaspoon sugar
  Salt and pepper
- 1 ripe avocado, halved, pitted, and chopped coarse
- 1 (2½-pound) rotisserie chicken, skin and bones discarded, meat shredded into bite-size pieces (3 cups)
- 8 slices hearty wheat sandwich bread, toasted
- 1 head Bibb lettuce (8 ounces), leaves separated
- 2 tomatoes, cored and sliced thin

1. Combine buttermilk, lime juice, oil, sugar, ½ teaspoon salt, and ½ teaspoon pepper in medium bowl. Add avocado and mash into dressing with fork. Stir in chicken until fully combined. Season with salt and pepper to taste.

2. Place heaping ½ cup chicken salad on each of 4 bread slices. Divide and arrange lettuce and tomatoes over chicken salad, then top with remaining bread slices. Serve.

TEST KITCHEN NOTE: For best results, be sure to use a very ripe avocado.

ORECCHIETTE WITH PEAS, PINE NUTS, AND RICOTTA

Serves 4

✓ **WHY THIS RECIPE WORKS:** To maximize flavor, we season the ricotta with mint, fresh lemon zest and juice, and spices.

- 4 ounces (½ cup) part-skim ricotta cheese
- 3 tablespoons chopped fresh mint
- 1 teaspoon grated lemon zest plus 1 tablespoon juice
  Salt and pepper
- ¼ teaspoon red pepper flakes
- ¼ cup extra-virgin olive oil, plus extra for drizzling
- 3 shallots, sliced thin
- 1 cup frozen peas
- 1 pound orecchiette
- ¼ cup pine nuts, toasted

1. Combine ricotta, 2 tablespoons mint, lemon zest and juice, ½ teaspoon salt, ½ teaspoon pepper, and pepper flakes in bowl; set aside. Heat oil in 10-inch skillet over medium-high heat until shimmering. Add shallots, ¼ teaspoon salt, and ¼ teaspoon pepper and cook until lightly browned, 3 to 5 minutes. Off heat, stir in peas and set aside.

2. Meanwhile, bring 4 quarts water to boil in large pot. Add pasta and 1 tablespoon salt and cook, stirring often, until al dente. Reserve ½ cup cooking water, then drain pasta and return it to pot.

3. Stir shallot mixture and reserved cooking water into pasta. Season with salt and pepper to taste. Transfer to serving platter and dollop with ricotta mixture. Sprinkle with pine nuts and remaining 1 tablespoon mint. Drizzle with extra oil. Serve.

TEST KITCHEN NOTE: Our favorite ricotta cheese is Calabro Part Skim Ricotta Cheese.

CRISP PARMESAN PORK CUTLETS WITH TOMATO SAUCE

Serves 4

✓ **WHY THIS RECIPE WORKS:** We add an extra flour dip to the classic three-step breading method here to ensure that the coating sticks and cooks up crisp.

- 1 cup plus 2 tablespoons all-purpose flour
- 3 large eggs
- 4 ounces Parmesan cheese, grated (2 cups), plus extra for serving
  Salt and pepper
- ½ teaspoon dried oregano
- 8 (3-ounce) boneless pork cutlets, ½ inch thick, trimmed
- ¼ cup vegetable oil
- 1 cup jarred marinara sauce, warmed
- 2 tablespoons chopped fresh basil

1. Place 1 cup flour in shallow dish. Beat eggs in second shallow dish. Combine Parmesan, 1 teaspoon salt, 1 teaspoon pepper, oregano, and remaining 2 tablespoons flour in third shallow dish. Pat cutlets dry with paper towels and season with salt and pepper. One at a time, coat cutlets lightly with flour, dip in egg mixture, dredge in Parmesan mixture, and return to flour, pressing to adhere.

2. Heat 2 tablespoons oil in 12-inch nonstick skillet over medium heat until just smoking. Cook 4 cutlets until golden brown and cooked through, 3 to 5 minutes per side. Transfer to paper towel–lined plate. Wipe out skillet and repeat with remaining 2 tablespoons oil and remaining 4 cutlets. Arrange cutlets on serving platter and top with marinara sauce. Sprinkle with basil and extra Parmesan. Serve.

TEST KITCHEN NOTE: Serve with pasta or over polenta.

STRIP STEAKS WITH SAUTÉED ONION AND MUSHROOMS

Serves 4

✓ **WHY THIS RECIPE WORKS:** Searing the steaks in a traditional skillet allows for the buildup of fond, the flavorful browned bits in the bottom of the skillet. Cooking the mushrooms and onion in the same skillet with a splash of balsamic vinegar makes for a complex accompaniment.

- 2 (1-pound) boneless strip or rib-eye steaks, 1 to 1½ inches thick
  Salt and pepper
- 2 tablespoons vegetable oil
- 8 ounces cremini mushrooms, trimmed and sliced thin
- 1 onion, halved and sliced thin
- 2 garlic cloves, minced
- ¼ cup balsamic vinegar
- 3 tablespoons chopped fresh chives
- 2 tablespoons unsalted butter

1. Pat steaks dry with paper towels and season with salt and pepper. Heat 1 tablespoon oil in 12-inch skillet over medium-high heat until just smoking. Cook steaks until well browned and meat registers 125 degrees (for medium-rare), about 5 minutes per side. Transfer to carving board, tent loosely with foil, and let rest for 5 minutes.

2. Heat remaining 1 tablespoon oil in now-empty skillet over medium-high heat until just smoking. Add mushrooms, onion, ½ teaspoon salt, and ½ teaspoon pepper and cook until vegetables are well browned, about 5 minutes. Add garlic and cook until fragrant, about 30 seconds.

3. Stir vinegar and any accumulated beef juices into skillet and simmer, scraping up any browned bits, until sauce has thickened, about 1 minute. Off heat, stir in 2 tablespoons chives and butter. Season with salt and pepper to taste. Slice steaks and transfer to platter. Top with sauce and sprinkle with remaining 1 tablespoon chives. Serve.

**JERK PORK TENDERLOIN
WITH ARUGULA AND PINEAPPLE SALAD**

SEAFOOD AND CHORIZO STEW

**CHICKEN TOSTADAS
WITH SPICY MASHED BLACK BEANS**

SESAME-HOISIN-GLAZED FLANK STEAK

SEAFOOD AND CHORIZO STEW
Serves 4

✓ **WHY THIS RECIPE WORKS:** We start by cooking the chorizo and onion together to infuse this bold flavor combination into the base of the stew.

- 1 tablespoon extra-virgin olive oil, plus extra for drizzling
- 6 ounces chorizo sausage, quartered lengthwise and sliced ½ inch thick
- 1 onion, chopped fine
- 4 garlic cloves, minced
- 1 tablespoon chopped fresh oregano
- 2 (14.5-ounce) cans diced tomatoes
- 1 (8-ounce) bottle clam juice
- 1 pound extra-large shrimp (21 to 25 per pound), peeled, deveined, and tails removed
- 2 (6-ounce) skinless cod fillets, 1 to 1½ inches thick, cut into 1-inch chunks
  Salt and pepper

1. Heat oil in large saucepan over medium-high heat until shimmering. Add chorizo and onion and cook until both are lightly browned, 7 to 9 minutes. Stir in garlic and 1 teaspoon oregano and cook until fragrant, about 30 seconds. Add tomatoes and their juice and clam juice, scraping up any browned bits, and bring to simmer. Cook until slightly thickened, about 10 minutes.

2. Pat shrimp and cod dry with paper towels and season with salt and pepper. Gently stir seafood into stew and cook until opaque and cooked through, about 5 minutes. Stir in remaining 2 teaspoons oregano and season with salt and pepper to taste. Portion stew into individual bowls and drizzle with extra oil. Serve.

TEST KITCHEN NOTE: Our favorite clam juice is Bar Harbor Clam Juice.

JERK PORK TENDERLOIN WITH ARUGULA AND PINEAPPLE SALAD
Serves 4

✓ **WHY THIS RECIPE WORKS:** To build layers of flavor, we make the warm pineapple salad in the skillet after cooking the tenderloins.

- 2 (12-ounce) pork tenderloins, trimmed
- 3 tablespoons jerk seasoning
- 2 tablespoons vegetable oil
- 2 cups ½-inch pineapple pieces
- ½ cup finely chopped red onion
- ¼ cup orange juice
  Pinch cayenne pepper
- 2 ounces (2 cups) baby arugula
  Salt and pepper

1. Adjust oven rack to middle position and heat oven to 450 degrees. Set wire rack in rimmed baking sheet. Pat pork dry with paper towels and season with 2 tablespoons jerk seasoning. Heat 1 tablespoon oil in 12-inch skillet over medium-high heat until just smoking. Cook pork until browned on all sides, 5 to 7 minutes; transfer pork to prepared wire rack. Roast until meat registers 140 degrees, about 15 minutes. Transfer to carving board, tent with foil, and let rest for 5 minutes.

2. Heat remaining 1 tablespoon oil in now-empty skillet over medium-high heat until shimmering. Add pineapple, onion, orange juice, cayenne, and remaining 1 tablespoon jerk seasoning and cook, scraping up any browned bits, until onion is just softened, about 3 minutes. Off heat, stir in arugula. Season with salt and pepper to taste. Slice pork, transfer to platter, and top with pineapple mixture.

TEST KITCHEN NOTE: Buy tenderloins that are of equal size and weight so that they cook at the same rate; make sure that they are no larger than 12 ounces, as bigger tenderloins won't fit in the skillet together.

SESAME-HOISIN-GLAZED FLANK STEAK
Serves 4

✓ **WHY THIS RECIPE WORKS:** The complex flavors of hoisin sauce, rice vinegar, toasted sesame oil, and Sriracha give the sauce a kick, while a little cornstarch produces a velvety texture.

- ¼ cup hoisin sauce
- 2 tablespoons rice vinegar
- 1 tablespoon toasted sesame oil
- 2 teaspoons Sriracha sauce
- 1 teaspoon cornstarch
- 1 (1½-pound) flank steak, trimmed
- 1 tablespoon vegetable oil
- ¼ cup chopped fresh cilantro
- 2 teaspoons toasted sesame seeds

1. Whisk hoisin, vinegar, sesame oil, Sriracha, and cornstarch together in bowl. Pat steak dry with paper towels. Heat oil in 12-inch skillet over medium-high heat until just smoking. Cook steak until well browned and meat registers 125 degrees (for medium-rare), 5 to 7 minutes per side. Transfer to carving board, tent loosely with foil, and let rest for 5 minutes.

2. Stir hoisin mixture into now-empty skillet and cook over medium-high heat, scraping up any browned bits, until sauce has thickened, about 2 minutes. Slice steak thin on bias against grain and transfer to platter. Stir any accumulated meat juices into sauce and spoon over meat. Sprinkle with cilantro and sesame seeds. Serve.

TEST KITCHEN NOTE: Serve with rice.

CHICKEN TOSTADAS WITH SPICY MASHED BLACK BEANS
Serves 4

✓ **WHY THIS RECIPE WORKS:** We add Ro-tel Diced Tomatoes & Green Chilies and fresh cilantro to the mashed black beans to contribute both texture and flavor.

- 2 (6- to 8-ounce) boneless, skinless chicken breasts, trimmed, halved lengthwise, and sliced crosswise ½ inch thick
- 1 tablespoon ground cumin
  Salt and pepper
- 2 tablespoons vegetable oil
- 1 (15-ounce) can black beans, rinsed
- 1 (10-ounce) can Ro-tel Diced Tomatoes & Green Chilies
- ¼ cup coarsely chopped fresh cilantro
- 8 (5-inch) corn tostadas, warmed
- 2 ounces feta cheese, crumbled (½ cup)
- 2 radishes, trimmed, halved, and sliced thin

1. Pat chicken dry with paper towels and toss with cumin, ½ teaspoon salt, and ½ teaspoon pepper. Heat oil in 12-inch nonstick skillet over medium-high heat until just smoking. Cook chicken until browned and cooked through, 5 to 7 minutes. Transfer to plate and tent loosely with foil.

2. Return now-empty skillet to medium-high heat and add beans, tomatoes, and 2 tablespoons cilantro. Cook, mashing beans with potato masher, until mixture is thickened and liquid has evaporated, about 5 minutes. Season with salt and pepper to taste.

3. Arrange tostadas on serving platter. Spoon ½ cup bean mixture onto each tostada. Evenly distribute chicken, feta, radishes, and remaining 2 tablespoons cilantro over bean mixture. Serve.

TEST KITCHEN NOTE: Serve with sour cream and lime wedges.

Matzo Ball Soup

Tender dumplings and savory broth make a happy pair. Just don't introduce them too soon. BY DIANE UNGER

MATZO BALL SOUP is not complicated—it's simply chicken broth with vegetables and tender boiled dumplings made from matzo meal. But ask one lifelong fan what makes a perfect version and then ask another, and you'll find yourself with completely different answers.

One thing fans can agree on: Matzo balls—made from matzo meal (ground matzo), eggs, and water or broth—should be substantial but not too heavy. Also, they must be poached in water and then added to the soup later; if you cook the balls directly in the soup, they leave it starchy and sludgy.

I tried five different existing recipes for matzo balls to get my bearings. Some were heavy, dense sinkers. Others were too delicate and fell apart.

The difference was in the ratio of the ingredients. After trial and error, I settled on 1 cup of matzo meal, four large eggs, and 5 tablespoons of water plus a bit of chopped, cooked onion and minced dill. After an hour's rest in the fridge, the dough was delicate but strong enough to hold together.

I added 12 matzo balls to boiling, salted water. After 10, 20, 30, 40, and 50 minutes, I pulled a few of the balls out and set them aside to cool. I then cut them in half to compare their interiors. Thirty minutes yielded the most consistent texture from edge to center.

Other ingredients in the soup vary by family tradition. Chicken broth, celery, onion, and carrot are common, but from there on it's a free-for-all; rutabaga, parsnip, parsley, dill, and thyme are all options. I was sold on parsnip after a side-by-side test revealed that even committed parsnip haters loved its subtle sweetness. To deepen the chicken flavor, I added two whole chicken legs, which I removed after they cooked through. (The chicken meat may be added back in if you like.)

MATZO BALL SOUP Serves 6

Chicken fat, or schmaltz, is available in the refrigerator or freezer section of most supermarkets. Note that the matzo batter needs to be refrigerated for at least 1 hour before shaping.

MATZO BALLS

- ¼ cup chicken fat (schmaltz) or vegetable oil
- 1 onion, chopped fine
- 4 large eggs
- 1 teaspoon minced fresh dill
  Salt and pepper
- 1 cup (4 ounces) matzo meal

SOUP

- 1 tablespoon chicken fat (schmaltz) or vegetable oil
- 1 onion, chopped
- 2 carrots, peeled and cut into ½-inch chunks
- 2 celery ribs, chopped
- 1 parsnip, peeled and cut into ½-inch chunks
  Salt and pepper
- 8 cups chicken broth
- 1½ pounds chicken leg quarters, trimmed
- 1 teaspoon minced fresh dill

1. FOR THE MATZO BALLS: Heat chicken fat in Dutch oven over medium heat until shimmering. Add onion and cook until light golden brown and softened, about 5 minutes. Transfer onion to large bowl and let cool for 10 minutes. (Do not clean pot.)

2. Whisk eggs, 5 tablespoons water, dill, ¾ teaspoon salt, and ½ teaspoon pepper into cooled onion mixture. Fold in matzo meal until well combined. Cover with plastic wrap and refrigerate for at least 1 hour or up to 2 hours. (Batter will thicken as it sits.)

3. Bring 4 quarts water and 2 tablespoons salt to boil in now-empty Dutch oven. Divide batter into 12 portions (about 1 heaping tablespoon each) and place on greased plate. Roll portions into smooth balls between your wet hands and return to plate. Transfer matzo balls to boiling water, cover, reduce heat to

medium-low and simmer until tender and cooked through, about 30 minutes.

4. Using slotted spoon, transfer matzo balls to colander and drain briefly. Transfer balls to clean plate and let cool to firm up, about 10 minutes. Discard cooking water. (Do not clean pot.)

5. FOR THE SOUP: Meanwhile, heat chicken fat in large saucepan over medium heat until shimmering. Add onion, carrots, celery, parsnip, and ½ teaspoon salt and cook, covered, until vegetables begin to soften, about 5 minutes. Add broth, chicken, and dill and bring to boil. Cover, reduce heat to low, and cook until chicken is tender, 35 to 45 minutes. Remove from heat and transfer chicken to plate. (Chicken can be used for soup or reserved for

another use. If adding to soup, shred with 2 forks into bite-size pieces; discard skin and bones.) Season soup with salt and pepper to taste.

6. Transfer soup to now-empty Dutch oven and bring to simmer over medium heat. Carefully transfer matzo balls to hot soup (along with shredded chicken, if using). Cover and cook until matzo balls are heated through, about 5 minutes. Serve.

TO MAKE AHEAD

Soup and matzo balls can be fully cooked, cooled, and refrigerated separately in covered containers for up to 2 days. To serve, return soup to simmer over medium heat, add matzo balls, and cook until heated through, about 7 minutes.

Our flavorful matzo balls are tender and light but sturdy enough to hold together in the soup.

Breakfast Pizza

Eggs and bacon on a cheese pizza? Sounds like an excellent breakfast to us.
If only we could get the crust to crisp and the eggs to cooperate. BY CECELIA JENKINS

PIZZA, SIMPLY PUT, is bread with stuff on it. Who's to say that stuff can't be breakfast—bacon and eggs? I wanted to create a simple but satisfying breakfast pizza with a crisp crust, crunchy bacon, golden-yolked eggs, and, instead of a red sauce, a creamy, breakfast-friendly layer of cheese to kick off a weekend morning.

My challenge was to achieve a crisp, golden-brown crust without overcooking the eggs—two contrasting goals.

Pizza parlors use specialized ovens that reach temperatures of 700 degrees or more to get perfect crisp-chewy crust in a short burst of time, but I knew that I was limited to a home oven, where 500 degrees is the max. My coworkers suggested a pizza stone, which can help an oven maintain consistently high temperatures and help a home cook produce a crisp crust, but I didn't want to spend the extra time heating one up. I was determined to do this on a baking sheet, but I was concerned that the store-bought pizza dough I chose for convenience would take 15 minutes to cook—much too long for the soft egg yolks I wanted.

But I had to start somewhere. So I pressed and rolled my pizza dough and patted it into a lightly oiled baking sheet. I sprinkled on some seasoned ricotta for creaminess, a few crumbles of cooked bacon, and some grated mozzarella. I carefully broke eggs on top and slid the whole thing into the oven to bake for 15 minutes. This routine was a bust: I had blond, flabby crust topped with chalky eggs.

I picked bits of crisp bacon off the pizza and considered my next move. What if I prebaked a pizza with everything except the eggs, giving the cheese a chance to melt and the crust more time to crisp up, and then added the eggs for the last few minutes? Another fail. Cracking the eggs over partially melted cheese was nearly impossible. They just slid right off.

I took a step back and considered. Maybe it wasn't just a problem of timing, but of architecture, too. What if I built a solid foundation by parbaking the dough first? I'd do this on the lowest rack, closest to the heating element, to help ensure crispness. Then, after a few minutes, when the dough was

The spiced cottage cheese melts in the oven, adding a creamy, savory base layer. You'd never know that it was cottage cheese.

puffed and firm, I would add my toppings. Introducing the shredded cheese at this stage allowed me to shape it into wells where I could safely nestle the eggs. With some finessing (and several pizzas), I determined that 5 minutes was all I needed to parbake the naked crust, plus another 9 to 12 minutes for the toppings.

I still faced a lingering texture problem. The ricotta that I'd hoped would create a creamy layer between the pizza crust and the other toppings was separating in the heat of the oven, becoming grainy and dry. A colleague offered a bold suggestion for a solution: cottage cheese.

Wait, what? I was not eager to vandalize this pizza with lumpy white glop. But we've tried stranger things in the test kitchen, and I couldn't think of a compelling reason not to try it. Cottage cheese is cheese after all—and a creamy one at that.

I popped open a tub and spread ½ cup over the parbaked dough before piling on the other toppings. To my surprise and delight, the curds melted and the cottage cheese transformed into a creamy, silky layer, deftly tethering everything together. Even professed cottage cheese haters found this pizza, and the variations I created, irresistible.

BREAKFAST PIZZA Serves 6

Small-curd cottage cheese is sometimes labeled "country-style." Room-temperature dough is much easier to shape than cold, so pull the dough from the fridge about 1 hour before you start cooking.

- 3 tablespoons extra-virgin olive oil, plus extra for drizzling
- 6 slices bacon
- 8 ounces mozzarella cheese, shredded (2 cups)
- 1 ounce Parmesan cheese, grated (½ cup)
- 4 ounces (½ cup) small-curd cottage cheese
- ¼ teaspoon dried oregano
  Salt and pepper
  Pinch cayenne pepper
- 1 pound store-bought pizza dough, room temperature
- 6 large eggs
- 2 scallions, sliced thin
- 2 tablespoons minced fresh chives

1. Adjust oven rack to lowest position and heat oven to 500 degrees. Grease rimmed baking sheet with 1 tablespoon oil.

2. Cook bacon in 12-inch skillet over medium heat until crisp, 7 to 9 minutes.

Building a Breakfast Pizza
For a crisp crust, we parbake the dough for 5 minutes, until the bottom is just beginning to brown. We then add the toppings, creating wells to keep the eggs in place.

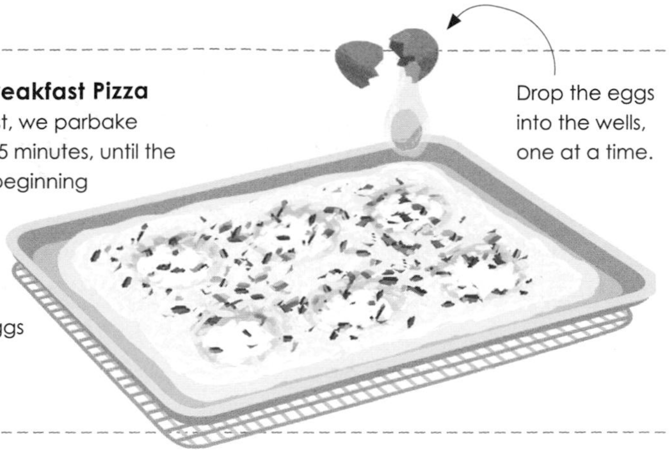

Drop the eggs into the wells, one at a time.

Transfer to paper towel–lined plate; when cool enough to handle, crumble bacon. Combine mozzarella and Parmesan in bowl; set aside. Combine cottage cheese, oregano, ¼ teaspoon pepper, cayenne, and 1 tablespoon oil in separate bowl; set aside.

3. Press and roll dough into 15 by 11-inch rectangle on lightly floured counter, pulling on corners to help make distinct rectangle. Transfer dough to prepared sheet and press to edges of sheet. Brush edges of dough with remaining 1 tablespoon oil. Bake dough until top appears dry and bottom is just beginning to brown, about 5 minutes.

4. Remove crust from oven and, using spatula, press down on any air bubbles. Spread cottage cheese mixture evenly over top, leaving 1-inch border around edges. Sprinkle bacon evenly over cottage cheese mixture.

5. Sprinkle mozzarella mixture evenly over pizza, leaving ½-inch border. Create 2 rows of 3 evenly spaced small wells in cheese, each about 3 inches in diameter (6 wells total). Crack 1 egg into each well, then season each with salt and pepper.

6. Return pizza to oven and bake until crust is light golden around edges and eggs are just set, 9 to 10 minutes for slightly runny yolks or 11 to 12 minutes for soft-cooked yolks, rotating sheet halfway through baking.

7. Transfer pizza to wire rack and let cool for 5 minutes. Transfer pizza to cutting board. Sprinkle with scallions and chives and drizzle with extra oil. Slice and serve.

CHORIZO AND MANCHEGO BREAKFAST PIZZA
Substitute 6 ounces chorizo sausage, halved lengthwise and cut into ½-inch slices, for bacon and 1 cup shredded Manchego cheese for Parmesan. Cook chorizo in 12-inch skillet over medium heat until lightly browned, 7 to 9 minutes. Let cool completely before proceeding.

SAUSAGE AND RED BELL PEPPER BREAKFAST PIZZA
Substitute 6 ounces bulk breakfast sausage for bacon and extra-sharp cheddar for mozzarella. Combine sausage; 1 stemmed, seeded, and chopped red bell pepper; 1 chopped onion; and ¼ teaspoon salt in 12-inch skillet. Cook over medium heat, breaking up sausage with spoon, until sausage begins to brown and bell pepper and onion are translucent, about 6 minutes. Transfer to paper towel–lined plate. Let mixture cool completely before proceeding.

THE KINDEST CUT: WE TESTED 15 PIZZA CUTTERS TO FIND THE BEST

When our winning pizza wheel was discontinued, we promoted the runner-up, a classic 4-inch wheel from OXO. But we'd recently noticed more options on the market, so we decided to test them to see if any could make precise, even slices in a range of pizza styles while also being comfortable, safe, and easy to clean.

We started with 15 cutters in five different styles, priced from $9.99 to $37.95, and an easy test: thin-crust cheese pizzas. We chose the six best cutters—two handled wheels, one hand wheel, a scissor-style cutter, one that resembles a sharp-sided pie server, and one long straight blade—and compared them cutting pepperoni pizza, Sicilian pizza, deep-dish pizza, and pizzas loaded with toppings.

The straight blade cutter couldn't get through crusts, and testers had to rock it back and forth, which battered the toppings, cheese, sauce, and crust into a messy pulp.

The hand wheel was disappointing, too. It worked on the thin crusts, but with bulkier pizzas its wheel swept food up under the case and testers had to disassemble it to clean it out, a dicey task with a wet, soapy blade.

The pie server–shaped cutter and the scissors were both sharp and easy to use. The pie server didn't have a place to brace a second hand when we needed more force, so we docked points. But the scissors sliced through even deep-dish pizza with ease. The downside: Both required testers to make a series of shorter cuts instead of one long continuous slice, which made for wonky slices.

Finally, we turned back to the classic handled wheels. We evaluated the top two and found one annoying to clean (its fixed case trapped toppings).

The best was our old favorite, the OXO Good Grips 4" Pizza Wheel ($12.99); it had a sharp wheel and a comfortable handle and was easy to clean. Read the full story and chart at **CooksCountry.com/may15**.

—HANNAH CROWLEY

HIGHLY RECOMMENDED	CRITERIA		TESTERS' NOTES
OXO Good Grips 4" Pizza Wheel **Price:** $12.99 **Model:** 26681 **Style:** Handled wheel **Dishwasher-Safe:** Yes	Cutting Comfort Cleanup	★★★ ★★★ ★★★	This wheel did it all—it was comfortable to hold and allowed for a powerful grip. Its streamlined design didn't trap food, and it still looked brand new after 10 rounds in the dishwasher. Its blade was sharp and visible for precise, straight cuts. The blade was tall, too, at 4 inches, so it rolled right over stacked toppings and towering crusts with ease.
RECOMMENDED			
DREAMFARM Scizza **Price:** $24.04 **Model:** DFSC2010 (Black) **Style:** Scissor **Dishwasher-Safe:** Yes	Cutting Comfort Cleanup	★★ ★★★ ★★★	With their extra-long blades, these pizza scissors were sharp and exact, even with saucy and cheesy deep-dish pizza and heavy toppings. They were easy to use and clean but cut somewhat crookedly because you have to make multiple cuts to get across the pizza. However, for easy and tidy (albeit slightly crooked) slices, they were great.
RECOMMENDED WITH RESERVATIONS			
KUHN RIKON Flexi Slice and Serve **Price:** $20 **Model:** 22877 **Style:** Pie server **Dishwasher-Safe:** Yes	Cutting Comfort Cleanup	★★ ★★ ★★★	This cutter was sharp and made clean, precise cuts, but they weren't straight because you have to make multiple cuts to get across the pizza. And testers wanted a place to brace a second hand: Because this model lacked the smooth forward motion of a wheel, we needed more force.
NOT RECOMMENDED			
TRUDEAU Stress Less Pizza Cutter **Price:** $14.95 **Model:** 0990012 **Style:** Handled wheel **Dishwasher-Safe:** Yes	Cutting Comfort Cleanup	★½ ★★★ ★	This cutter had a great grip, but it wasn't very sharp and it struggled to get through most crusts. Its wheel pulled food up under its hood and the hood wasn't removable, so cheese and sauce were stranded and impossible to reach while cleaning.
MICROPLANE Pizza Cutter **Price:** $11.95 **Model:** 48105 **Style:** Hand wheel **Dishwasher-Safe:** Yes	Cutting Comfort Cleanup	★★ ★★ ★½	This hand wheel had a tall handle that was too far from the wheel and felt unsteady—"like riding a unicycle," said one tester. Its blade was shorter and struggled to get through deep-dish crust. And while its wheel snapped out for easier cleaning, it was still an extra step.
PIZZACRAFT Soft Grip Handled Rocking Pizza Cutter **Price:** $19.99 **Model:** PM0213 **Style:** Straight blade **Dishwasher-Safe:** No	Cutting Comfort Cleanup	★½ ★★ ★★	This was the most comfortable and sharp straight blade, but it still didn't work very well. The blade wasn't sharp enough to neatly sever any of the crusts on the first try, so testers had to rock it back and forth again and again, which mashed the cheese and sauce and made ragged, uneven slices.

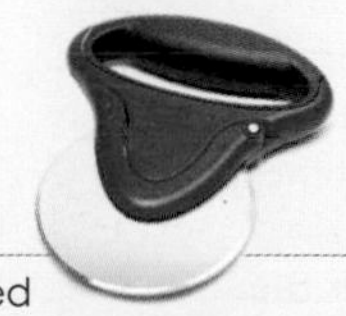

Butter Fan Rolls

These multilayered buns are more than cute—they pack an outsize punch of buttery flavor.
But they're very particular about one thing: location. BY CRISTIN WALSH

I F EVER A roll was aptly named, it's the butter fan roll: buttery layers of yeasty bread fanned out like, well, a fan—designed to be fancy enough for a dinner party but begging to be pulled apart and slathered with butter and jam for breakfast, too. After seeing these cute, tender, buttery little buns in bread baskets and bakery store windows throughout the Northeast, I set out to make my own homemade version.

Just looking at them, I had a feeling these rolls would take some doing—after all, you don't get such striking, layered, fanned-out mini loaves like these without a little countertop construction work. But how, exactly, is this unique shape achieved? I turned to a handful of existing recipes to find out.

After spending an afternoon in the kitchen, I had a wide range of rolls to sample. Some were tiny and tightly stacked. Others were big and floppy, with wings rather than fans. Some had robust buttery flavor, while others were bland. Some were soft and cakey, others dry and almost crunchy. But all followed a similar procedure: Mix and briefly knead the dough and let it rise once. Then punch down the dough, roll it out, cut it into strips, stack the strips, nestle them into muffin tins, let the dough rise again, and bake them off.

This all sounds like a lot of work, and they do take some attention, but butter fan rolls aren't nearly as taxing or complicated as their appearance led me to expect.

Where I tripped up, however, was in the baking. My early experiments became games of chance: I produced rolls that were sometimes undercooked in the middle, sometimes overcooked at the ends, often too brown on the bottom, at times soggy in the center— never perfect. Having nailed many dinner rolls in my day, I was vexed.

The beautiful fanned-out shape that defines these rolls was creating a problem of texture and consistency. I wanted soft, tender rolls that were completely cooked throughout, with faintly crisp—not crunchy—tips. After a few experiments baking the rolls on the center rack of the oven at a range

▶ What makes a great muffin tin? Read our testing story—and see our winner—at **CooksCountry. com/muffintins.**

Because they're made with plenty of butter and baked in a muffin tin, these rolls pick up lots of flavorful browning in the oven.

of temperatures (I tried 325, 350, and 375 degrees), and for a range of times (I tried 12, 15, and 18 minutes), I just couldn't crack the consistency code. When the oven was too hot, I'd have crisp tips but overcooked rolls. When it was too cool, I'd have nicely baked rolls but with soft tips.

Setting aside questions of temperature, I focused on location, moving the oven rack from the middle position to the upper-middle position. Placing the muffin tins just a bit farther from the heating element allowed the rolls to cook through a bit more gently, while the radiant heat reflected from the roof of the oven created the lightly crisp edges I was looking for. I'd found the sweet spot.

Satisfied, but still curious, I wanted to try one more adjustment for convenience's sake. Even though these buns are sometimes called Yankee buttermilk rolls, I couldn't help wondering whether the buttermilk was really necessary. Could these rolls be made with regular whole milk, or even skim?

Answer: Yes in both cases. In fact, my tasters had to work hard to discern any more than a very slight difference. When pressed, they preferred the slightly less-tangy flavor of the rolls made with whole milk.

BUTTER FAN ROLLS
Makes 12 rolls

Do not overflour the counter when rolling out the dough in step 3, and use a bench scraper to square off the edges of the rectangle. Make sure to plan ahead: This dough takes about 3 hours to rise before baking.

- ¾ cup warm milk (110 degrees)
- ¼ cup (1¾ ounces) sugar
- 1 large egg plus 1 large yolk, room temperature
- 1 tablespoon instant or rapid-rise yeast
- 3½ cups (17½ ounces) all-purpose flour
- 2 teaspoons salt
- 8 tablespoons unsalted butter, cut into 8 pieces and softened, plus 4 tablespoons unsalted butter, melted

1. In bowl of stand mixer, combine milk, sugar, egg and yolk, and yeast and let sit until foamy, about 3 minutes. Add flour and salt. Fit stand mixer with dough hook and knead on medium-low speed until dough is shaggy, about 2 minutes.

2. With mixer running, add softened butter 1 piece at a time until incorporated. Continue to knead until dough is smooth, about 5 minutes. Transfer dough to greased large bowl, cover tightly with plastic wrap, and let rise at room temperature until doubled in size, about 1½ hours.

3. Grease 12-cup muffin tin. Press down on dough to deflate and transfer to lightly floured counter (do not overflour counter). Divide dough into 2 equal balls (about 1 pound each). Roll one dough ball into 15 by 12-inch rectangle with long side parallel to counter's edge.

4. Using pizza wheel, cut dough vertically into 6 (2½-inch-wide by 12-inch-long) strips. Brush tops of 5 strips evenly with 1 tablespoon melted butter, leaving 1 strip unbuttered. Stack strips squarely on top of each other, buttered to unbuttered side, finishing with unbuttered strip on top.

5. Using sharp knife, cut stacked dough strips crosswise into 6 equal stacks. Place stacks, cut side up, in each of 6 muffin cups. Repeat with remaining dough ball and 1 tablespoon melted butter. Cover tin loosely with plastic and let dough rise at room temperature until doubled in size, 1¼ to 1½ hours. Adjust oven rack to upper-middle position and heat oven to 350 degrees.

6. Bake until golden brown, 20 to 25 minutes, rotating muffin tin halfway through baking. Brush rolls with remaining 2 tablespoons melted butter. Let cool in muffin tin for 5 minutes. Remove rolls from muffin tin and transfer to wire rack. Serve warm or at room temperature.

TEST KITCHEN TECHNIQUE
Shaping Butter Fan Rolls

After making the dough and pressing it down, divide it into two equal balls. Then follow these easy instructions.

1. ROLL AND CUT
Roll one of the balls into a rectangle and cut it into six strips. Brush five of the strips with melted butter.

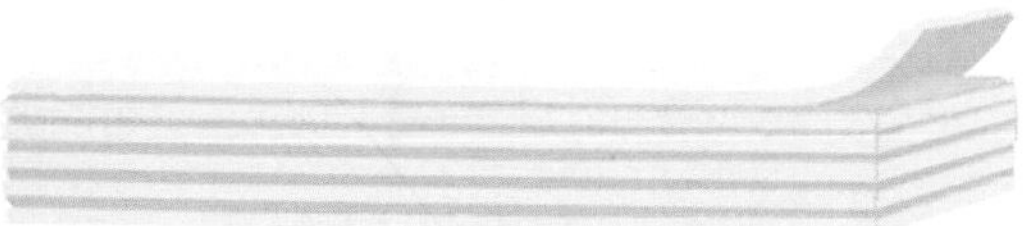

2. STACK Place the six strips in a stack, ending with the unbuttered one on top.

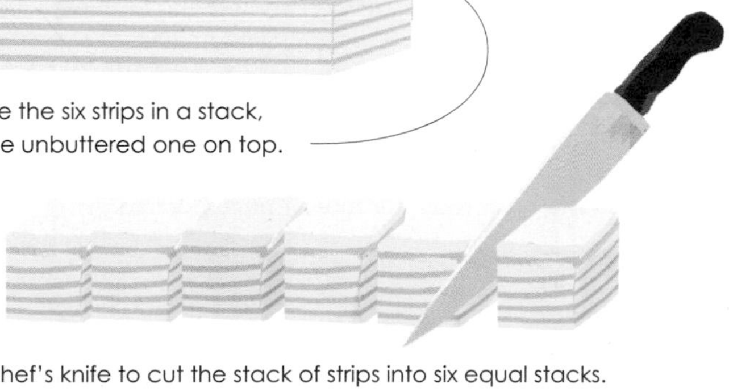

3. CUT Use a chef's knife to cut the stack of strips into six equal stacks.

4. PLACE IN TIN
Carefully transfer each stack to a cup of a muffin tin, cut side up. Repeat with remaining dough ball to fill the tin, let rise, and bake.

Skillet Turkey Meatballs with Lemony Rice

A smack of citrus provides a wake-up call for this easy, one-pan weeknight supper.

BY ASHLEY MOORE

MEATBALLS AND RICE sounds like a smart combination, until you're stuck with a pile of dirty pots and pans. I wanted tender meatballs and perfect rice, all in one skillet.

After forming the meatballs, I browned them and set them aside (they weren't done yet, but I'd begun to build flavor). I then turned to the pilaf method for the rice, toasting the grains for 2 minutes before adding liquid, a test kitchen technique that helps prevent the rice from clumping. I added broth, returned the meatballs to the pan, covered it, and crossed my fingers: Twenty minutes later, the rice and meatballs were done. But something was missing: pizzazz.

Cue lemon. I added 1½ teaspoons of lemon zest to the meatballs and another 1½ teaspoons of lemon zest plus 2 tablespoons of lemon juice to the cooking liquid—just enough to add some zing.

Our tender turkey meatballs are flavored with scallion, parsley, and lemon.

SKILLET TURKEY MEATBALLS WITH LEMONY RICE Serves 4
A 12-inch nonstick skillet with a tight-fitting lid is essential. Turn the meatballs gently in step 2 so they don't break.

- 2 slices hearty white sandwich bread, torn into 1-inch pieces
- 1¼ pounds ground turkey
- 6 scallions, white and green parts separated and sliced thin
- 1 large egg
- 3 tablespoons chopped fresh parsley
- 1 tablespoon grated lemon zest plus 2 tablespoons juice, plus lemon wedges for serving
  Salt and pepper
- 2 tablespoons olive oil
- 1½ cups long-grain white rice
- 3 garlic cloves, minced
- 3¼ cups chicken broth
- 1 ounce Parmesan cheese, grated (½ cup)

1. Pulse bread in food processor to fine crumbs, 10 to 15 pulses; transfer to large bowl. Add turkey, 2 tablespoons scallion greens, egg, 2 tablespoons parsley, 1½ teaspoons lemon zest, ½ teaspoon salt, and ½ teaspoon pepper and mix with your hands until thoroughly combined. Divide mixture into 20 portions (about 1 heaping tablespoon each). Roll into meatballs, transfer to plate, and refrigerate for 15 minutes.

2. Heat oil in 12-inch nonstick skillet over medium-high heat until shimmering. Cook meatballs until well browned all over, 5 to 7 minutes. Transfer meatballs to paper towel–lined plate, leaving fat in skillet.

3. Return skillet to medium-high heat and add rice. Cook, stirring frequently, until edges of rice begin to turn translucent, about 1 minute. Add scallion whites, garlic, and ½ teaspoon salt and cook until fragrant, about 1 minute. Add broth, lemon juice, and remaining 1½ teaspoons lemon zest and bring to boil.

4. Return meatballs to skillet, cover, and reduce heat to low. Cook until rice is tender and meatballs are cooked through, about 20 minutes. Remove from heat and let sit, covered, for 5 minutes. Sprinkle with Parmesan, remaining scallion greens, and remaining 1 tablespoon parsley. Serve with lemon wedges.

North Carolina Lemon Pie

This light, bright lemon pie has a perfect balance of sweet, salty, and sour.
Best of all? It's dead simple to make. BY BRYAN ROOF

WHEN IT ENJOYED a fleeting moment of Internet stardom recently, Atlantic Beach pie was tied to Crook's Corner restaurant in Chapel Hill, North Carolina. But while Crook's Corner does serve a deservedly popular example, versions of this pie can be found at many restaurants, mostly along the North Carolina coast, where menus often just call it "lemon pie."

In the handful of existing recipes I found in my initial research, most shared a few common elements: a crunchy, slightly salty cracker crust; a dense, opaque lemon custard, usually made with sweetened condensed milk; and a lavish pile of whipped cream on top. After a few rounds of testing, I zeroed in on the traits I loved most about this pie: the three-fer combination of salty, sour, and sweet; the intense lemon flavor; and the ease of making it.

The foundation of any great pie is its crust, and I found several variations in my research. Capt. Bill's Waterfront Restaurant in Morehead City, North Carolina, serves a lemon pie with a Ritz Cracker crust (and calls it "Down East Lemon Pie"); other pie shops and home cooks prefer a lightly salted graham cracker crust.

My tasters were happiest with a saltine crust, which is what Crook's Corner uses. But I fumbled with the construction: Mixing saltine crumbs with softened butter and a bit of sugar before pressing them into the pie plate was awkward—instead of a cohesive crust, I had a sandy mess when I sliced and served pieces of pie. By switching to melted butter to help the crumbs adhere to one another, and by adding in a bit of corn syrup to give some elasticity to the mix, I created a more pliable crust that stayed together and was much easier to press into my pie dish. After parbaking, my reworked crust set up cleanly, smoothing my way to less-sloppy slices.

Crust sorted, I turned my sights to the filling. Lemon, for all its obvious virtues, can be a tricky fruit to bake with; in a baked custard like this one, a sour, almost bitter sharpness sometimes overrides the vibrant citrus flavor you're looking for.

I set to tinkering with two specific (and, at first glance, opposing) goals: to increase the overall lemon flavor while concurrently tempering, but not losing,

Saltines in the crust? You bet. They add a welcome savory touch to this sweet-and-sour pie.

the sourness (and without losing the ease of this pie's dump, stir, and bake process; the last thing I wanted to do was create a stovetop custard ahead of baking).

While most recipes use just lemon juice in the custard, I wondered if lemon zest, which test kitchen experiments have shown holds up well to baking, would be my salve. After a few rounds of trial and error, I settled on a tablespoon of fragrant lemon zest for more citrus zing. I added ¼ cup of heavy cream to soften the lemon's sharper edges without compromising the overall texture of the custard.

I finished off my pie with a generous topping of sweetened whipped cream and served it up, and though my tasters

were enthusiastic, there was something lacking: salt. What sets this pie apart from other lemon pies is a slightly saline note, and despite the salt from the crackers in the crust, there was room for more here.

For my next round, I added a bit of salt to the whipped cream—a daring gamble that pleased some surprised tasters but left others less enthusiastic. So instead I closed the gap by adding salt to the other components: ⅛ teaspoon to the crust and another ⅛ teaspoon to the filling.

The pie was now in balance. One thing didn't change during my experiments with this recipe: its simplicity. This rewarding lemon pie is still as easy as . . . you know.

NORTH CAROLINA LEMON PIE
Makes one 9-inch pie
You will need about 53 saltines, roughly one-and-a-half sleeves, to equal 6 ounces.

CRUST
- 6 ounces saltines
- ⅛ teaspoon salt
- 10 tablespoons unsalted butter, melted
- ¼ cup light corn syrup

FILLING
- 1 (14-ounce) can sweetened condensed milk
- 4 large egg yolks
- ¼ cup heavy cream
- 1 tablespoon grated lemon zest plus ½ cup juice (3 lemons)
- ⅛ teaspoon salt

TOPPING
- ½ cup heavy cream, chilled
- 2 teaspoons sugar
- ½ teaspoon vanilla extract

1. FOR THE CRUST: Adjust oven rack to middle position and heat oven to 350 degrees. Combine saltines and salt in food processor and pulse to coarse crumbs, about 15 pulses. Add melted butter and corn syrup and pulse until crumbs are broken down into oatmeal-size pieces, about 15 pulses.

2. Transfer saltine mixture to greased 9-inch pie plate. Using bottom of dry measuring cup, press crumbs into even layer on bottom and sides of plate, using your hand to keep crumbs from spilling over plate edge. Place plate on baking sheet and bake until light golden brown and fragrant, 17 to 19 minutes.

3. FOR THE FILLING: Whisk condensed milk, egg yolks, cream, lemon zest, and salt in bowl until fully combined. Whisk in lemon juice until fully incorporated.

4. With pie plate still on sheet, pour filling into crust (crust needn't be cool). Bake pie until edges are beginning to set but center still jiggles when shaken, 15 to 17 minutes. Place pie on wire rack and let cool completely. Refrigerate pie until fully chilled, about 4 hours.

5. FOR THE TOPPING: Using stand mixer fitted with whisk, whip cream, sugar, and vanilla on medium-low speed until foamy, about 1 minute. Increase speed to high and whip until stiff peaks form, 1 to 3 minutes. Spread whipped cream over top of pie. Serve.

Toffee Squares

How do you replicate the buttery-sweet flavor of toffee without making it from scratch? With a few tricks and some smart shopping. BY MORGAN BOLLING

HERE'S THE THING about toffee: While its buttery flavor and crunchy texture are incredibly appealing, it can be a pain in the neck to make. Most recipes require the cook to carefully and constantly stir a bubbling-hot mixture of sugar and butter while using a candy thermometer to keep tabs on its temperature. Minor issues like a 5-degree difference in temperature, insufficient stirring, or a too-humid kitchen can ruin it. So it comes as no surprise that most home recipes for toffee treats rely on the flavor of brown sugar and/or store-bought toffee bits. No shame in this game: Commercial toffee bits can be great.

I made a handful of published recipes for toffee squares that were quite varied. Some called for using crushed graham crackers in the crust, while others produced crusts closer to shortbread. The toppings ranged from a buttery sugar syrup to caramel, melted chocolate, and melted toffee bits.

My tasters and I quickly discovered that these recipes produced bars that lacked not just toffee flavor but also a solid balance of the sweet, salty, and crunchy elements that should define them. Determined to make toffee squares that would bridge these gaps, I combined our favorite elements of these recipes to put together a baseline working recipe that I could then break down into components to perfect.

I started by baking a simple brown sugar–shortbread crust (made with flour, granulated and brown sugars, salt, and butter) to provide a toffee-like base flavor. When the crust was hot out of the oven, I sprinkled it with chocolate chips, smoothed out the melting chips, and then added chopped almonds. Not bad, but it was a little tough and short on toffee. Switching the granulated sugar for confectioners' sugar (which contains a little cornstarch) was an easy fix for a more-tender crust. Adding store-bought toffee bits to the crust upped the toffee flavor considerably.

Crust settled, I focused on chocolate. I did several side-by-side tests with different types of chocolate (semisweet, milk, and white) melted over the base. Tasters preferred the sweet and mild milk chocolate chips. I increased the amount to a full cup so the thicker layer of melted chocolate would better anchor the almonds to the top of the squares.

I was almost there, but my tasters wanted more crunch. For my next test, I toasted the almonds to simultaneously amplify both their flavor and crunch. And since I was already using toffee bits in the crust, I tried adding ¼ cup on top of the bars for more impact. Sweet victory: I'd achieved deep buttery, salty, sweet toffee flavor without having to pull out a saucepan or candy thermometer.

TOFFEE SQUARES Makes 24 bars

There are two kinds of toffee bits sold at the market; be sure to buy the ones without chocolate. Note that the squares need to cool for about 3 hours in order to set the chocolate; if you're in a hurry, you can put the bars in the refrigerator for 1 hour. But don't store them in the fridge much longer than that because the crust can become too hard.

- 1½ cups (7½ ounces) all-purpose flour
- ½ teaspoon salt
- 10 tablespoons unsalted butter, softened
- ⅓ cup packed (2⅓ ounces) dark brown sugar
- ⅓ cup (1⅓ ounces) confectioners' sugar
- ½ cup plain toffee bits
- 1 cup (6 ounces) milk chocolate chips
- ¾ cup whole almonds, toasted and chopped coarse

1. Adjust oven rack to middle position and heat oven to 350 degrees. Make foil sling for 13 by 9-inch baking pan by folding 2 long sheets of aluminum foil; first sheet should be 13 inches wide and second sheet should be 9 inches wide. Lay sheets of foil in pan perpendicular to each other, with extra foil hanging over edges of pan. Push foil into corners and up sides of pan, smoothing foil flush to pan. Spray lightly with vegetable oil spray.

2. Combine flour and salt in bowl. Using stand mixer fitted with paddle, beat butter, brown sugar, and confectioners' sugar on medium-high speed until light and fluffy, about 3 minutes. Reduce speed to low and add flour mixture in 3 additions, scraping down bowl as needed, until dough becomes sandy with large pea-size pieces, about 30 seconds. Add ¼ cup toffee bits and mix until combined.

3. Transfer dough to prepared pan and press into even layer using bottom of dry measuring cup. Bake until golden brown, about 20 minutes, rotating pan halfway through baking.

4. Remove crust from oven, sprinkle with chocolate chips, and let sit until softened, about 5 minutes. Spread softened chocolate into even layer over crust using small offset spatula. Sprinkle almonds and remaining ¼ cup toffee bits evenly over chocolate, then press gently to set into chocolate. Let bars sit at room temperature until chocolate is set, about 3 hours.

5. Using foil overhang, lift bars out of pan. Cut into 24 pieces and serve. (Toffee squares can be stored in airtight container at room temperature for up to 2 days.)

TEST KITCHEN TECHNIQUE
Easy Chocolate Layer

We sprinkle chips onto the hot baked crust. In just 5 minutes, the chocolate is soft enough to spread.

A double dose of toffee bits transforms these easy treats.

Cooking Class Italian-Style Meat Sauce

Meat sauce is often uninspired—or worse, features rubbery meat. Here's how to make it right. BY BRYAN ROOF

ITALIAN-STYLE MEAT SAUCE

Makes about 6 cups sauce, enough for 2 pounds pasta

Except for ground round (which tasters found spongy and bland), this recipe will work with most types of ground beef, as long as it is 85 percent lean. (Eighty percent lean beef will turn the sauce greasy; 90 percent will make it fibrous.) If using dried oregano, add the entire amount with the reserved tomato juice in step 2. Leftover sauce can be refrigerated for up to three days or frozen for up to one month.

- 4   ounces white mushrooms, trimmed and broken into rough pieces
- 1   slice hearty white sandwich bread, torn into quarters
- 2   tablespoons whole milk
-   Salt and pepper
- 1   pound 85 percent lean ground beef
- 1   tablespoon olive oil
- 1   large onion, chopped fine
- 6   garlic cloves, minced
- 1   tablespoon tomato paste
- ¼   teaspoon red pepper flakes
- 1   (14.5-ounce) can diced tomatoes, drained with ¼ cup juice reserved
- 1   tablespoon minced fresh oregano or 1 teaspoon dried
- 1   (28-ounce) can crushed tomatoes
- ¼   cup grated Parmesan cheese

1. Process mushrooms in food processor until finely chopped, about 8 pulses, scraping down sides of bowl as needed; transfer to bowl. Add bread, milk, ½ teaspoon salt, and ½ teaspoon pepper to now-empty processor and process until paste forms, about 8 pulses. Add beef and pulse until mixture is well combined, about 6 pulses.

2. Heat oil in large saucepan over medium-high heat until just smoking. Add onion and mushrooms and cook, stirring frequently, until vegetables are browned and dark bits form on pan bottom, 6 to 12 minutes. Stir in garlic, tomato paste, and pepper flakes; cook until fragrant and tomato paste starts to brown, about 1 minute. Add reserved tomato juice and 2 teaspoons oregano (if using dried, add full amount), scraping up any browned bits. Add meat mixture and cook, breaking meat into small pieces with spoon, until beef loses its raw color, 2 to 4 minutes, making sure that meat does not brown.

3. Stir in crushed tomatoes and diced tomatoes and bring to simmer. Reduce heat to low and gently simmer until sauce has thickened and flavors have blended, about 30 minutes. Stir in Parmesan and remaining 1 teaspoon oregano; season with salt and pepper to taste.

STEP BY STEP **Ten Steps to Simple Meat Sauce**

1. PROCESS MUSHROOMS
Finely chop the mushrooms in the food processor.
WHY? The smaller mushroom pieces release more flavor and contribute to the potent fond on the bottom of the saucepan.

2. MAKE PANADE
Process the bread and milk to form a panade.
WHY? A panade helps keep the ground beef tender and moist when it is cooked to medium and beyond.

3. PROCESS BEEF
Add the beef to the panade in the food processor.
WHY? This helps quickly and thoroughly incorporate the panade into the meat.

4. BROWN VEGETABLES
Cook the mushrooms and onion until dark bits form on the saucepan bottom.
WHY? These browned bits (fond) add flavor and complexity to the sauce.

5. ADD TOMATO PASTE
Brown the tomato paste.
WHY? This drives off some of the paste's moisture and develops its flavor.

Good Ideas

Make a Panade

A panade is a mixture of starch and liquid—most commonly white bread and whole milk. You'll often see panades in meatball and meatloaf recipes, where they help the ground meat stay moist and hold its shape. But a panade also serves a critical purpose in our Italian-Style Meat Sauce. The starch in the bread absorbs liquid from the milk, which in turn forms a coating around the protein molecules in the meat, preventing them from linking together in a tough matrix. The result? Meat that is tender, not rubbery.

on't Brown the Beef

ith larger cuts of meat, we often call for browning on the stovetop before roasting r braising to add an extra layer of flavor. But we don't recommend this step for most round meat sauces because the extra cooking up front can toughen the small ieces of meat, leaving you with chewy little nuggets rather than soft, tender beef.

ocus on the (Vegetable) Fond

ond is a French word that refers to the deeply avorful browned bits that stick to the bottom f the pan when you sear meat or vegetables. o not waste it. For many sauces or stews, you'll ant the flavor locked in these bits to find its ay to your fork. Here's how: After creating fond, you deglaze the pan by pouring quid over its hot surface and scraping up the rowned bits to distribute them throughout the ixture. Because we don't recommend browning the meat for this recipe, the fond omes from the chopped onion and minced mushrooms. You'll see browned bits uck to the bottom of the pot after you sauté the mushrooms; using the juice from e diced tomatoes to scrape up the fond ensures that none of the flavor gets lost.

Key Ingredients

The Right Ground Beef

The U.S. Department of Agriculture forbids the sale of packaged ground beef with more than 30 percent fat by weight. We call for 85 percent lean (15 percent fat) beef for this recipe. Unfortunately, most prepackaged ground beef in the meat case won't identify the cut, which means it may be any cut or combination of cuts. Your best bet? Ask the butcher to freshly grind a pound of chuck, which has the right ratio of fat to lean meat. Avoid round, which is much too lean and often gristly.

Triple Up on Tomatoes

Unlike most canned produce, good-quality canned tomatoes offer flavors that, in cooked applications, taste as good as (and sometimes better than) fresh in-season tomatoes. In a sauce like this, they're irreplaceable. We use three kinds of canned tomato products in this sauce: The browned tomato paste adds depth and body, while the crushed and diced tomatoes, which break down to different degrees during the cooking, give the sauce a range of textures. Our favorite canned tomato paste is Goya Tomato Paste. For canned diced tomatoes, we like Hunt's Diced Tomatoes. And for canned crushed tomatoes, our taste test winner was Tuttorosso Crushed Tomatoes in Thick Puree with Basil.

| OUR FAVORITE PASTE | OUR FAVORITE DICED | OUR FAVORITE CRUSHED |

Savory Flavor Boosters

To intensify the overall meatiness in a sauce, we often turn to ingredients high in umami (savory) flavors. For this sauce, browned minced mushrooms and Parmesan cheese both contribute umami richness. Also adding savory depth: six cloves of minced garlic, which transform from sharp to sweet during the slow simmer, and red pepper flakes for a hit of spice.

. DEGLAZE
dd the tomato juice and crape up the fond from the ottom of the pot.
HY? The juice helps loosen he fond and incorporate it into he sauce.

7. GENTLY COOK BEEF
Add the meat mixture, breaking it into small pieces, and cook until it loses its raw color. Take care not to let it brown.
WHY? Browning the meat can cause it to dry out and become chalky and pebbly.

8. ADD TOMATOES
Stir in crushed and drained diced tomatoes.
WHY? Using two types of tomato adds textural variety to the sauce.

9. SIMMER
Let the sauce bubble gently over low heat.
WHY? Simmering allows the flavors to marry, and the relatively short 30-minute cooking time helps keep the meat tender.

10. FINISH
Stir in Parmesan and fresh oregano.
WHY? The Parmesan adds flavor and subtle creaminess while the oregano adds brightness.

Slow Cooker Chicken Stock

Nothing beats homemade chicken stock, but it requires attention.
We appealed to the slow cooker for help. BY DIANE UNGER

EVERY FREEZER, IN my opinion, should be filled with homemade chicken stock, at the ready for soups, stews, pan sauces, or any recipes that need a rich, deep, meaty base of flavor that's impossible to replicate any other way.

Homemade stock tastes so much better than even the best store-bought broth, but while it's not complicated to make, it does require a bit of attention—monitoring the temperature, skimming the foam that rises to the surface, standing at the stove. The last time I was standing in front of a simmering pot on the stovetop, I caught sight of my trusty slow cooker on the counter and wondered whether I could use it to make even these minor inconveniences disappear. It was worth a try, but I was adamant that the slow-cooker stock had to taste as good as the stovetop version.

One great thing about chicken stock is that it can be made with ingredients that you'd otherwise throw away: in this case, chicken bones. Whether they're bones left over from chickens you've roasted or from rotisserie chickens you've purchased, there's gold in them. I stockpiled 2½ pounds of bones (about three rotisserie chickens' worth) for each batch and started testing.

The usual suspects for a basic stock (celery, carrot, and onion) joined the leftover chicken bones (broken up into smaller pieces to release more of their flavor and body-giving properties) in the slow cooker. The amount of water to add took some trial and error. I had to have enough water to barely cover the bones but not so much that the stock would emerge from the slow cooker watery and pale.

I found that 3 quarts of fresh cold

The slow cooker does most of the work of making this rich, savory stock.

water did the trick, keeping the bones submerged—essential for a good stock and, as it turns out, actually easier to do in a slow cooker, where evaporation is a nonissue. (With stovetop stocks, you often have to add liquid to keep the bones submerged.)

To season the stock, I added a bay leaf, whole black peppercorns, and salt. With the basic ingredients safely nestled in the slow cookers, time was the next piece of the puzzle to solve. After testing my stock at intervals from 4 hours to

12 hours, I found that I got the best, richest, most chicken-y flavor by setting my slow cooker to high and cooking for 8 to 10 hours.

For good measure, I tried this stock with meat-on chicken parts and chicken feet. They, too, produced a lovely stock. But the value of using bones that were destined for the garbage bin makes this a remarkably thrifty endeavor.

With no up-front cooking, this is also a remarkably easy slow-cooker recipe: Just pile the ingredients into the slow

cooker, add water, set it to cook, and go on about your day (or night of sleep). All you have to do at the end of cooking is strain the stock and skim the fat. The easiest way to skim the fat is to let the stock cool completely, refrigerate it, and then pop the chicken fat off the top in one piece.

SLOW-COOKER CHICKEN STOCK
Makes about 3 quarts

This stock is great to use in our recipe for Matzo Ball Soup (page 17) or in any of our recipes calling for chicken broth. You can freeze chicken carcasses one at a time until you have the 2½ pounds needed for this recipe; three to four rotisserie chicken carcasses or one 6-pound roasted carcass will weigh about 2½ pounds. This recipe was developed using bones from cooked chicken.

- 3 quarts water
- 2½ pounds roasted chicken bones
- 1 onion, chopped
- 2 carrots, peeled and cut into 1-inch chunks
- 2 celery ribs, chopped
- 1 teaspoon black peppercorns
- 1 teaspoon salt
- 1 bay leaf

1. Place all ingredients in slow cooker. Cover and cook on high for 8 to 10 hours.

2. Let stock cool slightly, then strain through fine-mesh strainer set over large bowl. Use immediately or let cool completely, then refrigerate until cold. (When cold, surface fat will solidify and can be easily removed with spoon.) Stock will keep, refrigerated, for up to 5 days, or frozen for up to 2 months.

TEST KITCHEN TIP **Stock Storage**
Frozen homemade chicken stock lasts for up to two months. Freeze small and medium amounts in ice cube trays or muffin tins; once frozen, pop out the stock blocks and keep them in zipper-lock bags for easy access when making pan sauces or gravy. Freeze larger amounts in plastic quart containers or zipper-lock bags, which are easy to stack in crowded freezers.

LARGE
Perfect for soups.

MEDIUM
Just right for gravy.

SMALL
Best for pan sauces.

LARGE
Easy to stack and store.

Recipe Makeover Chicken and Cheese Enchiladas

Reduced-fat enchiladas sound like a bad idea, right? Wrong.

BY CRISTIN WALSH

NORMALLY, A SUPPER of enchiladas stuffed and smothered with everything good leads to a belt-loosening sense of regret. The caloric construction of meat, cheese, tortillas, and sauce is enough to make a cardiologist weep (or rejoice, as he fills her appointment calendar with cholesterol-screening visits). Except on rare occasions, dishes like this are off-limits for health-minded eaters. Common wisdom says you can look, but you can't eat.

But the thing about common wisdom, I've found, is this: It's almost always ripe for revision. I was determined to create a new, healthier take on this fan favorite so I could even serve it to a table of health-conscious guests.

The first order of business was also the most obvious (and the most worrisome): swapping out the full-fat cheese for a lower-fat version. No matter how you slice it, lower-fat cheese doesn't have as rich a profile on the plate or in the mouth. It simply has less flavor. But the lower-fat cheese we chose still performs a vital role: It's cheesy in the best sense, forming strings that swing from the fork as you raise each bite. After experimenting with various low-fat cheeses, including Monterey Jack, Colby Jack, American, and cheddar, I found that low-fat cheddar, ounce for ounce, delivered the most flavor and the best meltiness.

Next up, the chicken. While many enchilada recipes call for flavorful (and relatively fatty) chicken thighs, I went for chicken breasts, which have a much lower fat content. The dish was still meaty, but the switch, like the cheese switch, dialed down the flavor a level or two. My tasters found the chicken breast enchiladas "pleasant," but I knew that pleasant wouldn't do. I wanted my tasters to be knocked out.

When flavor goes missing, it's my mission to replace it. Knowing a return to full-fat cheese or chicken thighs was a nonstarter, I doubled down on high-impact, aromatic ingredients like garlic and onion and looked to the pantry for a wider range of flavors than a typical chili powder–based enchilada sauce offers.

The answer came in canned chipotles packed in adobo sauce, which offered not just peppery, spicy heat but also a subtle smokiness—chipotle's calling card. Mincing just a tablespoon of the chipotle and tossing it with the chicken,

Poaching chicken breasts in our flavor-packed sauce proves a smart route to deep flavor.

along with 1 teaspoon of its accompanying garlicky adobo sauce, gave our enchiladas muscle and depth without setting off fire alarms. Happier but not satisfied, I went for yet another layer of complexity with 2 teaspoons of ground cumin in the sauce and, for freshness, a toss of cilantro at the end.

Low-fat enchiladas? Put away your sad trombone. With this recipe makeover I saved 220 calories and 20 grams of fat per serving, but because the enchiladas had such vibrant, exciting flavors, my tasters were none the wiser.

The Numbers

All nutritional information is for one serving of two enchiladas.

Traditional Chicken Enchiladas
CALORIES **560**
FAT **31 g** SATURATED FAT **17 g**

***Cook's Country* Reduced-Fat Chicken and Cheese Enchiladas**
CALORIES **340**
FAT **11 g** SATURATED FAT **4.5 g**

KEY INGREDIENT
Chipotles in Adobo
Talk about bang for buck: This little can contains smoky peppers, tangy vinegar, pungent spices, and more.

ONE INGREDIENT, MANY FLAVORS

REDUCED-FAT CHICKEN AND CHEESE ENCHILADAS Serves 6

Microwaving the tortillas makes them more pliable for rolling. Shred the chicken into small pieces so it won't tear through the tortillas. Cracker Barrel makes our favorite reduced-fat cheddar. Serve these enchiladas with lime wedges, low-fat sour cream, diced avocado, shredded lettuce, and hot sauce.

- 1 onion, chopped fine (1 cup)
- 1 teaspoon vegetable oil
  Salt and pepper
- 1 tablespoon minced canned chipotle chile in adobo sauce plus 1 teaspoon adobo sauce
- 3 garlic cloves, minced
- 2 teaspoons ground cumin
- 2 teaspoons chili powder
- 1 (15-ounce) can tomato sauce
- 1 cup water
- 1 pound boneless, skinless chicken breasts, trimmed
- 8 ounces 50 percent light cheddar cheese, shredded (2 cups)
- ½ cup minced fresh cilantro
- 12 (6-inch) corn tortillas

1. Adjust oven rack to middle position and heat oven to 350 degrees. Combine ½ cup onion, oil, and ½ teaspoon salt in large saucepan. Cover and cook over medium-low heat, stirring often, until onions have softened, 5 to 8 minutes.

2. Stir in chipotle and adobo sauce, garlic, cumin, and chili powder and cook until fragrant, about 30 seconds. Stir in tomato sauce and water and bring to simmer. Add chicken and return to simmer. Reduce heat to low, cover, and cook until chicken registers 160 degrees, 10 to 15 minutes, flipping chicken halfway through cooking.

3. Off heat, transfer chicken to plate and let cool slightly. Using 2 forks, shred into small pieces. Season sauce with salt and pepper to taste. Combine 1 cup cheddar, cilantro, shredded chicken, ½ cup sauce, and remaining ½ cup onion in bowl. Season with salt and pepper to taste.

4. Spread ½ cup sauce in bottom of 13 by 9-inch baking dish. Stack tortillas on plate, cover with damp towel, and microwave until warm and pliable, about 1 minute. Spread half of warm tortillas on counter. Spread level ⅓ cup chicken mixture across center of each tortilla, roll up tortillas tightly, and arrange crosswise, seam side down, in prepared dish. Repeat with remaining 6 tortillas and filling.

5. Cover enchiladas with remaining sauce. Sprinkle remaining 1 cup cheddar evenly over top. Cover dish with aluminum foil and bake until enchiladas are hot throughout, 20 to 25 minutes. Let cool for 10 minutes. Serve.

Cooking for Two Weeknight Pork Stew

Could we make a light-yet-complex spring stew with tender vegetables and savory pork—in less than an hour? BY AARON FURMANEK

A SPRING DAY is just as likely to be a lion as a lamb, and sometimes a warm stew is exactly what you need for a soothing, satisfying lunch or dinner at this time of year. But stews often require hours of sautéing and simmering, and when it's just two for dinner, the leftovers can be a little much. I wanted a stew that was both complex and light, something that featured tender vegetables and deeply flavored pork and that could be on the table in less than an hour. Was I asking too much?

Our sister magazine, *Cook's Illustrated*, published a recipe for French-Style Pork Stew a couple of years ago; it's a fantastic recipe, but it takes more than 3 hours to make. I was after a similar return in much less time. Choosing the right cut of pork was my first priority. I knew that I couldn't use a traditional stew cut like pork shoulder because it takes too long to become tender. Instead, I chose two quicker-cooking, lean cuts for my first tests: pork loin and tenderloin. I cut the meat into ¾-inch pieces, browned them, added chicken broth, and simmered until the meat was cooked through. Unfortunately, neither performed well with this technique—both were tough and chewy. But my tasters preferred the tenderloin, so I decided to go with that cut. I'd just need to find a more gentle cooking method.

Thinking about how a number of Asian soups are made, I wondered: Could I build the stew base first and then add the raw cubes of pork to the simmering liquid? I made a quick but flavorful broth by sautéing sliced kielbasa (which is precooked and has a ton of flavor) with onion and carrots, and then adding chicken broth, stirring in cubed potatoes, and simmering. After a few tests I found that I could add the potatoes up front with everything else to no ill effect (which saved time) and that garlic and herbes de Provence contributed fantastic supporting flavors with a minimum of fuss.

A spring stew needs something green, so I tried adding spinach (too slimy), escarole (too bitter), and kale (too strong) before landing on sliced savoy cabbage. The cabbage contributed just enough flavor and texture without taking over the stew.

The small chunks of pork tenderloin cook through off heat to ensure that they stay tender.

Only now that I had a flavorful broth and tender vegetables did I add the pork tenderloin. It took me a few tests to nail down the timing: It was best to add the raw pork pieces to the pot when the vegetables had cooked to just-tender, simmer everything for just 30 seconds, and then take the pot off the burner to let the pork finish cooking in the residual heat.

This stew was shaping up, but one problem remained: The broth was too loose. I found an easy fix using an item already in the pot: the potatoes. Borrowing a technique from another test kitchen recipe, I stirred the potato mixture constantly for 3 minutes as it was sautéing. This helped release starch from the potatoes; the starch, in turn, helped thicken the stew once the broth was added. For good measure, I mashed some of the potatoes right in the broth, adding even more body.

I now had succulent bits of pork and sausage, tender vegetables, and a savory broth full of bright flavors. A sprinkle of chives offered a touch of freshness, a final nod to spring.

TEST KITCHEN DISCOVERY
Shortcuts to Big Flavor

KIELBASA
Adds garlicky meatiness.

HERBES DE PROVENCE
One jar, many herbs.

PORK TENDERLOIN CHUNKS
Short cooking time.

COUNTRY-STYLE PORK STEW FOR TWO

It's important to stir the potato mixture continuously in step 1 to release the potato starch that will help give body to the stew. Green cabbage can be substituted for the savoy cabbage, but it should be added to the pot with the broth in step 2 and simmered for 15 minutes total.

 1 (12-ounce) pork tenderloin, trimmed and cut into ¾-inch chunks
    Salt and pepper
 1 tablespoon vegetable oil
 8 ounces Yukon Gold potatoes, unpeeled, cut into 1-inch chunks
 4 ounces kielbasa sausage, halved lengthwise and sliced ½ inch thick
 2 carrots, peeled and cut into ½-inch chunks
 ¼ cup finely chopped onion
 1 garlic clove, minced
 ½ teaspoon herbes de Provence
 2 cups chicken broth
 ¼ head savoy cabbage, cored and cut into 1-inch pieces (1 cup)
 1 tablespoon minced fresh chives

1. Pat pork dry with paper towels and season with ¼ teaspoon salt and ¼ teaspoon pepper; set aside. Heat oil in large saucepan over medium heat until shimmering. Add potatoes, kielbasa, carrots, and onion and cook, stirring constantly, until potato starch begins to release and coat other ingredients, about 3 minutes. Add garlic and herbes de Provence and cook until fragrant, about 30 seconds.

2. Add broth and bring to boil. Cover, reduce heat to medium-low, and simmer until vegetables are tender, about 10 minutes. Add cabbage, cover, and cook for 5 minutes longer.

3. Increase heat to high and bring to boil. Stir in pork and cook until no longer pink, about 30 seconds. Remove from heat, cover, and let sit until pork is cooked through, about 7 minutes.

4. Using back of spoon, mash about one-third of potatoes against side of saucepan until stew is slightly thickened. Season with salt and pepper to taste. Serve, sprinkled with chives.

Five Easy Recipes Tuna Salads

Right out of the can, tuna is chalky and bland—you need to fix those problems before your tuna salad can be any good. BY ASHLEY MOORE

DO YOU REALLY need a recipe for tuna salad? After all, don't you just open the can and dump the tuna into a bowl with some mayonnaise, salt and pepper, and maybe a little chopped onion or celery?

Well, yes and no: While this simple dump-and-stir method produces passable tuna salad, it tends to be bland, chalky, and, sometimes, if the tuna's not completely drained and dried, watery. And we were after something better than just passable—we wanted great.

We tasted every variety of canned tuna sold in supermarkets—packed in oil and water; salted and unsalted; solid, chunk, and flaked; white and light. The runaway winner for clean flavor was solid white tuna packed in water.

Working with three cans' worth of solid white tuna (enough for four hefty sandwiches), we found that blotting the tuna dry with paper towels—before adding anything else—ensured that the finished tuna salad was not squishy and watery. Mashing the dried tuna with a fork made for a nice, uniform consistency. Mixing onion-infused olive oil (which we quickly and easily make in the microwave) into the dried, mashed tuna not only moistened the salad but took care of the blandness. Adding lemon juice and a bit of sugar with the mayo rounded out the flavor.

With such a strong foundation, why not build up? Incorporating crunchy apple, walnuts, and tarragon brings tuna salad into Waldorf territory—a delicious revelation. A variation with cornichons and whole-grain mustard highlights the brininess of the tuna. Curry and grapes, a combination most often reserved for chicken salad, work together to bring a warm sweetness to the mix. And finally, hard-cooked eggs, radishes, and capers yield a tuna salad reminiscent of one served at my favorite deli in Brooklyn.

It may sound odd, but the key to great texture is to dry the canned tuna before dressing it.

CLASSIC TUNA SALAD

Makes 2 cups; enough for 4 sandwiches
For slightly milder salads, use an equal amount of shallot instead of onion.

- ¼ cup finely chopped onion
- 2 tablespoons olive oil
- 3 (5-ounce) cans solid white tuna in water
- ½ cup plus 2 tablespoons mayonnaise
- 1 celery rib, minced
- 2 teaspoons lemon juice
- ½ teaspoon sugar
  Salt and pepper

1. Combine onion and oil in small bowl and microwave until onion begins to soften, about 2 minutes. Let onion mixture cool for 5 minutes. Place tuna in fine-mesh strainer and press dry with paper towels. Transfer tuna to medium bowl and mash with fork until finely flaked.

2. Stir mayonnaise, celery, lemon juice, sugar, ½ teaspoon salt, ½ teaspoon pepper, and onion mixture into tuna until well combined. Season with salt and pepper to taste. Serve. (Salad can be refrigerated for up to 24 hours.)

TUNA SALAD WITH CURRY AND GRAPES

Add 1 teaspoon curry powder to bowl with onion and oil before microwaving. Add 1 cup green grapes, halved, to salad.

TUNA SALAD WITH HARD-COOKED EGGS, RADISHES, AND CAPERS

Substitute 2 tablespoons extra-virgin olive oil for olive oil and 6 tablespoons extra-virgin olive oil for mayonnaise. Add 2 thinly sliced hard-cooked eggs; 2 trimmed, halved, and thinly sliced radishes; and ¼ cup capers, minced, to salad.

TUNA SALAD WITH APPLE, WALNUTS, AND TARRAGON

Add 1 apple, cored and cut into ½-inch pieces; ½ cup walnuts, toasted and chopped coarse; and 1 tablespoon minced fresh tarragon to salad.

TUNA SALAD WITH CORNICHONS AND WHOLE-GRAIN MUSTARD

Add ¼ cup finely chopped cornichons, 1 tablespoon minced fresh chives, and 1 tablespoon whole-grain mustard to salad.

Taste Test Supermarket Sharp Cheddar Cheese

Does aging make for better sharp cheddar? Turns out, it's complicated.

BY LAUREN SAVOIE

YOU DON'T HAVE to go to a fancy shop to find great cheddar. In recent years, inexpensive supermarket cheddars—like Cracker Barrel, Cabot, and Tillamook—have taken top honors in international cheese competitions, beating out much-pricier artisan brands. Supermarket cheddar comes in a few varieties—mild, medium, sharp, extra-sharp—but we reach for sharp cheddar when we need a cheese that's complex enough for snacking but versatile enough for cooking.

But what exactly is "sharp" cheddar? In general, cheese gets sharper the longer it ages, but the U.S. Department of Agriculture (USDA) doesn't regulate cheddar labeling, and it's up to the manufacturer to determine what's sharp. We've found that most manufacturers consider the aging time frame for sharp cheddar to be six to 12 months.

We selected seven nationally available products to test: five cheeses labeled sharp cheddar and two "aged" cheddars that fall within the six-to-12-month time frame. Since many brands offer both orange and white sharp cheddars (see "The Color of Cheddar"), we asked each manufacturer to identify its best-selling color and ended up with an almost equal mix of orange and white cheeses. Twenty-one America's Test Kitchen staffers tasted the cheeses plain and in grilled cheese sandwiches.

Texture was a nonissue: Most products were "creamy" and slightly "crumbly," just how we like sharp cheddar; in grilled cheese they were pleasantly "melty" and "gooey." Flavor differences were more apparent when we tasted the cheeses plain. While we liked most of the cheddars, a few fell to the bottom of the pack for "funky," "sweet" flavors that, while not necessarily unpleasant, were unexpected. We preferred products with the familiar "bright" and "buttery" flavor of "classic" cheddar.

Tasters preferred sharper cheeses. But when we contacted manufacturers to find out how long each product is aged, we learned that our top-ranked cheeses actually age three months less than lower-ranked products, for nine versus 12 months. While time is one factor in flavor, how well a cheese ages also depends on how it was made and stored. Most cheesemakers weren't willing to share those secrets, so we sent the cheeses to an independent lab to learn why some younger cheeses tasted sharper and more complex.

Here, things started to line up: The longer-aged cheddars at the bottom of our rankings had higher pH values (meaning they were less acidic) than top-ranked cheddars. According to Dean Sommer, cheese and food technologist at the University of Wisconsin-Madison, a high pH is a good indication that the product didn't age well. Many factors during production can influence the pH of a cheddar—what the cows were fed, the type of bacteria used to culture the cheese, how long the milk was heated and to what temperature. Whatever the cause, Sommer said cheddar that begins life at a high pH will typically end up overfermented, off-flavored, and sweet by the time it's ready for sale.

When the cheeses were melted into grilled cheese, however, the funky flavors mellowed. In fact, tasters thought that the "fruity" and "grassy" flavors of lower-ranked cheeses added a nuanced complexity to an otherwise mild sandwich. Only one product, Boar's Head Sharp Wisconsin Cheddar, which tasters found mild when tasted plain, mellowed even more when melted, becoming "boring" and "bland." Here, moisture was the problem. According to our lab tests, it contained the highest percentage of moisture in the group—roughly 37 percent moisture compared with 34 percent to 36 percent moisture in winning products. High moisture content, like high pH, can prevent the development of flavor and cause the cheese to age poorly. With the exception of this one product, most cheeses made grilled cheese that was "nutty," "buttery," and "rich" enough for our tasters.

Ultimately, we ended up recommending six of the seven cheddars we tried. Our former winner, Cabot Vermont Sharp Cheddar ($3.78 for 8 ounces), once again took top honors for its complex nutty flavor and balanced sharpness.

RECOMMENDED

CABOT Vermont Sharp Cheddar
Price: $3.78 for 8 oz ($0.47 per oz)
Color: White
pH: 5.4
Moisture: 35.8%
Aged for: 9 months

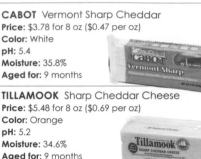

TASTERS' NOTES

This white cheddar took top honors for its "nutty," "almost smoky" "caramel" notes and "complex" sharpness. Tasters loved its "buttery," "creamy" texture that "completely satisfied comfort food cravings" when it was melted for grilled cheese.

TILLAMOOK Sharp Cheddar Cheese
Price: $5.48 for 8 oz ($0.69 per oz)
Color: Orange
pH: 5.2
Moisture: 34.6%
Aged for: 9 months

This faintly orange cheddar was deemed "bright" and "almost citrusy" for its "zesty" tang and "bold" sharpness. When melted, its "gooey," "buttery" texture earned this cheddar recognition as "a perfect cheese for grilled cheese."

CRACKER BARREL Sharp Cheddar Cheese
Price: $3.89 for 8 oz ($0.49 per oz)
Color: Orange
pH: 5.2
Moisture: 35.2%
Aged for: Proprietary

This popular block cheese was "salty," "acidic," "balanced," and "punchy," with a "quintessential sharp cheddar" flavor that made it "great for snacking." In grilled cheese, tasters found this cheddar "friendly" and "tame."

KRAFT Natural Sharp Cheddar Cheese
Price: $4.79 for 8 oz ($0.60 per oz)
Color: Orange
pH: 5.2
Moisture: 35.2%
Aged for: Proprietary

"Mild," "bright," and "waxy," this orange cheddar had a "rich," "elegant sharpness" and "smooth" texture that made for "gooey," "melty" grilled cheese. "Tastes like childhood," said one taster, who thought this product's "classic" flavor would be popular with kids.

KERRYGOLD Aged Cheddar
Price: $5 for 7 oz ($0.71 per oz)
Color: White
pH: 5.6
Moisture: 36.6%
Aged for: 12 months

With a "mild" sharpness, this Irish import earned comparisons with Swiss cheese for its "slightly funky," "tangy" flavor. Its subtle "grassy," "onion" notes added "complexity" to grilled cheese, though a few tasters felt that it had "too many unexpected flavors" for cheddar.

SARGENTO Tastings Aged Wisconsin Cheddar Cheese
Price: $2.79 for 3.95 oz ($0.71 per oz)
Color: Orange
pH: 5.7
Moisture: 35.3%
Aged for: 12 months

This petite orange wedge was "thick" and "chewy," with "toasty" "butterscotch" notes that became "sweet" and "slightly nutty" when the cheese was melted. A few tasters thought that this cheddar had an unusual "tannic," "tart flavor," "like port wine cheese."

RECOMMENDED WITH RESERVATIONS

BOAR'S HEAD Sharp Wisconsin Cheddar Cheese
Price: $4.50 for 10 oz ($0.45 per oz)
Color: White
pH: 5.2
Moisture: 37.1%
Aged for: 9 months

Tasters enjoyed this product's "mild," "creamy" flavor and "smooth" texture for snacking, but a higher moisture content caused this white cheddar to become "bland" and "boring" when melted into grilled cheese. Summarized one taster: "more reminiscent of Monterey Jack than cheddar."

The Color of Cheddar

Cheddar is naturally white or pale yellow, depending on what the cows eat; orange cheddar has annatto extract, a flavorless plant colorant, added. White cheddar is more popular in the eastern United States, while the rest of the country favors orange. But is there any difference aside from color?

To find out, we pitted one brand's white and orange sharp cheddars against each other in a blindfolded tasting. Surprisingly, all tasters were able to identify the color of the cheese via taste alone. The white cheddar was more acidic and sharper, while the orange cheese had a softer texture and milder flavor. Why? We learned that some manufacturers actually make their orange and white cheddars differently, altering moisture, fat, and aging to reflect regional preferences.

A true blind tasting of sharp cheddar.

One smart new opener kicked the rest to the curb.

BY HANNAH CROWLEY

KEY **Good** ★★★ **Fair** ★★ **Poor** ★

EZRA J. WARNER patented the first U.S. can opener in Connecticut in 1858, made from a bayonet and a sickle lashed together. At the time, most cans were about ³⁄₁₆ inch thick and were typically opened with a hammer and chisel. Luckily for our equipment testers, technology has improved.

Our past winners have been discontinued or redesigned, so we took a fresh look. In our last testing, we looked at safety openers and traditional models. The former cuts into the side of the can, leaving dull "safe" edges; the latter cuts into the top of the can, leaving jagged edges. We didn't prefer one style to the other, so we again included both in our lineup of seven openers, priced from roughly $15 to $30. Our goal: to find one that attached and detached easily, was comfortable to operate, and dealt safely and easily with the severed lid.

We enlisted testers—large and small, lefty and righty—to open hundreds of cans: squat cans of tuna fish, small cans of tomato paste, medium cans of chickpeas, and large cans of whole tomatoes. We evaluated each model during every step. First, attaching: All the traditional openers attached the same way—their two straight arms opened and clamped the gears onto the can. Having grown up with this style, our testers found these openers intuitive.

As for the safety openers, there were two different designs. The first housed the circular blades that clamp onto the can underneath the head; the second housed them on the side. The openers with blades underneath were harder to attach because the blades are hidden, so it often took multiple attempts to correctly align the openers. The side-style openers solved this problem—the blades were visible for easy alignment, and a thin metal railing propped the opener at the correct height.

Next, smoothness and ease of operation, or how easy it was to drive the openers around the cans. If the handles were too thin or round, they cramped our hands. We preferred straight, oval handles. We also liked textured handles or those coated in a tacky rubber for traction; one opener made of slick plastic felt like a slippery fish.

The rotating handle that you turn to move the opener around the can is called the driving handle. The best were longer for better leverage and easier turning, with ergonomic grooves that

HIGHLY RECOMMENDED

FISSLER Magic Smooth-Edge Can Opener
Model: FIS7570
Price: $29
Style: Safety
Dishwasher-Safe: Yes
Lid Disposal: Automatic

CRITERIA	
Attaching	★★★
Ease of Operation	★★★
Lid Disposal	★★★

TESTERS' NOTES: Sleek, smart, and comfortable, this opener's visible gears were easy to attach. The straight, textured handle fit comfortably and securely in hand, and the ergonomic driving handle was longer for better leverage and easier turning. It pulled off the lid when it was finished for safe and easy disposal.

RECOMMENDED WITH RESERVATIONS

ZYLISS Lock 'N Lift Can Opener
Model: 20362
Price: $15.99
Style: Traditional
Dishwasher-Safe: No
Lid Disposal: Magnet

Attaching	★★★
Ease of Operation	★★★
Lid Disposal	★

This opener attached readily with an obvious click and turned easily, with grippy plastic handles. While it did have a lid-lifting magnet, it was often too strong to readily release the lid; also, it was located on the front, so testers had to dip the head of the opener into the can's contents to retrieve the lid.

J.A. HENCKELS Twin Pure Can Opener
Model: 12914-000
Price: $19.99
Style: Safety
Dishwasher-Safe: Yes
Lid Disposal: Automatic

Attaching	★★★
Ease of Operation	★
Lid Disposal	★★★

This opener had an intuitive and visible attaching mechanism and seamless lid disposal, just like our winner. But it was heavier, with uncomfortable handles that were round, short, and without any ergonomic grooves, which made it physically much harder to turn.

NOT RECOMMENDED

KUHN RIKON Auto Safety Master Opener
Model: 2266 (black)
Price: $18
Style: Safety
Dishwasher-Safe: No
Lid Disposal: Pincers

Attaching	★★
Ease of Operation	★★
Lid Disposal	★

This opener was hard to attach because its head blocked its gears. It had pincers for lid disposal, but they were finicky. Designed to be a five-purpose opener—cans, jars, tabs, and two kinds of bottle caps, its other uses hindered basic can opening—namely the large spike at the end of the handle for opening tabs that poked testers in the belly with each rotation.

SAVORA Can Opener
Model: 5099588 (crimson)
Price: $19.03
Style: Traditional
Dishwasher-Safe: No
Lid Disposal: None

Attaching	★
Ease of Operation	★★★
Lid Disposal	★

This opener was easy to turn, but its smooth, hard, plastic handles were slippery to use with damp hands. Thanks to a stiff latch, it was also hard to clip on and off. It doesn't have a lid disposal device, and while the company said that it was dishwasher-safe, ours rusted in the machine overnight.

OXO Smooth Edge Can Opener
Model: 1049953V1
Price: $21.99
Style: Safety
Dishwasher-Safe: No
Lid Disposal: Pincers

Attaching	★
Ease of Operation	★★
Lid Disposal	★

This opener had grippy handles but also a bulky head that blocked our view and made it hard to latch onto the can. It was difficult to tell when the lid was severed, and you have to use the pincers on the side of the opener to pry off the lid, an annoying additional step worsened by the bulky head's blocking our view of the tiny pincers.

CHEF'N EZ Squeeze Can Opener
Model: 102-150-001
Price: $15.88
Style: Traditional
Dishwasher-Safe: No
Lid Disposal: Magnet

Attaching	★
Ease of Operation	★
Lid Disposal	★

There was nothing "EZ" about this can opener. Intended to be operated using just one hand, it was hard even using two. Its lid-lifting magnet was weak and only worked half the time, and you had to dip the whole front of the opener into the can to retrieve the top—messy and inconvenient.

securely braced our thumbs.

Finally, we evaluated detaching, safety, and lid disposal. We docked safety points from the one traditional opener that didn't have a lid disposal device. The others all did: Two had small pincers, two had magnets, and two used their blades to pull off the lid. The pincers were finicky. The magnets were inconsistent; one was too weak and the second too strong. Testers preferred the two whose blades and gears automatically clamped onto the lid and removed

it when it was completely severed—safe, clean, and simple.

We asked a lot of our lineup, and almost all the contenders failed. But one tester summed up our thoughts on the sole successful model, asking: "Can you be in love with a can opener?" We think so. The Fissler Magic Smooth-Edge Can Opener ($29) is a safety-style opener. It was easy to attach and operate, tidily and safely disposed of lids, and is dishwasher-safe. Compared with a sickle and bayonet, this opener practically *is* magic.

SAFETY FIRST
By reorienting the cutting blade, our winner removes tops leaving no sharp edges.

Heirloom Recipe

We're looking for recipes that you treasure, that have earned a place at your table and in your heart, through many years of meals. Send us the recipes that spell home to you. Visit **CooksCountry.com/magazines/home** (or write to Heirloom Recipes, *Cook's Country*, P.O. Box 470739, Brookline, MA 02447); click on Heirloom Recipes and tell us a little about the recipe. Include your name and mailing address. **If we print your recipe, you'll receive a free one-year subscription to** *Cook's Country.*

PICKLED SHRIMP Serves 6 to 8

Sheila Williams from Escondido, Calif., writes, "Growing up in Atlanta, my mother never threw a party without serving these mild pickled shrimp as a passed hors d'oeuvre, leaving the tails on to make them easy to eat with fingers. Today, I make them myself for a light lunch or first course served on Boston lettuce leaves."

The shrimp need to be refrigerated for at least 3 hours before serving.

- 2 pounds extra-large shrimp (21 to 25 per pound), peeled and deveined
- Salt
- 8 cups ice
- 1 cup cider vinegar
- ¼ cup sugar
- 2 garlic cloves, smashed and peeled
- 3 bay leaves
- 1 teaspoon allspice berries
- 1 teaspoon coriander seeds
- ½ teaspoon red pepper flakes
- 1 cup extra-virgin olive oil
- ¼ cup capers, minced
- 2 tablespoons Dijon mustard
- 2 tablespoons minced fresh dill
- 1 tablespoon hot sauce
- 1 tablespoon Worcestershire sauce
- 1 cup thinly sliced red onion
- 1 lemon, cut into 6 wedges

1. Combine 4 cups cold water, shrimp, and 2 teaspoons salt in Dutch oven. Set pot over medium-high heat and cook, stirring occasionally, until water registers 170 degrees and shrimp are just beginning to turn pink, 5 to 7 minutes. Remove from heat, cover, and let sit until shrimp are completely pink and firm, 5 to 7 minutes.

Stir ice into pot and let shrimp cool completely, about 5 minutes. Drain shrimp in colander. Transfer shrimp to paper towel–lined baking sheet and pat dry.

2. Combine vinegar, sugar, garlic, bay leaves, allspice, coriander seeds, and pepper flakes in large bowl and microwave until hot, about 2 minutes. Stir to dissolve sugar. Let cool completely. Whisk in oil, capers, mustard, dill, hot sauce, Worcestershire, and 1 teaspoon salt until combined.

3. Stir onion, lemon wedges, and shrimp into vinegar mixture until thoroughly combined. Push to submerge shrimp in marinade, then place small plate on top to keep submerged. Cover and refrigerate, stirring occasionally, for at least 3 hours or up to 48 hours. To serve, remove shrimp from marinade using slotted spoon.

COMING NEXT ISSUE

Our June/July issue features grill-ready **Smoked Beef Tenderloin** and **BBQ Chicken Thighs**. We'll hit the beach with **Hawaiian Dinner Rolls**, take a road trip to Rhode Island for **Dynamite Sandwiches,** swing by South Carolina for **Shrimp and Grits**, and visit Tennessee for **Pulled Pork Shoulder.** Still hungry? Have a slice of **French Coconut Pie.**

RECIPE INDEX

RC = Recipe Card

FIND THE ROOSTER!

A tiny version of this rooster has been hidden in the pages of this issue. Write to us with its location and we'll enter you in a random drawing. The first correct entry drawn will win our top-rated can opener, and each of the next five will receive a free one-year subscription to *Cook's Country*. To ent[er] visit **CooksCountry.com/rooster** by May 31, 2015 or write to Rooster AM15[ ] *Cook's Country*, P.O. Box 470739, Brookline, MA 02447. Include your nam[e] and address. Lisa Samec of Forest Lak[e] Minnesota, found the rooster in the December/January 2015 issue on pag[e] 4 and won our winning handheld mixe[r]

WEB EXTRAS

Free for 4 months online at
CooksCountry.com

Boneless Buffalo Chicken
Classic Pound Cake
Cranberry-Apple-Orange Relish
Easy Fresh Fruit Tart
Five easy fruit chutneys
Homemade Apple Butter
Homemade Peach Mostarda
Homemade Seville Orange Marmalade
Muffin Tin Testing
Peanut Butter and Jam Cake
Pizza Cutter Testing

READ US ON iPAD

Download the *Cook's Country* for iPad and star[t a] free trial subscrip[tion] or purchase a single issue of the magazine. All issu[es] are enhanced with full-color Cooking Mode slide show[s] that provide step-by-step instructions for completing recipes, plus expanded rev[iews] and ratings. Go to **CooksCountry.com/**[ ] to download our app through iTunes.

Follow us on **Pinterest**
pinterest.com/TestKitchen

Follow us on **Twitter**
twitter.com/TestKitchen

Find us on **Facebook**
facebook.com/CooksCountry

Lemon Meringue Cake

What's better than lemon meringue pie? Cake, of course. Buttery pound cake, tangy lemon curd, and swaths of fluffy, burnished meringue make this a winner.

3 tablespoons plus ½ cup lemon juice (4 lemons)

½ teaspoon unflavored gelatin

4 large eggs (2 whole, 2 separated)

1½ cups (10½ ounces) sugar
Salt

4 tablespoons unsalted butter, cut into 4 pieces and chilled

1 recipe Classic Pound Cake* (or 1 store-bought pound cake)

1 tablespoon light corn syrup

½ teaspoon vanilla extract

FOR THE LEMON CURD: Place 1 tablespoon lemon juice in small bowl; sprinkle gelatin over top. Heat ½ cup lemon juice in small saucepan over medium heat until hot but not boiling. Whisk 2 whole eggs and 2 yolks together in medium bowl; whisk in ¾ cup sugar and pinch salt. Whisking constantly, slowly pour hot lemon juice into egg mixture. Return lemon-egg mixture to saucepan and cook over medium heat, stirring constantly with wooden spoon, until mixture registers 170 degrees and is thick enough to coat spoon, about 3 minutes. Immediately remove pan from heat and stir in butter and gelatin mixture until dissolved. Strain through fine-mesh strainer set over medium bowl; set aside.

FOR THE CAKE: Using serrated knife, split cake horizontally about 2 inches from bottom. Using paring knife or fork, remove inside of cake bottom, leaving ¾-inch border along sides and bottom. Pour lemon curd into cake cavity, replace top, and wrap tightly with plastic wrap. Refrigerate for at least 6 hours or up to 24 hours.

FOR THE MERINGUE: In bowl of stand mixer, combine corn syrup, remaining ¾ cup sugar, remaining 2 egg whites, remaining 2 tablespoons lemon juice, and pinch salt. Place over medium saucepan filled with 1 inch barely simmering water, making sure that water does not touch bottom of bowl. Cook, stirring constantly, until mixture registers 160 degrees, 5 to 10 minutes. Attach bowl to mixer fitted with whisk and add vanilla. Whip on medium-high speed until stiff peaks form, 5 to 10 minutes.

Adjust oven rack to middle position and heat oven to 425 degrees. Unwrap cake and place on wire rack set in rimmed baking sheet. Using spatula, spread meringue on cake. Bake until tips of meringue are light golden brown, about 5 minutes. Transfer to cake platter. Serve.

*Go to CooksCountry.com/classicpoundcake for our Classic Pound Cake recipe.

Inside This Issue

Cook's Country

JUNE/JULY 2015

CooksCountry.com
$5.95 U.S./$6.95 CANADA

Sweet corn is a natural for grilling, but there are dozens of different approaches. We tested every one and came up with an easy two-step method that gives you perfect corn every time. PAGE 10

07> 7 25274 05251 6

Dear Country Cook,

When I lived in Connecticut, I often lunched at Rawley's in Fairfield—a henhouse-size shack selling hot dogs that are deep fried and finished on the griddle. Cheese dogs, chili dogs, bacon—nothing fancy but everything delicious. Even Martha Stewart is a fan.

I am also fond of the classic Chicago dog, with bright green relish, onions, and tomato wedges, plus a hot pepper or two. Perfect pairings for a soft bun and a beefy dog.

I remember the dogs of my youth—the ones on buttered, toasted buns, the dogs split and griddled—and have also had hot dogs in Copenhagen—bright reddish-orange with a nice snap.

Fast food used to be good food. Diners, shacks, and roadside stands. It was local, but you always knew that you might meet a stranger.

This summer I'm going to drive down to Rawley's and order a chili cheese dog. Maybe Martha Stewart might want to come along. I dunno, I'll ask!

Cordially,

Christopher Kimball
Founder and Editor, Cook's Country

Cook'sCountry

Founder and Editor Christopher Kimball
Editorial Director Jack Bishop
Editorial Director, Magazines John Willoughby
Executive Editor Tucker Shaw
Managing Editor Scott Kathan
Executive Food Editor Bryan Roof
Senior Editors Hannah Crowley,
Lisa McManus, Diane Unger
Test Kitchen Director Erin McMurrer
Associate Editor Christie Morrison
Test Cooks Morgan Bolling, Aaron Furmanek,
Katie Leaird, Ashley Moore
Assistant Test Cook Cecelia Jenkins
Assistant Editors Lauren Savoie, Kate Shannon
Senior Copy Editor Megan Ginsberg
Copy Editor Krista Magnuson
Executive Assistant Christine Gordon
Assistant Test Kitchen Director Leah Rovner
Senior Kitchen Assistants Michelle Blodget,
Alexxa Grattan
Kitchen Assistants Maria Elena Delgado,
Ena Gudiel, Jason Roman
Executive Producer Melissa Baldino
Co-Executive Producer Stephanie Stender
Associate Producer Kaitlin Hammond

Consulting Creative Director Amy Klee
Contributing Editors Erika Bruce, Eva Katz, Jeremy Sauer
Consulting Editors Anne Mendelson, Meg Ragland
Science Editor Guy Crosby, PhD
Executive Food Editor, TV, Radio & Media
Bridget Lancaster

Managing Editor, Web Christine Liu
Senior Editor, Cooking School Mari Levine
Associate Editors, Web Jill Fisher, Roger Metcalf
Assistant Web Editor Terrence Doyle
Senior Video Editor Nick Dakoulas

Design Director, Print Greg Galvan
Photography Director Julie Cote
Art Director Susan Levin
Associate Art Director Lindsey Timko
Art Director, Marketing Jennifer Cox
Staff Photographer Daniel J. van Ackere
Color Food Photography Keller + Keller
Styling Catrine Kelty, Marie Piraino
Deputy Art Director, Marketing Melanie Gryboski
Associate Art Director, Marketing Janet Taylor
Designer, Marketing Stephanie Cook
Associate Art Director, Photography Steve Klise

VP, Print & Direct Marketing David Mack
Circulation Director Doug Wicinski
Circulation & Fulfillment Manager Carrie Fethe
Partnership Marketing Manager Pamela Putprush
Marketing Coordinator Marina Tomao

Director, Business Systems Alice Carpenter
Manager, Business & Content Systems Dustin Brandt
Project Manager Britt Dresser
Development Manager Mike Serio

Chief Operating Officer Rob Ristagno
VP, Digital Products Fran Middleton
VP, New Product Development Michael Burton
Production Director Guy Rochford
Senior Color & Imaging Specialist Lauren Robbins
Production & Imaging Specialists Heather Dube,
Dennis Noble
Director, Marketing & Sales Operations Deborah Fagone
Client Services Manager Kate Zebrowski
Sponsorship Sales Associate Morgan Mannino
Senior Controller Theresa Peterson
Customer Loyalty & Support Manager Amy Bootier
Customer Loyalty & Support Reps Rebecca Kowalski,
Andrew Straaberg Finfrock, Juliet Tierney

Director, Retail Book Program Beth Ineson
Human Resources Manager Adele Shapiro
Publicity Deborah Broide

ON THE COVER: *Easy Grilled Corn*, Keller + Keller,
Catrine Kelty
ILLUSTRATION: Greg Stevenson

Follow us on **Pinterest**
pinterest.com/TestKitchen

Follow us on **Twitter**
twitter.com/TestKitchen

Find us on **Facebook**
facebook.com/CooksCountry

Cook's Country magazine (ISSN 1552-1990), number 63, published bimonthly by Boston Common Press Limited Partnership, 17 Station St., Brookline, MA 02445. Copyright 2015 Boston Common Press Limited Partnership. Periodicals postage paid at Boston, MA, and additional mailing offices, USPS #023453. Publications Mail Agreement No. 40020778. Return undeliverable Canadian addresses to P.O. Box 875, Station A, Windsor, ON N9A 6P2. POSTMASTER: Send address changes to Cook's Country, PO Box 6018, Harlan, IA 51593-1518. For subscription and gift subscription orders, subscription inquiries, or change of address notices, visit americasTestKitchen.com/support, call 800-526-8447 in the U.S. or 515-248-7684 from outside the U.S., or write to us at Cook's Country, P.O. Box 6018, Harlan, IA 51593-1518. PRINTED IN THE USA.

Contents

JUNE/JULY 2015

TENNESSEE PULLED PORK SANDWICHES, 4

PEACH AND TOMATO SALAD, 7

FRENCH COCONUT PIE, 22

Features

Departments

Make It Mexican (Here's How)

In our new cookbook *The Best Mexican Recipes*, we demystify the core techniques and surprising secrets of Mexican home cooking so you can use supermarket staples to create vibrant, flavorful Mexican dishes with ease. Contains 175 foolproof recipes highlighting the real flavors of Mexico.

America's Test Kitchen is a very real 2,500-square-foot kitchen located just outside Boston. It is the home of *Cook's Country* and *Cook's Illustrated* magazines and the workday destination of more than three dozen test cooks, editors, and cookware specialists. Our mission is to test recipes until we understand how and why they work and arrive at the best version. We also test kitchen equipment and supermarket ingredients in search of products that offer the best value and performance. You can watch us work by tuning in to *Cook's Country from America's Test Kitchen* (CooksCountry.com) and *America's Test Kitchen* (AmericasTestKitchen.com) on public television.

Ask Cook's Country

BY MORGAN BOLLING

Microgreen Primer

What are microgreens? Are they the same as sprouts?
Eric Williams, Palmdale, Calif.

Microgreens, once found primarily on fancy restaurant plates, have recently become more widely available in specialty stores and supermarkets. They are the first early, tiny shoots of herbs, lettuces, or other greens. Some of the most common options are arugula, beet greens, cilantro, basil, mustard greens, or salad mix varieties.

These young greens are not the same as sprouts. Most sprouts, such as alfalfa, are grown hydroponically in water and take just a couple of days to grow. Microgreens are grown in soil, often in greenhouses. They can be harvested between seven and 14 days old, when they're 1½ to 2 inches tall and their leaves have spread open. Most varieties have to be cut by hand with scissors. Because of the labor involved, they often come with a hefty price tag, typically ranging between $2 and $4 per ounce.

We tasted a handful of different microgreen varieties and found that they have similar flavors to the plants they would have eventually grown into, but the flavors are much more intense.
THE BOTTOM LINE: Microgreens are the delicate, flavorful baby leaves of herbs, lettuces, or salad greens.

Reheating French Fries

Is it possible to bring leftover French fries home and reheat them?
Marcia Yeager, Chestertown, Md.

Common wisdom says that French fries must be eaten right away; old, cold fries are fit only for the trash bin. But is this really true? We hoped not. We brought in French fries from a few local restaurants, let them cool, and tried several methods of reviving them with a goal of crisp, hot fries that, if they didn't taste exactly the same as those straight out of the fry basket, came close.

Microwaving them, unsurprisingly, resulted in soggy fries. And even at a variety of temperatures, the oven left fries dry, leathery, and decidedly uncrisp. We turned our attention to the stovetop. We tried heating the cold fries through in a dry skillet, in ½ inch of oil, and in a lightly oiled skillet. In a side-by-side tasting, this last method worked especially well.

To use our method, heat 1 tablespoon of vegetable oil in a 12-inch non-stick skillet until nice and hot (it should just start smoking). Add the fries in a single layer just covering the bottom of the skillet and stir frequently until they darken slightly in color and are fragrant, 2 to 3 minutes. Drain them on a paper towel–lined plate to absorb any excess oil. If you'd like, sprinkle them with a little salt for extra seasoning.

When using a 12-inch skillet, we were able to effectively reheat 6 ounces of fries, or about the amount in a large order of McDonald's fries. This method worked well for standard, shoestring, and steak fries.
THE BOTTOM LINE: Reheating restaurant French fries in a preheated, lightly oiled skillet yields the crispest results.

THE BEST REHEATING METHOD
A tablespoon of oil in a nonstick skillet.

Sizing Garlic Cloves

When you call for one garlic clove, what size should I be using?
Tamara Martfield, Sacramento, Calif.

In the test kitchen, we use the guideline that one clove of garlic yields 1 teaspoon of minced garlic. This translates to a clove of garlic weighing 5 grams, which in turn translates to 1¼ inches by ¾ inch by ½ inch. While we do not expect you to pull out a scale or ruler each time you mince a clove, this is relatively close in size to a Jordan almond.
THE BOTTOM LINE: A clove that's 1¼ inches long and ¾ inch by ½ inch should yield about 1 teaspoon minced. Or you can use multiple small cloves or part of a larger one—just measure after you've minced. Cloves are shown true to size.

Extra-Large Clove	Large Clove	Medium Clove	Small Clove
Yield: 1 tablespoon minced	Yield: 2 teaspoons minced	Yield: 1 teaspoon minced	Yield: ½ teaspoon minced

Should You Pack Your Herbs?

When measuring fresh basil for pesto, should I pack the leaves down in my measuring cup?
Brenda McCaffrey, Kansas City, Mo.

We had 26 staff members measure out 1 cup of basil in a dry measuring cup and then weighed the leaves. Samples were all over the place—those measuring gingerly ended up with 10 grams of basil; those who aggressively packed in the basil ended up with 29 grams. The average was 18.7 grams.

Based on these weights, we made three batches of our Classic Pesto, which calls for 2 cups of fresh basil leaves (and doesn't specify packed or unpacked). Tasters liked all three samples. The pesto with more basil tasted, unsurprisingly, more like basil, while the samples with less basil tasted more of garlic, Parmesan cheese, or olive oil. But when pressed to pick a favorite, most tasters agreed: The pesto made with the average amount of basil (18.7 grams) tasted the most balanced and, as one taster put it, "how pesto should taste."

We went back to the measuring cup with 18.7 grams of basil. We found that laying the leaves in the cup and pressing down just slightly, ensuring that there were no large air pockets, filled the cup just to its brim.
THE BOTTOM LINE: For the best results, measure basil by laying the leaves in the cup and pressing down slightly to remove any large air pockets. Do not pack the leaves down firmly into the cup. Use the same technique for all herbs.

Knife Disposal

How do I safely dispose of a spent kitchen knife?
Brenda Cicero, Boston, Mass.

Many home cooks have old or unused knives lurking in the back of kitchen drawers, taking up space and posing a safety risk. Just tossing knives in the trash creates a hazard for sanitation workers, so we contacted a handful of professional knife manufacturers and waste disposal companies for advice on getting rid of them safely. Many suggested donating the knife if there's still life in it. You could take it to a thrift store, soup kitchen, or school cafeteria in your area.

If donating isn't possible, carefully wrapping the knife for disposal is important for the safety of waste management workers. Christopher Costa, director of product management and packaging at Victorinox Swiss Army (maker of our winning Victorinox 8" Swiss Army Fibrox Chef's Knife), told us that the knife should be placed between layers of corrugated cardboard and clearly marked "sharp knife."

Here's how to do it: Use two 9-inch strips of 2-inch wide electrical tape to cover the tip end and butt end of the blade in a double layer. Then fold an 8 by 10-inch piece of cardboard lengthwise around the blade to cover it entirely. Secure this in place with more heavy-duty tape and write "SHARP KNIFE" on both sides of the package. From there you can take it to a recycling center or waste management center for safe disposal and/or recycling.

Brian Coughlin from the City of Boston Public Works Department cautioned us against ever throwing a knife directly into the trash, lest it cause injury; instead, he instructed us to hand-deliver it.
THE BOTTOM LINE: To dispose of an old kitchen knife, consider donating it. Otherwise, wrap it carefully and hand-deliver it to a recycling center or waste management center.

FAREWELL, TRUSTY BLADE
Hand it over at the dump.

To ask us a cooking question, visit **CooksCountry.com/ask**. Or write to Ask Cook's Country, P.O. Box 470739, Brookline, MA 02447. Just try to stump us!

Kitchen Shortcuts

COMPILED BY SHANNON FRIEDMANN HATCH

COOL TRICK Saving Bacon Grease
Cary Bauer, Madison, Wis.

I like the smoky pork flavor that bacon fat adds to everything from eggs to corn-bread, so I always save it after frying bacon. First, I pour the fat into a heatproof bowl and let it cool completely before refrigerating. Once it is solid, I scoop it into tablespoon-size balls and freeze them in a zipper-lock freezer bag for future use.

TIDY TIP
Easier Broccoli Trimming
Brandt McMillan, Nashville, Tenn.

I find trimming the florets off broccoli with a chef's knife awkward. I think it's easier to position the stalk upside down on a cutting board and snip each branch off the stem with kitchen shears.

RECYCLE IT
Soaking Solution
Emil Orth, Germantown, Tenn.

When I need to soak wooden skewers for grilling to prevent charring, I place them in an empty wine bottle and fill it with water. The vessel is just the right size to hold the skewers and allow the water to soak through.

HANDY TIP
Even Coverage
Claire Beighle, Redmond, Wash.

My husband and I often finish grilled or roasted vegetables with balsamic or cider vinegar, but we've found that drizzling can cover the food unevenly, leaving bare spots or bracing pools. Instead, we use a small spray bottle for even coverage.

COOL TRICK Better Ice Bath
Charles Lake, Greenville, S.C.

If I'm making a big batch of hard-cooked eggs, I need a large ice bath to stop the cooking. I don't always want to empty my ice trays, so I've started using ice gel packs in the water. They work just as well and are reusable.

CLEVER TIP
A Snip for Snappy Opening
Margaret Barre, Seneca, S.C.

Zipper-top closures on packaged items like shredded cheese aid in ensuring a tight seal but can be difficult to open later. I cut one edge a bit lower than the other with kitchen shears and find that it's easier to separate them.

SMART TIP Sizing Up Bulk Chicken Breasts
Laura Korte, Tucson, Ariz.

I buy chicken breasts in bulk and freeze them for convenience, but they often vary in size, which can throw off a recipe. Before I freeze them, I weigh each one and divide them into 1-, 1½-, and 2-pound portions, recording the weight on the bag. That way, I can grab similar-size pieces with no guesswork.

Submit a tip online at **CooksCountry.com/kitchenshortcuts** or send a letter to Kitchen Shortcuts, *Cook's Country*, P.O. Box 470739, Brookline, MA 02447. Include your name, address, and phone number. If we publish your tip, you will receive a free one-year subscription to *Cook's Country*. Letters may be edited for clarity and length.

Tennessee Pulled Pork Sandwiches

To re-create this supremely flavorful, finely textured pulled pork, we had to call in the heavy equipment. BY MORGAN BOLLING

WHEN I PICTURE pulled pork, I imagine ropey, tender strands of smoky meat studded with savory-sweet "bark," the crunchy bits from the exterior of the meat. But when our executive food editor described a style of pulled pork he'd had at Papa KayJoe's barbecue restaurant in central Tennessee—bark-less and shredded so fine it almost resembled pâté—I was intrigued, if skeptical. "I promise," my editor assured me, "it's great."

Lacking the custom setup that proprietor Devin Pickard built at Papa KayJoe's (see "On the Road"), I started a well-seasoned, bone-in pork butt on the grill, adding wood chip packets to mimic the smokiness Pickard draws from his hickory wood. After about 2 hours, I brought the pork inside to finish it in the even heat of the oven.

I can't say I was disappointed with the rich, meaty flavor, but the thing that really concerned me was the process of "pulling." After 30 minutes of shredding the meat with forks (our usual method), I still could not get the pork as fine as I wanted. In the test kitchen, we typically cook pork butt for pulled pork to 190 degrees, a temperature at which the fat and collagen would be completely broken down, ensuring tender, moist strands of meat. But for a superfine shred, a higher temperature is in order: Pickard takes his meat to 210 degrees. So I set my timer for an extra hour and I was rewarded for my patience with a soft roast, just right for shredding.

When Pickard shreds his pork, he slips on a pair of heatproof firefighter gloves and shreds the pork by hand. Lacking such specialty gloves, I first tried shredding the hot meat with tongs and then with a potato masher. But with 5 pounds of meat, this process took forever.

I tossed caution to the wind and dropped my hot pork shoulder right into the bowl of a stand mixer. I flipped the switch to low and stood back while the steam rose from the bowl. Bingo: After just 90 seconds in the mixer, the pork had the finely shredded consistency I had been seeking. It was a bit dry, though, so I harvested 1½ cups of the juices that had accumulated in the roasting pan and stirred them back into the meat. Promise fulfilled: I took a tip from Pickard and sandwiched the meat in a pair of hoecakes for the best sandwich of the season.

We serve our sandwich just like they do at Papa KayJoe's: on sturdy cornmeal hoecakes.

TENNESSEE PULLED PORK SANDWICHES
Serves 8 with leftovers

The roast must be seasoned at least 18 hours before cooking. In step 8, shred the pork while it's still hot. We prefer to serve the pork on hoecakes, but it's great on hamburger buns, too. Leftover pork can be refrigerated for up to three days. Find our favorite creamy coleslaw recipe at **CooksCountry.com/creamycoleslaw**.

PORK
- 1 (5- to 6-pound) bone-in pork butt roast, trimmed
  Kosher salt
- 2 cups wood chips
- 1 (13 by 9-inch) disposable aluminum roasting pan

BARBECUE SAUCE
- 1 cup ketchup
- ¼ cup cider vinegar
- ¼ cup water
- 2 tablespoons yellow mustard
- 1 tablespoon Worcestershire sauce
- 1 teaspoon granulated garlic
- 1 teaspoon pepper

- 1 recipe Hoecakes (recipe follows)
  Dill pickle chips
  Coleslaw

1. FOR THE PORK: Using sharp knife, cut 1-inch crosshatch pattern about ¼ inch deep in fat cap of roast, being careful not to cut into meat. Pat roast dry with paper towels. Place roast on large sheet of plastic wrap and rub 2 tablespoons salt over entire roast and into slits. Wrap tightly with plastic and refrigerate for 18 to 24 hours.

2. Just before grilling, soak wood chips in water for 15 minutes, then drain. Using large piece of heavy-duty aluminum foil, wrap soaked chips in foil packet and cut several vent holes in top.

3A. FOR A CHARCOAL GRILL: Open bottom vent completely. Light large chimney starter three-quarters filled with charcoal briquettes (4½ quarts). When top coals are partially covered with ash, pour evenly over half of grill. Place wood chip packet on coals. Set cooking grate in place, cover, and open lid vent completely. Heat grill until hot and wood chips are smoking, about 5 minutes.

3B. FOR A GAS GRILL: Remove cooking grate and place wood chip packet directly on primary burner. Set cooking grate in place, turn all burners to high, cover, and heat grill until hot and wood chips are smoking, about 15 minutes. Turn primary burner to medium-high and turn off other burner(s). (Adjust primary burner as needed to maintain grill temperature of 300 degrees.)

4. Unwrap pork and place fat side down in disposable pan. Place disposable pan on cooler side of grill. Cover grill (with lid vent directly over pork for charcoal) and cook until pork registers 120 degrees, about 2 hours. Thirty minutes before pork comes off grill, adjust oven rack to middle position and heat oven to 300 degrees.

5. Transfer disposable pan from grill to rimmed baking sheet. Cover pan tightly with foil and transfer to oven (still on sheet). Cook until fork inserted in pork meets little resistance and meat registers 210 degrees, about 3 hours.

6. FOR THE BARBECUE SAUCE: Meanwhile, combine all ingredients in medium saucepan and bring to boil over medium-high heat. Reduce heat to medium-low and simmer, whisking constantly, until slightly thickened, about 3 minutes. Transfer sauce to bowl and let cool completely.

7. Carefully remove foil from disposable pan (steam will escape). Remove blade bone from roast using tongs. Immediately transfer hot pork to bowl of stand mixer fitted with paddle attachment. Strain accumulated juices from pan through fine-mesh strainer set over separate bowl; discard solids.

8. Mix pork on low speed until meat

A 30-Year Journey to Pulled Pork Perfection

is finely shredded, about 1½ minutes. Whisk pork juices to recombine, if separated, and add 1½ cups juices to shredded pork. Continue to mix pork on low speed until juices are incorporated, about 15 seconds longer. Season with salt to taste, adding more pork juices if desired. Serve pork on hoecakes with barbecue sauce, pickles, and coleslaw.

HOECAKES Makes 16 hoecakes
Papa KayJoe's makes their hoecakes with bacon fat.

- 3 cups (15 ounces) white cornmeal
- 2 tablespoons sugar
- 2 teaspoons baking powder
- 1½ teaspoons salt
- 2 cups buttermilk
- 2 large eggs
- 2 tablespoons bacon fat or vegetable oil

1. Adjust oven rack to middle position and heat oven to 200 degrees. Set wire rack in rimmed baking sheet and place in oven. Whisk cornmeal, sugar, baking powder, and salt together in large bowl. Beat buttermilk and eggs together in separate bowl. Whisk buttermilk mixture into cornmeal mixture until combined.

2A. FOR A SKILLET: Heat 1 teaspoon fat in 12-inch nonstick skillet over medium heat until shimmering. Using level ¼-cup dry measuring cup, drop 3 evenly spaced scoops of batter into skillet, smoothing tops slightly if necessary.

2B. FOR A GRIDDLE: Heat 1 tablespoon fat on 400-degree nonstick griddle until shimmering. Using level ¼-cup dry measuring cup, drop 8 evenly spaced scoops of batter onto griddle, smoothing tops slightly if necessary.

3. Cook until small bubbles begin to appear on surface of cakes and edges are set, about 2 minutes. Flip and cook until second side is golden brown, about 2 minutes longer. Transfer hoecakes to prepared sheet in oven. Repeat with remaining fat and batter: 5 additional batches for skillet or 1 additional batch for griddle. Serve.

PAPA KAYJOE'S IN Centerville, Tennessee, is a weathered gray wood building with a red tin roof at the end of a steep, rocky driveway. In the spare dining room, patrons, most of them regulars, tuck into Papa KayJoe's signature sandwiches—pulled pork on cornmeal griddle cakes—and share local news.

The cozy scene belies the rough setup out back, where each morning owner Devin Pickard feeds armloads of hickory sticks into an outdoor furnace (really a converted oil drum), where they slowly burn down to coals. Pickard then carries the hot embers, a shovelful at a time, to a nearby dirt-floored barbecue shack where a pair of cinder block pits sit waiting. The building is well worn; a recent fire left the roof and walls charred. "This is just what I imagine a barbecue shack should be," Pickard says. He's been performing this task daily for 30 years.

At 11 a.m., Pickard lines up 24 heavily salted pork butts on the thick, black metal grate that sits over the pit and covers them with sheets of corrugated steel to trap the heat. The pork spends 6 to 8 hours on the grill, picking up the woodsy

Clockwise from top left: The chairs on Papa KayJoe's roof, a remnant of a prank played on Pickard by friends; stacks of aromatic hickory; Pickard salting pork butts on the grill; glowing hickory coals; Pickard hand-shredding the meat; hickory sticks burning down into coals for the pit.

aroma of the smoldering hickory.

After a day on the grill, the pork butts are packed into large aluminum roasting pans and transferred to a low oven where they'll spend the night. The next morning, Pickard slips on a pair of thick fireproof rubber gloves, picks out a pork butt, removes the blade bone (after nearly 24 hours of cooking, it snaps like chalk in his hands) and attacks the meat. In a clapping motion he brings his fingertips together, pinching the pork; in less than a minute, the pork is in tiny shreds. He works in cupfuls of the juices that have accumulated in the roasting pan, moistening the pork with its own essence. The result is silky and rich, as much pâté as pulled pork.

Inside, Pickard's mother (Debbie) and daughter (Ruby) help pile the pork onto hot cornmeal griddle cakes ("hoecakes") made to order with buttermilk and bacon fat. They'll produce dozens of these sandwiches today, and every day—including one for Pickard. "I would eat a barbecue sandwich every day of my life, that's how much I love it." –BRYAN ROOF

Smoked Beef Tenderloin

A whole beef tenderloin is an impressive roast that's perfect for entertaining. How do you make it even better? Adding smoke is a good start. BY DIANE UNGER

LUXURIOUS AND GRAND, beef tenderloin is best for special occasions. Its expense calls for careful attention, but don't sweat it: Because it has a relatively uniform shape once trimmed and tied, this pricey cut is a cinch to cook evenly. It's also easy to carve, since there are no bones to navigate. These are significant advantages for a cut of meat that, as fans of filet mignon know, has a buttery texture that is as tender as it gets.

So, what's its downside? Flavor. Beef tenderloin is a mild-tasting cut (and that's putting it mildly). My move this round: to ramp up the flavor by smoking the roast on the grill.

The test kitchen has grilled whole tenderloins before, but adding smoke was uncharted territory. Drawing on past test kitchen experience, I knew I'd start with a trimmed tenderloin, which has the small, fatty side muscle—the "chain," in butcherspeak—and the chewy silverskin removed. (Doing this at home can save you several dollars per pound; see "Preparing an Untrimmed Tenderloin.") I tucked the narrow end under to create a uniform shape and tied the roast with kitchen twine at 1-inch intervals. Then I hit it aggressively with salt and pepper and let the roast sit with the seasoning for 2 hours (it would be fine for up to 24 hours) so that the seasoning could work its way deep inside the roast.

I prepared a two-level fire (that is, a fire with both a hotter and a cooler side) on the grill and then wrapped some soaked wood chips in a foil packet and laid it on the hot coals. Once the chips were smoking, I followed our past grilling method and seared the roast directly over the smoldering chips until it was nice and brown on all sides, which took about 10 minutes. Then I moved the beef to the cooler side of the grill so that it could finish cooking evenly in the smoky, gentle heat. I took the roast off the grill when the center reached 125 degrees (for medium-rare) and tented it with foil so that the meat would stay warm while it rested for 30 minutes before slicing. I collected my colleagues to taste: Really good, they said, but not great. The smoke added depth and nuance, but it was a little harsh, and while the meat was well seasoned, it could use another jolt of flavor.

I looked at the way I was adding

For an extra hit of smoke, we grill the scallions for the herb sauce alongside the beef.

smoke. After some consultation with my colleagues, I realized that placing the foil packet of chips on top of the charcoal was hurting me: Because the tenderloin has such a mild flavor, this wood-chip arrangement was infusing the meat with too much smoke, giving the meat a harsh edge. I achieved a much more measured, subtle smoke flavor when I placed the packet on the bottom of the grill and then poured the hot charcoal on top. This way the smoke flavor was less aggressive, more nuanced.

As for other flavorings, I looked at my initial seasoning of salt and pepper. I tested adding different herbs, spices, and other ingredients to the mix to augment, but not overwhelm, the smoke flavor. On the tested-and-rejected list:

cayenne, canned chipotles in adobo, sage, steak sauce, dried porcini mushrooms, and oregano. A combination of fragrant fresh rosemary and thyme, rubbed into the salt to extract the herbs' full flavor, worked best for the initial seasoning of the beef.

But I didn't want to stop there. I decided to make a sauce to serve alongside. I simmered a healthy handful of chopped garlic in olive oil with pepper flakes and more rosemary and thyme. Then I discarded the herbs and added minced parsley, a little balsamic vinegar, pepper, and some reserved herb salt. To build layers of flavor, I used some of this potent mixture to baste the meat while it smoked, and I threw two bunches of scallions on the grill with the

beef. I finely chopped the smoky scallions and stirred them into the sauce.

I called my tasters again, and they couldn't believe how deeply flavored the beef—sliced, seasoned with more herb salt, and topped with the potent green sauce—now was. This recipe is poised to steal the show at your next big summer gathering.

SMOKED BEEF TENDERLOIN
Serves 12 to 16

For the most economical choice, buy a whole, untrimmed tenderloin and trim it yourself. Note that the roast needs to sit for at least 2 hours or up to 24 hours after seasoning but before cooking. If you'd like to use wood chunks instead of wood chips when using a charcoal grill, substitute two medium wood chunks, soaked in water for 1 hour, for the wood chip packet.

HERB SALT
- 2 tablespoons kosher salt
- 1 tablespoon minced fresh rosemary
- 2 teaspoons minced fresh thyme

BEEF AND SCALLIONS
- 1 (6- to 7-pound) whole beef tenderloin, trimmed
- 2 bunches scallions, trimmed
  Pepper
- 1½ cups wood chips

SAUCE
- ¾ cup extra-virgin olive oil
- 6 garlic cloves, chopped
- 1 sprig fresh rosemary
- 1 sprig fresh thyme
- ¼ teaspoon red pepper flakes
- ¼ cup minced fresh parsley
- 1 tablespoon balsamic vinegar
  Kosher salt and pepper

1. FOR THE HERB SALT: Rub salt, rosemary, and thyme together in bowl using your fingers.

2. FOR THE BEEF AND SCALLIONS: Tuck tail end of tenderloin under by 2 to 4 inches to create more even shape, then tie with kitchen twine to secure. Tie remainder of tenderloin at 1-inch intervals. Sprinkle tenderloin all over with 2 tablespoons herb salt (reserve remaining herb salt in covered container for later use). Wrap tenderloin in plastic wrap and refrigerate for at least 2 hours or up to 24 hours. Tie scallions into 2 separate bunches with kitchen twine.

3. FOR THE SAUCE: Combine oil, garlic, rosemary sprig, thyme sprig, and pepper flakes in small saucepan. Bring to gentle simmer over low heat, stirring occasionally, and cook until garlic just begins to brown and herbs are fragrant, 8 to 10 minutes. Remove from heat, transfer to bowl, and let cool completely. Discard rosemary and thyme sprigs. Stir in parsley, vinegar, 1 teaspoon pepper, and 1 teaspoon reserved herb salt.

4. Brush tenderloin all over with 3 tablespoons sauce, then sprinkle with 1 tablespoon pepper. Brush scallion bunches with 1 tablespoon sauce. Reserve remaining ¾ cup sauce for serving.

5. Soak wood chips in water for 15 minutes, then drain. Using large piece of heavy-duty aluminum foil, wrap soaked wood chips in foil packet and cut several vent holes in top.

6A. FOR A CHARCOAL GRILL: Open bottom vent halfway. Light large chimney starter three-quarters filled with charcoal briquettes (4½ quarts). Place wood chip packet on 1 side of grill. When top coals are partially covered with ash, pour evenly over half of grill on top of wood chip packet. Set cooking grate in place, cover, and open lid vent halfway. Heat grill until hot and wood chips are smoking, about 5 minutes.

6B. FOR A GAS GRILL: Remove cooking grate and place wood chip packet directly on primary burner. Set grate in place, turn all burners to high, cover, and heat grill until hot and wood chips are smoking, about 15 minutes. Leave primary burner on high and turn off other burners. (Adjust primary burner as needed to maintain grill temperature of 350 to 375 degrees).

7. Clean and oil cooking grate. Place tenderloin and scallions on hotter side of grill. Cook (covered if using gas) until scallions are lightly charred, about 3 minutes, and meat is browned on first side, about 5 minutes. Flip scallions and tenderloin and continue to cook on second sides until scallions are lightly charred, about 3 minutes, and meat is browned, about 5 minutes. Transfer scallions to plate. Move tenderloin to cooler side of grill. Cover, positioning lid vent over meat for charcoal, and cook for 30 minutes.

8. Move thicker part of tenderloin over hotter side of grill and continue to cook, covered, until tenderloin registers 125 degrees for medium-rare, 10 to 20 minutes longer. Transfer tenderloin to carving board, tent loosely with foil, and let rest for 30 minutes.

9. Chop scallions and stir into reserved sauce. Season with salt and pepper to taste. Remove twine and carve meat into ¼-inch-thick slices. Season meat lightly with herb salt and pepper and drizzle with sauce. Serve.

TEST KITCHEN TECHNIQUE **Preparing an Untrimmed Tenderloin**
Save money by buying an untrimmed roast and doing the simple butchering yourself. Here's how.

1. REMOVE CHAIN
The chain is the fatty strip that runs along the side of a tenderloin. Use a boning or chef's knife to remove it.

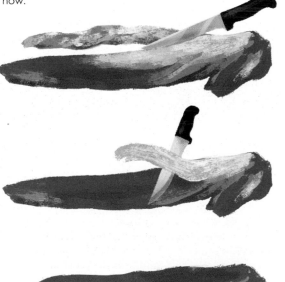

2. REMOVE SILVERSKIN
Insert the tip of your knife under the sinewy silverskin, and then grab it with a paper towel and cut upward against the silverskin to remove it.

3. TUCK NARROW END UNDER
Fold the narrow end under to make an even shape that will cook more consistently.

4. TIE WITH TWINE
Tie the roast at 1-inch intervals with kitchen twine. Now you're ready to season, let rest, and grill.

Peach and Tomato Salad

The key to making these summer ingredients sing in harmony is proper seasoning.

BY CHRISTIE MORRISON

Mint adds a vibrant element to this summery salad.

COMBINING PEACHES AND tomatoes into a salty-sweet salad is not a new idea. But judging by the recipes for this salad that I found and prepared, it is an idea that could use improving. The versions I made and tasted with my colleagues in the test kitchen were by turns watery, bland, mushy, or—worst of all—overloaded with everything from nuts to distracting vegetables like corn, zucchini, and green beans.

I wanted to keep the salad simple to let the fresh flavors of the peak-season peaches and tomatoes shine. The first step was ridding the tomatoes of excess liquid that would water down the salad. I cut the tomatoes into chunks and tossed them with salt before letting them drain in a colander. In just 30 minutes the tomatoes released a good bit of water, making the drained chunks more concentrated and lightly seasoned; by ridding the tomatoes of their extra moisture up front, I was ensuring that they wouldn't release too much moisture into the salad.

Since the peaches and tomatoes were contributing plenty of sweetness, I decided to play up savory flavors in the dressing. I tried a number of different vinegars and citrus juices in the vinaigrette and found that a combination of cider vinegar and lemon juice was the best match—sharp enough to balance the sweetness with a slight fruitiness and depth that complemented the fruit. A bit of lemon zest added a fresh note.

Wanting to keep the salad simple but not boring, I added thin shallot rings and some torn mint for a cool contrast to the fruit. The finished dish looked fantastic—chunks of fruit in shades of orange and red flecked with a generous amount of mint—and the flavor was bright, sweet, and tangy.

PEACH AND TOMATO SALAD
Serves 4 to 6
Perfectly ripe peaches and tomatoes are essential to this recipe.

- 1 **pound ripe tomatoes, cored, cut into ½-inch-thick wedges, and wedges halved crosswise Salt and pepper**
- 3 **tablespoons extra-virgin olive oil, plus extra for drizzling**
- 2 **tablespoons cider vinegar**
- ½ **teaspoon grated lemon zest plus 1 tablespoon juice**
- 1 **pound ripe peaches, halved, pitted, cut into ½-inch-thick wedges, and wedges halved crosswise**
- 1 **shallot, sliced into thin rings**
- ⅓ **cup fresh mint leaves, torn**

1. Combine tomatoes and ½ teaspoon salt in bowl and toss to coat; transfer to colander and let drain in sink for 30 minutes.

2. Whisk oil, vinegar, lemon zest and juice, ½ teaspoon salt, and ½ teaspoon pepper together in large bowl. Add peaches, shallot, and drained tomatoes to dressing and toss gently to coat. Season with salt and pepper to taste. Transfer to platter and sprinkle with mint. Drizzle with extra oil. Serve.

PEACH AND TOMATO SALAD WITH PANCETTA AND BASIL
Increase oil to ¼ cup. Cook 4 ounces pancetta, cut into ½-inch cubes, in 1 tablespoon oil in 10-inch skillet over medium heat until crisp, 7 to 9 minutes. Transfer pancetta to paper towel–lined plate to drain. Substitute 2 scallions, sliced thin on bias, for shallot and basil for mint. Sprinkle pancetta over salad with basil.

The Ultimate Barbecued Chicken

We stole a few tricks from the competition barbecue circuit to create the best grilled chicken thighs you've ever tasted. BY MATTHEW CARD

BRISKET AND RIBS hog the attention on the barbecue competition circuit, while chicken thighs take second billing. But aficionados spare no amount of creativity in creating stunning versions. Barbecue champ Myron Mixon's winning recipe involves "smoke-braising" spice-rubbed thighs in chicken broth in a customized muffin tin (he drills a hole in each cup) and then removing them from the tin, smoking them, and glazing them with a sticky-sweet sauce. The recipe requires specialty equipment and a lot of time, but the results are remarkable. Much of the skin's thick layer of fat renders during the braising process and the combination of moist and smoky dry heat ensures that the dark meat is as juicy as can be and tastes terrific. Mixon proves that chicken thighs—spice-rubbed, smoke-tinged, moist and juicy inside, and slicked with tangy sauce—are one of the true joys of summer.

But thighs can be tricky to grill. The irregular shape, dark meat that can still look pink even when it's done, and fatty skin mean that existing recipes for barbecued chicken thighs range wildly in method and result.

I hoped that I could simplify Mixon's complicated competition method for the home cook. My idea was to "grill-braise" the seasoned chicken in a disposable 13 by 9-inch roasting pan (there was no sense in sacrificing a muffin tin) until its fat rendered, and then finish the meat directly on the grill grate over the dry heat of briquettes paired with wood chips—no smoker required.

I added enough broth to partially submerge, but not fully cover, 4 pounds of seasoned thighs (placed skin side down). Location proved crucial. Positioned directly over a hot fire (and a foil packet of soaked wood chips), the skin stuck fast to the pan. Making a fire with both a hotter side and a cooler side and cooking the thighs on the cooler side (opposite the coals) solved the problem. After about 30 minutes, the chicken's fat had rendered and the meat was nearly cooked.

I transferred the thighs from the pan (discarding the now-fatty broth), positioned them skin side up—still opposite the coals—and swiped them with glaze to finish cooking in the dry heat of the cooling coals and wood chips. In 40 minutes, the thighs were perfectly moist

Our potent, glossy glaze is made with apple jelly, bottled barbecue sauce, fresh garlic, brown sugar, and hot sauce.

and capped with tender, rendered skin.

With a basic cooking method settled, I turned to flavorings. My spice rub started with kosher salt, black pepper, and brown sugar and included paprika for color and garlic powder for depth. Pungent white pepper added complexity. Seasoning the meat an hour ahead of cooking gave the rub a chance to penetrate and deeply flavor the meat. On a hunch, I reserved a portion of the rub

and reseasoned the thighs after braising. It turned out to be a good move, improving the chicken's flavor.

I used bottled barbecue sauce (Bull's Eye, the test kitchen's favorite) to keep things easy, however it didn't glaze as well as I had hoped. I doctored it with a little brown sugar and apple jelly to ensure that it would tighten into a shiny glaze. A splash of hot sauce and some minced garlic gave it more oomph.

With the spice rub, pumped-up barbecue sauce, and smoke, the chicken tasted pretty good, but I wanted just a little more depth. I'd been braising the meat in plain chicken broth; adding a bit of barbecue sauce, minced garlic, hot sauce, and Worcestershire sauce to the broth brought the chicken to a new level. These pitch-perfect barbecued chicken thighs took a little bit of work, but they were well worth it.

BARBECUED CHICKEN THIGHS

Serves 4 to 6

The seasoned chicken thighs need to sit for 1 hour before grilling. We prefer Frank's RedHot Original Cayenne Pepper Sauce for this recipe. If you use Tabasco, reduce the amount to 2 teaspoons in the broth mixture and 1 teaspoon in the glaze.

- 2 tablespoons packed brown sugar
- 1 tablespoon kosher salt
- 1 tablespoon paprika
- 1 teaspoon pepper
- 1 teaspoon white pepper
- ¾ teaspoon granulated garlic
- 4 pounds bone-in chicken thighs, trimmed
- 1 (13 by 9-inch) disposable aluminum roasting pan
- ½ cup plus 2 tablespoons bottled barbecue sauce
- ½ cup chicken broth
- 7 garlic cloves (6 sliced thin, 1 minced)
- 3 tablespoons Worcestershire sauce
- 3 tablespoons hot sauce
- 2 tablespoons apple jelly
- 1½ cups wood chips

1. Combine 1 tablespoon sugar, salt, paprika, pepper, white pepper, and granulated garlic in bowl. Set aside 4 teaspoons spice mixture. Place chicken in disposable pan and season all over with remaining spice mixture. Flip chicken skin side down and let sit at room temperature for 1 hour.

2. Meanwhile, whisk ½ cup barbecue sauce, broth, sliced garlic, Worcestershire sauce, and 2 tablespoons hot sauce together in bowl; set aside. In separate bowl, microwave jelly until melted, about 30 seconds. Stir minced garlic, remaining 2 tablespoons barbecue sauce, remaining 1 tablespoon sugar, and remaining 1 table-spoon hot sauce into jelly; set glaze aside.

3. Just before grilling, soak wood chips in water for 15 minutes, then drain. Using large piece of heavy-duty aluminum foil, wrap soaked chips in foil packet and cut several vent holes in top.

4A. FOR A CHARCOAL GRILL: Open bottom vent completely. Light large chimney starter mounded with charcoal briquettes (7 quarts). When top coals are partially covered with ash, pour into steeply banked pile against side of grill. Place wood chip packet on coals. Set cooking grate in place, cover, and open lid vent completely. Heat grill until hot and wood chips are smoking, about 5 minutes.

4B. FOR A GAS GRILL: Remove cooking grate and place wood chip packet directly on primary burner. Set grate in place, turn all burners to high, cover, and heat grill until hot and wood chips are smoking, about 15 minutes. Leave primary burner on high and turn off other burners. (Adjust primary burner as needed to maintain grill temperature of 350 to 375 degrees.)

5. Pour broth mixture over chicken in pan. Place pan on cooler side of grill, cover (positioning lid vent over chicken for charcoal), and cook for 30 minutes (chicken will be about 140 degrees).

6. Remove pan from grill. Using tongs, transfer chicken skin side up to cooler side of grill. (Discard cooking liquid.) Brush chicken skin with half of glaze, then sprinkle with reserved spice rub. Cover and cook for 15 minutes.

7. Brush chicken skin with remaining glaze. Cover and cook until glaze has set and chicken registers 175 degrees, 25 to 30 minutes longer. Transfer chicken to platter, tent loosely with foil, and let rest for 15 minutes. Serve.

AT A GLANCE Attaining the Ultimate

After seasoning our chicken thighs with a flavorful rub and letting them sit for an hour, we set up our grill with a cooler side for cooking and wood chips for smoke. The thighs cook in three phases.

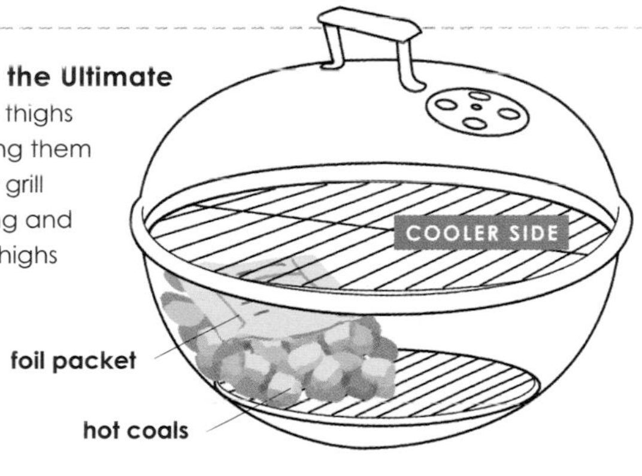

COOLER SIDE

foil packet

hot coals

1. Braise in a Pan
We submerge the chicken in our potent braising liquid in a disposable aluminum pan set on the cooler side of the grill.
30 MINUTES

2. Glaze on the Grate
We remove the thighs from the pan and set them skin side up on the grate. We glaze, add more rub, cover, and cook.
15 MINUTES

3. Reglaze and Rest
We glaze the chicken once more and cook it 30 minutes longer. We then give the meat a 15-minute rest before serving.
45 MINUTES

Iceberg Lettuce Slaw

An unexpected encounter down South provided a fresh take on this much-maligned leaf.

BY AARON FURMANEK

WHEN OUR EXECUTIVE food editor, Bryan Roof, returned from a research and tasting trip to Tennessee with tales of an iceberg lettuce slaw he'd tried and enjoyed—surreptitiously, behind the scenes at a local food festival—I wondered whether he'd been dipping too deeply into the local moonshine. Iceberg lettuce slaw? One of the hallmarks of traditional cole-slaw, made with shreds of relatively rigid cabbage, is its crunch, which holds firm even in a creamy dressing. I just couldn't picture iceberg lettuce doing the same—and the image of soggy, watery slaw is not appealing.

I hit the books and, to my surprise, found a slew of slaw recipes that centered on iceberg. They all warned against the water that the lettuce exudes when shredded. Some called for salting the shredded leaves to draw out any excess moisture and then draining this liquid away; others called for simply dressing the finely shredded leaves and serving the slaw right away, before the water had a chance to exude.

I tried the first proposal, salting the shredded lettuce and setting it in a colander to drain for 30 minutes. Then I spun the lettuce dry in a salad spinner before dressing it. But this process left the lettuce translucent, with a limp, rubbery texture akin to the lettuce on a day-old sandwich. Simply dressing the finely shred-ded leaves, on the other hand, left a watery mess.

The fix was unexpectedly simple. I'd been shredding the leaves on a box grater as the recipes suggested, but this method just created a watery pulp. What if I cut the leaves by hand, leaving them in larger pieces? I grabbed my knife. To my relief, I found that slicing the leaves into ¼-inch-wide strips kept most of the water where it belonged—inside the leaves. Even after I tossed them with dressing, the sliced leaves were plump and crunchy, and my salad stayed more crisp longer.

A few accents (sunflower seeds, peas, and a bit of chopped bacon) rounded out the flavors for a light, cooling iceberg slaw.

Lemon juice brightens this unconventional slaw.

ICEBERG LETTUCE SLAW

Serves 4

Dress the slaw just before serving.

- 4 slices bacon
- ½ cup mayonnaise
- 1 tablespoon lemon juice
- 1 tablespoon minced fresh parsley
  Salt and pepper
- 1 head iceberg lettuce (2 pounds), cored, cut into 6 equal wedges, and sliced crosswise into ¼-inch-wide strips
- 1 carrot, peeled and shredded (½ cup)
- ¼ cup thinly sliced onion
- 2 tablespoons frozen peas, thawed
- 2 tablespoons sunflower seeds, toasted

1. Cook bacon in 10-inch skillet over medium heat until crisp, 7 to 9 minutes. Transfer to paper towel–lined plate. When cool enough to handle, crumble into ½-inch pieces.

2. Whisk mayonnaise, lemon juice, parsley, ¼ teaspoon salt, and ¼ tea-spoon pepper together in large bowl. Add lettuce, carrot, onion, peas, and sunflower seeds and toss to combine. Season with salt and pepper to taste. Transfer to serving dish, sprinkle with bacon, and serve.

Grilled Corn

Grilled corn seldom tastes as good as it sounds.
We wanted grilled corn that's moist, smoky, and deeply flavorful. BY DIANE UNGER

CORN IS THE perfect vegetable to grill: Its sweet flavor loves a smoky accent. Plus, its large size means that you don't have to chop it and it doesn't fall through the grate. But what is the best grilling method? There are as many techniques as there are kernels on a cob—grilling ears shucked or unshucked, brushing them with butter or oil before cooking, presoaking, brining, using various heat levels and cooking times, and on it goes. But with all these variables, two constants remain: Corn grilled in the husk doesn't pick up any grill flavor, and shucked corn dries on the grill by the time it's cooked. I wanted grilled corn that was moist, smoky, and sweet.

After some testing, it became clear that corn grilled in the husk was much more moist than corn grilled naked, so that's where I started. I cut the protruding silk from a half-dozen unshucked ears (so it wouldn't ignite) and put the ears over the glowing charcoal. I turned the ears every few minutes to ensure even cooking and pulled them off when the husks were nicely charred, which took about 12 minutes over a hot fire. This corn was tender and very moist but, as expected, it lacked grill flavor.

I decided to keep this test going by carefully shucking the hot grilled corn (the husks come off grilled corn very easily) and tossing the ears back on the grill. After about 4 minutes, the corn had taken on some nice browning, so I took the ears off the grill and slathered on some butter. My tasters and I were impressed by this still-tender, moist, and smoky corn, but I wondered if I could make the butter flavor more than just superficial. What if I applied the butter to the husk-steamed and shucked corn before it hit the grill, as well as after? Grilling the shucked corn with butter helped the corn brown faster and really upped its flavor. For easier application, I made a little foil boat to hold the butter—I just rolled each shucked ear in my butter boat before and after grilling.

With my method down, I decided that I would give the butter more impact by adding some flavorful ingredients that would complement—but not overwhelm—the sweet, smoky corn. This was the best grilled corn any of us had ever tasted.

We first grill the corn in the husk. Then we shuck it, roll the ears in seasoned butter, and slap them back on the grill to caramelize.

HUSK-GRILLED CORN
Serves 6
The flavored butter can be made ahead and refrigerated for up to three days; bring it to room temperature before using. Set up a cutting board and knife next to your grill to avoid traveling back and forth between the kitchen and grill.

- 6 ears corn (unshucked)
- 6 tablespoons unsalted butter, softened
- ½ teaspoon salt
- ½ teaspoon pepper

1. Cut and remove silk protruding from top of each ear of corn. Combine butter, salt, and pepper in bowl. Fold one 14 by 12-inch piece heavy-duty aluminum foil in half to create 7 by 12-inch rectangle; then crimp into boat shape long and wide enough to accommodate 1 ear of corn. Transfer butter mixture to prepared foil boat.

2A. FOR A CHARCOAL GRILL: Open bottom vent completely. Light large chimney starter mounded with charcoal briquettes (7 quarts). When top coals are partially covered with ash, pour evenly over half of grill. Set cooking grate in place, cover, and open lid vent completely. Heat grill until hot, about 5 minutes.

2B. FOR A GAS GRILL: Turn all burners to high, cover, and heat grill until hot, about 15 minutes.

3. Clean and oil grate. Place corn on grill (over coals, with stem ends facing cooler side of grill, for charcoal). Cover and cook, turning corn every 3 minutes, until husks have blackened all over, 12 to 15 minutes. (To check for doneness, carefully peel down small portion of husk. If corn is steaming and bright yellow, it is ready.) Transfer corn to cutting board. Using chef's knife, cut base from corn. Using dish towel to hold corn, peel away and discard husk and silk with tongs.

4. Roll each ear of corn in butter mixture to coat lightly and return to grill (over coals for charcoal). Cook, turning as needed to char corn lightly on each side, about 5 minutes total. Remove corn from grill and roll each ear again in butter mixture. Transfer corn to platter. Serve, passing any remaining butter mixture.

Creole Potato Salad

To give this potato salad real Creole flavor, we had to find the right sauce.

BY CHRISTIE MORRISON

HUSK-GRILLED CORN WITH BROWN SUGAR–CAYENNE BUTTER

Stir 2 tablespoons packed brown sugar and ¼ teaspoon cayenne pepper into butter mixture in step 1.

HUSK-GRILLED CORN WITH CILANTRO-LIME BUTTER

Stir ¼ cup minced fresh cilantro, 2 teaspoons grated lime zest plus 1 tablespoon juice, and 1 minced small garlic clove into butter mixture in step 1.

HUSK-GRILLED CORN WITH MUSTARD-PAPRIKA BUTTER

Stir 2 tablespoons spicy brown mustard and 1 teaspoon smoked paprika into butter mixture in step 1.

HUSK-GRILLED CORN WITH ROSEMARY-PEPPER BUTTER

Increase pepper to 1 teaspoon. Stir 1 tablespoon minced fresh rosemary and 1 minced small garlic clove into butter mixture in step 1.

I'VE TRIED A lot of potato salads, but Creole potato salad was a new one for me. I was expecting bold flavors and some subtle heat, but most of the recipes I found were underwhelming. These recipes shared a common set of ingredients: mayonnaise, Creole mustard (a spicy brown variety), pickle relish or dill pickles, hard-cooked eggs, and the classic Louisiana trinity of green peppers, onions, and celery. This combination lacked the bold flavor I associate with Creole dishes like étouffée or gumbo; in fact, it tasted like regular old potato salad. A few recipes included more regional ingredients like andouille sausage or Creole seasoning, but they tended to overpower the salad.

Thinking of other ingredients or recipes that seemed representative of Creole cooking, I made my way to rémoulade, the creamy, tangy, paprika-spiked sauce commonly served with Creole dishes. While the sauce is derived from the classical French sauce (mayonnaise mixed with mustard, capers, anchovies, and chopped gherkins), the version served throughout Louisiana is spicy and assertive. Its ingredient list shares items in common with the salads I tried, but it includes things like hot sauce, Worcestershire sauce, lemon juice, and sometimes horseradish for extra kick. I whipped up a quick Louisiana rémoulade and tossed it with some cooked, cooled potatoes and the other salad ingredients. The difference was remarkable; what had previously been a rather uninspired, mayonnaise-heavy potato salad now had impressive depth, a looser texture (thanks to the additional liquids), and just the right level of heat. A few tablespoons of ketchup added some sweetness and, along with the paprika, contributed the pinkish hue traditionally associated with the sauce. Scallions and fresh parsley added welcome freshness.

I paired a number of potato varieties with the rémoulade, quickly rejecting russets (too starchy) and Red Bliss (too waxy) in favor of creamy Yukon Golds. To keep the potatoes firm, I added a couple of tablespoons of vinegar to the water as they cooked; I knew from previous tests that the acid in the vinegar would slow down the release of starch molecules, helping the potatoes hold their shape. Now *this* was Creole potato salad, no doubt about it.

Horseradish, spicy mustard, garlic, and cayenne bring the heat to this lively salad.

CREOLE POTATO SALAD
Serves 8

You can use dill pickles in place of the cornichons. This rémoulade is great on sandwiches or as a dip for crudités.

POTATO SALAD

- 3 **pounds Yukon Gold potatoes, peeled and cut into ¾-inch chunks**
- ¼ **cup white wine vinegar**
  Salt and pepper
- 3 **hard-cooked large eggs, chopped**
- 1 **celery rib, chopped fine**
- ½ **green bell pepper, chopped fine**
- 2 **tablespoons minced fresh parsley**

RÉMOULADE

- 1¼ **cups mayonnaise**
- ⅓ **cup cornichons, drained and chopped**
- 4 **scallions, sliced thin**
- 1 **tablespoon prepared horseradish**
- 2 **teaspoons spicy brown mustard**
- 2 **teaspoons ketchup**
- 2 **teaspoons lemon juice**
- 2 **garlic cloves, minced**
- 1 **teaspoon paprika**
- ¾ **teaspoon Worcestershire sauce**
- ½ **teaspoon sugar**
- ½ **teaspoon salt**
- ½ **teaspoon pepper**
- ¼ **teaspoon cayenne pepper**

1. FOR THE POTATO SALAD: Combine potatoes, 8 cups water, 2 tablespoons vinegar, and 1 tablespoon salt in Dutch oven and bring to boil over high heat. Reduce heat to medium and simmer until potatoes are just tender, 14 to 17 minutes.

2. Drain potatoes thoroughly in colander, then transfer to large bowl. Drizzle remaining 2 tablespoons vinegar over hot potatoes and toss gently to coat. Let potatoes cool at room temperature for 30 minutes; then refrigerate until cool, about 30 minutes longer, stirring halfway through chilling.

3. FOR THE RÉMOULADE: Whisk all ingredients in bowl until combined.

4. Add eggs, celery, bell pepper, parsley, and rémoulade to chilled potatoes and fold gently to combine. Season with salt and pepper to taste. Cover and refrigerate to let flavors blend, about 30 minutes. Serve. (Salad can be covered and refrigerated for up to 2 days.)

Shrimp and Grits

Many modern versions of this Carolina favorite add too many frills.
We set out to bring it back to basics. BY MORGAN BOLLING

TODAY THE SAVORY Southern dish known as shrimp and grits is ubiquitous on restaurant menus and, increasingly, in home kitchens around the United States. But until recently, it was unknown outside a small swath of the southeastern U.S. coast. There, the entrenched combination was an inevitable outcome of abundance— the Carolina shores teemed with shrimp, and grits were plentiful and cheap. Together, they've been known locally for generations as "breakfast shrimp."

Early versions of this dish, including the first known published recipe in *Two Hundred Years of Charleston Cooking* (1930), called for little more than butter, shrimp, and grits. Though countless adaptations have been explored over the years (see "Shrimp Jumps the Shark"), I planned to keep it simple. I prepared five existing recipes, including the *Charleston Cooking* version. Some were better than others, but none was exactly what I sought. I wanted to taste shrimp above anything else, I wanted creamy grits, and I wanted a lively, relatively light sauce.

The recipes were split on what liquid to use for the sauce. Some called for chicken stock, others clam juice. The shrimpiest used a simple, flavorful stock made by simmering shrimp shells in water for just a few minutes. I was happy to follow suit, for flavor and thrift; my shrimp shells were otherwise destined for the trash bin.

I used a butter-and-flour roux to thicken the stock and reduced it to the silky consistency I wanted. I added the shrimp partway through so they could poach in the sauce and then finished with two standard add-ins: a squirt of lemon juice for brightness and some crumbled bacon.

Easy, yes, but rife with potholes, too. Finicky shrimp can overcook in a matter of seconds and turn from supple to rubbery. What's more, while the shrimp poached in the sauce, they released liquid, thinning it out and compromising its structure.

I decided to try a two-step process, rendering chopped bacon in the pan and lightly sautéing the shrimp in this fat until just pink for a base of flavor. I removed the shrimp well before they were cooked through and in the same skillet stirred together a tablespoon of butter and 2 tablespoons of flour to

We use the shells from shell-on shrimp to make the stock that forms the base of our sauce.

cook for 1 minute. Then I whisked in shrimp stock to simmer and reduce. When the stock reached the correct consistency (just thick enough to coat the back of a spoon), I returned my shrimp to the skillet to cook through.

Success. Parcooking the shrimp this way prevented them from releasing too much liquid in my sauce, and I could finish them off right before I was ready to serve the dish.

The well-known Southern formula to cook grits is to start with a 4:1 ratio of liquid to grits. You boil the liquid and slowly whisk in the grits, stirring often and cooking them until they're soft and creamy before finishing with butter, salt, and pepper. But I wanted to explore other options for creaminess, corniness, and texture. In the end, I made only one tweak to the tried-and-true: Toasting the grits in butter before adding

the liquid (a mix of water and milk was best) helped coax out the corn flavor I was after. I also went with a little more liquid, a covered pot, and a slightly longer cooking time to arrive at just the right creamy texture.

My final recipe had few bells and whistles, but the result thrilled my tasters. This dish was simple to prepare and entirely satisfying. Exactly what I was after.

SHRIMP AND GRITS Serves 4

We prefer untreated shrimp—those without added sodium or preservatives like sodium tripolyphosphate. Most frozen E-Z peel shrimp have been treated (the ingredient list should tell you). If you're using treated shrimp, do not add the salt in step 4. If you use our winning grits (Anson Mills Pencil Cob) or other fresh-milled grits, you will need to increase the simmering time by 25 minutes.

GRITS

- 3 tablespoons unsalted butter
- 1 cup grits
- 2¼ cups whole milk
- 2 cups water
- Salt and pepper

SHRIMP

- 3 tablespoons unsalted butter
- 1½ pounds extra-large shrimp (21 to 25 per pound), peeled and deveined, shells reserved
- 1 tablespoon tomato paste
- 2¼ cups water
- 3 slices bacon, cut into ½-inch pieces
- 1 garlic clove, minced
- Salt and pepper
- 2 tablespoons all-purpose flour
- 1 tablespoon lemon juice
- ½ teaspoon Tabasco sauce, plus extra for serving
- 4 scallions, sliced thin

1. **FOR THE GRITS:** Melt 1 tablespoon butter in medium saucepan over medium heat. Add grits and cook, stirring often, until fragrant, about 3 minutes. Add milk, water, and ¾ teaspoon salt. Increase heat to medium-high and bring to boil. Reduce heat to low, cover, and simmer, whisking often, until thick and creamy, about 25 minutes. Remove from heat, stir in remaining 2 tablespoons butter, and season with salt and pepper to taste. Cover and keep warm.

2. **FOR THE SHRIMP:** Meanwhile, melt 1 tablespoon butter in 12-inch nonstick skillet over medium heat. Add shrimp shells and cook, stirring occasionally, until shells are spotty brown, about 7 minutes. Stir in tomato paste

Fresh versus Frozen

Just because shrimp are raw at the store doesn't mean they're fresh; roughly 90 percent of the shrimp sold in the United States comes from outside the country. So unless you live near a coastal area, you can bet the shrimp you're seeing were frozen and then defrosted. The problem is, once shrimp have been defrosted, their quality deteriorates quickly—and there is no way of telling how long they've been sitting in the case. We prefer to buy frozen shrimp and defrost them ourselves.

and cook for 30 seconds. Add water and bring to boil. Reduce heat to low, cover, and simmer for 5 minutes.

3. Strain shrimp stock through fine-mesh strainer set over bowl, pressing on solids to extract as much liquid as possible; discard solids. You should have about 1½ cups stock (add more water if necessary to equal 1½ cups). Wipe out skillet with paper towels.

4. Cook bacon in now-empty skillet over medium-low heat until crisp, 7 to 9 minutes. Increase heat to medium-high and stir in shrimp, garlic, ½ teaspoon salt, and ½ teaspoon pepper. Cook until edges of shrimp are just beginning to turn pink, but shrimp are not cooked through, about 2 minutes. Transfer shrimp mixture to bowl.

5. Melt 1 tablespoon butter in now-empty skillet over medium-high heat. Whisk in flour and cook for 1 minute. Slowly whisk in shrimp stock until incorporated. Bring to boil, reduce heat to medium-low, and simmer until thickened slightly, about 5 minutes.

6. Stir in shrimp mixture, cover, and cook until shrimp are cooked through, about 3 minutes. Off heat, stir in lemon juice, Tabasco, and remaining 1 tablespoon butter. Season with salt and pepper to taste. Serve over grits, sprinkled with scallions, and passing extra Tabasco.

Backstory
Shrimp Jumps the Shark

For decades, "shrimp and grits" was little known outside the Carolinas. But its profile grew after influential *New York Times* writer Craig Claiborne (above) visited Crook's Corner restaurant in Chapel Hill, North Carolina, in 1985. There, Chef Bill Neal's Brunswick stew, hoppin' John, and shrimp and grits inspired Claiborne to write that Neal "considers the regional dishes of this country as important and worthy of preservation as the nation's monuments and architecture." But as the dish took off, preservation was quickly set aside in favor of improvisation: Choose the right (or wrong) restaurant today, and you'll find yourself in front of a "shrimp and grits" plate that's actually a grits soufflé draped with panko-crusted crawfish.

TESTING SHRIMP PEELING TOOLS

Shelling shrimp and removing their veins can be laborious. We typically use a knife to remove the shell and fish out the vein. But we found a handful of new tools that promised to make this chore easier.

We tested these five, priced from roughly $6 to $17, against our winning seafood scissors, The RSVP International Endurance Seafood Scissors (about $8; these are also helpful with crab and lobster). We also included our winning paring knife, the Wüsthof Classic with PEtec, 3½-inch ($39.99): To earn our favor, a tool had to be significantly faster, easier, and better than the knife.

We shelled piles of small, medium, and large shrimp, removing the shells and veins and leaving the tails on. We timed how long it took each tool to shell 10 of each size shrimp, considering how easy they were to use, how precisely they severed the shells, how the shrimp looked afterward, and how versatile they were.

The six tools came in four different styles. The first and worst style is what testers called the "expansion" model. These tools get inserted between the shell and the meat and expand, forcing the two apart so that you can pull off the shell. At best, these tools didn't complete the task. At worst, they shredded the meat to ribbons.

The second style is shaped like a two-tined fork; one tine fits between the shell and the meat and pushes back toward the tail to sweep the shell and vein off. It worked, but it mangled the meat.

Two deveiners came in a third design that looks like a paring knife with a curved blade, which you thread between the shell and the meat and pull upward.

The fourth and sole successful style was our trusty pair of seafood scissors. They were precise and efficient, removing the shell and splaying open the meat so we could pluck out the entire vein with a single tug. On average, the scissors were 32 percent faster than a paring knife—which translates to roughly 5 minutes of prep time saved per 1½ pounds of shrimp. –HANNAH CROWLEY

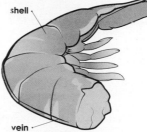

TWO TASKS, ONE TOOL
Prepping shrimp means removing both the shell and the vein.

KEY Good ★★★   Fair ★★   Poor ★

HIGHLY RECOMMENDED	CRITERIA		TESTERS' NOTES
RSVP INTERNATIONAL Endurance Seafood Scissors **Model:** SEA-J **Price:** $8.09	Ease of Use End Result Versatility	★★★ ★★★ ★★★	The scissors' curved blades neatly snipped off the shells of shrimp large and small. They were intuitive and both faster and more precise than a paring knife.

RECOMMENDED WITH RESERVATIONS			
LAMSONSHARP Shrimp Deveiner **Model:** 39468 **Price:** $16.80	Ease of Use End Result Versatility	★★ ★★ ★★★	This shrimp tool resembled a paring knife with a thin curved blade. It worked well and was precise, but it required focus and wasn't faster than a paring knife.

NOT RECOMMENDED			
BENDAL'S SEAFOOD UTENSILS Mr. Crab Zipper Deluxe Shellfish Opener and Shrimp Deveiner **Model:** 87 **Price:** $5.99	Ease of Use End Result Versatility	★★ ★ ★★★	This tool was faster than a paring knife but tore the shell off in pieces, marred the meat, and smashed the veins into smaller bits so that we had to fish out each individual piece. We'd rather use a knife.
OXO Good Grips Shrimp Cleaner **Model:** 35881 **Price:** $6.99	Ease of Use End Result Versatility	★½ ★½ ★★	This plastic deveiner's blunt serrated edge was too dull and required multiple attempts to get through the whole shell. It marred the meat and chopped the vein into pieces that were tough to remove.
CHEF'N Hightailer Shrimp Deveiner **Model:** 102-184-005 **Price:** $11.05	Ease of Use End Result Versatility	★ ★ ★★	This deveiner had three linked metal slats that laid flush when closed and expanded into a triangle. It couldn't pull off the whole shell, so testers had to finish with a paring knife. They also had to use the knife to fish out the vein.
HIC 2-in-1 Devein and Peel ShrimpMaster **Model:** 1744 **Price:** $6.14	Ease of Use End Result Versatility	½ ½ ★★	This tool mangled shrimp in several messy steps. Following instructions, testers inserted its two prongs between the shell and meat and squeezed the arms closed, but the lower prong shredded the meat to a shaggy pulp.

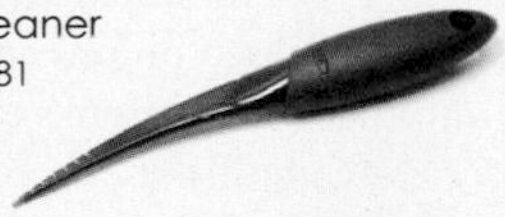

Rhode Island Dynamites

Meaty, spicy "dynamite" sandwiches are the pride of Woonsocket, Rhode Island.
We wanted to do "Woonie" proud. BY ASHLEY MOORE

TAKE A TRIP to Woonsocket, Rhode Island, or "Woonie" as locals call it, and you'll likely come across a dynamite sandwich, which bears a resemblance to the more widely known Sloppy Joe. Restaurants and convenience stores in town sell the sandwiches—a sweet-spicy ground beef and tomato filling on a soft torpedo roll—every day of the week.

In the 1920s, Woonsocket was a booming New England mill town with a thriving textile industry. Dynamites, easy to wrap up and carry, were a popular lunch for the laborers; before long, passengers on the New Haven Railroad, which stopped in downtown Woonsocket, discovered them, too.

The test kitchen is only about an hour away from Woonsocket, so a colleague and I took a drive down to see this sandwich in its natural habitat and to meet with dynamite expert Diane Frenette, owner of The Castle Luncheonette. The restaurant, originally a food cart, has used the same dynamite recipe for nearly 50 years. Frenette's cooks start by browning ground beef. They then add peppers, onions, celery, and tomato paste and cook it all down for a couple of hours. While most patrons order a sandwich, Frenette told us that many people like the dynamite filling over pasta or potatoes (some even eat it straight out of a bowl). After trying Frenette's and a few other versions of dynamites, I had a solid idea of just how delicious the sandwich was supposed to be. I went back to the test kitchen to parse out a recipe.

I started by making five different versions of the sandwich from existing recipes. They ranged from saucy to dry and from mild to very spicy. Some recipes called for browning the beef first; others the vegetables. One recipe included an interesting ingredient: jarred hot cherry peppers. Not only did the cherry peppers add some heat, but they also added a sharp vinegar note from their brine.

Testing notes in hand, I set to work. After settling on 85 percent lean, which provided the best texture, I browned it for 10 minutes until the liquid had evaporated and the meat was sizzling. Although tasters liked the extra boost of flavor that browning gave, the beef was a bit pebbly and tough. I turned to a tenderizing trick from the test kitchen and stirred together baking soda, water,

and salt to shower over the beef before browning it. No more pebbles.

In went chopped onions and bell peppers, cut into 1-inch chunks, along with garlic, red pepper flakes, cherry peppers with their brine, and a 15-ounce can of tomato sauce (we left out the celery that the luncheonette uses; tasters deemed it unnecessary).

One colleague suggested adding some tomato paste for even more depth, as well as some Italian seasoning. We don't often use herb blends in the test kitchen, but it works here; with just 1 tablespoon, I got four herbs: dried basil, oregano, rosemary, and thyme. After simmering my dynamite filling for 45 minutes, I stuffed some rolls and called down my tasters. Smiles all around.

Dynamites have a little heat, but that's not their defining characteristic: Depth of flavor is.

KEY INGREDIENT
Jarred Hot Cherry Peppers
These peppers—which are sold with the jarred Italian products in supermarkets—add texture, heat, and vinegar tang to our dynamite sandwiches.

HOT CHERRY PEPPERS
Light the fuse.

RHODE ISLAND DYNAMITE SANDWICHES
Serves 10

If you would like to reduce the spiciness of these sandwiches, substitute sweet cherry peppers for the hot cherry peppers and reduce the amount of red pepper flakes.

- 3 tablespoons water
- 1 teaspoon baking soda
- Salt and pepper
- 2 pounds 85 percent lean ground beef
- 1 tablespoon vegetable oil
- 2 onions, chopped
- 2 green bell peppers, stemmed, seeded, and cut into 1-inch pieces
- ¼ cup finely chopped jarred hot cherry peppers plus 2 tablespoons brine
- ¼ cup tomato paste
- 5 garlic cloves, minced
- 1 tablespoon Italian seasoning
- 1 teaspoon red pepper flakes
- 1 (15-ounce) can tomato sauce
- 10 (6-inch) Italian sub rolls, split lengthwise

1. Stir water, baking soda, ½ teaspoon pepper, and ¼ teaspoon salt together in medium bowl until baking soda and salt are dissolved. Add beef and mix until thoroughly combined. Set aside for 15 minutes.

2. Heat oil in Dutch oven over medium-high heat until shimmering. Add beef and cook, breaking up pieces with spoon, until all liquid has evaporated and meat begins to sizzle, about 10 minutes.

3. Add onions, bell peppers, ¼ teaspoon salt, and ¼ teaspoon pepper and cook, stirring frequently, until vegetables are softened, 5 to 7 minutes. Add cherry peppers and brine, tomato paste, garlic, Italian seasoning, and pepper flakes and cook until tomato paste is rust-colored and fragrant, about 3 minutes.

4. Stir in tomato sauce, scraping up any browned bits, and bring to simmer. Reduce heat to low and cook at bare simmer, stirring occasionally, until thickened (wooden spoon should leave trail when dragged through sauce), about 45 minutes. Season with salt and pepper to taste. Spoon filling into rolls and serve.

Grilled Panzanella Salad

Stale bread is the traditional foundation of this summery salad.
But who wants to wait around for bread to go stale? BY DIANE UNGER

PANZANELLA, THE CLASSIC summertime salad with roots in Tuscany, is traditionally a marriage of stale bread and vegetables at their peak, tossed together with vinaigrette for a colorful, multitextured side dish or light lunch or supper. It's important that the bread be stale so that it doesn't go completely soggy when dressed.

The problem with stale bread, of course, is that you have to have it on hand. But I'm not the type to set out bread today for a salad later in the week. The answer? My grill. By slicing a fresh baguette into 1-inch-thick slices, brushing the slices with extra-virgin olive oil with a little minced garlic whisked in, and grilling them, I had bread that could stand up to dressing and had a bonus layer of summery, grill-marked flavor.

You can't call it a salad without vegetables, and at the height of summer, you have your pick of the best. A traditional take would (likely) include fresh tomatoes and cucumber, but any summer vegetable is fair game. With the grill already on, I decided to double down on grilled flavor; I settled on grilled red onion, zucchini, and red bell pepper. Eggplant proved too slimy, fennel too pungent, broccoli too tough.

To season the vegetables, I brushed them with the garlic oil I'd made for the bread. I grilled them until just tender, removing them in stages as they finished. I cut the grilled bread and vegetables into bite-size pieces and tossed them with cut-up cucumber and halved cherry tomatoes.

To bring everything together, I created a simple vinaigrette. I started with a bit more of the garlic oil and then whisked in white wine vinegar, a teaspoon of Dijon mustard, and a few salty minced capers with some of their brine. I quickly tossed the salad and finished it with a sprinkle of Parmesan and fresh basil. I had a substantial side dish or a light supper to eat al fresco. Ah, summer.

GRILLED PANZANELLA SALAD
Serves 4 to 6

The dressing can be made up to a day in advance, but the salad is best eaten the day it is made.

DRESSING
- 1 cup extra-virgin olive oil
- 3 garlic cloves, minced
- ⅓ cup white wine vinegar
- 2 tablespoons capers, minced, plus 1 tablespoon brine
- 1 teaspoon Dijon mustard
- ½ teaspoon salt
- ½ teaspoon pepper

SALAD
- 1 red onion, halved and cut into ½-inch-thick wedges through root end
- 1 red bell pepper, stemmed, seeded, and cut into 2-inch planks
- 1 zucchini, trimmed and quartered lengthwise
- 1 (12-inch) baguette, cut on bias into 4-inch-long, 1-inch-thick slices Salt and pepper
- ½ seedless English cucumber, cut into ½-inch chunks
- 1 cup cherry tomatoes, halved
- ½ cup chopped fresh basil
- 1½ ounces Parmesan cheese, shredded (½ cup)

1. FOR THE DRESSING: Whisk oil and garlic together in bowl. Set aside ⅓ cup garlic oil for brushing vegetables and bread. Whisk vinegar, capers and brine, mustard, salt, and pepper into remaining ⅔ cup garlic oil until combined.

2. FOR THE SALAD: Place onion, bell pepper, zucchini, and bread on rimmed baking sheet and brush all over with reserved garlic oil.

3A. FOR A CHARCOAL GRILL: Open bottom vent completely. Light large chimney starter mounded with charcoal briquettes (7 quarts). When top coals are partially covered with ash, pour evenly over grill. Set cooking grate in place, cover, and open lid vent completely. Heat grill until hot, about 5 minutes.

3B. FOR A GAS GRILL: Turn all burners to high, cover, and heat grill until hot, about 15 minutes. Turn all burners to medium.

4. Clean and oil cooking grate. Transfer onion, bell pepper, and zucchini to grill and cook (covered if using gas) until well-browned and tender, 6 to 12 minutes, flipping and turning as needed for even cooking. Return vegetables to sheet as they finish grilling and season with salt and pepper.

5. Arrange bread slices on grill and cook, uncovered, until golden brown and lightly charred, 1 to 2 minutes per side. Return to sheet and season with salt and pepper.

6. Cut grilled vegetables and bread slices into ¾-inch chunks and transfer to large bowl. Add cucumber, tomatoes, basil, and ¾ cup dressing and toss to combine. Let sit for 10 minutes for flavors to blend, then season with salt and pepper to taste. Transfer salad to serving platter and sprinkle with Parmesan. Serve, passing remaining ¼ cup dressing separately.

Capers, garlic, and Dijon mustard give the dressing enough backbone to stand up to the smoky flavor of the grilled bread and vegetables.

TEST KITCHEN TECHNIQUE
Prepping Ingredients for the Grill
Some simple knife work gets the vegetables and bread in shape for the grill. Here's how we prep everything into uniform shapes that won't fall through the grates.

RED ONION
Peel and cut into wedges, leaving the root end intact.

RED BELL PEPPER
Remove stem and seeds and cut into planks.

ZUCCHINI
Trim ends and quarter lengthwise.

BAGUETTE
Slice on the bias.

More than 27,000 types of fish exist in the world, but these 12 routinely appear in your local grocery store.

❶ Atlantic Salmon
OMEGA-3 POWERHOUSE

Most supermarket Atlantic salmon is farmed and is available year-round whole, in fillets, or as cross-cut steaks. Atlantic salmon has a meaty texture and mild flavor that pairs well with fragrant herbs like dill or chives.

BEST FOR: Grilling, roasting, or broiling, as in our Glazed Salmon with Dilly Mustard Sauce (**CooksCountry.com/glazedsalmon**).

❷ Pacific Salmon
WILD CATCH

Most Pacific salmon—including sockeye, coho, and Chinook (also called king)—are caught in the wild. Wild salmon is available seasonally between late spring and early fall (although frozen can be found year-round). Wild salmon has a stronger flavor than Atlantic salmon and deep red flesh.

BEST FOR: Grilling, broiling, or roasting.

❸ Cod
WHITEFISH KING

Fresh cod is available year-round from cold North American and European waters. In recent years, shrinking stocks have been closely monitored. Cod's medium-size flakes and mild flavor make it very versatile.

BEST FOR: Sautéing, poaching, steaming, or baking, as in our Grilled Cod and Summer Squash Packets (a Recipe Card in this issue).

❹ Catfish
SOUTHERN STAPLE

Most catfish sold in the U.S. are farmed in the Mississippi delta, although imports from Asia are on the rise. Wild catfish can have a muddy flavor, but farmed catfish tastes cleaner and milder. Fillets should be white to off-white; avoid fish that is yellow.

BEST FOR: Sautéing or frying, as in our Fried Catfish with our Comeback Sauce (**CooksCountry.com/friedcatfish**).

❺ Haddock
THIS FISH AND CHIPS

A member of the cod family, haddock has firm, mild flesh that is perfect for fried fish and chips. Finnan haddie, or cold-smoked haddock, is particularly popular in Scotland.

BEST FOR: Pan frying, deep frying, or baking, as in our Oven-Fried Fish Sticks with Old Bay Dipping Sauce (**CooksCountry.com/ovenfishsticks**)

❻ Trout
FRESHWATER TREAT

Common types of this mostly freshwater fish include rainbow, lake, brown, and brook trout. Available wild or farmed, trout has a soft texture and delicate flavor. Trout is often prepared whole (look out for translucent pinbones) but is also available in fillets. The freshest trout has clear, bright eyes.

BEST FOR: Grilling (whole fish) or pan frying (fillets).

❼ Flounder
BOTTOM DWELLER

Flat fish like flounder swim along the ocean floor and have fillets on the top and bottom of their bodies. Many flounder species are sold as sole (not to be confused with Dover sole, a more expensive fish). Look for pure, milky-white flesh. The faintly sweet, delicate flesh works best with gentle cooking methods.

BEST FOR: Baking or steaming.

❽ Tuna
RARE FIND

While bluefin tuna is prized and used primarily for sushi, yellowfin (or ahi) tuna is the type you're likely to find in your local fish market, usually cut into steaks. The uncooked flesh is a bright ruby red with a firm texture. Tuna is best when cooked to rare or medium-rare; well-done tuna turns gray and loses its moisture.

BEST FOR: Grilling or pan frying.

❾ Tilapia
FARMED FLIPPER

One of the most extensively farmed fish in the world, tilapia thrives in warm freshwater environments. Tilapia's lean meat, which should be white to pinkish-white when purchased, stays moist when cooked. It has an oily texture and muddy flavor; in general, we prefer flounder or catfish.

BEST FOR: Baking, braising, or poaching.

❿ Swordfish
SWIMMING SWASHBUCKLER

Swordfish caught off the Atlantic coast is available fresh year-round, although its peak season is summer. Most swordfish is sold in steaks. It has a slightly sweet flavor and meaty texture. Look for firm flesh without discolored edges.

BEST FOR: Grilling, as in our Grilled Swordfish with Eggplant Salad (**CooksCountry.com/grilledswordfish**).

⓫ Snapper
RED BEAUTY

Snapper varieties abound in the Atlantic, but only one variety (*L. campechanus*) is recognized by the FDA as "red snapper." With beautiful, deep-red skin, it is often sold whole, but snapper is also available in firm, pink fillets. Be sure to remove the gills (bright red gills are an indicator of freshness) when preparing this fish whole.

BEST FOR: Roasting or grilling.

⓬ Halibut
JUST FOR THE . . .

Halibut is a flat fish that can grow to several hundred pounds, yielding fillets and steaks that are firm, meaty, and mild. Look for flesh that is almost translucent, without a yellowish cast. Halibut's low fat content makes it prone to overcooking.

BEST FOR: Baking, as in our Potato-Crusted Halibut with Tartar Sauce (**CooksCountry.com/potatocrustedhalibut**).

GRILLED COD AND SUMMER SQUASH PACKETS

RICE NOODLES WITH CRISP TOFU AND CABBAGE

GRILLED SKIRT STEAK AND SWEET POTATOES

SEARED CHICKEN WITH SAFFRON COUSCOUS

RICE NOODLES WITH CRISP TOFU AND CABBAGE Serves 4

✓ **WHY THIS RECIPE WORKS:** For optimal flavor, we season the tofu by tossing it with savory fish sauce before coating it in cornstarch.

- 8 ounces (¼-inch-wide) rice noodles
- 14 ounces firm tofu, cut into 1-inch cubes
- 6 tablespoons fish sauce, plus extra for drizzling
- ¼ cup lime juice (2 limes)
- ¼ cup (1¾ ounces) packed brown sugar
- 6 tablespoons cornstarch
- ¼ cup vegetable oil
- 3 cups (8¼ ounces) shredded green coleslaw mix
- ¼ cup chopped fresh mint
  Sriracha sauce

1. Place noodles in large bowl, cover with boiling water, and let sit until softened, about 15 minutes. Press tofu dry between paper towels. Toss tofu with 2 tablespoons fish sauce. Combine lime juice, sugar, ¼ cup water, and remaining ¼ cup fish sauce in bowl. Place cornstarch in shallow dish. Heat 2 tablespoons oil in 12-inch nonstick skillet over medium-high heat until shimmering. Dredge tofu in cornstarch, shake off any excess, and add to hot oil. Cook tofu until golden brown and crisp all over, about 5 minutes; transfer to paper towel–lined plate. Discard oil in skillet.

2. Heat remaining 2 tablespoons oil in now-empty skillet over medium-high heat. Drain noodles and add to skillet along with coleslaw mix and lime juice mixture. Cook until coleslaw mix is just wilted, about 5 minutes. Divide noodles evenly among 4 bowls and top with tofu and mint. Drizzle with Sriracha and extra fish sauce before serving.

TEST KITCHEN NOTE: Look for rice noodles in the international aisle of your supermarket.

GRILLED COD AND SUMMER SQUASH PACKETS Serves 4

✓ **WHY THIS RECIPE WORKS:** Summer squash and tomatoes cook at the same rate as the fish. An easy microwave garlic oil adds depth.

- ½ cup extra-virgin olive oil, plus extra for drizzling
- 2 shallots, sliced thin
- 6 garlic cloves, sliced thin
  Salt and pepper
- 1 pound yellow summer squash, sliced ¼ inch thick
- 12 ounces plum tomatoes, sliced ½ inch thick
- ¼ cup capers, rinsed
- 4 (6-ounce) skinless cod fillets, 1 to 1½ inches thick
- 1 lemon, sliced ¼ inch thick
- 2 tablespoons minced fresh parsley

1. Spray centers of four 18 by 14-inch sheets of heavy-duty foil with vegetable oil spray. Microwave oil, shallots, garlic, 1 teaspoon salt, and 1 teaspoon pepper in small bowl until garlic begins to brown, about 2 minutes. Combine squash, tomatoes, capers, and garlic oil in large bowl.

2. Pat fish dry with paper towels and season with salt and pepper. Divide vegetable mixture evenly among centers of each piece of foil. Top vegetables with fish, then top fish with lemon slices. Bring short sides of foil together and crimp to seal tightly. Crimp remaining open ends of packets.

3. Grill packets over hot fire, squash side down, until fish is cooked through and vegetables are tender, about 10 minutes. Let rest for 5 minutes. Cut packets open, sprinkle with parsley, and drizzle with extra oil. Serve.

TEST KITCHEN NOTE: You can substitute vine-ripened tomatoes for the plum tomatoes in this recipe.

SEARED CHICKEN WITH SAFFRON COUSCOUS SERVES 4

✓ **WHY THIS RECIPE WORKS:** We cook the couscous in the same skillet as the chicken to infuse it with extra flavor from the browned bits in the pan.

- 4 (6- to 8-ounce) boneless, skinless chicken breasts, trimmed
  Salt and pepper
- 2 tablespoons extra-virgin olive oil, plus extra for drizzling
- 1 onion, chopped fine
- 1½ cups chicken broth
- ¼ teaspoon saffron threads
- 1 cup couscous
- 1 cup pitted green olives, chopped, plus 2 tablespoons brine
- ½ cup dried apricots, chopped
- ¼ cup chopped fresh cilantro

1. Pat chicken dry with paper towels and season with salt and pepper. Heat 1 tablespoon oil in 12-inch skillet over medium-high heat until just smoking. Cook chicken until golden brown and registers 160 degrees, about 6 minutes per side. Transfer to plate; tent loosely with foil.

2. Heat remaining 1 tablespoon oil in now-empty skillet over medium-high heat until shimmering. Add onion and cook until softened, about 5 minutes. Add broth and saffron and bring to simmer. Stir in couscous, olives and brine, and apricots. Cover and remove from heat. Let stand for 5 minutes. Fluff couscous with fork and season with salt and pepper to taste. Sprinkle with cilantro and drizzle with extra oil. Serve with chicken.

TEST KITCHEN NOTE: The test kitchen prefers Columela Extra Virgin Olive Oil.

GRILLED SKIRT STEAK AND SWEET POTATOES Serves 4

✓ **WHY THIS RECIPE WORKS:** Thin skirt steak cooks quickly. Microwaving the sweet potatoes ensures that they cook evenly on the grill.

- 1½ pounds sweet potatoes, unpeeled, sliced lengthwise into ½-inch-thick planks
- ¼ cup extra-virgin olive oil
  Salt and pepper
- 1½ pounds skirt steak, trimmed and cut into 4 pieces
- 1 tablespoon smoked paprika
- ¼ teaspoon cayenne pepper
- ¼ cup chopped fresh cilantro
- 2 tablespoons red wine vinegar
- 2 garlic cloves, minced

1. Combine potatoes, 2 tablespoons oil, ½ teaspoon salt, and ½ teaspoon pepper in large bowl. Microwave, covered, until softened, 6 to 8 minutes, stirring halfway through microwaving. Pat steak dry with paper towels and sprinkle with paprika, cayenne, 1 teaspoon salt, and 1 teaspoon pepper. Combine cilantro, vinegar, garlic, ½ teaspoon salt, ½ teaspoon pepper, and remaining 2 tablespoons oil in separate bowl; set aside.

2. Grill steak over hot fire until well browned and meat registers 125 degrees (for medium-rare), 2 to 4 minutes per side. Grill potatoes until browned and tender, 2 to 4 minutes per side. Transfer steak to carving board and potatoes to platter and tent both loosely with foil. Let steak rest for 5 minutes. Slice steak thin against grain and arrange next to potatoes. Drizzle sauce over steak and potatoes. Serve.

TEST KITCHEN NOTE: Be sure to slice the skirt steak thin against the grain to ensure tenderness.

RIGATONI WITH SAUSAGE AND CHIVES

STIR-FRIED PORK WITH GREEN BEANS AND CASHEWS

**MOZZARELLA CHICKEN
WITH ARUGULA-PESTO SALAD**

GRILLED BALSAMIC BEEF SKEWERS

STIR-FRIED PORK WITH GREEN BEANS AND CASHEWS Serves 4

✓ **WHY THIS RECIPE WORKS:** "Velveting" the pork with oil and cornstarch before browning keeps it tender and encourages the sauce to cling.

- 1 cup chicken broth
- ¼ cup mirin
- ¼ cup soy sauce
- 3 tablespoons cornstarch
- 1 (1-pound) pork tenderloin, trimmed, halved lengthwise, and sliced thin crosswise
- 3 tablespoons vegetable oil
- 8 ounces green beans, trimmed and cut into 2-inch pieces
- 6 garlic cloves, minced
- 1 tablespoon grated fresh ginger
- ¼ cup roasted cashews, chopped coarse

1. Whisk broth, mirin, soy sauce, and 1 tablespoon cornstarch together in bowl; set aside. Toss pork, 1 tablespoon oil, and remaining 2 tablespoons cornstarch together in large bowl. Heat 2 teaspoons oil in 12-inch nonstick skillet over medium-high heat until just smoking. Brown half of pork, 3 to 5 minutes; transfer to plate. Repeat with 2 teaspoons oil and remaining pork.

2. Add green beans and remaining 2 teaspoons oil to now-empty skillet and cook until bright green, about 1 minute. Add garlic and ginger and cook until fragrant, about 30 seconds. Whisk broth mixture to recombine and add to skillet. Cook until thickened, about 2 minutes. Return pork and any accumulated juices to skillet and cook until heated through, about 1 minute. Sprinkle with cashews and serve.

TEST KITCHEN NOTE: You can use dry sherry in place of the mirin.

RIGATONI WITH SAUSAGE AND CHIVES Serves 4

✓ **WHY THIS RECIPE WORKS:** We simmer the wine until it's nearly evaporated to soften its edge and cook off the alcohol.

- 1 pound rigatoni
  Salt and pepper
- 1 pound hot or mild Italian sausage, casings removed
- 2 shallots, minced
- ½ cup white wine
- 1 cup heavy cream
- ¾ cup chicken broth
- 1 ounce Parmesan cheese, grated (½ cup), plus extra for serving
- ¼ cup finely chopped chives

1. Bring 4 quarts water to boil in large pot. Add pasta and 1 tablespoon salt and cook, stirring often, until al dente. Reserve ½ cup cooking water, then drain pasta and return it to pot.

2. Meanwhile, cook sausage in 12-inch nonstick skillet over medium heat, breaking up pieces with spoon, until cooked through, about 8 minutes. Using slotted spoon, transfer sausage to paper towel–lined plate. Add shallots to fat left in pan and cook over medium-high heat until softened, about 3 minutes.

3. Add wine and simmer until almost evaporated, about 2 minutes. Add cream and broth and simmer until sauce is slightly thickened, about 7 minutes. Stir in sausage and cook to let flavors meld, about 2 minutes. Remove from heat, stir in Parmesan, and season with salt and pepper to taste. Add sauce and chives to pasta and toss to combine. Adjust consistency with reserved cooking water as needed. Serve with extra Parmesan.

TEST KITCHEN NOTE: You can use other short pastas such as orecchiette or penne in this recipe.

GRILLED BALSAMIC BEEF SKEWERS Serves 4

✓ **WHY THIS RECIPE WORKS:** We use steak tips for these grilled skewers because they are quick cooking, easy to butcher, and very tender.

- ½ cup balsamic vinegar
- ¼ cup extra-virgin olive oil
- 2 tablespoons Dijon mustard
- 4 garlic cloves, minced
  Salt and pepper
- ½ teaspoon red pepper flakes
- 2 pounds sirloin steak tips, cut into 1-inch chunks
- 1 red onion, cut through root end into 8 equal wedges

1. Whisk vinegar, oil, mustard, garlic, 1 teaspoon salt, 1 teaspoon pepper, and pepper flakes together in large bowl. Set aside ½ cup vinegar mixture in small saucepan for basting. Add beef to remaining vinegar mixture, toss to coat, and let marinate for 10 minutes.

2. Meanwhile, cook reserved vinegar mixture over medium heat until slightly thickened, about 2 minutes; set aside basting sauce.

3. Thread 1 onion wedge onto each of four 12-inch metal skewers, followed by beef and then remaining 4 onion wedges to cap each skewer. Grill skewers over hot fire, turning every 2 minutes and basting with sauce until well charred on all sides and meat registers 125 degrees (for medium-rare), 10 to 12 minutes. Transfer to platter, tent loosely with foil, and let rest for 5 minutes. Season with salt and pepper to taste. Serve.

TEST KITCHEN NOTE: You will need four 12-inch metal skewers for this recipe.

MOZZARELLA CHICKEN WITH ARUGULA-PESTO SALAD

Serves 4

✓ **WHY THIS RECIPE WORKS:** Balsamic vinegar adds brightness to this pesto and lets it double as a vinaigrette.

- 2 cups fresh basil leaves
- ½ cup plus 2 tablespoons extra-virgin olive oil
- 2 tablespoons balsamic vinegar
- 2 garlic cloves, peeled
  Salt and pepper
- 4 (6-ounce) boneless, skinless chicken breasts, trimmed
- 1 (4-ounce ball) fresh mozzarella, sliced into 4 equal pieces
- 6 ounces grape tomatoes, halved
- 2 ounces (2 cups) baby arugula

1. Process basil, ½ cup oil, vinegar, garlic, ¾ teaspoon salt, and ½ teaspoon pepper in food processor until smooth, about 1 minute. Set aside ¼ cup pesto for serving. Transfer remaining pesto to large bowl. Pat chicken dry with paper towels and season with salt and pepper.

2. Heat remaining 2 tablespoons oil in 12-inch nonstick skillet over medium-high heat until shimmering. Cook chicken until golden brown and registers 160 degrees, about 6 minutes per side. Top each breast with 1 piece mozzarella, cover skillet, and let sit off heat until cheese is melted, about 4 minutes.

3. Add tomatoes and arugula to bowl with pesto and toss to combine. Season with salt and pepper to taste. Arrange salad on serving platter, top with chicken, and drizzle with reserved pesto. Serve.

TEST KITCHEN NOTE: Be sure to buy fresh mozzarella cheese packed in liquid, not the low-moisture blocks in plastic.

Lemon Thins

To give these thin, delicate wafers the intense flavor we wanted,
we needed more than just lemon juice. BY MORGAN BOLLING WITH AARON FURMANEK

SMALL AND DELICATE, the humble lemon thin doesn't cut an especially imposing figure. But in days past, teatime cookies like this had legions of fans—grocery store shelves, particularly in the South, were crowded with regional versions and even Nabisco marketed a lemon thin until the early 1980s. But the cookie zeitgeist now favors bigger, bolder biscuits, and lemon thins are hard to find. So we decided to make our own.

Tests of a half-dozen existing recipes for lemon thins (all using a similar list of ingredients like flour, butter, sugar, and lemon juice and/or zest) delivered cookies that didn't satisfy. They were too thick, too soft, too crumbly, or too chewy. And all were desperately short on lemon flavor.

Texture was the first puzzle to solve. After flirting with icebox-style cookies (in which the dough is shaped into a log, chilled, and sliced thin before being baked) and more familiar drop cookies (dough is spooned into small mounds on a baking sheet), I found I got the most consistent thickness by rolling the dough out to a thin ⅛ inch and then cutting out rounds with a cookie cutter. The cookies were thin and crisp, with a faint golden hue around the edges.

But after they cooled, they moved from crisp to tough. Baking them for a shorter time just left them soft. Increasing the butter only made the dough more difficult to work with. The answer was in an old test kitchen trick for lighter cookies: subbing in cornstarch for some of the flour in the dough. The cookies stayed crisp even after fully cooling.

Still missing? Bold lemon flavor. Experiments ensued, using various combinations and amounts of lemon juice and lemon zest—one batch, which thrilled my tasters with its bright, sour sweetness, used the zest of 10 lemons. But zesting 10 lemons is going too far. And any more than 2 tablespoons of lemon juice rendered the dough too wet to work with.

The solution was lurking in the spice cabinet: lemon extract. A teaspoon of this intense liquid coupled with 2 tablespoons of lemon juice gave the cookies the perfect level of lemon flavor. After the final batch was glazed, tasters gathered round. "Bright and lemony," they pronounced, and "delicately crisp."

LEMON THINS Makes 40 cookies

You will need at least two lemons for this recipe. If you do not have a 2-inch round cookie cutter, you can use a 3-inch round cutter, but you'll need to increase your baking time by 1 to 2 minutes. A rasp-style grater (our favorite is the Microplane Classic Zester Grater) makes quick work of zesting lemons.

COOKIES

- 1½ cups (7½ ounces) all-purpose flour
- 2 tablespoons cornstarch
- ¼ teaspoon salt
- ¼ teaspoon baking powder
- ⅛ teaspoon baking soda
- 10 tablespoons unsalted butter, softened
- ½ cup (3½ ounces) granulated sugar
- 2 tablespoons lemon juice
- 1 large egg yolk
- 1½ teaspoons lemon extract

GLAZE

- 1 cup (4 ounces) confectioners' sugar
- 1 tablespoon grated lemon zest plus 7 teaspoons juice, plus extra juice if needed
  Pinch salt

1. **FOR THE COOKIES:** Combine flour, cornstarch, salt, baking powder, and baking soda in medium bowl; set aside. Using stand mixer fitted with paddle, beat butter and sugar on medium-high speed until pale and fluffy, about 3 minutes. Add lemon juice, egg yolk, and lemon extract and beat until combined.

2. Reduce speed to low and add flour mixture in 3 additions until just combined, scraping down bowl as needed. Turn out dough onto counter and divide in half. Form each half into 5-inch disk, wrap disks tightly in plastic wrap, and refrigerate for at least 1 hour or up to 24 hours.

3. Adjust oven rack to middle position and heat oven to 325 degrees. Line 2 baking sheets with parchment paper. Remove 1 dough disk from refrigerator and knead dough for 3 to 5 turns to make more pliable. Roll into 10-inch circle, about ¼ inch thick, on lightly floured counter.

4. Using 2-inch round cookie cutter, cut 14 to 15 rounds from dough. Reroll scraps up to 2 times to similar thickness and cut out remaining 5 to 6 rounds to yield 20 cookies. Space cookies 1 inch apart on 1 prepared sheet.

5. Bake cookies, 1 sheet at a time, until edges are lightly browned, 12 to 14 minutes, rotating sheet halfway through baking. Let cookies cool on sheet for 5 minutes, then transfer to wire rack to cool completely. Repeat with second dough disk and second baking sheet.

6. **FOR THE GLAZE:** Whisk sugar, lemon zest and juice, and salt together in bowl. Working with 1 cookie at a time, dip top of cookie into glaze, then drag top lightly against rim of bowl to remove excess glaze. Repeat. (If glaze thickens as it sits, add extra lemon juice as needed to maintain proper consistency.) Let glazed cookies set fully before serving, about 15 minutes.

These cookies are easy: Mix, roll out the dough, stamp the rounds, bake, let cool, and glaze.

TEST KITCHEN DISCOVERY
The Secret to Big Lemon Flavor

Pure lemon extract is an oil derived from lemon peel; the oil is mixed with alcohol and water before bottling. Because it's so potent, we never use more than a few teaspoons in a recipe, and we prefer to use it in conjunction with fresh lemon juice and zest.

LEMON EXTRACT
Easier than zesting 10 lemons.

Hawaiian Sweet Rolls

Was replicating the distinct flavor and texture of a popular supermarket bread a fruitless endeavor?

BY REBECCAH MARSTERS

K ING'S HAWAIIAN STARTED in the 1950s as a family bakery in Hilo, on the big island of Hawaii, where sweet bread was already popular thanks to Portuguese immigrants (see "A Hawaiian History of Sweet Breads"). King's breads, a perfect accompaniment for Hawaiian-style pork and other local dishes, found fans across the archipelago and the company soon expanded to California in the 1970s; after all, why should mainlanders be deprived of the breads they fell in love with while on vacation? Today the rolls—their signature product—have an almost cult-like following across the United States.

King's rolls are soft and fluffy—not as eggy as challah bread, not as buttery as brioche. They are decidedly sweet but not cloying, and the flavor is distinct but elusive: tangy, fruity, almost earthy. Always game for a challenge, I set out to develop my own Hawaiian sweet roll recipe and learn just what made King's reign supreme. The ingredient list on the package yielded no clues.

It wasn't hard to find copycat recipes claiming to be just like King's. None were illuminating to read, but a few did call for a curious ingredient: pineapple juice. There is none of the stuff in King's, but I was intrigued. So I baked a few batches of rolls and set up a blind tasting alongside a package of King's. Some were indistinguishable from plain old dinner rolls; others were so sweet and cakey that all they needed was a layer of frosting. After identifying my favorites, I shuffled back through my notes and, sweet surprise: The rolls that used pineapple juice were the best.

I drafted a working recipe based on these early tests. Flour, sugar, yeast, and salt composed the dry ingredients; pineapple juice, milk, and half a stick of melted butter made up the wet. I mixed the dough in a stand mixer, set it aside to rise, shaped the rolls into rounds, nestled them (18 of them) into a 13 by 9-inch baking dish to rise again, and baked them. A few tests with varying ratios of juice to milk showed the ideal amount of pineapple juice to be 1 cup,

▶ Do you know what would be great stuffed inside these rolls? Some of our Hawaiian-Style Smoked Pork (Kalua Pork). Visit **CooksCountry.com/kaluapork** for our recipe.

Brushing the warm rolls with softened butter adds richness and an attractive sheen.

supplemented by ½ cup of whole milk for richness. The rolls were tangy and flavorful but not quite sweet enough.

I inched up on sugar in a few successive tests until I reached ½ cup; now the sweetness was there, but the rolls still lacked complexity. A simple switch from sugar to honey did the trick, adding a subtle earthiness to the overall sweetness. And since honey is sweeter than sugar, I had to use only ⅓ cup. I added

an egg for structure, and for even more richness, I increased the butter to 6 tablespoons in the dough, plus 2 more tablespoons brushed on the just-baked rolls for good measure.

I was nearly there, but my rolls lacked some of the brightness of King's. Pineapple juice is fairly acidic and added some zing to my rolls, but tests had proved that any more than a cup tipped the flavor balance into piña colada

territory. Extra acidity without extra flavor was what I needed: Cue white vinegar. Just 2 teaspoons did it. And 2 teaspoons of vanilla enhanced the flavor without distracting from it; a bit more salt brought everything into balance.

Soft, fluffy, and subtly sweet like the original, these rolls were irresistible whether pulled warm from the oven and slathered with salted butter or stuffed with pulled pork or ham.

The American Table
A Hawaiian History of Sweet Breads

By the time Mrs. M.F. de Rego took top honors in the "Portuguese sweet bread" category at the 1919 Maui Fair, sweet rolls and breads were as Hawaiian as slow-roasted pork and plate lunches. But like many popular Hawaiian foods, they weren't exactly native.

Sweetened breads came to the islands with the Portuguese immigrants who flooded Hawaii in the mid-to-late 19th century to work the livestock ranches and sugarcane plantations. The newcomers were embraced by the business community—as Honolulu newspaper *The Pacific Commercial Advertiser* dubiously editorialized in 1878, "Those employing [the Portuguese immigrants] prefer them to any other laborers because they never get drunk . . ."

By 1910, another Honolulu newspaper, *The Democrat*, counted the number of Portuguese immigrants in Hawaii at more than 20,000. Many of these families baked their own breads using recipes brought from home, but when refined sugar was scarce or expensive (most of the sugar produced on the islands was destined for export), they used local ingredients like honey and pineapple juice as sweeteners.

Shortly before Hawaii became a state in 1959, Japanese American Robert Taira opened Robert's Bakery in Hilo, where bakers specialized in sweet Portuguese-style breads. A move to King Street in Honolulu a decade later prompted a name change to King's Bakery, and distribution soared. Mainlanders took to transporting the breads home as souvenirs; they became so popular in California that King's eventually moved its center of operations to Torrance, California, spurring another name change to King's Hawaiian.

Today, a few families continue to bake Portuguese-style sweetened breads in large, hive-shaped outdoor ovens built by hand, particularly in the Kona region on the Big Island. Local kiawe wood, which burns hot and slow, is the preferred fuel.

Portuguese, Japanese, Chinese, and Mexican workers joined native Hawaiians to help establish Hawaii's pineapple and sugar plantations in the early 1900s. At left, Robert Taira at Robert's Bakery in Hilo, shortly before his move to King Street in Honolulu.

HAWAIIAN SWEET ROLLS

Makes 18 rolls

Use a mild-flavored honey (like clover honey) and not an assertive one (like buckwheat honey) in this recipe. These rolls are best eaten warm the day they are baked. Plan ahead: The dough needs two rises of 1 to 1½ hours each before baking.

- 1 cup pineapple juice
- ½ cup whole milk
- 6 tablespoons unsalted butter, melted, plus 2 tablespoons softened
- ⅓ cup honey
- 5½ cups (27½ ounces) all-purpose flour
- 1 tablespoon instant or rapid-rise yeast
- 2½ teaspoons salt
- 1 large egg
- 2 teaspoons distilled white vinegar
- 2 teaspoons vanilla extract

1. Grease large bowl and 13 by 9-inch baking dish. Combine pineapple juice, milk, melted butter, and honey in 4-cup liquid measuring cup and microwave until mixture registers 110 degrees, about 1 minute. (Mixture may appear curdled.)

2. Using stand mixer fitted with dough hook, mix flour, yeast, and salt on low speed until combined, about 5 seconds. Slowly add pineapple juice mixture, followed by egg, vinegar, and vanilla and knead until cohesive mass starts to form, about 2 minutes. Increase speed to medium-low and knead until dough is smooth and elastic, 5 to 7 minutes. (Dough should clear sides of bowl but will stick to bottom.)

3. Turn dough onto lightly floured counter and knead briefly to form smooth, cohesive ball. Transfer dough to prepared bowl and turn to coat with grease. Cover tightly with plastic wrap and let rise at room temperature until almost doubled in size and fingertip depression in dough springs back slowly, 1 to 1½ hours.

4. Gently press down on center of dough to deflate. Place dough on clean counter and divide into thirds. Cut each third into 6 equal pieces (about 2¾ ounces per piece). Form each piece into rough ball by pinching and pulling dough edges under so that top is smooth. On counter, cup each ball with your palm and roll in circular motion into smooth, tight ball.

5. Arrange into 6 rows of 3 in prepared dish and cover loosely with plastic. Let rise at room temperature until doubled in size, 1 to 1½ hours (rolls should almost reach top of dish and edges should be touching). Adjust oven rack to lower-middle position and heat oven to 375 degrees.

6. Remove plastic, transfer rolls to oven, and bake until golden brown and centers register 190 degrees, 20 to 23 minutes, rotating dish halfway through baking. Let rolls cool in dish on wire rack for 10 minutes. Using spatula, slide rolls out onto wire rack, brush with softened butter, and let cool for 20 minutes. Serve warm. (To reheat room-temperature rolls, wrap in aluminum foil, place on baking sheet, and bake in 350-degree oven for 20 minutes.)

STEP BY STEP Shaping Dough into Rolls

These rolls aren't hard to shape if you follow these easy instructions.

1. Divide the dough into thirds. Use a bench scraper to cut each portion into six equal pieces, for 18 pieces altogether.

2. Working with one piece of dough at a time, pinch and pull the dough down to create a smooth top.

3. Cup each dough ball in your hand and roll it on the counter while applying even pressure to create a smooth, tight ball.

4. Place the dough balls in a greased 13 by 9-inch dish, making three even rows of six balls.

KEY INGREDIENTS
Pineapple Juice? What Gives?

Hawaiian sweet rolls have a sweet-tangy-floral signature. To get it, we turned to three unexpected ingredients.

Pineapple juice helps give these rolls a fruity sweet character, which in turn is balanced by **white vinegar's** subtle sharpness. And 2 teaspoons of **vanilla extract** enhances the floral, tropical flavor of the pineapple.

Taken together, these ingredients help make our Hawaiian Sweet Rolls pleasantly sweet—but not cloying.

Chilaquiles

We aimed to capture the deep flavor and chewy-crisp texture of traditional *chilaquiles* while turning this side dish into a meal. BY CHRISTIE MORRISON

Our version of *chilaquiles* uses fresh ingredients to reinvigorate a dish often made with leftovers.

CHILAQUILES, A MEXICAN comfort-food dish of fried tortilla wedges tossed in chili sauce, is all about contrasts: chewy chips with crisp edges, spicy sauce with cooling sour cream and cheese, smoky chiles with fresh cilantro and lime. Sometimes constructed with leftovers, other times made from scratch, it's often served on the side at breakfast or lunch. I wanted to turn it into a main course while keeping the ease that's part of the dish's appeal.

Sorting through and cooking a number of chilaquiles recipes revealed that using store-bought tortilla chips, though a convenient plan, was a bad idea. The texture of the chips varied wildly from brand to brand and yielded chilaquiles that either turned to mush or never adequately softened. For better control, I'd have to make my own chips from corn tortillas.

Frying wedges of corn tortillas in oil until they're crisp is a labor-intensive process that I wanted to avoid. Instead, I moved the operation to the oven. I cut tortillas into wedges, divided the wedges between two baking sheets, tossed them with oil and salt, and slid them into a hot oven until they were golden brown and crisp. Stirring the chips and rotating the sheets halfway through cooking helped the chips brown evenly.

Chips crisped, I began work on the sauce. While tomato-based red sauce and tomatillo-based green sauce are both common in chilaquiles across the Southwest, my tasters preferred the bolder flavor of the red, so I chose that lane. I was inspired by the earthy intensity of recipes that called for toasting a few dried chiles (a critical step to develop their deep flavors) before pureeing them with tomatoes, sautéed onion, garlic, and other aromatic ingredients. A side-by-side test showed that the sautéing step was superfluous; since the aromatic vegetables would simmer with the tomatoes for 15 to 20 minutes, they had plenty of time to cook through and flavor the sauce. I could just add the raw vegetables to the blender with the ground chiles and tomatoes and puree the lot. I transferred the mixture to a Dutch oven to simmer and reduce slightly.

With the sauce on the stove, I had some time to think about additional ingredients. To make this a main course I'd need some kind of fortifying protein.

Chilaquiles are often served with scrambled or fried eggs (similar to Tex-Mex *migas*) or Mexican chorizo sausage, but based on my tasters' preferences, I ultimately settled on boneless, skinless chicken breasts, which I poached right in the sauce while it reduced on the stovetop. Once the chicken was cooked through, I removed it, shredded it, and added it back into the reduced sauce.

I mixed in the toasted chips, covered the pot, and let it sit off the heat for a few moments to give the chips a chance to soften. Some tasters liked it when I almost forgot about the chips and they bordered on mush; I liked them best after just a couple of minutes of standing time when they still had a bit of chew and slightly crisp edges. Either way, though, an assortment of garnishes like chopped avocado, sliced radishes, and cilantro adds freshness and crunch to the dish, while sour cream and crumbly *queso fresco* balance the heat of the sauce with creamy richness.

CHICKEN CHILAQUILES
Serves 6

New Mexican or Anaheim chiles can be substituted for the guajillo chiles. If *queso fresco* is unavailable, you can substitute farmer's cheese or a mild feta. When baking the tortillas, stir them well to promote even browning.

- 16 (6-inch) corn tortillas, each cut into 8 wedges
- ¼ cup olive oil
  Salt
- 5 dried guajillo chiles, stemmed and seeded
- 1 (28-ounce) can whole peeled tomatoes
- 1 cup finely chopped onion
- 1 poblano chile, stemmed, seeded, and chopped
- 1 jalapeño chile, stemmed, seeded, and chopped
- 8 sprigs fresh cilantro, plus 2 tablespoons chopped
- 3 garlic cloves, chopped
- 1½ cups chicken broth
- 1½ pounds boneless, skinless chicken breasts, trimmed
- 4 ounces queso fresco, crumbled (1 cup)
- 1 avocado, halved, pitted, and cut into ½-inch chunks
- 2 radishes, trimmed and sliced thin
  Sour cream
  Lime wedges

KEYS TO **Entrée-Worthy Chilaquiles**

Use Three Types of Chiles
We pair dried guajillo chiles (toasted and ground) with fresh poblanos and jalapeños.

Make Easy Homemade Chips
These chips are easy and far better than bagged. Just cut corn tortillas into wedges, toss with oil and salt, and bake.

Cook Chicken in Sauce
We poach boneless breasts in the sauce for maximum flavor.

Finish with Fresh Garnishes
Traditional garnishes include cheese, avocado, radishes, cilantro, onion, and lime.

Fried Zucchini Sticks

Since these crisp, salty bar snacks just may be the best use of summer's ubiquitous vegetable, we created an easy home version. BY DIANE UNGER

1. Adjust oven racks to upper-middle and lower-middle positions and heat oven to 425 degrees. Divide tortillas evenly between 2 rimmed baking sheets and drizzle each with 2 tablespoons oil and ¼ teaspoon salt. Toss until tortillas are evenly coated with oil. Bake until golden brown and crisp, 15 to 20 minutes, stirring chips and switching and rotating sheets halfway through baking.

2. Toast guajillos in Dutch oven over medium heat until fragrant and slightly darkened, about 5 minutes. Transfer to blender and process until finely ground, 60 to 90 seconds, scraping down sides of blender jar as needed.

3. Add tomatoes and their juice, ¾ cup onion, poblano, jalapeño, cilantro sprigs, garlic, and ¾ teaspoon salt to guajillos and process until very smooth, 60 to 90 seconds. Transfer sauce to now-empty Dutch oven and stir in broth. Bring sauce to boil over medium-high heat. Add chicken breasts; reduce heat to low and simmer, uncovered, until chicken registers 160 degrees, 15 to 20 minutes, flipping halfway through cooking.

4. Using tongs, transfer chicken to large plate. Increase heat to medium and continue to simmer sauce until thickened and reduced to about 4½ cups, about 5 minutes longer. While sauce simmers, shred chicken into bite-size pieces using 2 forks. Return chicken to sauce and cook until warmed through, about 2 minutes.

5. Add chips to pot and toss to coat. Remove from heat and season with salt to taste. Cover and let stand for 2 to 5 minutes, depending on how soft you like your chips.

6. Transfer chilaquiles to serving dish and top with queso fresco, avocado, radishes, remaining ¼ cup onion, and chopped cilantro. Serve with sour cream and lime wedges.

▶ Visit CooksCountry.com/ frozenstrawberrymargaritas to learn how to make our sweet-tart Frozen Strawberry Margaritas.

ZUCCHINI STICKS ARE common in pubs and family restaurants as an irresistible way to consume summer's most abundant vegetable. But the recipes I found for fried zucchini sticks all produced results that were entirely resistible: "Bland," "limp," and "mushy" were a few of my tasters' complaints.

I set out to solve each of these problems. For the breading, I found that a simple beer batter of flour, cornstarch (for extra crispness), and lager, plus granulated garlic and cayenne (for flavor), produced a better coating than bread crumbs (too stiff) or plain flour (not enough crunch). And for firmer zucchini inside, a few tests showed that removing the watery seedbeds was more effective (and took less time) than salting and resting the zucchini to draw off its moisture. A vegetable peeler made easy work of this task.

What are fried zucchini sticks without a dipping sauce? I made a simple one here, stirring together mayonnaise, lemon, hot sauce, garlic, and salt and pepper.

FRIED ZUCCHINI STICKS Serves 4 to 6

Dredge the zucchini just before frying for the best texture. You may not need the full ¾ cup of beer to achieve the correct pancake batter–like consistency in step 2. This recipe can easily be doubled.

- 2 zucchini, trimmed
- ¾ cup plus 1 tablespoon (4 ounces) all-purpose flour
- ¼ cup (1 ounce) cornstarch
- 1 teaspoon baking powder
- 1 teaspoon granulated garlic
  Salt and pepper
- ¾ teaspoon cayenne pepper
- ¾ cup lager, such as Budweiser
- 2 quarts peanut or vegetable oil

1. Quarter zucchini lengthwise. Using vegetable peeler, shave seeds from inner portion of each quarter. Halve each quarter lengthwise, then cut in half crosswise. (You should have 32 pieces total.)

2. Whisk flour, cornstarch, baking powder, granulated garlic, 1 teaspoon salt, ¾ teaspoon pepper, and cayenne together in large bowl. Reserve ½ cup flour mixture. Slowly whisk beer into remaining flour mixture until consistency of pancake batter (you may have leftover beer).

3. Set wire rack inside rimmed baking sheet and line with triple layer of paper

A little cornstarch in the beer batter helps these sticks fry up nice and crisp.

towels. Add oil to large Dutch oven until it measures about 1½ inches deep and heat over medium-high heat to 375 degrees.

4. Toss half of zucchini in bowl with reserved flour mixture until evenly coated. Set fine-mesh strainer over second bowl of similar size and transfer zucchini and flour mixture to strainer; shake to remove all excess flour mixture from zucchini (catching excess in second bowl).

5. Transfer zucchini to batter and stir to coat. Using tongs, drop each spear into hot oil and stir quickly to prevent pieces from clumping together. Cook until light golden brown, about 4 minutes. Adjust burner, if necessary, to maintain oil temperature between 350 and 375 degrees.

6. Transfer spears to prepared wire rack and season with salt. Return oil to 375 degrees and repeat with remaining zucchini spears, flour mixture, and batter. Serve.

SPICY AÏOLI
Makes ½ cup
Use Frank's RedHot Original Cayenne Pepper Sauce for this aïoli.

- ½ cup mayonnaise
- 1½ teaspoons lemon juice
- 1 teaspoon hot sauce
- 1 small garlic clove, minced
  Salt and pepper

Combine all ingredients in bowl and season with salt and pepper to taste.

French Coconut Pie

Balancing the flavor in this Southern favorite (no, it's not from France) was all about using the right coconut. BY CHRISTIE MORRISON

FRENCH COCONUT PIE, sometimes called Tennessee coconut pie or Florida Everglades coconut pie, is a delicious coconut-custard pie that has been popular in the American South for generations. A survey of existing recipes for this pie showed that most use the same basic ingredients: coconut (usually sweetened), eggs, sugar, melted butter, dairy, vanilla, and vinegar or buttermilk. You whisk the ingredients together, pour the mixture into a prepared pie crust, and bake for up to an hour. I made a counterful of pies; I knew my tasters wanted to like them, but they complained that the pies were too sweet or too eggy or lacked coconut flavor. But they held promise, so I set to work.

Most pies called for two to four eggs to give the custard the proper set and richness. I started with three eggs, 1 cup of sugar, 8 tablespoons of butter, ½ cup of buttermilk, 1 cup of sweetened shredded coconut, and 2 tablespoons of flour to thicken the custard. The resulting custard was nicely dense but had an eggy flavor that detracted from the coconut. Reducing the number of eggs gave me a diminished filling more appropriate for a tart than a pie. Since the egg whites contain the sulfur that contributes the eggy flavor, I tried another pie using two whole eggs and one extra yolk. This pie had just the right amount of richness and a clean, sweet (albeit too sweet) custard flavor.

Correcting for the sweetness was a little more difficult, since both the sugar and sweetened coconut were factors. The recipes I tried required anywhere from ¾ cup to 2 cups of sugar. Our preferred pie used 1 cup of sugar, but it also contained sweetened coconut. The combination was too sweet, for sure, but I didn't know which variable to change.

I started by substituting unsweetened coconut. What a surprise: Not only did the unsweetened coconut bring the sweetness in check, but without the extra sugar to mask it, the unsweetened coconut pie also packed more intense coconut flavor. Since I could now add more coconut without making the pie too sweet, I went up to 1¼ cups of the flaky stuff.

The only problem was the texture of the coconut on top of the pie; since the custard was so dense, the coconut rose and created a dry, chewy crust on top. I tried soaking the coconut in water and

The sugary crust that forms atop the coconut-buttermilk custard adds a pleasant textural contrast to the pie.

draining it before adding it to the pie, but that method drained away flavor. What if I soaked it in the liquid I was using in the pie? I tossed the coconut in the buttermilk and vanilla, covered it, and let it soak for 15 minutes while I assembled the rest of the ingredients. The extra step paid off; the moistened coconut was more evenly distributed throughout the custard and had a markedly softer texture.

Most recipes for this pie don't call for prebaking the crust, but I found that both premade and homemade crusts benefited from some alone time in the oven. Blind-baking the pie with pie weights for 18 to 25 minutes helped dry out the crust and set the bottom and sides (eliminating slumping). Keeping the temperature lower (at 325 degrees instead of our usual 375 degrees) ensured that the crust

wouldn't overcook after we added the filling and baked the pie for another 40 minutes or so.

The finished pie was golden brown from edge to edge—from the pie crust to the lovely sugar crust that formed on top of the custard. I let it cool to room temperature (a lesson in patience) before digging in for a bite. One taster described it as a little like biting into a macaroon.

FRENCH COCONUT PIE Serves 8 to 10

Look for shredded unsweetened coconut, about ¼ inch in length, in the natural foods section of the supermarket. It sometimes goes by the name "coconut flakes." Do not use large flaked coconut in this recipe. Our favorite shredded unsweetened coconut is NOW Real Food Organic Unsweetened Coconut, Shredded.

- 1 (9-inch) store-bought pie dough round
- 1¼ cups (3¾ ounces) unsweetened shredded coconut
- ½ cup buttermilk
- 1 teaspoon vanilla extract
- 1 cup (7 ounces) sugar
- 8 tablespoons unsalted butter, melted and cooled
- 2 large eggs plus 1 large yolk
- 2 tablespoons all-purpose flour
- ¼ teaspoon salt

1. Adjust oven rack to lower-middle position and heat oven to 325 degrees. Roll dough into 12-inch circle on lightly floured counter. Loosely roll dough around rolling pin and gently unroll it onto 9-inch pie plate, letting excess dough hang over edge. Ease dough into plate by gently lifting edge of dough with your hand while pressing into plate bottom with your other hand.

2. Trim overhang to ½ inch beyond lip of plate. Tuck overhang under itself; folded edge should be flush with edge of plate. Crimp dough evenly around edge of plate using your fingers. Wrap dough-lined plate loosely in plastic wrap and freeze until dough is firm, about 15 minutes.

3. Line chilled pie shell with two 12-inch squares of parchment paper, letting parchment lie over edges of dough, and fill with pie weights. Bake until lightly golden around edges, 18 to 25 minutes. Transfer to wire rack and carefully remove parchment and weights. (Pie shell needn't cool completely before proceeding.)

4. Meanwhile, combine coconut, buttermilk, and vanilla in bowl. Cover with plastic and let sit for 15 minutes.

5. Whisk sugar, butter, eggs and yolk, flour, and salt together in large bowl. Stir in coconut mixture until fully incorporated. Pour coconut-custard mixture into warm pie shell. Bake until custard is set and golden-brown crust forms on top of pie, 40 to 55 minutes.

6. Transfer pie to wire rack and let cool completely, about 4 hours. Serve at room temperature. (Cooled pie can be covered with plastic and refrigerated for up to 2 days. Let come to room temperature before serving.)

▶ Is it better to use real or imitation vanilla extract? Read our tasting at **CooksCountry. com/vanillatasting** to find the answer.

TEST KITCHEN TECHNIQUE Crimping a Single Crust Pie Shell
Our easy crimping technique makes a decorative, sturdy edge.

1. Use scissors to trim the overhanging dough to a uniform ½ inch.

2. Tuck the dough under to form a thick, even edge on the lip of the pie plate.

3. Use both of your hands to pinch the dough into ridges, working your way around the perimeter.

TASTING UNSWEETENED SHREDDED COCONUT

There are two types of shredded coconut—sweetened and unsweetened. We save the sweetened stuff to use as a form of added sugar in desserts like macaroons or coconut cake and use the unsweetened variety when we want to maximize coconut flavor without making the recipe too sweet. We focused on unsweetened coconut for this tasting. To find the best unsweetened shredded coconut, 21 America's Test Kitchen staffers tasted four products plain, in toasted coconut icing, and in our French Coconut Pie.

Flavor was hardly an issue. Coconut has plenty of natural sugar, and all the products were slightly sweet with tropical, nutty notes. There was a larger disparity in texture. Tasters preferred shreds that were visibly larger, especially when used in recipes.

Top-ranked shreds weren't just larger; they were also more uniform in shape and size; we did a sifting test to prove it. We found that large, uniformly shaped shreds made for better, prettier pies and icing.

FLUFFY STUFF
We liked large, uniform bits.

Our winner was NOW Real Food Organic Unsweetened Coconut, Shredded; it had a strong coconut flavor and thick, fibrous pieces. Visit **CooksCountry.com/july15** for the full tasting story and chart. –LAUREN SAVOIE

RECOMMENDED

	TASTERS' NOTES
NOW REAL FOOD Organic Unsweetened Coconut, Shredded **Price:** $6.20 for 10 oz ($0.62 per oz) **Particle Consistency:** 93% large, 7% small	Tasters loved this product's "nutty," "tropical" flavor and "naturally sweet" fruitiness. In icing and pie, these "thick," "fluffy" shreds lent a "flaky" texture that was "crisp" and "crunchy" but not too fibrous or dry. It's available in natural foods stores, including Whole Foods.
WOODSTOCK FOODS Organic Shredded Coconut **Price:** $2.88 for 7 oz ($0.41 per oz) **Particle Consistency:** 83% large, 17% small	This product had "rich," "complex" coconut flavor, with "slightly savory," "grassy" notes. Tasters thought that these "big, firm shreds" added a "lacy" crispness to pie and "pleasant chew" to toasted coconut icing.

RECOMMENDED WITH RESERVATIONS

	TASTERS' NOTES
BOB'S RED MILL Shredded Coconut **Price:** $3.59 for 12 oz ($0.30 per oz) **Particle Consistency:** 70% large, 30% small	In pie and icing, these medium-size shreds were "snappy" and "chewy," with "just the right amount of sweetness" and a "nutty," "toasted" flavor. A few tasters picked up on a slight astringent aftertaste when sampling this product plain.
LET'S DO . . . Organic Shredded Coconut **Price:** $5.64 for 8 oz ($0.71 per oz) **Particle Consistency:** 30% large, 70% small	While tasters appreciated this product's "nutty" flavor and "delicate" texture when sampled plain, a few thought that these "powdery," "fine" shreds got lost when used as an ingredient. Icing was slightly "grittier," while pie had a "less distinct" coconut topping.

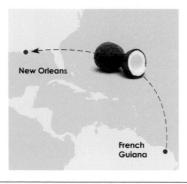

The world's best breakfast can go south fast if you don't follow the rules. BY BRYAN ROOF

BUTTERMILK PANCAKES Makes sixteen 4-inch pancakes; serves 4 to 6

The pancakes can be cooked on an electric griddle. Set the griddle temperature to 350 degrees and cook as directed.

- 2 cups (10 ounces) all-purpose flour
- 2 tablespoons sugar
- 1 teaspoon baking powder
- ½ teaspoon baking soda
- ½ teaspoon salt
- 2 cups buttermilk
- ¼ cup sour cream
- 2 large eggs
- 3 tablespoons unsalted butter, melted and cooled slightly
- 1–2 teaspoons vegetable oil

1. Adjust oven rack to middle position and heat oven to 200 degrees. Spray wire rack set inside rimmed baking sheet with vegetable oil spray; place in oven.

2. Whisk flour, sugar, baking powder, baking soda, and salt together in medium bowl. In second medium bowl, whisk buttermilk, sour cream, eggs, and melted butter together. Make well in center of dry ingredients and pour in wet ingredients; gently stir until just combined (batter should remain lumpy with few streaks of flour). Do not overmix. Let batter sit 10 minutes before cooking.

3. Heat 1 teaspoon oil in 12-inch nonstick skillet over medium heat until shimmering. Using paper towels, carefully wipe out oil, leaving thin film on bottom and sides of pan.

4. Using ¼-cup dry measuring cup, portion batter into pan in 4 places. Cook until edges are set, first side is golden brown, and bubbles on surface are just beginning to break, 2 to 3 minutes. Using thin, wide spatula, flip pancakes and continue to cook until second side is golden brown, 1 to 2 minutes longer. Serve pancakes immediately, or transfer to wire rack in preheated oven. Repeat with remaining batter, using remaining oil as necessary.

BLUEBERRY BUTTERMILK PANCAKES
Sprinkle 1 tablespoon fresh blueberries over each pancake before flipping. (If using frozen berries, thaw and rinse the berries and spread them out on paper towels to dry.)

CORNMEAL BUTTERMILK PANCAKES
Substitute 1½ cups cornmeal for 1 cup flour.

GRAHAM BUTTERMILK PANCAKES
Substitute 1 cup graham cracker crumbs plus 2 tablespoons cornmeal for 1 cup flour.

▶ Visit **CooksCountry.com/syruptasting** to read our tasting story on maple and pancake syrup.

STEP BY STEP **Ten Steps to Buttermilk Pancakes**

1. COMBINE DRY
Whisk the flour, sugar, baking powder, baking soda, and salt together.
WHY? Whisking the dry ingredients together helps evenly distribute the baking soda and baking powder to make these pancakes fluffy.

2. WHISK WET
Whisk the buttermilk, sour cream, eggs, and melted butter together.
WHY? Whisking the wet ingredients fully incorporates the thick sour cream, eliminating clumps.

3. COMBINE WET AND DRY
Make a well in the center of the dry ingredients and pour in the wet ingredients; gently stir until just combined.
WHY? Using the well method allows you to combine the wet and dry in a uniform manner without overmixing.

4. DON'T OVERMIX
Mix until the wet and dry ingredients are just incorporated and the mixture is still slightly lumpy with a few streaks of flour.
WHY? Mixing causes gluten formation. Too much gluten development in pancake batter leads to tough pancakes.

5. LET IT REST
Allow the batter to sit for 10 minutes before cooking.
WHY? Letting the batter rest gives the gluten time to relax, yielding more tender pancakes.

Good to Know

TIPS FOR ANY BUTTERMILK PANCAKE

Keep It Tender

You'll be tempted to mix the batter until it's completely smooth and no lumps remain, but fight the urge and stir gently. If you overmix the batter, you'll overdevelop the gluten (the protein strands that form when flour and liquid meet) and end up with tough, not tender, pancakes. Pancake batter should have a few lumps still visible. Also, let the batter rest for 10 minutes before you cook to give the minimal gluten that does develop from the light mixing a chance to relax before it hits the pan.

Leaven Twice

For the lightest, fluffiest buttermilk pancakes with the most flavor, both baking soda and baking powder are essential. Baking powder, when exposed to heat, releases carbon dioxide, creating tiny bubbles that help leaven the batter. Before that happens, baking soda (an alkali) has already been hard at work—when it meets up with buttermilk and sour cream (acids), it too produces pockets of carbon dioxide to create a lighter, airier pancake. But that's not all; baking soda also promotes the flavorful golden-brown edges of the pancakes for more complexity and a faintly crisp texture.

Double Dairy

Buttermilk pancakes should have a mild tanginess. Way back when, "churned" buttermilk was the liquid left over after cream was churned into butter, and it had a strong, tangy flavor. Today, most commercial buttermilk is "cultured"—made from skim milk and cultured bacteria—and has much less flavor. We wanted tangy pancakes, but simply adding more buttermilk creates a batter with too much acid, causing the baking soda to overreact and produce collapsed cakes. Instead, we add ¼ cup of sour cream—just enough to bring back the tang without radically affecting the makeup or consistency of the batter.

Troubleshooting

| TOO COLD | JUST RIGHT | TOO HOT |

The Wrong Temperature

It's important to have your skillet or griddle surface at the right temperature for pancakes. To test, drop 1 tablespoon of batter in the center of the pan. If the pancake is golden brown on the bottom after 1 minute, the pan is ready. If it remains pale and blond, the pan is too cool; if it has dark, uneven marks, the pan is too hot.

Too Little Rest

If you don't allow the prepared batter to rest for 10 minutes before cooking (which allows the gluten in the batter to relax), you'll have tough, not tender, pancakes.

Overlapping in the Oven

It's important to lay the pancakes in a single layer on a wire rack—with no overlapping—when keeping them warm in the oven. If you stack the pancakes, you'll end up with soggy, limp cakes.

Too Much Oil

It's essential to cook the pancakes in the thinnest layer of oil; if you have pools of oil in your pan, it'll seep into the pancakes and leave you with greasy rounds. To create this thin film of oil, we add 1 to 2 teaspoons to the pan, heat it until shimmering, and then carefully wipe it out with paper towels before cooking the pancakes. If more oil is needed for subsequent batches, repeat the process.

ESSENTIAL GEAR Nonstick Skillet

A nonstick skillet is the best vessel for pancakes, creating golden-crisp edges and speeding up cleanup. Our favorite is the T-fal Professional Non-Stick Fry Pan, which at $34.99 outperformed much more expensive pans in a battery of tests including durability and evenness of cooking.

6. HEAT THE OIL

Heat the oil in a 12-inch nonstick skillet over medium heat until shimmering.

WHY? The right pan temperature is crucial to avoiding blond or burnt pancakes; when the oil shimmers, the pan's at the right temperature.

7. WIPE THE PAN

Carefully wipe out the oil with paper towels, leaving just a thin film of oil on the bottom and sides of the pan.

WHY? A thin coat of oil allows the pancakes to release from the pan without becoming greasy.

8. PORTION EQUALLY

Using a ¼-cup dry measuring cup, portion the batter into the pan in four places.

WHY? Using a measuring cup will ensure evenly sized pancakes that will cook evenly and won't overcrowd the pan.

9. BROWN AND FLIP

Cook until the edges are set, the first side is golden brown, and bubbles on the surface are just beginning to break.

WHY? Browning increases flavor. The bubbles tell you that the baking powder has been activated.

10. KEEP WARM

Serve pancakes immediately or transfer to the greased wire rack in the preheated oven.

WHY? If you're not serving the pancakes immediately, a low oven will keep them warm. Nobody likes cold pancakes.

Five Easy Recipes Milkshakes

Milkshakes these days tend to be so thick that you need a spoon.
We wanted a shake to sip through a straw. BY ASHLEY MOORE

MILKSHAKES ARE RIDICULOUSLY easy to make, right? You put some ice cream and a bit of milk in a blender, give it a whirl, and boom—it's done. But after making dozens of milkshakes with a variety of ingredients, I was consistently getting a thick, icy milkshake that required a spoon to consume. My tasters gladly gobbled them down, but what I really wanted was an old-fashioned soda fountain–style milkshake that I could suck through a straw.

I assembled a handful of milkshake recipes and fired up the blender. But my milkshakes were coming out with an inconsistent texture every time: Pockets of thick ice cream surrounded by liquid. Simply adjusting the ratios of ice cream to milk didn't solve the problem. Experiments with gelato and ice milk also failed. I needed a radical fix.

One of my colleagues suggested that maybe my problem wasn't my ingredients but my equipment. Why not ditch the blender and use a food processor? Who makes a milkshake in a food processor? But experimenting is what we do in the test kitchen, and I had plenty of ice cream on hand. So I set up a side-by-side test, blender versus food processor. To my surprise, tasters unanimously preferred the milkshake made in the food processor. It was easy to sip through a straw and had a silky-smooth texture.

I reached out to our science editor for some insight and he explained: The larger bowl of the food processor exposes more ice cream to air and to the walls of the basin; this results in extra air being incorporated into the milkshakes, which makes them lighter, frothier, and easier to sip through a straw. Also, the slightly higher heat generated by the food processor blade causes more of the ice cream's tiny ice crystals to melt slightly, creating a smoother milkshake that remains cold but fluid.

It was smooth and sippable through a straw, but the flavor of my vanilla milkshake needed a shake-up. I found that adding a pinch of salt amplified the vanilla just enough and brought everything into focus, inspiring me to explore even more milkshake flavors.

After a quick team survey (which revealed how opinionated milkshake lovers can be), I settled on four more options: chocolate-banana, coffee, salted caramel, and strawberry. Rather than just switching to flavored ice cream, I decided to add flavors to my original vanilla recipe; doing so would give me more control over the intensity of flavor.

For the chocolate-banana milkshake, I processed a ripe banana until smooth and then added some cocoa powder and malted milk powder for a complex, round chocolate flavor. (Chocolate sauce was much too sweet.) I turned to instant espresso powder for a coffee variation—the espresso gave the milkshake a strong coffee flavor without being too sweet or bitter. Some extra salt and caramel sauce gave me a tasty salted caramel milkshake. And frozen strawberries, thawed and added to the processor, made a vibrant strawberry shake.

One last trick: Serving milkshakes in chilled glasses helps the shakes stay colder longer.

SHAKE IT UP
Use your food processor for the smoothest shakes.

Our easy shakes might be the best you've ever tasted.

VANILLA MILKSHAKE
Makes about 4 cups; serves 2
Our favorite vanilla ice cream is Ben & Jerry's Vanilla.

    4   cups vanilla ice cream
    ½   cup milk
        Pinch salt

Let ice cream soften on counter for 15 minutes. Combine all ingredients in food processor and process until smooth, about 1 minute, scraping down sides of bowl as needed. Pour into chilled glasses and serve.

CHOCOLATE-BANANA MILKSHAKE
Process 1 ripe banana, peeled and halved crosswise, in food processor until smooth, about 1 minute, scraping down sides of bowl as needed. Reduce ice cream to 18 ounces (3 cups) and milk to ¼ cup. Add ice cream, milk, ¼ cup malted milk powder, and 1 tablespoon unsweetened cocoa powder to food processor with pureed banana.

COFFEE MILKSHAKE
Add 2 teaspoons instant espresso powder to food processor with other ingredients.

SALTED CARAMEL MILKSHAKE
Increase salt to ¼ teaspoon. Add ¼ cup caramel sauce or topping to food processor with other ingredients.

STRAWBERRY MILKSHAKE
Process 1 pound (3½ cups) thawed frozen strawberries in food processor until smooth, about 1 minute, scraping down sides of bowl as needed. Reduce ice cream to 12 ounces (2 cups) and milk to ¼ cup, and add to processor with pureed strawberries.

Slow Cooker Brunch Casserole

You need bold ingredients to make a slow-cooker brunch casserole that actually tastes like something more than mush. BY DIANE UNGER

SLOW COOKERS WERE once relegated to long-cooked braises and stews, but we've found that this handy appliance can be used for cooking virtually everything. So we decided that it was time to try our hand at a slow-cooker version of brunch casserole (also known as strata), a kind of savory, eggy, creamy bread pudding. After all, what would be better than a brunch dish you could put in the slow cooker at breakfast time and forget about until your guests arrive hours later?

The Internet is peppered with recipes for this dish, so I collected a handful of the most promising and got to cooking. These test recipes all followed the same basic blueprint: Add toasted or staled bread to the cooker, pour in a mixture of beaten eggs and milk or cream, and top with cheese, cover, and cook. Some recipes also called for various vegetables or breakfast meats. The results were wholly unappetizing; greasy, burnt and dry, curdled, mushy, and sorely lacking flavor.

I decided to tackle the core elements first: the bread, eggs, and dairy. The bread component we liked the most in the initial tests was a cubed baguette that was toasted in a 300-degree oven until dry and crisp, so I'd go with that for now. Using 12 beaten eggs, I tested adding milk and cream in various amounts. After a few tests I settled on 3 cups of liquid dairy as the right quantity, but there were problems with both the cream (too rich) and milk (which curdled). The solution was something in between: half-and-half, which had just enough richness to taste good, while also being stable enough to withstand 4 hours of cooking without curdling.

Most recipes call for sharp cheddar cheese, but the cheese separated in the cooker and made the dish greasy. Tangy Jack cheese—a great melter—proved to be a better choice. Stirring 1 cup of shredded cheese into the bread distributed the cheese flavor throughout the casserole, while a generous 2 cups sprinkled on top melted into a beautifully gooey top layer. As for additional components, my tasters liked bulk sausage browned in a skillet with sliced onions and peppers. I added more oomph by way of a southwestern profile by stirring in some minced garlic, canned chipotle chile,

and ground cumin and sprinkling sliced scallions on top before serving.

I was making good progress, but I had one remaining problem: The cooked casserole was sticking to the insert. I tried coating the insert with vegetable oil spray, and while it helped a little with the sticking, it didn't work as well as using 2 tablespoons of butter to grease the insert. The butter had the added benefits of contributing flavor and helping the outside get uniformly crisp.

The strata was really good, but since I had added the step of cooking the sausage and vegetables in a skillet up front, I wanted to find a way to trim a little prep time from the recipe. On a whim I tried skipping the step of toasting the bread; thanks to the crisp, buttery exterior of the casserole, my tasters couldn't tell the difference. Finally, I had perfected the ultimate tasty, hearty brunch dish that can feed a crowd with no last-minute work. Mimosa, anyone?

SLOW-COOKER BRUNCH CASSEROLE
Serves 8 to 10

Baguettes vary in size so you may need to purchase two for this recipe, depending on their size and weight.

- 2 tablespoons unsalted butter, softened
- 12 ounces bulk breakfast sausage
- 2 onions, chopped fine
- 2 red bell peppers, stemmed, seeded, and chopped
- 1 tablespoon minced canned chipotle chile in adobo sauce, plus 1 teaspoon adobo sauce
- 2 garlic cloves, minced
- 1 teaspoon ground cumin
- 14 ounces baguette, cut into ½-inch pieces (12 cups)
- 12 ounces pepper Jack cheese, shredded (3 cups)
- 3 cups half-and-half
- 12 large eggs
  Salt and pepper
- 4 scallions, sliced thin

1. Grease slow-cooker insert with butter. Cook sausage, onions, and bell peppers in 12-inch nonstick skillet over medium-high heat until well browned, about 10 minutes, breaking up sausage with spoon. Stir in chipotle and adobo sauce, garlic, and cumin and

cook until fragrant, about 30 seconds. Transfer sausage mixture to large bowl, add bread, and stir until thoroughly combined.

2. Arrange half of bread mixture in even layer in prepared slow cooker. Sprinkle 1 cup pepper Jack over bread mixture. Arrange remaining bread mixture in even layer over cheese.

3. Whisk half-and-half, eggs, 1 teaspoon salt, and ¼ teaspoon pepper together in bowl, then pour custard evenly over casserole. Using spatula, press gently on bread mixture to partially submerge in custard. Sprinkle remaining 2 cups pepper Jack over casserole. Cover and cook until center of casserole is set and registers 160 degrees, 2½ to 4 hours on low.

4. Let casserole cool, uncovered, for 30 minutes. Sprinkle scallions over top and serve.

TO MAKE AHEAD
The casserole can be made through step 2, covered, and refrigerated for up to 24 hours. Add custard and cheese just before cooking.

Bell pepper, chipotle, garlic, and cumin give our casserole a southwestern accent.

Slow-Cooker Roulette
Since some models run hotter or cooler than others, working with a slow cooker isn't an exact science. That's why our slow-cooker recipes have time ranges for when the food is done. It's important to track the cooking times for your slow cooker; if recipes are done on the low or high ends of our ranges, you know your cooker runs relatively hot or cool, respectively, and you'll know when to start checking for doneness the next time you use it. If you're using a slow cooker for the first time, check the food on the early side.

OUR FAVORITE SLOW COOKER
KitchenAid 6-Quart Slow Cooker

Recipe Makeover Chicken Noodle Casserole

We've made a from-scratch version of this American favorite that's rich and creamy. Could we trim fat and calories without losing the cheesy appeal? BY CHRISTIE MORRISON

THERE'S SOMETHING BEYOND comforting about a plate of hot, cheesy chicken noodle casserole. Whether it's the flavor itself or the memories it invokes, it's just plain good food. But with a whopping 530 calories and 23 grams of fat per serving, this casserole can leave you needing a nap. Since we had been able to upgrade this dish from a repository of canned products to a fresher, homemade (if calorie-dense) casserole, it seemed like we could make it healthier, too. I was ready to give it a try.

Chicken noodle casserole comprises five components: chicken, egg noodles, vegetables, sauce, and topping. Boneless, skinless chicken breasts were the natural starting point for a makeover. While rotisserie chicken promised a shortcut, it meant a mix of light and dark meat that was likely to be overcooked before I assembled the casserole. Poaching the chicken in the sauce (for now, I was using our full-fat sauce of chicken broth thickened with a butter-and-flour roux and enriched with 2½ cups of half-and-half) allowed me to monitor the doneness of the meat while the chicken juices flavored the sauce.

Egg noodles, while an important component of the dish, were also the biggest contributor of calories. Since opting for egg-free noodles made a minimal impact in terms of fat and calories, I stuck with regular egg noodles, but I looked at the amount of noodles I was using. A typical recipe called for anywhere from 12 ounces to 1 pound of noodles. What if I reduced the amount of noodles but bulked up the casserole with vegetables? I cut the noodles back to 8 ounces and added 8 ounces of chopped mushrooms

Slicing the chicken in half lengthwise ensures that the chicken remains covered by the sauce during cooking and reduces the poaching time.

and a chopped carrot to the red bell pepper and onion that were already in the recipe. This step saved about 50 calories per serving and added not only flavor but also meaty texture—from the mushrooms. Best of all, my tasters still thought that the casserole tasted great.

The bulk of the dish's remaining fat was in the sauce. The earliest version of chicken noodle casserole used Campbell's condensed cream of chicken soup (the recipe was part of a marketing effort by the Campbell's company to boost sales in the 1940s). Our original recipe uses chicken broth, half-and-half, and a flour-and-butter roux—tasty, but not exactly light. In a past recipe for a reduced-fat cream sauce, we substituted a can of low-fat evaporated milk for the half-and-half. This was an improvement, but the sauce still wasn't quite thick enough. I made a slurry of cornstarch and water and added it to the sauce at the end of cooking, which worked great.

On to the cheese. Our original recipe calls for 4 ounces of both sharp cheddar (for flavor) and American cheese (its stabilizers prevent it from breaking and becoming greasy). In this case, switching to an equal amount of low-fat versions of each of these cheeses proved the best path to good flavor and a creamy consistency.

Finally, a cheesy casserole like this is nothing without a crunchy topping. Toppings range from Ritz Crackers (as in our original recipe) and saltines to bread crumbs, panko, and potato chips. In side-by-side tastings, nothing really compared with the buttery richness of crumbled Ritz Crackers. So while I tried a number of low-fat alternatives, I found that reduced-fat Ritz were really the best solution.

When the finished casserole came out of the oven, it had half the fat and 130 fewer calories per serving than the original version. But more important, it was thick with chicken, noodles, and vegetables and enriched with a cheesy cream sauce that lived up to its name.

REDUCED-FAT CHICKEN NOODLE CASSEROLE Serves 8
Cooking the egg noodles until just al dente and then shocking them in cold water prevents them from overcooking when baked in the casserole. To keep the sauce from breaking, be sure to remove the Dutch oven from the heat before adding the cheese.

- 8 ounces wide egg noodles
  Salt and pepper
- 1 tablespoon vegetable oil
- 8 ounces white mushrooms, trimmed and chopped
- 1 red bell pepper, stemmed, seeded, and chopped fine
- 1 onion, chopped fine
- 1 carrot, peeled and chopped fine
- 1½ teaspoons minced fresh thyme
- 3 tablespoons cornstarch
- 3 cups chicken broth
- 1 (12-ounce) can 2 percent low-fat evaporated milk
- 1 pound boneless, skinless chicken breasts, trimmed and halved lengthwise
- 4 ounces 50 percent light cheddar cheese, shredded (1 cup)
- 4 ounces reduced-fat American cheese, chopped (1 cup)

A Fresher Take on a Fatty Classic
Losing calories and fat often means losing flavor. We avoid this trap by packing our made-over chicken noodle casserole with flavorful vegetables. Chopped mushrooms, onion, carrot, and red bell pepper, plus plenty of peas and fresh thyme, more than make up the difference.

The Numbers
All nutritional information is for one serving.
Traditional Chicken Noodle Casserole
CALORIES **530**
FAT **23 g** SAT FAT **12 g**

Cook's Country Reduced-Fat Chicken Noodle Casserole
CALORIES **400**
FAT **12 g** SAT FAT **4.5 g**

Cooking for Two Roast Lemon Chicken

To get maximum lemon flavor into a quick dinner for two, we gave bone-in breasts a double dose of zest and juice. BY AARON FURMANEK

1½ cups frozen peas
20 reduced-fat Ritz Crackers, crushed coarse

1. Adjust oven rack to upper-middle position and heat oven to 425 degrees. Bring 2 quarts water to boil in Dutch oven. Add noodles and 1½ teaspoons salt and cook until just al dente, about 3 minutes. Drain noodles in colander and rinse under cold running water until cool, about 2 minutes. Drain again thoroughly and set aside.

2. Heat oil in now-empty pot over medium-high heat until shimmering. Add mushrooms, bell pepper, onion, carrot, and ¼ teaspoon salt and cook until beginning to brown, 5 to 7 minutes. Stir in thyme and cook until fragrant, about 30 seconds. Transfer to bowl.

3. Whisk cornstarch together with 3 tablespoons broth in small bowl; set aside. Combine evaporated milk and remaining broth in now-empty pot and bring to boil over high heat. Add chicken, reduce heat to medium-low, and cook until chicken registers 155 degrees, 8 to 10 minutes. Transfer chicken to plate.

4. Whisk cornstarch mixture into sauce, return to boil, and cook until thickened, about 1 minute. Remove pot from heat and whisk cheddar and American cheeses into sauce until smooth. Shred chicken into bite-size pieces using 2 forks. Stir peas, shredded chicken, noodles, mushroom mixture, 1½ teaspoons salt, and 1¼ teaspoons pepper into cheese sauce until combined.

5. Transfer mixture to 13 by 9-inch baking dish and top with crackers. Bake until golden brown and bubbling, about 15 minutes. Let casserole cool on wire rack for 10 minutes. Serve.

TO MAKE AHEAD

Casserole can be prepared through step 4, transferred to baking dish, and refrigerated without cracker topping for up to 24 hours. To serve: Heat casserole in microwave until hot throughout, about 5 minutes; then top with crackers and bake as directed.

WE'VE ROASTED THOUSANDS of chickens over the years, many of them infused with lemon. But when it came to a weeknight meal for two that achieved moist meat, crisp skin, and vibrant lemon aroma and flavor using just chicken breasts, we had to start from scratch.

Our favorite method for roasting chicken breasts is to first sear them skin side down on the stovetop to give the skin a head start on crisping and then flip them over before finishing them off in the more even heat of the oven. Though I considered using boneless, skinless breasts, past experience has shown us that bone-in breasts are best for this method; the bone helps keep the chicken from drying out and promotes more even cooking. But how to give these bone-in, skin-on breasts ample lemony flavor?

One favorite technique in the test kitchen is to rub lemon zest and herbs underneath the skin, so I thought that would be a good place to begin. After stirring together a mix of grated lemon zest, minced parsley, and salt, I used my fingers to carefully separate the skin from the meat (without tearing into it) and rubbed ½ teaspoon of the mixture under the skin of each breast. I seared the breasts, skin side down, in a skillet for 6 minutes before transferring them to a 450-degree oven to reach 160 degrees. After a short post-oven rest (about 5 minutes), I took a taste.

The lemon was present in the dish, but it didn't have much punch. So instead of cooking the seasoned breasts right away, I let the rub sit on the chicken for 30 minutes before cooking and resting. This extra time allowed the salt and seasonings to penetrate the meat. My chicken was now flavorful and moist.

Still, something was missing: A pan sauce would amplify the lemon flavor even more. While the chicken was resting, I whisked together 1 teaspoon of cornstarch and 1 cup of chicken broth and cooked it down in the same skillet I'd used for the chicken. I added back the accumulated juices from the resting chicken, plus a tablespoon of lemon juice, a teaspoon of parsley, a little thyme, and a bit of butter to finish. For the minimal extra effort this required, my dish was infinitely more special.

We cook deeply seasoned chicken breasts on the bone to help ensure that they stay moist and then remove the bone before serving for a nicer presentation.

ROAST LEMON CHICKEN FOR TWO

If the skin detaches when you're putting the seasoning under it, use a toothpick or two to secure it before searing. Be careful when making the sauce in step 4 as the skillet handle will be hot.

2 teaspoons minced fresh parsley
½ teaspoon grated lemon zest plus 1 tablespoon juice
Salt and pepper
2 (10- to 12-ounce) bone-in split chicken breasts, trimmed
1 teaspoon vegetable oil
1 teaspoon cornstarch
1 cup chicken broth
2 tablespoons unsalted butter
1 teaspoon minced fresh thyme

1. Combine 1 teaspoon parsley, lemon zest, and ¼ teaspoon salt in bowl. Using your fingers, gently loosen skin from breast along rib side, taking care to not remove it completely. Divide zest mixture evenly beneath skin of each breast. Season breasts all over with salt and pepper. Transfer to plate, cover with plastic wrap, and refrigerate for at least 30 minutes or up to 24 hours.

2. Adjust oven rack to middle position and heat oven to 450 degrees. Pat chicken dry with paper towels. Heat oil in 10-inch ovensafe skillet over medium-high heat until just smoking. Cook chicken, skin side down, until well browned, 6 to 8 minutes.

3. Flip chicken skin side up and transfer skillet to oven. Roast until chicken registers 160 degrees, 15 to 20 minutes. Transfer chicken to plate, tent loosely with aluminum foil, and let rest while preparing sauce.

4. Whisk cornstarch into broth. Add broth mixture to now-empty skillet and bring to boil over medium-high heat, scraping up any browned bits. (Skillet handle will be hot.) Cook until slightly thickened and reduced to about ⅓ cup, about 6 minutes. Pour any accumulated juices from plate into sauce. Off heat, whisk in butter, thyme, lemon juice, and remaining 1 teaspoon parsley. Season with salt and pepper to taste.

5. Carve chicken from bone and cut crosswise into ½-inch-thick slices. Serve, passing sauce separately.

Equipment Review Innovative Potholders

Svelte silhouettes, high-heat silicone, and innovative designs—how does the next generation of potholders stack up against the classic terry-cloth square? BY HANNAH CROWLEY

KEY **Good** ★★★ **Fair** ★★ **Poor** ★

EVERY HOME KITCHEN should have a few good potholders. We saw several new designs trying to improve on the classic cotton square, and wondered: Could any raise the bar for protection and ease of use?

To find out, we pitted five new potholders against new copies of our old winner, a classic terry-cloth square called the Ritz Basic Potholder; the six ranged in price from $7.99 to $19.98 for a set. The new designs included two all-silicone models: One had a special woven grid pattern designed to improve flexibility and strength, while the other was a set of dainty pinch grips that covered just the tips of your fingers. The third and fourth potholders used both silicone and cotton; one was a standard size and the other a slimmer hourglass shape. The fifth and final new model was a small oval shape made of cotton.

To assess our six potholders, large- and small-handed testers moved hot oven racks and loaded, rotated, and unloaded full baking sheets, cake pans, and pie plates. We also maneuvered 6.5-quart Dutch ovens filled with hot water in and out of 500-degree ovens and did the same with screaming-hot stainless-steel skillets, first empty and then loaded with sizzling whole chickens. We stained each potholder with tomato soup, left it overnight, and then washed and dried each five times (per manufacturer specifications), after which we assessed staining, wear, and shrinkage.

We looked first at the most important factor: how well the potholders protected us from the heat. Size was a deciding issue here. Two of the three smaller holders weren't sufficiently protective. Two were too small; one was small but well designed. The sole successful smaller design was an oval, with two small pockets for fingers. At 7 by 5 inches, it was trim, but perfectly tailored to protect hands large and small.

The three larger potholders—our old winner, the all-silicone square, and the standard size silicone and cotton combo—ranged from 7 to 10 inches tall and from 7 to 8 inches wide. They were big enough to cover our hands, but only the combo model was fully protective. Here it came down to material. The combo potholder was thicker and made of layered cotton and silicone topped with an additional layer of silicone bars that disseminated the heat effectively. The all-silicone square and the old winner, made of thin cotton, were sufficient for cakes, cookies, and the like (all baked at 400 degrees or less), but for anything hotter, they were too flimsy.

After protection, we looked at the maneuverability of each potholder. The all-silicone square was an absolute wrecking ball. It was so stiff and floppy that it smashed cookies left and right, belly flopped into cake batter, and pulverized pie crusts. The old winning cotton square and the new cotton and silicone hourglass-shaped holder weren't as destructive, but they were still too unstructured and bulky. We had to constantly tuck them out of the way or else they also ended up in the food. The silicone pinch grips were actually quite deft at rotating pans in the oven but were too small to hold hot things safely, and they put testers' hands in such a pinched position that it was impossible to hold anything heavier than a pound or so.

The two most nimble potholders were also the two most protective. First, the sole successful small holder from Le Creuset. Its trim, smart design was incredibly maneuverable because it had zero extra fabric to bunch up and get in the way. And its small pockets covered our fingers but still allowed us to nimbly pinch, pull, and turn. As when using a folded dish towel, we had to be mindful when using these because there's no extra buffer, but testers appreciated their agility.

Our overall favorite potholder was from OXO. It had a deep, secure pocket that gave testers excellent control along with layers of cotton and silicone and silicone bars that kept testers' hands safe and cool. For this combination of full protection and maneuverability (plus the handy magnet and loop, and its durability in washing tests), we named the OXO Good Grips Silicone Pot Holder with Magnet ($9.99) our winning potholder.

	CRITERIA	TESTERS' NOTES
HIGHLY RECOMMENDED		
OXO GOOD GRIPS Silicone Pot Holder with Magnet **Model:** 1148607 (licorice) **Price:** $9.99 each **Innovation:** Silicone/cotton combo **Dimensions:** 10 by 8 in **Material:** Silicone and cotton **Cleanup:** Machine wash/dry 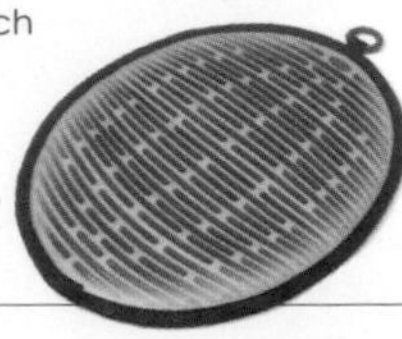	**Protection** ★★★ **Dexterity** ★★★ **Cleanup** ★★★	Whether maneuvering a screaming-hot stainless-steel skillet or a Dutch oven filled with boiling water, we always felt safe and confident using this potholder. It had cotton for flexibility and comfort and grippy, high-heat silicone for protection. At 10 by 8 inches, it was big enough for full coverage but also nimble, thanks to a pocket that allowed testers to precisely pinch thin baking sheet rims and to rotate cake pans with ease.
RECOMMENDED		
LE CREUSET Fingertip Potholders **Model:** TH5004 **Price:** $15 for two (sold as set) **Innovation:** Small size **Dimensions:** 7 by 5 in **Material:** Cotton **Cleanup:** Machine wash/air dry 	**Protection** ★★½ **Dexterity** ★★★ **Cleanup** ★★★	These trim potholders wowed testers with their dexterity, comfort, and protection. Small but precise, they made rotating baking sheets, cake pans, and pie plates a cinch, and they still protected testers wielding 500-degree stainless-steel skillets. Like a folded dish towel, they required a smidge more mindfulness because their trim design left more hand exposed.
RECOMMENDED WITH RESERVATIONS		
RITZ Basic Potholder **Model:** 30024 (federal blue) **Price:** $9.99 for two (sold as set) **Innovation:** N/A **Dimensions:** 9 by 8 in **Material:** Cotton **Cleanup:** Machine wash/dry 	**Protection** ★★ **Dexterity** ★★ **Cleanup** ★★★	Our old favorite, a simple cotton square, was protective enough for handling baking sheets, cake pans, and pie plates—at 400 degrees or less. But any higher and it was too thin and left testers challenging the boundaries of work-appropriate language. It was cumbersome, too. Testers were constantly tucking away the excess fabric to avoid mashing cookies and denting cakes.
NOT RECOMMENDED		
CALPHALON 6 x 10-in Pot Holder **Model:** 32178 (biscotti) **Price:** $9.99 each **Innovation:** Silicone/cotton combo, smaller size **Dimensions:** 10 by 5 in **Material:** Cotton and silicone **Cleanup:** Machine wash/air dry 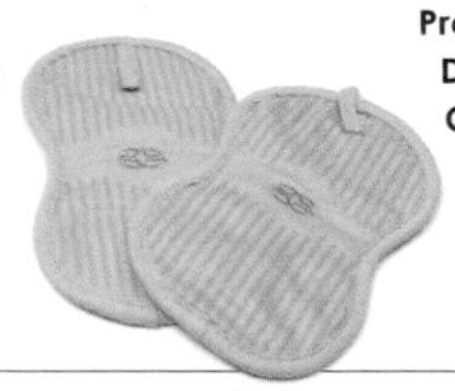	**Protection** ★½ **Dexterity** ★½ **Cleanup** ★★★	This potholder slimmed down the classic square, but the shape didn't work. It was narrower in the middle, and where it was natural to grip the lower palm was exposed, and testers burnt themselves more than once. Lengthwise, it was floppy and unwieldy; it got pinned under a hot skillet and keeled over, smashing cookies and dunking into cake batter.
SILICONEZONE Soft Cell Grid Potholders **Model:** SZ11-KA-11426 **Price:** $9.99 each **Innovation:** Silicone grid design **Dimensions:** 7¼ by 7¼ in **Material:** Silicone **Cleanup:** Dishwasher-safe 	**Protection** ★★ **Dexterity** ★ **Cleanup** ★★★	Even with a new grid design, an all-silicone potholder still proved too stiff. It couldn't fold away like fabric, so it smashed into cookies, crumbled pie crusts, and dove into cake batter. It was so stiff that it even thwacked a crater into a fully baked cake. It also wasn't protective enough to safely remove a skillet or a Dutch oven from a 500-degree oven.
TRUDEAU Stay Cool Silicone Pinch Grips **Model:** 998500 **Price:** $7.99 for two (sold as set) **Innovation:** Small size **Dimensions:** 2½ by 2½ in **Material:** Silicone **Cleanup:** Dishwasher-safe 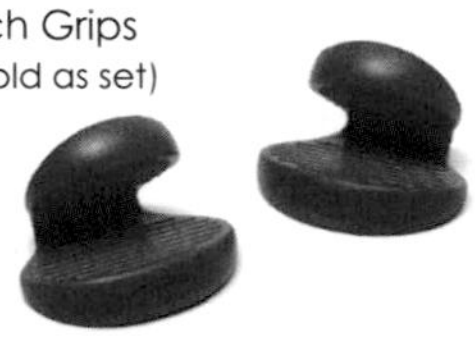	**Protection** ½ **Dexterity** ★ **Cleanup** ★★★	These small pinch grips excelled at rotating hot pans, but that was it. They only held three fingertips, which made handling anything heavy impossible, hot or cold. Protection-wise, they were useless, too. Testers didn't trust them near hot oven racks, skillets, baking sheets, cake pans, pie plates, or Dutch ovens. "I value my hands too much," said one.

Taste Test American Cheese

Hate to love it or love to hate it? We slice through the stigma surrounding American cheese. BY LAUREN SAVOIE

AMERICAN CHEESE IS polarizing. A good American cheese is mild, but not bland, and melts like a dream in grilled cheese sandwiches and atop burgers. But in this age of slow food, plastic-wrapped cheese slices have become a symbol of hyperprocessing. Could we find a product that we actually liked?

To find out, we asked 21 America's Test Kitchen staffers to sample seven nationally available American cheeses plain and in grilled cheese sandwiches.

Tasters didn't like bland cheeses, so we examined salt levels, but we saw no clear trend. Instead we noticed a different pattern: The shorter the ingredient list, the better-tasting the cheese. Our top product listed just five ingredients—cheese, water, cream, sodium phosphates, and salt—and was praised by tasters for its cheddar-like sharpness, while the bland bottom-ranked cheeses contained up to 20 ingredients, many of them processed dairy derivatives like whey or milk protein.

We reached out to experts to figure out what impact these ingredients might have on cheese flavor. They told us that some manufacturers cut costs by using less actual cheese in their products and more comparatively cheap dairy

ingredients like milk, whey, or milk protein concentrate. While these dairy products contain many of the proteins found in cheese, they lack the bacterial cultures that contribute sharp, nutty flavors. This explained why products with whey or milk protein concentrate tasted bland and boring, while top-ranked brands were complex and tangy.

To confirm that our top-ranked products contain more actual cheese, we sent the products to an independent lab for analysis. Since cheese is higher in fat and protein than other dairy products, products with more natural cheese will also usually have significantly more fat and protein than products that use whey or milk concentrates. This held true in our lab results—lower-ranked cheeses that use alternate dairy products contained as little as 8 percent fat and 14 percent protein, while our recommended cheeses contained more than 27 percent fat and 19 percent protein.

Lab results also helped explain textural differences. Experts told us that replacing natural cheese with other dairy adds moisture to the final product. Our bottom-ranked cheeses did have higher moisture percentages (up to 51 percent, compared with 40 percent moisture in top products), and many of them were watery and wet when melted. Some products attempted to counteract excessive moisture by adding gelatin or other thickeners, but tasters thought that these additives made for grilled cheese that was too gummy and stiff.

So how can you tell if you're getting a product with more real cheese? Turns out, the answer is right on the front of the package. In 1950, the U.S. Food and Drug Administration (FDA) ruled that American cheese must be labeled clearly on its packaging as "process cheese," "cheese food," or "cheese product." What do they mean?

We didn't see any brands using the term "cheese food," only "process cheese" and "cheese product." In order for a product to be labeled as "process cheese," it has to meet strict FDA specifications (which parallel our tasters' preferences): Products must have less than 43 percent moisture and contain no whey, milk protein concentrates, or thickeners. By contrast, the FDA does not have standards for the term "cheese product," and manufacturers are free to make these products as they desire. Our top two American cheeses were the only

What Is That Stuff?

In 1914, a cheese factory owner named James L. Kraft began experimenting with ways to expand cheese's shelf life and reduce factory waste. By heating leftover scraps of cheddar and mixing in emulsifying salts, Kraft created (and patented) what we now know as American cheese. By 1930, Kraft's American cheese accounted for more than 40 percent of cheese sales in the United States.

Today the perception among consumers is that American cheese is not technically cheese. So what exactly is it? The most basic of American cheeses are made from a blend of natural cheese (usually cheddar), emulsifying salts, and water or cream. But many manufacturers also add ingredients to extend shelf life and improve meltability. These additives are anything from powdered milk protein, whey, and emulsifiers to chemical preservatives, gelatin, and anticaking agents.

HIGHLY RECOMMENDED

BOAR'S HEAD American Cheese
Price: $5.49 for 8 oz ($0.69 per oz)
Classification: Process cheese
Protein: 19.1%
Fat: 30.7%
Moisture: 40.1%

TASTERS' NOTES

Our winning cheese, which is made from a blend of cheddar cheeses, had "nutty," "sharp" tanginess and a "slightly soft," "tender" texture. These "superthin" slices melted perfectly.

RECOMMENDED

KRAFT Deli Deluxe American Cheese
Price: $5.99 for 12 oz ($0.50 per oz)
Classification: Process cheese
Protein: 19.1%
Fat: 31.2%
Moisture: 39.3%

These "crumbly" slices made "molten" and "melty" grilled cheese that was "rich," "sharp," and "cheddary," with "balanced" notes of "cream" and "butter."

LAND O'LAKES Deli American Cheese Product
Price: $4.49 for 8 oz ($0.56 per oz)
Classification: Cheese product
Protein: 19.6%
Fat: 27.8%
Moisture: 39.7%

Though this "cheese product" contains added whey and milk protein concentrates, a lower moisture level made these "thicker" slices "crumbly" like "aged" cheese, with "cheddar-like sharpness" to match. This product's "tangy" acidity made for "rich" and "assertive" grilled cheese.

RECOMMENDED WITH RESERVATIONS

KRAFT Singles
Price: $3.49 for 12 oz ($0.29 per oz)
Classification: Cheese product
Protein: 18.7%
Fat: 22.1%
Moisture: 41.9%

Most tasters agreed that this product had "classic" flavor, though a few found it too bland: "good for kids, but boring for adults." It melted well, but was "plasticky" and "rubbery" when tasted plain.

NOT RECOMMENDED

BORDEN American Cheese Singles
Price: $3.49 for 12 oz ($0.29 per oz)
Classification: Cheese product
Protein: 16.9%
Fat: 21.4%
Moisture: 44.6%

"Bland," "greasy," and "waxy," these high-moisture slices melted into a "slimy," "wet" mass that coated tasters' mouths and teeth. Many also thought that this cheese had a "funky," "artificial" sourness.

CRYSTAL FARMS American Cheese
Price: $3.40 for 12 oz ($0.28 per oz)
Classification: Cheese product
Protein: 18.7%
Fat: 23.2%
Moisture: 45.2%

Another "mouth-coating" cheese, this product was "rubbery" and "gummy" when melted and had a "superprocessed," "plastic wrapper" flavor. Sampled plain, this cheese was "really bland," "boring," and "oily."

VELVEETA Slices
Price: $2.99 for 12 oz ($0.25 per oz)
Classification: Cheese product
Protein: 13.6%
Fat: 8.1%
Moisture: 51.8%

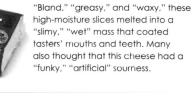

One of the few products without any natural cheese, these "vibrant yellow" slices were "thick," "tacky," and "gluey" from added gelatin. Tasters were turned off by their "sickening" sweetness and "microwave popcorn flavor."

---

products in the lineup labeled as "process cheese." Unfortunately, quality also added to the price. Since real cheese is a more expensive ingredient than fillers, our top products cost two to three times as much as lower-rated entries.

In the end, Boar's Head American Cheese led the pack with its complex sharpness and nutty, rich flavor. This process cheese costs almost twice as much as cheese products, but tasters thought that the extra money was worth it for perfectly "creamy" cheese that was "familiar," yet "sophisticated." Visit **CooksCountry.com/july15** for the full tasting chart.

Heirloom Recipe

We're looking for recipes that you treasure—the ones that have been handed down in your family for a generation or more; that always come out for the holidays; that have earned a place at your table and in your heart, through many years of meals. Send us the recipes that spell home to you. Visit CooksCountry.com/magazines/home (or write to Submit a Recipe, *Cook's Country*, P.O. Box 470739, Brookline, MA 02447); click on "Submit a Recipe" and tell us a little about the recipe. Include your name and mailing address. **If we print your recipe, you'll receive a free one-year subscription to *Cook's Country*.**

OZARK PUDDING

Serves 4 to 6

Verna Lawrence of Pine Bluff, Arkansas, writes: "Although this comforting dessert is usually served warm, my family used to make it year-round. Family legend has it that someone on our family tree got the recipe directly from Bess Truman. I don't know for sure, but it's fun to think about when digging into this pudding." Ben & Jerry's is our favorite supermarket brand of vanilla ice cream.

- ½ cup (2½ ounces) all-purpose flour
- 2 teaspoons baking powder
- ½ teaspoon salt
- 2 Granny Smith apples, peeled, cored, halved, and cut into ½-inch pieces
- 1½ cups pecans, toasted and chopped
- 2 cups (14 ounces) plus 1 teaspoon sugar
- 4 large eggs
- 1 tablespoon vanilla extract
  Vanilla ice cream

1. Adjust oven rack to middle position and heat oven to 350 degrees. Grease and flour 8-inch square nonstick baking pan.

2. Whisk flour, baking powder, and salt together in large bowl. Stir in apples and pecans. Whisk 2 cups sugar, eggs, and vanilla together in separate bowl until pale yellow, about 1 minute. Stir sugar mixture into flour mixture until thoroughly combined. Scrape batter into prepared pan and sprinkle with remaining 1 teaspoon sugar.

3. Bake until golden brown and toothpick inserted in center of pudding comes out with few crumbs attached, 45 to 50 minutes. Transfer to wire rack and let cool for 30 minutes. Spoon pudding into bowls and top with ice cream before serving.

COMING NEXT ISSUE

In the August/September edition of *Cook's Country*, we're traveling across the country, from western Kentucky for a plate of spicy **Monroe County–Style Pork Steaks** with **Vinegar Slaw** and **Barbecue White Beans** to Denver, Colorado, for the story behind that city's popular **Sugar Steaks**. We'll visit the Pacific Northwest to discover the secrets of **Cedar-Planked Salmon** on the grill and rural New England to learn more about **Mixed Berry Scones**. We'll top it all with a scoop of **Old-Fashioned Frozen Custard**. Join us.

FIND THE ROOSTER!

A tiny version of this rooster has been hidden in the pages of this issue. Write to us with its location and we'll enter you random drawing. The first correct entry will win a set of our winning potholders, each of the next five will receive a free year subscription to *Cook's Country*. To visit CooksCountry.com/rooster by July 2015, or write to Rooster JJ15, *Cook's Co* P.O. Box 470739, Brookline, MA 02447. In your name and address. Susan Rhood Purcellville, Virginia, found the rooster in February/March 2015 issue on page 18 won our winning citrus juicer.

WEB EXTRAS

Free for 4 months online at
CooksCountry.com
American Cheese Tasting
Comeback Sauce
Creamy Coleslaw
Fried Catfish
Frozen Strawberry Margaritas
Glazed Salmon with Dilly Mustard Sauce
Grilled Swordfish with Eggplant Salad
Hawaiian-Style Smoked Pork (Kalua Por
Maple and Pancake Syrup Tasting
Oven-Fried Fish Sticks with Old Bay Dipp Sauce
Potato-Crusted Halibut with Tartar Sauce
Single White Cake Round
Unsweetened Shredded Coconut Tasting
Vanilla Tasting

READ US ON iPAD

Download the *Cook's Country* for iPad and start free trial subscrip or purchase a single issue of the magazine. All issu are enhanced w full-color Cooking Mode slide show that provide step-by-step instructions for completing recipes, plus expanded revi and ratings. Go to CooksCountry.com/i to download our app through iTunes.

Follow us on **Pinterest**
pinterest.com/TestKitchen

Follow us on **Twitter**
twitter.com/TestKitchen

Find us on **Facebook**
facebook.com/CooksCountry

Watermelon Ice Cream Cake

Our refreshing, frozen "watermelon" cake features raspberry sorbet studded with chocolate "seeds," tender white cake, and tangy lime frosting.

To make this cake, you will need:

- 1 **(9-inch) round white cake***
- 2½ **cups raspberry sorbet**
- 2 **ounces semisweet chocolate, chopped fine**
- 12 **tablespoons unsalted butter, softened**
- 3 **tablespoons lime juice (2 limes)**
- ½ **teaspoon vanilla extract**
- ⅛ **teaspoon salt**
- 2 **cups (8 ounces) confectioners' sugar**
   Green food coloring

FOR THE CAKE: Line 6-cup-capacity mixing bowl with plastic wrap. Using serrated knife, cut off domed top of cake so that remaining cake

measures ¾ inch thick (reserve top for another use). Cut remaining cake into 8 wedges and line bowl with wedges, arranging as closely as possible to achieve snug fit. Scoop raspberry sorbet into separate bowl and mash with wooden spoon until softened; gently fold in chopped chocolate. Fill cake-lined bowl with sorbet mixture and smooth top. Cover surface with plastic wrap and freeze until very firm, about 6 hours.

FOR THE FROSTING: Using stand mixer fitted with whisk, whip butter, lime juice, vanilla, and salt on medium-low speed until combined. Slowly add sugar and continue to whip until smooth, about 2 minutes. Increase speed to

medium-high and whip until light and fluffy, about 5 minutes. Add 6 drops food coloring and mix until combined. Transfer ½ cup frosting to small bowl, add 6 more drops food coloring, and whisk until combined.

TO FINISH: Remove plastic from cake and turn out onto chilled plate or cake pedestal; remove remaining plastic wrap. Cover cake with even layer of light green frosting. Spread 8 vertical stripes of dark green frosting evenly around cake. Freeze until frosting is firm, at least 30 minutes. Serve.

▶ Go to **CooksCountry.com/whitecakeround** for our Single White Cake Round recipe or use your own.

Inside This Issue

Cook's Country

AUGUST/SEPTEMBER 2015

CooksCountry.com
$5.95 U.S./$6.95 CANADA

A random stop at a Massachusetts antique store—which turned out to be a bakery as well—provided the inspiration for these sweet, crumbly mixed berry scones. Three weeks in the test kitchen perfected them. PAGE 17

09>

7 25274 05251 6

Cook's Country

Dear Country Cook,

In the late 1950s, our Vermont cabin had a fieldstone barbecue under two large apple trees, just up from the garden. It wasn't used that often—the adults were usually enjoying sunset cocktails instead of grilling—but my sister Kate and I always liked outdoor cooking. It was a change in the routine, a bit of smoky adventure with heat, sparks, and sizzle. And, as the coals died down, it was also perfect for marshmallows skewered on long whips of apple branch, snapped from the tree above.

Those were summers of corn silk smoked in corncob pipes, burn barrels, homemade peach ice cream, and pond water so cold it grabbed your breath. There were frogs and crayfish, brook trout and rabbits, woodchucks and crows. There were tree stands, roofless barns, and a small copse of sun-dappled fern hidden deep in the woods.

A barbecue is one small step outside, but when you keep on walking, you find bits and pieces of the forgotten: broken pottery, pickle jars, rusted horse-drawn mowers, and abandoned cellar holes.

Kate and I ventured out beyond the edges of the known and found a world unexpected, a landscape that is still familiar today.

Christopher Kimball

Christopher Kimball
Founder and Editor, Cook's Country

Cook's Country

Founder and Editor Christopher Kimball
Editorial Director Jack Bishop
Editorial Director, Magazines John Willoughby
Executive Editor Tucker Shaw
Managing Editor Scott Kathan
Executive Food Editor Bryan Roof
Executive Tastings & Testings Editor Lisa McManus
Senior Editors Hannah Crowley,
Christie Morrison, Diane Unger
Test Kitchen Director Erin McMurrer
Associate Editor Ashley Moore
Test Cooks Morgan Bolling, Cecelia Jenkins,
Katie Leaird
Assistant Editors Lauren Savoie, Kate Shannon
Senior Copy Editor Megan Ginsberg
Copy Editor Krista Magnuson
Executive Assistant Christine Gordon
Assistant Test Kitchen Director Leah Rovner
Senior Kitchen Assistants Michelle Blodget,
Alexxa Grattan
Kitchen Assistants Blanca Castanza,
Maria Elena Delgado, Ena Gudiel
Executive Producer Melissa Baldino
Co-Executive Producer Stephanie Stender
Associate Producer Kaitlin Hammond

Consulting Creative Director Amy Klee
Contributing Editors Erika Bruce, Eva Katz, Jeremy Sauer
Consulting Editors Anne Mendelson, Meg Ragland
Science Editor Guy Crosby, PhD
Executive Food Editor, TV, Radio & Media
Bridget Lancaster

Managing Editor, Web Christine Liu
Senior Editor, Cooking School Mari Levine
Social Media Manager Jill Fisher
Senior Editor, Web Roger Metcalf
Assistant Editor, Web Terrence Doyle
Senior Video Editor Nick Dakoulas

Design Director, Print Greg Galvan
Photography Director Julie Cote
Art Director Susan Levin
Associate Art Director Lindsey Timko
Art Director, Marketing Jennifer Cox
Staff Photographer Daniel J. van Ackere
Color Food Photography Keller + Keller
Styling Catrine Kelty, Marie Piraino
Deputy Art Director, Marketing Melanie Gryboski
Associate Art Director, Marketing Janet Taylor
Designer, Marketing Stephanie Cook
Associate Art Director, Photography Steve Klise

VP, Print & Direct Marketing David Mack
Circulation Director Doug Wicinski
Circulation & Fulfillment Manager Carrie Fethe
Partnership Marketing Manager Pamela Putprush
Marketing Coordinator Marina Tomao

Director, Business Systems Alice Carpenter
Manager, Business & Content Systems Dustin Brandt
DAM Systems Manager Ian Matzen
Project Manager Britt Dresser

Chief Operating Officer Rob Ristagno
VP, Digital Products Fran Middleton
VP, New Product Development Michael Burton
Production Director Guy Rochford
Imaging Manager Lauren Robbins
Production & Imaging Specialists Heather Dube,
Dennis Noble
Director, Marketing & Sales Operations Deborah Fagone
Client Services Manager Kate Zebrowski
Sponsorship Sales Associate Morgan Mannino
Senior Controller Theresa Peterson
Customer Loyalty & Support Manager Amy Bootier
Customer Loyalty & Support Reps Caroline Augliere,
Rebecca Kowalski, Andrew Straaberg Finfrock

Director, Retail Book Program Beth Ineson
Human Resources Manager Adele Shapiro
Publicity Deborah Broide

ON THE COVER: *Mixed Berry Scones*, Keller + Keller,
Catrine Kelty
ILLUSTRATION: Greg Stevenson

Follow us on **Pinterest**
pinterest.com/TestKitchen

Follow us on **Twitter**
twitter.com/TestKitchen

Find us on **Facebook**
facebook.com/CooksCountry

Cook's Country magazine (ISSN 1552-1990), number 64, is published bimonthly by Boston Common Press Limited Partnership, 17 Station St., Brookline, MA 02445. Copyright 2015 Boston Common Press Limited Partnership. Periodicals postage paid at Boston, MA, and additional mailing offices, USPS #023453. Publications Mail Agreement No. 40020778. Return undeliverable Canadian addresses to P.O. Box 875, Station A, Windsor, ON N9A 6P2. POSTMASTER: Send address changes to Cook's Country, P.O. Box 6018, Harlan, IA 51593-1518. For subscription and gift subscription orders, subscription inquiries, or change of address notices, visit americastestkitchen.com/support, call 800-526-8447 in the U.S., or 515-248-7684 from outside the U.S., or write to us at Cook's Country, P.O. Box 6018, Harlan, IA 51593-1518. PRINTED IN THE USA.

Contents

AUGUST/SEPTEMBER 2015

SLOW-COOKER CARNITAS, 26

SWEET GLAZED PEACHES, 21

GRILLED PORK BURGERS, 14

Features

Departments

No-Fail Recipes from Across the USA

We traveled the country to sample the best dishes America has to offer, from New England Clam Chowder to Hawaiian Fried Rice. The result? Our newest book, *Cook's Country Eats Local*, with 150 of our best regional recipes. No matter where you live, you should be making these.

America's Test Kitchen is a very real 2,500-square-foot kitchen located just outside Boston. It is the home of *Cook's Country* and *Cook's Illustrated* magazines and the workday destination of more than three dozen test cooks, editors, and cookware specialists. Our mission is to test recipes until we understand how and why they work and arrive at the best version. We also test kitchen equipment and supermarket ingredients in search of products that offer the best value and performance. You can watch us work by tuning in to *Cook's Country from America's Test Kitchen* (CooksCountry.com) and *America's Test Kitchen* (AmericasTestKitchen.com) on public television.

Ask Cook's Country

BY MORGAN BOLLING

The Color of Cornmeal

Can I use white and yellow cornmeal interchangeably in recipes? Do they taste the same?
–Sandy Smith, Deep Run, N.C.

The color of cornmeal comes from the variety of corn from which it is milled. Besides the common white and yellow kinds you find at most grocery stores, some companies mill red and blue varieties, too. To see if there is a noticeable flavor difference, we made our Old-Fashioned Corn Muffins, Hushpuppies, and Easy Baked Polenta with yellow cornmeal and then with white cornmeal.

With the corn muffins, a few tasters did detect sweeter notes, stronger corn flavor, and a slightly more delicate crumb in the batch made with yellow cornmeal. However, in the tastings of the hushpuppies and polenta, we did not find strong flavor or textural differences (though visually many tasters preferred the look of the yellow cornmeal).

While most of our recipes work with yellow or white cornmeal, our testing here did confirm a more important distinction: Coarseness is key. When a recipe calls for a specific grind of cornmeal, be sure to use what's called for, as it can greatly affect the texture of the final product. If the recipe does not specify, use finely ground. The test kitchen's favorite finely ground cornmeal is Arrowhead Mills Organic Yellow Cornmeal.

THE BOTTOM LINE: Feel free to use white and yellow cornmeal interchangeably in recipes since flavor differences are minor. Just be sure to pay attention to the grind.

Heavy Cream Substitute?

I try to avoid dairy. Can I substitute coconut cream for heavy cream in chocolate ganache?
–Betty Schoenegge, Denver, Colo.

At its most basic, chocolate ganache is a simple formula of two ingredients: melted chocolate and heavy cream. Would coconut cream make a reasonable substitution for those who avoid dairy? To find out, we made side-by-side batches of dark chocolate ganache, one with heavy cream and one with coconut cream. The samples were surprising. In the batch made with coconut cream, tasters did detect slight coconut flavor. They also noticed slightly muted chocolate flavor and a somewhat less luxurious texture. These were minor, however, and overall most tasters thought that the coconut cream worked well as a substitute.

Out of curiosity we also tried coconut cream as a substitute in other applications, including creamy tomato soup, creamed onions, and crème brûlée. None of these applications worked nearly as well as the dark chocolate ganache. Both the tomato soup and onions tasted oddly sweet and oily, and the crème brûlée using coconut cream never fully set up. Given these results, we'd stick with just using it in ganache.

THE BOTTOM LINE: You can substitute coconut cream for heavy cream in dark chocolate ganache. But it does not work in other applications we tried.

Does Time Equal Balance?

Why do certain recipes call for you to let flavors meld in a soup or dressing? Does this actually do anything?
–Teddy Sue White, Barksdale, Texas

Have you ever noticed that many dishes taste better the next day? To understand why, I asked our science editor. He explained that when a food contains both water and fat, it takes time for fat-soluble flavors to diffuse into the water and water-soluble flavors to diffuse into the fat to form a uniform blend of flavors.

To test this, we made two batches each of hummus, green goddess dressing, and chili that all had directions to let flavors meld. For each test, we tasted one batch immediately and gave the other time to meld. Tasters detected strong differences between the samples

Shades of Onion

What does it mean to cook an onion to soft or golden? How do I know when it's there?
–Bob Wigand, Beltsville, Md.

In recipes we call for onions cooked to a handful of different descriptions: softened, translucent, golden brown, and dark brown.

Sautéing onions causes their cell walls to break down, releasing moisture. It also causes the complex starches within the onion's cells to slowly turn into simple sugars and concurrently release sulfur compounds (which cause the harsh taste in raw onions)—the combined effect leaves sweeter and less pungent onions in the pan. When we direct you to cook onions to a specific stage, we do so based on the flavor and texture we want from the onions in that dish.

We've created a visual guide to help you determine when your onions reach each stage. We tested with 2 cups of sliced onions and 1 tablespoon of vegetable oil in a 12-inch skillet over medium-high heat.

THE BOTTOM LINE: Follow our visual chart to know when your onions have reached the desired color.

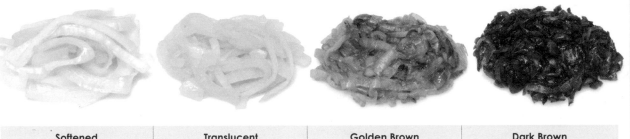

Softened	Translucent	Golden Brown	Dark Brown
2 to 4 minutes	3 to 5 minutes	5 to 7 minutes	20 minutes
Still crunchy, slightly softened.	Softer, raw onion flavor gone.	Slight caramel flavors, sweeter.	Very dark, sweet, and rich.

in all three tests. With the hummus and green goddess dressing, the just-mixed versions tasted more "sharp" and "pungent," whereas the melded ones tasted more "balanced." For the chili, the freshly made version tasted flatter in comparison with the more flavorful cooled-and-reheated version.

THE BOTTOM LINE: When a recipe calls for you to let flavors meld, do it: It allows time for all the flavors to blend together, giving you a more balanced dish.

Proper Tenting

I've read that tenting meat can ruin its crust. Is this true? Is there a "best way" to tent meat?
–Steve O'Neill, Chicago, Ill.

Here in the test kitchen, we often call for tenting meat with foil to keep it warm while it rests. And because it can affect carryover cooking (meat's temperature continues to rise for a few minutes after it's pulled from the oven), we often build it into our recipe times.

We tested different cuts of meat not tented, tented, and with the foil tightly crimped around the plate the meat was resting on. Our results depended on the roast in question. We do not suggest tenting skin-on chicken or turkeys when you're looking for crispy skin, because tenting traps steam and sogs out the skin. We do, however, suggest tenting steaks, beef roasts, and pork roasts, so long as they don't have a glaze. These meats are often cooked to

lower temperatures, so the foil plays a bigger role in keeping the temperature of the meat from dropping. And in our testing, the crusts on these meats did not soften significantly when tented. When the meats were glazed, however, the foil often hit and damaged the glaze, and the trapped steam compromised the glazy texture.

Unless a recipe calls for something more specific, we found that tenting works best when the foil is loosely placed on top of the meat in an upside-down V. You shouldn't crimp the edges of the foil around the meat or the plate that the meat is resting on because air should be able to circulate under the foil. It does not matter if the shiny side of the foil is up or down.

THE BOTTOM LINE: Tent meat loosely with one sheet of aluminum foil in an upside-down V. Do not crimp the edges as this can trap steam and sog out a crust.

To ask us a cooking question, visit **CooksCountry.com/ask.** Or write to Ask Cook's Country, P.O. Box 470739, Brookline, MA 02447. Just try to stump us!

Kitchen Shortcuts

COMPILED BY SCOTT KATHAN

SMART TIP
Thrifty Sifter
Brian O'Rourke, Mercersburg, Pa.

Very coarse salt for garnishes and baked goods (like pretzels) can be hard to find and expensive. So I've taken to passing Diamond Crystal kosher salt through a fine-mesh strainer, sifting out the small flakes, and leaving just the large ones behind. They aren't quite as big as the giant crystals found on a commercial pretzel, but they are a big improvement over table salt or unsifted kosher salt.

COOL TIP
Smoothie Starter
Seth Branin, San José, Calif.

Rather than scrounging bleary-eyed through the kitchen in the morning, I put all my healthy smoothie ingredients—yogurt, berries, seeds, and juice—in the blender jar the night before and then stick the jar in the fridge. Come morning, all I have to do is put the jar on the base and hit "puree" and my breakfast is ready.

CLEVER COOKING
Rustic Cupcakes
Dorrine Esposito, Hamilton, N.J.

When I was baking cupcakes for my daughter's birthday recently, I discovered that I didn't have enough cupcake papers. I came up with an idea on the spot. I cut parchment paper into 4-inch squares and placed them in the wells. It worked wonderfully and I liked the down-home, rustic look of the parchment paper.

Submit a tip online at CooksCountry.com/kitchenshortcuts or send a letter to Kitchen Shortcuts, *Cook's Country*, P.O. Box 470739, Brookline, MA 02447. Include your name, address, and phone number. If we publish your tip, you will receive a free one-year subscription to *Cook's Country*. Letters may be edited for clarity and length.

SMART TIP
Parmesan Primer
Darlene Daly, Boulder, Colo.

I always toss my just-drained, piping-hot pasta with some freshly grated Parmesan cheese before saucing it. The melted cheese helps the sauce cling to the noodles and boosts the flavor at the same time.

HELPFUL HINT **Butter Float**
Audrey Thompson, Barnesville, Pa.

I was baking cookies recently and the recipe required room-temperature eggs and softened butter. I hadn't planned ahead and my ingredients were still in the refrigerator, so I ran a bowl of warm water to warm the eggs and accidentally put the wrapped stick of butter in the bowl as well. Minutes later I had room-temperature eggs and butter. I have been using this trick ever since. The waxed-paper wrapping keeps the butter dry in the water.

CLEVER TIP
Shake It Up
Lesley Ellis, Ann Arbor, Mich.

Peeling garlic is such a pain. But I've found that if I put two or three garlic cloves in a Mason jar, close it tightly, and shake vigorously for 15 seconds, the papery skins come right off the cloves.

COOL TRICK **Taming Curled Parchment**
Jill March, Otisfield, Maine

I'm always annoyed when parchment paper doesn't lie flat on a baking sheet. I started spraying the baking sheet with vegetable oil spray first and then cutting the right-size piece of parchment and laying it in the sprayed baking sheet. All the edges stay down and don't keep rolling up.

Monroe County Pork Steaks

Paper-thin pork "steaks" cooked on the grill? Sounds like a recipe for shoe leather. But a trip to Monroe County, Kentucky, showed us the light. BY ASHLEY MOORE

WHEN OUR EXECUTIVE food editor, Bryan Roof, recently arrived home from a visit to Monroe County in southern Kentucky, all he could talk about was the grilled pork "steaks" he'd found there. Spicy, tender, smoky, intoxicating—when anyone waxes so enthusiastically about a dish, I know it's worth learning more about.

The cooks Roof met in Kentucky begin by slicing frozen pork butt into thin steaks. The steaks are generously seasoned with salt and pepper and then grilled and smoked over hickory wood for a few minutes—or in some cases longer. The pork steaks get sopped continually with a fiery, crimson-colored sauce of distilled vinegar, black and red peppers, and plenty of lard, butter, or both. If you like it hot (as in, you like your lips numb), then you order your pork "dipped," which means the meat is either drizzled with or dunked in the sauce (see "On the Road").

I'm handy with a knife, but there's no way to slice such thin steaks from a bone-in pork butt without industrial equipment, so I hit the meat counter to find a reasonable replacement. After experiments with pork rib chops and boneless loin chops, I found that thin bone-in pork blade chops made the best substitution because they contain a good amount of shoulder muscle along with fat. Another plus to using blade chops was that they are sold precut—no significant home butchery required.

Because the steaks are cut from the forgiving shoulder, they can stay on the fire for 20 minutes or longer without turning tough. The blade chops I was working with, though, needed less time on the grill. A side-by-side (by side) test of chops cooked over a medium fire, a cooler fire, and a hot fire revealed that chops cooked over a hot fire for 3 to 5 minutes per side had the best color and were the most tender.

But the chops were curling up at the edges. I wanted flat steaks, not peaks and valleys. The remedy was easy: I cut two slits in the fat surrounding the loin portion of each chop. This quick fix kept the meat from curling and allowed the chops to hold their shape.

Now about that crazy-hot hot sauce. It needed a few slight tweaks. I didn't want it to be so spicy that it required a warning sign, so I decided to slightly

Our take on this fiery sauce is made with browned butter, vinegar, cayenne, and plenty of black pepper.

dial back on the cayenne and black pepper amounts. I melted butter, cooking it until it was golden brown to bring out its nutty flavor, and then added the black and cayenne peppers, paprika (for color), and white vinegar. I brought the mixture to a simmer and then took it off the heat. I poured the sauce over the quick-cooking chops when they came off the grill. Tasters ranging from spice fanatics to those with tamer palates all loved this sauce.

TEST KITCHEN TECHNIQUE Snip the Fat

We use blade chops here because they're very flavorful and are often sold cut thin. They do, however, require a little prep. Using kitchen shears, snip the interior portion of fat surrounding the loin muscle of each chop in two places, about 2 inches apart, to prevent the chops from buckling (and thus cooking unevenly) when they hit the heat of the grill.

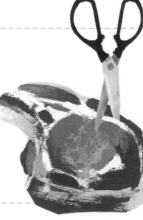

Fans of Collins Bar-B-Q swear by the screaming hot "dip" served with thin pork steaks.

Barbecue in Monroe County, Kentucky, is known (or rather not known) for being a little different. Take the 'cue found at Collins Bar-B-Q in Gamaliel. There, you won't find the slow-smoked fall-apart-tender hunk of pork prevalent at most Southern barbecue joints. Instead, you'll find slices of bone-in pork shoulder, cut thin on the butcher's band saw and quickly grilled over hickory coals.

The sauce, which doubles as the basting liquid, is atypical, too. Known locally as "dip"—basting or saucing is thus "dipping"—it's more spicy than traditional barbecue sauce. Made with lard, butter, vinegar, and black and cayenne peppers, it's thin, oily, and potent. It comes together in a tall pot that's left to sit

on the back of the stove where the oily portion naturally rises to the top and the vinegary spice-laden part sinks to the bottom. Since much of the capsaicin in the peppers is oil-soluble, that's where most of the heat resides. If you like your shoulder spicy, the pit master will dip from the top of the pot; less spicy and he dives the ladle to the bottom where it collects more of the spent pepper and sharp vinegar. It's as much about the dip as it is the pork. The shoulder is mopped with dip on the grill, smothered with dip on your plate, and then served with more dip on the side for dunking. And while this is essentially a bone-in pork chop, this is 100 percent finger food. Tear off a piece, dip, eat, repeat. –BRYAN ROOF

Kentucky White Beans and Vinegar Slaw

These flavorful sides make a meal out of pork steaks.
BY ASHLEY MOORE

MONROE COUNTY–STYLE PORK CHOPS Serves 4

Thin pork chops buckle during cooking. To prevent this, we snip the fat surrounding the loin portion of each chop. In Monroe County, these chops are considered finger food.

- 2 tablespoons kosher salt
- 2 tablespoons pepper
- 1 tablespoon paprika
- ¾ teaspoon cayenne pepper
- 1 tablespoon cornstarch
- 8 (6-ounce) bone-in blade-cut pork chops, ½ inch thick, trimmed
- 8 tablespoons unsalted butter
- ½ cup distilled white vinegar

1. Combine salt, pepper, paprika, and cayenne in bowl. Transfer 2 tablespoons spice mixture to separate bowl and stir in cornstarch. Using kitchen shears, snip interior portion of fat surrounding loin muscle of each chop in 2 places, about 2 inches apart. Season chops all over with cornstarch mixture. Reserve remaining spice mixture for sauce.

2. Heat butter in small saucepan over medium-low heat. Cook, swirling pan constantly, until butter turns dark golden brown and has nutty aroma, 4 to 5 minutes. Add reserved spice mixture and cook until fragrant, about 30 seconds. Carefully add vinegar (mixture will bubble up), bring to quick simmer, then remove from heat. Let cool completely, but do not let butter solidify.

3A. FOR A CHARCOAL GRILL: Open bottom vent completely. Light large chimney starter mounded with charcoal briquettes (7 quarts). When top coals are partially covered with ash, pour evenly over grill. Set cooking grate in place, cover, and open lid vent completely. Heat grill until hot, about 5 minutes.

3B. FOR A GAS GRILL: Turn all burners to high, cover, and heat grill until hot, about 15 minutes. Leave all burners on high.

4. Clean and oil cooking grate. Place chops on grill and cook without moving them (covered if using gas) until well charred on first side, 3 to 5 minutes. Flip chops and continue to cook on second side until well charred and meat registers 140 degrees, 3 to 5 minutes longer.

5. Transfer chops to rimmed baking sheet. Pour sauce over chops, flipping to evenly coat. Tent with aluminum foil and let rest for 5 minutes, flipping chops halfway through resting. Serve.

KENTUCKY-STYLE WHITE BEANS
Serves 4 to 6
We prefer the flavor and texture of Goya canned cannellini beans. Use the meat from the ham hock within a few days to flavor another dish. Our favorite brand of liquid smoke is Wright's.

- 1 (8-ounce) ham steak, rind removed
- 1 tablespoon vegetable oil
- 1 onion, chopped fine
- 2 garlic cloves, minced
- 3 (15-ounce) cans cannellini beans, rinsed
- 5 cups water
- 1 (12-ounce) smoked ham hock
- ¼ teaspoon liquid smoke
  Salt and pepper

1. Using 2 forks, shred ham steak into 1-inch pieces; set aside. Heat oil in Dutch oven over medium heat until shimmering. Add onion and cook until softened and beginning to brown, about 5 minutes. Stir in garlic and cook until fragrant, about 30 seconds.

2. Add beans, water, ham hock, liquid smoke, and ham steak pieces to pot and bring to boil over high heat. Reduce heat to medium-low and simmer until beans are very tender and mixture is thickened slightly, about 35 minutes, stirring occasionally.

3. Remove ham hock. Season beans with salt and pepper to taste. Serve.

KENTUCKY-STYLE VINEGAR SLAW Serves 4
Shred the carrot on the large holes of a box grater.

- 1 (14-ounce) bag shredded green and red coleslaw mix
- ½ cup finely chopped onion
- 1 carrot, peeled and shredded
- 1 cup distilled white vinegar
- ½ cup sugar
- 1 tablespoon vegetable oil
  Salt and pepper

1. Combine coleslaw mix, onion, and carrot in large bowl. Bring vinegar, sugar, oil, 1 teaspoon salt, and ½ teaspoon pepper to simmer in small saucepan over medium heat, stirring to dissolve sugar. Once simmering, pour hot vinegar mixture over coleslaw mixture and toss to combine.

2. Refrigerate until fully chilled and coleslaw mix is wilted, about 2 hours. Season with salt and pepper to taste. Serve, using slotted spoon.

Fried Pizza

Fried pizza sounds like novelty food. But when it's properly done, this centuries-old tradition produces a pie that is crisp, chewy, and far from greasy. BY CHRISTIE MORRISON

FRIED PIZZA, ALSO called *pizza montanara* or *pizza fritta*, has become something of a sensation in New York pizzerias over the past several years. But, not unexpectedly, this pizza's roots run deeper, all the way back to Italy. In the rural, mountainous areas outside Naples, home cooks who lacked ovens have been frying pizza for centuries. This tradition traveled with Italians as they came to the New World and has been passed down through generations.

When word spread through the test kitchen that I was making fried pizza, several staff members shared childhood memories of their grandmothers' New York or New Jersey kitchens. They described a puffed, golden-brown crust with a crisp, chewy texture. And despite being deep-fried, the crust wasn't greasy. This was something I'd have to see to believe.

I hit the books, where I found interesting stories about the dish itself but few instructions on how to make it. One thing I knew for sure: If I was going to fry the crust, I wanted the rest of the pizza to come together easily. With that in mind, I blitzed a few batches of our no-cook pizza sauce in the food processor, shredded some fresh mozzarella, tore a bunch of basil leaves, and grabbed some store-bought pizza dough.

While traditional pizza montanara is deep-fried (most restaurants that serve it have dedicated deep-fry equipment), I was hoping to obtain the same results—a puffed texture and crisp crust—using a shallower pool of oil. I heated ½ inch of vegetable oil (about ½ quart) to 350 degrees in a high-sided Dutch oven (our favorite pan to fry in because its high sides contain splatter). In the meantime, I divided a pound of room-temperature pizza dough into two 8-ounce balls and began working them into 10-inch rounds on a floured counter.

Once the oil reached 350 degrees—hot enough to ensure the crust cooked up crisp, not greasy—I carefully added one dough round. It began to puff immediately, and I had to press down on it with a spider skimmer to keep it submerged. Unfortunately, the oil didn't cover enough of the dough, so the middle stayed raw. I increased the oil depth until I was able to fully submerge the dough and found that 6 cups, which yielded a depth of about 1¼ inches, was sufficient (and 2 cups less oil than

The crust is deep-fried (and then broiled), but it won't be greasy if you fry it at the correct temperature.

we usually use for deep frying). About 90 seconds per side gave me a golden-brown crust with a nice chew.

I spread ½ cup of my quick pizza sauce on each fried crust and scattered fresh mozzarella on top. Some recipes call for finishing the pizzas in the oven on a preheated pizza stone or in a cast-iron skillet to melt the cheese and heat the sauce, but both of those options meant I could finish only one pizza at a time, and I wanted two. I had better luck with a wire rack set in a rimmed baking sheet. Elevating the pies this way had the added benefit of allowing hot air to circulate underneath, ensuring that the bottoms of the pies stayed nice and crisp. Broiling the pizzas for about 5 minutes provided faster browning than baking, and warming the sauce first helped protect against sogginess.

If crowd reaction counts for anything, I had a hit on my hands. My sudden popularity among my colleagues made it clear, however, that two pizzas would not suffice for this recipe, so I tweaked my sauce and added a second ball of dough. I found that I could fry all four crusts in quick succession and then assemble the second two pies while the first two were broiling. No wonder my colleagues spoke so fondly of the pizza fritta from their childhoods.

FRIED PIZZA MONTANARA

Serves 4 to 6

Room-temperature dough is much easier to shape than cold dough, so pull the dough from the fridge about 1 hour before you plan to start cooking. Shred the mozzarella on the large holes of a box grater.

SAUCE

- 1 (28-ounce) can whole peeled tomatoes, drained
- 1 tablespoon extra-virgin olive oil
- 2 garlic cloves, minced
- 1 teaspoon red wine vinegar
- 1 teaspoon dried oregano
- 1 teaspoon salt
- ¼ teaspoon pepper

PIZZA

- 2 (1-pound) balls pizza dough, room temperature
- 6 cups vegetable or peanut oil
- 1 ounce Pecorino Romano cheese, grated (½ cup)
- 8 ounces fresh mozzarella cheese, shredded (2 cups)
- ¼ cup fresh basil leaves, torn
- Extra-virgin olive oil for drizzling

1. FOR THE SAUCE: Process all ingredients in food processor until smooth, about 30 seconds. Transfer to small saucepan, cover and set over low heat to warm (sauce needn't be cooked, just warmed).

2. FOR THE PIZZA: Place 2 wire racks in 2 rimmed baking sheets. Cut four 12-inch squares of parchment paper.

3. Divide each dough ball into two 8-ounce balls and cover with greased plastic wrap. Press and roll 1 dough ball into 10-inch circle on lightly floured counter. Transfer to floured parchment square, dust top of dough round with flour, and set aside on counter. Press and roll second dough ball into 10-inch circle, transfer to floured parchment square, and stack on top of first dough round. Repeat with remaining 2 dough balls, creating second stack. Lightly cover dough round stacks with clean dish towel.

4. Add vegetable oil to large Dutch oven until it measures about 1¼ inches deep and heat over medium-high heat to 350 degrees. Gently lower 1 dough round into oil, keeping it as flat as possible as it enters oil. Fry first side, carefully pressing down with spider or slotted metal spatula to keep submerged, until puffed and golden brown, 1½ to 2 minutes. Adjust burner, if necessary, to maintain oil temperature between 325 and 350 degrees.

5. Using tongs, carefully flip dough round and continue to fry until second side is golden brown, 1½ to 2 minutes longer. Transfer to prepared wire rack. Repeat with remaining dough rounds. (You should have 2 fried crusts on each rack; crusts may extend slightly beyond edges of racks.)

6. Adjust oven rack 10 inches from broiler element and heat broiler. Spread ½ cup warm sauce over each crust, leaving 1-inch border. Sprinkle each crust with 2 tablespoons Pecorino, followed by ½ cup mozzarella. Broil 1 sheet of pizza until cheese melts and crusts begin to brown in spots, 4 to 6 minutes. Repeat with second sheet. Transfer pizzas to cutting board; sprinkle each with basil and drizzle with olive oil. Slice and serve.

TEST KITCHEN TECHNIQUE How to Make Fried Pizza

1. SHAPE Divide each dough ball in half. Roll each half into an even 10-inch round.

2. STACK This recipe makes four pizzas; stack the dough rounds on parchment.

3. FRY Place each dough round in the hot oil, pressing down to keep it submerged.

4. TOP AND BROIL Ladle on our easy sauce, add cheese, and broil two pizzas at a time.

TESTING SPLATTER SCREENS

KEY Good ★★★ Fair ★★ Poor ★

Splatter screens promise to help contain grease during stovetop cooking. Our current winning model, from Amco Houseworks, blocks larger, potentially painful (and messy) flying drops of oil but still lets through a fine mist. Could we find a better option?

We assembled seven models, priced from $7 to $21.55. We used them while searing chicken thighs and browning bacon, ranking each on how easy it was to use, how well it contained splatter, how it affected the food, and how it cleaned up. We tried the screens on small, medium, and large skillets and saucepans, as well as Dutch ovens.

Models made from silicone and perforated metal blocked our view of the food, making it difficult to monitor. The silicone models were too dense, too; they blocked oil but trapped steam, so when we lifted them, condensation dripped back into the oil, causing major splatters. And because the steam couldn't escape, the food browned more slowly.

The catch-22 of splatter screens is this: Steam and oil rise off the pan together, so no splatter screen can contain all the oil but still release the steam. Nothing worked perfectly, but fine mesh worked best, allowing steam to escape and letting us see the food.

Fit was the defining factor, and our best model was our old favorite, the Amco Houseworks Splatter Screen ($19.51). It released steam and tidied up easily, and while it won't keep your kitchen splatter-free, it will help. Read the full testing story and results chart at **CooksCountry.com/sept15.**

–HANNAH CROWLEY

RECOMMENDED

AMCO Houseworks Splatter Screen
Model: 881
Price: $19.51
Diameter: 13 in
Dishwasher-Safe: Yes

CRITERIA	
Ease of Use	★★★
Splatter Containment	★★½
Cooking Results	★★★
Cleanup	★★★

TESTERS' NOTES No splatter screen was perfect, but this one did the best job of containing grease, blocking larger, dangerous oil blobs. It laid flat atop every pan we tried it on and didn't need constant adjusting to stay flush with the rim. Also, we could see through its fine-mesh face to monitor the food, and it didn't change cooking times or prohibit browning.

RECOMMENDED WITH RESERVATIONS

PROGRESSIVE
Prepworks Splatter Screen
Model: GT-7113
Price: $11.67
Diameter: 13 in
Dishwasher-Safe: Yes

CRITERIA	
Ease of Use	★★½
Splatter Containment	★★
Cooking Results	★★★
Cleanup	★★★

This fine-mesh screen blocked larger oil splatters but still let through a fine mist. Its metal feet and handle meant we had to fiddle to get it to lay flush atop pans, and when it didn't, more oil escaped. But we liked that we could see through the fine mesh to monitor the food, and it allowed steam to escape freely.

NOT RECOMMENDED

NORPRO
Grip-EZ Silicone Splatter Screen
Model: 2061
Price: $17
Diameter: 13 in
Dishwasher-Safe: Yes

CRITERIA	
Ease of Use	★½
Splatter Containment	★
Cooking Results	★
Cleanup	★★★

This guard's thick, perforated silicone face trapped moisture inside the pan, altering cooking time. Condensation underneath the splatter guard ran off into the pan, and together the water and oil exploded in a splatter. It also blocked our view of the food.

NORPRO
Nonstick Splatter Guard
Model: 2063
Price: $7
Diameter: Three 9 by 10-in panels
Dishwasher-Safe: No

CRITERIA	
Ease of Use	★
Splatter Containment	½
Cooking Results	★★★
Cleanup	★★

This guard was made up of three connected metal rectangles that stood around the pan vertically to block splatters. Food was fine, because the guard didn't cover the top of the pan, but oil flew over its 9-inch walls. And one side was always left unprotected. Worse still, it blocked the three surrounding burners from use.

KEY INGREDIENT
Fresh Mozzarella

It's important to use fresh mozzarella—and not block mozzarella—in this recipe. The fresh cheese, sometimes sold in water or wrapped in plastic, has a distinct texture that holds its shredded shape and won't melt into a puddle. Pat the cheese dry and shred it on the large holes of a box grater, but use a gentle hand and work with the cheese when it is cold.

FRESH MOZZ IS A MUST
Don't use block cheese here.

Ranch Fried Chicken

Hot oil is the key to crunchy fried chicken, but it's deadly to fresh herbs.
Or is it? BY KATIE LEAIRD

SAVORY, CRUNCHY CRUST and irresistibly juicy meat make fried chicken one of our favorite foods in the test kitchen. For a summery twist, I set out to make fried chicken with all its beloved attributes, plus the aroma and flavor of bright, lively fresh herbs.

First, I had to pick a flavor lane. The woody herbs traditionally paired with poultry—rosemary, thyme, and sage—reminded me of winter. But chive, dill, and cilantro recalled a summery American flavor: ranch. Buttermilk, already one of fried chicken's best friends, would provide ranch's signature tang.

To start, I brined my chicken pieces, as we usually do in the test kitchen, and then dipped them in buttermilk and a few different herbed coatings (flour, cornstarch, bread crumbs, and combinations thereof) and used our tried-and-true frying methods. But batch after batch tasted more or less the same—fried. The herbs were undetectable in the final product.

I tried treating the chicken to a bath in an herby marinade. I tried rubbing dried spices directly on the chicken before coating it with flour. I even infused the frying oil with herbs. But still I had only faintly green chicken to prove that I had used any fresh herbs at all.

Why were the herb flavors disappearing? Our science editor explained that the flavor compounds in herbs become unstable and volatile when exposed to heat. Some compounds start to chemically break down while others simply evaporate at hot temperatures. The breading helped protect the herbs from the heat but for only a short time.

Aha: So the issue wasn't how I introduced the herbs to the chicken, but rather how long I let them stay in the hot oil. With this knowledge, I tried precooking the chicken, poaching it before coating it with the herbs. Less than a minute in the hot oil and this chicken was crispy. And, at last, I could taste the herbs. But I lost the juicy decadence. And who wants to cook chicken twice?

Another look at the cut of chicken I was using revealed a loophole. If I used smaller boneless thighs instead of thicker bone-in parts, I could reduce the frying time by half. And with the increased surface area on boneless, skinless thighs, I could increase the amount of herby coating per piece. What's more, thigh meat is naturally juicier than breast meat so I could forgo the standard brining step and shave off an hour of prep time. Plus, chicken thighs are cheaper.

After a few tests, I'd settled on a three-part technique for the chives, dill, and cilantro. I whisked them into buttermilk along with the other ranch components (vinegar, garlic, salt and pepper, and mayonnaise) to make an herby liquid coating. I mixed the herbs into the flour coating along with some cornstarch for extra crunch. And I used the herbs in a ranch-style dipping sauce.

The final analysis? Not one, but two American classics found a place at my summer table. And with boneless pieces, I can fork-and-knife them if I'm feeling fancy or just grab and gobble by hand.

Flavorful, juicy boneless thighs are thin enough to fry quickly.

KEY INGREDIENTS
Three Herbs, Three Ways
We use the defining herbs of ranch flavor—chives, cilantro, and dill—in three ways for this chicken: in the buttermilk dip, in the flour coating, and in the serving sauce.

RANCH FLAVORS
Chives, cilantro, and dill.

RANCH FRIED CHICKEN Serves 4 to 6
Use a Dutch oven that holds 6 quarts or more for this recipe.

CHICKEN
- 8 (5- to 7-ounce) boneless, skinless chicken thighs, trimmed
  Salt and pepper
- 2 quarts peanut or vegetable oil

BUTTERMILK MIXTURE
- 1 cup buttermilk
- 2 tablespoons minced fresh chives
- 2 tablespoons minced fresh cilantro
- 2 teaspoons minced fresh dill
- 2 teaspoons distilled white vinegar
- 1 garlic clove, minced
- ½ teaspoon salt
  Pinch cayenne pepper

COATING
- 1¼ cups all-purpose flour
- ½ cup cornstarch
- 3 tablespoons minced fresh chives
- 3 tablespoons minced fresh cilantro
- 1 tablespoon minced fresh dill
- 1½ teaspoons garlic powder
- 1½ teaspoons salt
- ¾ teaspoon pepper

RANCH SAUCE
- ½ cup mayonnaise
  Salt and pepper

1. FOR THE CHICKEN: Pat chicken dry with paper towels and season with salt and pepper.

2. FOR THE BUTTERMILK MIXTURE: Whisk all ingredients together in bowl. Set aside ¼ cup buttermilk mixture for ranch sauce.

3. FOR THE COATING: Whisk all ingredients together in large bowl.

4. Set wire rack in rimmed baking sheet. Set second wire rack in second rimmed baking sheet and line half of rack with triple layer of paper towels.

5. Working with 1 piece at a time, dip chicken in remaining buttermilk mixture to coat, letting excess drip back into bowl; then dredge in coating, pressing to adhere. Transfer chicken to first wire rack (without paper towels). (At this point, coated chicken may be refrigerated, uncovered, for up to 2 hours.)

6. Heat oil in large Dutch oven over medium-high heat until it reaches 350 degrees. Add half of chicken to hot oil and fry until golden brown and registers 175 degrees, 7 to 9 minutes. Adjust

...urner, if necessary, to maintain oil tem-...erature between 325 and 350 degrees.

7. Transfer chicken to paper towel–...ined side of second wire rack to drain ...n each side for 30 seconds, then ...nove to unlined side of rack. Return ...il to 350 degrees and repeat with ...emaining chicken.

8. FOR THE RANCH SAUCE: ...Vhisk mayonnaise into reserved ...uttermilk mixture. Season with salt ...nd pepper to taste.

9. Transfer chicken to platter and ...erve with ranch sauce.

Sweet Potato Cornbread

Adding sweet potatoes to crumbly cornbread isn't a new idea, but it sure is a good one. BY CHRISTIE MORRISON

SWEET POTATO CORNBREAD marries two Southern staples—sweet potatoes and cornbread—to take the latter into a colorful, flavorful new direction. But introducing cooked sweet potatoes to cornbread affects the bread's texture and not always in a good way. I wanted sweet potato flavor and no soggy mess.

After experiments with a handful of recipes, I learned that precooking the sweet potato is a must. My test recipes varied in their precooking methods (boiling, roasting, microwaving), but I found that drier methods of cooking made it easier to control the added moisture in the cornbread. Microwaving won out for ease and efficiency. After poking each potato to allow steam to escape (I was using 1½ pounds of potatoes to start), I zapped them for about 15 minutes, flipping them every 5 minutes for even cooking. I let them cool a bit before scooping the softened flesh from the skins.

After several tests with different ratios of cornmeal and flour, I landed on 1½ cups cornmeal to just ½ cup flour for a light-yet-sturdy bread.

Tasters preferred samples made with whole milk to those with buttermilk. They also shied away from warm spices like cinnamon and nutmeg. And just ¼ cup of brown sugar helped the bread develop deeper color and enhanced the delicate sweet potato flavor.

Cast-iron cornbread is great, but I found that an ovensafe nonstick skillet was a low-fuss replacement. I melted a tablespoon of butter in the skillet until the foaming subsided (nonstick or not, fat is essential for crisp brown edges), poured in the batter, and transferred the operation to a 425-degree oven for 30 minutes. I let the cornbread cool in the pan for about an hour before sliding it from the skillet. At once crumbly and cohesive, savory and sweet, this sweet potato version—with a browned crust and brilliant orange-gold interior—was in a league of its own.

SWEET POTATO CORNBREAD
Serves 10 to 12

You can make this cornbread in a 10-inch cast-iron skillet or in an ovensafe nonstick skillet. Light or dark brown sugar works equally well in this recipe. Note that the cornbread needs to cool for 1 hour before being removed from the pan.

Microwaving the sweet potatoes saves time and is much easier than roasting them.

1½	pounds sweet potatoes, unpeeled
½	cup whole milk
8	tablespoons unsalted butter, melted, plus 1 tablespoon unsalted butter
4	large eggs
1½	cups (7½ ounces) yellow cornmeal
½	cup (2½ ounces) all-purpose flour
¼	cup packed (1¾ ounces) brown sugar
1	tablespoon baking powder
½	teaspoon baking soda
1¾	teaspoons salt

1. Adjust oven rack to middle position and heat oven to 425 degrees. Prick potatoes all over with fork. Microwave on large plate until potatoes are very soft and surfaces are slightly wet, 10 to 15 minutes, flipping every 5 minutes. Immediately slice potatoes in half to release steam.

2. When potatoes are cool enough to handle, scoop flesh into bowl and mash until smooth (you should have about 1¾ cups); discard skins. Whisk in milk, melted butter, and eggs. Whisk cornmeal, flour, sugar, baking powder, baking soda, and salt together in separate large bowl. Stir sweet potato mixture into cornmeal mixture until combined.

3. Melt remaining 1 tablespoon butter in 10-inch ovensafe nonstick skillet over medium-high heat until bubbling, about 3 minutes. Swirl butter to coat bottom and sides. Pour batter into hot skillet and smooth top with rubber spatula. Bake until cornbread is golden brown and toothpick inserted in center comes out clean, 25 to 30 minutes. Let cornbread cool in skillet on wire rack for 1 hour. Loosen edges of cornbread from skillet with spatula and slide out onto cutting board. Cut into wedges and serve.

Grilled Sugar Steak

The sugar adds a hint of sweetness and helps create the ultimate charred crust.

BY CECELIA JENKINS

STEAK GRILLED WITH a sugar crust? Really? Really. At Bastien's, a historic family-owned restaurant in Denver, Colorado, grilled sugar steak has been the signature dish and a customer favorite for decades. Their strip steak is a juicy medium-rare on the inside (a warning on the menu disclaims any steak cooked further) and delicately crusty on the outside, delivering a fleeting moment of sweetness followed by a flood of meaty flavors. I set out to create an equally captivating version in the test kitchen.

Though famous for it, Bastien's doesn't have a lock on sugar steak: A little research turned up recipes from New Orleans, Kansas City, and California. Most called for rubbing the steaks with a combination of sugar and salt. Some used brown sugar, which we quickly discounted because of its strong molasses flavor. Others called for so much sugar that the steaks did nothing but burn and turn bitter. Some introduced ingredients like bourbon or cayenne pepper to the mix, but these additions muddied the waters. I wanted a clean, faintly sweet steak with a delicate crust. To get it, I'd need to find the right amount of sugar for sweetness, and just enough salt for seasoning. After cooking through five recipes and compiling notes from my tasters, a 2:1 ratio of sugar to salt seemed like a good starting point.

My first problem revealed itself straight out of the gate: When I applied the sugar-salt mixture to the steaks (strips, just like Bastien's uses), it mostly just slid off the meat when it hit the grill. Whatever coating managed to stick melted off as it heated, leaving no trace of crust or flavor. This never happens with just salt; was the sugar creating an unexpected moisture problem?

Observing the coated steaks more closely, I saw that they started to moisten within a few minutes of being rubbed. The salt in the mixture pulled moisture out of the meat, which dissolved the sugar, creating a thin syrup. Not good. Moist steaks wouldn't give me the crust I wanted because once they were on the grill, the moisture would create steam, discouraging browning. (Patting them dry, our normal fix for too much moisture, would have removed the coating.)

I thought that maybe instead of

The key to sugar steak's crust is deep browning without burning, which means the cook has to pay attention and move the steaks around the grill.

fighting this natural process, I could put it to work in my favor. To find out, I sprinkled the sugar-salt mixture onto my steaks and let them rest at room temperature for an hour. I removed them from the dish, applied more of the mixture, and found that, to my delight, the moisture on the steaks' surfaces allowed it to stick beautifully.

I reconsidered my 2:1 ratio of granulated sugar to salt. I hoped to forestall

any burnt bitter flavors by switching to a 1:1 ratio, but then I couldn't detect sweetness at all. Adjusting the ratio to 4 parts sugar to 3 parts salt created the delicate crust and clean sweetness I wanted without any bitterness.

One last detail needed smoothing out: heat. When I cooked steaks over a fire that was too cool, I never got a crust. Too hot, and the steaks just burned. I wanted char on the outside

and juiciness on the inside.

To get it, I rotated the steaks once they started to caramelize and also swapped their positions over the coals (depending on how quickly some were coloring). We rarely suggest fussing with your steaks on the grill in this way, but keeping them moving helped me minimize the hot spots and even out the heavy browning caused by the sugar. Sweet success.

Shaped like a circus tent, Bastien's Restaurant sits prominently on Colfax Avenue, a 50-odd-mile street that bisects Denver. It's a notorious street of contrasts (one stretch abuts the state capital while the next teems with unlawful trade, and gentrification mixes with grit along its entire stretch), but as Denver's defining throughway, it was granted Heritage Corridor status in the late 1990s to help protect and preserve Bastien's and many other midcentury architectural gems.

GRILLED SUGAR STEAK
Serves 4 to 6

Plan ahead: These steaks need to sit for at least 1 hour after seasoning. You will have about 1 teaspoon of sugar mixture left over after the final seasoning of the steaks in step 3. If your steaks are more than 1 inch thick, pound them to 1 inch.

- ¼ cup sugar
- 3 tablespoons kosher salt
- 4 (9- to 11-ounce) boneless strip steaks, 1 inch thick, trimmed
  Pepper

1. Mix sugar and salt together in bowl. Pat steaks dry with paper towels and place in 13 by 9-inch baking dish. Evenly sprinkle 1½ teaspoons sugar mixture on top of each steak. Flip steaks and sprinkle second side of each steak with 1½ teaspoons sugar mixture. Cover with plastic wrap and let sit at room temperature for 1 hour or refrigerate for up to 24 hours.

2A. FOR A CHARCOAL GRILL: Open bottom vent completely. Light large chimney starter mounded with charcoal briquettes (7 quarts). When top coals are partially covered with ash, pour evenly over half of grill. Set cooking grate in place, cover, and open lid vent completely. Heat grill until hot, about 5 minutes.

2B. FOR A GAS GRILL: Turn all burners to high, cover, and heat grill until hot, about 15 minutes. Turn all burners to medium-high.

3. Clean and oil cooking grate. Transfer steaks to plate. (Steaks will be wet; do not pat dry.) Sprinkle steaks with 1 teaspoon sugar mixture on each side, then season with pepper.

4. Place steaks on hotter side of grill (if using charcoal) and cook (covered if using gas) until evenly charred on first side, 3 to 5 minutes, rotating and switching positions for even cooking. Flip steaks and continue to cook until meat registers 120 to 125 degrees (for medium-rare), 3 to 5 minutes, rotating and switching positions for even cooking.

5. Transfer steaks to wire rack set in rimmed baking sheet and let rest for 5 minutes. Slice and serve.

KEYS TO The Best Sugar Steaks
To get the right mix of sweet and savory, follow these steps.

1. Start with thick strip steaks.

1 inch

2. Sprinkle with sugar and salt mixture, let them rest, and sprinkle again.

3. Watch them carefully and keep the steaks moving on the grill to prevent burning.

Broiled Tomatoes

Cooking juicy summer tomatoes seemed fruitless, but this old-school technique pays off.

BY MORGAN BOLLING

AS ANYONE WHO'S ever had one knows, nothing beats a plump, juicy, fresh-off-the-vine tomato, sprinkled with salt and devoured in the heat of high summer. Why, then, have Americans been messing with perfection for so many years, gilding those fruits with a crusty topping and sliding them into the oven?

I looked for answers in a collection of vintage and modern broiled tomato recipes. Most followed a pretty basic formula: Top tomato halves with something creamy or crunchy and broil. I didn't fall in love, but I started to see the promise in a soft, warm tomato with a topping that amplified and complemented its complex flavors.

Improvising, I topped a few supermarket tomato halves with a basic mix of dried bread crumbs, basil, garlic, olive oil, and a bit of sugar for balance. I broiled them until the crumbs were just golden brown (about 4 minutes). But the tomato halves were only partly cooked through.

Switching to smaller vine-ripened tomatoes helped. And rather than using halves, I tried slicing each tomato into three thick slices. This gave me a more consistently cooked tomato—soft and warm and summery—and the added bonus of more crunchy topping per bite. Plus, since vine-ripened tomatoes are available year-round, I knew I'd be able to make this summery dish any time.

With my basic ingredients and techniques settled, I looked for ways to punch up the vibrancy in the topping. I added parsley for freshness. I also mixed in some capers and Parmesan cheese for savory depth.

Thick slices of vine-ripened tomatoes warm through but don't get mushy.

BROILED TOMATOES
Serves 4 to 6

Look for tomatoes that are 2½ to 3 inches in diameter.

- 4 vine-ripened tomatoes (6 to 8 ounces each), cored
- ½ teaspoon sugar
  Salt and pepper
- 1 slice hearty white sandwich bread, torn into 1-inch pieces
- ¼ cup grated Parmesan cheese
- 2 tablespoons chopped fresh basil
- 2 tablespoons chopped fresh parsley
- 1 tablespoon capers, rinsed and patted dry
- 1 tablespoon extra-virgin olive oil, plus extra for drizzling
- 1 garlic clove, minced

1. Remove and discard thin slice from tops and bottoms of tomatoes (so rounds will sit flat). Slice tomatoes crosswise into thirds to create ½- to ¾-inch-thick rounds. Combine sugar, ½ teaspoon salt, and ½ teaspoon pepper in bowl. Season both sides of tomato slices with sugar mixture. Place tomatoes on wire rack set in rimmed baking sheet.

2. Pulse bread, Parmesan, basil, parsley, capers, oil, garlic, ½ teaspoon pepper, and ⅛ teaspoon salt in food processor until coarsely ground, about 10 pulses.

3. Adjust oven rack 6 inches from broiler element and heat broiler. Divide bread-crumb mixture evenly among tops of tomato slices (about 1 tablespoon each) and press gently to adhere. Broil until crumbs are golden brown and crispy, 3 to 5 minutes. Transfer tomatoes to platter. Serve, drizzled with extra oil.

Cedar-Planked Salmon

Why bother cooking salmon on wooden planks? Preventing sticking is just one reason. There's also flavor. BY MORGAN BOLLING

TO THOSE WHO have never tried it, grilling salmon on a cedar plank may seem unnecessarily showy. That's what we used to think, too. But in recent years the test kitchen has experimented with this technique, and we've found that it just may be the best way to grill salmon. Soft fish, big flavor, easy cleanup. A stellar midsummer supper.

The planks aren't showy; they're practical. Because of salmon's delicate flesh, it can easily stick to the grill or, worse, fall through the grate. But inserting a wooden plank between the fish and the grill grate defuses these dangers because, wait for it, the fish never actually touches the grill.

What's more, the subtle smoky flavor that cedar smoke contributes—woodsy, earthy, outdoorsy, summery—is just plain fantastic (see "Made for Each Other"). And the rustic presentation is a knockout at the table.

Untreated cedar planks for cooking used to be an expensive specialty item that was difficult to procure in many parts of the country, but today you can find planks in supermarkets, hardware stores, and big-box stores coast to coast (look near the charcoal and other grilling supplies). I picked up a dozen packages of planks, ordered in 20 pounds of salmon, poured myself a big cup of coffee, and sat down in our cookbook library to pore over recipes for cedar-planked salmon.

The recipes I found called for all sorts of cures, sauces, marinades, and rubs for the fish and a multitude of different set-ups for the grill. And while all called for me to soak the planks for an hour or so before cooking to help forestall any flare-ups over the fire, they otherwise treated the planks very differently. Some called for preheating the plank before laying the fish fillets on it. One even required you to place the plank directly on the hot coals to jump-start its smoking process, a daunting option that took just one flame-filled test for me to eliminate. (Thankfully I had my fire extinguisher nearby when I took this one for a spin.)

After a few hours at the grill, I concluded that while some of these recipes showed promise, there was one common shortcoming: The cedar, so rich and rewarding as an aroma during the cooking process, was barely

This smoky, succulent salmon is surprisingly easy to make.

discernible once the salmon reached the plate. I didn't want a piece of fish that tasted like a campfire, but I did want to get some character out of the planks I'd picked up.

I decided to tone down my approach on the front end, skipping the elaborate rubs and marinades I found in my initial research and instead taking a quieter approach with a simple mixture of brown sugar, salt, and dill rubbed onto

four ½-pound skin-on fillets (enough to feed four). The salt helped season the fish, while the sugar would add flavor and, I hoped, would help the fillets achieve a nice lightly browned color. I let the seasoned fish rest while I soaked my plank for an hour.

Based on my initial tests, I knew that preheating the soaked plank on the grill before adding the fish was important for a present but balanced cedar flavor,

one that complemented, rather than clobbered, the fish. Without this step, it would take 5 minutes before the cedar would even start smoking. Because the fish is done within 12 to 15 minutes, by the time the cedar flavor had sufficiently infused the fish, the fillets would be tragically overcooked and my dinner would go straight to the cat.

Preheating the plank on the grill made a big difference in my next couple of rounds, but I still wasn't satisfied. The fish wasn't taking on quite as much cedar flavor as I wanted.

I tried covering the salmon and plank with an inverted disposable aluminum pan to help trap the smoke. But this took me too far in the other direction; the intense cedar flavor was so strong that the fillets tasted like a moth-proof closet; the delicate salmon flavor didn't stand a chance. I started wondering whether chasing this cedar flavor was just an exercise in futility.

A fellow test cook saw my distress and, after closely inspecting my work, wondered whether the skin on the salmon was inhibiting the development of smoky flavor. I was skeptical. I worried that removing it was removing a thin layer of protection, and I might end up with dried-out salmon, more like smoked or cured fish than a fresh fillet.

But I tried a side-by-side test with skin-on versus skinless fillets. My co-worker was right: Removing the skin had little effect on the moistness of the salmon, while concurrently opening the door for just enough cedar flavor.

To seal the deal, I served my tender, smoky salmon with a classic Greek *tzatziki* sauce of yogurt and cucumber. The acidity of the yogurt and lemon in the sauce balanced the richness of the fish, and the herbs echoed the cure. The cucumber added texture without overwhelming the fish's delicate nature.

Score. After rigorous testing and plenty of trial and error, my tasters were finally satisfied. Rich, deeply seasoned, and full of earthy, woodsy cedar flavor, this salmon was a hit. Even avowed fish-haters liked it.

And perhaps the best part of all, especially for cooks who've lived through the misery of cleaning up after grilling fish at home: I spent exactly 0 minutes scouring my pristine grill grates.

CEDAR-PLANKED SALMON
Serves 4

Be sure to buy an untreated cedar plank specifically intended for cooking. To ensure uniform pieces of fish, we prefer to purchase a whole center-cut salmon fillet and cut it into four equal pieces. Note that the seasoned fillets must be refrigerated for at least 1 hour before grilling. When preheating the cedar plank, you will know it's ready when it is just giving off wisps of smoke. It should not ignite. Serve with lemon wedges and our Cucumber-Yogurt Sauce (recipe follows).

- 1 (2-pound) center-cut, skinless salmon fillet, about 1½ inches thick
- 2 tablespoons packed brown sugar
- 1½ tablespoons kosher salt
- 1 tablespoon chopped fresh dill
- 1 teaspoon pepper
- 1 (16 by 7-inch) cedar plank
- 1 teaspoon vegetable oil
  Lemon wedges

1. Cut salmon crosswise into 4 equal fillets. Combine sugar, salt, dill, and pepper in bowl. Pat salmon dry with paper towels. Sprinkle salmon all over with sugar mixture, place on plate, and refrigerate, uncovered, for at least 1 hour or up to 24 hours. One hour before grilling, soak cedar plank in water for 1 hour (or according to manufacturer's directions).

2A. FOR A CHARCOAL GRILL: Open bottom vent completely. Light large chimney starter filled with charcoal briquettes (6 quarts). When top coals are partially covered with ash, pour evenly over grill. Set cooking grate in place. Place cedar plank in center of grill. Cover and open lid vent completely. Heat grill until plank is lightly smoking and crackling (it should not ignite), about 5 minutes.

2B. FOR A GAS GRILL: Place cedar plank in center of grill. Turn all burners to medium-low, cover, and heat grill until plank is smoking and crackling (it should not ignite), about 15 minutes. Leave all burners on medium-low. Adjust burners as needed to maintain grill temperature between 300 and 325 degrees.

3. Brush skinned side of salmon fillets with oil, then place skinned side down on plank. Cover grill and cook until center of salmon is translucent when checked with tip of paring knife and registers 125 degrees (for medium-rare), 12 to 15 minutes. Using tongs, transfer plank with salmon to baking sheet, tent with aluminum foil, and let rest for 5 minutes. Serve with lemon wedges.

Back Story
Made for Each Other

Cedar and salmon are a match for the ages.

Using cedar to smoke salmon has been done for centuries by indigenous people in the Pacific Northwest, where both cedar and salmon are abundant. Local cedar trees were relatively easy to cut into planks large enough to anchor whole sides of salmon. The sides were then placed around a fire to smoke. During the yearly salmon runs, local communities would smoke scores of fish to preserve.

The unique flavor produced by the pairing is an added bonus with a scientific basis. Cedar contains high levels of flavor-rich compounds called "sesquiterpenes" (try saying that five times fast) that salmon's natural fats eagerly embrace. As the cedar wood smokes, these flavorful compounds infuse the fish, giving it a deeply satisfying, woodsy flavor.

TEST KITCHEN TECHNIQUE **How to Soak a Cedar Plank**

To keep your cedar plank from catching fire, you must soak it for an hour before grilling. We set the plank in a rimmed baking sheet, cover it with water, and weigh it down with a measuring cup to keep the plank submerged. You can find cedar planks near the charcoal in most grocery, big box, and hardware stores; one plank will easily hold four portions.

PREVENTING FLARE-UPS
A good long soak keeps the flames at bay.

CUCUMBER-YOGURT SAUCE Makes about ¾ cup

A spoon makes easy work of removing the cucumber seeds. Using Greek yogurt here is key; don't substitute regular plain yogurt, or the sauce will be very watery.

- ½ cucumber, peeled, halved lengthwise, and seeded
- ½ cup plain whole-milk Greek yogurt
- 1 tablespoon extra-virgin olive oil
- 1 tablespoon chopped fresh mint
- 1 tablespoon chopped fresh dill
- 1 small garlic clove, minced
- ¼ teaspoon pepper
- ⅛ teaspoon salt

Shred cucumber on large holes of box grater. Combine yogurt, oil, mint, dill, garlic, pepper, salt, and shredded cucumber in bowl. Cover and refrigerate until chilled, about 20 minutes. Serve.

This bright, fresh sauce (which is sometimes called *tzatziki*) helps balance the richness of the smoky salmon.

Grilled Pork Burgers

Ground pork makes for tender, mild-yet-savory burgers— if you add the right ingredients. BY MATTHEW CARD

WHILE PORK USUALLY shines on the grill, there is one glaring exception: pork burgers, which, when cooked carelessly, tend to be tough, dry, and bland. This is because, due to lingering but outdated health concerns, the U.S. Department of Agriculture recommends that ground pork be cooked to 160 degrees, which wrings out the flavor- and texture-enhancing juices (and fat) from the meat, constricting it into a tough, unappetizing hockey puck.

But pork burgers can be, and should be, so much more. Pork has a nuanced, slightly sweet flavor that makes a fine canvas for seasonings, sauces, and add-ins. But to keep it tender, a successful pork burger needs an extra hit of moisture in the mix.

Most existing recipes attempt to do just that by adding a host of flavorful, and typically fatty, ingredients. Bacon tops the list. While I rarely find fault with bacon, I did in this instance: The smoky-sweet flavor, even when used judiciously, ran roughshod over the sweet, mild pork flavor—and its fat rendered out during grilling, causing serious flare-ups. Pork patties laden with cheese or butter suffered the same sooty fate.

A handful of recipes that I tested kept their list of ingredients as simple as could be—just ground pork, salt, and pepper—but toyed with the grill's temperature in an attempt to preserve the meat's moisture. High heat, low heat, and combo heat, I tried them all, but each yielded the same sad results: dry, bland burgers.

Looking beyond burgers for inspiration, I shifted my focus toward their closest cousin, meatballs. The most obvious difference between the two (aside from the shape) is how meatballs are typically enriched with a panade of bread mashed to a paste with a liquid, often milk, and sometimes egg. Simple, yes, but a panade works a minor miracle by both adding and trapping moisture (juices and fat), allowing meatballs to be thoroughly cooked without drying out. I whipped up a batch of burgers enhanced with a few spoonfuls of panade and was rewarded with the most moist, "porky" burgers to date.

But the burgers were far from perfect. The texture was dense and the flavor was bland—they were veering

Our savory, creamy burger sauce gets its kick from horseradish, fresh garlic, and whole-grain mustard.

into meatloaf territory. In successive batches, I abandoned the egg to loosen things up and made my next panade with just one slice of white sandwich bread (about 1 ounce) mashed with 4 tablespoons of milk (mixed into 1½ pounds of ground pork). This worked much better in terms of texture but did little for the flavor of my burgers. To build deeper flavor, I thought back to a recent test kitchen discovery in which

we determined that you can use liquids more flavorful than milk in a panade to good effect. After days of testing various ratios of ingredients, I landed on keeping half the milk (2 tablespoons) for richness but replacing the rest with a combination of two of our favorite meaty-flavor enhancers: Worcestershire and soy sauces. A minced shallot, a spoonful of fresh minced thyme, and a hefty full teaspoon of black pepper

rounded out the seasonings.

As for grilling the burgers, a full chimney of briquettes spread in an even layer (or medium heat on a gas grill) provided just the right heat. To reach the necessary 150-degree internal temperature without burning their crusts, I found that I needed to flatten the burgers to about ¾ inch thick, or 4 inches in diameter (which perfectly fills out a standard hamburger bun).

Pressing a dimple into the center of each burger ensured that the patties wouldn't bulge and be awkward to eat. To gild the lily, I made up a quick mayonnaise-based burger sauce flavored with horseradish, whole-grain mustard, and garlic.

Sandwiched between toasted buns, these moist and juicy pork burgers can easily go toe-to-toe with the best beef burger. The basic recipe also proved the perfect platform for additional flavorings to match any backyard barbecue menu.

GRILLED PORK BURGERS

Serves 4

We developed this recipe with whole milk, but low-fat will work, too.

- 1 slice hearty white sandwich bread, torn into pieces
- 1 shallot, minced
- 2 tablespoons milk
- 4 teaspoons soy sauce
- 1 tablespoon Worcestershire sauce
- 1¼ teaspoons minced fresh thyme
- 1 teaspoon pepper
- ½ teaspoon salt
- 1½ pounds 80 to 85 percent lean ground pork
- 4 hamburger buns, toasted and buttered
- 1 recipe Horseradish Burger Sauce (optional)

Building Better Burgers

PROBLEM Bulging Burgers
A flat raw patty will mound during cooking, creating a shape more like a baseball than a burger. Rounded burgers can be awkward to serve and eat. We think burgers should be flat, not bulging.

SOLUTION Make a Divot
Pressing a divot into the center of each patty before cooking ensures that the cooked burgers will be flat.

---

1. Combine bread, shallot, milk, soy sauce, Worcestershire, thyme, pepper, and salt in large bowl. Mash to paste with fork. Using your hands, add pork and mix until well combined.

2. Divide pork mixture into 4 equal balls. Flatten balls into even ¾-inch-thick patties, about 4 inches in diameter. Using your fingertips, press centers of patties down until about ½ inch thick, creating slight divot.

3A. FOR A CHARCOAL GRILL: Open bottom vent completely. Light large chimney starter filled with charcoal briquettes (6 quarts). When top coals are partially covered with ash, pour evenly over grill. Set cooking grate in place, cover, and open lid vent completely. Heat grill until hot.

3B. FOR A GAS GRILL: Turn all burners to high and heat grill until hot, about 15 minutes. Turn all burners to medium.

4. Clean and oil cooking grate. Grill patties (covered if using gas), until browned on first side, 5 to 7 minutes. Flip and continue to grill until burgers register 150 degrees, 5 to 7 minutes longer. Serve burgers on buns with sauce, if using.

GRILLED PARMESAN PORK BURGERS

Add ½ cup grated Parmesan, 1 tablespoon minced fresh sage, 1 teaspoon ground fennel, and ½ teaspoon red pepper flakes to pork mixture in step 1.

GRILLED SOUTHWEST PORK BURGERS

Add 2 tablespoons minced jarred hot pepper rings, 1½ teaspoons chili powder, and ½ teaspoon minced fresh rosemary to pork mixture in step 1.

GRILLED THAI-STYLE PORK BURGERS

Substitute fish sauce for soy sauce. Add 3 tablespoons minced fresh cilantro, 2 teaspoons Sriracha sauce, and 1 teaspoon grated lime zest to pork mixture in step 1.

HORSERADISH BURGER SAUCE

Makes ½ cup

Buy refrigerated prepared horseradish, not the shelf-stable kind, which contains preservatives and additives. Horseradish strength varies, so add it according to your taste.

- ¼ cup mayonnaise
- 2 tablespoons sour cream
- 1–2 tablespoons prepared horseradish
- 1 tablespoon whole-grain mustard
- 1 garlic clove, minced
  Pinch sugar
  Salt and pepper
  Hot sauce

Whisk mayonnaise, sour cream, horseradish, mustard, garlic, and sugar together in bowl. Season with salt, pepper, and hot sauce to taste.

Fresher Creamed Corn

Who says creamed corn has to be gray or gloppy? We set out to freshen up this classic side dish.

BY CECELIA JENKINS

With creamed corn, the simpler, the better.

Corn and cream should be a fantastic combination, sweet flavors mingling to bring out the best in each other. But many people dread creamed corn because they've had only the canned versions, most of which contain no cream at all—only water, thickeners, sugar, and who-knows-what suspended in a grayish, brownish, gelatinous, gloppy goo. I hoped to rescue what should be a simple, satisfying side dish and return it to its rightful place at the summertime table.

To start, I carefully stripped plump, yellow kernels from a stack of husked corn cobs and simmered the kernels gently in cream seasoned with salt and pepper. I expected to get corn kernels that were tender inside but still fairly crisp on the outside, providing a satisfying little pop with each bite.

But as my corn cooked, I found a glaring problem. When I peeked under the lid of my saucepan, I was distressed to find my mixture looked curdled. How could this be? Cream has so much fat that it rarely curdles, and I hadn't introduced any acid (like lemon or vinegar) that would hasten or encourage curdling. I tried both half-and-half and light cream, and they too curdled (and didn't taste as good as the cream). What was going on here?

I gave a shout to our science editor, who explained that enzymes naturally present in the fresh corn may react with cream to cause curdling. To solve the curdling problem, I would need to deactivate the enzymes by cooking the corn before adding the cream. I simmered nine ears' worth of kernels in water and added cream in at the end and found that the liquid turned into a surprisingly flavorful concentrated corn broth. It didn't curdle, so that was progress, but the dish was too watery. I wanted a thicker dish.

Cooking down the corn liquid to thicken it took too much time; starting with less water resulted in unevenly cooked corn (because all of the kernels weren't evenly submerged). Instead, I blended a portion of the kernels with ¼ cup of cream until smooth and then added the puree back to the rest of the corn in the saucepan, which gave me the perfect texture.

One last detail: Recent experiments in the test kitchen revealed that cooking certain vegetables in salted water can toughen their skins. A side-by-side test showed that cooking the corn in unsalted water and then seasoning later produced noticeably softer kernels. Kick the can, because fresh creamed corn is back.

CREAMED CORN

Serves 4 to 6

This recipe is best made with fresh corn cut from the cob. If making this recipe ahead of time, rewarm it gently over low heat, adjusting the consistency with water as needed.

- 9 ears corn, kernels cut from cobs (6¾ cups)
- 1¼ cups water
- ¼ cup heavy cream
  Salt and pepper

1. Combine corn and water in large saucepan and bring to boil over high heat (bubbles will be noticeable around sides of saucepan). Reduce heat to low, cover, and cook until corn is crisp-tender, about 20 minutes, stirring occasionally.

2. Remove saucepan from heat and transfer 1½ cups corn mixture to blender. Add cream, 1⅛ teaspoons salt, and ¼ teaspoon pepper and process until smooth, about 1 minute. Stir pureed corn mixture into corn mixture in saucepan. Season with salt and pepper to taste. Serve. (If your creamed corn looks thin, return it to low heat and cook gently until thickened slightly, about 3 minutes.)

Getting to Know Fermented Foods

BY CHRISTIE MORRISON

You might be surprised to learn that familiar items like bread, coffee, beer, and chocolate wouldn't exist without fermentation. This ancient, natural process—which relies on the transformative powers of friendly bacteria—not only helps preserve food but also alters its textures, flavors, and aromas.

❶ Miso
UMAMI PASTE

Miso is made by mashing cooked soybeans with salt; grains like rice, barley, or rye; flavorings; and koji, which is rice that has grown a healthy mold that produces a sweet, delicate fragrance. In the United States, you're most likely to find the mild, sweet white *shiromiso* (pictured); intense red *aka*; and pungent, dark-colored *hatcho*. We like the first two to deepen the flavor of salad dressings, glazes, and marinades.

❷ Sauerkraut
REUBEN ESSENTIAL

True sauerkraut is the result of wild fermentation (meaning that it uses lactic acid bacteria already present in and on the vegetable). It is often flavored with either juniper berries or caraway seeds. It's bacteria, though, that lends sauerkraut its trademark flavor. Sauerkraut can be served piled on a Reuben sandwich or used as an ingredient in cooked dishes like our Kielbasa Casserole (**CooksCountry.com/kielbasacasserole**).

❸ Fish Sauce
SIGNATURE SMELL

Fish sauce is called *nuoc nam* in Vietnam and *nam pla* in Thailand, but its pungent, fishy aroma is unmistakable. Made from salted, fermented fish, water, salt, and sometimes sugar, it's a highly concentrated liquid that adds complexity to foods—and when used carefully, no trace of fishiness. And it's not just for Asian dishes: We use it for depth in our Gumbo (**CooksCountry.com/gumbo**). Find it in most supermarkets near the soy sauce.

❹ Yogurt
PERFECTLY CULTURED

This fermented milk product comes from the Turkish word for "condense." Milk is heated and then cooled to just over 100 degrees before a bacteria culture is added. After 4 to 8 hours, the mixture thickens into yogurt. You can use yogurt in sauces, in salad dressings, or as a topping as you would sour cream. Yogurt adds moisture and tangy flavor to our Lemon–Poppy Seed Muffins (**CooksCountry.com/lemonpoppymuffins**).

❺ Kimchi
FUNKY VEGETABLES

While this spicy, crunchy Korean pickle is most commonly made with napa cabbage, it can be made with radish, cucumber—even watermelon rind. The vegetables are chopped and then salted (to pull out moisture) or packed in a liquid brine. Since the vegetables release carbon dioxide as they ferment, kimchi often has an effervescent quality; some versions have chiles for heat.

❻ Sour Pickles
INTENSE PUCKER

Unlike sweet pickles, which are preserved in a vinegar solution, true sour pickles (and half-sours, which use less salt) are the product of fermentation. Herbs and spices like dill, mustard seed, coriander, or garlic add dimension. After as little as a week in solution, the lactic acid bacteria have done their work and the pickles are salty, sour, and crisp.

❼ Chocolate
SECRET STEP

Without fermentation, products made from the cacao plant would taste acrid. After the cacao pods are picked, the beans and pulp inside are scooped out and left to sit outdoors for four to seven days, often in wooden crates. Naturally occurring yeasts grow on the pulp, helping decrease the overall pH level. The pulp is discarded and the beans are dried in the sun before being refined into cocoa.

❽ Kefir
TRANSFORMATIVE GRAINS

Kefir, which is becoming more widely available in supermarkets, is akin to a drinkable yogurt. Kefir cultures are added to milk and left to ferment at room temperature for as little as 24 hours and then refrigerated for a few days. As the milk ferments, it becomes thicker and takes on a tart, sometimes bubbly quality. You can drink kefir straight or blend it with fruits or vegetables for a smoothie.

❾ Soy Sauce
SALTY BREW

Made from soybeans and wheat, salty, pungent soy sauce is left to ferment anywhere from two days to four years, which can explain the widely divergent flavors and quality of different commercial brands. We take advantage of its flavor-boosting qualities to intensify beef stew, meatloaf, and even pot pies. Our favorite is Lee Kum Kee Table Top Premium Soy Sauce.

❿ Preserved Lemons
MELLOW RIND

This savory take on citrus has Middle Eastern origins. Lemons are scored deeply, packed with coarse salt and lemon juice, and left to ferment for six to eight weeks. As the lemons ferment, the rinds soften in texture and mellow in flavor. Once preserved, the rinds (as well as the flesh, if desired) can be chopped to add a tart, salty-sweet note to braises, pan sauces, vinaigrettes, and more.

⓫ Vinegar
WINE GONE BAD

Vinegar is the last stop on grape juice's fermentation adventure. Its initial fermentation turns it into wine, of course, but if left undrunk and exposed to air and room temperature, over time bacteria and yeasts in the wine convert the sugars into acid. To speed things up, manufacturers often use a vinegar "mother," a thick blob of cellulose and acetic acid–forming bacteria.

⓬ Salami
AIR-DRIED

Salting and drying is essential for any cured meat, but salami recipes also typically include a starter culture of lactic acid–producing bacteria that acts as a preservative and lends a signature, faintly sour flavor. The lactic acid feeds on carbohydrates in the mix (often sugar) while the salted meat rests, ferments, and dries in cool storage over several months.

BUCATINI WITH BROCCOLINI, CAPERS, AND LEMON

BEEF AND BEAN BURRITOS

**SEARED SCALLOPS
WITH PICKLED PEPPERS AND COUSCOUS**

**PEPPER-CRUSTED PORK TENDERLOIN WITH
ASPARAGUS AND GOAT CHEESE**

BEEF AND BEAN BURRITOS Serves 4

✓ **WHY THIS RECIPE WORKS:** Combining mashed and whole beans adds textural variety to these burritos.

- ½ cup water
- 1 (15-ounce) can pinto beans, rinsed
- 1 tablespoon vegetable oil
- 1 onion, chopped fine
- 1 tablespoon ground cumin
- 1 teaspoon chipotle chile powder
- 1½ pounds 90 percent lean ground beef
- 1 teaspoon salt
- 4 (10-inch) flour tortillas
- 4 ounces sharp cheddar cheese, shredded (1 cup)
- 2 cups shredded iceberg lettuce

1. Combine water and half of beans in medium bowl and coarsely mash with potato masher. Heat oil in 12-inch nonstick skillet over medium heat until shimmering. Add onion and cook until just beginning to brown, about 5 minutes. Stir in cumin and chile powder and cook until fragrant, about 1 minute. Add beef, breaking up pieces with wooden spoon, and cook until no longer pink, about 10 minutes. Stir mashed bean mixture into meat mixture. Cook, stirring constantly, until nearly all liquid has evaporated, about 3 minutes. Stir in remaining whole beans and salt. Remove from heat, cover, and set aside.

2. Wrap tortillas in clean dish towel and microwave until soft and pliable, about 1 minute. Arrange tortillas on counter. Divide beef-and-bean filling, cheddar, and lettuce evenly among tortillas. Fold sides of tortillas over filling, fold bottoms of tortillas over sides and filling, and roll tightly. Slice in half on bias and serve.

TEST KITCHEN NOTE: Serve with sour cream, hot sauce, and lime.

BUCATINI WITH BROCCOLINI, CAPERS, AND LEMON Serves 4

✓ **WHY THIS RECIPE WORKS:** We sauté the broccolini with garlic, salt, and pepper until just tender to ensure that it doesn't overcook when added to the pasta.

- 1 pound bucatini
  Salt and pepper
- 2 tablespoons extra-virgin olive oil, plus extra for drizzling
- 12 ounces broccolini, trimmed and cut into 2-inch pieces
- 4 garlic cloves, sliced thin
- 2 cups chicken broth
- ½ cup dry white wine
- 2 ounces Pecorino Romano cheese, grated (1 cup), plus extra for serving
- ½ cup capers, rinsed and minced
- 1 tablespoon lemon juice

1. Bring 4 quarts water to boil in large pot. Add pasta and 1 tablespoon salt and cook, stirring often, until al dente. Reserve ½ cup cooking water, then drain pasta and return to pot.

2. Meanwhile, heat oil in 12-inch skillet over medium-high heat until shimmering. Add broccolini, garlic, ½ teaspoon salt, and ½ teaspoon pepper and cook until broccolini is just tender, about 4 minutes. Transfer broccolini mixture to plate; set aside.

3. Add broth and wine to now-empty skillet and bring to simmer. Cook until sauce is reduced to 2 cups, about 7 minutes. Add sauce to pasta and toss to combine, adjusting consistency with reserved cooking water as needed. Stir in Pecorino, capers, lemon juice, and broccolini mixture and season with salt and pepper to taste. Drizzle with extra oil. Serve with extra Pecorino.

TEST KITCHEN NOTE: You can use other long pastas, such as spaghetti or linguine, in this recipe.

PEPPER-CRUSTED PORK TENDERLOIN WITH ASPARAGUS AND GOAT CHEESE Serves 4

✓ **WHY THIS RECIPE WORKS:** To build layers of flavor, we cook the asparagus in the flavorful pan drippings the tenderloins leave behind.

- 1 tablespoon minced fresh rosemary
  Salt and coarsely ground pepper
- 2 (12-ounce) pork tenderloins, trimmed
- 2 tablespoons extra-virgin olive oil
- 2 pounds asparagus, trimmed and cut on bias into 2-inch lengths
- ¼ cup chicken broth
- 2 ounces goat cheese, crumbled (½ cup)
- ¼ cup balsamic vinegar
- 2 tablespoons unsalted butter

1. Adjust oven rack to middle position and heat oven to 450 degrees. Set wire rack in rimmed baking sheet. Combine rosemary, 1 tablespoon pepper, and 1 teaspoon salt in bowl. Pat pork dry with paper towels and sprinkle with spice mixture.

2. Heat 1 tablespoon oil in 12-inch skillet over medium-high heat until just smoking. Cook pork until browned on all sides, 5 to 7 minutes. Transfer pork to prepared wire rack and roast until 140 degrees, about 15 minutes. Transfer to carving board, tent with foil, and let rest for 5 minutes.

3. Heat remaining 1 tablespoon oil in now-empty skillet over medium-high heat until shimmering. Add asparagus, broth, ¼ teaspoon salt, and ¼ teaspoon pepper and cook, covered, until tender, about 5 minutes; transfer asparagus to platter and top with goat cheese. Reduce heat to medium-low, add vinegar to now-empty skillet, and simmer until thickened, scraping up any browned bits, about 1 minute. Off heat, whisk in butter. Slice pork, arrange on platter with asparagus, and drizzle with sauce. Serve.

SEARED SCALLOPS WITH PICKLED PEPPERS AND COUSCOUS Serves 4

✓ **WHY THIS RECIPE WORKS:** Searing the scallops for just 3 minutes enhances their flavor without overcooking them.

- ½ cup finely chopped pepperoncini plus 2 tablespoons brine
- ½ cup extra-virgin olive oil
- 4 scallions, sliced thin
- 1 teaspoon grated orange zest plus 2 tablespoons juice
  Salt and pepper
- 1 tablespoon unsalted butter
- 1 cup couscous
- 1 cup water
- 2 tomatoes, cored and cut into ¼-inch pieces
- ½ cup chopped fresh parsley
- 1½ pounds large sea scallops, tendons removed

1. Combine pepperoncini and brine, 2 tablespoons oil, scallions, orange zest and juice, and ¼ teaspoon pepper in bowl; set aside. Melt butter in medium saucepan over medium-high heat. Add couscous and cook, stirring frequently, until grains are just beginning to brown, about 4 minutes. Add water, ¾ teaspoon salt, and ½ teaspoon pepper; stir to combine, cover, and remove pan from heat. Let stand until tender, about 7 minutes. Uncover, add tomatoes, parsley, and ¼ cup oil and fluff with fork.

2. Meanwhile, pat scallops dry with paper towels and season with salt and pepper. Heat 1 tablespoon oil in 12-inch nonstick skillet over medium-high heat until just smoking. Add half of scallops in single layer and cook without moving them until well browned, about 1½ minutes. Flip scallops and cook without moving them until second side is well browned, about 1½ minutes longer. Transfer scallops to plate and tent loosely with foil. Repeat with remaining 1 tablespoon oil and remaining scallops. Arrange scallops over couscous and top with pepperoncini mixture. Serve.

**PORK CHOPS WITH SAUTÉED ZUCCHINI
AND MUSTARD BUTTER**

APRICOT-BASIL CHICKEN SALAD

FLANK STEAK WITH RED CURRY POTATOES

**PAN-SEARED CHICKEN BREASTS
WITH MARINATED TOMATOES**

APRICOT-BASIL CHICKEN SALAD Serves 4

✓ **WHY THIS RECIPE WORKS:** For a fresh take on chicken salad, we added apricots and basil. Lemon juice and Dijon mustard provide brightness and complexity.

- ¾ cup mayonnaise
- ½ cup dried apricots, chopped fine
- ¼ cup chopped fresh basil
- 2 tablespoons minced shallot
- 2 tablespoons lemon juice
- 1 teaspoon Dijon mustard
  Salt and pepper
- 1 (2½-pound) rotisserie chicken, skin and bones discarded, meat shredded into bite-size pieces (3 cups)
- 2 heads Bibb lettuce (1 pound), leaves torn into bite-size pieces
  Extra-virgin olive oil

1. Combine mayonnaise, apricots, basil, shallot, lemon juice, mustard, ½ teaspoon salt, and ½ teaspoon pepper in large bowl. Stir in chicken until fully combined. Season with salt and pepper to taste.

2. Evenly distribute lettuce among 4 plates. Drizzle lettuce with oil and season with salt and pepper. Place heaping ½ cup chicken salad on each plate of lettuce. Serve.

TEST KITCHEN NOTE: If you can't find Bibb lettuce, substitute red or green leaf lettuce.

PORK CHOPS WITH SAUTÉED ZUCCHINI AND MUSTARD BUTTER Serves 4

✓ **WHY THIS RECIPE WORKS:** A flavorful compound butter of chives, whole-grain mustard, and lemon juice melts quickly on the hot pork chops.

- 4 tablespoons unsalted butter, softened
- 2 tablespoons minced fresh chives
- 1 tablespoon whole-grain mustard
- 1 teaspoon lemon juice
- ⅛ teaspoon cayenne pepper
  Salt and pepper
- 4 (8- to 10-ounce) bone-in pork rib chops, ½ inch thick, trimmed
- 1 tablespoon vegetable oil
- 1½ pounds zucchini, trimmed and sliced ¼ inch thick

1. Combine butter, chives, mustard, lemon juice, cayenne, and ⅛ teaspoon salt in small bowl; set aside.

2. Pat pork dry with paper towels and season with salt and pepper. Heat oil in 12-inch skillet over medium-high heat until just smoking. Add pork and cook until well browned and cooked through, about 4 minutes per side; transfer to plate and tent with foil.

3. Add zucchini, ½ teaspoon salt, and ½ teaspoon pepper to now-empty skillet and cook, stirring occasionally, over medium-high heat until tender, 5 to 7 minutes. Transfer zucchini to large platter and top with pork chops. Dollop mustard butter over pork. Serve.

TEST KITCHEN NOTE: To make sure they cook at the same rate, look for rib chops of similar thickness.

PAN-SEARED CHICKEN BREASTS WITH MARINATED TOMATOES Serves 4

✓ **WHY THIS RECIPE WORKS:** Letting the tomatoes and fennel sit with salt for 15 minutes not only seasons the vegetables but also helps extract any unwanted moisture.

- 4 tomatoes, cored and cut into ½-inch-thick wedges
- ½ fennel bulb, stalks discarded, cored and sliced thin
  Salt and pepper
- 4 (6- to 8-ounce) boneless, skinless chicken breasts, trimmed
- ¼ cup extra-virgin olive oil
- 2 ounces feta cheese, crumbled (½ cup)
- ¼ cup chopped fresh parsley
- 1 shallot, halved and sliced thin
- 2 tablespoons white wine vinegar
- 1 garlic clove, minced

1. Toss tomatoes, fennel, and ½ teaspoon salt in bowl, then place in colander in sink and let sit for 15 minutes.

2. Meanwhile, pat chicken dry with paper towels and season with salt and pepper. Heat 2 tablespoons oil in 12-inch nonstick skillet over medium-high heat until just smoking. Cook chicken until golden brown and meat registers 160 degrees, about 6 minutes per side. Transfer chicken to plate, tent with foil, and let rest for 5 minutes.

3. Transfer drained tomatoes and fennel to large bowl and toss with feta, parsley, shallot, vinegar, garlic, remaining 2 tablespoons oil, ¼ teaspoon salt, and ¼ teaspoon pepper. Transfer tomato mixture to platter and top with chicken. Serve.

TEST KITCHEN NOTE: Serve with rice or crusty bread.

FLANK STEAK WITH RED CURRY POTATOES Serves 4

✓ **WHY THIS RECIPE WORKS:** We make a potent curry sauce using only a few pantry items—all in just 3½ minutes.

- 1½ pounds small Yukon Gold potatoes, unpeeled, quartered
- 3 tablespoons vegetable oil
- 1 (1½-pound) flank steak, trimmed and halved lengthwise
  Salt and pepper
- ¼ cup red curry paste
- 1 tablespoon grated fresh ginger
- 2 garlic cloves, minced
- 1 cup canned coconut milk
- 2 teaspoons fish sauce
- 2 tablespoons fresh cilantro leaves

1. Combine potatoes and 2 tablespoons oil in large bowl. Cover and microwave until potatoes are nearly tender, about 7 minutes; set aside.

2. Pat steak dry with paper towels and season with salt and pepper. Heat remaining 1 tablespoon oil in 12-inch nonstick skillet over medium-high heat until just smoking. Cook steak until well browned and meat registers 125 degrees (for medium-rare), 5 to 7 minutes per side. Transfer to carving board, tent with foil, and let rest for 5 minutes. Wipe out skillet with paper towels.

3. Add curry paste, ginger, and garlic to now-empty skillet and cook over medium-high heat until fragrant, about 30 seconds. Stir in coconut milk, fish sauce, and parcooked potatoes, and bring to simmer. Cook until potatoes are tender, about 3 minutes. Slice steak thin on bias against grain. Serve with curried potatoes and sprinkle with cilantro.

TEST KITCHEN NOTE: Use Yukon Gold potatoes measuring 1 to 2 inches in diameter.

Mixed Berry Scones

What does an antique store in rural western Massachusetts have to offer the test kitchen? Inspiration for big, bold, berry-filled scones. BY MORGAN BOLLING

A COOK'S INSPIRATION CAN strike in unlikely spots. Case in point: Freight House Antiques in Erving, Massachusetts, where our executive food editor Bryan Roof stopped a few months back. Turns out that the place has an attached coffee shop, where each day proprietor Rita Dubay sets out a display of pies, muffins, and more baked goods—including massive, sweet, crumbly mixed berry scones that Roof loved so much he raced back to the test kitchen determined that we should create a version ourselves.

We have company recipes for scones that vary from traditional, dense English scones to cakey, sweet American styles. I baked and sampled my way through several American-style recipes trying to imitate Dubay's scones, to no avail. So I headed out to Freight House myself to learn her tricks. But like many great cooks, while she gave us some clues, Dubay's recipe would remain a secret.

Determined nonetheless, I returned to the test kitchen and started grating frozen butter into flour, sugar, salt, and baking powder—several recipes agreed that this technique helps produce a flaky scone—and then mixed in milk, eggs, and frozen berries before shaping the dough into scones and baking them off.

The frozen berries were causing me issues right off the bat, bleeding into my batter and leaving me with blue-marbled scones. Plus, the berry flavor was more tart than sweet. I found that tossing the frozen berries with confectioners' sugar before mixing them into the other dry ingredients controlled the bleed and beat back the tartness.

I still had some issues, though. The grated butter left nice buttery pockets in my scones, but grating frozen sticks of butter was a pain. I wondered if I could get the same effect with the food processor. I pulsed the chilled butter into the dry ingredients, leaving pea-size chunks, but when I baked this batch, the butter pieces didn't fully incorporate into the dough and leached out onto the baking sheet. I tried processing in the butter until it was fully incorporated, but these scones lacked richness.

Another cook in the kitchen suggested combining the two methods, processing in half the butter until fully incorporated and then pulsing in the second half for larger chunks. Now I had rich scones packed with biscuit-like butter pockets. A brushing of honey butter on top of the scones before the final 5 to 8 minutes of baking gave them a nice sheen and sweet finish.

With a few adjustments (see "To Make Ahead") I found that I could freeze the unbaked scones without sacrificing flavor or texture. I could make a batch of dough on Sunday, freeze the shaped scones, and bake them off one at a time throughout the week.

MIXED BERRY SCONES Makes 8 scones

Work the dough as little as possible, just until it comes together. Work quickly to keep the butter and berries as cold as possible for the best results. Note that the butter is divided in this recipe. An equal amount of frozen blueberries, raspberries, blackberries, or strawberries (halved) can be used in place of the mixed berries.

SCONES

- 1¾ cups (8¾ ounces) frozen mixed berries
- 3 tablespoons confectioners' sugar
- 3 cups (15 ounces) all-purpose flour
- 12 tablespoons unsalted butter, cut into ½-inch pieces, chilled
- ⅓ cup (2⅓ ounces) granulated sugar
- 1 tablespoon baking powder
- 1¼ teaspoons salt
- ¾ cup plus 2 tablespoons whole milk
- 1 large egg plus 1 large yolk

GLAZE

- 2 tablespoons unsalted butter, melted
- 1 tablespoon honey

For convenience, these scones are engineered to work with frozen berries.

1. FOR THE SCONES: Adjust oven rack to upper-middle position and heat oven to 425 degrees. Line rimmed baking sheet with parchment paper. If your berry mix contains strawberries, cut them in half. Toss berries with confectioners' sugar in bowl; freeze until needed.

2. Combine flour, 6 tablespoons butter, granulated sugar, baking powder, and salt in food processor and process until butter is fully incorporated, about 15 seconds. Add remaining 6 tablespoons butter and pulse until butter is reduced to pea-size pieces, 10 to 12 pulses. Transfer mixture to large bowl. Stir in berries.

3. Beat milk and egg and yolk together in separate bowl. Make well in center of flour mixture and pour in milk mixture. Using rubber spatula, gently stir mixture, scraping from edges of bowl and folding inward until very shaggy dough forms and some bits of flour remain. Do not overmix.

4. Turn out dough onto well-floured counter and, if necessary, knead briefly until dough just comes together, about 3 turns. Using your floured hands and bench scraper, shape dough into 12 by 4-inch rectangle, about 1½ inches tall. Using knife or bench scraper, cut dough crosswise into 4 equal rectangles. Cut each rectangle diagonally into 2 triangles (you should have 8 scones total). Transfer scones to prepared sheet. Bake until scones are lightly golden on top, 16 to 18 minutes, rotating pan halfway through baking.

5. FOR THE GLAZE: While scones bake, combine melted butter and honey in small bowl.

6. Remove scones from oven and brush tops evenly with glaze mixture. Return scones to oven and continue to bake until golden brown on top, 5 to 8 minutes longer. Transfer scones to wire rack and let cool for at least 10 minutes before serving.

TO MAKE AHEAD

Unbaked scones can be frozen for several weeks. After cutting scones into triangles in step 4, freeze them on baking sheet. Transfer frozen scones to zipper-lock freezer bag. When ready to bake, heat oven to 375 degrees and extend cooking time in step 4 to 23 to 26 minutes. Glaze time in step 6 will remain at 5 to 8 minutes.

Four-at-a-Time Quesadillas

You can fit only one or two quesadillas in a skillet at once. We wanted to find a way to make four tasty quesadillas with perfectly melted cheese in one go. BY MORGAN BOLLING

YOU MAY BE asking yourself, "Do I really need a recipe for tortillas stuffed with cheese?" Answer: Yes, especially if you're making quesadillas for a small crowd of four to six hungry diners.

Traditionally, quesadillas are cooked on a metal *comal*, a type of Mexican griddle. Because of the direct contact with the hot surface (and a coating of butter, oil, or lard), quesadillas cooked on a comal crisp beautifully around the edges, staying just supple enough to eat. Most home cooks today use a skillet, but who has a skillet big enough to fit four quesadillas? Not I. So I turned my attention to the oven.

I found several recipes for oven-baked quesadillas but was disheartened to learn that the dry heat of a 350-degree oven (the temperature most recipes called for) made for dry, pale, and all-around inferior quesadillas. Cranking the heat to 450 degrees and flipping the quesadillas—stuffed with nothing more than shredded Monterey Jack cheese for now—halfway through cooking gave me nice, even, flavorful browning.

But the tortillas were still dry. One of the best stovetop recipes I found called for shallow-frying the quesadillas in a hefty dose of oil. Could I get the same effect by using more fat in the oven? After testing various types and amounts of fats, I found that coating the rimmed baking sheet with 3 tablespoons of vegetable oil worked wonders for creating a crisp—but not dry—exterior. Now I could focus on the fillings.

In Mexico the most common option is Oaxaca ("wa-HA-ka") cheese, named after the central Mexican state it comes from. The salty, buttery cheese melts beautifully but can be hard to find in the States. I ordered a pound of it from a specialty shop and tested it against six widely available varieties: the Monterey Jack I had been using, along with various

The hardest part of this recipe is letting the quesadillas cool for 5 minutes before you dig in.

cheddars, American, mozzarella, and provolone. After much munching, we decided a combination of provolone and mozzarella was the best approximation for Oaxaca cheese. Provolone gave a nutty richness, while creamy mozzarella melted perfectly. Some minced jarred

jalapeños gave the filling a little spark.

These cheese tests showed me that a full cup of shredded cheese was the best amount for each 10-inch flour tortilla. But by the time the tortillas were browned, the cheese was bubbling out onto my baking sheet. I tried adding a little cornstarch to the shredded cheese to slow its melting. This helped but made the cheese chalky. When a colleague saw that I was pulling the sheet out of the oven to flip the tortillas at the halfway point, she suggested that I try adding the cheese at the flip stage rather than at the beginning. I browned four folded tortillas on one side; then after flipping them, I filled each with cheese. With this new method the cheese was in the oven for only the final 4 to 6

minutes of baking—the ideal amount of time to melt without leaking out.

It's not a hard or time-consuming process, but yes, the best quesadillas do require a little technique—and a recipe. This recipe.

QUESADILLAS FOR A CROWD
Serves 4 to 6
Letting the quesadillas cool before cutting them is important; straight from the oven the cheese is molten and will ooze out. Serve the quesadillas with pico de gallo, guacamole, and/or sour cream.

- 3 tablespoons vegetable oil
- 8 ounces provolone cheese, shredded (2 cups)
- 8 ounces whole-milk mozzarella cheese, shredded (2 cups)
- ¼ cup minced jarred jalapeños
- 4 (10-inch) flour tortillas

1. Adjust oven rack to middle position and heat oven to 450 degrees. Brush rimmed baking sheet with oil.

2. Combine provolone, mozzarella, and jalapeños in bowl. Fold tortillas in half. Arrange folded tortillas in single layer on prepared sheet with rounded edges facing center of sheet.

3. Bake until tortilla tops and edges begin to turn spotty brown, 5 to 7 minutes. Remove sheet from oven. Flip tortillas over. Using tongs, open each tortilla and fill each with equal amount cheese mixture (about 1 cup each), leaving 1-inch border. Close tortillas and press firmly with spatula to compact.

4. Return quesadillas to oven and continue to bake until crisp around edges and golden brown on second side, 4 to 6 minutes longer. Remove from oven and press quesadillas gently with spatula to deflate any air bubbles. Transfer to wire rack and let cool for 5 minutes. Slice each quesadilla into 4 wedges and serve.

CHORIZO QUESADILLAS FOR A CROWD
Cook 4 ounces chorizo sausage, cut into ¼-inch pieces, in 10-inch skillet over medium heat until lightly browned, 5 to 7 minutes. Let cool completely, then add to cheese mixture.

CILANTRO AND SCALLION QUESADILLAS FOR A CROWD
Add ¼ cup minced fresh cilantro and 2 thinly sliced scallions to cheese mixture.

TEST KITCHEN DISCOVERY
Wait on the Cheese
To prevent the cheese from liquefying and running onto the baking sheet, we add it only after the first side of each quesadilla has been browned. This arrangement on the baking sheet isn't random: It's the best way to fit four large quesadillas at once.

Stuffed Chicken Breasts

For stuffed chicken breasts worth the bother, you need to start with the right cut. BY REBECCAH MARSTERS

THE APPEAL OF stuffed chicken breasts is clear: The impressive presentation elevates a weeknight dish, and the filling adds flavor to bland breasts. But too many versions don't deliver on the flavor part. I set out to change that.

Some initial research revealed potential potholes. Vegetable fillings I tested tasted grassy and steamed, bread stuffings gummy and bland, oozy cheese-based fillings lackluster, as most cheeses that melt well are mild in flavor.

Two points of promise: Bone-in breasts, I found, delivered much more flavor when roasted, and salty, high-impact fillings like salami and Parmesan packed the most punch. What's more, the best way to get browned skin was with a pre-oven sear in a skillet.

▶ Visit **CooksCountry. com/sept15** for a spicy feta variation of these stuffed chicken breasts.

After a few tests, my tasters and I landed on a combination of salami, Parmesan, and capers, enlivened with herbal notes from fresh rosemary and thyme. A little sautéed onion brought depth, and some Dijon mustard, garlic, and lemon zest rounded out the filling.

To seal the deal, I wanted a sauce. When making my next batch of stuffing mixture, I set aside some garlic, mustard, chopped herbs, and extra-virgin olive oil and mashed it together to create a flavorful paste.

Once the chicken was cooked, I moved it to a carving board and stirred the reserved herb paste into the drippings in the pan along with a tablespoon of lemon juice. I took the breasts off the bone, sliced them into rounds, and drizzled my pan sauce over the top.

HERB-AND-PARMESAN-STUFFED CHICKEN BREASTS Serves 4
High-quality Parmesan makes a difference here.

- 4 **(12-ounce) bone-in, skin-on split chicken breasts, trimmed**
  Salt and pepper
- ¼ **cup extra-virgin olive oil**
- ½ **cup finely chopped onion**
- 2 **teaspoons grated lemon zest plus 1 tablespoon juice**
- 2 **garlic cloves, minced**
- 2 **teaspoons minced fresh thyme**
- 2 **teaspoons Dijon mustard**
- 1 **teaspoon minced fresh rosemary**
- 2 **ounces sliced Genoa salami, chopped fine**
- 2 **ounces Parmesan cheese, grated (1 cup)**
- 2 **tablespoons capers, chopped**
- ½ **cup chicken broth**

1. Adjust oven rack to middle position and heat oven to 400 degrees. Using kitchen shears, remove any rib bones that extend beyond each breast. Working with 1 breast at a time, place skin side down on counter with breastbone side facing your knife hand. Press on breast with your opposite hand to flatten slightly and, using sharp paring knife, cut 3-inch-long horizontal pocket in breastbone side of breast, stopping ½ inch from rib side so halves remain attached. Using your fingers and tip of knife, make interior of pocket wider without increasing 3-inch opening. Season breasts inside and out with salt and pepper; set aside.

2. Heat 1 tablespoon oil in 12-inch ovensafe nonstick skillet over medium heat until shimmering. Add onion and ⅛ teaspoon salt and cook until softened and browned around edges, 4 to 6 minutes. Remove from heat and set aside to cool slightly, about 5 minutes.

3. Combine lemon zest, garlic, thyme, mustard, rosemary, and 2 tablespoons oil in bowl; set aside 2 teaspoons oil mixture for sauce. Stir salami, Parmesan, capers, onion, 1 teaspoon pepper, and ¼ teaspoon salt into remaining oil mixture, mashing against side of bowl with back of spoon until stuffing mixture clumps together.

4. Place about 3 tablespoons stuffing mixture into pocket of each breast, pressing into ends of pockets with your fingers to fill completely and evenly. Fold breast over to enclose. Secure each breast with 3 evenly spaced pieces of kitchen twine. Wipe skillet clean with paper towels.

5. Heat remaining 1 tablespoon oil in now-empty skillet over medium-high heat until just smoking. Cook breasts skin side down until well browned, about 7 minutes, moving as needed for evenly browned skin.

6. Flip breasts skin side up, add broth to skillet, and transfer to oven. Roast until thickest part of stuffing registers 160 degrees, 30 to 37 minutes. Transfer breasts to carving board, tent with aluminum foil, and let rest for 15 minutes.

7. Meanwhile, pour pan juices into liquid measuring cup (skillet handle will be hot) and skim off fat. Stir in lemon juice and reserved oil mixture; season with salt and pepper to taste. Remove twine, then carve breasts from bones. Slice ½ inch thick, transfer to serving platter, and drizzle with sauce. Serve.

TEST KITCHEN TECHNIQUE
Cutting Pockets in Chicken Breasts

Place breast skin side down on a cutting board with the breastbone side facing your knife hand. Press on the breast with your opposite hand to flatten it slightly, and use a sharp paring knife to cut a 3-inch-long horizontal pocket in the breastbone side of the breast, stopping ½ inch from the rib side so the halves remain attached. Then use your fingers and the tip of the knife to make the pocket wider without increasing the 3-inch opening.

You can serve the chicken on the bone, but we prefer to remove the bones and slice the breasts before serving.

Old-Fashioned Frozen Custard

You won't need to dust off your ice cream maker for our version of this rich, supremely creamy frozen treat. BY CHRISTIE MORRISON

FROZEN CUSTARD ISN'T just a fancy name for ice cream; it's actually a lovely frozen treat in its own right—as refreshing on a hot summer afternoon as it is soothing on a cool autumn evening. The popular regional sweet treat (Wisconsin, New York, and Arkansas all claim versions as their own) takes its name from a custard base that includes egg yolks and heavy cream for a luxurious texture.

Commercial frozen custard—the thick, soft serve–like treat made famous by the Kohr Brothers in Coney Island and Kopp's in Milwaukee—requires an industrial condenser to produce its almost taffy-like consistency. But through research, I found recipes for frozen custard in cookbooks written as far back as the late 19th century, long before ice cream makers. I decided to pursue this old-fashioned technique.

Taking a cue from several of these old recipes, I started my testing with a custard: specifically, crème anglaise, a classic French cooked custard of cream, milk, sugar, egg yolks, and vanilla. After the mixture reached 180 degrees, I transferred it to a bowl set inside a bigger bowl of ice to quickly cool. Then I followed an approach common to early ice cream recipes and poured the mixture into a baking dish for freezing (the extra surface area this vessel creates helps it freeze quickly). The flavor was excellent. But the texture? Riddled with ice crystals.

The key to supersmooth frozen custard is limiting the buildup of ice crystals as it freezes. How do you do this? Incorporating and churning air reduces the effect of ice crystals—the enemy of smooth ice cream or frozen custard—on the tongue. Machines add this air, and break down the ice crystals, by constantly churning the mixture as it freezes. Most machine-free recipes mimic this action by asking the cook to stir or whisk the mixture periodically during freezing. But I wanted a mostly hands-off approach. What would happen, I wondered, if I incorporated air into the mixture before I froze it? I whipped my custard in a stand mixer, testing varying lengths of whipping time, and achieved a relatively smooth custard after about 3 minutes.

But I wanted better than "relatively" smooth. I wanted perfect. I experimented with different amounts and combinations of dairy ingredients, including heavy cream, half-and-half, whole milk, sweetened condensed milk, and evaporated milk. I found that a combination of heavy cream and whole milk was best. (A little nonfat dry milk powder enhanced the dairy flavor.)

Sugar plays a dual role in frozen custard: as a sweetener and as further insurance against ice crystals. So does corn syrup, but because it's only 40 percent as sweet as white sugar, corn syrup does the job without adding unneeded sweetness. After whipping in plenty of air and freezing the custard, I found its texture silky and creamy.

With a freezer full of baking dishes, I was delighted to find that the custard froze just perfectly in a quart-size plastic container.

Our smooth, creamy frozen custard is made with a stand mixer, not an ice cream maker.

Steps to Smooth Frozen Custard

1. TEMPER
Heating the cream mixture before slowly adding it to the cold yolk mixture prevents the eggs from curdling.

2. STRAIN
Pouring the warm custard through a strainer removes any pieces of cooked egg.

3. CHILL
Cooling the custard on ice primes it for adding air.

4. WHIP
Finally, whipping the cooled custard adds air to make the final texture especially creamy.

Frozen Custard vs. Ice Cream: Cracking Open the Difference

According to guidelines administered by the U.S. Food and Drug Administration, both ice cream and frozen custard must contain at least 10 percent milk fat (along with milk, cream, sweeteners, flavorings, and so forth). The main difference between them is eggs: While egg yolks are optional in ice cream bases (and occasionally do appear on ingredient lists), they are absolutely required in frozen custard. Frozen custards must contain at least 1.4 percent yolks by weight. The resulting frozen treat is eggier and richer than ice cream.

OLD-FASHIONED VANILLA FROZEN CUSTARD

Makes about 1 quart

One teaspoon of vanilla extract can be substituted for the vanilla bean; stir the extract into the strained custard in step 3. Use an instant-read thermometer for the best results.

- **6** large egg yolks
- **¼** cup (1¾ ounces) sugar
- **2** tablespoons nonfat dry milk powder
- **1** cup heavy cream
- **½** cup whole milk
- **⅓** cup light corn syrup
- **⅛** teaspoon salt
- **1** vanilla bean

1. Whisk egg yolks, sugar, and milk powder in bowl until smooth, about 30 seconds; set aside. Combine cream, milk, corn syrup, and salt in medium saucepan. Cut vanilla bean in half lengthwise. Using tip of paring knife, scrape out vanilla seeds and add to cream mixture, along with vanilla bean. Heat cream mixture over medium-high heat, stirring occasionally, until it steams steadily and registers 175 degrees, about 5 minutes. Remove saucepan from heat.

2. Slowly whisk heated cream mixture into yolk mixture to temper. Return cream-yolk mixture to saucepan and cook over medium-low heat, stirring constantly, until mixture thickens and registers 180 degrees, 4 to 6 minutes.

3. Immediately pour custard through fine-mesh strainer set over large bowl; discard vanilla bean. Fill slightly larger bowl with ice and set custard bowl in bowl of ice. Transfer to refrigerator and let chill until custard registers 40 degrees, 1 to 2 hours, stirring occasionally.

4. Transfer chilled custard to stand mixer fitted with whisk and whip on medium-high speed for 3 minutes, or until mixture increases in volume to about 3¾ cups. Pour custard into airtight 1-quart container. Cover and freeze until firm, at least 6 hours, before serving. (Frozen custard is best eaten within 10 days.)

OLD-FASHIONED CHOCOLATE FROZEN CUSTARD

Use 60 percent cacao bittersweet chocolate.

Omit vanilla bean. Add ½ ounce finely chopped bittersweet chocolate and 1 tablespoon Dutch-processed cocoa to cream mixture in step 1 before cooking. Add ½ teaspoon vanilla extract to strained custard in step 3.

Sweet Glazed Peaches

True, it might seem impossible to improve on a perfect peach. But we didn't let that stop us from trying. BY DIANE UNGER

HOW DO YOU eat your way through an overabundance of ripe, in-season peaches? Some folks grill them for a side dish; others chop them into a fruit salad. I wanted something different: A warm, summery dessert with just enough added sweetness to amplify the peaches' complex, soothing flavors.

I found dozens of recipes for glazed peaches, and after a few days in the kitchen, I'd learned that most cover up fruit with cloyingly sweet syrup. What's more, some peaches turned to mush in the oven. None had the light-handed sweetness or velvety texture I wanted.

I gathered another pile of peaches and hit the kitchen. I peeled several peaches (a serrated vegetable peeler made this a breeze), halved and pitted them, tossed the halves with sugar,

Visit **CooksCountry. com/sept15** for our Honey-Glazed Peaches and Raspberry-Glazed Peaches.

and baked them at 300 degrees for 40 minutes, thinking that the low temperature would gently caramelize the sugar into a sticky-sweet glaze.

Wrong. By the time the peaches took on any color, there was nothing but mush in the dish. And the sugar had turned bitter during its long stay in the dry heat. I needed a complete rethink.

For my next round, I tossed the peaches with sugar and a little lemon juice for balance and tried a 450-degree oven. The peaches held their shapes, but by the time they were warm all the way through, the sugar had burned. I switched to broiling, thinking that the direct heat might give me a little color on top before the peaches overcooked. Adding a bit of water to the pan helped prevent sticking.

I was right. The three small adjustments gave me the soft-but-firm texture I wanted after about 18 minutes in the oven. To boost the flavor, I took the next batch of peaches out after about 11 minutes and brushed them with a mixture of melted butter and red currant jelly before returning them to the broiler. Five more minutes was all it took to get a beautiful, lightly browned batch of peaches with a sticky glaze. A bit more glaze drizzled over, plus a few nuts for texture, and I had a simple, sweet summertime dessert.

Toasted, chopped pistachios add a burst of color and a nice crunch to the silky peaches.

SWEET GLAZED PEACHES Serves 6

Use a serrated peeler to peel the peaches. These peaches are best served warm with vanilla ice cream or frozen custard.

- **2** tablespoons lemon juice
- **1** tablespoon sugar
- **¼** teaspoon salt
- **6** firm, ripe peaches, peeled, halved, and pitted
- **⅓** cup water
- **¼** cup red currant jelly
- **1** tablespoon unsalted butter
- **¼** cup pistachios, toasted and chopped

1. Adjust oven rack 6 inches from broiler element and heat broiler. Combine lemon juice, sugar, and salt in large bowl. Add peaches and toss to combine, making sure to coat all sides with sugar mixture.

2. Transfer peaches, cut side up, to 12-inch ovensafe skillet. Pour any remaining sugar mixture into peach cavities. Pour water around peaches in skillet. Broil until peaches are just beginning to brown, 11 to 15 minutes.

3. Combine jelly and butter in bowl and microwave until melted, about 30 seconds, then stir to combine. Remove peaches from oven and brush half of jelly mixture over peaches. Return peaches to oven and continue to broil until spotty brown, 5 to 7 minutes.

4. Remove skillet from oven, brush peaches with remaining jelly mixture, and transfer peaches to serving platter, leaving juices behind. Bring accumulated juices in skillet to simmer over medium heat and cook until syrupy, about 1 minute. Pour syrup over peaches. Sprinkle with pistachios and serve.

Honey Cake

This holiday cake often tastes mostly of spices or fruit.
Shouldn't honey cake taste like honey? BY MORGAN BOLLING

HONEY CAKE, BESIDES being a sweet treat as good for breakfast as it is for dessert, is a staple at dinners celebrating Rosh Hashanah, the Jewish New Year, as a symbol of a sweet new year. As I found in my research, traditions and recipes for this yearly treat vary from family to family—and cooks have very strong opinions about what makes a good one (or a bad one).

To learn more about this cake firsthand, I headed into our cookbook library, found six promising recipes, and baked samples. The cakes smelled great coming out of the test kitchen ovens, so as soon as they were cool, I eagerly grabbed a slice of each.

My enthusiasm quickly dwindled. These cakes were not pleasant to eat, as they were by turns greasy, gummy, or dry. The biggest problem, though, was that even the ones with passable textures had dominant flavors of warm spices, citrus, or liquor—everything but honey. They all had honey in them, all right, but we just couldn't taste it.

I decided to hit the reset button and start from scratch with a simple *Cook's Country* Bundt cake (though honey cakes come in all shapes and sizes from loaves to sheets, Bundt cakes are big and festive, perfect for the holidays). For my first test, I replaced half the sugar with honey and, to make the cake compatible with kosher dietary laws, used vegetable oil instead of butter (most honey cake recipes do the same). A straight swap of oil for butter didn't work, though, as it made for exactly the kind of greasy cake we rejected in the initial testing.

I tried reducing the oil in various amounts, but my tasters were never satisfied with the results: Cakes were still either too greasy, gummy, or dry, with no apparent sweet spot. Trying to brainstorm other ingredients that could add moisture, I considered applesauce. Could this trick, usually reserved for "healthier" desserts, work here?

After trying various amounts in combination with a bit of oil, I landed on 6 tablespoons of applesauce and 4 tablespoons of vegetable oil. The applesauce lent moisture and a subtle, fruity background sweetness but, I was happy to discover, didn't make the cake taste like apples at all. This combination, along with both baking soda and baking

While honey is the dominant flavor in the cake, the batter also contains orange juice and applesauce.

powder, gave me a tender, tall cake with plenty of moisture.

On to the honey. All the recipes I tried early on called for at least some sugar in addition to the honey, but I was determined to use honey as the cake's sole source of sweetness. I baked through a slew of sticky tests where I slowly subbed out the sugar for honey ¼ cup at a time. I was pleased that the cake that traded all the sugar for honey

turned out to be our favorite—it had a strong honey flavor.

But as is often the case in cooking (and particularly in baking), solving one problem created another. Honey is sweeter than sugar and browns more quickly, so now the cake was turning too brown, too quickly, in the oven. After several tests at various temperatures, I found that backing down just slightly from my 350-degree baking

temperature, to 325 degrees, evened out the cooking for the best well-browned but moist cake.

I whisked together a simple vanilla-flavored glaze to dress up the cake with minimal effort.

When I cut a slice, I knew I'd achieved the holiday-worthy cake I had initially envisioned. Most important, it tasted how we thought honey cake should taste: like honey.

HONEY CAKE Serves 12

Make sure to use unsweetened applesauce in this cake. If you plan to make this cake ahead of time, hold off on glazing it until 30 minutes before serving. You'll need 20 ounces of honey for this recipe. This cake is sticky; baking spray with flour provides the cleanest release, but if you have only regular cooking spray, apply a heavy coat and then dust the inside of the pan with flour.

CAKE

- 2½ cups (12½ ounces) all-purpose flour
- 1¼ teaspoons salt
- 1 teaspoon baking powder
- ½ teaspoon baking soda
- ½ cup water
- 4 large eggs
- ¼ cup plus 2 tablespoons unsweetened applesauce
- ¼ cup vegetable oil
- ¼ cup orange juice
- 1 teaspoon vanilla extract
- 1¾ cups honey

GLAZE

- 1 cup (4 ounces) confectioners' sugar
- 4½ teaspoons water
- 1 teaspoon vanilla extract
- Pinch salt

1. FOR THE CAKE: Adjust oven rack to middle position and heat oven to 325 degrees. Heavily spray 12-cup nonstick Bundt pan with baking spray with flour. Whisk flour, salt, baking powder, and baking soda together in large bowl. Whisk water, eggs, applesauce, oil, orange juice, and vanilla together in separate bowl until combined. Whisk honey into egg mixture until fully incorporated.

2. Whisk honey mixture into flour mixture until combined. Scrape batter into prepared pan. Bake until skewer inserted into middle of cake comes out clean, 45 to 55 minutes, rotating pan halfway through baking.

3. Let cake cool in pan on wire rack for 30 minutes. Using small spatula, loosen cake from sides of pan and invert onto rack. Let cool completely, about 2 hours. (Cooled cake can be wrapped with plastic wrap and stored at room temperature for up to 3 days.)

4. FOR THE GLAZE: Whisk together all ingredients. Drizzle glaze evenly over top of cake. Let sit until glaze is firm, about 30 minutes. Serve.

The Buzz About Honey

Honey cakes are typically sweetened with sugar and use just a little honey—no wonder most don't taste like honey. We ditch the sugar completely in favor of a whopping 1¾ cups of honey for bold flavor.

LOTS OF HONEY
1¾ cups gives maximum honey flavor.

DON'T MAKE THIS MISTAKE
A Bundt Cake that Sticks

Thoroughly greasing the pan is especially important for cakes baked in Bundt pans, because the accordion edges of these pans hold stubbornly to cakes, making it uncomfortably likely for cakes to stick and crumble. Our Honey Cake recipe calls for coating the pan with baking spray with flour, which we found did the best job of providing a clean release after baking and cooling. If you only have regular baking spray on hand, apply a liberal coat and then dust the pan with flour, tipping out the excess before adding the batter.

SOME CAKE COMES OUT

SOME DOESN'T

For the easiest, cleanest release, we grease the pan with baking spray and flour.

WHAT'S THE BEST SUPERMARKET HONEY?

America has a sky-high demand for honey: According to the National Honey Board, we eat more than 400 million pounds of the stuff every year. Considering that the average honeybee produces only ½ of a teaspoon of honey over its lifetime, that's a lot of bees.

To keep up with the demand, manufacturers source honey from all over the globe. Today, the average jar of honey on supermarket shelves is actually a mix of honeys from many hives that's been carefully blended and processed to engineer a preferred flavor and color. ("Single-source" honeys are a different breed entirely.)

Most supermarket honey is processed one of two ways. Traditional honey is usually heated to thin it enough so that it can pass under high pressure through fine strainers to remove pollen and give the honey a clear appearance, which consumers prefer. Raw honey, by contrast, is usually heated only high enough (about 120 degrees) to prevent it from crystallizing on store shelves. The honey is then lightly strained to remove debris and leftover wax, but it's not filtered under high pressure and retains most of its pollen.

To find the best supermarket honey, we selected five top-selling honeys—three traditional and two raw. Twenty-one America's Test Kitchen staffers tried each product plain and in honey cake.

In both tastings, we universally preferred the two raw honeys, calling them "complex," with "slight bitterness" and "strong floral notes." Traditional honeys, by contrast, were "one-note" and "aggressively sweet." Some were so "cloying" that tasters thought the samples were corn syrup. What accounts for the flavor difference?

Our science editor explained that pollen contains alkaloids and phenolics—chemicals that add complex, slightly bitter flavors. Tasters liked how these tempered the sweetness of honey. The fact that raw honey is also heated more gently likely helps preserve its delicate, nuanced flavors. These flavors showed through when we used the honey as an ingredient in cake, too: Tasters deemed cakes made with raw honey "more complex" than cakes made with traditional honey.

Flavor is also influenced by what the bees feed on, and most manufacturers list the primary diet of their bees on honey jars. The traditional honeys in our lineup were primarily sourced from clover-eating bees, while the raw brands were mixtures from bees that feasted on all sorts of grasses and flowers. Tasters noted strong floral and grassy notes in raw honeys and milder flavors in clover honey.

So when shopping for honey, look for the word "raw" on the label and choose a product that comes from bees with a varied diet. Our favorite product, Nature Nate's 100% Pure Raw and Unfiltered Honey, sources its honey from bees that feed on a blend of wildflowers, clover, Chinese tallow, and vetch; it was slightly bitter and floral, with a deep, balanced sweetness. –LAUREN SAVOIE

RECOMMENDED | TASTERS' NOTES

NATURE NATE'S 100% Pure Raw and Unfiltered Honey
Price: $12.63 for 16 oz ($0.79 per oz)
Type: Raw
Bee Diet: Wildflowers, clover, Chinese tallow, and vetch

This raw honey had "big flowery flavor," with "rich," "bold" notes of "citrus," "clover," and "anise." Tasters loved this "complex" product's "mild" sweetness and "slight acidity," which added "brightness" to honey cake.

AUNT SUE'S Raw-Wild Honey
Price: $8.92 for 16 oz ($0.56 per oz)
Type: Raw
Bee Diet: Wildflowers

"Sweet" and "smoky," this raw wildflower honey balanced "nutty" notes of "caramel" and "cocoa" with "spicy," "herby," "floral" flavors. Tasters liked the "hint of bitterness" in this honey, which tempered the sweetness of the cake.

SUE BEE Clover Honey
Price: $3.54 for 8 oz ($0.44 per oz)
Type: Traditional
Bee Diet: Clover

This "light," "mild" honey was "sweet" and "fruity" with just a touch of bitterness. Though some tasters found this offering "a tad boring" when sampled on its own, most enjoyed its "delicate," "mellow" sweetness in honey cake.

RECOMMENDED WITH RESERVATIONS

BURLESON'S Pure Clover Honey
Price: $5.98 for 24 oz ($0.25 per oz)
Type: Traditional
Bee Diet: Clover

Though many tasters equated this product's "supersweet," "pure sugar" flavor with the "classic" honey profile, others thought this honey was "one note" and "cloyingly sweet." In cake, most found it "just fine."

GUNTER'S Pure Clover Honey
Price: $7.59 for 12 oz ($0.63 per oz)
Type: Traditional
Bee Diet: Clover

Tasters didn't mind this "supersweet" honey as an ingredient in cake, but when sampled plain it was "one-dimensional," "toothache-inducing," and "overpoweringly sweet." "Is this corn syrup?" asked one taster.

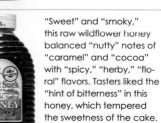

Cooking Class How to Make a Frittata

With a little finesse, you can make a golden, tender frittata every time. BY CHRISTIE MORRISON

PARMESAN AND BASIL FRITTATA Serves 4

You can substitute parsley or chives for the basil.

12	**large eggs**
1½	**ounces Parmesan cheese, grated (¾ cup)**
3	**tablespoons chopped fresh basil**
3	**tablespoons half-and-half**
1½	**teaspoons salt**
½	**teaspoon pepper**
2	**tablespoons extra-virgin olive oil**

1. Adjust oven rack to upper-middle position and heat oven to 450 degrees. Whisk eggs, Parmesan, basil, half-and-half, salt, and pepper together in bowl until well combined, about 30 seconds; set aside.

2. Heat oil in 10-inch ovensafe nonstick skillet over medium heat until shimmering. Add egg mixture and cook, using rubber spatula to stir and scrape bottom of skillet, until large curds form and spatula begins to leave wake but eggs are still very wet, about 2 minutes. Shake skillet to distribute eggs evenly; cook, without stirring, for 30 seconds to let bottom set.

3. Bake until surface of frittata is puffy and golden, about 5 minutes. (When cut into with paring knife, eggs should be slightly wet.) Remove skillet from oven and let stand for 5 minutes to finish cooking. Using spatula, loosen frittata from skillet and slide onto platter or cutting board. Cut into wedges and serve.

ASPARAGUS, HAM, AND GRUYÈRE FRITTATA

Substitute ¾ cup shredded Gruyère for Parmesan and omit basil. Cook 8 ounces trimmed asparagus, cut on bias into ¼-inch pieces, in oil in step 2 (before adding eggs) until lightly browned and almost tender, about 3 minutes. Add 4 ounces deli ham, cut into ½-inch pieces, and 1 minced shallot and cook until shallot softens slightly, about 2 minutes. Add egg mixture and proceed with recipe.

LEEK, PROSCIUTTO, AND GOAT CHEESE FRITTATA

Substitute 1 cup crumbled goat cheese for Parmesan and increase basil to ¼ cup. Cook white and light green parts of 2 halved, thinly sliced, and washed leeks in oil in step 2 (before adding eggs), covered, until softened, 6 to 8 minutes, stirring occasionally. Add 3 ounces thinly sliced prosciutto, cut into ½-inch-wide strips, with egg mixture and proceed with recipe.

MUSHROOM AND CHIVE FRITTATA

Substitute ¼ cup minced fresh chives for basil. Cook 10 ounces thinly sliced cremini mushrooms, 6 ounces thinly sliced stemmed shiitake mushrooms, and 1 finely chopped onion in oil in step 2 (before adding eggs) until dry and lightly browned, 12 to 15 minutes. Stir in 2 minced garlic cloves and cook until fragrant, about 30 seconds. Add egg mixture and proceed with recipe.

STEP BY STEP **Ten Steps to a Perfect Frittata**

1. ADD DAIRY
Add 3 tablespoons of half-and-half to the eggs.
WHY? The water in half-and-half provides steam to help the eggs puff up, while the fat adds richness and keeps the curds tender.

2. WHISK IT
Whisk the eggs, cheese, basil, half-and-half, salt, and pepper together.
WHY? Whisking ensures that the yolks are broken and that the whites and yolks are evenly distributed.

3. HEAT OIL
Heat oil in 10-inch nonstick skillet until shimmering.
WHY? Extra-virgin olive oil adds flavor and helps prevent sticking. A 10-inch skillet produces a thicker frittata.

4. STIR AND SCRAPE
Use a spatula to stir and scrape the bottom of the skillet to form large curds.
WHY? Creating large curds keeps the eggs from becoming tough and ensures quicker, more even cooking.

5. SHAKE IT
Gently shake skillet side to side.
WHY? After you've scraped the eggs into large curds, shaking the pan helps the curds settle and distribute evenly across the pan.

Good to Know

What's My Size?

The contents of a chicken egg can vary widely depending on the size of the bird. Bigger hens lay bigger eggs. In the test kitchen, we typically use "large" eggs. These have about 2 ounces of contents—egg and yolk—by weight, according to U.S. Department of Agriculture (USDA) guidelines and our own scales. Eggs labeled "medium" weigh about 1.75 ounces, "extra large" come in at 2.25 ounces, and "jumbo" eggs weigh 2.5 ounces—sometimes more. ("Small" and "peewee" eggs, at 1.5 ounces and 1.25 ounces, respectively, are rarely found in stores.)

Does "Sell By" Mean "Use By"?

All egg cartons are marked with a sell-by date, which is the legal limit until which eggs may be sold. According to the USDA, eggs are still fit for consumption for an additional three to five weeks past the sell-by date if they're refrigerated. Store eggs in their carton on a shelf in your fridge—not on the door, where temperatures can climb well over the recommended 40 degrees. In addition to blocking off-flavors (which can be an issue because eggshells are porous), the carton also helps maintain humidity, which slows down evaporation of the eggs' contents. Use your discretion, though: If the eggs smell odd or display discoloration, pitch them.

Frittata 101

Frittata versus Omelet

In terms of ingredients, frittatas are very similar to omelets—but they're much easier to make. Classic French omelets involve rolling the egg around the filling, while diner-style omelets use a folding technique that requires a strong wrist. Frittatas, on the other hand, are served open-faced with the filling stirred into the egg base. The most important thing is to ensure that the top and bottom of the frittata are evenly cooked. While some recipes have you flip the frittata (a hot, sometimes messy technique) for even cooking, we skip the acrobatics by cooking the bottom of the frittata on the stovetop (for optimal browning) before transferring the pan to the upper rack of a hot oven to finish the top.

Curd's the Word

The best way to ensure a tender, not tough, frittata is to create large curds—much as you'd do for a scrambled egg dish—before the eggs are completely set. Setting the heat to medium keeps the eggs from cooking too quickly, allowing curds to build up. Moving the eggs to the center of the pan in slow, easy swipes will help you create large, tender curds before the eggs fully set.

KEY EQUIPMENT Large Silicone Spatula

To ensure easy release of your frittata after cooking, it's essential to use an ovensafe nonstick pan. That means you also need a strong but flexible heatproof silicone spatula to stir and scrape the frittata without scratching the nonstick surface. We like the Rubbermaid Professional 13½-inch High-Heat Scraper because it is a no-nonsense tool that aced all our cooking tests—including making eggs. It also withstood all our attempts to stain or melt it.

**RUBBERMAID PROFESSIONAL
13½-INCH HIGH-HEAT SCRAPER**
Our favorite silicone spatula.

6. LET IT BE

Cook the eggs without stirring for 30 seconds.
WHY? The bottom needs to set into a smooth, cohesive layer, so it can develop browning and provide structure.

7. BAKE

Bake on the upper-middle rack of a 450-degree oven.
WHY? The high heat (and upper position) helps the top of the frittata puff slightly and set without overcooking the bottom.

8. TEST FOR DONENESS

Use a knife to cut into the center of the frittata (be careful not to scrape the nonstick surface).
WHY? The eggs should be set but still slightly wet in the center.

9. LET REST IN PAN

Transfer the pan to a wire rack and let rest for 5 minutes.
WHY? Letting the frittata finish cooking off the heat in the pan instead of in the oven prevents overcooking.

10. RELEASE AND SLIDE

Use a spatula to release the frittata and slide it onto a serving platter.
WHY? The spatula will gently release any cooked-on egg mixture without disturbing the frittata.

Slow Cooker Carnitas

For great slow-cooker carnitas, you need to rethink the braise.

BY DIANE UNGER

RICH AND SILKY WITH crisp, flavorful edges, carnitas are Mexico's version of pulled pork. They're great tucked into warm tortillas, draped over nachos, or eaten with your hands over the sink when no one is watching—when they're good, they're that good.

Like pulled pork, carnitas start with pork butt, a well-marbled cut from the shoulder of the hog that requires a long cooking time to melt out the fat and tough connective tissue and become tender. But where pulled pork calls for smoking the butt whole, recipes for carnitas usually call for cutting the butt into chunks and braising it to tenderness before finishing it on a griddle or under the broiler to create its signature crisp edges. And as you might imagine, the seasonings are different: Carnitas use citrus and Mexican seasonings instead of a barbecue rub.

The test kitchen has a carnitas recipe that is out of this world. It calls for cutting a 4-pound boneless pork butt into 2-inch chunks and braising it (in a covered Dutch oven in a 300-degree oven) in a mixture of orange juice, lime juice, and 2 cups of water seasoned with salt, pepper, cumin, oregano, and bay leaves until tender, which takes about 2 hours. Then the pork pieces are coarsely pulled apart, moistened with some of the reduced braising liquid, and quickly broiled on both sides until crisp. Fantastic. I wanted to reproduce these same great carnitas using my slow cooker.

I knew going in that I'd have to make

KEY INGREDIENTS
Orange and Lime
Pork butt is a rich, flavorful cut. To help balance some of that heft of flavor, carnitas recipes usually employ some type of citrus. We found that a combination of fresh orange and lime juices and zests really made our carnitas sing.

a few adjustments. I upped the citrus juice by a few tablespoons, knowing that long cooking in a covered environment has a tendency to mute its flavors. Similarly, I increased the amounts of cumin and oregano so that the finished dish would have plenty of seasoning. But the pork pieces were swimming in liquid by the time they were fork-tender (which took about 9 hours on low), and all that liquid was washing out the flavor. I tried another test in which I omitted the 2 cups of water up front, and now I was in business. The meat gave up just enough of its own deliciously porky juices during cooking to leave me with sufficient liquid to moisten the shreds before crisping them.

Since the slow cooker should be all about ease, I wanted to find a way around using forks to pull apart each chunk of cooked pork. I found that a few quick strokes with a potato masher did the trick. As for the crisping step, broiling worked just fine, but I wanted to be able to monitor the browning without having to peek inside the oven every 30 seconds. Instead, I browned the meat (with 1 cup of its juices added to keep things moist) in a 12-inch nonstick skillet, which took only about 12 minutes and gave me great results. Make sure to serve this pork with tortillas and plenty of garnishes like chopped onion, cilantro, radishes, sour cream, and lime wedges. Although if no one is looking, all you'll need to eat these carnitas are your hands.

We tuck carnitas into warmed tortillas and top them with vibrant garnishes.

TEST KITCHEN TECHNIQUE
Crisping Carnitas
Once the meat has finished braising in the slow cooker, you also need to crisp it up. We like to do this in a nonstick skillet with some of the braising liquid added to keep the pork from drying out as it crisps.

SLOW-COOKER PORK CARNITAS
Serves 6 to 8
Remove the lime and orange zest with a vegetable peeler. Pork butt roast is often labeled Boston butt. Do not overtrim the pork; this extra fat is essential to keeping the pork moist and helping it brown when sautéed in step 3. We like to serve carnitas with warmed corn tortillas and a variety of toppings, like finely chopped onion, fresh cilantro leaves, thinly sliced radishes, sour cream, and lime wedges.

- 1 (3- to 3½-pound) boneless pork butt roast, lightly trimmed and cut into 2-inch chunks
- 1 small onion, peeled and halved
- 3 (2-inch) strips orange zest plus ½ cup juice
- 3 (2-inch) strips lime zest plus 2 tablespoons juice
- 5 garlic cloves, minced
- 1 tablespoon ground cumin
- 1 tablespoon dried oregano
  Salt and pepper
- 2 bay leaves
- 2 tablespoons vegetable oil

1. Combine pork, onion, orange zest and juice, lime zest and juice, garlic, cumin, oregano, 2½ teaspoons salt, 1½ teaspoons pepper, and bay leaves in slow cooker. Cover and cook until fork slips easily in and out of pork, 5 to 7 hours on high or 8 to 10 hours on low.

2. Using slotted spoon, transfer pork from slow cooker to large bowl. Using potato masher, smash pork until coarsely shredded. Strain cooking liquid from slow cooker through fine-mesh strainer set over separate bowl and discard solids.

3. Heat oil in 12-inch nonstick skillet over medium-high heat until shimmering. Add pork to skillet. Whisk cooking liquid to recombine, then add 1 cup to skillet with pork. Cook, stirring occasionally, until liquid has evaporated and pork is evenly browned and crispy in spots, 10 to 15 minutes.

4. Season with salt and pepper to taste. Transfer pork to serving platter and moisten with ¼ cup remaining cooking liquid, or more as needed. Serve.

One-Pan Dinner Chicken Legs with Cauliflower and Tomatoes

Sometimes the key to the perfect one-pan dinner is making the right incision. BY CHRISTIE MORRISON

CHICKEN LEG QUARTERS MIGHT just be the most woefully underused cuts of the bird. But why? Leg quarters are cheap, easy to work with, full of flavor, and hard to overcook   drumsticks, especially, become more tender with prolonged cooking. I wanted to roast the chicken legs simultaneously with cauliflower, another often-neglected ingredient that is superb roasted, for an easy weeknight dinner with minimal cleanup. My goals: ease and great flavor.

Leg quarters have thicker and fattier skin than breasts, and you need to render that fat during cooking so the skin isn't rubbery. I followed the lead of a fantastic *Cook's Country* recipe for grilled leg quarters where we slashed the meat to the bone four times on each leg quarter. The slashing not only encourages the fat to render but also helps the seasoning get deeper into the meat, creates more surface area to carry flavor, and exposes more of the dark meat so it cooks faster. To add flavor, I whisked lemon, garlic, and chopped sage into olive oil and brushed it on the slashed chicken leg quarters.

Cauliflower needs some moisture to help it soften without drying out in the oven. I cut a head of cauliflower into large wedges and tossed the wedges with a few halved shallots. Instead of covering the cauliflower for the first part of cooking to steam it (as some

recipes suggest), I found that the chicken contributed enough moisture to help the cauliflower wedges cook through and brown at the same time without becoming leathery. Arranging the vegetables in the middle of the sheet (where it's cooler) and positioning the chicken legs around the perimeter (where it's hotter) ensured that everything cooked at the same rate.

The recipe was coming along, but the chicken skin, while rendered, was lacking crispness, and the dish as a whole was missing something. Looking for an intense blast of heat to help crisp the skin, I preheated the broiler. But before I broiled, I grabbed a handful of grape tomatoes and tossed them onto the pan. After about 5 minutes under the broiler, the chicken skin had crisped, the top of the cauliflower had browned in spots, and the tomatoes were just barely blistered and wilted, the perfect fresh complement to my hearty chicken dinner.

ONE-PAN ROAST CHICKEN WITH CAULIFLOWER AND TOMATOES
Serves 4

Note that this recipe calls for kosher salt, not table salt. Some leg quarters are sold with the backbone attached. Be sure to remove it (we like to use a heavy chef's knife for this task) before cooking to make serving easier. If you substitute cherry tomatoes for the grape tomatoes, cut them in half before adding them to the sheet in step 5.

We position the slashed chicken legs around the outside of the baking sheet, where it's hottest.

- 1 head cauliflower (2 pounds)
- 6 shallots, peeled and halved
- ¼ cup extra-virgin olive oil
- 2 tablespoons chopped fresh sage
  Kosher salt and pepper
- 4 (10-ounce) chicken leg quarters, trimmed
- 2 garlic cloves, minced
- 1 teaspoon grated lemon zest
- 7½ ounces grape tomatoes
- 1 tablespoon coarsely chopped fresh parsley
  Lemon wedges

1. Adjust 1 oven rack to lower-middle position and second rack 6 inches from broiler element and heat oven to 475 degrees. Trim outer leaves of cauliflower and cut stem flush with bottom of head.

Cut head into 8 equal wedges, keeping core and florets intact.

2. Gently toss cauliflower, shallots, 2 tablespoons oil, 1 tablespoon sage, 1 teaspoon salt, and ½ teaspoon pepper together on rimmed baking sheet to combine. Position vegetables cut sides down in single layer in center of sheet.

3. Pat chicken dry with paper towels. Leaving drumsticks and thighs attached, make 4 parallel diagonal slashes in chicken: 1 across drumsticks, 1 across leg joints, and 2 across thighs (each slash should reach bone). Season chicken with salt and pepper. Place 1 piece of chicken, skin side up, in each corner of sheet (chicken should rest directly on sheet, not on vegetables).

4. Whisk garlic, lemon zest, remaining 2 tablespoons oil, and remaining 1 tablespoon sage together in bowl. Brush skin side of chicken with seasoned oil mixture (use all of it). Transfer sheet to lower-middle oven rack and bake until cauliflower is browned, shallots are tender, and chicken registers at least 175 degrees, 25 to 30 minutes.

5. Remove sheet from oven and heat broiler. Scatter tomatoes over vegetables and place sheet on upper oven rack. Broil until chicken skin is browned and crisp and tomatoes have started to wilt, 3 to 5 minutes.

6. Transfer sheet to wire rack and let rest for 5 minutes. Sprinkle with parsley and serve with lemon wedges.

KEY STEP
Slashing Chicken Legs

Making deep slashes in each chicken leg has several benefits. It helps the seasoning penetrate deeply, creates more surface area to hold seasoning, allows more fat to render, and helps the dark-meat legs cook faster and more evenly.

Paella, with its long list of ingredients, can be a production. But does it have to be? BY CECELIA JENKINS

PAELLA IS A RICE dish from the coastal city of Valencia, Spain, traditionally prepared in its namesake shallow, flat-bottomed pan. It is composed of a flavorful base of onion, tomato, and garlic (called *sofrito*); a mix of poultry, game, snails, sausage, and, in more modern interpretations, seafood; pricey saffron threads; and short-grain rice, cooked until the much-coveted brown crust (called *socarrat*) develops on the bottom. It's a labor-intensive process, and when expensive saffron is added to the mix, potentially bank-breaking. We wanted a fast, weeknight version for two that still recognized tradition.

Paellas typically contain several meats browned individually in batches according to their specific cooking times, and the sofrito is created in the flavorful brown bits they leave behind in the pan. I went down this road, browning the chorizo and strips of chicken breast in a 12-inch skillet (the closest thing most of us have to a paella pan) but found it tedious: Did I really need to brown the chicken breast and chorizo? In a side-by-side test, my tasters could tell little difference between a paella that started with searing the sausage and chicken and one in which those proteins were stirred into the sofrito with the rice and broth. So that saved me a little work.

About that sofrito. I made three of them: one using fresh tomatoes, one with canned, and one with tomato paste. My tasters preferred the version with tomato paste, which, when it caramelized, made a beautiful, dark, flavorful sofrito base.

After coating the rice in the sofrito and adding broth, I introduced the meat: chopped chorizo and one boneless chicken breast cut into large pieces so it wouldn't dry out. Unfortunately, not all the breast meat was submerged, which meant the meat cooked unevenly. Flipping the pieces would disturb the rice (a serious paella blunder; rice must be left alone to form the signature socarrat crust) and smaller pieces cooked up tough and dry, so I switched to dark meat in the form of boneless thighs, which stayed put and, because their dark meat is more moist and forgiving, cooked evenly into juicy morsels.

I carefully nestled in the quick-cooking shrimp, which only bothered the rice slightly, and soon the paella began to

crackle and pop, indicating browning on the bottom. With patience and a few tries, I discovered that moving the skillet around the flame as the paella sizzled not only helped the crust evenly brown on the bottom but allowed the edges to accurately reflect browning, as well. As they turned from golden to brown, I let the paella rest off the heat, covered, to finish cooking everything through. With a sprinkle of lemon, I enjoyed my paella after less than 50 minutes. I made versions with and without saffron; tasters enjoyed both, so I leave the decision to use it up to you and your accountant.

PAELLA FOR TWO

Spanish varieties of rice, while traditional in paella, are sometimes difficult to find, which is why we offer the more widely available Arborio rice as a substitute. Each type of rice requires a slightly different amount of liquid, so note the difference in the recipe. Make sure to use cured Spanish chorizo, not the fresh Mexican sausage, here.

Smoked paprika and chorizo sausage add a pleasantly smoky depth to this paella.

2	tablespoons extra-virgin olive oil, plus extra for drizzling
1	small onion, chopped
¼	cup dry white wine
1	tablespoon tomato paste
2	garlic cloves, minced
½	teaspoon smoked paprika
1	bay leaf
¾	cup Valencia or Arborio rice
8	ounces boneless, skinless chicken thighs, trimmed and cut into 1-inch pieces
	Salt and pepper
2½–2¾	cups chicken broth
3	ounces Spanish dry-cured chorizo sausage, cut into ½-inch chunks
	Pinch saffron threads (optional)
6	ounces extra-large shrimp (21 to 25 per pound), peeled, deveined, and tails removed
2	teaspoons minced fresh parsley
	Lemon wedges

1. Heat oil in 12-inch nonstick skillet over medium heat until shimmering. Add onion and cook until lightly browned, 3 to 5 minutes. Stir in wine, tomato paste, garlic, paprika, and bay leaf and cook until liquid evaporates and mixture looks oily, 2 to 4 minutes.

2. Stir in rice and cook until grains are well coated with tomato mixture,

about 1 minute. Season chicken with salt and pepper. Stir in broth (2½ cups for Valencia rice, 2¾ cups for Arborio); chorizo; saffron, if using; chicken; and ⅛ teaspoon salt.

3. Bring to strong simmer and continue to cook, uncovered, over medium heat until liquid level falls just below surface of rice but paella still looks wet, 10 to 14 minutes. (After first 5 minutes of simmering, do not stir or paella will become starchy.)

4. Season shrimp with salt and pepper and nestle halfway into rice. Continue to cook until shrimp are mostly pink and all

liquid has been absorbed, 4 to 7 minutes longer (paella will crackle and pop when liquid is absorbed).

5. To develop crust (socarrat) on bottom of paella, continue to cook until crackling and popping sounds become more pronounced, while occasionally rotating skillet over heat for even browning, 3 to 5 minutes. At this point, shrimp should be almost completely pink and paella should look dry on top.

6. Remove from heat, cover, and let sit for 3 minutes. Discard bay leaf. Sprinkle with parsley. Serve with lemon wedges and drizzle with extra oil.

Preparing Paella for a Crowd: Bigger Is Better

Paella is a popular party food, and not just in Spain. To maximize *socarrat*, the crunchy bits from the bottom of the pan, banquet cooks (like these Miami chefs) use huge, shallow paella pans to ensure everyone gets some crunch. The drama is just a bonus.

Five Easy Recipes Potato Salads

We packed these potato salads with as much flavor as possible by seasoning them in three different stages. BY ASHLEY MOORE

MANY POTATO SALADS FALL victim to one of two cooking crimes: underseasoning or improperly cooked potatoes. We've made enough potato salads to know that it's critical to season them not only after cooking but during, as well. And the cooking needs to be closely monitored to get potatoes with a tender, not mushy, texture.

The first round of seasoning happens before the potatoes—in this case flavorful Yukon Golds—even hit the heat. We start the potatoes in cold, salted water, then we bring it up to just a gentle simmer to ensure that the potatoes cook gently and evenly throughout. A high, rolling boil would cook the outsides of the potatoes before the interiors became tender and result in torn-up, rather than tidy, potatoes.

The next step is crucial: drizzling the cooked, drained, still-hot potatoes with a quick dressing of mustard and salty dill pickle brine. This—you guessed it—is the second phase of seasoning. As the potatoes cool in the refrigerator, they absorb these savory flavors.

Once the potatoes are cool, we mix some mayonnaise with celery, red onion, and more pickle brine. We add celery seeds to boost the celery flavor and some chopped dill pickles and white vinegar for punch. Then we season this mixture with salt and pepper before stirring it into the potatoes for the final seasoning step.

With a base salad this good, why not doctor it up? I created four variations, including a smoky and spicy one with scallions, cilantro, and chipotle in adobo. With a little garlic and a generous helping of herbs like chives, parsley, and tarragon, I brought the potato salad into green goddess territory. Another, with a hefty amount of prepared horseradish, was nippy and pungent. And finally, adding some ketchup and brown sugar was our ode to Thousand Island dressing.

Clockwise from top: Potato Salad, Green Goddess Potato Salad, Horseradish Potato Salad, Chipotle Potato Salad, and Thousand Island Potato Salad.

POTATO SALAD
Serves 4 to 6
Red Bliss potatoes can be substituted for the Yukon Gold potatoes.

- 2 pounds Yukon Gold potatoes, unpeeled, cut into ¾-inch chunks
  Salt and pepper
- ¼ cup finely chopped dill pickles, plus 3 tablespoons brine
- 1 tablespoon yellow mustard
- ¾ cup mayonnaise
- ½ cup finely chopped red onion
- 1 celery rib, minced
- 2 tablespoons distilled white vinegar
- ½ teaspoon celery seeds

1. Place potatoes and 1 teaspoon salt in large saucepan and cover with cold water by 1 inch. Bring to boil over high heat, reduce heat to medium-low, and simmer until potatoes are tender, 10 to 15 minutes.

2. Drain potatoes thoroughly in colander, then spread out on rimmed baking sheet. Mix 2 tablespoons pickle brine and mustard together in bowl, then drizzle over potatoes, carefully tossing until evenly coated. Refrigerate potato mixture until cooled slightly, about 15 minutes.

3. Combine mayonnaise, onion, celery, vinegar, celery seeds, pickles, remaining 1 tablespoon pickle brine, ½ teaspoon salt, and ¼ teaspoon pepper in large bowl. Add cooled potato mixture and toss to combine. Cover and refrigerate until well chilled, about 30 minutes. (Salad can be refrigerated for up to 2 days.)

CHIPOTLE POTATO SALAD
Add 4 thinly sliced scallions, ¼ cup chopped fresh cilantro, 1 tablespoon minced canned chipotle in adobo sauce plus 1 teaspoon adobo sauce, 1 minced garlic clove, and 1 teaspoon lime juice to mayonnaise mixture in step 3.

GREEN GODDESS POTATO SALAD
Add ¼ cup chopped fresh chives, ¼ cup chopped fresh parsley, 2 tablespoons chopped fresh tarragon, and 1 minced garlic clove to mayonnaise mixture in step 3.

HORSERADISH POTATO SALAD
Add ¼ cup prepared horseradish to mayonnaise mixture in step 3.

THOUSAND ISLAND POTATO SALAD
Add ½ cup ketchup and 1½ teaspoons packed brown sugar to mayonnaise mixture in step 3.

Equipment Review Water Bottles

Smart, durable, and spill-proof, one bottle clobbers the competition.

BY HANNAH CROWLEY

KEY Good ★★★ Fair ★★ Poor ★

	CRITERIA		TESTERS' NOTES

HIGHLY RECOMMENDED

NATHAN LittleShot
Model: 4313TN
Price: $11.99
Capacity: 24 oz (BigShot is 32 oz)
Material: Tritan
Dishwasher-Safe: yes

Ease of Use ★★★
Durability ★★★
Cleanup ★★★

This bottle's clear plastic sides made it easy to fill, and its bi-level twist-on lid was secure and easy to sip from. Its tether stayed out of the way and folded into a handy carrying loop.

RECOMMENDED

NALGENE Wide Mouth
Model: 32 Ounce Wide Mouth
Price: $10.50
Capacity: 32 oz
Material: Tritan
Dishwasher-Safe: Yes

Ease of Use ★★½
Durability ★★★
Cleanup ★★★

This basic clear bottle was simple to fill, carry, and clean. It was easy to open and close and aced our durability testing. The only drawback: Its wide mouth was harder to drink from.

CAMELBAK Chute .75L
Model: 53540 (lime)
Price: $13
Capacity: 24 oz
Material: Tritan
Dishwasher-Safe: Yes

Ease of Use ★★
Durability ★★★
Cleanup ★★★

This clear bottle had a bi-level screw-on cap, with one opening for filling and one for sipping. Its cap was on a stiff plastic leash and bonked us between the eyes while we drank. But it aced our abuse tests.

VAPUR Element Anti-Bottle
Model: N/A
Price: $11.99
Capacity: 23 oz
Material: Triple-ply BPA-free plastic
Dishwasher-Safe: Yes

Ease of Use ★½
Durability ★★★
Cleanup ★★★

This soft pouch was durable and spill-proof and had a nice drinking spout. Its soft sides were awkward, and we felt in constant peril of squeezing too hard and sending up a geyser. However, it was light and handy for traveling.

RECOMMENDED WITH RESERVATIONS

THERMOS Hydration Bottle with Rotating Meter on Lid
Model: HP4100MGTRI6 (magenta)
Price: $12.20
Capacity: 24 oz
Material: Tritan
Dishwasher-Safe: Yes

Ease of Use ★★
Durability ★★
Cleanup ★★★

This clear bottle didn't hold on to smells or stains and had a nice drinking spout. But its finicky latch and cheap plastic button were hard to open; during abuse testing it leaked and the meter for recording water intake broke.

NOT RECOMMENDED

CONTIGO Autoseal Cortland Water Bottle
Model: 70601
Price: $11.99
Capacity: 24 oz
Material: Tritan
Dishwasher-Safe: Yes

Ease of Use ★½
Durability ★★
Cleanup ★★★

This bottle's small drinking spout and cap were too fussy. You had to unlock the lid, flip the cap open, and hold a slippery button while drinking. It was complicated, and the cap broke off during abuse testing.

KLEAN KANTEEN "The Original" Classic
Model: K27CPPS-GF (green fatigue)
Price: $19.95
Capacity: 27 oz
Material: Stainless steel
Dishwasher-Safe: Yes (except painted bottles)

Ease of Use ★★
Durability ★★
Cleanup ★★

This bottle had an exposed drinking spout made of tacky rubber that collected dust. Its steel body meant that we couldn't see inside, and it dented during the dropping test.

STANLEY Adventure One Hand H20
Model: 10-01152-065
Price: $20
Capacity: 24 oz
Material: Stainless steel
Dishwasher-Safe: No

Ease of Use ★½
Durability ★½
Cleanup ★½

This steel bottle had an exposed drinking spout, and we had to hold down a button to release water. The button isn't covered, so if something nudged it, say, a shoe in a gym bag, the spout opened. It also dented when we dropped it.

THE ALLEY BEHIND the test kitchen isn't exactly a bucolic place to spend a breezy afternoon, but I, along with a photographer and videographer, had important work to do: dropping refillable water bottles onto the pavement, over and over again, to test their durability. Call it a cold, hard real-world test.

We were evaluating eight different water bottles. There are thousands for sale, so we narrowed our lineup to stick with a few key parameters.

First, we focused on basic single-walled bottles and considered only BPA-free models. (BPA stands for bisphenol A, an industrial chemical used in some plastics. It's currently under review by the FDA, but critics claim that it can leach into food and cause health problems.) Also, we nixed straws because they're difficult to clean thoroughly and tend to get funky fast. We avoided bottles made from glass, too, because it's heavy and, of course, breakable. And we were strict on price; anything north of twenty bucks was out. Our final lineup of eight bottles, each costing between $10 and $20, was made up of five plastic bottles, two stainless-steel ones, and a soft plastic pouch.

We wanted a bottle that was easy to fill, open, close, carry, clean, and sip from. It also had to be spill-proof and exceptionally durable. Before each bottle plummeted toward the pavement, a succession of testers evaluated its basic functionality. We then filled them with an electric-yellow sports drink and let them sit for 24 hours to check for unwanted staining. Some were dishwasher-safe, while others weren't; we hand-washed or ran each through the machine 10 times, depending on manufacturer instructions, to check for wear and tear.

We bought extras of each bottle and assigned them to staffers, with the stipulation that they use them every day for two weeks and take them wherever they go. The bottles went to work in the test kitchen and at local restaurants; they went on long walks around the city, hiking in the mountains, to the gym, and to yoga; they rode in cars, trains, and buses and sat on the couch through Netflix marathons; one even took a weekend trip to Cape Cod.

Meanwhile, we ventured into the alley with our eight testing copies. We shook each full bottle vigorously upside down for 10 seconds and then dropped

The best test for durability? Dropping water bottles onto rock-hard asphalt.

each from shoulder height onto the hard pavement—upside down, right side up, and sideways. Only half the bottles survived.

Of the three materials the bottles were made from, the soft plastic pouch was too squishy and awkward for everyday use. The stainless-steel canisters were problematic, too; testers sometimes spilled while filling them because they couldn't see inside, and they dented easily. Our favorite canisters were made of Tritan, a clear, hard plastic. We could see through them for easy filling, and they aced the dropping tests, bouncing off the pavement with nary a scratch.

Testers liked protected mouthpieces, which felt clean on the lips; exposed ones got dirty or dusty. And testers didn't like complex bottles with fussy buttons or finicky, hard-to-undo latches. These complicated bottles were also less durable: More external doodads meant more to break off.

As far as being spill-proof and durable, nothing beat the classic screw-on lid. But some bottles were too wide to drink from easily, while others were so narrow that they were hard to fill and clean. Two bottles with screw-on lids

Taste Test Tortilla Chips

Can you judge a chip by its color? BY LAUREN SAVOIE

tackled this catch-22 by mounting a second, smaller twist-off cap on top of the lid. One bonked us in the face while we sipped—less than ideal. But the final bottle nailed it.

Our favorite was clear: the Nathan LittleShot. It was made of strong, clear BPA-free Tritan and had a smaller twist-on cap that opened and closed smoothly and was easy to drink from; its large opening was great for filling and made cleaning a cinch. It smacked down onto the pavement again and again without spilling a drop and looked nearly brand-new afterward. It comes in 24- and 32-ounce (BigShot) sizes; the former fit easily in larger cup, bike, and backpack holders. Whether you're hiking, lounging, or squished on a bus, the Nathan LittleShot is the best water bottle for staying hydrated on the go.

SALSA IS NOW America's best-selling condiment, so it's not surprising that tortilla chips are poised to soon overtake potato chips as America's favorite salty snack. According to data from IRi, a Chicago-based market research firm, tortilla chip sales grew at nearly double the rate of potato chip sales in 2014.

Tortilla chips are traditionally made from yellow or white corn, but we've noticed an increase in products made with blue corn. We reached out to manufacturers and learned that—for some smaller, health-focused brands—these blue corn products are just as popular as traditional white or yellow corn chips. We gathered seven nationally available tortilla chip products: three made from blue corn and four made from white or yellow corn (if a company made multiple products, we selected its most popular variety). Twenty-one America's Test Kitchen staffers sampled the chips plain and—to see how well they could scoop—with salsa and guacamole.

To our surprise, blue corn chips universally sank to the bottom of the pack. Many tasters detected "slightly bitter," "burnt," or "beany" notes in blue corn chips that stood in stark contrast to the "sweet," "mild" flavor of white and yellow corn chips. How did these pretty chips end up at the bottom of our rankings? Blue corn gets its vibrant hue from large concentrations of pigment-producing chemicals called anthocyanins in its kernels; the same chemicals responsible for the bright color of eggplants, blackberries, and grapes. In addition to a blue hue, anthocyanins can contribute a slightly bitter, astringent flavor to foods, particularly when they're cooked.

Blue chips were also universally lacking in salt, with most having between 60 and 80 milligrams of sodium per serving, compared with 110 to 115 milligrams of sodium in higher-ranked products. Chips with less than 110 milligrams (including one white corn product) were "bland" and "overly sweet." Tasters thought that saltier chips were more "authentic," "fresh," and "bright." We tried salting one of the blue corn chip products to see if it would improve the flavor, but it wasn't enough to mask the beany aftertaste.

Testers dipped the chips in our winning medium chunky salsa and our Hearty Guacamole to evaluate how well each held its shape. While most chips maintained their structure, a few

RECOMMENDED

ON THE BORDER Café Style Tortilla Chips
Price: $3 for 12 oz ($0.25 per oz)
Type of Corn: Yellow and white
Sodium: 110 mg
Thickness: 3.28 mm

TOSTITOS Original Restaurant Style Tortilla Chips
Price: $4.29 for 13 oz ($0.33 per oz)
Type of Corn: White
Sodium: 115 mg
Thickness: 2.39 mm

SANTITAS White Corn Tortilla Chips
Price: $2 for 11 oz ($0.18 per oz)
Type of Corn: White
Sodium: 115 mg
Thickness: 1.98 mm

RECOMMENDED WITH RESERVATIONS

GARDEN OF EATIN' Blue Corn Tortilla Chips
Price: $3.99 for 8.1 oz ($0.49 per oz)
Type of Corn: Blue
Sodium: 60 mg
Thickness: 2.72 mm

MISSION Tortilla Triangles
Price: $3.49 for 13 oz ($0.27 per oz)
Type of Corn: White
Sodium: 90 mg
Thickness: 2.06 mm

FOOD SHOULD TASTE GOOD Blue Corn Tortilla Chips
Price: $3.29 for 5.5 oz ($0.60 per oz)
Type of Corn: Blue (also contains rice flour, quinoa, sesame seeds, sunflower seeds, and flaxseeds)
Sodium: 80 mg
Thickness: 1.78 mm

NOT RECOMMENDED

XOCHITL Blue Corn Chips
Price: $5.29 for 12 oz ($0.44 per oz)
Type of Corn: Blue
Sodium: 103 mg
Thickness: 0.88 mm

TASTERS' NOTES

This recently reformulated product was praised for its "traditional," "buttery" sweetness and "bright corn flavor." Tasters found these big "flaky" chips "light and airy," with a "bubbly," "crisp" exterior that was "the perfect counterpart to salsa." "I could eat a whole bag of these," said one taster.

"Oh, hi, old friend," said one taster, who identified this top-selling product's "familiar," "very salty" seasoning and "large," "sturdy" shape. These "coarse," "crunchy" chips were "built for heavy dipping" and had "simple, straightforward flavor" that tasters loved.

Our former favorite, this product was "very salty" and "grainy," with "mellow corn flavor" and "light roasted notes." Though a little too thin for some tasters, these chips were "crisp but strong," with "satisfying crunch" and a "slightly bubbly" exterior.

With the lowest levels of salt in our lineup, these "rustic" blue corn chips were "a little bland" for some tasters, though most appreciated their "mild" earthiness and "grainy" flavor. Tasters also liked the "dense," "thick" texture of these chips, which were good for "sturdy," "supported dipping."

This product, made from all white corn, was "sweet," "mild," and "inoffensive" but was "bordering on too bland" for some tasters. Though these chips could hold a good scoop of dip, many testers noted that the chips quickly turned "soft" and "soggy" under the weight of salsa and "crumbled like a stale tortilla."

These "hearty," hexagonal-shaped chips are made from blue corn, other grains like quinoa and rice flour, and flaxseeds. While many tasters appreciated this product's "slight sweetness" and "sturdy" texture, others were turned off by its "smoky," "earthy" flavor and "lack of authentic feel."

These "fragile," "paper-thin" chips had "razor-sharp" edges that cut tasters' mouths and shattered in salsa. Most tasters couldn't get past the "burnt toast" bitterness and "beany" blue corn flavor, but those that could noted unpleasant "stale" and "cardboardy" aftertastes.

products turned soggy under salsa or crumbled on a drag through guacamole. Tasters preferred thick chips with curved or curled edges that could trap dips. A thicker chip didn't necessarily mean a denser chip, though. We favored chips with large air pockets, which added structural support while still maintaining a crispy, flaky texture

that wasn't too dense or stiff.

Our new favorite chips, On The Border Café Style Tortilla Chips, were reformulated right before our tasting, and while the manufacturer wouldn't disclose exactly what it changed, it's certainly doing something right. These chips were light, flaky, and crispy, with a bright corn taste.

Heirloom Recipe

We're looking for recipes that you treasure—the ones that have been handed down in your family for a generation or more; that always come out for the holidays; that have earned a place at your table and in your heart, through many years of meals. Send us the recipes that spell home to you. Visit **CooksCountry.com/magazines/home** (or write to Heirloom Recipes, *Cook's Country*, P.O. Box 470739, Brookline, MA 02447); click on Heirloom Recipes and tell us a little about the recipe. Include your name and mailing address. **If we print your recipe, you'll receive a free one-year subscription to *Cook's Country*.**

SWITCHEL Makes about 2 quarts
Harriet Barnstable, New Hope, Pa.

"My grandfather told us that when he was growing up in upstate New York, he'd often sip on this sharp, gingery drink during the fall harvest months."

This recipe can be easily doubled. Do not substitute pancake syrup for the maple syrup. Use a rasp grater for the ginger and the lemon zest. The longer you let the switchel chill before straining, the stronger the ginger flavor will be. Feel free to adjust the tartness with water to suit your taste.

- 6 cups water
- ¾ cup cider vinegar
- ½ cup pure maple syrup
- ¼ cup old-fashioned rolled oats
- 2 tablespoons grated fresh ginger
- 1 teaspoon grated lemon zest
- ¼ teaspoon salt

1. Bring all ingredients to simmer in large saucepan over medium-high heat. Once simmering, remove from heat and let cool completely.
2. Transfer switchel to bowl, cover, and refrigerate for at least 6 hours or up to 24 hours. Strain switchel through fine-mesh strainer set over 2-quart pitcher. Serve over ice.

COMING NEXT ISSUE

Our October/November issue kicks off the holiday season with a **No-Fuss Roast Turkey**, but that's just the start—we'll fill out the table with **Sourdough Stuffing**, **Cornmeal Drop Biscuits**, and a **Brussels Sprout Gratin** good enough to convert the most stubborn sprout skeptics. For your sweet tooth, we've got **Cranberry Pound Cake**, **Chocolate-Cherry Brownies**, and perfect **Apple Pie**. Still hungry? How about **San Antonio Puffy Tacos**, **Wisconsin Butter Burgers**, or **St. Louis Steak Modiga**? Pull up a chair.

FIND THE ROOSTER!

A tiny version of this rooster has been hidden in the pages of this issue. Write to us with its location and we'll enter you in a rand... drawing. The first correct entry drawn will win our winning water bottle, and each of the next five will receive a free one-year subscription to *Cook's Coun...* To enter, visit **CooksCountry.com/roost...** by September 30, 2015, or write to Roo... AS15, *Cook's Country*, P.O. Box 470739 Brookline, MA 02447. Include your nam... and address. Ronald Hertzog of Sinkin... Spring, Pennsylvania, found the rooste... the May 2015 issue on page 12 and w... our winning can opener.

WEB EXTRAS

Free for 4 months online at CooksCountry.com

Gumbo
Honey-Glazed Peaches
Kielbasa Casserole
Lemon–Poppy Seed Muffins
Pastry Cream
Raspberry-Glazed Peaches
Spicy Feta-Stuffed Chicken Breasts
Splatter Screens Testing
White Layer Cake

READ US ON iPAD

Download the *Cook's Country* for iPad and star... free trial subscrip... or purchase a single issue of the magazine. All iss... are enhanced w... full-color Cookin... Mode slide show... that provide step-by-step instructions fo... completing recipes, plus expanded rev... and ratings. Go to **CooksCountry.com/...** to download our app through iTunes.

Follow us on **Pinterest**
pinterest.com/TestKitchen

Follow us on **Twitter**
twitter.com/TestKitchen

Find us on **Facebook**
facebook.com/CooksCountry

Toasted Almond Cake

Layers of tender white cake are filled with creamy, almond-tinged custard and covered with fluffy amaretto buttercream and crunchy caramelized almonds.

To make this cake, you will need:

- 1 **tablespoon unsalted butter, plus 16 tablespoons unsalted butter, softened**
- 2 **cups sliced almonds**
- 3 **tablespoons granulated sugar**
- 3 **cups pastry cream***
- 2 **tablespoons amaretto**
- ½ **cup heavy cream, whipped to soft peaks**
- 1 **teaspoon almond extract**
- 2 **(9-inch) white layer cake rounds***
  Confectioners' sugar

FOR THE ALMONDS: Line rimmed baking sheet with parchment paper. Melt 1 tablespoon butter in 12-inch nonstick skillet over medium heat. Add almonds and cook until light golden brown, about 5 minutes, stirring frequently. Add granulated sugar and continue to cook, stirring constantly, until sugar has caramelized and almonds are deep golden brown, about 3 minutes longer. Transfer to prepared sheet, spread in even layer, and let cool completely.

FOR THE FROSTING: Transfer 1 cup pastry cream to small bowl and let come to room temperature. Using stand mixer fitted with paddle, beat softened butter on medium speed until smooth and light, about 3 minutes. Add room-temperature pastry cream in 3 additions, beating for 30 seconds after each addition. Add amaretto and continue to beat until light and fluffy, about 5 minutes longer, scraping down bowl as needed.

FOR THE FILLING: Using rubber spatula, fold whipped cream and almond extract into remaining 2 cups pastry cream.

TO ASSEMBLE: Cut each cake round in half horizontally. Spread each bottom half with 1 cup filling and replace top. Place one filled cake on cake plate or pedestal. Top with remaining 1 cup filling and place second filled cake on top. Spread frosting in even layer over top and sides of cake. Gently press candied almonds into frosting all over cake. Dust top of cake with confectioners' sugar. Serve.

*Use your recipes or visit **CooksCountry.com/sept15** for our **Pastry Cream** and **White Layer Cake** recipes.

Inside This Issue

Cook's Country

OCTOBER/NOVEMBER 2015

Easy One-Pan Pork Dinner

Puffy Tacos

Mustard Chicken

Two-Hour Roast Turkey
Start to Finish, No Kidding

Wisconsin Butter Burgers
Plus: Tasting Burger Buns

Cornmeal Drop Biscuits
Quick and Pantry-Friendly

Cooking Class: Apple Pie

Pork and Ricotta Meatballs
Lighter, Cleaner Flavor

Chocolate-Cherry Brownies
Solving the Texture Problem

Easy Breakfast Scrambles
Five Flavor Variations

Brussels Sprout Casserole
Rich and Creamy, Not Bitter

Rating Slicing Knives
Should You Buy One?

CooksCountry.com
$5.95 U.S./$6.95 CANADA

Roasting pork tenderloin, potatoes, and green beans all together in one pan seemed like a great idea for a weeknight dinner. After two weeks in the test kitchen, we figured out how to get it all cooked perfectly every time. PAGE 27

Cook's Country

Dear Country Cook,

Every year at the Washington County Fair, the agricultural exhibits display vegetables dressed in various disguises: an ear of corn as a fashion model in a bikini, an eggplant as a fanged monster, and a butternut squash as a bird (the stem is the beak). Of course agriculture is a serious endeavor, and so this odd business of animating vegetables at harvest time is a puzzler.

Perhaps it is the one bit of fun we allow ourselves, as Puritan descendants, after the long growing season? Or maybe we view vegetables as living beings—after all, we did raise them up from the soil—and therefore want to give them a face?

The Vermont farmers I grew up with were, for the most part, serious people, but they were also fond of a practical joke. Shaking hands with an unsuspecting flatlander and then grabbing hold of an electric fence. Or tickling a sleeping farmhand on the nose with a stalk of timothy after having loaded up his outstretched hand with a pile of dried cow manure.

Farmers are serious people, to be sure, but sometimes, just sometimes, you do have to laugh. You might just say that it's the nature of things.

Cordially,

Christopher Kimball
Founder and Editor, Cook's Country

Cook's Country

Founder and Editor Christopher Kimball
Editorial Director Jack Bishop
Editorial Director, Magazines John Willoughby
Executive Editor Tucker Shaw
Managing Editor Scott Kathan
Executive Food Editor Bryan Roof
Executive Tastings & Testings Editor Lisa McManus
Senior Editors Hannah Crowley, Christie Morrison, Diane Unger
Test Kitchen Director Erin McMurrer
Associate Editor Ashley Moore
Test Cooks Morgan Bolling, Cecelia Jenkins, Katie Leaird
Assistant Editors Lauren Savoie, Kate Shannon
Senior Copy Editor Megan Ginsberg
Copy Editors Jillian Campbell, Krista Magnuson
Executive Assistant Christine Gordon
Assistant Test Kitchen Director Leah Rovner
Senior Kitchen Assistants Michelle Blodget, Alexxa Grattan
Kitchen Assistants Blanca Castanza, Maria Elena Delgado, Ena Gudiel
Executive Producer Melissa Baldino
Co-Executive Producer Stephanie Stender
Associate Producer Kaitlin Hammond

Consulting Creative Director Amy Klee
Contributing Editors Erika Bruce, Eva Katz, Jeremy Sauer
Consulting Editors Anne Mendelson, Meg Ragland
Science Editor Guy Crosby, PhD
Executive Food Editor, TV, Radio & Media Bridget Lancaster

Managing Editor, Web Christine Liu
Senior Editor, Cooking School Mari Lovino
Social Media Manager Jill Fisher
Senior Editor, Web Roger Metcalf
Assistant Editor, Web Terrence Doyle
Senior Video Editor Nick Dakoulas

Design Director, Print Greg Galvan
Photography Director Julie Cote
Art Director Susan Levin
Associate Art Director Lindsey Timko
Art Director, Marketing Jennifer Cox
Staff Photographer Daniel J. van Ackere
Color Food Photography Keller + Keller
Styling Catrine Kelty, Marie Piraino
Deputy Art Director, Marketing Melanie Gryboski
Associate Art Director, Marketing Janet Taylor
Designer, Marketing Stephanie Cook
Associate Art Director, Photography Steve Klise

VP, Print & Direct Marketing David Mack
Circulation Director Doug Wicinski
Circulation & Fulfillment Manager Carrie Fethe
Partnership Marketing Manager Pamela Putprush
Marketing Coordinator Marina Tomao

Director, Business Systems Alice Carpenter
Manager, Business & Content Systems Dustin Brandt
DAM Systems Manager Ian Matzen
Project Manager Britt Dresser

Chief Operating Officer Rob Ristagno
VP, Digital Products Fran Middleton
VP, New Product Development Michael Burton
Production Director Guy Rochford
Imaging Manager Lauren Robbins
Production & Imaging Specialists Heather Dube, Dennis Noble
Director, Marketing & Sales Operations Deborah Fagone
Client Services Manager Kate Zebrowski
Sponsorship Sales Associate Morgan Mannino
Senior Controller Theresa Peterson
Customer Loyalty & Support Manager Amy Bootier
Customer Loyalty & Support Reps Caroline Augliere, Rebecca Kowalski, Andrew Straaberg Finfrock

Director, Retail Book Program Beth Ineson
Human Resources Manager Adele Shapiro
Publicity Deborah Broide

ON THE COVER: *One-Pan Pork Tenderloin with Green Beans and Potatoes*, Keller + Keller, Catrine Kelty
ILLUSTRATION: Greg Stevenson

Follow us on **Pinterest**
pinterest.com/TestKitchen

Follow us on **Twitter**
twitter.com/TestKitchen

Find us on **Facebook**
facebook.com/CooksCountry

OCTOBER/NOVEMBER 2015

Contents

TWO-HOUR TURKEY, 18

PUFFY TACOS, 8

DEEP-DISH APPLE PIE, 24

Features

Departments

Just the Essentials

Do an Internet search for the word "recipe," and you'll get more than 50 million hits. Overwhelmed? Our new title, *100 Recipes: The Absolute Best Ways to Make the True Essentials*, is the antidote: a focused collection of no-fail recipes designed to make you a master in the kitchen.

America's Test Kitchen is a very real 2,500-square-foot kitchen located just outside Boston. It is the home of Cook's Country and Cook's Illustrated magazines and the workday destination of more than three dozen test cooks, editors, and cookware specialists. Our mission is to test recipes until we understand how and why they work and arrive at the best version. We also test kitchen equipment and supermarket ingredients in search of products that offer the best value and performance. You can watch us work by tuning in to Cook's Country from America's Test Kitchen (CooksCountry.com) and America's Test Kitchen (AmericasTestKitchen.com) on public television.

Ask Cook's Country

BY MORGAN BOLLING

Make-Ahead Mashed Potatoes

Can I make mashed potatoes ahead of time, freeze them, and then defrost and reheat them right before a big dinner?
Selma Clark, Detroit, Mich.

In order to find the answer to your question, we made five batches of our Creamy Mashed Potatoes (find the recipe at **CooksCountry.com/creamymashedpotatoes**), which are made with Yukon Gold potatoes, butter, heavy cream, and salt. We froze them and tried reheating them in a water bath, on the stovetop, and in the microwave at different power levels.

The most consistently successful technique was to freeze the mashed potatoes, covered with plastic wrap, in a microwave-safe bowl. When you're ready to reheat them, remove the plastic, cover the bowl with an overturned plate, and microwave the potatoes at 50 percent power, stirring occasionally. With a fully frozen batch of our Creamy Mashed Potatoes, this took 15 to 17 minutes. Next to a fresh batch of mashed potatoes, tasters noted that the thawed potatoes tasted somewhat less rich and luxurious, but overall they were very similar. And you could add richness back with a little cream or butter.

Note that when at room temperature the previously frozen potatoes can look soupy, but as they heat up, they will return to their original consistency. This is because the potato starches bond with water as they heat.

THE BOTTOM LINE: You can make and freeze your mashed potatoes in advance. Freeze them, covered, in a microwave-safe bowl and thaw them at 50 percent power in the microwave. And you may want to add a little extra butter.

DEFROSTED, ROOM TEMPERATURE
Looks like potato soup.

DEFROSTED AND HEATED
Please pass the gravy.

Sour Situation

I don't tend to keep sour cream on hand, but I always have Greek yogurt at home. In a pinch, can I substitute Greek yogurt for sour cream in recipes?
David Wilson, Albany, N.Y.

Greek yogurt and sour cream are both sour-tasting, thick dairy products, so it's not crazy to think they could be interchangeable. To test this, we tried Greek yogurt in our Sour Cream Drop Biscuits, in a sour cream–based horseradish sauce, and in beef stroganoff. In the biscuits and the cream sauce we thought that the Greek yogurt was a fine substitute; it felt slightly leaner than the sour cream in both applications, but overall it was acceptable. However, the Greek yogurt broke when it was added to the hot sauce in the beef stroganoff. While tasters said it was fine—albeit less rich—it was visually unappealing. The lower fat content of Greek yogurt is the reason it broke in the stroganoff. While 1 cup of sour cream has 40 grams of fat, the same amount of whole-fat Greek yogurt has only 11 grams of fat, making it much less stable when exposed to high heat.

THE BOTTOM LINE: In a pinch, go ahead and substitute whole-fat Greek yogurt for sour cream. Just be wary of using it in recipes that require high heat.

A Nutty Product

I've recently seen powdered peanut butter in the grocery store. What is it?
Gretta Everett, Santa Fe, N.M.

Powdered peanut butter is a byproduct of peanut oil production: Roasted peanuts are pressed to extract the peanut oil, and the leftover, defatted peanut bits are dried and ground into a powder, which can be reconstituted if desired.

We ordered four brands of powdered peanut butter and followed their package directions to reconstitute them with water. We matched these against our winning creamy peanut butter, Skippy, plain, in peanut butter cookies, in milkshakes, and in peanut butter sandwiches. Tasters were easily able to pick out the powdered varieties. The cookies were noticeably leaner. In the milkshakes, the peanut flavor was less pronounced, and the texture was decidedly chalky. The sandwiches, according to tasters, seemed like they were made with diet peanut butter. These comments made sense when we compared nutrition labels. While 2 tablespoons of Skippy have 190 calories and 16 grams of fat, 2 tablespoons of powdered peanut butter have about 45 calories and 1.5 grams of fat.

Knowing that peanut oil is removed from powdered peanut butter, we tried reconstituting the powder using peanut oil instead of water. It made the product much more similar to peanut butter.

THE BOTTOM LINE: Powdered peanut butter reconstituted with water, per manufacturers' instructions, tastes like a weak imitation of the real thing. It's much better when reconstituted with peanut oil.

Metallic Cheese

The other day I was out of plastic wrap and wrapped some cheese in aluminum foil. But when I unwrapped it, the cheese had several gray spots and I thought that it tasted metallic. What gives?
Helen Clapsaddle, Yakima, Wash.

Aluminum foil is much more highly reactive than paper and plastic (which are only slightly reactive) or stainless steel and glass (which are not at all reactive). This is especially an issue with acidic foods like tart fruits or cheese.

To store cheese, we suggest first wrapping it in waxed or parchment paper before wrapping it loosely in aluminum foil. The paper prevents any reaction or flavor transfer, and the foil helps prevents the cheese from losing moisture and drying out.

THE BOTTOM LINE: Aluminum foil can react with acidic foods like cheese if there is direct contact. To avoid this, wrap the cheese first in waxed or parchment paper and then loosely in foil.

How You Slice It

I just bought ham, and its label says, "Water Added." What does that mean, and why am I paying for added water?
Maris White, Creston, Ohio

The U.S. Department of Agriculture (USDA) grades cooked ham products. "Ham, Water Added" is one of the four categories used in classifying ham. The others are "Ham," "Ham with Natural Juices," and "Ham and Water Product."

Cooked ham is commonly wet-cured with a brining solution (often water, salt, phosphates or nitrates, and sugar). This makes the meat more seasoned and less likely to dry out when reheated at home. It also allows the producer to make more money by increasing the weight of the ham with water.

Officially, a cooked ham product is labeled by the percentage of protein by weight. The added water affects the weight: The more water you add, the lower the percentage of protein in the meat. The USDA bases its grading scale on this protein percentage.

THE BOTTOM LINE: "Ham, Water Added" is one of the four categories of cooked ham products as determined by the USDA. The labels stem from a process called "wet curing" in which ham is treated with a brining solution, affecting both its water and protein contents.

Ham	Ham with Natural Juices	Ham, Water Added	Ham and Water Product
At least 20.5% protein by weight	18.5% to 20.5% protein by weight	17% to 18.5% protein by weight	Less than 17% protein by weight
0% to 2% added water	7% to 8% added water	No more than 10% added water	More than 10% added water
$8.33 per lb	$6.00 per lb	$3.99 per lb	$2.49 per lb
Meatier, with the most flavor, but a little dry when cooked. Often has to be special-ordered.	Smoky and strongly pork-flavored. Saltier and moister than "Ham" and a favorite when cooked.	Dulled but still acceptable ham flavor. Very moist, which some tasters preferred but some thought felt rubbery.	Spongy, bouncy, salty, and processed-tasting.

To ask us a cooking question, visit **CooksCountry.com/ask**. Or write to Ask Cook's Country, P.O. Box 470739, Brookline, MA 02447. Just try to stump us!

Kitchen Shortcuts

COMPILED BY SCOTT KATHAN

SMART TRICK
More Juice
Scott Sullivan, Charlestown, Mass.

I have one of those hinged lime juicers—the kind where you open it, put in a halved lime, and squeeze it closed—that is a staple of my home bar. I've found I get more juice out of each fruit if I quarter, not halve, the limes. This trick is a lifesaver when I'm making margaritas for a crowd.

DOUBLE DUTY
Tortilla Cooker
Carole Berkoff, Carmen, Idaho

I don't have a micro-wave, but I love to cook with tortillas. I've discovered that I can use my panini maker to heat tortillas. I can do four at a time, and I can make them soft for tacos or (with a little oil and more time in the press) crisp enough for tostadas.

Submit a tip online at CooksCountry.com/kitchenshortcuts or send a letter to Kitchen Shortcuts, Cook's Country, P.O. Box 470739, Brookline, MA 02447. Include your name, address, and phone number. If we publish your tip, you will receive a free one-year subscription to Cook's Country. Letters may be edited for clarity and length.

DOUBLE DUTY
Chimney Starter Hack
Larry Webster, Plano, Texas

A few weeks ago I was helping my friend break in his new charcoal grill—turns out he forgot to buy a chimney starter. I spotted one of those big rectangular olive oil cans in his recycling bin and cut out the top and bottom panels of the tin. I made a few vent holes on the sides near the bottom and stuffed it with crumpled newspaper and charcoal. The tin doesn't hold a lot of charcoal, so you have to add charcoal to the pile once it's lit, and since there's no handle, you have to move it with tongs. Still, it works pretty well.

SMART TIP
Improving the Oil
Jonathan Hayden, Dover, Del.

We eat a lot of salad in our house, always with home-made vinaigrette made with extra-virgin olive oil. When I ran out of extra-virgin a few weeks ago, I came up with an idea to improve the flavor of regular olive oil, which I keep around but don't use very much because I usually find it pretty bland. I ran a pitted kalamata olive through my garlic press and into the oil: The small bits of olive were undetectable in the dressed salad, but there was a strong olive flavor in the dressing.

NEAT TRICK
Bean Saver
Robin Burgess, Grants Pass, Ore.

Whenever I open a can of kidney or black beans, I find that many of the beans remain stuck to the bottom of the can. I've discovered that vigorously shaking the can before opening it helps release the beans from the bottom, so they all pour out together after I open the can.

WASTE NOT, WANT NOT
Celery Saver
Denise Muldoon, Warwick, R.I.

Most recipes that call for chopped celery make no mention of the leaves; most people just throw them out. I've found that the leaves have a ton of herby celery flavor. I store them in a plastic bag in the fridge and add a few to recipes that call for chopped celery, and it really boosts the flavor.

COOL TRICK
Chill Out
Amy Eckel, Biddeford, Maine

Whenever I try to cover a bowl or plate with plastic wrap, static electricity causes the wrap to cling to itself and make a mess of the job. There's an easy work-around: I keep the wrap in the door of my refrigerator. The humidity helps tame the static, and the plastic wrap is much easier to use.

Wisconsin Butter Burgers

Why should Wisconsin have all the fun? We wanted butter on our burgers, too. BY ASHLEY MOORE

ARE YOU REALLY putting butter on a burger?"
Questions like this came at me every time I made a batch of Wisconsin butter burgers in the test kitchen. But the minute the skeptics tried a bite, they were persuaded that the folks over at Solly's Grille in Glendale (a suburb of Milwaukee) were doing something right. Since 1936, when Kenneth "Solly" Salmon opened the joint, they've been serving these burgers at all three meals every day—yep, some patrons even eat these for breakfast (see "On the Road").

The small restaurant consists of two yellow U-shaped counters, an open kitchen, and most important, a well-seasoned flattop grill. Grab a stool and watch the cooks pull the well-done, crispy-edged burgers from the griddle; stack them onto bun bottoms; and top each with a slice of American cheese, a small pile of stewed onions, and a toasted bun top that's been lavishly slathered with butter. Even before you grab one, you know that butter is destined to run down your chin in the most satisfying way.

I was determined to create these burgers in the test kitchen, no flattop required. I found a handful of recipes for butter burgers inspired by Solly's, but after cooking through a few of these, I determined that the test kitchen's tried-and-true recipe for the Best Old-Fashioned Burgers was my best inspiration for the burger base. I flattened each patty to ½ inch thick, sprinkled each with salt and pepper, and set them all in the fridge while I prepared the onions.

These "stewed" onions, softened and just barely taking on color (never caramelized), are a mandatory component. At Solly's, the onions are cooked slowly on the flattop grill, but I approximated their color and texture in a saucepan with a bit of water, salt, and, naturally, butter. I covered the pot to let them stew until soft and then removed the lid and allowed them to cook a little longer until they were just barely beginning to brown.

Onions done, I seared my patties in a hot skillet for 3 minutes on the first side without moving them—a crucial step for those crisp edges. After a flip, just 1 minute on the other side finished them off. (I set a slice of American cheese on each and tacked on 30 seconds to give it time to melt.) These burgers were ready

for their toppings.
I stacked a burger on each lightly toasted bun bottom and piled on some onions. I spread each bun top with 2 tablespoons of softened salted butter (tasters preferred this to unsalted), capped each burger, and called my tasters. Together we huddled, hunched over our plates to prevent any butter dribbles, and devoured the burgers. Not one taster failed to ask for seconds.

In Milwaukee, they'll tell you that butter makes a burger better. And you know what? They're right.

When Ham Became Beef
Before World War II, according to late food historian Josh Ozersky, a "hamburger" could be most anything: beef, pork, sausage, you name it. But in 1946, the powerful beef lobby successfully petitioned the USDA to set strict pro-beef rules: To call your product "hamburger," it could contain only beef and beef fat. "Even the slightest bit of pork or pork fat disqualified it." The sweeping decree solidified beef's preeminence in the American marketplace; because White Castle and other chains had made hamburger the nation's top meat product, the move effectively "demoted pork to second-place (later third-place) status forever."

WISCONSIN BUTTER BURGERS

Serves 4

Our favorite domestic salted butter is Kate's Homemade.

- 9 tablespoons salted butter, softened
- 1 onion, chopped
- 1 tablespoon water
  Salt and pepper
- 1 pound 90 percent lean ground beef
- 4 hamburger buns, toasted
- ½ teaspoon vegetable oil
- 4 slices American cheese

1. Melt 1 tablespoon butter in medium saucepan over medium heat. Add onion, water, and ¼ teaspoon salt and cook, covered, until tender, about 5 minutes. Remove lid and continue to cook until translucent and just beginning to brown, about 3 minutes. Cover and keep warm.

2. Transfer beef to rimmed baking sheet and separate into 4 equal mounds. Gently shape each mound into 4½-inch-wide by ½-inch-thick patty. Combine ¾ teaspoon salt and ¾ teaspoon pepper in bowl and sprinkle both sides of patties with mixture. Refrigerate until ready to cook, up to 30 minutes.

3. Spread 2 tablespoons butter onto each bun top; set aside. Heat oil in 12-inch skillet over high heat until just smoking. Using spatula, transfer patties to skillet and cook without moving them for 3 minutes. Flip patties and cook for 1 minute. Top each burger with 1 slice of American cheese and continue to cook until cheese is melted, about 30 seconds longer.

4. Transfer burgers to bun bottoms. Divide onion mixture among burgers and cover with buttered bun tops. Serve immediately.

▶ Want some fries with that? Visit **CooksCountry.com/frozenfrytasting** to read our tasting of frozen French fries.

On the Road
Solly's Grille, Milwaukee

The gold standard of butter burgers can be found at Solly's Grille in Glendale, Wisconsin. From the outside, the restaurant looks more like a new-construction home than old-fashioned diner (according to George Motz, author of *Hamburger America*, the original 1936 Solly's was relocated in 2000 to make room for, of all things, an outpatient heart clinic), but the yellow laminate countertops and milkshake machines confirm: This is a diner, and burgers are served all day.

Though other outlets serve variations on butter burgers (including the regional fast food chain Culver's), true butter burger aficionados seek out Solly's for owner Glenn Fieber's thin, crisp-edged burgers under salty American cheese, creamy stewed onions, and a shameless slather of Wisconsin butter. Fieber is modest but proud of his burgers, saying only as much as needs to be said; when I asked what he puts in the stewed onions that come on every burger, he replied, "I just told you. Stewed onions." For more on our trip to Milwaukee, visit **CooksCountry.com/fieldnotesmilwaukee**.

–BRYAN ROOF

KEY STEPS To Making Butter Burgers
Here are the three essential steps for making these Wisconsin favorites.

1. COOK ONIONS
"Stew" the onions in butter and water in a covered saucepan. Then remove the lid and brown them.

2. BUTTER BUNS
Slather 2 tablespoons of softened salted butter onto each bun top.

3. SEAR BURGERS
Cook the burgers hard and fast to create a flavorful dark brown crust.

WHICH BURGER BUN IS THE BEST?
We want soft, not soggy.

When it comes to hamburgers, the patty tends to hog all the glory—but we think a great burger deserves an equally great bun. To find the best, we asked 21 America's Test Kitchen staffers to taste four top-selling products plain and with hamburgers.

What separates a good bun from a great bun? First, subtle flavor that doesn't overpower the patty. Burgers generally have a hearty dose of salt, so tasters preferred buns with minimal sodium and a dash of sweetness.

We preferred slightly wider buns with at least a 3.5-inch diameter, which comfortably accommodated moderately sized patties. One lower-ranked product was only 3.35 inches wide and our 4-ounce burgers hung awkwardly off its sides. What's more, buns with bottoms that were less than ½ inch thick turned soggy under the weight of the burger.

But the key component was texture. Though every product was tender, one product took the crown for being the fluffiest and moistest of the bunch. Its secret? While traditional hamburger buns use water to hydrate the dough, Martin's Sandwich Potato Rolls replace the water with potato flakes, milk, and butter (essentially mashed potatoes). Potatoes are rich in starches that prevent tough, chewy proteins from forming in the bun. The result? A bun with a delicate crumb that is moist but still extremely fluffy.

Though the second-most-popular hamburger bun brand in the country, Martin's is found primarily on supermarket shelves in the eastern United States. Fortunately, these buns can be ordered online and stored in the freezer. Our tasters noticed no measurable difference in flavor or texture between a bun that was thawed and one that was fresh, but if you'd rather buy from the store and can't find Martin's, Pepperidge Farm White Hamburger Buns are a good backup choice.

–LAUREN SAVOIE

RECOMMENDED

TASTERS' NOTES

MARTIN'S Sandwich Potato Rolls
Price: $3.69 for 8 buns ($0.46 per bun)
Sodium: 170 mg
Sugar: 4.72 g
Height of Bun Top: 0.9 in
Height of Bun Bottom: 0.9 in
Diameter: 3.5 in

"This is my ideal bun," said one taster about our winning product, which is made with potato starch for a "soft," "moist" crumb. Tasters loved the "tender," "fluffy" texture of these buns and thought that their "rich" sweetness nicely "complemented the saltiness of the burger." Though a top-selling product, it is primarily available in East Coast grocery stores or online.

PEPPERIDGE FARM White Hamburger Buns
Price: $2.99 for 8 buns ($0.37 per bun)
Sodium: 205 mg
Sugar: 3.92 g
Height of Bun Top: 0.7 in
Height of Bun Bottom: 0.5 in
Diameter: 3.6 in

These "soft," "squishy" buns condensed easily to "hug the burger," and their wide, thin shape made for a "good ratio of bun to patty" in each bite. Tasters thought that this product was "slightly sweet" and had a "nice honey-like aftertaste."

ARNOLD'S White Hamburger Buns
Price: $3.69 for 8 buns ($0.46 per bun)
Sodium: 220 mg
Sugar: 3.51 g
Height of Bun Top: 0.8 in
Height of Bun Bottom: 0.4 in
Diameter: 3.5 in

These "soft," "buttery" buns had big, "pillowy" tops and a "doughy," Wonder Bread–like texture. Tasters liked that this "airy" product compressed nicely for easy eating, though a few lamented that the "thinner" bottoms "quickly sogged out" from burger juices.

BALL PARK Hamburger Buns
Price: $2.50 for 8 buns ($0.31 per bun)
Sodium: 240 mg
Sugar: 4 g
Height of Bun Top: 0.9 in
Height of Bun Bottom: 0.6 in
Diameter: 3.35 in

This product was "slightly sweet" with a "light," "airy" crumb and "firmer," "chewier" crust. A few tasters noted that larger patties dwarfed these slightly smaller buns. Most deemed this product "perfectly acceptable for any cookout."

All serving sizes were adjusted to 50 grams. Nutritional information was recalculated accordingly.

Pork and Ricotta Meatballs

For a fresher take on meatballs, boot the beef in favor of pork—
and add ricotta cheese. BY CHRISTIE MORRISON

WHAT'S NOT TO love about meatballs? They are staples in cuisines around the world. And the variations—meats, seasonings, binders—are endless. During a recent perusal of Italian cookbooks, I was reminded of an old trick for extra-tender meatballs: adding ricotta cheese.

Most meatball recipes include a mixture of milk and bread. Called a panade, this combination adds moisture to the mix and helps the meatballs stay tender. So why not ricotta cheese instead of milk? And why not all pork instead of a mix of meats? The combination of sweet, mild ground pork and fluffy, creamy ricotta suggested a meatball delicate in flavor and texture. I couldn't wait to give it a try. I quickly discovered a wealth of existing recipes to use for inspiration.

I gathered a handful of these recipes and got to work in the test kitchen. Many of them were fine (if not spectacular), but even the failures were instructive—I learned, for instance, that too much garlic nixed any porky flavors, that substituting chopped shallot for traditional onion helped highlight the meat's natural sweetness, and that sharp flavors like orange peel, which I found in a Sicilian-inspired recipe, were far too dominant a flavor for these comforting meatballs. Using what I'd learned, as well as past experience in the test kitchen, I stitched together a working recipe for pork and ricotta meatballs: a starting point.

To bolster the flavor of the pork, I added garlic, shallot, and Parmesan (not too much, as I didn't want to overwhelm the other flavors). Some chopped parsley and lemon zest provided a fresh note. I mixed in an egg and some fresh bread crumbs and formed balls. I seared a batch in a skillet, finishing them by pouring over some jarred tomato sauce (I'd work on the real thing later) and simmering until the meatballs were cooked through.

The results were impressive: These meatballs were tender, juicy, and flavorful, and they had an unexpected lightness that my tasters loved.

Why so tender and light? I asked our science editor to explain. He explained that the water in ricotta is tightly trapped in coagulated protein, so it doesn't leach out and make the bread crumbs soggy. Plus, the ricotta doesn't

Chopped fresh basil adds a burst of flavor and color to the finished meatballs.

dissolve inside the meatballs, which means it forms lots of little barriers that keep the meat proteins from binding into a dense, tough ball. The result? An uncommonly tender meatball.

What's more, the ricotta added a savory richness that provoked comments of "More, please."

Traditional recipes often call for pan-frying the meatballs as I had done before adding the sauce, but this

method can make a greasy mess of the stovetop. I found that assembling the meatballs on a wire rack set in a rimmed baking sheet and roasting them in the oven was an easier, cleaner option—elevating the meatballs this way allowed air to circulate around them, producing evenly browned (but still not fully cooked) meatballs in about 30 minutes. Plus, using the oven meant that I could double my recipe without having to

brown the balls in batches.

Jarred tomato sauce has its merits, but I wanted a brighter, fresher take here. I kept things simple by gently cooking smashed garlic cloves in extra-virgin olive oil until just golden brown to infuse the sauce with subtle garlic flavor. I added some red pepper flakes and crushed tomatoes to the golden garlic and gently simmered the mixture while the meatballs browned in the oven.

The sauce reduced slightly, bringing out the tomatoes' natural sweetness.

To finish the dish, I transferred the browned meatballs to my big pot of sauce and baked them at 300 degrees for 30 minutes so the flavors could meld. Gently braising the meatballs in the sauce made them even more tender and infused the sauce with sweet, meaty flavor. It also made the kitchen smell terrific.

PORK AND RICOTTA MEATBALLS
Serves 6 to 8

It takes about 10 minutes of occasional mashing with a fork for the ricotta to fully wet the bread enough for the panade to achieve the desired paste consistency. Use a greased ¼-cup dry measuring cup or equal-size portion scoop to divvy up the meatballs, and use slightly wet hands when shaping them to minimize sticking. This recipe makes enough sauce to coat 1½ pounds of pasta.

MEATBALLS
- 4 slices hearty white sandwich bread, crusts removed, torn into small pieces
- 8 ounces (1 cup) whole-milk ricotta cheese
- 2 pounds ground pork
- 1 ounce Parmesan cheese, grated (½ cup), plus extra for serving
- ½ cup chopped fresh parsley
- 2 large eggs
- 2 shallots, minced
- 4 garlic cloves, minced
- 1 tablespoon salt
- 1½ teaspoons pepper
- 1 teaspoon grated lemon zest

SAUCE
- ¼ cup extra-virgin olive oil
- 10 garlic cloves, smashed and peeled
- 1 teaspoon red pepper flakes
- 2 (28-ounce) cans crushed tomatoes
  Salt and pepper
- 2 tablespoons chopped fresh basil

1. FOR THE MEATBALLS: Adjust oven rack to lower-middle position and heat oven to 450 degrees. Set wire rack in aluminum foil–lined rimmed baking sheet and spray evenly with vegetable oil spray. Combine bread and ricotta in large bowl and let sit, mashing occasionally with fork, until smooth paste forms, about 10 minutes.

2. Add pork, Parmesan, parsley, eggs, shallots, garlic, salt, pepper, and lemon zest to bread mixture and mix with your hands until thoroughly combined. Divide meat mixture into 24 portions (about ¼ cup each) and place on platter. Roll meat between your wet hands to form meatballs and space evenly on prepared wire rack. Roast meatballs until browned, 30 to 35 minutes, rotating sheet halfway through roasting. Remove from oven and reduce oven temperature to 300 degrees.

3. FOR THE SAUCE: Meanwhile, combine oil and garlic in Dutch oven set over low heat and cook until garlic is soft and golden on all sides, 12 to 14 minutes, stirring occasionally. Add pepper flakes and cook until fragrant, about 30 seconds. Stir in tomatoes and 1 teaspoon salt. Cover, with lid slightly ajar, and bring to simmer over medium-high heat. Reduce heat to medium-low and simmer until sauce has thickened slightly, about 30 minutes. Season with salt and pepper to taste.

4. Nestle meatballs into sauce, cover, and transfer pot to oven. Bake until meatballs are tender and sauce has thickened, about 30 minutes. Transfer meatballs and sauce to serving platter. Sprinkle with basil and serve, passing extra Parmesan separately.

Spinach Salad with Gorgonzola and Pear

A punch of pear was just the thing to liven up this simple spinach salad. BY KATIE LEAIRD

SPINACH SALAD IS an appealing idea: a deep green, fresh-tasting toss. But often the dressing is too aggressive, overwhelming the delicate, fresh flavor of the spinach—or too wimpy, leaving you with nothing but a mouthful of spinach. I was determined to create a balanced, vibrant salad suitable for the holiday table.

Walnuts, blue cheese, and pears were the ingredients I set out, hoping that they'd elevate these humble baby leaves (which we prefer to less-tender curly leaves) into a holiday-worthy dish. The first two ingredients needed very little help: Lightly toasting the walnuts would bring out their flavor, and a nice wedge of Gorgonzola would add creaminess, savoriness, and tang. So I turned my focus to the pears.

If your pears aren't quite ripe, they'll be mealy. If they are overripe, they'll just squish. But a just-right ripe pear, one that gives slightly at the base of the stem when you press your thumb into it, is glorious. (When in doubt at the grocery store, choose pears that are slightly less ripe and let them sit for a day or two in a brown paper bag that you've folded over at the top.)

In addition to scattering slices on top of each salad, I blended half a pear into the vinaigrette. The added sweetness from the fresh fruit, along with red wine vinegar, shallots, mustard, and oil, gave me a balanced dressing that highlighted the grassy, slightly minerally flavor of the spinach. A sprinkle of ruby-red pomegranate seeds added a little holiday flair.

SPINACH SALAD WITH GORGONZOLA AND PEAR
Serves 4

To make a smooth dressing, be sure the pear is completely ripe. Make sure to use baby, not curly, spinach here.

- 1 ripe Anjou pear, halved and cored
- 3 tablespoons red wine vinegar
- 1 tablespoon minced shallot
- 1 teaspoon Dijon mustard
- 1 teaspoon packed brown sugar

Pomegranate seeds add a pop of bright flavor and color to this fall salad.

- Salt and pepper
- ¼ cup canola oil
- 1 tablespoon lemon juice
- 8 ounces (8 cups) baby spinach
- 3 ounces Gorgonzola cheese, crumbled (¾ cup)
- ½ cup walnuts, toasted and chopped coarse
- ¼ cup pomegranate seeds

1. Cut 1 pear half into large chunks and place in food processor. Add vinegar, shallot, mustard, sugar, ¼ teaspoon salt, and ¼ teaspoon pepper and process until smooth, about 15 seconds. With processor running, slowly pour in oil and process until emulsified, about 30 seconds.

2. Thinly slice remaining pear half crosswise, toss with lemon juice, and set aside. Toss spinach and ½ cup dressing together in large bowl. Season with salt and pepper to taste. Divide salad among individual plates and top each with Gorgonzola, walnuts, pomegranate seeds, and sliced pear. Drizzle remaining ¼ cup dressing over top. Serve.

Introducing Puffy Tacos

San Antonio's been enjoying these light, crisp taco shells in restaurants for years. Could we create a home version for the rest of us? BY MORGAN BOLLING

RESIDENTS OF SAN Antonio, Texas, have strong feelings about puffy tacos—deep-fried, light, crisp, emphatically corn-flavored shells that encase savory meat fillings. They're a regional take on tacos that deserves a spot on menus, and in home kitchens, everywhere.

Many San Antonio fans of the dish cite Diana Barrios-Treviño's restaurant, Los Barrios, as having the best in the city. So when our executive food editor, Bryan Roof, was in San Antonio last year, he visited Barrios-Treviño to see her technique firsthand. As you might expect, Barrios-Treviño starts with fresh *masa de maíz*, finely ground hominy, to create a moist masa dough. She uses a tortilla press to stamp portions of masa dough into 6-inch tortillas and then drops them one at a time into the deep-fryer. The tortillas puff up with air, ballooning as Barrios-Treviño flips and shapes them with two spatulas into the familiar taco-shell shape—except a bit puffier. She pulls the shells from the oil to drain upside down before stuffing them with a simple ground meat filling.

Back in the test kitchen, with Roof's guidance, I started to put together a working recipe. I knew this recipe would have a few steps: I'd be making a dough and frying taco shells, plus creating a filling. But I wanted to make it as simple as possible. Since fresh masa is not available in most grocery stores, I made a dough using much more widely available masa harina (dried masa), salt, and water (see "Masa Harina"). Rather than use a tortilla press, I pressed out disks using a clear pie plate; this simple technique produced a tortilla of even thickness and was easier and more consistent than using a rolling pin. And since you can see through the plate, it's easy to gauge when you have a perfect 6-inch disk.

I brought some oil to 375 degrees in a Dutch oven (our go-to frying vessel in the test kitchen) and dropped in a masa disk. It puffed just as expected. But when I flipped it, the bottom burst and the shell split in two. I attempted again with both lower and higher oil temperatures but had the same issue.

Realizing that I needed some expert advice, I reached out to Barrios-Treviño, who told me I probably had too much water in my dough. When frying, the heat of the oil rapidly pushes water out of the masa dough. The **excess water**

Our from-scratch fried taco shells contain only three ingredients: masa harina, salt, and water. They're worth every minute it takes to make them.

was converting to steam rapidly, causing the shells to puff so much that they exploded. After a series of tests, I found the balance. A ratio of 1⅔ cups water to 2½ cups masa harina was the sweet spot for a workable dough that didn't explode.

I was using a hefty 3 quarts of oil to be able to fully submerge the shells in a Dutch oven. But manipulating the shells in the deep Dutch oven was an awkward process. Would a shallower vessel make the process easier? I tried 2 cups of oil in an 8-inch skillet to see if shallow frying would be a feasible option, but the oil splattered and the oil temperature dropped almost 100 degrees after I added each tortilla. I switched to a large saucepan; by doing so I could get away with using just 2 quarts of oil, and the saucepan's smaller profile made shaping the tacos easier.

A favorite filling for San Antonio puffy tacos is a Texas take on *picadillo*—browned ground beef cooked with potatoes, onion, and green peppers and flavored with garlic, cumin, salt, and black pepper. I lined up 12 crisp, light puffy taco shells; stuffed them with my picadillo; and topped them with shredded lettuce, cheese, and tomatoes. Tasters tore into them with unbridled **pleasure.**

PUFFY TACOS Serves 6 to 8

We used Maseca Brand Instant Masa Corn Flour for our taco shells. The dough should not be sticky and should have the texture of Play-Doh. If the dough cracks or falls apart when pressing the tortillas, just reroll and press again.

PICADILLO

- 12 ounces 85 percent lean ground beef
- ½ russet potato (4 ounces), peeled and cut into ¼-inch pieces
- Salt and pepper
- 1 onion, chopped fine
- 1 small green bell pepper, stemmed, seeded, and chopped fine
- 3 garlic cloves, minced
- 1½ teaspoons ground cumin
- 2 teaspoons all-purpose flour
- ¾ cup water

TACO SHELLS

- 2½ cups (10 ounces) masa harina
- 1 teaspoon salt
- 1⅔ cups warm water
- 2 quarts vegetable oil

Shredded iceberg lettuce
Chopped tomato
Shredded sharp cheddar cheese
Hot sauce

1. FOR THE PICADILLO: Combine beef, potato, 1 teaspoon pepper, and ¾ teaspoon salt in 12-inch nonstick skillet. Cook over medium-high heat until meat and potatoes begin to brown, 6 to 8 minutes, breaking up meat with spoon. Add onion and bell pepper and cook until softened, 4 to 6 minutes. Add garlic and cumin and cook until fragrant, about 30 seconds.

2. Stir in flour and cook for 1 minute. Stir in water and bring to boil. Reduce heat to medium-low and simmer until thickened slightly, about 1 minute. Season with salt and pepper to taste. Remove from heat, cover, and keep warm.

3. FOR THE TACO SHELLS: Mix masa harina and salt together in medium bowl. Stir in warm water with rubber spatula. Using your hands, knead mixture in bowl until it comes together fully (dough should be soft and tacky, not sticky), about 30 seconds. Cover dough with damp dish towel and let rest for 5 minutes.

4. Divide dough into 12 equal portions, about ¼ cup each, then roll each into smooth ball between your hands. Transfer to plate and keep covered with damp dish towel. Cut sides of 1-gallon zipper-lock bag, leaving bottom seam intact.

5. Set wire rack in rimmed baking sheet and line rack with triple layer of paper towels. Add oil to large saucepan until it measures 2½ inches deep and heat over medium-high heat to 375 degrees.

6. When oil comes to temperature, enclose 1 dough ball at a time in split bag. Using clear pie plate (so you can see size of tortilla), press dough flat into 6-inch circle (about ⅛ inch thick).

7. Carefully remove tortilla from plastic and drop into hot oil. Fry tortilla until it puffs up, 15 to 20 seconds. Using 2 metal spatulas, carefully flip tortilla. Immediately press down in center of tortilla with 1 spatula to form taco shape, submerging tortilla into oil while doing so. Using second spatula, spread top of tortilla open about 1½ inches. Fry until golden brown, about 60 seconds. Adjust burner, if necessary, to maintain oil temperature between 350 and 375 degrees.

8. Transfer taco shell to prepared rack and place upside down to drain. Return oil to 375 degrees and repeat with remaining dough balls.

9. Divide picadillo evenly among taco shells, about ¼ cup each. Serve immediately, passing lettuce, tomato, cheddar, and hot sauce separately.

The American Table
Puffy, Crisp, Crunchy, Crumbly

Ask an outsider about San Antonio's charms, and you'll likely hear about the downtown Riverwalk, the vibrant nightlife, and of course, the iconic Alamo. But ask a local and you'll get an earful about puffy tacos.

The ubiquitous tacos are so important here that the mascot for the San Antonio Missions minor league baseball team is, yes, Henry the Puffy Taco. But until prefab taco shells became the national Tex-Mex norm in the 1960s, most tacos in South Texas were of a similar puffy ilk. Cooks in Houston, Corpus Christi, Austin, and many other, smaller south Texas towns have been dropping fresh tortillas into frying oil and forming them into pockets for ground meat fillings for generations, sometimes calling them "crispy" or "crunchy" tacos—both equally apt descriptors.

Or they just call them tacos. When author Robb Walsh sampled a version at Caro's Restaurant in Rio Grande City on the Texas-Mexico border a decade ago, owner Juan Caro told him, "Up in San Antonio they are making a big deal about puffy tacos. I say: 'What's the difference? We have always made them this way.'" Read about our recent trip to Texas at **CooksCountry.com/fieldnotessanantonio**.

Top: The Alamo. Bottom: Henry the Puffy Taco rallies baseball fans.

MASA HARINA
Tortilla base

KEY INGREDIENT Masa Harina

Masa harina, also called dried masa flour on some supermarket labels, is the base ingredient for most home-kitchen tortilla recipes. The direct translation is "dough flour," which makes sense when you understand how it's made: Dried corn kernels are soaked in an alkaline solution to remove the hulls and then ground into a dough, called masa. This dough is then washed, dried again, and powdered into fine-grained flour that, when mixed with warm water and salt, makes a simple tortilla dough. You can find masa harina in the Mexican foods section of your local grocery store.

TEST KITCHEN TECHNIQUE Creating Puffy Taco Shells

After mixing the dough, dividing it into 12 equal balls, and setting up the draining rack, heat the oil to 375 degrees. Then begin shaping and frying the dough.

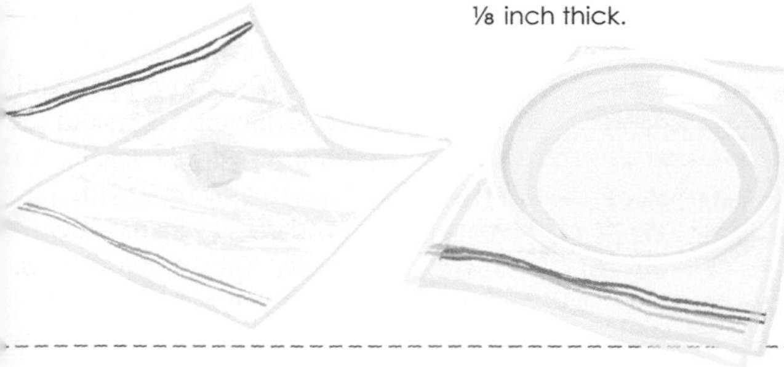

1. Cut open the sides of a 1-gallon zipper-lock bag and place a ball of dough inside. Fold the plastic over the top.

2. Press down on plastic with a clear pie plate to flatten each ball into a 6-inch circle. It should be ⅛ inch thick.

3. Lower the tortilla into the hot oil. Don't splash, and watch carefully: In about 15 to 20 seconds, the tortilla will begin to puff up in the middle.

4. Use two metal spatulas to grip the tortilla and flip it over in the oil. Be gentle here: You don't want to pierce or tear the tortilla.

5. Use spatulas to shape the tortilla into a taco shell with a wide mouth. Nudge shell down into the oil and fry until golden brown.

Pennsylvania Dutch Chicken-Corn Soup

Deep chicken and corn flavors make this soup delicious.
Rivels make it memorable. BY CHRISTIE MORRISON

WITH ITS SATISFYING flavors and hearty, stick-to-your-ribs feel, chicken-corn soup is typical of Pennsylvania Dutch recipes. The soup is traditionally made by simmering a whole chicken for hours to create a rich broth in which to showcase the sweet, tender bite of local corn kernels. But what really makes it special are its tiny *rivels*, a cross between dumplings and German spaetzle, which add an unexpected chewy component. As a girl, I spent many a Saturday afternoon watching my grandmother make this soup in her central Pennsylvania home. I wanted to capture all the slow-cooked flavor and texture I remembered without devoting an entire day to the process.

Re-creating the soup with an eye toward efficiency meant starting with chicken parts instead of a whole bird. I decided to go with bone-in, skin-on breasts and thighs, which provided a nice mix of light and dark meat. Since I didn't need to brown the chicken, I discarded the skin before cooking to prevent the broth from becoming greasy. To build long-cooked flavor without overcooking the lean white meat, I started by sautéing onion and celery, pouring in chicken broth, and then poaching the thighs—only adding the chicken breasts after the thighs were partially cooked (since thighs take longer). This technique yielded meat that was perfectly moist and a reinforced broth that tasted as if it had been simmering for hours.

Because corn is so important to this soup, I wanted to find a way to deepen the corn flavor. I departed from tradition and added the stripped cobs to the broth while the chicken poached; then I added the kernels to cook for the last 15 minutes to keep the flavor fresh. But this short cooking time left the kernels too starchy and firm. Extending the cooking time to 25 minutes yielded more tender corn. To get at even more of the flavor inside the corn kernels, I grated two of the four ears I was using on the large holes of a box grater; this had the added advantage of releasing starch that helped thicken this hearty soup.

The chicken and corn may pack all the flavor in this soup, but the dense, chewy rivels supply the texture that made my tasters go back for a second bowl. Traditional recipes call for a

ratio of 2 cups flour to 2 eggs and no additional milk or water to loosen the dough, making it quite dry and very hard to work together. The drier the rivels, the more they disintegrated into the soup, leaving me with floury sludge. I eased back on the flour to 1¼ cups, at which point I could easily work together the flour and egg (and some minced chives for added flavor). But the rivels were still a little tough. Letting the dough rest while I prepared the soup was the answer; this extra time gave the dough a chance to relax.

When my soup was done, I stirred in some fresh parsley and topped each bowl with chopped hard-cooked egg, a traditional garnish that adds richness and texture.

This homey soup is studded with pleasantly chewy rivels, small dumplings pinched from a flour, egg, and chive dough and poached in the pot.

PENNSYLVANIA DUTCH CHICKEN AND CORN SOUP

Serves 6

Fresh corn kernels (plus the stripped cobs) give this soup its flavor; do not substitute frozen corn. Our favorite store-bought broth is Swanson Chicken Stock. Note that the chicken thighs and breast are added to the soup at different points. This soup cooks for about 90 minutes.

- 1¼ cups (6¼ ounces) all-purpose flour
- 2 tablespoons minced fresh chives
  Salt and pepper
- 2 large eggs, lightly beaten, plus 2 hard-cooked large eggs, chopped
- 4 ears corn, husks and silk removed
- 2 tablespoons unsalted butter
- 1 onion, chopped fine
- 2 celery ribs, chopped fine
- 8 cups chicken broth
- 2 (5- to 7-ounce) bone-in chicken thighs, skin removed, trimmed
- 1 (10- to 12-ounce) bone-in split chicken breast, skin removed, trimmed
- 2 tablespoons minced fresh parsley

1. Combine flour, chives, and ¾ teaspoon salt in bowl. Form well in center and add beaten eggs. Using fork, slowly work flour into eggs, using your hands when stirring becomes difficult. (Dough will be very firm.) Knead dough on lightly floured counter until smooth, about 1 minute. Return dough to bowl, cover with plastic wrap, and let sit at room temperature while assembling soup.

Spaghetti Squash Salad

Sure, you can toss it with butter (yawn) or pretend it's pasta (it's not).
But we wanted a more flavorful approach. BY ASHLEY MOORE

SPAGHETTI SQUASH IS making a comeback. This squash, whose cooked flesh scrapes into noodle-like strands, is now showing up on trendy restaurant menus and piled high in bins at the supermarket. While some insist on positioning its string-like strands as a vegetable alternative to pasta, I wanted to meet this squash on its own merits and create an unexpected, fresh-tasting, room-temperature salad that would highlight its grassy, nutty sweetness.

With this direction in mind, I began my testing with the cooking method. Boiling introduced too much liquid and gave me soggy squash. Roasting held more promise, and after playing with various oven temperatures, cooking times, and precooking preparations, I zeroed in on the best technique: I cut the squash in half lengthwise, removed the seeds, positioned it cut side down on a baking sheet (to maximize browning), and let it ride in a 375-degree oven for 40 to 45 minutes. This gave me soft, non-soggy strings of squash with just a hint of caramelization.

Once the squash halves had cooled for about an hour, I took a fork to their interiors and began to scrape out the flesh into individual strands. The strands were tender but firm enough to hold their shape. Even better, they didn't release any excess liquid. The delicate but distinct nutty, squashy flavor stood out. I had a fine base with which to build a salad.

I wanted this salad to feature light, nutty flavors to echo the flavor of the squash, so I went in a Mediterranean direction. I tossed the squash with some chickpeas, salty feta cheese, chopped parsley, chopped scallions, and toasted pistachios. A fresh lemon vinaigrette added a final note of brightness.

SPAGHETTI SQUASH SALAD WITH CHICKPEAS AND FETA
Serves 4 to 6
Plan ahead: The squash needs to cool for 1 hour after roasting.

- 1 (2½-pound) spaghetti squash, halved lengthwise and seeded
- 6 tablespoons extra-virgin olive oil, plus extra for drizzling
  Salt and pepper
- 2 teaspoons grated lemon zest plus 7 teaspoons juice
- 1 (15-ounce) can chickpeas, rinsed
- 2 ounces feta cheese, crumbled (½ cup)
- ½ cup coarsely chopped fresh parsley
- 4 scallions, sliced thin on bias
- 2 tablespoons chopped toasted pistachios

1. Adjust oven rack to middle position and heat oven to 375 degrees. Brush cut sides of squash with 2 tablespoons oil and season with salt and pepper. Place squash, cut side down, on rimmed baking sheet. Roast squash until just tender and tip of paring knife can easily be slipped into flesh, 40 to 45 minutes. Transfer squash to wire rack, cut side up, and let cool completely, about 1 hour.

2. Combine lemon zest and juice, remaining ¼ cup oil, ½ teaspoon salt, and ½ teaspoon pepper in large bowl. Holding squash over bowl, use fork to scrape flesh from skin into strands; discard skin.

3. Add chickpeas to bowl with squash and toss gently to coat with dressing. Transfer to serving platter and sprinkle with feta, parsley, scallions, and pistachios. Drizzle with extra oil before serving.

▶ Visit CooksCountry.com/nov15 for two variations: one with radishes and *queso fresco*, the other with tomatoes and Pecorino.

Chickpeas and feta cheese add substance and flavor to this hearty room-temperature salad.

INGREDIENT SPOTLIGHT
Spaghetti Squash
Yellow, oblong, and slightly ridged spaghetti squash has flesh that, once cooked, can be forked into the thin strands that give this squash its name. We roast the halved squash and let it cool before scraping out the flesh.

Baked Mustard Chicken

We made 46 variations before we finally got the two best parts of this recipe—
the mustard flavor and the crunchy breading—to play nice together. BY CECELIA JENKINS

TALK ABOUT AN appealing supper: chicken, infused with sharp mustard flavor and baked in a crunchy crust. Who wouldn't love that?

Well, me, at least not after pulling what felt like the millionth sheet of chicken parts out of the oven and digging in only to find them completely lacking in mustard flavor, with breading sliding off like sand down a dune.

But I knew there had to be a way. After all, I'd researched thoroughly and found dozens of existing recipes for baked mustard chicken, many of which seemed straightforward and simple: Dunk chicken in mustard, press on some bread crumbs, and bake until done. But while some held promise, none produced the deep mustard flavor and perfectly crunchy crust that I wanted. I realized that to achieve my goal, I'd have to chart new territory.

I patted dry 3 pounds of chicken parts, enough to feed four to six people, and put them through a quick dredge in flour, a dip in beaten egg (fortified with some Dijon mustard), and a roll in panko bread crumbs. I slid them into the oven and waited, hopeful.

Letdown. While the chicken cooked perfectly (in just 35 to 40 minutes), it was desperately short on the whole point of this dish: mustard flavor. And the bread crumbs, though adhering to each other, stubbornly refused to stay stuck to the chicken; instead, they formed a sheath that peeled right off.

My first move to address the wimpy mustard flavor was to ditch the egg yolk in the egg dip; the flavorful yolk was obscuring the dip's mustardiness. I whisked up an egg white–only dip and added even more mustard to it. But when I baked this batch, the coating again slid right off.

After close inspection, I concluded that mustard makes a lousy adhesive. Because it was adding moisture to the coating, the bread crumbs were just steaming off the chicken. So I cut back on the amount of Dijon in the egg white dip. This did help the coating stick but robbed the chicken of precious mustard flavor.

A promising salve lurked in the pantry: dry mustard powder. Adding it to the egg white dip and to the bread crumbs contributed some mustardy heat but not enough. This dish needed yet more mustard, but where to fit it in?

I turned to the bread crumbs themselves. I'd already tossed some mustard powder in with them, but could I doctor them up in a way that would bring even more mustard to the party? I fired up the food processor and pulsed some mustard into the crumbs (not too much; just 5 tablespoons was enough to saturate them), along with melted butter, white wine vinegar, and some fresh tarragon. After I toasted the mix, the bread crumbs took on a lovely mustard flavor.

With mustard in my egg dip and in my crumbs, I went in for the hat trick: a quick, creamy Dijon sauce to seal the deal with a third vibrant, vigorous mustard punch.

BAKED MUSTARD CHICKEN

Serves 4 to 6

Ian's Panko Breadcrumbs, Original Style won a recent test kitchen taste test of bread crumbs. The seasoned bread crumbs brown quickly; stir them frequently for even browning. You will need two rimmed baking sheets for this recipe.

MUSTARD SAUCE

¼	cup Dijon mustard
¼	cup sour cream
1	tablespoon water
2	teaspoons white wine vinegar
2	teaspoons minced fresh tarragon
⅛	teaspoon pepper
	Pinch salt

CHICKEN

7	tablespoons unsalted butter, melted
7	tablespoons Dijon mustard
2½	tablespoons white wine vinegar
2½	tablespoons dry mustard
½	teaspoon granulated garlic
	Salt and pepper
2⅓	cups panko bread crumbs
1¼	teaspoons minced fresh tarragon
3	pounds bone-in chicken pieces (2 split breasts cut in half crosswise, 2 drumsticks, and 2 thighs), skin removed, trimmed
¼	cup all-purpose flour
3	large egg whites
½	teaspoon paprika
¼	cup grated Parmesan cheese

1. FOR THE MUSTARD SAUCE: Whisk all ingredients together in bowl; set aside. (Sauce can be refrigerated for up to 2 days.)

2. FOR THE CHICKEN: Adjust oven rack to middle position and heat oven

For big, layered mustard flavor, we use both dry mustard and Dijon in the crumbs and more Dijon in the wet dip and sauce.

to 350 degrees. Process melted butter, 5 tablespoons Dijon mustard, vinegar, 1½ tablespoons dry mustard, granulated garlic, ½ teaspoon pepper, and ¼ teaspoon salt in food processor until combined, about 5 seconds, scraping down sides of bowl as needed. Add panko and tarragon and pulse until mixture resembles wet sand, about 8 pulses.

3. Spread bread-crumb mixture in even layer on rimmed baking sheet, breaking up any clumps. Bake, stirring every 5 minutes, until golden brown, 14 to 16 minutes. Let cool slightly and crumble larger clumps with your fingers. Increase oven temperature to 400 degrees.

4. Set wire rack in second rimmed baking sheet and spray with vegetable oil

spray. Pat chicken dry with paper towels and season with salt and pepper. Spread flour in shallow dish. Whisk egg whites, paprika, remaining 2 tablespoons Dijon mustard, and remaining 1 tablespoon dry mustard in second shallow dish. Transfer cooled crumbs to third shallow dish and stir in Parmesan.

5. Working with 1 piece at a time, dredge chicken pieces in flour, shaking off excess; dip into egg white mixture to thoroughly coat, letting excess drip back into dish; then coat with crumbs, pressing gently to adhere. Transfer chicken pieces to prepared wire rack. Bake until breasts register 160 degrees and drumsticks/thighs register 175 degrees, 35 to 40 minutes. Let rest for 5 minutes. Serve with mustard sauce.

Shrimp Creole

To create an authentic Creole dish without using every spice on the rack, we looked to the past for inspiration. BY KATIE LEAIRD

SHRIMP CREOLE, ONCE an elegant New Orleans dish of sweet-savory shrimp poached in a tomato-based sauce, has evolved over the years into an unbridled spice cabinet raid. Recipes call for a dozen or more different dried herbs and spices to achieve an "authentic" Creole flavor. Why? Does this dish have to be a riot of flavor? Isn't there room for subtlety?

A thorough search of our vintage cookbook library gave me hope. While some of the old recipes I found were too bare-bones, and others plain reckless (including a 1959 gem that had me boiling shrimp for 90 minutes), I found some that promised what I wanted: a complex but refined sauce that would highlight the tender, savory shrimp without an epic ingredient list. A middle ground.

Following New Orleans culinary tradition, I started the sauce with a roux, sautéing flour and oil to create a thickening base. I added the "holy trinity" of Louisiana cooking—onions, celery, and green bell peppers, all finely chopped—to create a solid base of flavor. After the vegetables had softened and begun to brown, I stirred in a restrained mix of Creole spices, including paprika, garlic powder, and cayenne, among others, and then doused the sizzling veggies with dry white wine. Once the wine was mostly cooked off, I introduced a can of diced tomatoes.

I'd need more liquid to submerge the shrimp, so naturally I tried chicken broth and vegetable broth, but both, to my surprise, seemed to muddy the cooking liquid and mask the sweet, delicate shrimp flavor. I ditched the stock for more white wine, but that took things in a far-too-boozy direction.

Could the answer be as simple as water? Yes: A quarter cup of water, plus a bit of Worcestershire for depth and sugar for sweetness, gave me a lovely poaching liquid and sauce.

Once the peeled and deveined shrimp were cooked (just 5 to 7 minutes in the liquid for perfectly tender shrimp), I added a little lemon juice and parsley for freshness. Once I spooned the shrimp and sauce over rice (which thirstily soaked up the juices), I had a lovely, beautifully balanced, multifaceted and invigorating Louisiana-style supper, at once elegant and simple. You can add hot sauce if you want, but I think this Shrimp Creole is perfect just as it is.

SHRIMP CREOLE Serves 4 to 6
Serve this dish over white rice.

CREOLE SEASONING
- 2 teaspoons paprika
- 1 teaspoon garlic powder
- ½ teaspoon salt
- ¼ teaspoon dried thyme
- ¼ teaspoon dried basil
- ¼ teaspoon pepper
- ⅛ teaspoon cayenne pepper

SHRIMP
- 3 tablespoons vegetable oil
- 2 tablespoons all-purpose flour
- 1 onion, chopped fine
- 1 green bell pepper, stemmed, seeded, and chopped fine
- 2 celery ribs, chopped fine
  Salt and pepper
- ½ cup dry white wine
- 1 (14.5-ounce) can diced tomatoes
- ¼ cup water
- 1 tablespoon Worcestershire sauce
- 1 teaspoon sugar
- 2 pounds large shrimp (26 to 30 per pound), peeled, deveined, and tails removed
- 2 tablespoons lemon juice
- 2 tablespoons chopped fresh parsley
- 2 scallions, sliced thin

1. FOR THE CREOLE SEASONING: Combine all ingredients in bowl and set aside.

2. FOR THE SHRIMP: Heat oil in Dutch oven over medium heat until shimmering. Add flour and cook, stirring constantly, until light brown, 3 to 5 minutes. Add onion, bell pepper, celery, and ½ teaspoon salt and cook, stirring often, until vegetables are softened and beginning to brown, 10 to 12 minutes, scraping up any browned bits.

3. Stir in Creole seasoning and cook until fragrant, about 30 seconds. Add wine and cook until nearly evaporated, 4 to 6 minutes, scraping up any browned bits. Add tomatoes and their juice, water, Worcestershire, and sugar. Bring to boil, reduce heat to low, and simmer, covered and stirring occasionally, until slightly thickened, about 30 minutes.

4. Add shrimp, increase heat to medium, and return to simmer. Cook until shrimp are opaque and just cooked through, 5 to 7 minutes. Stir in lemon juice and parsley. Season with salt and pepper to taste, sprinkle with scallions, and serve.

Diced tomatoes—and plenty of paprika—give our Shrimp Creole its rich red color.

KEY STEPS Building Fond and Deglazing
Many cooks think about fond—the concentrated browned bits on the bottom of your cooking vessel—as a meat-based phenomenon (as when making gravy or a pan sauce for seared steaks), but it happens with vegetables, too. But fond is useless if it doesn't dissolve into the sauce. To make sure this happens, gently scrape the bottom of the pot (we like to use a wooden spoon) after adding liquid so the fond's flavor is incorporated into the dish.

FOND

Cranberry–Sour Cream Pound Cake

Traditional pound cake is all about balance, so what happens when you throw two untraditional ingredients into the mix? BY REBECCAH MARSTERS

I'M SOMEWHAT OF a pound cake purist: no tangerine rind, maple-bourbon glaze, or butterscotch in my pound cake, please. To me, the beauty of pound cake is in its simplicity: a velvety, tender, fine crumb and straightforward vanilla flavor. But I recently enjoyed a slice of cranberry–sour cream pound cake at my local coffee shop; it was good enough to get me rethinking my purist bias. While the cake was a little gummy and too sour, the bright combination had great potential. I set out to develop a recipe for cranberry–sour cream pound cake that had the cake's signature tight and sturdy crumb, sported a crisp and golden top crust, and was enriched—but not overwhelmed—with sour cream and tart cranberries.

I combed through baking books in the test kitchen's cookbook library and found recipes for sour cream pound cake calling for anywhere from a few tablespoons to a whole cup of sour cream. Butter, sugar, eggs, and flour (all-purpose or cake) amounts varied. While traditional pound cake relies on creaming (beating the butter and sugar together to incorporate air pockets) to help with leavening, many modern recipes call for baking soda or baking powder. I'd try both techniques. I gathered a half-dozen promising recipes and headed into the test kitchen.

While some cakes tasted good, most had texture issues. Cake flour promised a more delicate crumb, but it buckled under the moisture from the sour cream. Baking powder helped lighten the texture and produce an impressive rise. And as for the sour cream, I found ⅓ cup to be perfect—lesser amounts didn't register; any more and the cake was too dense and sour.

I also learned that 2 tablespoons of milk mixed into the sour cream made it easier to incorporate evenly into the batter. Two sticks of butter, 1½ cups of sugar, five eggs (up from the three or four most recipes call for—the extra eggs help lift the heavy batter), and 2 teaspoons of vanilla rounded out my ingredient list.

I had a tasty cake, but the texture still wasn't quite perfect—it was a little gummy. I suspected that the wet sour cream was the culprit. After a series of tests, I found that I could back off just

a bit on two other moisture-adding ingredients—butter and sugar (both of which melt into a liquid state in the oven)—without my tasters being any the wiser, and this eliminated the gumminess. Now that I had the perfect sour cream pound cake base, it was time to add the cranberries.

Starting with the simplest approach, I stirred a cup of whole cranberries into the batter and baked. Of course, nothing's that simple: The berries were too big, leaving unsightly red craters in each slice and creating explosions of mouth-puckering tartness. Chopping the cranberries solved the first problem, distributing slivers of berry evenly throughout the cake. To take the sting out of the tart berries, I tossed them with a tablespoon of confectioners' sugar, and now the cake was really good—moist, velvety, and very flavorful.

CRANBERRY–SOUR CREAM POUND CAKE
Serves 8

If you're using frozen cranberries for this recipe, there's no need to thaw them first. The ideal temperature for the eggs and butter is 60 degrees. The test kitchen's preferred loaf pan measures 8½ by 4½ inches; if you use a 9 by 5-inch loaf pan, start checking for doneness 5 minutes earlier than advised in the recipe. This cake bakes for almost 2 hours and must cool for 2 hours more.

To make sure the tart cranberries don't overpower the cake, we chop them into smaller pieces and toss them with confectioners' sugar before folding them into the batter.

- 5 large eggs, room temperature
- 2 teaspoons vanilla extract
- 1¾ cups (8¾ ounces) all-purpose flour
- Salt
- ½ teaspoon baking powder
- ⅓ cup sour cream
- 2 tablespoons milk
- 14 tablespoons unsalted butter, softened but still cool
- 1¼ cups (8¾ ounces) granulated sugar
- 4 ounces (1 cup) fresh or frozen cranberries, chopped coarse
- 1 tablespoon confectioners' sugar

1. Adjust oven rack to lower-middle position and heat oven to 300 degrees. Spray 8½ by 4½-inch loaf pan with baking spray with flour. Whisk eggs and vanilla together in 2-cup liquid measuring cup. Sift flour, ¾ teaspoon salt, and baking powder into bowl. Whisk sour cream and milk together in second bowl.

2. Using stand mixer fitted with paddle, beat butter on medium-high speed until smooth and creamy, 2 to 3 minutes, scraping down bowl once. Reduce speed to medium and gradually pour in granulated sugar. Increase speed to medium-high and beat until pale and fluffy, 3 to 5 minutes, scraping down bowl as needed.

3. Reduce speed to medium and gradually add egg mixture in slow, steady stream. Scrape bottom and sides of bowl and continue to mix on medium speed until uniform, about 1 minute (batter may look slightly curdled).

4. Reduce speed to low and add flour mixture in 3 additions, alternating with sour cream mixture in 2 additions,

scraping down bowl as needed. Give batter final stir by hand.

5. Toss cranberries with confectioners' sugar and ⅛ teaspoon salt in bowl until evenly coated, then gently but thoroughly fold into batter. Transfer batter to prepared pan and tap pan on counter twice to release air bubbles. Bake until toothpick inserted in center comes out clean, 1¾ hours to 1 hour 55 minutes, rotating pan halfway through baking.

6. Let cake cool in pan on wire rack for 15 minutes. Remove cake from pan and let cool completely on rack, about 2 hours, before serving. (Cooled cake can be wrapped tightly in plastic wrap and stored at room temperature for up to 3 days.)

Chocolate-Cherry Brownies

Adding cherries to brownies seemed like a brilliant idea—until we sampled batch after batch of soggy brownies. BY MORGAN BOLLING

CHOCOLATE AND CHERRIES are a common pairing—think Black Forest cake or chocolate-covered cherries. The richness of chocolate is a perfect match for the sweet-tart fruitiness of cherries. I wanted to find the best way to add bright cherry flavor to chewy chocolate brownies.

To start, I baked six existing recipes for chocolate-cherry brownies. As my colleagues and I tasted them, it became apparent that incorporating the cherries without ruining the texture of the brownies was going to be my biggest challenge. A few of the recipes called for simply spooning cherry pie filling or cherry preserves on top of brownies: It was easy, sure, but way too sweet. Recipes that used chopped fresh or frozen cherries were too wet, and the pieces of fruit were gummy inside the brownies. Those that used cherry extract tasted medicinal, and cherry liqueur is a bit obscure for a brownie recipe. To add insult to injury, none of the base brownies were very good.

Since I wasn't making any progress with existing recipes, I decided to start somewhere solid—with a favorite test kitchen recipe for chewy brownies. This recipe uses both cocoa powder and chopped unsweetened chocolate for richness and depth. As for the cherries, I hoped I could sprinkle chopped fresh cherries with sugar and leave

them to drain off some of their liquid before stirring them into the brownie batter; unfortunately, this didn't work, as the slimy cherry bits still made the brownies too wet. I turned to dried cherries. They added a ton of fruit flavor (both sweetened and unsweetened worked fine here) and didn't make the brownies soggy, but their texture was a bit leathery.

I knew just what to do: I'd soak the dried cherries in hot liquid to soften them. I ran tests rehydrating the dried cherries in red wine, port, and water. The wine and port added distinct flavors that didn't taste right, and the cherries plumped with water were fine but underwhelming. I tried using different sodas and juices, but nothing tasted right. Then a colleague suggested using what seemed like an odd ingredient, almond extract, explaining that almonds share similar flavor compounds with stone fruit—including cherries. For my next batch, I rehydrated my 6 ounces of dried cherries in ¼ cup of water bolstered by a teaspoon of the potent almond extract. These cherries, once stirred into the batter (with their liquid) and baked, gave the brownies a deep, rounded, fruity complexity.

DARK CHOCOLATE–CHERRY BROWNIES Makes 24 brownies

Do not cut the brownies until they're fully cooled. Either sweetened or unsweetened dried cherries can be used in this recipe. Droste Cocoa is the test kitchen's highest-rated Dutch-processed brand.

- 1½ cups (6 ounces) dried cherries, chopped
- ¼ cup plus ⅓ cup water
- 1 teaspoon almond extract
- 2 ounces unsweetened chocolate, chopped fine
- 4 tablespoons unsalted butter, cut into 4 pieces
- 6 tablespoons vegetable oil
- ⅓ cup (1 ounce) Dutch-processed cocoa powder
- 2 large eggs plus 2 large yolks
- 2 teaspoons vanilla extract
- 2¼ cups (15¾ ounces) sugar
- ¾ teaspoon salt
- 1¾ cups (8¾ ounces) all-purpose flour

1. Adjust oven rack to lowest position and heat oven to 350 degrees. Make foil sling for 13 by 9-inch baking pan by folding 2 long sheets of aluminum foil; first sheet should be 13 inches wide and second sheet should be 9 inches wide. Lay sheets of foil in pan perpendicular to each other, with extra foil hanging over edges of pan. Push foil into corners and up sides of pan, smoothing foil flush to pan. Spray lightly with vegetable oil spray.

2. Combine cherries, ¼ cup water, and almond extract in small bowl. Microwave, covered, until hot, about 1 minute. Let stand, covered, until cherries are soft, about 5 minutes. Microwave chocolate and butter in separate large bowl at 50 percent power, stirring occasionally, until melted, about 45 seconds. Whisk in oil, cocoa, and remaining ⅓ cup water. (Mixture may look curdled.)

3. Whisk eggs and yolks and vanilla into chocolate mixture until smooth. Whisk in sugar and salt until fully incorporated. Stir in flour until just combined. Stir in softened cherries and their liquid.

4. Pour batter into prepared pan, spread into corners, and smooth top with rubber spatula. Bake until slightly puffed and toothpick inserted in center comes out with few moist, fudgy crumbs attached, 25 to 30 minutes, rotating pan halfway through baking.

5. Let brownies cool in pan on wire rack for 1 hour. Using foil overhang, lift brownies out of pan. Return brownies to wire rack and let cool completely, about 1 hour. Cut into squares and serve.

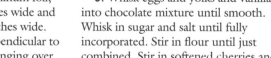
Rehydrated dried cherries give these brownies the best mix of bold cherry flavor and texture.

INGREDIENT SPOTLIGHT
Almond Extract

It's no mere coincidence that cherries and almonds taste good together: Almonds are genetically related to all stone fruit, and thus they share some of the same chemical makeup.

FLAVOR FRIENDS
Almonds and cherries taste good together because they share flavor compounds.

Getting to Know Leaveners

Leaveners add lift and lightness to lots of different foods. But they work in different ways. BY CHRISTIE MORRISON

Baking Soda
ACID REQUIRED

Sodium bicarbonate—baking soda—produces carbon dioxide when activated with moist, acidic ingredients like buttermilk, lemon juice, or sour cream. This gas physically causes batters to rise, and the heat of the oven sets the risen batter. Use too little and you don't get enough lift; use too much and the bubbles will burst, leaving your baked goods flat. Baking soda also makes doughs more alkaline, which encourages browning.

Baker's Ammonia
CLASSIC LIFTER

Ammonium carbonate—also called baker's ammonia or hartshorn—isn't used much in this country anymore, but it's still common in Greek and Scandinavian baking. It adds lift to thin items that benefit from a lighter texture (like crackers) and don't need to grow much in size. It gives off an initial ammonia odor during baking, but the odor dissipates quickly, leaving no off-flavor in the baked goods.

Baking Powder
POWER TRIO

Baking powder is a combination of baking soda, acid salt (such as cream of tartar), and cornstarch. Since baking powder contains acid already, it only needs moisture to activate. We recommend using double-acting baking powder, which reacts immediately when mixed with liquid and then a second time when exposed to heat. Date your baking powder when you open it; its leavening power declines noticeably after 6 months.

Steam
VAPOR-RISE

How does puff pastry rise without leaveners? Steam. In a very hot environment, butter spread between layers of dough melts, and the liquid turns to steam. The dough is elastic enough to rise before becoming a stable crust. Ditto for popovers and cream puffs. Just as the trapped steam makes these items rise, it is apt to let them fall if the heat drops before the dough has a chance to set, so resist opening the oven door prematurely.

Instant Yeast
RAPID RISER

Also known as rapid-rise yeast, instant yeast is dehydrated to the same concentration as active dry, but by a gentler, less-damaging method. As a result, rapid-rise yeast can be mixed directly into other ingredients, and you can use less without a reduction in leavening. We prefer rapid-rise yeast in the test kitchen for its potency, convenience, and clean flavor. This yeast has a long shelf life and can be stored, unopened, for up to two years.

Fresh Yeast
IT'S ALIVE!

Yeast is a living microorganism that leavens by ingesting sugars in the flour and expelling carbon dioxide. This process takes time, whereas chemical leaveners can work immediately. Also called cake or compressed yeast, fresh yeast has a crumbly, soft texture that dissolves easily in warm liquid. Fresh yeast is a powerful leavener, but its short shelf life (about two weeks in the fridge) makes it impractical for most home uses.

Natural Yeast
SOURDOUGH STARTER

A mix of flour and water provides a home for wild, naturally occurring yeasts and bacteria to collect and grow. Over about 10 days, with daily doses of flour and water "refreshments," the yeasts and bacteria ferment, transforming sugars in the flour into carbon dioxide gas and lending complex flavor and tang to the mix. A portion of this starter is then added to bread recipes. True sourdough breads contain no other leaveners.

Active Dry Yeast
DIRECT PROOF

Active dry yeast has been 95 percent dehydrated into tiny granules. This intense process damages some of the cells while others become dormant, so we "proof" the yeast in warm (about 110 degrees) water before adding it to the rest of the ingredients; the yeast will start to bubble when it activates. To substitute rapid-rise yeast in recipes that call for active dry, use 25 percent less than called for. All types of dry yeast stay fresh longer when stored in the refrigerator or freezer.

Cream of Tartar
MERINGUE MAKER

While not a leavener per se, cream of tartar (or potassium acid tartrate) is the acidic component in baking powder that allows it to activate without an additional acid. Cream of tartar is a helpful pantry ingredient in its own right; its acidic nature lowers the pH of egg whites, which creates more volume, greater stability (they're less likely to weep), and a glossier appearance when they're whipped for **soufflés and meringues.**

Beer
BATTER UP

Beer's carbonation makes it a good choice for leavening batters for fried onion rings and tempura-style vegetables. The carbon dioxide bubbles add lift to the batter as they escape and evaporate in the hot oil environment. Beer's acidity also keeps these batters tender, since the low pH inhibits gluten formation. We use beer in the light batter for our California Fish Tacos (**CooksCountry.com/fishtacos**).

Egg Whites
AIR TRAP

As you whip egg whites, their proteins loosen and stretch, trapping air inside a fluffy foam. While air is the actual leavener that gives angel food cakes, sponge cakes, and some pound cakes their lift, egg whites or whole eggs are usually necessary to provide the foaming ingredient that captures the air and traps it in the batter. See for yourself in our Rolled Soufflé for a Crowd (**CooksCountry.com/rolledsouffle**).

Seltzer
TINY BUBBLES

Like beer, seltzer is full of bubbles that can add lift to foods. We've used seltzer in place of whipped egg whites in waffle recipes and also love the way it lightens our Maryland Crab Fluff (**CooksCountry.com/crabfluff**). It's important to use fresh, highly carbonated unflavored seltzer or club soda in recipes. Sparkling waters like Perrier don't have the same amount of carbonation and will cause your recipe **to fall flat.**

BRATWURST REUBEN

TURKEY CUTLETS WITH BARLEY AND SWISS CHARD

**PAN-ROASTED SALMON
WITH FENNEL AND ORANGE SALAD**

QUICK BEEF AND VEGETABLE SOUP

TURKEY CUTLETS WITH BARLEY AND SWISS CHARD Serves 4

✓ **WHY THIS RECIPE WORKS:** Caramelizing the lemon infuses the cooking oil (and, thus, the cutlets) with flavor.

- 3 tablespoons extra-virgin olive oil
- 1 cup quick-cooking barley
- ¼ cup finely chopped onion
- 2 garlic cloves, minced
- 1¾ cups chicken broth
- 12 ounces Swiss chard, stems chopped, leaves cut into 1-inch pieces
- 1 teaspoon grated lemon zest, plus 1 lemon, halved and seeded
  Salt and pepper
- 1½ ounces Parmesan cheese, shredded (½ cup)
- 6 (4-ounce) turkey cutlets, trimmed

1. Heat 2 tablespoons oil in large saucepan over medium-high heat until shimmering. Add barley, onion, and garlic and cook until barley is toasted and onion is softened, about 3 minutes. Stir in broth and bring to boil; reduce heat to medium-low, cover, and simmer until barley is almost tender, about 8 minutes.

2. Add chard stems and cook, covered, until softened, about 3 minutes. Add chard leaves, lemon zest, and ½ teaspoon salt; increase heat to medium-high and cook, uncovered, until barley is tender, about 2 minutes. Stir in ¼ cup Parmesan, transfer to serving platter, and tent with foil.

3. Pat cutlets dry with paper towels and season with salt and pepper. Heat remaining 1 tablespoon oil in 12-inch nonstick skillet over medium-high heat until shimmering. Add lemon halves, cut side down, and cook until browned, about 2 minutes; set aside. Cook cutlets in now-empty skillet until well browned, about 2 minutes per side. Arrange cutlets on top of barley mixture and squeeze lemon halves over cutlets. Sprinkle with remaining ¼ cup Parmesan and serve.

BRATWURST REUBEN Serves 4

✓ **WHY THIS RECIPE WORKS:** We remove the casings and brown bratwurst sausages for a quick, supermeaty Reuben-style sandwich.

- 3 tablespoons unsalted butter, softened
- 8 slices hearty rye bread
- 4 cooked bratwurst sausages, halved lengthwise
- ¼ cup mayonnaise
- 2 tablespoons whole-grain mustard
- 2 tablespoons ketchup
- 1 tablespoon dill pickle relish
- ¼ teaspoon salt
- 8 thin slices deli Swiss cheese (8 ounces)
- 1 cup sauerkraut, drained

1. Adjust oven rack to upper-middle position and heat oven to 400 degrees. Spread 1 teaspoon butter on 1 side of each bread slice. Place bread slices, buttered side down, on baking sheet; set aside.

2. Melt remaining 1 teaspoon butter in 12-inch nonstick skillet over medium heat. Add bratwurst in single layer, weigh down with Dutch oven, and cook until well browned, about 2 minutes per side.

3. Whisk mayonnaise, mustard, ketchup, relish, and salt together in bowl and spread evenly on facing sides of each bread slice. Place 1 slice cheese on each of 4 bread slices, then layer each with one-quarter of sauerkraut and browned bratwurst, finishing with 1 slice cheese. Top with remaining 4 bread slices, buttered side up; press down to flatten. Bake until golden brown on both sides and cheese is melted, about 12 minutes, flipping sandwiches halfway through baking. Serve.

TEST KITCHEN NOTE: Make sure to buy fully cooked bratwurst, which is usually sold near the hot dogs, for this recipe.

QUICK BEEF AND VEGETABLE SOUP Serves 4

✓ **WHY THIS RECIPE WORKS:** Quick-cooking ground beef is a great alternative to beef cubes for a meaty, satisfying soup that's ready in half an hour.

- 1 pound 90 percent lean ground beef
- 1 onion, chopped
- 2 carrots, peeled and cut into ½-inch pieces
- 1 teaspoon dried oregano
  Salt and pepper
- 4 cups beef broth
- 1 (14.5-ounce) can diced tomatoes
- 8 ounces Yukon Gold potatoes, peeled and cut into ½-inch pieces
- 6 ounces green beans, trimmed and cut on bias into 1-inch lengths
- 2 tablespoons chopped fresh parsley

1. Cook beef, onion, carrots, oregano, 1 teaspoon salt, and ½ teaspoon pepper in Dutch oven over medium-high heat, breaking up beef with spoon, until no longer pink, about 6 minutes. Add broth, tomatoes and their juice, and potatoes. Bring to boil, reduce heat to low, and simmer, covered, until potatoes are almost tender, about 10 minutes.

2. Add green beans and cook, uncovered, until vegetables are tender and soup has thickened slightly, 10 to 12 minutes. Season with salt and pepper to taste. Serve, sprinkled with parsley.

TEST KITCHEN NOTE: You can substitute chicken broth for the beef broth if you prefer.

PAN-ROASTED SALMON WITH FENNEL AND ORANGE SALAD Serves 4

✓ **WHY THIS RECIPE WORKS:** The brightness of the citrus balances the richness of the seared salmon. The crunch of the fennel adds textural contrast.

- 2 oranges
- 1 fennel bulb, 1 tablespoon fronds minced, stalks discarded, bulb quartered, cored, and sliced thin crosswise
- 3 tablespoons extra-virgin olive oil
- 1 tablespoon white wine vinegar
  Salt and pepper
- 4 (6-ounce) skinless center-cut salmon fillets, 1¼ inches thick
- ½ cup pitted kalamata olives, sliced thin

1. Cut away peel and pith from oranges. Quarter oranges, then slice thin crosswise. Combine orange slices and their juice, sliced fennel, 2 tablespoons oil, vinegar, ½ teaspoon salt, and ¼ teaspoon pepper in bowl. Transfer salad to platter.

2. Pat salmon dry with paper towels and season with salt and pepper. Heat remaining 1 tablespoon oil in 12-inch nonstick skillet over medium-high heat until just smoking. Cook salmon until well browned and temperature registers 125 degrees, 4 to 6 minutes per side. Transfer salmon to platter with salad. Sprinkle olives over salad and fennel fronds over both. Serve.

TEST KITCHEN NOTE: Add the olives just before serving so they don't discolor the salad.

FLANK STEAK WITH PEANUT SLAW

**ROASTED CHICKEN THIGHS
WITH CREAMED SHALLOTS AND BACON**

**SKILLET PORK CHOPS
WITH APPLES AND MAPLE-SAGE BUTTER**

**PENNE WITH BUTTERNUT SQUASH
AND BROWN BUTTER SAUCE**

ROASTED CHICKEN THIGHS WITH CREAMED SHALLOTS AND BACON Serves 4

WHY THIS RECIPE WORKS: Browning the chicken in a skillet on the stovetop and then finishing it on a baking sheet in the oven leaves the skillet free for caramelizing the shallots.

- 8 (5- to 7-ounce) bone-in chicken thighs, trimmed
  Salt and pepper
- 1 tablespoon vegetable oil
- 4 slices bacon, cut into 1-inch pieces
- 8 shallots, peeled and halved lengthwise
- ½ cup brandy
- ¼ cup water
- ½ cup heavy cream
- 1 tablespoon minced fresh thyme

1. Adjust oven rack to upper-middle position and heat oven to 450 degrees. Line rimmed baking sheet with foil. Pat chicken dry with paper towels and season with salt and pepper. Heat oil in 12-inch skillet over medium-high heat until just smoking. Cook chicken, skin side down, until well browned, about 8 minutes. Transfer chicken to prepared sheet, skin side up, and roast until chicken registers 175 degrees, 15 to 20 minutes.

2. Meanwhile, pour off fat from skillet. Add bacon and cook over medium heat until crisp, 6 to 8 minutes. Using slotted spoon, transfer bacon to paper towel–lined plate. Add shallots to now-empty skillet, cut side down. Cover and cook until well browned, about 3 minutes. Off heat, add brandy and water. Return skillet to heat and cook, covered, until shallots are tender, about 5 minutes.

3. Stir in cream and thyme and simmer, uncovered, until thickened, about 3 minutes. Season with salt and pepper to taste. Transfer creamed shallots to serving platter, arrange chicken on top, and sprinkle with bacon. Serve.

FLANK STEAK WITH PEANUT SLAW Serves 4

WHY THIS RECIPE WORKS: We reserve a portion of the slaw's peanut dressing and reduce it to make an intense sauce for the steak.

- 5 tablespoons peanut oil
- ¼ cup chopped fresh cilantro
- 2 tablespoons crunchy peanut butter
- 4 teaspoons packed brown sugar
- 1 tablespoon soy sauce
- 2 teaspoons grated fresh ginger
- 1 teaspoon grated lime zest plus ¼ cup juice (2 limes)
- 1 (14-ounce) bag coleslaw mix
  Salt and pepper
- 1 (2-pound) flank steak, trimmed

1. Whisk ¼ cup oil, cilantro, peanut butter, sugar, soy sauce, ginger, and lime zest and juice together in large bowl until emulsified. Set aside ¼ cup dressing. Toss coleslaw mix with remaining ½ cup dressing to coat. Season with salt to taste; set aside.

2. Cut steak lengthwise with grain into 3 equal pieces. Pat pieces dry with paper towels and season with salt and pepper. Heat remaining 1 tablespoon oil in 12-inch nonstick skillet over medium-high heat until just smoking. Cook steaks until well browned and meat registers 125 degrees (for medium-rare), 5 to 7 minutes per side. Transfer to carving board, tent with foil, and let rest for 5 minutes.

3. Combine ¼ cup water with reserved dressing in now-empty skillet and simmer over medium-low heat until thickened slightly, about 2 minutes, scraping up any browned bits. Slice steaks thin on bias against grain and drizzle with sauce. Serve with slaw.

PENNE WITH BUTTERNUT SQUASH AND BROWN BUTTER SAUCE Serves 4

WHY THIS RECIPE WORKS: Covering the squash speeds up its cooking while still allowing for browning.

- 1 pound penne, fusilli, or other short, tubular pasta
  Salt and pepper
- 1 tablespoon olive oil
- 1 pound butternut squash, peeled, seeded, and cut into ½-inch pieces (3 cups)
- 2 tablespoons fresh sage leaves, torn
- 3 garlic cloves, minced
- 4 tablespoons unsalted butter, cut into 4 pieces
- ¼ cup hazelnuts, toasted, skinned, and chopped coarse
- 1 tablespoon lemon juice
- 2 ounces Parmesan cheese, grated (1 cup)

1. Bring 4 quarts water to boil in large pot. Add pasta and 1 tablespoon salt to boiling water and cook, stirring often, until al dente. Reserve ½ cup cooking water, then drain pasta and return it to pot.

2. Heat oil in 12-inch skillet over medium-high heat until shimmering. Add squash, 1 teaspoon salt, and ½ teaspoon pepper. Cover and cook until squash is softened and browned, about 5 minutes. Add sage and garlic and cook until fragrant, about 30 seconds; add squash mixture to pasta.

3. Add butter and hazelnuts to now-empty skillet and cook over medium-high heat until both are browned and fragrant, about 2 minutes. Remove skillet from heat and stir in lemon juice and ¼ cup reserved cooking water (butter will foam and sizzle). Stir hazelnut mixture and ½ cup Parmesan into pasta and season with salt and pepper to taste. Adjust consistency with remaining reserved cooking water as needed. Serve, sprinkled with remaining ½ cup Parmesan.

SKILLET PORK CHOPS WITH APPLES AND MAPLE-SAGE BUTTER Serves 4

WHY THIS RECIPE WORKS: The fresh sage and maple syrup butter melts on the hot chops, forming a flavorful sauce without any extra cooking.

- 4 tablespoons unsalted butter, softened, plus 1 tablespoon unsalted butter
- 2 tablespoons maple syrup
- 1 tablespoon minced fresh sage
  Salt and pepper
- 4 (6- to 8-ounce) boneless pork chops, ¾ to 1 inch thick, trimmed
- 2 Granny Smith apples, peeled, cored, halved, and cut into ½-inch-thick wedges
- 1 red onion, halved and sliced thin
- 1 tablespoon red wine vinegar

1. Combine softened butter, 1 tablespoon maple syrup, sage, ¼ teaspoon salt, and ¼ teaspoon pepper in bowl; set aside. Pat chops dry with paper towels and season with salt and pepper. Melt remaining 1 tablespoon butter in 12-inch skillet over medium-high heat. Cook chops until well browned and meat registers 140 degrees, about 5 minutes per side. Transfer to platter and tent with foil.

2. Pour off all but 1 tablespoon fat from skillet. Add apples, onion, and ¼ teaspoon salt and cook, covered, over medium-high heat until softened, about 6 minutes. Stir in vinegar and remaining 1 tablespoon maple syrup and cook, uncovered, until apples start to brown, 2 to 4 minutes.

3. Stir any accumulated pork juices into apple-onion mixture and spoon around chops. Dollop chops with maple-sage butter. Serve.

TEST KITCHEN NOTE: You can also use Gala or Fuji apples here.

Steak Modiga

This St. Louis specialty features a juicy steak topped with crunchy bread crumbs and a buttery, cheese-enriched sauce. BY ASHLEY MOORE

VISIT THE ITALIAN neighborhood known as "The Hill" in St. Louis, Missouri, and you'll find steak modiga on many restaurant menus. What is it? A steak (usually strip or filet mignon) that's piled with seasoned bread crumbs and grilled or broiled until juicy inside and crunchy on top. It's served with a buttery, white wine–and–mushroom sauce enriched with a local specialty: salty, smoky Provel cheese.

I searched regional cookbooks and found a handful of recipes for this unusual steak treatment, all of which were grilled outdoors, and decided to give them a try. The results were disappointing. In almost every version, most of the breading either stuck to the grate or fell off and burned in the fire, and the sauces were too thin and oily. I wanted breading that stuck to the steak, not to mention a silky sauce. And I wanted to make it inside, not outdoors.

I tried employing the broiler (using a simple but flavorful topping of crunchy panko bread crumbs, garlic, parsley, and salt and pepper), but the crumbs burned by the time the steak was cooked. I tried baking the steaks in a hot oven, flipping them halfway through cooking for even browning, but the crumbs didn't adhere well and the steaks didn't have any char.

The next option was to move to the stovetop and use a grill pan. The grill pan gave me pretty much the same results as the grill—crumbs that fell off the steak and burned.

A colleague suggested browning the steaks crumb side down in a nonstick skillet. Following her advice, I brushed the steaks with olive oil and then pressed the seasoned crumbs onto one side. I then seared the steaks on both sides, starting with the breaded side, in a nonstick skillet.

Since the searing didn't fully cook the steaks, I transferred them (breaded side up) to a wire rack set in a rimmed baking sheet and finished them in a 400-degree oven, which took about 5 minutes. After a few tests, I learned that letting the raw, breaded steaks rest for just 5 minutes before searing gave the crumb coating a chance to set up and stick better.

Now for the sauce. I knew I wanted a flavorful, cheesy sauce with a luxurious, creamy texture that wasn't too heavy— the sauce is there to complement the steak, not overshadow it. Tradition dictates a sauce made with mushrooms, white wine, garlic, cream, chicken broth, and cheese.

I started by browning mushrooms and then adding white wine and reducing it. I incorporated minced garlic and a bit of flour for thickening, followed by chicken broth and heavy cream. I cooked it down for a few minutes and was ready to stir in some cheese. But what kind? Provel is not widely available outside of St. Louis, so I tested American, cheddar, Swiss, and provolone, with the latter winning out for its mild tang and smooth melting.

After arranging the steaks on a serving platter, I spooned the sauce over the top and finished it all with a sprinkle of verdant fresh parsley. Cheesy sauce, tender steak, and crisp crumbs—my modiga was a winner.

ITALIAN STEAK MODIGA
Serves 4
Note that only one side of the steak is coated with bread crumbs; the other sides remain bare.

- 4 (10- to 12-ounce) boneless strip steaks, about 1 inch thick, trimmed Salt and pepper
- 1 tablespoon unsalted butter
- 8 ounces white mushrooms, trimmed and sliced thin
- ¼ cup dry white wine
- 1 tablespoon all-purpose flour
- 4 garlic cloves, minced
- 1 cup chicken broth
- ¼ cup heavy cream
- ¼ cup plus 1 teaspoon olive oil
- 1 cup panko bread crumbs
- ¼ cup chopped fresh parsley
- 2 slices deli provolone cheese (2 ounces), torn into 1-inch pieces

1. Adjust oven rack to middle position and heat oven to 400 degrees. Set wire rack in rimmed baking sheet. Pat steaks dry with paper towels and season with salt and pepper; set aside.
2. Melt butter in large saucepan over medium-high heat. Add mushrooms, ½ teaspoon salt, and ½ teaspoon pepper and cook until liquid has evaporated and mushrooms begin to brown, 5 to 7 minutes. Add wine and cook until evaporated, about 3 minutes.
3. Stir in flour and half of garlic and cook until mushrooms are well coated and garlic is fragrant, about 1 minute. Stir in broth and cream, scraping up any browned bits. Bring to boil and cook until slightly thickened, about 3 minutes. Remove from heat, cover, and keep warm.
4. Pour ¼ cup oil into shallow dish. Process panko in food processor until finely ground, about 10 seconds. Combine 3 tablespoons parsley, ground panko, remaining garlic, ¾ teaspoon salt, and ¾ teaspoon pepper in second shallow dish.
5. Working with 1 steak at a time, add to oil and turn to coat on all sides. Transfer oiled steak to panko mixture and press firmly to coat only 1 side of steak with mixture. Transfer steak, breaded side up, to prepared wire rack and let sit for 5 minutes.
6. Heat remaining 1 teaspoon oil in 12-inch nonstick skillet over medium-high heat until shimmering. Place steaks in skillet, breaded side down, and cook until well browned, about 3 minutes. Flip steaks and continue to cook until well browned on second side, about 3 minutes. Return steaks to wire rack, breaded side up.
7. Roast until meat registers 120 to 125 degrees (for medium-rare), 4 to 7 minutes. Let steaks cool on wire rack for 5 minutes while finishing sauce.
8. Return sauce to simmer over medium heat. Whisk in provolone until melted, about 1 minute. Serve steaks with sauce, sprinkled with remaining 1 tablespoon parsley.

Why should cutlets have a lock on crunch? Crisp bread crumbs are great on thick steaks, too.

Two-Hour Turkey

With two small cuts, we cooked a juicy roast turkey for the holidays in just 2 hours.

BY MORGAN BOLLING

HERE IN THE test kitchen, we've cooked turkey in dozens of ways: We've brined, glazed, smoked, spatchcocked, and even fired up the deep-fryer. And we've cooked some marvelous turkeys. But this year, we wanted a recipe that many home cooks, particularly those who cook turkey just once a year, might find helpful during the busy holiday season. Besides juicy, flavorful meat and crisp skin, we also wanted ease, with a side of speed.

In a perfect world, all you'd do is tie on an apron, slide a whole turkey into the oven, and a couple of hours (and a glass of sherry) later, pull out a beautiful, golden-brown, Norman Rockwell–esque centerpiece. And since it'd be done so quickly, you'd set it aside to rest—a necessary step for juicy meat—and fill the now-empty oven with dressing, green bean casserole, dinner rolls, and the rest of the requisite side dishes. Wishful thinking? Perhaps. But I was determined.

I bought a 14-pound turkey, big enough for a 10-person feast. To save time and effort, I chose a prebrined bird, meaning that it was already injected with a saltwater solution to help season the meat and keep it moist. I nestled the bird into a roasting rack, and since I wanted it to cook quickly, I started it in a high 450-degree oven.

The breast reached 160 degrees—our test kitchen target for juicy white meat—in just 1 hour and 35 minutes. However, large roasts continue to cook after they come out of the oven, a phenomenon known as carryover cooking, and in this case, the breast meat climbed to 180 degrees: cardboard.

I kept closer tabs on the temperature during my next test, checking it every few minutes. Once the breast meat hit 120 degrees I turned my oven down to a low 250 degrees, hoping that the reduction would finish cooking my bird more gently and stave off overcooking during the resting phase. It worked, mostly: I had juicy breast meat under lovely, crackly skin. And the bird was still in and out of the oven in less than 2 hours.

But the crux of all turkey woes loomed: White meat cooks faster than dark meat, and my dark meat wasn't done. Dark meat (legs and thighs) needs to reach at least 175 degrees to be fully cooked—long after the point at which

Our two-hour turkey cooks fast but looks a bit akimbo when cooked. We suggest carving it in the kitchen and bringing the platter to the table.

the white meat goes dry.

We have a few techniques in the test kitchen to help keep the breast from overcooking, including icing down the breast before it cooks or flipping the turkey over partway through cooking—but while these tricks helped, they were more work than I was willing to do. I tried covering the breast with aluminum foil, but the difference was minimal.

I flipped my thinking. Rather than protecting the breast meat, I wondered, could I expose the dark meat to more heat more quickly? For my next test, I cut into the skin on both sides of the bird, just between the breast and the thigh, to open up that area. This caused the legs to spread away from the breast, giving them more surface area and exposing them to more oven heat faster. Success: The thighs reached 175 degrees at approximately the same time as the breast hit 160. I set the turkey aside to rest (uncovered, to keep the skin crisp).

What's turkey without gravy? A prom queen without a date, that's what. So I tossed some vegetables and the turkey neck under the turkey while it roasted, letting them take on deep, caramelized flavors. After the bird came out, I used these roasting pan goodies, along with white wine, sage, thyme, and water, to make a simple, flavorful gravy.

Turkey Yoga

A little up-front prep helps ensure that the dark meat (thighs and legs) cooks at the same rate as the white meat (breasts). Use a sharp knife to slice through just the skin (not the meat) between the breast and leg on each side. This cut loosens the leg so it splays out slightly, exposing more dark meat to direct heat, accelerating its cooking.

The browned, slightly splayed finished bird.

TWO-HOUR TURKEY AND GRAVY

Serves 10 to 12

If you can't find a self-basting turkey (Butterball makes our favorite self-basting bird), a kosher turkey can be substituted. Avoid opening the oven too frequently to take the turkey's temperature. If your turkey is on the smaller side of the weight range, follow the lower end of the time ranges given, and vice versa.

- 2 onions, quartered through root end
- 2 carrots, peeled and cut into 3-inch pieces
- 1 celery rib, cut into 3-inch pieces
- 1 (12- to 14-pound) prebrined turkey, neck reserved, giblets discarded
- 3 tablespoons extra-virgin olive oil
  Kosher salt and pepper
- 3 cups water, plus extra as needed
- 1 tablespoon unsalted butter
- ¼ cup dry white wine
- ¼ cup all-purpose flour
- 4 sprigs fresh thyme
- 1 sprig fresh sage

1. Adjust oven rack to lowest position and heat oven to 450 degrees. Scatter onions, carrots, celery, and turkey neck in bottom of large roasting pan. Set V-rack over vegetables in roasting pan. Pat turkey dry with paper towels and tuck wingtips behind back. Transfer turkey, breast side up, to V-rack.

2. Using sharp knife, slice through skin between breast and leg on each side of turkey to expose entire underside of thigh without cutting into meat. Combine oil, 1 tablespoon salt, and 1½ teaspoons pepper in small bowl. Brush turkey all over with oil mixture.

3. Roast turkey until thickest part of breast registers 120 degrees and thickest part of thighs registers at least 135 degrees, 60 to 70 minutes.

4. Reduce oven temperature to 250 degrees and continue to roast turkey until breast registers 160 degrees and thighs register 175 degrees, 35 to 45 minutes longer. Transfer turkey to carving board and let rest for 45 minutes.

5. While turkey rests, transfer vegetables and turkey neck from roasting pan to bowl, leaving turkey juices behind. Add water to roasting pan with turkey juices and scrape up any browned bits from pan bottom. Transfer deglazed juices to 4-cup liquid measuring cup; add extra water, if needed, to equal 4 cups.

6. Melt butter in Dutch oven over medium-high heat. Add vegetables and turkey neck and cook until any liquid has evaporated and browned bits begin to form on bottom of pot, 3 to 5 minutes. Add wine and cook until nearly evaporated, about 2 minutes, scraping up any browned bits.

7. Sprinkle flour over top and cook, stirring constantly, for 1 minute. Add thyme sprigs, sage sprig, deglazed pan juices, ½ teaspoon salt, and ½ teaspoon pepper. Bring to boil, then reduce heat to medium-low and simmer until thickened to gravy consistency, 12 to 15 minutes.

8. Strain gravy through fine-mesh strainer set over medium saucepan; discard solids. Season with salt and pepper to taste. Carve turkey and serve with gravy.

Gravy Master

There are many ways to thicken gravy: You can start with a roux; you can add a cornstarch slurry to the drippings; you can add a paste of flour and butter to the roasting pan. Our method makes full use of the vegetables and turkey neck that roast under the bird: We brown them in butter, deglaze with wine, and sprinkle with flour. Then we add seasonings and the pan juices and simmer for a thick, full-flavored accompaniment to our easy turkey.

WHAT'S THE BEST ROASTING RACK?

A good roasting rack securely holds a roast, elevating it so it doesn't sit in fat while cooking. It should allow hot air to circulate around the meat—key for accurate cooking and a perfectly rendered exterior. We've often disliked the racks that come bundled with roasting pans; even our winning pan's rack is slightly unstable. What's more, many roasting pans don't come with a rack in the first place, and racks occasionally go astray. For years, we've turned to a nearly $25 rack from All-Clad.

But a slew of new models have entered the market, with snazzy silicone shapes and intriguing designs. To compare, we tested our favorite All-Clad against six newcomers, priced from roughly $8.50 to nearly $26, by roasting 250 pounds of chicken, beef, and turkey. We looked for stability, capacity, cleanup, design, and—most important—excellent roasted meat.

Some racks were too small: Plump turkeys bulged over their sides as if they were trying to squeeze into their high school jeans, and the racks skittered around the pan. In general, bigger was better, providing both capacity and stability.

Side support was key, too. Those with U- or V-shaped baskets cradled the roasts securely; on flat racks, the birds were unstable. Handles factored heavily too: Loaded racks are heavy, and large handles made them easier to maneuver.

The silicone models looked great but didn't have handles. What's more, they didn't raise the meat enough, so the food steamed on the bottom. In fact, half the models we tested didn't allow for proper air circulation, an issue which was further illustrated when we tried to roast vegetables below a chicken, as we sometimes do when we want an easy one-pan meal. Models without enough clearance turned out pasty potatoes that literally paled in comparison to the crisp, caramel-hued tubers produced by racks with open, raised bottoms. Loads of space wasn't necessary—our winning model had just ½ inch of clearance, but its open slats ensured that hot air had full, even access to the meat. Visit **CooksCountry.com/nov15** for the full story and chart. –HANNAH CROWLEY

HIGHLY RECOMMENDED	CRITERIA	TESTERS' NOTES
 **ALL-CLAD** Nonstick Large Rack **Price:** $24.95 **Model:** 3016 **Dimensions:** 14.5 in by 11.2 in by 5 in Cooking ★★★ Capacity ★★★ Stability ★★★ Handles ★★★ Cleanup ★★★ Versatility ★★★	This broad rack had very little wiggle room between it and the roasting pan, so it always felt supremely secure, even when holding a 22-pound turkey. It handled everything we set inside it and had handles that were easy and secure to grab. It allowed for proper 360-degree air circulation, so its food was always perfectly browned and evenly rendered.

RECOMMENDED

 **CUISIPRO** Dual Roaster **Price:** $25.13 **Model:** 74 6791 **Dimensions:** 13.8 in by 10.2 in by 4.6 in Cooking ★★★ Capacity ★★★ Stability ★★½ Handles ★★ Cleanup ★★★ Versatility ★★½	This rack fit chicken, turkey, and roast beef nicely. Its adjustable center slats swing up to hold two upright chickens for side-by-side roasting. It was fairly stable, but its handles are located right where most roasting pans position their handles, so they were hard to grab at times. But it raised its contents up off the pan for circulation and turned out nicely rendered meat.	

| 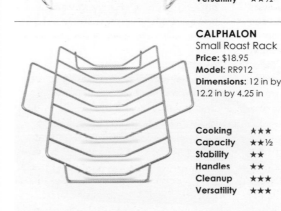 **CALPHALON** Small Roast Rack **Price:** $18.95 **Model:** RR912 **Dimensions:** 12 in by 12.2 in by 4.25 in

Cooking ★★★
Capacity ★★½
Stability ★★
Handles ★★
Cleanup ★★★
Versatility ★★★ | This rack worked well for chicken and beef, but a 12-pound turkey blocked its handles, rendering them useless. Its smaller frame slid around in the pan; we had to take extra care. (Even though it's called the "small rack," Calphalon doesn't currently sell a larger model.) Otherwise, it cleaned up readily and allowed for proper air circulation for optimal browning. |

Sourdough Dressing

Sourdough bread's characteristic tang and chewy texture liven up any sandwich. Our goal was to add the same punch to our holiday dressing. BY CHRISTIE MORRISON

ORDINARY WHITE SANDWICH bread gets its yearly brush with greatness in holiday dressing, coming to life when toasted and tossed with a savory mix of melted butter, onion, celery, and herbs. But what if we ditched the white bread in favor of complex, tangy sourdough?

I wasn't surprised to find several recipes for sourdough dressing in cookbooks from sourdough's home turf, California. What was unexpected, though, was their use of extra-flavorful vegetables like turnips and kale, presumably to stand up to the sourdough. I was inspired.

The usual process for dressing is to first dry out cubed bread in the oven so the cubes can soak up the liquid. Next, you sauté onion and garlic with herbs and butter on the stovetop. Finally, you combine it all with a binder—broth, eggs, or a creamy custard—before baking in a casserole dish.

But since I was already tossing convention to the wind by exiling the white bread, why should I be tied to the usual process? I decided to roast my vegetables (including the onion and garlic) on a rimmed baking sheet rather than sauté them on the stovetop, since I could do this at the same time as I dried out the bread. I auditioned a long list of vegetables. Though we liked the way sweet root vegetables like carrots and parsnips balanced the sour bread, they took too long to cook. Mushrooms (we preferred meaty shiitakes to cremini) and chopped curly kale, however, were a good fit in both flavor and texture—and they cooked perfectly in my allotted time.

The result was promising, but a bit wimpy. To give the dish some muscle, I topped the tray of vegetables with small pieces of Italian sausage. As the sausage cooked, its fat rendered into the vegetables. A few plumped golden raisins added after roasting contributed sweet notes; sage and chopped onion gave a nod to Thanksgiving tradition.

After tossing the roasted vegetables and dried bread with chicken broth and three eggs, I scooped the dressing into a buttered casserole dish. I covered it with foil and baked it on the lower-middle rack for 15 minutes to brown the bottom and then removed the foil for the final 15 minutes needed to crisp the top. Dotting the top with butter ensured some nice brown bits.

SOURDOUGH DRESSING WITH KALE AND MUSHROOMS
Serves 8 to 10

For a meatless variation, omit the sausage and use vegetarian broth. You will need two rimmed baking sheets for this recipe.

- 3½ tablespoons unsalted butter
- ½ cup golden raisins
- ½ cup water
- 1½ pounds sourdough bread, cut into 1-inch pieces
- ½ cup extra-virgin olive oil
- Salt and pepper
- 12 ounces shiitake mushrooms, stemmed and sliced ¼ inch thick
- 8 ounces kale, stemmed and chopped coarse
- 1 onion, chopped
- 5 garlic cloves, smashed and peeled
- 2 tablespoons minced fresh sage
- 8 ounces sweet Italian sausage, casings removed
- 2½ cups chicken broth
- 3 large eggs, lightly beaten

1. Adjust oven racks to upper-middle and lower-middle positions and heat oven to 400 degrees. Grease 13 by 9-inch baking dish with 1 tablespoon butter. Grease one 15 by 11-inch sheet of aluminum foil with ½ tablespoon butter. Combine raisins and water in bowl and microwave for 30 seconds. Set aside and let raisins soften for at least 15 minutes; drain.

2. Meanwhile, toss bread, ¼ cup oil, and ½ teaspoon salt together in large bowl; spread evenly on rimmed baking sheet. Combine mushrooms, kale, onion, garlic, sage, remaining ¼ cup oil, ½ teaspoon salt, and ½ teaspoon pepper in now-empty bowl; spread on second rimmed baking sheet. Break sausage into ½-inch pieces and distribute evenly over vegetables.

3. Bake bread mixture on upper rack and vegetable mixture on lower rack until bread is golden brown but still tender inside and vegetables and sausage are golden, about 30 minutes, stirring halfway through baking. Transfer sheets to wire racks and let cool slightly, about 10 minutes. Combine toasted bread and vegetable mixture in large bowl.

4. Stir broth, eggs, and drained raisins into bread-vegetable mixture until liquid is absorbed. Transfer dressing to prepared dish. Cut remaining 2 tablespoons butter into ¼-inch pieces and sprinkle evenly over dressing. Cover tightly with prepared foil.

5. Bake dressing on lower rack for 15 minutes. Uncover and continue to bake until top is golden and crisp, about 15 minutes longer. Let cool for 10 minutes before serving.

TO MAKE AHEAD

Dressing can be made through step 4 and refrigerated for up to 24 hours. Increase covered baking time by 5 minutes.

The bold flavors of sourdough, kale, sausage, and shiitake mushrooms are balanced by sweet golden raisins in this hearty dressing.

TEST KITCHEN TECHNIQUE **Skip the Stovetop**

Making dressing usually requires sautéing vegetables on the stovetop before stirring in toasted bread cubes. We avoid the stovetop by simultaneously toasting the bread and roasting the vegetables in the oven before combining them in a baking dish to finish.

Candied Sweet Potatoes

No more marshmallow topping.
We were looking for balanced sweetness without the toothache. BY CECELIA JENKINS

CANDIED SWEET POTATOES are a classic holiday side dish, but too often they border on dessert territory, clobbering you with sweetness (hello, marshmallows) and totally shortchanging the sweet potato's deep, earthy flavor. I set out to reclaim the pure flavors in this dish with a simple, balanced take in which the "candy" would provide a sweetly delicate counterpoint to the stalwart sweet potatoes.

I started with a handful of recipes found in our cookbook library, many of which called for baking or boiling whole sweet potatoes before slicing and glazing them—and then baking them again. And for all the work involved, too many of these recipes yielded mushy sweet potatoes cloaked in sticky, tooth-rattling syrups. Where was the subtle flavor of the potatoes themselves?

But these initial tests did make a number of things clear. For one thing, I learned that cutting the sweet potatoes too thin inevitably resulted in mush, but cutting them carefully into ¾-inch-thick rounds produced a soft texture that still held together. I also learned that roasting the cut pieces in a single layer on a rimmed baking sheet and then flipping them before glazing them and finishing them off gave me attractively browned edges and provided plenty of space to prepare enough for a crowd. Finally, I found that slathering the partially cooked sweet potato pieces with syrup for the last stretch of oven time gave me a richer flavor with a glaze that adhered.

I tried out a long list of glaze flavors to see what would best complement the sweet potatoes without covering them up. I wanted sweetness, but it had to stay in balance. Tangy apple cider was too overpowering, whereas orange juice was distracting, too specifically citrusy. Brown sugar and warm holiday spices were too reminiscent of sweet potato pie and, of course, marshmallows were out.

Maple syrup and butter were the most promising, providing a woodsy sweetness and always-welcome butteriness, but the combo can be overly rich; I needed something to temper and restrain them. The fix? Water, the most neutral ingredient in the world. Cutting the maple syrup with an equal amount of water lightened the load without hijacking the flavor, and stirring in cornstarch helped absorb any unwanted wetness. While the spuds were roasting,

Rich, woodsy maple syrup gives our glaze more depth than most.

I simply combined the glaze ingredients in a saucepan and boiled them for just a few minutes to thicken up.

One last detail to smooth out: a neat appearance. Transferring the fully cooked, glazed sweet potatoes from the rimmed baking sheet to a serving dish made for a messy presentation—potatoes fell apart as I was transferring them to the dish, leaving me with what resembled a mash. No: Though this is a dish of rustic flavors, I wanted to give it a neat appearance at the table.

Since I was going into the oven to flip the sweet potatoes as soon as they'd achieved good browning on one side, why not flip them at that point into a table-friendly but also oven-safe baking dish? Now I could arrange the

medallions, still only partially cooked, just so. I added the glaze and returned the sweet potatoes to the oven to finish. Glossy, glazy, earthy, rich, and just sweet enough—this was a holiday side dish to be proud of.

TEST KITCHEN TECHNIQUE
Brown and Then Braise
Start the rounds of sweet potato on a rimmed baking sheet. Once the bottoms are brown, transfer the potatoes to a baking dish with the glaze to finish.

CANDIED SWEET POTATOES
Serves 6 to 8
Whisk the syrup frequently to keep it from boiling over. A broiler-safe dish (not Pyrex) is important because of the high heat.

- 3 **pounds sweet potatoes, peeled, ends trimmed, and sliced ¾ inch thick**
- 2 **tablespoons vegetable oil**
  Salt and pepper
- ½ **cup maple syrup**
- ½ **cup water**
- 4 **tablespoons unsalted butter**
- 1 **teaspoon cornstarch**

1. Adjust oven rack to lowest position and heat oven to 450 degrees. Toss potatoes, oil, and 1 teaspoon salt together in bowl. Evenly space potatoes in single layer on rimmed baking sheet. Bake until potatoes are tender and dark brown on bottom, 18 to 22 minutes, rotating sheet halfway through baking.

2. Meanwhile, combine maple syrup, water, butter, cornstarch, and ⅛ teaspoon salt in small saucepan. Bring to boil over medium-high heat and cook, whisking frequently, until thickened and reduced to 1 cup, 3 to 5 minutes.

3. Place potatoes in broiler-safe 13 by 9-inch baking dish, browned side up, shingling as necessary if you have larger potatoes. Pour syrup mixture over potatoes and bake until bubbling around sides of dish, 8 to 10 minutes. Transfer dish to wire rack and let cool for 10 minutes. Season with pepper to taste. Serve.

TO MAKE AHEAD
Potatoes and syrup can be prepared through step 2, placed in baking dish, and kept at room temperature for up to 2 hours. In step 3, extend the baking time to 11 to 13 minutes.

Brussels Sprout Gratin

Brussels sprouts can send some folks running for the exit.
We wanted our take to win over even the harshest skeptics. BY MORGAN BOLLING

ASK A BRUSSELS sprouts–hater why sprouts are so bad and you'll hear some colorful language: "Slimy, stinky, and sulfurous," they'll say, and that's just the complaints beginning with *s*. But there's nothing inherently wrong with Brussels sprouts themselves; it's just the way they've been cooked over the years. I wanted to develop a recipe that would convert even the most ardent anti-sprouter—not by covering up their flavor but by casting them in a new light. My plan: a gratin.

After cooking a half-dozen Brussels sprout gratins from existing recipes, I knew I had my work cut out for me. None was great, but each had something going for it: One had sprouts that held their shape, one had a nicely balanced cream sauce, and one had a successfully crunchy topping. Could I cobble together the best aspects of each gratin into a single, easy, Thanksgiving-worthy dish?

One thing I learned from this initial round of testing: Since Brussels sprouts come in a variety of sizes, precooking them would allow me to customize the cooking time depending on their heft. I tried boiling and microwaving the sprouts, but doing so left them tasting too cabbagey. Roasting at 450 degrees (for 30 to 35 minutes, depending on their sizes) proved a much better option; the dry heat of the oven brings out the very best nutty, roasty flavors that Brussels sprouts have to offer. What's more, roasting them in the same dish that I'd finish the gratin in saved on cleanup.

I'd need something to bring my gratin together, so while the sprouts precooked, I made a Mornay sauce—a creamy cheese sauce (in this case, melty Gruyère and salty Parmesan) thickened by flour and butter. I tossed my sauce with the sprouts in the baking dish and cooked them together until everything bubbled. After tasting these and finding them somewhat dull, I decided to boost the flavors in the sauce with nutmeg, cayenne, a minced garlic clove, and some sweet-sharp minced shallot.

To me, the best part of a gratin is the crusty top. I began by topping mine with panko bread crumbs and broiling it for the final minutes of cooking. But in the time it took for the panko to become a nice golden brown, the Brussels sprouts on top of the gratin were getting too dark—some were borderline burnt. I nixed the broiler and simply added the crumbs for just the final few minutes of roasting—but this left my crusty topping pale. Jump-starting the panko by sautéing it in a tablespoon of butter before sprinkling it over the top was the fix. A bit of Gruyère helped tie the crumbs to the rest of the dish.

Nutty, roasted sprouts; a bubbling, creamy cheese sauce; and a crusty topping—sure to win over even the most committed members of the anti–Brussels sprouts brigade.

BRUSSELS SPROUT GRATIN
Serves 6 to 8

Look for smaller Brussels sprouts, no bigger than a golf ball, as they're likely to be sweeter and more tender than large sprouts. If you can find only large sprouts, quarter them. A broiler-safe dish is important because the sprouts cook at such a high temperature.

2½	pounds Brussels sprouts, trimmed and halved through stem
1	tablespoon vegetable oil
	Salt and pepper
3	tablespoons unsalted butter
¼	cup panko bread crumbs
1	shallot, minced
1	garlic clove, minced
1	tablespoon all-purpose flour
1¼	cups heavy cream
¾	cup chicken broth
2	ounces Gruyère cheese, shredded (½ cup)
1	ounce Parmesan cheese, grated (½ cup)
	Pinch ground nutmeg
	Pinch cayenne pepper

1. Adjust oven rack to middle position and heat oven to 450 degrees. Grease 13 by 9-inch broiler-safe baking dish. Toss Brussels sprouts, oil, ½ teaspoon salt, and ¼ teaspoon pepper together in prepared baking dish. Bake until sprouts are well browned and tender, 30 to 35 minutes. Transfer to wire rack and set aside to cool for at least 5 minutes or up to 30 minutes.

2. Meanwhile, melt 1 tablespoon butter in medium saucepan over medium heat. Add panko and cook, stirring frequently, until golden brown, about 3 minutes. Transfer to bowl and stir in ¼ teaspoon salt and ¼ teaspoon pepper; set aside. Wipe saucepan clean with paper towels.

3. Melt remaining 2 tablespoons butter in now-empty saucepan over medium heat. Add shallot and garlic and cook until just softened, about 1 minute. Stir in flour and cook for 1 minute. Whisk in cream and broth and bring to boil over medium-high heat. Once boiling, remove from heat and whisk in ¼ cup Gruyère, Parmesan, nutmeg, cayenne, ¼ teaspoon pepper, and ⅛ teaspoon salt until smooth.

4. Pour cream mixture over Brussels sprouts in baking dish and stir to combine. Sprinkle evenly with panko mixture and remaining ¼ cup Gruyère. Bake until bubbling around edges and golden brown on top, 5 to 7 minutes. Transfer dish to wire rack and let cool for 10 minutes. Serve.

We don't add the cream sauce and crumbs until after we've roasted the halved sprouts to draw out their sweet, nutty flavors.

TEST KITCHEN TIP
Choose the Right Size Sprouts
For this recipe, the Brussels sprouts should be relatively small, no larger than a golf ball. Larger sprouts can be tougher and more bitter.

Cornmeal Drop Biscuits

Cornmeal should add flavor and a pleasant corny crunch to biscuits.
Could we find the right formula for tasty, tender success? BY ASHLEY MOORE

IN MY HOUSE, biscuits are usually for the weekends—when I have time to carefully mix, knead, roll, and stamp them out. But drop biscuits, which are as easy as stirring together the ingredients and portioning them on the baking sheet, come together so quickly that they are a staple on weeknights and perfect for holidays when there's so much more to concentrate on. But as easy as they are to make, they still deliver homemade flavor, something unattainable in every store-bought biscuit I've ever tried.

Our dependable buttermilk drop biscuit recipe produces tender, tasty biscuits and uses the cool trick of stirring together cold buttermilk and melted (and cooled) butter until the butter clumps. These clumps of butter create steam during baking, and that steam helps make the biscuits light and airy. I wanted something similar but different, something that kept the butter clumps but also incorporated the rustic, earthy flavor and lightly crunchy texture of cornmeal.

I started by simply introducing cornmeal into the mixture, swapping out half of the flour and substituting cornmeal in its place. But the result was a dry, unpleasantly dense biscuit. I needed something more tender and light. After a few more swings with varying quantities of cornmeal, I landed at a 1:3 ratio of ½ cup cornmeal to 1½ cups flour, which gave me a biscuit texture I was happy with.

The cornmeal presence was strong in these biscuits, but the flavor wasn't quite in balance. When working with cornmeal in the past, in cornbreads and muffins and so forth, we've often turned to sweeteners to draw out the corn flavor. My recipe had a small amount of sugar, but I wondered whether more sugar would help—or, for that matter, if another sweetener would be preferable to plain white sugar.

I tried substituting maple syrup, honey, and brown sugar (both light and dark) for the granulated sugar, but each of these options contributed a strong, distinctive flavor that blurred rather than enhanced the corn flavor. I decided to stick with plain white sugar.

I increased the amount of sugar in the recipe. My initial tests were too sweet (I wanted a dinner-table biscuit, after all, not a dessert), but after another few rounds of test biscuits, I found that 3 tablespoons of granulated sugar gave me a balanced biscuit: savory and slightly sweet with pronounced cornmeal flavor.

My simple, pantry-friendly recipe stands on its own but has the added benefit of being a solid canvas for experimentation, welcoming to flavorful stir-ins to suit a range of tastes. Plenty of freshly cracked black pepper introduced a bit of refreshing pungency to one version, chopped green chiles added a bit of southwestern flair to another version, and finally, chopped fresh sage recalled the festive flavors of Thanksgiving, an excellent complement to turkey and gravy.

CORNMEAL DROP BISCUITS
Makes 12 biscuits
Be sure to chill the buttermilk so the melted-and-cooled butter clumps when the two are combined. These biscuits are best eaten still warm from the oven; try them spread with honey butter or pimento cheese.

1½	cups (7½ ounces) all-purpose flour
½	cup (2½ ounces) stone-ground cornmeal
3	tablespoons sugar
2	teaspoons baking powder
½	teaspoon baking soda
¾	teaspoon salt
1	cup buttermilk, chilled
8	tablespoons unsalted butter, melted and cooled

1. Adjust oven rack to middle position and heat oven to 450 degrees. Line rimmed baking sheet with parchment paper. Whisk flour, cornmeal, sugar, baking powder, baking soda, and salt together in large bowl. Stir buttermilk and melted butter together in separate bowl until butter forms clumps.

2. Add buttermilk mixture to flour mixture and stir with rubber spatula until just incorporated. Using greased ¼-cup dry measuring cup or equal-size portion scoop, drop scant ¼-cup scoops of batter 1½ inches apart on prepared sheet (use spoon to free batter from cup if necessary).

3. Bake until biscuit tops are golden brown, 12 to 14 minutes, rotating sheet halfway through baking. Transfer biscuits to wire rack and let cool for 5 minutes before serving. (To refresh day-old biscuits, heat them in 300-degree oven for 10 minutes.)

CORNMEAL DROP BISCUITS WITH BLACK PEPPER
Add 1½ teaspoons coarsely ground pepper to flour mixture in step 1.

CORNMEAL DROP BISCUITS WITH GREEN CHILES
Add ¼ cup canned diced green chiles, patted dry, to flour mixture in step 1.

CORNMEAL DROP BISCUITS WITH SAGE
Add 1 tablespoon minced fresh sage to flour mixture in step 1.

This version of our Cornmeal Drop Biscuits gets a kick from diced green chiles.

KEY STEP Clumping Butter
Stirring melted butter into buttermilk creates little butter clumps. They look funny, but these small "butter balls" melt and release steam in the oven to create light, fluffy biscuits.

Cooking Class Deep-Dish Apple Pie

A perfect apple pie with a sweet filling and tender crust is within anyone's reach—if you follow these guidelines.

BY CHRISTIE MORRISON

Pick Two Kinds of Apples
For a perfectly balanced apple pie filling, choose one variety from each group.

TART

Granny Smith   Empire   Cortland

SWEET

Golden Delicious   Fuji   Jonagold   Braeburn

Add Acid
A tablespoon of lemon juice (added after the apples cook) adds a sharp, bright note to contrast and balance the sweetness of the sugar and fruit.

Don't Make This Mistake
Using raw apples may seem like less work, but you risk a soupy pie with a giant air pocket between the top crust and the fruit. That's because apples shrink as they cook, oozing liquid. By cooking the apples before we put them in the pie, we can pack in more apples, control the amount of juice in the mix, and eliminate the crust gap. But don't rush the cooking or crank up the heat: The apples must be cooked gently (below 140 degrees) to keep them from becoming mushy when cooked further in the oven.

Good to Know

GOOD IDEAS FOR ANY FRUIT PIE

Chill Your Pastry
Cold dough is less sticky and much easier to roll.

Flour Your Counter
A floured counter helps minimize sticking. You can also place your dough disk between two pieces of plastic wrap or parchment paper to help keep it from sticking.

Roll in One Direction
Creating an even round of dough is easier when you roll in one direction only. Roll over the dough, rotate it a quarter turn, and then roll again. Repeat, adding flour as necessary, until you reach the desired diameter.

Take It Easy on the Dough
If you roll it too aggressively or too many times, you'll end up with a tough, not tender, crust.

Put Your Pie Plate on a Baking Sheet
Baking your pie on a baking sheet doesn't just save your oven from overflows; it also helps promote a nice, brown crust on the bottom of the pie.

Our Favorite Rolling Pin
We prefer a long, straight wooden rolling pin to one with handles; we find that it gives us a better "feel" for the dough. Our favorite, the **J.K. Adams Plain Maple Rolling Dowel**, has a slightly textured finish that holds a light dusting of flour to help keep the dough from sticking.

Our Favorite Pie Dish
We're crazy about the **Pyrex Bakeware 9 Inch Pie Plate**; its ½-inch rim is just the right size, and its see-through bottom leaves no mystery as to when the crust is brown.

STEP BY STEP Perfect Deep-Dish Apple Pie

1. COMBINE TART AND SWEET
Peel and slice 2½ pounds each of sweet and tart apples.
WHY? Using two varieties adds full, complex flavor. And because different apples break down at different rates, a mix adds textural interest, too.

2. PRECOOK THE APPLES
Cook the apples, sugars, and seasonings until the apples are tender but still hold their shape.
WHY? Precooking the apples removes excess moisture so they won't shrink during baking. It also concentrates their flavor.

3. COOL THE FRUIT
Spread the cooked apple mixture on a rimmed baking sheet to cool.
WHY? Adding hot apples to the crust will melt the butter prematurely, and the crust will be dense rather than flaky.

4. ROLL DOUGHS
Gently roll first dough into a 12-inch round and transfer to pie plate. Roll second dough to the same size and transfer to parchment-lined baking sheet.
WHY? A 12-inch round leaves just enough extra to seal and crimp together with the top crust.

5. CHILL OUT
Wrap both doughs loosely with plastic wrap and refrigerate for at least 30 minutes before filling and topping the pie.
WHY? Chilling the doughs before assembling and baking the pie ensures that the crusts won't heat too fast and slump in the oven.

DEEP-DISH APPLE PIE Serves 8

You can substitute Empire or Cortland apples for the Granny Smiths and Jonagold, Fuji, or Braeburn apples for the Golden Delicious. A regular 9-inch pie plate works great; a deep-dish pie plate is not needed. Buy ready-made pie doughs or go to CooksCountry.com/doublepiedough for our recipe.

FILLING AND CRUST
- 2½ pounds Granny Smith apples, peeled, cored, halved, and sliced ¼ inch thick
- 2½ pounds Golden Delicious apples, peeled, cored, halved, and sliced ¼ inch thick
- ½ cup (3½ ounces) granulated sugar
- ¼ cup packed (1¾ ounces) light brown sugar
- ½ teaspoon grated lemon zest plus 1 tablespoon juice
- ¼ teaspoon salt
- ⅛ teaspoon ground cinnamon
- 2 (9-inch) pie doughs

TOPPING
- 1 large egg white, lightly beaten
- 1 teaspoon granulated sugar

1. FOR THE FILLING AND CRUST: Toss apples, granulated sugar, brown sugar, lemon zest, salt, and cinnamon together in Dutch oven. Cover and cook over medium heat, stirring frequently, until apples are tender when poked with fork but still hold their shape, 15 to 20 minutes. Transfer apples and their juice to rimmed baking sheet and let cool completely, about 30 minutes.

2. Roll 1 dough into 12-inch circle on lightly floured counter. (If dough is soft and/or sticky, refrigerate until firm.) Loosely roll dough around rolling pin and gently unroll it onto 9-inch pie plate, letting excess dough hang over edge. Ease dough into plate by gently lifting edge of dough with your hand while pressing into plate bottom with your other hand. Leave any dough that overhangs plate in place. Wrap dough-lined plate loosely in plastic and refrigerate until dough is firm, about 30 minutes. Roll other dough into 12-inch circle on lightly floured counter, then transfer to parchment paper–lined baking sheet; cover with plastic and refrigerate for 30 minutes.

3. Adjust oven rack to lowest position and heat oven to 425 degrees. Drain cooled apples thoroughly in colander set over bowl and reserve ¼ cup of juice. Stir lemon juice into reserved juice. Spread apples in dough-lined plate, mounding them slightly in middle, and drizzle with apple juice mixture. Loosely roll remaining dough round around rolling pin and gently unroll it onto filling.

4. Trim overhang to ½ inch beyond lip of plate. Pinch edges of top and bottom crusts firmly together. Tuck overhang under itself; folded edge should be flush with edge of plate. Crimp dough around edge of plate using your fingers. Cut four 2-inch slits in top of dough.

5. FOR THE TOPPING: Brush surface with egg white and sprinkle with sugar. Set pie on parchment-lined rimmed baking sheet and bake until crust is light golden brown, about 30 minutes. Reduce oven temperature to 375 degrees, rotate baking sheet, and continue to bake until juices are bubbling and crust is deep golden brown, 30 to 40 minutes longer. Transfer pie to wire rack and let cool until filling has set, about 2 hours; serve slightly warm or at room temperature.

6. DRAIN AND FILL
Transfer the apples to a large colander and drain off all but ¼ cup of juice. Pour the drained apples into the chilled bottom pie dough.
WHY? Controlling the amount of juice makes the pie moist but not soupy.

7. SEAL THE DEAL
Top filling with second chilled dough, pinch the top and bottom doughs together, tuck the overhang under itself, and crimp the dough.
WHY? This creates a tight seal so the filling stays inside the pie.

8. CUT STEAM VENTS
Cut four 2-inch slits in the dough.
WHY? The vents allow excess steam to escape so the crust doesn't rupture.

9. BAKE ON LINED SHEET
Set the pie on a parchment-lined rimmed baking sheet and bake it at 425 degrees for 30 minutes.
WHY? The baking sheet conducts heat evenly to promote browning of the bottom crust and catches any overflows before they make a mess of the oven.

10. LOWER HEAT TO FINISH
Reduce the oven temperature to 375 degrees to finish baking.
WHY? Reducing the heat ensures that the pie is cooked through before the edges become too dark.

We set out to rescue this dish from leftovers land and return it to its creamy, cheesy roots—in a dish for two. BY KATIE LEAIRD

CHICKEN TETRAZZINI IS named for Luisa Tetrazzini, a celebrated Italian opera star. When critics questioned her fading talents during a United States tour in the early 1900s, she proclaimed, "I am old, I am fat, but I am still Tetrazzini." We wanted the same captivating but defiant grandeur, even in a simple weeknight dish for two.

Over the years, this cheesy, comforting suppertime casserole has deteriorated from an elegant dish of torn roasted chicken, broken strands of spaghetti, and flavorful shreds of cheese built on a velvety, sherry-spiked cream sauce into a sloppy mash-up of leftover poultry and canned cream of mushroom soup—an afterthought dish that mostly serves as a fridge clean-out supper. Filling, yes, but without much personality.

Luisa deserves better, so I set out to revitalize this dish with fresh ingredients and timesaving techniques while also scaling it back from a bulky crowd-feeder to a restrained but satisfying supper that would serve just two.

Easier said than done.

I knew that I couldn't count on leftover chicken being available in any given fridge, so I searched for the best way to cook the chicken. Poaching breasts in broth and shredding them took too much time. Sautéing thin slices of chicken took too much effort. Instead, I turned to one of the test kitchen's favorite convenience products: a freshly cooked rotisserie chicken from the grocery store; all I'd have to do was tear it into pieces.

The next order of business was the bread crumbs. Prefab crumbs were a no-go here; I wanted a fresh, tender bread-crumb topping. Easy: I dropped a slice of white sandwich bread into the food processor and spun it for just a few seconds, until it was finely ground. I stirred in a bit of melted butter and set the crumbs aside to await their fate.

I was on to the bigger challenge: an easy, flavorful cream sauce. I started by browning onions and mushrooms in a skillet, building a much-needed flavor base for the sauce. I added chicken broth and heavy cream and then dropped broken spaghetti strands directly into the mixture.

In less than 10 minutes, the spaghetti was cooked and the sauce had reduced; plus, the starch released by the cooking pasta thickened the cream sauce without the need for an extra step. Some fresh thyme gave the sauce an herbal note, and the sherry contributed a hint of elegance.

I added in the meat at the last minute so it wouldn't overcook and slid the skillet into the oven to brown. Tasters liked the result well enough, but there was room for another note of brightness—something to cut through the thickness of the sauce. But where to add it? I eyed the bread crumbs.

Though this dish is unequivocally American, it nonetheless has an Italian name. So I felt free to draw upon one of my favorite Italian add-ins: gremolata. This mixture of finely chopped garlic, lemon zest, and parsley is often used as a condiment or ingredient in Italian cooking to pep up creamy or meaty dishes. I added these ingredients to the food processor along with the bread and let it rip. Then I assembled another skillet of Tetrazzini. Once it was out of the oven, we dug in. Success: The sharp acid from the lemon, the mild astringency from the parsley, and the subtle heat from the garlic refreshed the dish, cutting through the rich sauce.

This simple but rich and satisfying chicken Tetrazzini, made with fresh ingredients and boasting full, round flavors, would make Luisa proud.

The pasta cooks right in the flavorful sauce for an easy (and tasty) weeknight dinner for two.

Gremolata: Adding Freshness
Rich, savory dishes like this one often benefit from a finish of something fresh and bright, like a squeeze of lemon or a sprinkling of fresh herbs. Gremolata, the classic Italian garnish for osso buco, adds garlic to the lemon and herb combination. For this recipe, we combine the gremolata ingredients (fresh parsley, lemon zest, and minced garlic) with bread crumbs to create a lively, crunchy topping.

A BURST OF FRESH FLAVOR
Parsley, lemon, garlic, and bread crumbs.

CHICKEN TETRAZZINI FOR TWO
You can use a rasp-style grater to mince the garlic and grate the lemon zest. To contain runaway pieces, wrap the spaghetti in a kitchen towel before you break it. The peas needn't be defrosted for this recipe.

- 1 **slice hearty white sandwich bread, torn into pieces**
- 1 **tablespoon chopped fresh parsley**
- 1 **small garlic clove, minced**
- ½ **teaspoon grated lemon zest**
  Salt and pepper
- 1 **tablespoon unsalted butter, melted, plus 1 tablespoon unsalted butter**
- 7 **ounces white mushrooms, trimmed and sliced thin**
- ½ **cup finely chopped onion**
- 2¼ **cups chicken broth**
- ½ **cup heavy cream**
- 4 **ounces spaghetti, broken into thirds**
- 1 **teaspoon minced fresh thyme**
- 2 **ounces Gruyère cheese, shredded (½ cup)**
- ½ **cup frozen peas**
- 1 **tablespoon dry sherry**
- 1½ **cups shredded rotisserie chicken**

1. Adjust oven rack to middle position and heat oven to 475 degrees. Process bread, parsley, garlic, lemon zest, and ⅛ teaspoon salt in food processor until finely ground, about 15 seconds. Transfer crumbs to bowl and stir in melted butter; set aside.

2. Melt remaining 1 tablespoon butter in ovensafe 10-inch skillet over medium heat. Add mushrooms, onion, and ¼ teaspoon salt and cook until any moisture has evaporated and mushrooms are golden brown, 7 to 9 minutes.

3. Stir in broth, cream, pasta, and thyme. Bring to simmer and cook, stirring often, until pasta is just tender and sauce is slightly thickened, about 9 minutes.

4. Off heat, stir in Gruyère, peas, and sherry until combined. Stir in chicken until fully incorporated. Season with salt and pepper to taste.

5. Sprinkle bread-crumb mixture over top. Transfer skillet to oven and bake until topping is golden brown and casserole is bubbling lightly around edges, about 10 minutes. Let rest for 10 minutes. Serve.

One-Pan Dinner Pork with Green Beans and Potatoes

An unexpected ingredient solved two problems in this easy weeknight dinner. BY CHRISTIE MORRISON

MILD-FLAVORED, LEAN PORK tenderloin makes a great weeknight meal because it is relatively inexpensive, cooks quickly, and takes well to a wide variety of flavors. I set out to make an easy-but-flavorful dinner of two pork tenderloins and a few vegetables on a single baking sheet—easy cooking, easy cleanup.

To start my testing, I looked for two vegetables that would cook at a similar rate to the pork. Since pork tenderloins can reach their optimal temperature of 140 degrees in as little as 20 minutes at 450 degrees, most root vegetables, which take much longer to cook, were out. Thin fingerling potatoes (halved lengthwise), however, worked well, cooking through in the same time it took to cook the pork. Now I needed a green vegetable to complete the meal.

Green beans, which are great roasted, came to mind; I was disappointed, then, when the green beans that I roasted with the pork and potatoes became tough and chewy from the intense dry heat. For my next test, I tried insulating the beans by positioning the tenderloins directly on top of them. This method effectively steamed the green beans to a crisp-tender texture.

When I removed the tenderloins from the baking sheet, however, I noticed that while the potatoes and beans had cooked through, they hadn't picked up much tasty browning. To remedy this lack of color, I returned the vegetables to the oven while the pork rested (a necessary post-roast step that ensures juiciness). Ten minutes later, both the spuds and the green beans were browned and tender, and the pork was ready for slicing.

But while the pork was moist and juicy, it needed a little help in the flavor department. It also looked a little pale without a browned crust. I could give it one by cooking it more (either under the broiler or in a sauté pan), but I knew that, while it would be brown, it would also be dry.

My fix: a sweet glaze. Since sugars caramelize and brown faster than meat, I knew that coating the meat with one would improve its appearance and flavor. But I came up short with maple syrup (too sweet), honey (too sticky), and brown sugar (too molasses-y). What's more, each provided sweetness but not much else. Inspiration appeared in a jar

of hoisin sauce. This thick, dark, potent Chinese sauce is made of soybeans, ginger, chiles, garlic, and sugar—it's a staple ingredient in stir-fries. I brushed some of it on the tenderloins. After 25 minutes in the oven, the pork picked up just the right amount of sweetness and a rounded, unexpected complexity from the hoisin. Tasters couldn't quite identify the secret flavor, but they sure liked it.

To give this dinner a little extra oomph, I mashed together softened butter, chives, and minced garlic and dotted the hot pork with this flavored butter while the meat was resting and the vegetables were finishing up in the oven. I saved some to toss with the browned potatoes and green beans, too.

Arrangement Counts

Placing the tenderloins directly over the green beans creates steam, which helps the beans cook through without drying out. The drippings from the meat also help flavor the green beans.

ONE-PAN PORK TENDERLOIN WITH GREEN BEANS AND POTATOES
Serves 4 to 6

Buy tenderloins that are of equal size and weight so they cook at the same rate. A rasp-style grater makes quick work of turning the garlic into a paste. Our favorite hoisin sauce is Kikkoman's.

- 4 tablespoons unsalted butter, softened
- 2 tablespoons minced fresh chives
- 1 garlic clove, minced to paste
  Salt and pepper
- 2 (1-pound) pork tenderloins, trimmed
- ¼ cup hoisin sauce
- 1 pound green beans, trimmed
- 3 tablespoons extra-virgin olive oil
- 1½ pounds fingerling potatoes, unpeeled, halved lengthwise

1. Adjust oven rack to lower-middle position and heat oven to 450 degrees. Combine butter, chives, garlic, ¼ teaspoon salt, and ¼ teaspoon pepper in bowl; set aside. Pat pork dry with paper towels and season with pepper. Brush tenderloins all over with hoisin sauce.

2. Toss green beans, 1 tablespoon oil, ¼ teaspoon salt, and ¼ teaspoon pepper together in large bowl. Arrange green bean mixture crosswise down center of rimmed baking sheet, leaving room on both sides for potatoes. Toss potatoes, remaining 2 tablespoons oil, ¼ teaspoon salt, and ¼ teaspoon pepper together in now-empty bowl. Arrange potatoes, cut side down, on both sides of green beans.

3. Lay tenderloins, side by side without touching, lengthwise on top of green beans. Roast until pork registers 140 degrees, 20 to 25 minutes. Transfer tenderloins to carving board and dot each with 1 tablespoon reserved herb butter. Tent with aluminum foil and let rest while vegetables finish cooking.

4. Gently stir vegetables on sheet to combine. Return sheet to oven and roast until vegetables are tender and golden brown, 5 to 10 minutes longer. Remove from oven, add remaining 2 tablespoons herb butter to sheet, and toss vegetables to coat. Transfer vegetables to platter. Cut pork into ½-inch-thick slices and place over vegetables, pouring any accumulated juices over top. Serve.

Hoisin sauce adds subtle depth of flavor and gives the pork a beautiful brown color.

This classic French braise features tender chicken and sweet (not harsh) garlic. Could we make it work in the slow cooker? BY CECELIA JENKINS

THIS TRADITIONAL FRENCH recipe consists of bone-in chicken pieces and garlic cloves braised in broth until tender. It's typically served with crusty bread, which is the perfect thing to smear with softened garlic cloves and use to mop up the sauce. The garlic in this dish mellows and turns sweet with the long cooking—surprisingly, it's not an excessively garlicky dish.

I did find some slow-cooker recipes for this dish in our cookbook library, but come tasting time, none of them turned out to be very good. The most glaring problem was garlic cloves that kept too much of their dragon-like bite. The next concern was that the sauces tasted wan and washed out; they were also either sludgy and too thick, or too brothy and thin. I knew I could do better.

I began my testing with the garlic, which, somewhat surprisingly, didn't lose its raw edge by the time the chicken was cooked through. Fortunately, past test kitchen recipes provided a possible solution: jump-starting the garlic in the microwave. I microwaved the garlic just until it had a slight give, which took about 4 minutes; this quick precooking step made for garlic that was mostly sweet and creamy in the finished dish. Adding a little sugar to this microwaving step gave the garlic (and thus the sauce) more complexity and roundness.

For the chicken, I had been using a mix of bone-in pieces, which were cooking irregularly. I switched to bone-in thighs, which all cooked at the same rate. Plus, their dark meat could stand up to longer cooking without drying out. Browning them in a skillet before adding them to the slow cooker left lots

Bone-in chicken thighs have great flavor and take well to braising.

of flavorful fond in the skillet. I added the microwaved garlic to the skillet so that it, too, could pick up some browning, and then I deglazed with sherry to incorporate the potent browned bits into the braising liquid. Next I added the broth, brought the mixture to a boil, and transferred it to the slow cooker. I was making progress, but the dish was a little bland and some of the garlic cloves weren't quite soft and mellow enough.

To ensure that the cloves cooked fully in the slow cooker, I layered them all in first and placed the chicken on top to keep the garlic submerged. This was also advantageous for the chicken skin, which now sat above the liquid and thus didn't become rubbery. Adding some sprigs of thyme to the braise and finishing the sauce with fresh parsley and lemon gave the dish the extra boost of flavor it needed. Pass the baguette, please.

SLOW-COOKER CHICKEN WITH 40 CLOVES OF GARLIC
Serves 4 to 6

You will need three or four heads of garlic to yield 40 cloves, or you can purchase prepeeled garlic instead. To avoid flare-ups, be sure to remove the skillet from the heat when adding the sherry. The chicken is only browned on the skin side.

- 40 garlic cloves, peeled
- 2 teaspoons olive oil
- ½ teaspoon sugar
- 8 (5- to 7-ounce) bone-in chicken thighs, trimmed
  Salt and pepper
- ⅔ cup dry sherry
- ½ cup chicken broth
- 4 sprigs fresh thyme
- 1 tablespoon lemon juice
- 1 tablespoon chopped fresh parsley
- 1 (12-inch) baguette, sliced ¾ inch thick on bias

1. Combine garlic, 1 teaspoon oil, and sugar in bowl. Cover and microwave until garlic is translucent and yields slightly when squeezed, about 4 minutes, stirring halfway through cooking. Pour off any liquid from garlic bowl and set garlic aside.

2. Pat chicken dry with paper towels and season with salt and pepper. Heat remaining 1 teaspoon oil in 12-inch skillet over medium-high heat until just smoking. Cook chicken skin side down until well browned, about 10 minutes. Transfer chicken to plate, skin side up. Pour off all but 2 tablespoons fat from skillet.

3. Add microwaved garlic to fat in skillet and cook over medium-high heat until lightly browned, 1 to 2 minutes. Off heat, stir in sherry; return skillet to heat and cook until nearly evaporated, about 4 minutes, scraping up any browned bits. Add broth and thyme sprigs and bring to boil.

4. Transfer garlic-broth mixture to slow cooker. Nestle chicken skin side up on top of garlic cloves (garlic should be completely covered). Cover and cook on low until chicken registers 175 degrees, about 3 hours.

5. Transfer chicken to platter. Discard thyme sprigs; add lemon juice, parsley, ¼ teaspoon salt, and ¼ teaspoon pepper to sauce. Pour sauce around chicken and serve with baguette slices.

KEY STEP Microwaving Garlic
To make sure they fully soften, we give the garlic cloves a head start by microwaving them briefly before browning them in chicken fat and adding them to the braising liquid.

JUST TRANSLUCENT
Precook the garlic until it looks like this.

TEST KITCHEN TECHNIQUE
A Smart Arrangement
We put the braising liquid—which includes the garlic cloves—in the insert first and then nestle the browned chicken on top. This keeps the garlic submerged so it can cook to tenderness evenly and prevents the chicken skin from getting too soggy.

The secret to no-fuss scrambled eggs is not what you put in them—it's what you leave out. BY CECELIA JENKINS

WHEN MY COLLEAGUES and chef friends are making themselves breakfast, more often than not they are making scrambled eggs with a bunch of, well, stuff in them.

And why not? Breakfast scrambles are less fussy than omelets (no fancy folding or rolling to potentially botch), and they happily serve as a blank canvas for just about anything you have around: leftover vegetables, herbs, cheeses, leftover meats, and so on. I set out to come up with a basic method and five hearty, great-tasting versions of breakfast scrambles.

First off, because we're adding other flavorful ingredients, there is no need to add milk, cream, half-and-half, extra egg yolks, or any other fatty, rich ingredient to the beaten eggs. But that doesn't mean there isn't a correct way to make a breakfast scramble.

After several days of cracking, beating, and scrambling, I came up with the basic technique to serve two. First, beat five eggs with nothing more than salt and pepper. Then, melt a tablespoon of unsalted butter in a 10-inch nonstick skillet over medium-high heat, add the eggs, and stir constantly with a heat-resistant rubber spatula until the eggs begin to clump, which takes about 2 minutes. Then—and this is important—reduce the heat to low, sprinkle in your add-ins, and gently and constantly fold the eggs until fully clumped but still slightly wet, just about 45 seconds more. Immediately transfer the eggs to warmed plates, where they will continue to firm up due to their residual heat, and serve.

I wanted to keep the add-ins simple and straightforward. Grated extra-sharp cheddar, minced scallion, and minced pickled jalapeños made for a scramble with richness and zip. Black Forest ham and shredded Gruyère cheese elevated a tried-and-true combination. Buttery Havarti cheese was a great match for fresh dill, and chopped chives brought freshness to a scramble starring smoked trout. My last variation featured the classic Greek pairing of briny feta cheese and spinach; for this one, I had to briefly wilt the spinach in the pan before adding the eggs, but it was still easy to throw together—even before my first cup of coffee.

Our breakfast scramble add-ins bring a lot of flavor without a lot of fuss.

CHEDDAR AND PICKLED JALAPEÑO BREAKFAST SCRAMBLE
Serves 2

It is important to follow visual cues, as pan thickness will affect cooking times. If using an electric stove, heat one burner on low heat and a second on medium-high heat; move the skillet between burners when it's time to adjust the heat.

- 5 large eggs
  Salt and pepper
- 1 tablespoon unsalted butter
- 1 ounce extra-sharp cheddar cheese, shredded (¼ cup)
- 1 scallion, minced
- 1 tablespoon minced pickled jalapeños

1. Beat eggs, ¼ teaspoon salt, and ⅛ teaspoon pepper with fork in bowl until eggs are thoroughly combined and mixture is pure yellow; do not overbeat.

2. Melt butter in 10-inch nonstick skillet over medium-high heat, swirling to coat pan. Add egg mixture and, using heat-resistant rubber spatula, constantly and firmly scrape along bottom and sides of skillet until eggs begin to clump and spatula leaves trail on bottom of skillet, 1½ to 2½ minutes.

3. Reduce heat to low and add cheddar, scallion, and jalapeños. Gently but constantly fold eggs until clumped and slightly wet, 30 to 60 seconds. Immediately transfer eggs to warmed plates and season with salt and pepper to taste. Serve immediately.

HAM AND GRUYÈRE BREAKFAST SCRAMBLE
Substitute ½ cup chopped Black Forest ham and ¼ cup shredded Gruyère for cheddar, scallion, and jalapeños.

HAVARTI AND DILL BREAKFAST SCRAMBLE
Substitute ½ cup shredded Havarti and 1½ teaspoons minced fresh dill for cheddar, scallion, and jalapeños.

SMOKED TROUT AND CHIVE BREAKFAST SCRAMBLE
Substitute ½ cup flaked smoked trout and 1 tablespoon minced fresh chives for cheddar, scallion, and jalapeños.

SPINACH AND FETA BREAKFAST SCRAMBLE
Omit scallion and jalapeños. Add 2 cups chopped baby spinach to melted butter in step 2 before adding eggs and cook until wilted, about 1 minute. Substitute ¼ cup crumbled feta cheese for cheddar.

Equipment Review Slicing Knives

Want perfect slices at your holiday table? Lose the chef's knife.

BY HANNAH CROWLEY

THERE YOU ARE at the head of the table, with family and friends arrayed expectantly on either side. You've got a carving fork in one hand and a chef's knife in the other. It doesn't end well: Before long, the rosy roast is reduced to a pitiful pile of slabs and shaggy slivers.

If you're spending time and money on a special meal, it's worth getting the right tool to serve it. Unlike shorter chef's knives and pointed, flexible carving knives, slicing knives are long and straight for smooth, even slicing. They have rounded tips so as to be less threatening for tableside serving.

For years, when we wanted perfect slices, we turned to a nearly $55 12-inch slicing knife from Victorinox. To see if it's still the best, we retested it against seven new knives, priced from roughly $28 to $118, by slicing more than 150 pounds of turkey breast and roast beef and rating each knife on its handle, blade, sharpness, and agility.

Comfortable, grippy handles were imperative, as was the right degree of flexibility: Bendy blades bailed out midcut, leaving behind ragged slices. Stiff blades went where they wanted, not where we asked. Subtle but present flexibility allowed for control and strength.

Length mattered, too. We had to insert shorter blades to the hilt to get a full slice, causing our knuckles to brush against the meat; longer blades gave us more room to work. We also liked taller blades because they put more distance between our fingers and the sharpened edge. Called a bevel, this edge tapers to a point like a V and ranged from 14 to 20 degrees wide on either side, depending on the knife. As in our chef's knife evaluations, we preferred narrower blades because they're sharper.

Lastly, when it came to those scalloped divots called Grantons that dot the side of many knives, we preferred blades with them. And we spoke to N. Brian Huegel, knife expert and owner of Country Knives Inc., in Intercourse, Pennsylvania, to understand why. According to Huegel, Grantons break up the resistance on the blade, and the reduced friction makes it easier to cut even slices, thick or thin.

In the end the Victorinox ($54.65) wowed us all over again. "I feel like I can do anything with this knife," said one tester. It was long, tall, sharp, and just flexible enough to give us utter control and perfect slices.

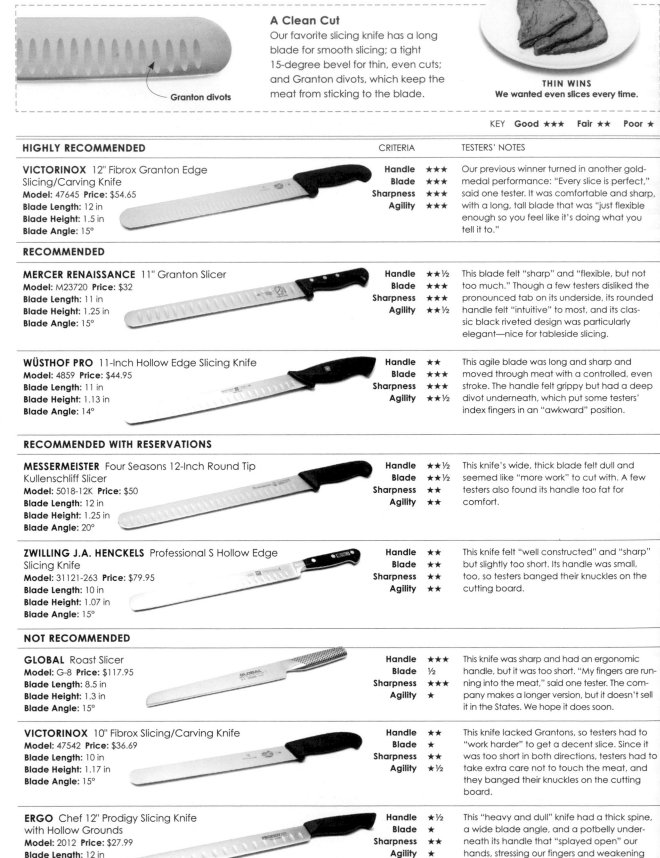

A Clean Cut
Our favorite slicing knife has a long blade for smooth slicing; a tight 15-degree bevel for thin, even cuts; and Granton divots, which keep the meat from sticking to the blade.

Granton divots

THIN WINS
We wanted even slices every time.

KEY **Good ★★★** **Fair ★★** **Poor ★**

	CRITERIA		TESTERS' NOTES
HIGHLY RECOMMENDED			
VICTORINOX 12" Fibrox Granton Edge Slicing/Carving Knife **Model:** 47645 **Price:** $54.65 **Blade Length:** 12 in **Blade Height:** 1.5 in **Blade Angle:** 15°	Handle Blade Sharpness Agility	★★★ ★★★ ★★★ ★★★	Our previous winner turned in another gold-medal performance: "Every slice is perfect," said one tester. It was comfortable and sharp, with a long, tall blade that was "just flexible enough so you feel like it's doing what you tell it to."
RECOMMENDED			
MERCER RENAISSANCE 11" Granton Slicer **Model:** M23720 **Price:** $32 **Blade Length:** 11 in **Blade Height:** 1.25 in **Blade Angle:** 15°	Handle Blade Sharpness Agility	★★½ ★★★ ★★★ ★★½	This blade felt "sharp" and "flexible, but not too much." Though a few testers disliked the pronounced tab on its underside, its rounded handle felt "intuitive" to most, and its classic black riveted design was particularly elegant—nice for tableside slicing.
WÜSTHOF PRO 11-Inch Hollow Edge Slicing Knife **Model:** 4859 **Price:** $44.95 **Blade Length:** 11 in **Blade Height:** 1.13 in **Blade Angle:** 14°	Handle Blade Sharpness Agility	★★ ★★★ ★★★ ★★½	This agile blade was long and sharp and moved through meat with a controlled, even stroke. The handle felt grippy but had a deep divot underneath, which put some testers' index fingers in an "awkward" position.
RECOMMENDED WITH RESERVATIONS			
MESSERMEISTER Four Seasons 12-Inch Round Tip Kullenschliff Slicer **Model:** 5018-12K **Price:** $50 **Blade Length:** 12 in **Blade Height:** 1.25 in **Blade Angle:** 20°	Handle Blade Sharpness Agility	★★½ ★★½ ★★ ★★	This knife's wide, thick blade felt dull and seemed like "more work" to cut with. A few testers also found its handle too fat for comfort.
ZWILLING J.A. HENCKELS Professional S Hollow Edge Slicing Knife **Model:** 31121-263 **Price:** $79.95 **Blade Length:** 10 in **Blade Height:** 1.07 in **Blade Angle:** 15°	Handle Blade Sharpness Agility	★★ ★★ ★★ ★★	This knife felt "well constructed" and "sharp" but slightly too short. Its handle was small, too, so testers banged their knuckles on the cutting board.
NOT RECOMMENDED			
GLOBAL Roast Slicer **Model:** G-8 **Price:** $117.95 **Blade Length:** 8.5 in **Blade Height:** 1.3 in **Blade Angle:** 15°	Handle Blade Sharpness Agility	★★★ ½ ★★★ ★	This knife was sharp and had an ergonomic handle, but it was too short. "My fingers are running into the meat," said one tester. The company makes a longer version, but it doesn't sell it in the States. We hope it does soon.
VICTORINOX 10" Fibrox Slicing/Carving Knife **Model:** 47542 **Price:** $36.69 **Blade Length:** 10 in **Blade Height:** 1.17 in **Blade Angle:** 15°	Handle Blade Sharpness Agility	★★ ★ ★★ ★½	This knife lacked Grantons, so testers had to "work harder" to get a decent slice. Since it was too short in both directions, testers had to take extra care not to touch the meat, and they banged their knuckles on the cutting board.
ERGO Chef 12" Prodigy Slicing Knife with Hollow Grounds **Model:** 2012 **Price:** $27.99 **Blade Length:** 12 in **Blade Height:** 1.2 in **Blade Angle:** 18°	Handle Blade Sharpness Agility	★½ ★ ★★ ★	This "heavy and dull" knife had a thick spine, a wide blade angle, and a potbelly underneath its handle that "splayed open" our hands, stressing our fingers and weakening our grip.

Taste Test Preshredded Parmesan Cheese

Shredding cheese is time-consuming. Is there an acceptable shortcut even skeptics can get behind?

BY LAUREN SAVOIE

NOTHING BEATS THE savory saltiness of real Parmigiano-Reggiano, the name-protected aged cheese made in Parma, Italy, according to strict traditional standards. Cheese made in the same style anywhere else or by less exacting standards is just called "Parmesan." The distinction can bring a drop in flavor but also a big drop in cost: Parmigiano-Reggiano often costs twice as much as domestic Parmesan.

We've recommended a number of domestic Parmesan wedges in the past, but when we polled our readers we learned that more than half use preshredded or grated Parmesan for topping weeknight pasta dinners or in cheese-heavy dishes like polenta or risotto. As Parm purists, we were skeptical—but if there was a good shortcut out there, we wanted to know about it. So we gathered seven nationally available preshredded Parmesans (we couldn't find preshredded Parmigiano-Reggiano that was widely available) and tasted each plain, atop sauced pasta, and melted into polenta.

Texture was the biggest issue. Compared with the fluffy strands of freshly shredded cheese, some preshredded Parmesans were stiff and fibrous. To get a closer look at shred size, we sifted equal amounts of each cheese through a strainer, weighing the small bits that fell through the 4-millimeter holes and the larger strands that remained. Brands with more than 75 percent large shreds left goopy strings in polenta, while products

with more small bits (up to 50 percent) were mealy on pasta. We preferred Parmesan that had one-third small shreds and two-thirds large. (When following recipes, we recommend measuring Parmesan by weight instead of volume to account for varying shred sizes.)

We also wanted flavor that matched the punch of real Parmigiano-Reggiano. Tasters chided lower-ranked products for their bland flavor. We examined ingredient labels thinking that salt might be the culprit, but while no product matched the 433 milligrams of sodium per ounce found in real Parmigiano-Reggiano, only one "too bland" product suffered from too little sodium (252 milligrams, compared with 336 milligrams and up in top-ranked cheeses).

We needed more information, so we sent the cheeses to a lab for analysis. According to the consortium that oversees its regulation, Parmigiano-Reggiano has 8 grams of fat and 8.7 grams of moisture per ounce. Our favorite preshredded product came back with results that almost matched: 7.9 grams of fat and 8.6 grams of moisture, which translated into the firm, crystalline bite and complex buttery richness we associate with real Parm. Lower-ranked cheeses varied from Parmigiano-Reggiano by up to 4 grams of fat and 2 grams of moisture and were, in turn, overly soft, stiff, or bland.

Which led us to the question: Could our favorite preshredded Parmesan stand a chance against real-deal Parmigiano-Reggiano? We held a final blind taste test with new batches of pasta and polenta. Most tasters still preferred the subtle tang and nutty flavor of Parmigiano-Reggiano, but our new winner held its own, especially in polenta, where tasters remarked that it was "rich," "cheesy," and "creamy."

When we have the time and money, we still prefer freshly grated Parmigiano-Reggiano, but we found acceptable shredded alternatives. Sargento Artisan Blends Shredded Parmesan Cheese came out on top for its "nutty," "rich" flavor and "softer," medium-size shreds. Though most manufacturers wouldn't disclose aging information, we learned that Sargento is made with a blend of 10- and 18-month aged Parmesan for extra "punchy" flavor. At $0.80 per ounce, it's only slightly cheaper than real Parmigiano-Reggiano ($1.00 per ounce) but requires less prep time for fairly comparable flavor.

What's the Deal with the Green Can?

Many of us grew up shaking piles of Kraft Grated Parmesan onto our pasta. Is nostalgia the only merit to the green can? We tried the powdered stuff (which is finely grated Parmesan that's been tossed with cellulose powder to prevent caking) on pasta and in polenta. Most tasters found it "bland," "powdery," and "dusty," even when mixed into hot polenta. On pasta, it was "like a mountain of sawdust" with "no discernible cheese flavor." While a few tasters gave Kraft "points for nostalgia," most agreed that this product was best left for "childhood pasta dinners."

RECOMMENDED

	TASTERS' NOTES
SARGENTO Artisan Blends Shredded Parmesan Cheese **Price:** $3.99 for 5 oz ($0.80 per oz) **Sodium:** 336 mg per oz **Fat:** 7.9 g per oz **Moisture:** 8.6 g per oz **Size of Shreds:** 34% small, 66% large	A mix of small and large shreds lent this blend of 10- and 18-month-aged Parmesan a "fluffy," "lighter" texture that was "perfectly smooth" and "creamy" in polenta. Atop pasta, this cheese's "mild sharpness" and "nutty" flavor were reminiscent of "freshly shredded" Parmesan.
KRAFT Natural Cheese Shredded Parmesan Cheese **Price:** $4.08 for 7 oz ($0.58 per oz) **Sodium:** 400 mg per oz **Fat:** 7.8 g per oz **Moisture:** 7.8 g per oz **Size of Shreds:** 40% small, 60% large	The more refined cousin of the ubiquitous green can, this refrigerated Parmesan was "bold" and "tangy," with a "slightly salty" kick. Tasters liked this product's smaller shreds, which distributed well in pasta and made for "silky" polenta.

RECOMMENDED WITH RESERVATIONS

DIGIORNO Shredded Parmesan **Price:** $3.84 for 5.04 oz ($0.76 per oz) **Sodium:** 400 mg per oz **Fat:** 7.6 g per oz **Moisture:** 8.0 g per oz **Size of Shreds:** 30% small, 70% large	In polenta, these moderately sized strands produced a "sharp," "distinctly Parmesan" flavor and "creamy" texture. While many tasters appreciated their "buttery," "nutty" notes on pasta, a few remarked that their texture was "a bit plasticky."
4C Homestyle Shredded Parmesan **Price:** $4.99 for 6 oz ($0.83 per oz) **Sodium:** 392 mg per oz **Fat:** 4.1 g per oz **Moisture:** 6.9 g per oz **Size of Shreds:** 50% small, 50% large	Small and "waxy," these shreds were "chewy" and "stiff" on pasta but melted easily in polenta for a "silky," "even" texture. Most tasters thought that this cheese was "sweet" and "nutty," though a few picked up on a "slight sour" aftertaste.
FRIGO Shredded Parmesan Cheese **Price:** $2.44 for 5 oz ($0.49 per oz) **Sodium:** 380 mg per oz **Fat:** 7.6 g per oz **Moisture:** 8.8 g per oz **Size of Shreds:** 23% small, 77% large	These "softer," "fluffy" strands nailed the ideal Parmesan texture but fell flat on flavor. Tasters noted that these shreds were "tart" and "slightly sour," with an aftertaste reminiscent of "Swiss cheese." Off-flavors were muted when mixed into polenta.
STELLA Shredded Parmesan Cheese **Price:** $3.99 for 5 oz ($0.80 per oz) **Sodium:** 380 mg per oz **Fat:** 7.5 g per oz **Moisture:** 9.0 g per oz **Size of Shreds:** 17% small, 83% large	While some tasters enjoyed the "mild," "slightly sweet" flavor of these shreds, others found this product "bland" and "boring." Most agreed that these strands were too large and "stiff," making for "stringy" pasta and "clumpy" polenta.

NOT RECOMMENDED

BELGIOIOSO Shredded Parmesan **Price:** $2.91 for 4.24 oz ($0.69 per oz) **Sodium:** 252 mg per oz **Fat:** 8.7 g per oz **Moisture:** 6.8 g per oz **Size of Shreds:** 7% small, 93% large	While this product is made from our favorite domestic wedge Parmesan, these "long" and "chewy" strands were compared to "candle wax" and "twigs" when sampled on pasta. They were no better in polenta, where they congealed into "gloppy," "stringy" masses. Tasters also noted that this cheese was "a little too bland" as a result of its lower salt level.

Heirloom Recipe

We're looking for recipes that you treasure—the ones that have been handed down in your family for a generation or more; that always come out for the holidays; that have earned a place at your table and in your heart, through many years of meals. Send us the recipes that spell home to you. Visit CooksCountry.com/magazines/home (or write to Heirloom Recipes, *Cook's Country*, P.O. Box 470739, Brookline, MA 02447); click on Heirloom Recipes and tell us a little about the recipe. Include your name and mailing address. **If we print your recipe, you'll receive a free one-year subscription to *Cook's Country*.**

BOURBON BALLS   Makes about 24 balls

Kent Burnet of Phoenix, Ariz., writes: "My parents always served these at holiday parties when I was a kid in Asheville, North Carolina. But I never understood the appeal until I grew up and began to appreciate bourbon."

Either Dutch-processed or natural cocoa powder can be used in this recipe. These bourbon balls can be refrigerated in an airtight container for up to one week.

2½	cups (6 ounces) vanilla wafers
1	cup pecans, toasted
½	cup (2 ounces) confectioners' sugar
6	tablespoons bourbon
3	tablespoons light corn syrup
1½	tablespoons unsweetened cocoa powder
½	cup (3½ ounces) granulated sugar

1. Process vanilla wafers and pecans in food processor until finely ground, about 15 seconds. Transfer to large bowl. Stir in confectioners' sugar, bourbon, corn syrup, and cocoa.

2. Working with 1 heaping tablespoon at a time, shape mixture into 1-inch balls and roll in granulated sugar. Transfer balls to large plate and refrigerate until firm, at least 1 hour. Serve.

COMING NEXT ISSUE

The menu is full in our December/January issue: Besides an excellent recipe for **Prime Rib and Potatoes** suitable for the holiday table, we scoured the country for regional favorites, from **Philadelphia Swiss Haus Hazelnut Cake** to **Michigan Cornish Pasties** to **Miami Coconut Shrimp**. We'll also show you the secrets to perfect **Herb-Roasted Chicken, One-Pot Baked Ziti with Sausage and Spinach,** and a full suite of supereasy, crowd-pleasing, and swap-ready **Holiday Cookies**.

FIND THE ROOSTER!

A tiny version of this rooster has been hidden in the pages of this issue. Write to us with its location and we'll enter you in a random drawing. The first correct entry drawn will win our winning slicing knife, and each of the next five will receive a free one-year subscription to *Cook's Country*. To enter, visit CooksCountry.com/rooster by November 30, 2015, or write to Rooster ON15, *Cook's Country*, P.O. Box 470739, Brookline, MA 02447. Include your name and address. Kate Kettles of Dallas, Texas, found the rooster in the June/July 2015 issue on page 10 and won a set of our favorite potholders.

WEB EXTRAS
Free for 4 months online

Basic Brownies
California Fish Tacos
Creamy Mashed Potatoes
Double-Crust Pie Dough
Field Notes: Milwaukee
Field Notes: San Antonio
Frozen French Fry Tasting
Maryland Crab Fluff
Roasting Rack Testing (full story and charts)
Rolled Soufflé for a Crowd
Spaghetti Squash Salad with Radishes and Queso Fresco
Spaghetti Squash Salad with Tomatoes and Pecorino

READ US ON iPAD

Download the *Cook's Country* app for iPad and start a free trial subscription or purchase a single issue of the magazine. All issues are enhanced with full-color Cooking Mode slide shows that provide step-by-step instructions for completing recipes, plus expanded reviews and ratings. Go to CooksCountry.com/iPad to download our app through iTunes.

B-52 Cake

It's bombs away with this spirited cake, a riff on the popular drink of layered liqueurs. The cake features layers of brownie, light Bailey's mousse, and Grand Marnier gelatin.

To make this cake, you will need:

- **1** recipe Basic Brownies batter*
- **2½** teaspoons unflavored gelatin
- **1** tablespoon water
- **6** ounces white chocolate, chopped
- **½** cup Bailey's Irish Cream
- **1½** teaspoons instant espresso powder
- **1½** cups heavy cream, chilled
- **1** cup orange juice
- **2** tablespoons sugar
- **2** tablespoons Grand Marnier
  Bittersweet chocolate curls*

FOR THE BASE: Adjust oven rack to middle position and heat oven to 325 degrees. Grease 9-inch springform pan. Pour brownie batter into pan and bake until toothpick inserted in center comes out with few crumbs attached, 22 to 27 minutes, rotating pan halfway through baking. Transfer pan to wire rack and let cool completely.

FOR THE FILLING: Combine 1 teaspoon gelatin and water in small bowl and let stand until gelatin softens, about 5 minutes. Place white chocolate in large bowl. Heat Bailey's and espresso powder in small saucepan over medium heat until just simmering. Pour Bailey's mixture over white chocolate, add gelatin mixture, and whisk until melted; let cool slightly, about 5 minutes. Using stand mixer fitted with whisk, whip cream on medium-low speed until foamy, about 1 minute. Increase speed to high and whip until soft peaks form, 1 to 3 minutes. Whisk one-third of whipped cream into white chocolate mixture. Using spatula, fold in remaining whipped cream. Spread evenly over brownie layer in pan. Refrigerate until set, about 2 hours.

FOR THE TOPPING: Combine orange juice, sugar, Grand Marnier, and remaining 1½ teaspoons gelatin in small saucepan and cook over medium-high heat, stirring frequently, until just simmering. Transfer to 2-cup liquid measuring cup and let cool completely, about 1 hour. Slowly pour juice mixture over cake and refrigerate until set, about 1 hour. Run thin knife between cake and side of pan; remove side of pan. Transfer cake to cake platter. Place chocolate curls in center of cake. Serve.

*Find our **Basic Brownies** recipe and learn how to make chocolate curls at **cookscountry.com/nov15**.

Inside This Issue

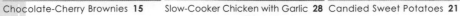

Cook's Country

DECEMBER/JANUARY 2016

Hazelnut Cake

Prime Rib with Roast Potatoes

Holiday Cookies

Almond Boneless Chicken
Simple, Crisp, Flavorful

Stuffed Acorn Squash
Wedges Are the Answer

Spicy Cheese Bread
Wisconsin Favorite Perfected

Easy Slow-Cooker Chicken and Rice Soup

Small Food Processors
Are They Worth Buying?

Apple-Cinnamon Muffins
Amp Up the Apple Flavor

Pork Saltimbocca
Make Your Own Cutlets

Cooking Class: Herb Roast Chicken

Crab Louis Salad
Bring Back the King of Salads

Testing Baking Powders
No, They Aren't All the Same

CooksCountry.com
$5.95 U.S./$6.95 CANADA

The Swiss Haus Bakery in Philadelphia has long been famous for its fluffy, delicate hazelnut cake. The recipe is a secret, but after a few weeks in the test kitchen, we created a rich, tender version you can make at home. PAGE 8

Cook's Country

Dear Country Cook,

Wild turkeys are everywhere! I see them almost every time I head into the woods. I've even seen them in Boston, crossing the street slowly, almost daring a car to get in the way. They rarely give ground.

A few years back, our neighbor Jean brought over a homegrown heirloom bird for the holidays; small breasts and legs so large I had to use a hacksaw to get it into the wood cookstove. Sometimes there is good reason why an heirloom variety is just that—a thing of the past.

My favorite turkey is Heri, the heirloom bird that Jean keeps as a pet. He is one-legged after an unfortunate car accident, but he still manages to hop around. He's white and large, about the size of pot-bellied pig, if pigs had wings.

Ben Franklin wanted to make the turkey the national bird. It was "more respectable" than the eagle, which he felt had "bad moral character" since it was apt to steal dinner from the fishing hawk. As a cook, I agree that the turkey would have been a better choice—a brined and roasted eagle is a poor offering for the hungry traveler.

But even though we think of turkeys as dinner, I still like to see them in the wild, scurrying across an open pasture when they hear me coming or marching across a road in single file, the last young hen rushing to catch up in a flurry of quick steps.

An eagle is a thing of beauty; a turkey is a throwback, a prehistoric heirloom that has become a culinary centerpiece. One bird appears on our money; the other on our dinner table.

There is a moral there somewhere, but I like sliced turkey with gravy too much to figure out what it is.

Christopher Kimball
Christopher Kimball
Founder and Editor, Cook's Country

Cook'sCountry

Founder and Editor Christopher Kimball
Editorial Director Jack Bishop
Editorial Director, Magazines John Willoughby
Executive Editor Tucker Shaw
Managing Editor Scott Kathan
Executive Food Editor Bryan Roof
Executive Tastings & Testings Editor Lisa McManus
Senior Editors Hannah Crowley,
Christie Morrison, Diane Unger
Test Kitchen Director Erin McMurrer
Associate Editor Ashley Moore
Test Cooks Morgan Bolling, Cecelia Jenkins,
Katie Leaird
Assistant Editors Lauren Savoie, Kate Shannon
Copy Editors Jillian Campbell, Krista Magnuson
Executive Assistant Christine Gordon
Assistant Test Kitchen Director Leah Rovner
Senior Kitchen Assistants Michelle Blodget,
Alexxa Grattan
Kitchen Assistants Blanca Castanza,
Maria Elena Delgado, Ena Gudiel
Executive Producer Melissa Baldino
Co-Executive Producer Stephanie Stender
Associate Producer Kaitlin Hammond

Creative Consultant Amy Klee
Contributing Editors Erika Bruce, Eva Katz, Jeremy Sauer
Consulting Editors Anne Mendelson, Meg Ragland
Science Editor Guy Crosby, PhD
Executive Food Editor, TV, Radio & Media
Bridget Lancaster

Managing Editor, Web Christine Liu
Senior Editor, Cooking School Mari Levine
Social Media Manager Jill Fisher
Senior Editor, Web Roger Metcalf
Assistant Editor, Web Terrence Doyle
Senior Video Editor Nick Dakoulas

Design Director, Print Greg Galvan
Photography Director Julie Cote
Art Director Susan Levin
Associate Art Director Lindsey Chandler
Art Director, Marketing Jennifer Cox
Staff Photographer Daniel J. van Ackere
Color Food Photography Keller + Keller
Styling Catrine Kelty, Marie Piraino
Deputy Art Director, Marketing Melanie Gryboski
Associate Art Director, Marketing Janet Taylor
Designer, Marketing Stephanie Cook
Associate Art Director, Photography Steve Klise

VP, Print & Direct Marketing David Mack
Circulation Director Doug Wicinski
Circulation & Fulfillment Manager Carrie Fethe
Partnership Marketing Manager Pamela Putprush
Marketing Coordinator Marina Tomao

Director, Business Systems Alice Carpenter
Manager, Business & Content Systems Dustin Brandt
DAM Systems Manager Ian Matzen
Project Manager Britt Dresser

Chief Operating Officer Rob Ristagno
VP, Digital Products Fran Middleton
VP, New Product Development Michael Burton
Production Director Guy Rochford
Imaging Manager Lauren Robbins
Production & Imaging Specialists Heather Dube,
Dennis Noble
Director, Marketing & Sales Operations Deborah Fagone
Client Services Manager Kate Zebrowski
Sponsorship Sales Associate Morgan Mannino
Senior Controller Theresa Peterson
Customer Loyalty & Support Manager Amy Bootier
Customer Loyalty & Support Reps Caroline Augliere,
Rebecca Kowalski, Andrew Straaberg Finfrock

Director, Retail Book Program Beth Ineson
Human Resources Manager Adele Shapiro
Publicity Deborah Broide

ON THE COVER: SWISS HAUS HAZELNUT CAKE,
Keller + Keller, Catrine Kelty
ILLUSTRATION: Greg Stevenson

Follow us on **Pinterest**
pinterest.com/TestKitchen

Follow us on **Twitter**
twitter.com/TestKitchen

Find us on **Facebook**
facebook.com/CooksCountry

Cook's Country magazine (ISSN 1552-1990), number 66,
published bimonthly by Boston Common Press Limited
Partnership, 17 Station St., Brookline, MA 02445. Copyright
2015 Boston Common Press Limited Partnership. Periodicals
postage paid at Boston, MA, and additional mailing offices,
USPS #023453. Publications Mail Agreement No. 40020778.
Return undeliverable Canadian addresses to P.O. Box
875, Station A, Windsor, ON N9A 6P2. POSTMASTER: Send
address changes to Cook's Country, P.O. Box 6018, Harlan,
IA 51593-1518. For subscription and gift subscription orders,
subscription inquiries, or change of address notices, visit
AmericasTestKitchen.com/support, call 800-526-8447 in
the U.S. or 515-248-7684 from outside the U.S., or write to
us at Cook's Country, P.O. Box 6018, Harlan, IA 51593-1518.
PRINTED IN THE USA.

Contents

SPICY CHEESE BREAD, 20   ITALIAN RAINBOW COOKIES, 11   ULTIMATE PRIME RIB AND POTATOES, 4

Features

Departments

Hack Your Kitchen

Save money and time, and get better results in your kitchen with our latest book, *Kitchen Hacks: How Clever Cooks Get Things Done*. It's full of tips for how to outsmart tricky tasks and face down kitchen challenges with innovative and ingenious ideas.

America's Test Kitchen is a very real 2,500-square-foot kitchen located just outside Boston. It is the home of *Cook's Country* and *Cook's Illustrated* magazines and the workday destination of more than three dozen test cooks, editors, and cookware specialists. Our mission is to test recipes until we understand how and why they work and arrive at the best version. We also test kitchen equipment and supermarket ingredients in search of products that offer the best value and performance. You can watch us work by tuning in to *Cook's Country from America's Test Kitchen* (CooksCountry.com) and *America's Test Kitchen* (AmericasTestKitchen.com) on public television.

Ask Cook's Country

BY MORGAN BOLLING

Sherry Substitute

Some of your recipes call for sherry. Are there any nonalcoholic ingredients I can use instead?
–Shawna Sullivan, Hickory, N.C.

Sherry is a Spanish fortified white wine, which means that the wine has liquor added. It has a distinctive caramel, earthy, often musky flavor that is typically both sweet and acidic. After a few days of experimenting in the test kitchen, we landed on a simple formula to imitate those qualities. To yield about a cup of nonalcoholic sherry substitute, combine ½ cup water, ⅓ cup apple juice, 3 tablespoons apple cider vinegar, and ¼ teaspoon soy sauce (to mimic sherry's muskiness). We tested this in our Sherry-Rosemary Pan Sauce, and it tasted very close to the sauce made with sherry. When testing our "mock sherry" in our Frozen Biscuit Tortoni dessert, we found that it was best to omit the soy sauce. Feel free to make this mixture in advance, as it will hold up to 1 week in the refrigerator.

THE BOTTOM LINE: For a nonalcoholic substitute for sherry, use our combination of water, apple juice, apple cider vinegar, and soy sauce (omit the soy sauce for sweet applications).

All About Alliums

What is the difference between green onions, spring onions, and scallions? Can they be used interchangeably?
–Emily Adams, Waterbury, Vt.

In the United States, green onions and scallions are two names for the same thing. We refer to them as scallions, as this is a slightly more widely used term.

Spring onions and scallions are species of the genus *Allium*, along with garlic, shallots, chives, ramps, and leeks. Scallions never form a bulb, so their white bases do not bulge. Spring onions look like scallions with small white bulbs; they are typically harvested in spring and are usually not available year-round.

We tried them both raw, roasted with oil and salt, in a compound butter (which we tossed with potatoes), and in our Honey-Scallion Barbecue Sauce (CooksCountry.com/honeybbqsauce).

They both tasted very similar. Tasters called both of them "strong and oniony," with the scallions being slightly more pungent and reminiscent of raw onion than the spring onions. The spring onions, however, fared the best in our roasting tests because of their sweetness and slightly larger size.

You can use spring onions and scallions interchangeably in raw applications where they are chopped. But be careful about using them in cooked applications, as the smaller size of scallions may affect cooking times.

Sweet Potato Rainbow

I recently saw purple and white sweet potatoes at the market. Can I substitute these for orange sweet potatoes in my sweet potato pie?
–Marchell Scott, Winston-Salem, N.C.

While you may typically see just one or two kinds of sweet potatoes at the grocery store, there are actually hundreds of varieties. Among these, both the flesh and skin color can vary. To determine what the differences were in flavor and texture, we tasted common varieties of white and purple sweet potatoes boiled, mashed, and in sweet potato pie next to their more common orange-fleshed cousins.

Overall, the white sweet potatoes we tried tasted citrusy and floral, while the purple sweet potatoes tasted more neutral. Both, however, shared some of the sweet, pumpkin-like flavors we're used to with orange sweet potatoes. But there were more noticeable differences in texture. Both white and purple sweet potatoes have lower moisture contents and are generally starchier—actually more akin to regular white or yellow potatoes. Because of this, they cooked differently. The mashed sweet potatoes made with white or purple sweet potatoes were thicker and needed to be thinned significantly with stock or cream to reach the texture of the mashed orange sweet potatoes. In the pie, both were denser than the control batch. And while the purple sweet potato pie was visually very interesting, tasters commented that it seemed "starchy" or even "gluey" or "mealy."

THE BOTTOM LINE: White and purple sweet potatoes have their own unique texture and flavor and so are worth trying. But do not substitute them for orange sweet potatoes in recipes because they are starchier, contain less water, and will cook differently.

ORANGE SWEET POTATOES
Fluffy, perfect pie.

WHITE SWEET POTATOES
Dense and starchy pie.

PURPLE SWEET POTATOES
Cool look, but also too dense.

THE BOTTOM LINE: Scallions and green onions are the same vegetable. In raw applications we found spring onions to be an acceptable substitute for scallions and vice versa.

Preshredded Cheese

I have better results with preshredded store-bought Parmesan than with freshly grated cheese when coating food for baking or frying. Why?
–Amy Grohman, St. Paul, Minn.

Most of the test kitchen's recipes that call for Parmesan cheese call for freshly grated. But your question intrigued us. We made our Parmesan-Crusted Asparagus (CooksCountry.com/parmasparagus) and our Crisp Parmesan Pork Cutlets (CooksCountry.com/parmporkcutlets) with both freshly grated Parmesan and store-bought preshredded Parmesan to see if we noticed a difference. In both tests, preshredded Parmesan produced a crispier coating.

Our science editor explained that

because pieces of preshredded cheese are exposed to air for a much longer time than freshly grated cheese is, the preshredded cheese loses more moisture to evaporation. The decreased moisture content leads to crispier, drier coatings.

What about the flavor? We still preferred the taste of the freshly grated cheese in both applications. But if you want to take a shortcut, or you are more focused on the crispiness, go ahead and use preshredded in frying and breading applications. Sargento won our recent taste test of preshredded Parmesans.

THE BOTTOM LINE: Preshredded Parmesan cheese yields crispier coatings than freshly grated because of its larger surface area and lower moisture content.

Walnut Oil 101

Someone gave me a bottle of unrefined walnut oil for Christmas, but I have no idea what to do with it. Can I use it as I would olive oil?
–Alex Fox, Sacramento, Calif.

Most nut oils (like walnut, hazelnut, and almond) are available in refined and unrefined versions. To answer your question, we tasted both refined and unrefined walnut oils against extra-virgin olive oil in our recipes for Basic Vinaigrette (CooksCountry.com/vinaigrette) Garlicky Croutons (CooksCountry.com/croutons), and Classic Hummus CooksCountry.com/hummus), as well as plain. To see how it would fare in cooked applications, we also tasted plain oil that had been heated to 350 degrees and then cooled.

We found the refined walnut oil to be neutral-tasting and not very interesting in all applications. The unrefined walnut oil, however, has a strong taste of roasted walnuts when tasted raw (it was especially fantastic in the vinaigrette). When heated, it loses much of its flavor—therefore, cooking with unrefined walnut oil is a waste of relatively expensive oil.

We repeated these tests with refined and unrefined hazelnut and almond oils and had similar results.

THE BOTTOM LINE: We suggest saving unrefined nut oils for raw applications, as heat destroys much of their flavor. Most nut oils, especially the unrefined versions, can go rancid quickly; store them in the refrigerator, and use them within a few months of purchase.

○ To ask us a cooking question, visit **CooksCountry.com/ask**. Or write to Ask *Cook's Country*, P.O. Box 470739, Brookline, MA 02447. Just try to stump us!

ONION COUSINS
Scallions, aka green onions (left), are slender. Spring onions have a small bulb.

Kitchen Shortcuts

COMPILED BY DIANE UNGER

FOILED AGAIN
Flatter Bacon
Tyler Swenson, Owensboro, Ky.

Years ago, someone gave me a small 6-inch cast-iron skillet as a gift. It was cute, but I had no idea what to use it for. It hit me one day when I was frying bacon in my big cast-iron pan: I wrapped the smaller pan in foil and used it as a bacon press. Now the goofy gift is actually useful.

NUTTY TIP
Freeze for Ease
Sarah Roland, Oak Park, Ill.

I have a recipe for Brazil nut cookies that I make every Christmas, and every year I wrestled with shelling the hard-to-crack nuts. I then found that the shells of the nuts come off much more easily—and their meat is much easier to extract—if I freeze them first. Just a few hours of freezer time saves me a lot of extra work.

TIMESAVER
Seasoned Flour, Anytime
Kate Foley, Jefferson City, Mo.

I frequently dredge chicken or pork in a deeply seasoned flour mixture before frying. To make my life easier, I mix up a big batch of flour seasoned with salt, black pepper, garlic powder, onion powder, and paprika and keep it in the pantry. It saves me a lot of time when I need to get dinner on the table fast.

Submit a tip online at **CooksCountry.com/kitchenshortcuts** or send a letter to Kitchen Shortcuts, *Cook's Country*, P.O. Box 470739, Brookline, MA 02447. Include your name, address, and phone number. If we publish your tip, you will receive a free one-year subscription to *Cook's Country*. Letters may be edited for clarity and length.

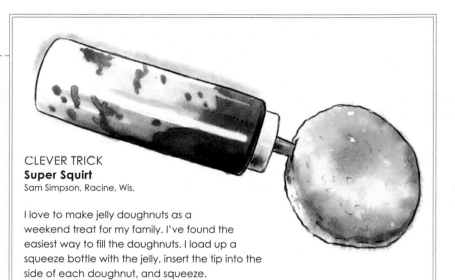

CLEVER TRICK
Super Squirt
Sam Simpson, Racine, Wis.

I love to make jelly doughnuts as a weekend treat for my family. I've found the easiest way to fill the doughnuts. I load up a squeeze bottle with the jelly, insert the tip into the side of each doughnut, and squeeze.

COOL TIP
Frost No More
Marilyn Clapsaddle, Chapel Hill, N.C.

To prevent freezer burn on things like meat sauce and chili that I freeze in pint containers, I first put them in the freezer for 1 hour. I then press plastic wrap down onto the food, then cover and freeze. This eliminates the frosty top that can give foods a nasty flavor.

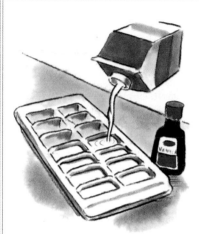

COOL IDEA
Cold and Creamy
Brenda Gorman, Salt Lake City, Utah

My kids love hot cereal in the morning. To keep these impatient eaters from burning their tongues, I use an ice cube tray to freeze low-fat milk (with a drop of vanilla extract for flavor) and then stir two cubes into the hot cereal. This cools it down quickly and adds a bit of creaminess. I often drop a cube into my morning tea, too.

DOUBLE DUTY
Squash Scoop
Kathy Wheeler, Saco, Maine

I love butternut and acorn squash, but I've always made a mess when scooping out the seeds with a soupspoon. So I was excited to find a better tool for the job: a standard ice cream scoop. The sturdy scoop has a sharp edge that cuts through the fibrous seed goop with ease.

Ultimate Prime Rib and Potatoes

We wanted potatoes with rich, beefy flavor. Would it prove to be as easy as just cooking them under the roast? BY MORGAN BOLLING

THE CULINARY FOLKLORE of boulangère potatoes is a well-spun yarn: Before French peasants had home ovens, they would bring their Sunday roasts, nestled on beds of potatoes, to the town bread baker (the boulangère) to cook in the residual heat of his oven. The tasty rendered fat would drip down onto the potatoes, infusing them with meaty flavor. I used this idea as inspiration for a simple but luxurious holiday meal.

Nothing beats a bone-in prime rib for a holiday centerpiece, and I knew that this cut's ample marbling (also known as fat) would render and flavor the potatoes. Following test kitchen protocol, I trimmed the roast of excess fat, made shallow crosshatch cuts in the remaining fat cap, and rubbed the roast all over with salt a full 24 hours before cooking. The long salting time gave the salt the chance to penetrate the meat, ensuring a well-seasoned, juicy roast. To serve eight to 10 people, I decided to use 4 pounds of Yukon gold potatoes, which are our favorites for roasting.

I placed the potatoes in a roasting pan, nestled a V-rack into them, and dropped the meat into the rack. We like to roast potatoes at a high temperature (425 to 475 degrees) to get crispy, brown exteriors and creamy interiors; we like to cook bone-in rib roasts slowly at a low temperature (200 to 250 degrees) for controlled, even cooking. I tried a middle ground of 350 degrees, but the potatoes were only pale and limp by the time the meat was medium-rare.

I dialed the oven back to 250 degrees. But when the roast was a perfect medium-rare, the potatoes were still hard. Cooking the meat and potatoes together was a bad idea.

But I wasn't ready to give up my dream of beefy potatoes. I cooked my next roast for just over 3 hours at the same 250 degrees. Then I removed the roast, cranked the heat to 450, tossed the potato chunks with the beef drippings, and roasted them on a rimmed baking sheet for about 40 minutes. They were crisp on the outside and fluffy within, but I wanted more flavor.

I added a little beef broth to the baking sheet, but that didn't do much for the flavor and greatly impeded browning. What about the fat I was trimming off the raw roasts at the beginning? With the next roast, I saved that trimmed fat and put it under the meat as it cooked; at the end of roasting I had more intensely flavored drippings in which to toss the potato chunks, and it made the potatoes taste much more beefy. Precooking the potatoes in the microwave until they just began to release moisture made their interiors creamier. A bit of chopped fresh rosemary brought everything together.

There was just one more problem to solve: The roast lacked exterior browning. Since the oven was on, I tried letting the roast brown in its dry heat, but the exterior overcooked by the time there was decent browning. It was better to sear the cooked roast in a little oil in a hot skillet, which did the job much faster and thus didn't overcook the meat. An easy red wine–orange sauce proved a nice, bright contrast to the savory beef and potatoes.

We cook the bone-in roast slowly for even cooking and then turn up the heat to cook the potatoes while the meat rests.

SHOPPING **Prime Rib**
Look for a prime rib roast with a **½-inch fat cap**. You'll use the fat.

PRIME RIB AND POTATOES

Serves 8 to 10

Look for a roast with an untrimmed fat cap, ideally ½ inch thick. The roast must be salted and refrigerated for at least 24 hours before cooking. Wait until the roast is done cooking before peeling and cutting the potatoes so they don't discolor. It is crucial to use a sturdy rimmed baking sheet for this recipe. Our favorite is the Wear-Ever Half Size Heavy Duty Sheet Pan (13 gauge) by Vollrath. Serve with Red Wine–Orange Sauce, if desired.

- 1 (7-pound) first-cut beef standing rib roast (3 bones), with untrimmed fat cap
  Kosher salt and pepper
- 4 pounds Yukon gold potatoes, peeled and cut into 1½-inch pieces
- 1 tablespoon minced fresh rosemary
- 1 tablespoon vegetable oil

1. Using sharp knife, trim roast's fat cap to even ¼-inch-thickness; reserve and refrigerate trimmings. Cut 1-inch crosshatch pattern in fat cap, being careful not to cut into meat. Rub 2 tablespoons salt over entire roast and into crosshatch. Transfer to large plate and refrigerate, uncovered, for at least 24 hours or up to 4 days.

2. Adjust oven rack to lower-middle position and heat oven to 250 degrees. Cut reserved trimmings into ½-inch pieces. Place 4 ounces (about 1 cup) of trimmings in rimmed baking sheet, then set wire rack in sheet. Season roast with pepper and place, fat side up, on wire rack.

3. Roast until meat registers 115 degrees for rare, 120 degrees for medium-rare, or 125 degrees for medium, 3 to 3½ hours. Transfer roast to carving board, tent with aluminum foil, and let rest for 1 hour. Carefully remove wire rack and reserve beef fat in baking sheet (there should be about ½ cup; if not, supplement with vegetable oil).

4. Increase oven temperature to 450 degrees. Microwave potatoes, covered, in large bowl until they begin to release moisture and surfaces look wet, about 7 minutes. Pat potatoes dry with paper towels. Toss potatoes with rosemary, 2 teaspoons salt, and ½ teaspoon pepper. Transfer potatoes to baking sheet and carefully toss with reserved fat (fat may be hot). Roast until tender and browned,

35 to 40 minutes, redistributing halfway through cooking. Season potatoes with salt and pepper to taste.

5. Pat roast dry with paper towels. Heat oil in 12-inch skillet over medium-high heat until just smoking. Sear all sides until browned, 6 to 8 minutes total. Transfer roast to carving board. Carve meat from bones and cut into ¾-inch-thick slices. Serve with potatoes.

RED WINE–ORANGE SAUCE

Makes about 1½ cups

Medium-bodied red wines, like Côtes du Rhône or Pinot Noir, are best for this sauce.

- 6 tablespoons unsalted butter, cut into 6 pieces and chilled
- 3 shallots, minced
- 1½ tablespoons tomato paste
- 1 tablespoon sugar
- 4 garlic cloves, minced
- 1 tablespoon all-purpose flour
- 3 cups beef broth
- 1½ cups red wine
- ⅓ cup orange juice
- 1½ tablespoons Worcestershire sauce
- 1 sprig fresh thyme
  Salt and pepper

1. Melt 2 tablespoons butter in medium saucepan over medium-high heat. Add shallots, tomato paste, and sugar and cook, stirring frequently, until deep brown, 4 to 5 minutes. Stir in garlic and flour and cook until garlic is fragrant and vegetables are well coated with flour, about 30 seconds.

2. Stir in broth, wine, orange juice, Worcestershire, and thyme, scraping up any browned bits. Bring to boil, reduce heat to medium, and cook at low boil until reduced to 2 cups, about 40 minutes.

3. Strain sauce through fine-mesh strainer set over bowl; discard solids. Return sauce to pot and place over low heat. Whisk in remaining 4 tablespoons butter, 1 piece at a time. Season with salt and pepper to taste. Serve.

TO MAKE AHEAD

Strained sauce can be cooled and then refrigerated in airtight container for up to 2 days. Bring sauce to simmer before reducing heat to low and whisking in butter to finish.

TEST KITCHEN TECHNIQUE **Using the Fat**

After trimming the roast, we use the fat to infuse big beefy flavor into the potatoes.

FIRST ROAST THE MEAT
with the fat scraps in the pan.

THEN ROAST THE POTATOES
in the rendered beef fat.

Sautéed Collards with Raisins and Nuts

Boiled collards taste great but don't look great. We wanted a fresh, elegant take for the holiday table. BY MORGAN BOLLING

COLLARD GREENS BOILED in the traditional Southern way take an hour to cook and, while tasty, can take on a muddy, pale hue. I wanted to dress up these humble greens for a vibrant, elegant holiday side.

I washed and dried a few bunches of collards, trimmed and discarded the stem pieces below the leaves, chopped the leaves (leaving the ribs intact), and hit the stove. I tried sautéing the chopped collards in olive oil, but it took about 40 minutes to soften the remaining stem pieces. Too long. Blanching them before sautéing helped but took two extra dishes.

For my next test, I didn't bother drying the chopped greens after washing them. I placed the wet leaves in a Dutch oven, hoping the clinging water would steam them. I covered the pot and cooked the greens for 15 minutes; I then removed the lid and stirred in plenty of extra-virgin olive oil, as well as some golden raisins and sliced almonds. The process was fast, but the collards tasted muddy. Next round, I thoroughly drained the excess liquid after the steaming stage; the flavor (and color) brightened.

For a punchy finish, I added some sliced shallot and a handful of salty grated Parmesan.

Sweet raisins and crunchy almonds elevate humble collard greens.

COLLARD GREENS WITH RAISINS AND ALMONDS

Serves 4 to 6

Kale can be substituted for the collard greens in this recipe.

- 2 pounds collard greens
  Salt and pepper
- 6 tablespoons extra-virgin olive oil
- ½ cup golden raisins
- 2 shallots, sliced thin
- 4 garlic cloves, sliced thin
- ⅛ teaspoon red pepper flakes
- ¼ cup grated Parmesan cheese, plus extra for serving
- ¼ cup sliced almonds, toasted
  Lemon wedges for serving

1. Trim collard stems to base of leaves; discard stems. Cut leaves into

1- to 2-inch pieces. Place collards in large bowl and cover with water. Swish with your hand to remove grit. Repeat with fresh water, as needed, until grit no longer appears in bottom of bowl. Drain collards in colander, but do not dry.

2. Add damp collards, 1 teaspoon salt, and ½ teaspoon pepper to Dutch oven. Cover and cook over medium-high heat until tender, 14 to 17 minutes, stirring occasionally. (If pot becomes dry, add ¼ cup water so collards continue to steam.) Drain collards in colander, pressing with rubber spatula to release excess liquid. Wipe out Dutch oven with paper towels.

3. Heat ¼ cup oil in now-empty Dutch oven over medium heat until shimmering. Add raisins, shallots, garlic, and pepper flakes and cook until just beginning to brown, 2 to 4 minutes. Add collards, ½ teaspoon salt, and ¼ teaspoon pepper and cook until warmed through, about 3 minutes. Off heat, stir in Parmesan. Season with salt and pepper to taste.

4. Transfer collards to platter. Drizzle with remaining 2 tablespoons oil and sprinkle with almonds. Serve with lemon wedges and extra Parmesan.

Cheesy Corn Casserole

Too many versions of this Midwestern favorite go wrong. It was time to set things right. BY MORGAN BOLLING

CHEESY CORN CASSEROLE, a common holiday side dish in the South and Midwest, falls somewhere on the spectrum between creamed corn and cornbread. Most recipes involve stirring together corn muffin mix, canned creamed corn, canned (or frozen) corn kernels, sour cream, cheese, and eggs. You just dump it into a casserole and bake.

Sound too good to be true? It is. The worst of the handful of existing recipes I tried didn't even justify this minimal effort. They ranged from goopy to greasy and from appallingly bland to unappealingly dense. I knew this dish could do with a makeover. I envisioned something substantial but light, with sweet corn and savory cheese flavors.

Prefab corn muffin mixes are good in a pinch but too sweet for this casserole. Instead, I made my own, stirring together flour, cornmeal, and baking powder—definitely worth the 2 minutes it took to put together. I also ditched the canned corn kernels and creamed corn, which rarely have any flavor and are often mushy. Instead I turned to frozen kernels. Pulsing half of them in the food processor released even more of their flavor and helped mimic the texture of creamed corn.

To these ingredients I added sour cream and a hefty dose of shredded cheddar. I stirred it all together and put it in the oven.

While the result was a substantive improvement, I found that the delicate corn was being overwhelmed by the cheddar. I tried American cheese but found the opposite problem: It was too mild. After casting about, I landed on a combination of Monterey Jack and Parmesan. Monterey Jack melts like a dream and gave me the creaminess I wanted,

Scallion whites add savory flavor to the interior of the casserole; we save the greens for the top.

while the Parmesan added deep cheese flavor without becoming overwhelming. A colleague suggested cutting some of the Monterey Jack into cubes instead of shredding all of it to create excellent gooey cheese pockets throughout.

My casserole, though tasty, needed one more note. I gave it two: a little

cayenne for heat and some scallions (white parts processed into the corn, green parts scattered on top) for bite. "A-maize-ing," one colleague joked. Talk about cheesy.

CHEESY CORN CASSEROLE
Serves 8 to 10
Two pounds of fresh corn kernels (from about 8 cobs) can be substituted for the frozen corn.

- 8 ounces Monterey Jack cheese
- ½ cup (2½ ounces) all-purpose flour
- ⅓ cup (1⅔ ounces) cornmeal
- 2 teaspoons baking powder
- 1 teaspoon salt
- ¼ teaspoon pepper
- ¼ teaspoon cayenne pepper
- 2 pounds frozen corn, thawed
- 4 scallions, white and green parts separated and sliced thin
- 1 cup sour cream
- 1 ounce Parmesan cheese, grated (½ cup)
- 2 large eggs, lightly beaten
- 4 tablespoons unsalted butter, melted

1. Adjust oven rack to middle position and heat oven to 350 degrees. Grease 13 by 9-inch baking dish. Cut 4 ounces of Monterey Jack into ½-inch cubes. Shred remaining 4 ounces of Monterey Jack on large holes of box grater; set aside. Whisk flour, cornmeal, baking powder, salt, pepper, and cayenne together in large bowl.

2. Pulse half of corn and scallion whites in food processor to coarse puree, about 10 pulses. Stir pureed corn mixture into flour mixture. Stir in sour cream, ¼ cup Parmesan, eggs, melted butter, remaining half of corn, and cubed Monterey Jack until combined. Transfer mixture to prepared baking dish. Sprinkle with shredded Monterey Jack and remaining ¼ cup Parmesan.

3. Bake until casserole is slightly puffy and cheese is golden brown, 45 to 50 minutes. Transfer casserole to wire rack and let cool for 10 minutes. Sprinkle with scallion greens and serve.

CHEESY CORN CASSEROLE WITH JALAPEÑOS AND CILANTRO
Add ¼ cup minced pickled jalapeños to batter in step 2. Sprinkle with 2 tablespoons chopped fresh cilantro before serving.

RECIPE MAKEOVER
Revamping a Prefab Favorite
Most memories of this rib-sticking classic are of bland, stodgy versions made with supermarket corn muffin mix and cans of creamed corn; when we cooked a handful of those versions we were totally unimpressed. To achieve a cleaner, more contemporary take, we ditched the corn muffin mix and canned corn and turned to frozen corn kernels, tangy sour cream, Monterey Jack cheese (cut into cubes for melty pockets inside and shredded for full coverage on top), nutty and flavorful grated Parmesan, and vibrant scallion greens and whites.

FRESH INGREDIENTS, FRESHER FLAVOR

Stuffed Acorn Squash

Our goal: to dress up this humble squash without weighing it down. BY ASHLEY MOORE

ACORN SQUASH, THOSE squat ridged numbers resembling giant acorns that appear every fall, are delicious simply roasted and mashed with butter. But come holiday time, we want to gussy them up a bit in a festive but not overburdened side dish.

Early tests of existing recipes, along with some research into our company's previous squash recipes, showed me that to get flesh that was velvety and soft but still stable enough to hold its shape, I'd have to precook the squash wedges before adding the stuffing. But precooking has a bonus: a bit of browning on the squash sides that adds a sweet, caramelized note. To maximize that browning, I positioned the squash wedges on their sides on a rimmed baking sheet and slid them into the oven to roast at 400 degrees. Twenty minutes later I flipped them over for even browning. In 15 more minutes they were soft enough that I could slip my knife easily into the flesh. Ready for the stuffing.

I'd been considering a wide range of options for that stuffing. It wasn't difficult to take too-filling grains like rice and barley out of the potential lineup. Meat was out, too—there'd be enough of that on the holiday table. I decided to focus on vegetables. But which ones?

Curly spinach and Swiss chard proved too slippery and insubstantial here, so I turned to sturdy, flavorful kale, cut into strips and sautéed in a skillet until just wilted. After spooning the precooked kale into the squash wedges and baking them for another 5 minutes, the kale had a pleasant texture.

But when I went to set the squash on a platter, the kale just tumbled right off. I needed a glue to make it stick. But what? A bunch of grated cheese? Some beaten egg? Nope: I wanted to avoid adding yet another ingredient. Instead, I found my glue right there on the sheet pan: roasted squash. For my next batch, I roasted eight wedges of squash (from two acorn squashes) and then scooped the flesh from two wedges and mashed it together with the kale. It baked up into a sturdy, cohesive filling.

To round out the flavors, I added some bright chopped apple, a bit of garlic and rosemary, a splash of cider vinegar, tangy crumbled goat cheese, and some crunchy nuts. I had a rustic but elegant holiday side dish that would leave plenty of room for, among other things, dessert.

STUFFED ACORN SQUASH
Serves 6

Of the eight wedges of squash, use the two that are least attractive for the stuffing. Any variety of kale will work in this recipe.

- 2 acorn squashes (1½ pounds each), quartered pole to pole and seeded
- ¼ cup extra-virgin olive oil, plus extra for drizzling
  Salt and pepper
- 6 ounces kale, stemmed and sliced into ¼-inch-thick strips
- 1 Fuji or Gala apple, peeled, cored, and cut into ¼-inch pieces
- 1 garlic clove, minced
- ½ teaspoon minced fresh rosemary
- 1 tablespoon cider vinegar
- 1 tablespoon unsalted butter
- 2 ounces goat cheese, crumbled (½ cup)
- 2 tablespoons whole blanched almonds, toasted and chopped coarse

1. Adjust oven rack to middle position and heat oven to 400 degrees. Toss squash wedges, 2 tablespoons oil, 1 teaspoon salt, and 1 teaspoon pepper together in bowl until thoroughly coated. Arrange wedges on rimmed baking sheet with 1 narrow cut side down. Roast until browned on first side, about 20 minutes. Flip wedges so other narrow cut side is down and continue to roast until browned on second side and tip of paring knife slips easily into flesh, about 15 minutes longer.

2. Remove sheet from oven and let wedges cool slightly. Once cool enough to handle, scoop flesh from 2 least attractive wedges into bowl; discard skins. (You should have about ¾ cup of scooped squash.) Turn remaining 6 wedges skin side down on sheet.

3. Heat 1 tablespoon oil in 12-inch nonstick skillet over medium heat until shimmering. Add kale, apple, and ¼ teaspoon salt and cook, covered, until kale is wilted, about 3 minutes. Uncover and continue to cook until any liquid has evaporated, about 30 seconds. Stir in scooped squash, mashing with spoon to incorporate, and cook until beginning to brown, about 1 minute.

4. Push squash mixture to sides of skillet. Add garlic, rosemary, and remaining 1 tablespoon oil to center of skillet and cook until fragrant, about 30 seconds. Stir garlic mixture into squash mixture. Stir in vinegar and cook until evaporated, about 1 minute. Off heat, stir in butter and season with salt and pepper to taste.

5. Divide filling evenly among wedges on sheet. Evenly sprinkle goat cheese and almonds over filling. Bake until cheese is softened and squash heated through, 5 to 7 minutes. Drizzle with extra oil before serving.

STUFFED ACORN SQUASH WITH PEAR AND HAZELNUT

Substitute 1 ripe pear for apple, fresh thyme for rosemary, and 2 tablespoons finely chopped toasted and skinned hazelnuts for almonds.

Goat cheese and almonds add texture and flavor to the stuffed squash wedges.

TEST KITCHEN DISCOVERY
Sacrificial Wedges

After searching high and low for the best binder for our stuffing, we found it under our noses: cooked squash scraped from two roasted wedges. It kept things cohesive without compromising the flavors.

PICK TWO
The roasted flesh from two wedges is incorporated into the filling.

Swiss Hazelnut Cake

This sweet, nutty, tender cake is famous in Philadelphia. We thought it deserved a bigger audience.

BY KATIE LEAIRD

A PHILADELPHIA GRANDMOTHER places a weathered black-and-white photograph on top of the bakery case at the Swiss Haus Bakery in the Center City neighborhood of Philadelphia. The faded picture shows her as a young bride a half-century ago, cutting through her Swiss Haus wedding cake. The woman wants to know if the bakery, which has been making the same recipes in the same building since 1923, can re-create this dessert for an upcoming celebration. The bakery can proudly fill this order, as a piece of Swiss Haus cake is a piece of living history.

When I visited the Swiss Haus Bakery to taste their famous hazelnut sponge cake, I found a beautiful cake frosted with a fluffy vanilla icing and covered in chocolate shavings. The cake itself was light and airy with a subtle nut flavor, the frosting delicate and sweet. I wanted to translate this local favorite into a cake anyone could make at home.

I started with the base cake. The Swiss Haus pastry chef, Donna Feldman, was trained decades ago by the founding family's baker and would not disclose the recipe. She did, however, give me a valuable tip: "It's all about the egg whites." I surmised that the cake was either a sponge or chiffon cake, as both of these use whipped egg whites to achieve their light, fluffy texture.

After testing, I settled on a chiffon base because it's simpler and more reliable than sponge: You just combine your wet and dry ingredients, fold in beaten egg whites, and bake. To get the signature nutty flavor, I tried adding hazelnut extract, but it tasted like hazelnut flavoring, not hazelnuts. I had better luck substituting toasted hazelnuts ground in a food processor into a flour-like texture for a portion of the flour. And there was no need to remove the nut skins after toasting, as they contributed to the cake's signature speckled look.

Swiss meringue buttercream, which is made by heating and whipping egg whites and sugar and then beating in softened butter, was the obvious frosting choice for its satiny texture. But this buttercream is a project and then some. Searching for a quicker path to a creamy, sweet frosting, I had a wacky idea: What if I replaced the Swiss buttercream's meringue base with marshmallow crème? Though it was intensely sweet

Swiss meringue buttercream frosting takes time to prepare. We found an excellent shortcut in marshmallow crème.

at first, adjusting the amounts of butter and powdered sugar and adding some hazelnut liqueur tempered the sweetness and made a perfectly pillowy frosting. This simple one-bowl method was a much easier approach.

Speaking of easy, shaving a block of chocolate to make the curls that adorn the cake was anything but. Watching me shake the cramps out of my hand, a colleague suggested trying the food

processor. I fitted the machine with the shredding disk and fed a standard chocolate bar through the top tube. It was the loudest noise in the kitchen that day, but it worked. However, by the time I processed a second bar, the mechanical friction started to melt the chocolate. So I slipped the shredding disk into the freezer for a bit. This temperature tweak allowed me to shave down two chocolate bars in mere seconds with no messy

melting, at least until I went to apply those curls to the cake. The heat from my hands instantly softened the delicate shards, ruining the look of the cake. Freezing the shaved chocolate and using a folded piece of parchment paper like a flexible putty knife to press the curls onto the cake solved the problem.

This tender, hazelnut-freckled cake is a tasty, beautiful reflection of its Philadelphia-born inspiration.

SWISS HAZELNUT CAKE

Serves 12 to 16

We toast and grind the hazelnuts with heir skins for better color and flavor. We developed this recipe with Fluff brand marshmallow crème. When working with he marshmallow crème, grease the nside of your measuring cup and spatula with vegetable oil spray to prevent ticking. Note that the shredding disk hould be placed in the freezer for 15 minutes before shaving the chocolate. You may use a vegetable peeler or the arge holes of a box grater to shave the chocolate. In step 9, it's important to handle the chocolate shavings using the olded parchment paper so they don't melt from the heat of your hands.

CAKE

- ½ **cup (2 ounces) skin-on hazelnuts, toasted and cooled**
- 1¼ **cups (5 ounces) cake flour**
- 1 **cup (7 ounces) granulated sugar**
- 1½ **teaspoons baking powder**
- ½ **teaspoon salt**
- ½ **cup vegetable oil**
- ¼ **cup water**
- 3 **large egg yolks, plus 5 large whites**
- 2½ **teaspoons vanilla extract**
- ¼ **teaspoon cream of tartar**

FROSTING

- 24 **tablespoons (3 sticks) unsalted butter, softened**
- ¼ **teaspoon salt**
- 1¾ **cups (7 ounces) confectioners' sugar**
- 12 **ounces (2⅔ cups) Fluff brand marshmallow crème**
- 2 **tablespoons hazelnut liqueur**
- 6 **ounces bittersweet bar chocolate**

1. **FOR THE CAKE:** Adjust oven rack o middle position and heat oven to 350 degrees. Line 2 light-colored 9-inch round cake pans with parchment paper; grease parchment but not pan sides.

2. Process hazelnuts in food processor until finely ground, about 30 seconds. Whisk flour, sugar, baking powder, salt, nd ground hazelnuts together in large bowl. Whisk oil, water, egg yolks, and vanilla together in separate bowl. Whisk gg yolk mixture into flour-nut mixture until smooth batter forms.

3. Using stand mixer fitted with whisk, whip egg whites and cream of tartar on medium-low speed until foamy, about minute. Increase speed to medium-high and whip until soft peaks form, 2 o 3 minutes. Gently whisk one-third of whipped egg whites into batter. Using rubber spatula, gently fold remaining gg whites into batter until incorporated.

4. Divide batter evenly between prepared pans and gently tap pans on counter to release air bubbles. Bake until tops are light golden brown and cakes spring back when pressed lightly in center, 25 to 28 minutes, rotating pans halfway through baking.

5. Let cakes cool in pans for 15 minutes. Run knife around edges of pans; invert cakes onto wire rack. Discard parchment and let cakes cool completely, at least 1 hour. (To prepare to make chocolate shavings, place food processor shredding disk in freezer.)

6. **FOR THE FROSTING:** Using clean stand mixer fitted with whisk, whip butter and salt on medium speed until smooth, about 1 minute. Reduce speed to low and slowly add sugar. Increase speed to medium and whip until smooth, about 2 minutes, scraping down sides of bowl as needed. Add marshmallow crème, increase speed to medium-high, and whip until light and fluffy, 3 to 5 minutes. Reduce speed to low, add hazelnut liqueur, return speed to medium-high, and whip to incorporate, about 30 seconds.

7. Line rimmed baking sheet with parchment paper. Fit food processor with chilled shredding disk. Turn on processor and feed chocolate bar through hopper. Transfer shaved chocolate to prepared baking sheet and spread into even layer. Place in freezer to harden, about 10 minutes.

8. Place 1 cake layer on cake stand. Spread 2 cups frosting evenly over top, right to edge of cake. Top with second cake layer, pressing lightly to adhere. Spread remaining 2 cups frosting evenly over top and sides of cake.

9. Fold 16 by 12-inch sheet of parchment paper into 6 by 4-inch rectangle. Using parchment rectangle, scoop up half of chocolate shavings and sprinkle over top of cake. Once top of cake is coated, scoop up remaining chocolate shavings and press gently against sides of cake to adhere, scooping and reapplying as needed. Serve.

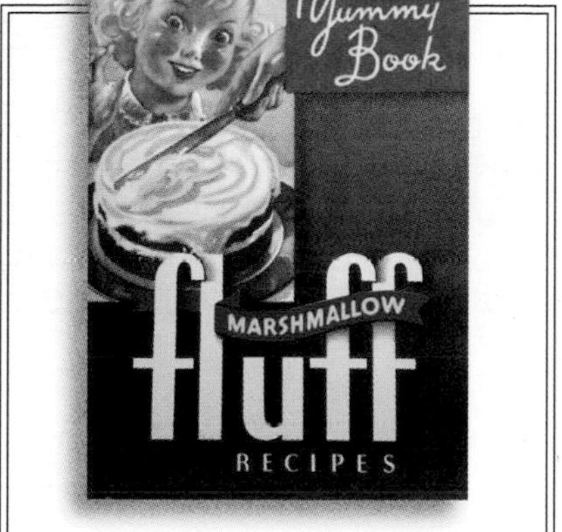

The American Table
A Sweet Deal

In 1920, after five years of selling his homemade marshmallow crème door-to-door, a weary Archibald Query sold his recipe to H. Allen Durkee and Fred L. Mower for just $500. The pair fired up production and radio promotion (the Flufferettes show aired just before Jack Benny) and made millions. More at **CooksCountry.com/fluffpiece**.

WHAT MAKES A GREAT CAKE STAND?

A good cake stand makes cake decorating faster and easier by elevating the cake for better visibility and by rotating for quick and even frosting application. We still like our previous winner from Ateco, but it's prone to rusting. We started wondering—is there a better option?

To find out, we tested seven new models, priced from about $23 to $80, against new copies of the Ateco. We rated height, weight, stability, surface, and rotation.

Height and stability were paramount: Shorter stands, about 3 inches tall, didn't give us a clear view of the cake; taller stands, 4.5 to 6 inches tall, made it much easier to see all angles of the cake.

One pricey model ($80) tilted for better access to the bottom edge of the cake, but it was jerky and unpredictable—it sent a whole cake crashing to the counter twice. Another stand with stability issues required a plate from our kitchen to hold the cake, which then sat atop the stand to spin but never felt secure.

Testers preferred surfaces with shallow circles etched in to help center cakes; some stands didn't have these guidelines, while others' guidelines were too pronounced and impeded frosting. Rotation was tricky—some stands were stiff, while others were loose; the best stands allowed us to stop the spin in one motion.

In the end we still liked our previous winner from Ateco, but we liked a model from Winco even more. At just under $30, it was about $20 cheaper than the Ateco and had two additional features we liked: an attached base and surface for easy transporting and rust-free washing, and guides on its surface for centering, helping make decorating like a pro that much easier. Read the full testing story and results chart at **CooksCountry.com/dec15**. –HANNAH CROWLEY

KEY **Good** ★★★ **Fair** ★★ **Poor** ★

HIGHLY RECOMMENDED	CRITERIA	TESTERS' NOTES
WINCO Revolving Cake Decorating Stand **Model:** CKSR-12 **Price:** $29.98 **Surface Diameter:** 11.5 in **Height:** 5.3 in **Weight:** 4.8 lb 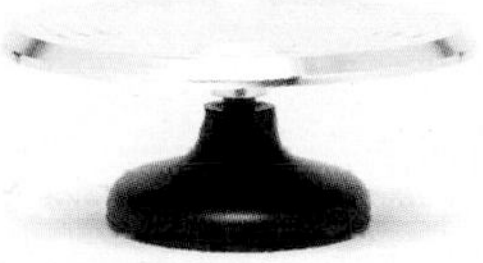	**Stability** ★★★ **Surface** ★★★ **Rotation** ★★★	This stand was tall, providing excellent visibility and comfort. It was solid but light, and its surface and base were attached, which made it easy to carry. It rotated quickly and smoothly yet stopped right where we asked it to, and it had three shallow circles etched onto its surface for easy centering.
RECOMMENDED		
ATECO Revolving Cake Stand **Model:** 612 **Price:** $49.38 **Surface Diameter:** 12 in **Height:** 4.7 in **Weight:** 5.6 lb 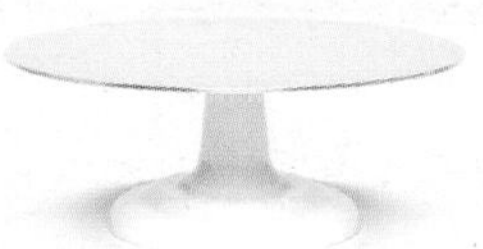	**Stability** ★★½ **Surface** ★★½ **Rotation** ★★★	Our previous winner still had a charming look, a smooth turning motion, and a precise stop. It was tall for excellent visibility, but it lacked guidelines for centering cakes. Its top and bottom came apart for easy cleanup, but if the parts weren't 100 percent dry when reassembled, they rusted together.
JOHNSON-ROSE Aluminum Cake Decorating Stand, Green Enamel **Model:** 4612 **Price:** $36.97 **Surface Diameter:** 11.75 in **Height:** 4.8 in **Weight:** 5.3 lb 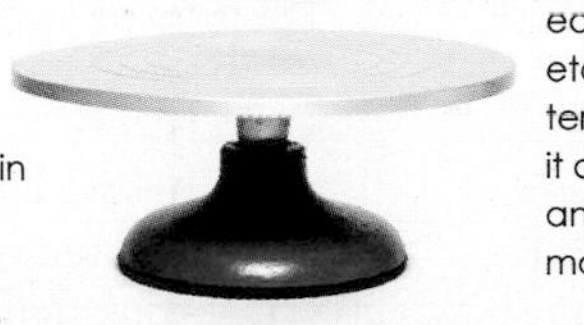	**Stability** ★★½ **Surface** ★★★ **Rotation** ★★	This stand was tall with a wide surface. It had a nice sturdy base lined with grippy rubber that clung to the counter. It was easy to spin and had shallow circles etched onto its surface—handy for centering cakes. But while it spun smoothly, it didn't stop very well. It shimmied left and right before settling down, which made it slightly harder to work with.

KEY STEPS **Producing Perfect Chocolate Shreds**

Temperature and timing are key factors in creating uniform chocolate shavings.

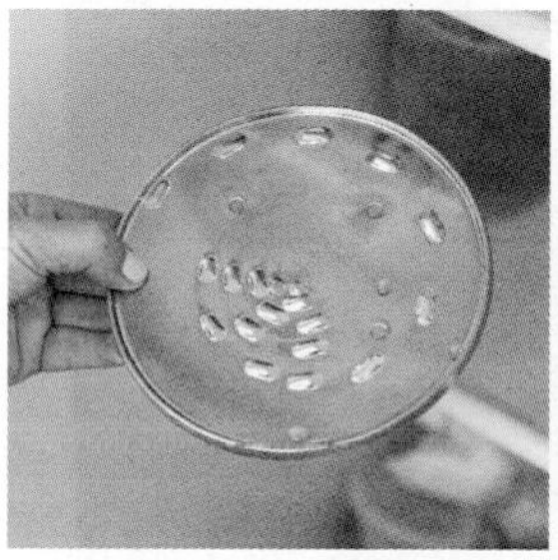

Place food processor's shredding disk in freezer for 15 minutes.

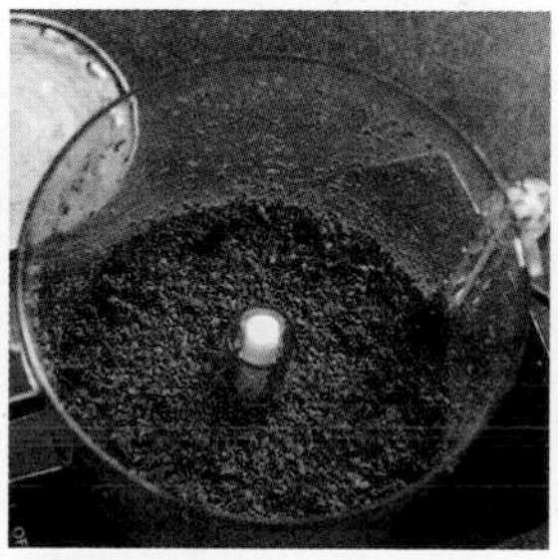

Quickly feed chocolate bar through shredder, then freeze shavings.

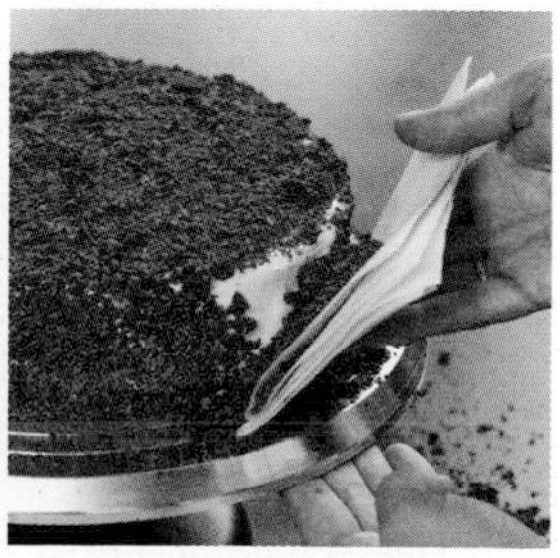

Use parchment to gently press frozen chocolate shreds into frosting.

Bonus! Find two more new holiday cookie recipes at CooksCountry.com/dec15.

New Holiday Cookies

We dug deep into the cookie jar this year and found some unexpected treats. BY ERIKA BRUCE

CHOCOLATE SALAMI

Makes 24 cookies

There's nothing savory about this confection rooted in Portuguese and Italian tradition. With a base akin to a chocolate truffle, it's typically chock-full of dried fruit, nuts, and crushed cookies. To complete the salami look, the dough is rolled into logs before being dredged in confectioners' sugar. We liked the combination of dried cherries (first macerated in Grand Marnier) and pistachios, and we used dried ladyfingers as the cookie component—although any dry, biscuit-like cookie will work.

- ½ cup dried cherries, chopped coarse
- 2 tablespoons Grand Marnier
- 4 ounces dried ladyfingers (savoiardi), cut into ½-inch chunks
- 1 cup (6 ounces) semisweet or bittersweet chocolate chips
- ⅓ cup heavy cream
  Pinch salt
- ⅔ cup pistachios, toasted
- ½ cup (2 ounces) confectioners' sugar

1. Combine cherries and Grand Marnier in small bowl and microwave until hot, about 30 seconds; let sit until cherries have softened and mixture is cool, about 15 minutes. Reserve 1 cup ladyfingers. Process remaining ladyfingers in food processor to fine crumbs, 15 to 20 seconds. (You should have about ¾ cup.)

2. Microwave chocolate chips and cream in medium bowl at 50 percent power, stirring frequently, until melted and smooth, 30 to 60 seconds. Add salt and ladyfinger crumbs and stir to combine. Add pistachios, reserved ladyfingers, and cherry mixture and stir until thick dough forms.

3. Divide dough in half and place each half on large sheet of plastic wrap. Use plastic to roll each dough into tight 6-inch log, twisting ends well to secure. Refrigerate dough logs until firm, at least 3 hours. (Chilled dough can be stored in refrigerator for up to 3 days.)

4. When ready to serve, place confectioners' sugar in shallow dish. Unwrap dough logs and roll in sugar until well coated, brushing off excess. Cut each log into ½-inch-thick slices. Serve.

BISCOCHITOS Makes about 40 cookies

A longtime New Mexican holiday tradition with Spanish roots, these crisp shortbread cookies are scented with anise seed and cinnamon. They are typically made with lard for a meltingly tender texture, but we opted for a combination of butter and shortening instead. Tossing the warm cookies in cinnamon sugar after baking gives them a sweet crunch.

- 1 cup (7 ounces) sugar
- 1 teaspoon ground cinnamon
- 1 tablespoon anise seeds
- 8 tablespoons unsalted butter, softened
- 8 tablespoons vegetable shortening, cut into 1-inch chunks
- ½ teaspoon salt
- 1 large egg yolk
- 1 teaspoon vanilla extract
- 2 cups (10 ounces) all-purpose flour

1. Line 2 baking sheets with parchment paper. Combine sugar and cinnamon in small bowl; reserve ½ cup cinnamon sugar in shallow dish. Grind anise seed in spice grinder until finely ground, about 10 seconds.

2. Using stand mixer fitted with paddle, beat butter, shortening, salt, remaining ½ cup cinnamon sugar, and ground anise on medium-high speed until light and fluffy, about 3 minutes, scraping down bowl as needed. Add yolk and vanilla and mix until combined.

3. Reduce speed to low, add flour, and mix until dough forms, about 10 seconds. Working on piece of parchment, roll dough into 9-inch circle, about ½-inch thick. Transfer dough on parchment to large plate, cover with plastic wrap, and refrigerate until firm, about 30 minutes. Adjust oven racks to upper-middle and lower-middle positions and heat oven to 350 degrees.

4. Transfer dough, still on parchment, to cutting board. Using knife or pizza cutter, cut dough lengthwise into 1-inch-wide strips, then cut diagonally into 1-inch-wide strips to form diamonds. Space them evenly on prepared sheets, about 20 per sheet.

5. Bake until set and just starting to brown, about 15 minutes, switching and rotating sheets halfway through baking. Let cookies cool on sheets for 5 minutes. Gently toss cookies, a few at a time, in reserved cinnamon sugar. Transfer cookies to wire racks and let cool completely, about 1 hour.

ITALIAN RAINBOW COOKIES

Makes 60 cookies

With their green, white, and red stripes, these cookies are meant to look like diminutive Italian flags. The multicolored layers of cake are made with almond paste, filled with raspberry jam, and topped with rich dark chocolate.

- 2 cups (8 ounces) cake flour
- ½ teaspoon baking powder
- 1½ cups (10½ ounces) sugar
- 8 ounces almond paste, cut into 1-inch pieces
- 7 large eggs
- 1 teaspoon vanilla extract
- ½ teaspoon salt
- 8 tablespoons unsalted butter, melted and cooled slightly
- ⅛ teaspoon red food coloring
- ⅛ teaspoon green food coloring
- ⅔ cup seedless raspberry jam
- 1 cup (6 ounces) bittersweet chocolate chips

1. Adjust oven rack to middle position and heat oven to 350 degrees. Grease 13 by 9-inch baking pan. Make parchment paper sling by folding 1 long sheet of parchment 13 inches wide and laying across width of pan, with extra parchment hanging over edges of pan. Push parchment into corners and up sides of pan, smoothing parchment flush to pan. Grease parchment.

2. Combine flour and baking powder and sift into bowl; set aside. Process sugar and almond paste in food processor until combined, 20 to 30 seconds. Transfer sugar mixture to bowl of stand mixer; add eggs, vanilla, and salt. Fit mixer with whisk and whip mixture on medium-high speed until pale and thickened, 5 to 7 minutes. Reduce speed to low and add melted butter. Slowly add flour mixture until just combined.

3. Transfer 2 cups batter to prepared pan and spread in even layer with offset spatula. Bake until top is set and edges are just starting to brown, 10 to 12 minutes. Let cool 5 minutes in pan. Using parchment overhang, lift cake out of pan and transfer to wire rack. Let cake and pan cool completely.

4. Divide remaining batter between 2 bowls. Stir red food coloring into first bowl and green food coloring into second bowl. Make new parchment sling for now-empty pan and repeat baking with each colored batter, letting pan cool after each batch.

5. Invert red layer onto cutting board and gently remove parchment. Spread ⅓ cup jam evenly over top. Invert plain layer onto red layer and gently remove parchment. Spread remaining ⅓ cup jam evenly over top. Invert green layer onto plain layer and gently remove parchment.

6. Microwave chocolate chips in bowl at 50 percent power, stirring occasionally, until melted, 2 to 4 minutes. Spread chocolate evenly over green layer. Let set for 2 minutes, then run fork in wavy pattern through chocolate. Let cool until chocolate has set, 1 to 2 hours. Using serrated knife, trim away edges. Cut lengthwise into 5 equal strips (about 1½ inches wide) and then crosswise into 12 equal strips (about 1 inch wide). Serve.

GINGERBREAD WHOOPIE PIES

Makes 24 sandwich cookies

This version of the beloved whoopie pie uses soft, cakey gingerbread for the cookies and tangy cream cheese frosting for the filling. Full of warm, seasonal spices with a nice gingery bite, these cookies will get you into the spirit.

- 2 cups (10 ounces) all-purpose flour
- 4 teaspoons pumpkin pie spice
- ¾ teaspoon baking soda
- ½ teaspoon salt
- ¾ cup packed (5¼ ounces) light brown sugar
- 8 tablespoons unsalted butter, melted, plus 6 tablespoons unsalted butter, softened
- ¼ cup molasses
- 3 tablespoons finely chopped crystallized ginger
- 1 large egg
- ¼ cup buttermilk
- 1½ cups (6 ounces) confectioners' sugar, plus extra for dusting
- 6 ounces cream cheese, cut into 6 pieces and softened

1. Whisk flour, pumpkin pie spice, baking soda, and salt together in bowl. Whisk brown sugar, melted butter, molasses, and ginger together in large bowl until combined. Whisk in egg and buttermilk until combined. Add flour mixture and stir with rubber spatula until dough just comes together. Cover bowl with plastic wrap and refrigerate for at least 1 hour or up to 24 hours.

2. Adjust oven rack to middle position and heat oven to 350 degrees. Line 2 baking sheets with parchment paper. Working with 1 scant tablespoon dough at a time, roll into 1-inch balls and space them evenly on prepared sheets, about 24 per sheet. Bake, 1 sheet at a time, until cookies have puffed and are just set, 11 to 13 minutes. Let cool on sheet for 5 minutes, then transfer to wire rack to cool completely.

3. Using stand mixer fitted with paddle, beat confectioners' sugar and remaining 6 tablespoons butter on medium-high speed until fluffy, about 2 minutes. With mixer running, add cream cheese, 1 piece at a time, and continue to beat until smooth, about 30 seconds. If frosting is very soft, refrigerate for 15 minutes before filling cookies. Spread or pipe 1 tablespoon frosting onto bottoms of half of cookies; sandwich frosting with remaining cookies, bottom side down, pressing gently to adhere. Dust with confectioners' sugar and serve.

Cider-Braised Pork Roast

Pork and apples are a tried-and-true combination. But cooking them together revealed some core problems. BY CECELIA JENKINS

W HETHER IT'S applewood-smoked bacon or pork chops served with applesauce, pork and apples are a classic combination. With this in mind, I set out to create a recipe for a pork roast slowly braised in cider.

I collected several recipes to test drive. They featured different cuts, different cooking times and temperatures, and supporting ingredients that ranged from onions and celery to orange and caraway. Out of the six recipes I prepared, not one was a success. The meat was bland and leathery in recipes that called for lean tenderloin or loin. Recipes that called for fattier cuts were greasy and produced tough, chewy meat. And they all had muddied flavors that didn't taste much like either pork or apples. I wanted a flavorful, tender roast infused with clean, bright, sweet-tart cider flavor.

I knew from experience that pork shoulder (also known as Boston butt or pork butt, the cut called for in recipes for pulled pork) is a good cut for braising—its fat and connective tissue break down over the long cooking time, resulting in silky, tender, flavorful meat. I tested bone-in versus boneless shoulder roasts, and my tasters preferred the moister meat that came off the bone-in roast; this made sense, because there is a lot of connective tissue around the bone that renders out during cooking, keeping the meat moist.

I rubbed the roast with a mixture of salt and brown sugar and refrigerated it overnight so the seasoning could penetrate it. This not only made the meat taste better, but the salt helped the muscle fibers hold onto moisture, which made the meat juicier, too. I seared the seasoned pork in a Dutch oven, poured in enough cider (1¾ cups) to come about halfway up the sides of the roast, and gently cooked it in a 300-degree oven until the meat registered 190 degrees and was completely tender. This pork was pretty good, but it was a little dry. Reducing the oven temperature to 275 degrees made for gentler cooking that kept the meat juicier. After about 2½ hours, the pork was perfect.

It was time to fine-tune. I tested cutting the cider with other flavorful ingredients like chicken broth, wine, apple juice, and apple liqueur. Each

We sear the apple wedges in flavorful pork fat to unite the elements of this hearty roast.

one diluted or distracted from the clean taste of the cider. Onions, garlic, bay leaf, cinnamon (for a subtle warm note that goes well with cider), and thyme were welcome additions that built a baseline of savory flavor without muting the cider. But when the pork was done, the braising liquid—which, after defatting, becomes the sauce—wasn't thick enough for serving.

Boiling the sauce down on the stovetop worked but took more effort than I wanted to expend. I tried stirring a cup of apple butter into the braising liquid to thicken it and reinforce the apple flavor; my tasters loved the flavor but not the slippery texture. I decided to keep ¼ cup of the apple butter for flavor. As for thickening, cornstarch

worked better here. I reserved ¼ cup of cider, and, once the roast was done, whisked it together with 1 tablespoon of cornstarch. I then added this mixture, called a slurry, to the pot. It thickened the sauce beautifully.

I was almost at the end of my journey but felt that something was missing. How about actual apples? I tried adding wedges of apples to the braise at various points—from the get-go, in the middle, at the end—but the apples were consistently too hard, too soft, or too mealy. Simply searing the apples in the flavorful pork fat that I'd separated out of the braising liquid was the solution. This made for deliciously porky-sweet apples that held their shape and texture alongside the sliced roast.

CIDER-BRAISED PORK ROAST
Serves 8

Pork butt roast is often labeled Boston butt in the supermarket. Plan ahead: This roast needs to cure for 18 to 24 hours before cooking. If you can't find Braeburn apples, substitute Jonagold. If you don't have a fat separator, strain the liquid through a fine-mesh strainer into a medium bowl in step 4 and wait for it to settle.

- 1 (5- to 6-pound) bone-in pork butt roast
- ¼ cup packed brown sugar Kosher salt and pepper
- 3 tablespoons vegetable oil
- 1 onion, halved and sliced thin
- 6 garlic cloves, smashed and peeled
- 2 cups apple cider
- 6 sprigs fresh thyme
- 2 bay leaves
- 1 cinnamon stick
- 2 Braeburn apples, cored and cut into 8 wedges each
- ¼ cup apple butter
- 1 tablespoon cornstarch
- 1 tablespoon cider vinegar

1. Using sharp knife, trim fat cap on roast to ¼ inch. Cut 1-inch crosshatch pattern, 1⁄16 inch deep, in fat cap. Place roast on large sheet of plastic wrap. Combine sugar and ¼ cup salt in bowl and rub mixture over entire roast and into slits. Wrap roast tightly in double layer of plastic, place on plate, and refrigerate for 18 to 24 hours.

2. Adjust oven rack to middle position and heat oven to 275 degrees. Unwrap roast and pat dry with paper towels, brushing away any excess salt mixture from surface. Season roast with pepper.

3. Heat oil in Dutch oven over medium-high heat until just smoking. Sear roast until well browned on all sides, about 3 minutes per side. Turn roast fat side up. Scatter onion and garlic around roast and cook until fragrant and beginning to brown, about 2 minutes. Add 1¾ cups cider, thyme sprigs, bay leaves, and cinnamon stick and bring to simmer. Cover, transfer to oven, and braise until fork slips easily in and out of meat and meat registers 190 degrees, 2¼ to 2¾ hours.

4. Transfer roast to carving board, tent with aluminum foil, and let rest for 30 minutes. Strain braising liquid through fine-mesh strainer into fat separator; discard solids and let liquid settle for at least 5 minutes.

5. About 10 minutes before roast is done resting, wipe out pot with paper towels. Spoon 1½ tablespoons of clear, separated fat from top of fat separator into now-empty pot and heat over medium-high heat until shimmering. Season apples with salt and pepper. Space apples evenly in pot, cut side down, and cook until well browned on both cut sides, about 3 minutes per side. Transfer to platter and tent with foil.

6. Wipe out pot with paper towels. Return 2 cups defatted braising liquid to now-empty pot and bring to boil over high heat. Whisk in apple butter until incorporated. Whisk cornstarch and remaining ¼ cup cider together in bowl and add to pot. Return to boil and cook until thickened, about 1 minute. Off heat, add vinegar and season with salt and pepper to taste. Cover sauce and keep warm.

7. To carve roast, cut around inverted T-shaped bone until it can be pulled free from roast (use clean dish towel to grasp bone if necessary). Slice pork and transfer to serving platter with apples. Pour 1 cup sauce over pork and apples. Serve, passing remaining sauce at table.

Removing the Bone

Using a long knife and holding onto the tip of the T-shaped bone, cut the meat away from all sides of the bone until it is loose enough to pull out of the roast.

Smothered Chicken

To do right by this simple dish, we smothered the pieces but not the flavor of the chicken. BY CHRISTIE MORRISON

TOO OFTEN, chicken dishes taste like whatever else is in the dish rather than the chicken itself. But smothered chicken is designed to coax out as much chicken flavor as possible and then bolster it with supporting—not distracting—ingredients.

I tried a handful of existing recipes from some of the South's best cooks (including Edna Lewis and John Folse) to get my bearings and set my goals: big chicken flavor and weekday ease.

To start, I tossed chicken parts in lightly seasoned flour and browned them in batches in a Dutch oven to render some of the fat and build a base of flavor.

Once the chicken pieces were browned, I set them aside and began to add the ingredients for my smothering sauce. I found that a simple mix of onions and celery, plus some garlic and dried sage, gave me a clean, savory base that enhanced, rather than challenged, the rich flavor of chicken.

Achieving the right consistency for the sauce took some tinkering. Working with 2 cups of chicken broth, I tried as little as 2 teaspoons of flour up to as much as 3 tablespoons. The best consistency came from 2 tablespoons, added along with the garlic and cooked for a minute with the vegetables before whisking in chicken broth.

I returned the chicken to the sauce, covered the pot, and set it to simmer. I removed the breast pieces once they'd hit 160 degrees, about 30 minutes later, and let the dark-meat pieces cook a bit longer, until they hit 175. I piled the chicken on a platter, splashed a bit of cider vinegar into the sauce, and doused the lot. Smothered satisfaction.

This simple braise isn't flashy, but its robust chicken flavor is deeply satisfying.

SOUTHERN-STYLE SMOTHERED CHICKEN Serves 4

This dish is best served with rice, but it's also good with potatoes. You may substitute ground sage for the dried sage leaves, but decrease the amount to ¼ teaspoon.

- 3 pounds bone-in chicken pieces (split breasts cut in half crosswise, drumsticks, and/or thighs), trimmed
  Salt and pepper
- ½ cup plus 2 tablespoons all-purpose flour
- ¼ cup vegetable oil
- 2 onions, chopped fine
- 2 celery ribs, chopped fine
- 3 garlic cloves, minced
- 1 teaspoon dried sage leaves
- 2 cups chicken broth
- 1 tablespoon cider vinegar
- 2 tablespoons minced fresh parsley

1. Pat chicken dry with paper towels and season with salt and pepper. Spread ½ cup flour in shallow dish. Working with 1 piece at a time, dredge chicken in flour, shaking off excess, and transfer to plate.

2. Heat oil in Dutch oven over medium-high heat. Add half of chicken to pot, skin side down, and cook until deep golden brown, 4 to 6 minutes per side; transfer to plate. Repeat with remaining chicken, adjusting heat if flour begins to burn.

3. Pour off all but 2 tablespoons fat and return pot to medium heat. Add onions, celery, 1 teaspoon salt, and ½ teaspoon pepper and cook until softened, 6 to 8 minutes. Stir in garlic, sage, and remaining 2 tablespoons flour and cook until vegetables are well coated with flour and garlic is fragrant, about 1 minute. Whisk in broth, scraping up any browned bits.

4. Nestle chicken into sauce, add any accumulated juices from plate, and bring to boil. Reduce heat to low, cover, and simmer until breasts register 160 degrees and drumsticks/thighs register 175 degrees, 30 to 40 minutes.

5. Transfer chicken to serving dish. Stir vinegar into sauce and season with salt and pepper to taste. Pour sauce over chicken, sprinkle with parsley, and serve.

Cornish Pasties

Upper midwesterners have divisive opinions about this coal miner's classic.
We wanted our version to bring people together. BY KATIE LEAIRD

CORNISH PASTIES SHOULD be great: tender beef and vegetables wrapped in a flaky handheld crust. So I was surprised when one of our editors who ate these as a child told me, "The best thing about a pasty is the ketchup on the side."

Pasties do evoke strong feelings. Some fans adamantly oppose any vegetables in the filling other than potatoes and onions. Some, equally adamantly, endorse turnips, carrots, and rutabagas. Some recipes call for lard, while others use butter. Where to begin?

The mining industry in Michigan's Upper Peninsula attracted immigrants from Cornwall, England, in the 19th century (see "The American Table"); they brought their pasties with them. The miners' pasties were as big as dinner plates, filled with enough food to fuel an entire day's labor. The crust was sturdy enough for carrying and, some legends suggest, for protecting the contents even when dropped down the mine shaft.

A vibrant image, but I wanted a hand pie with a tender, not impact-resistant, crust. After experimenting with flour doughs made with lard, shortening, and butter (and various combinations thereof), my tasters agreed that butter imparted the best flavor into the crust.

To make a pliable dough that would be easy to manipulate and shape, I added an egg and, instead of water, cold sour cream, which added a pleasant flavor. The food processor allowed me to mix quickly and avoid overworking the dough. I pressed it into a disk, wrapped it, and refrigerated it; the cold dough was much easier to work with.

In initial tests, my pasty fillings (beef, chopped onion, potato, and salt and pepper) were bland. I sautéed the onion in butter to deepen its flavor and added minced garlic and fresh thyme.

I chose cubed meat over ground (the latter gave me patties, not pasties), and after trying several cuts, I settled on skirt steak. It went, raw, into the cooled onions along with cubed potatoes and—after much testing and impassioned debate—earthy rutabaga. I seasoned the mixture with salt and pepper then tossed it with flour to help the meat create its own gravy while it baked.

The final hurdle was construction. I rolled the pieces of dough into ovals and spooned some filling into the center of each. I brushed their edges with water to help them stick and folded the ovals over the filling to create half-moon shapes. I pressed the edges together, then trimmed and crimped for a neat finish.

To create an escape vent for steam (and forestall any leakage in the oven), I cut a small slit in the top of each pie. After 45 minutes, the pies were golden brown, with the filling just bubbling up through the vents.

Like the original miners' fare, these pasties are hearty, but the crust is more flaky than fortified. I'm as likely to fork-and-knife one as I am to eat it out of my hands. Ketchup optional.

CORNISH PASTIES Serves 4

You can substitute turnips for rutabagas if you like. If you can't find skirt steak, you can use 1½ pounds of blade steak. The extra ¼ pound accounts for the trimming required with the blade cut. The pasties fit best on the baking sheet when placed crosswise in two rows of three. Serve the pasties with ketchup, if desired.

CRUST
- ⅔ cup sour cream, chilled
- 1 large egg, lightly beaten
- 3 cups (15 ounces) all-purpose flour
- 1¾ teaspoons salt
- 16 tablespoons unsalted butter, cut into ½-inch pieces and chilled

FILLING
- 1 tablespoon unsalted butter
- 1 onion, chopped fine
  Salt and pepper
- 1 tablespoon minced fresh thyme
- 2 garlic cloves, minced
- 1¼ pounds skirt steak, trimmed and cut into ½-inch pieces
- 10 ounces russet potatoes, peeled and cut into ½-inch pieces
- 10 ounces rutabaga, peeled and cut into ½-inch pieces
- ¼ cup all-purpose flour
- 1 large egg

1. FOR THE CRUST: Whisk sour cream and egg together in small bowl. Process flour and salt in food processor until combined, about 3 seconds. Add butter and pulse until only pea-size pieces remain, about 10 pulses. Add half of sour cream mixture and pulse until combined, about 5 pulses. Add remaining sour cream mixture and pulse until dough begins to form, about 15 pulses.

2. Transfer mixture to lightly floured counter and knead briefly until dough comes together. Form dough into 6-inch disk, wrap tightly in plastic wrap, and refrigerate for 30 minutes. (Dough can be refrigerated for up to 24 hours; let chilled dough sit on counter for 15 minutes to soften before rolling.)

3. FOR THE FILLING: Melt butter in 10-inch skillet over medium heat. Add onion and ¼ teaspoon salt and cook until softened, about 5 minutes. Add thyme and garlic and cook until fragrant, about 30 seconds. Let cool slightly, about 5 minutes. Combine cooled onion mixture, steak, potatoes, rutabaga, 2 teaspoons salt, and ¾ teaspoon pepper in bowl. Add flour and toss to coat.

4. Adjust oven rack to upper-middle position and heat oven to 375 degrees. Line rimmed baking sheet with parchment paper. Remove dough from refrigerator and cut into 6 equal pieces (about 5 ounces each); cover with plastic wrap. Divide filling into 6 equal portions, about 1 heaping cup each.

5. Working with 1 piece of dough at a time, roll into 10 by 8-inch oval (about ⅛ inch thick) on lightly floured counter. Place 1 portion filling in center of dough. Moisten edges of dough with water, then fold narrow end of oval over filling to form half-moon shape. Press dough around filling to adhere.

Sure, you can use a fork, but these savory, meaty pies are usually eaten by hand.

▶ Discover the pasty's Southern cousin, the Natchitoches meat pie.
CooksCountry.com/natchitochespies.

The American Table
Miners' Meals

Starting in 1843, the wilderness of Michigan's Upper Peninsula was the site of an epic copper boom. Miners flocked to the region from around the world; many came from Cornwall, England. By 1903 Red Jacket, the region's primary city, had a 50,000-volume library, an elaborate opera house where Caruso and Bernhardt performed, and eight separate foreign-language newspapers. Then, in 1913, a long, bloody strike started the city's slow but steady decline. Today Red Jacket, renamed Calumet, is a village of some 700 people in a region of ghost towns. Not everything has vanished, though; as is so often the case, food is the last tradition to die, and the Cornish pasty lives on to recall the glory days of King Copper. –JOHN WILLOUGHBY

TEST KITCHEN TECHNIQUE **Forming Pasties**
After chilling the dough for at least 30 minutes, it's ready to shape and fill.

Divide dough into 6 equal pieces. Roll each into an oval and place filling in the center.

Brush the edges of the dough with water and fold them over the filling to create a half-moon shape. Press the edges to seal.

For a tidy finish, trim the excess dough from the sealed edges with a pizza cutter and then crimp with a fork.

---

6. Trim any ragged edges, then crimp edges with fork to seal; transfer to prepared sheet. (For more decorative edge, trim any ragged edges and, starting at one end, pinch and slightly twist dough diagonally across seam between your thumb and index finger. Continue pinching and twisting dough around seam.) Repeat with remaining dough and filling.

7. Using paring knife, cut 1-inch vent hole on top of each pasty. Whisk egg and 2 teaspoons water in bowl. Brush pasties with egg wash. Bake until crust is golden brown and filling is bubbling up through vent hole, about 45 minutes, rotating sheet halfway through baking. Transfer pasties to wire rack and let cool for 10 minutes before serving.

TO MAKE AHEAD
Pasties can be prepared through step 6, then frozen on baking sheet. Once frozen, pasties can be stored in zipper-lock bag for up to 1 month. To cook from frozen, bake at 350 degrees for 1 hour 5 minutes to 1 hour 10 minutes.

The Best Way to Cook Broccoli

The secret to crisp-tender, brilliantly green broccoli? Nuke it. Yes, we're serious.

BY CHRISTIE MORRISON

When it comes to broccoli, roasting and sautéing have their advantages (brown edges, crisp florets) but for even cooking every time, quickly, we turn to the microwave.

The reason? Water. Unlike standard ovens, which cook food through the direct application of heat, a microwave uses electromagnetic waves to penetrate the food. When the food is mostly water (like broccoli, which is 91 percent water), the microwave steams it from the inside.

Careful cutting is essential to even cooking: I found that the broccoli was best when I cut the florets into 1-inch pieces and then used a vegetable peeler to remove the fibrous exterior from the very flavorful stem (too often discarded) and cut it into ½-inch cubes. I tossed everything with a bit of salt in a microwave-safe bowl, no added water necessary. Tests confirmed that tightly covering the bowl with plastic was no more effective than just laying a plate on top, so I covered the bowl with a plate, slipped it into the microwave, and pressed "cook."

Five minutes wasn't enough, and 10 minutes was too long: The Goldilocks timing in our 1,200-watt test kitchen microwaves was 7 minutes for perfectly tender, brightly colored broccoli. Some microwaves are stronger than others, though—power can range from 700 watts in older or smaller models to between 1,000 and 1,500 watts in newer, larger models—so I tested my method in several different ovens with different wattages. I found that ovens with under 1,000 watts needed around 10 minutes. My advice: The first time you make this recipe, check your broccoli about a minute before you think it's done, just in case.

This broccoli is tasty enough to eat straight from the microwave, but a quick toss with a flavored oil enhances its appeal.

Our technique is easy: cut, microwave, drain, and dress.

BROCCOLI WITH LEMON-OREGANO DRESSING
Serves 4

We developed this recipe in a full-size 1,200-watt microwave. If you're using a compact microwave with 800 watts or fewer, increase the cooking time to about 10 minutes.

- 1½ pounds broccoli
  Salt and pepper
- 3 tablespoons extra-virgin olive oil
- 2 teaspoons minced fresh oregano
- 1 garlic clove, minced
- ¾ teaspoon grated lemon zest

1. Trim broccoli florets from stalk. Cut florets into 1-inch pieces. Trim and discard lower 1 inch of stalk. Using vegetable peeler, peel away outer ⅛ inch of stalk. Cut stalk into ½-inch chunks.

2. Place broccoli in bowl and toss with ½ teaspoon salt. Microwave, covered, until broccoli is bright green and just tender, 6 to 8 minutes.

3. Meanwhile, whisk oil, oregano, garlic, lemon zest, and ¼ teaspoon salt together in bowl.

4. Drain broccoli in colander, then return to bowl. Add dressing and toss to combine. Season with salt and pepper to taste. Serve.

BROCCOLI WITH ANCHOVY-GARLIC DRESSING
Omit lemon zest. Substitute 2 rinsed and minced anchovy fillets for oregano and add ⅛ teaspoon red pepper flakes to dressing in step 3.

▶ For our variation featuring sesame-miso dressing, go to CooksCountry.com/dec15.

Getting to Know Beer

BY CHRISTIE MORRISON

It's not just for guzzling. We use beer's flavor and fizz in dozens of recipes.

What, exactly, is beer? It's the nectar created when malt (a grain, most often barley, that has germinated and then been dried and/or roasted) is mixed with water, strained, and the resulting liquid fermented. Fermentation is the process—triggered by yeast or bacteria—that converts the sugar in the malt into acid, gas, and/or alcohol. Many beers are flavored with hops, the seed cones of a climbing vine, which add flowery, bitter, and piney flavors to the mix.

Session
ALL-DAY SIPPER

Session beers were invented as a response to ever-increasing alcohol percentages in craft beers such as India Pale Ales. The addition of more hops doesn't just increase a craft beer's flavor, it also sends its alcohol content by volume (ABV) sky high (between 8 and 12 percent). Session beers are brewed with the same care for flavor as craft beers, but with an ABV usually between 4 and 5 percent.

Lager
GO-TO BREW

Unlike ales, which ferment at high temperatures for more yeast activity and flavor, lagers ferment at cool temperatures before aging to develop more subtle, crisp flavors. Lagers (such as Budweiser) tend to be light- to medium-bodied, which makes them ideal for use in cooking. We use lager for beer batters as well as for cooking our Beer-Braised Cabbage (**CooksCountry. com/beerbraisedcabbage**).

Pilsner
GOLDEN BUBBLES

This light, gold- to straw-colored beer gets its name from its birthplace in Pilsen, Bohemia (now Czech Republic). Though it's brewed like lager, it's lighter in color and body and has a floral, slightly spicy finish thanks to the Saaz hops that are traditionally used. True pilsners often have a high level of carbonation due to months of aging. Try it in our recipe for Almond Boneless Chicken (page 23).

Saison
MIXED HARVEST

In the Belgian tradition, seasonal workers who helped with the harvest were paid with beer made by the farmer's wife from leftover mixed grains. Folklore aside, *saisons* are funky, yeasty, hoppy ales made from mixed grains and noble hops. Saisons pair well with food, especially cheese. American beers brewed in the same style are often labeled "farmhouse" ales.

India Pale Ale
HOPPED AND LOADED

The extra hops in this style of beer were originally added as a preservative to help it survive the long trek from London to the colonies in India in the late 18th century. European noble hops lend vegetal, grassy flavors to some IPAs, while Cascade hops from North America introduce flavors of citrus and pine. Beware: the hoppier the beer, the higher the ABV.

Porter
WORKING MAN'S PINT

Relatively low-alcohol porters first became popular with London's transportation workers. They are known for their chocolate, toffee, and toasty flavors, which come from the malts used to make them—these dark malts are what make porter so dark. The roasted malt flavors make porter a great match for grilled meats.

Stout
IRISH FAVORITE

This dark, rich brew uses toasted malts, giving stouts roasted, sometimes bitter coffee-like notes. Since sugars are cooked off during roasting, the resulting stouts are usually lower in alcohol (and calories) than you'd expect. The deep flavor and full body of stout makes it a natural pairing with roasted and braised meats. Try our Guinness Beef Stew (**CooksCountry.com/guinnessbeefstew**).

Wheat Beer
WEIZ GUY

Wheat beers have a hazy, unfiltered look and taste of clove, banana, and citrus. Brewers rely on warm fermentation (most beers are fermented in cooler temperatures) and a particular strain of yeast to produce the yeasty, spicy flavor of what they call *Weissbier*, *Weizenbier*, or *Hefeweizen* (*hefe* is yeast, *weizen* is wheat). Try wheat beer in our Grill-Braised Short Ribs (**CooksCountry.com/grillbraisedshortribs**).

Lambic
WILD THING

Lambics are dry, sour, and tart Belgian wheat beers that are often infused with fruit. Before brewing, lambic wort (a mix of crushed grain and water) is fermented in the open air, where it develops flavor from wild yeasts. *Kreik* and framboise are lambics fermented with cherries and raspberries, respectively. The high acidity of lambics makes them pair well with shellfish or oily fish like salmon or bluefish.

Sour Beer
FOOD'S FRIEND

Sour beer starts with sweet malt that undergoes warm fermentation. The fermented beer is then placed in old wooden barrels full of wild yeasts and other yeast strains for a second or third fermentation. Bacteria in the barrels eat the sugars in the beer, which produces a beer that is tart and sour, though often sweeter than lambic. Like lambic, sour beers are excellent paired with rich or fatty foods.

Trappist
MONK-Y BUSINESS

More of a tradition than a specific style of beer, Trappist beers are produced by Cistercian monks in 11 European monasteries. The monks follow a brewing method known for its discipline and high standards. The beers are slightly sweet, hoppy, and spicy. Their alcohol levels vary, from around 7 percent to up to 9 percent. Secular brews that mimic the style of Trappist beers are often called "Abbey" ales.

PORK CUTLET CUBAN SANDWICH

PASTA WITH LENTIL-MUSHROOM RAGU

CHICKEN THIGHS WITH PANCETTA, WHITE BEANS, AND ROSEMARY

STEAMED MUSSELS WITH FENNEL, WHITE WINE, AND TARRAGON

PASTA WITH LENTIL-MUSHROOM RAGU Serves 4

✔ **WHY THIS RECIPE WORKS:** We use canned lentils instead of dried to make this Neapolitan pasta dish an easy weeknight supper.

- 2 tablespoons extra-virgin olive oil, plus extra for drizzling
- 2 large portobello mushroom caps, gills removed, caps cut into ½-inch pieces
- 1 onion, chopped fine
- 2 carrots, peeled and chopped fine
  Salt and pepper
- ½ cup red wine
- 1 (15-ounce) can lentils, rinsed
- 1 (14.5-ounce) can diced tomatoes
- 12 ounces ditalini
- 1½ ounces Pecorino Romano cheese, grated (¾ cup)

1. Heat 1 tablespoon oil in large saucepan over medium-high heat until shimmering. Add mushrooms, cover, and cook until mushrooms release their liquid, about 5 minutes. Add onion, carrots, ¾ teaspoon salt, ½ teaspoon pepper, and remaining 1 tablespoon oil and cook, uncovered, until softened, about 5 minutes. Add wine and cook until almost evaporated, about 2 minutes. Add lentils and tomatoes and their juice; reduce heat to medium-low and simmer until slightly thickened, 5 to 7 minutes.

2. Meanwhile, bring 4 quarts water to boil in large pot. Add pasta and 1 tablespoon salt and cook, stirring often, until al dente. Reserve ½ cup cooking water, then drain pasta and return to pot. Add lentil-mushroom mixture and ½ cup Pecorino and toss to combine. Adjust consistency with reserved cooking water as needed. Serve, sprinkled with remaining ¼ cup Pecorino and drizzled with extra oil.

TEST KITCHEN NOTE: You can substitute another small pasta for ditalini, such as tubettini or elbow macaroni.

PORK CUTLET CUBAN SANDWICH Serves 4

✔ **WHY THIS RECIPE WORKS:** For a twist on the classic Cuban sandwich, we start by browning a pork cutlet. Then we top it with ham, melted Swiss cheese, pickles, and a tangy orange-mustard sauce.

- 4 (3-ounce) boneless pork cutlets, ¼ inch thick, trimmed
  Salt and pepper
- 1 tablespoon vegetable oil
- ¾ cup orange juice
- ½ cup dill pickle chips, patted dry and chopped
- 2 tablespoons yellow mustard
- 4 kaiser rolls, split
- 4 thin slices deli Black Forest ham
- 8 thin slices deli Swiss cheese, folded in half
- 1 cup fresh cilantro leaves

1. Adjust oven rack to upper-middle position and heat oven to 450 degrees. Line rimmed baking sheet with parchment paper. Pat cutlets dry with paper towels and season with salt and pepper. Heat oil in 12-inch skillet over medium-high heat until just smoking. Cook cutlets until golden brown on both sides and cooked through, about 2 minutes per side. Transfer to plate and tent with foil.

2. Add orange juice to now-empty skillet, bring to simmer over medium-high heat, and cook until syrupy, about 5 minutes. Off heat, whisk in pickles and mustard. Season with salt and pepper to taste.

3. Place roll bottoms and tops, cut side up, on prepared sheet. Lay 1 slice ham and 1 slice cheese on each roll bottom. Lay 1 slice cheese on each roll top. Bake until cheese is melted, 3 to 4 minutes. Place 1 cutlet on each roll bottom and divide mustard mixture among sandwiches. Top with cilantro leaves, cover with roll tops, and press to secure. Serve.

STEAMED MUSSELS WITH FENNEL, WHITE WINE, AND TARRAGON Serves 4

✔ **WHY THIS RECIPE WORKS:** Simmering the broth for a few minutes before adding the mussels allows the fennel to soften and flavor the broth.

- 8 tablespoons unsalted butter, softened
- 6 garlic cloves, minced
- ¼ cup minced fresh tarragon
  Salt and pepper
- 1 (12-inch) baguette, cut on bias into 12 (1-inch-thick) slices
- 1 fennel bulb, stalks discarded, bulb quartered, cored, and chopped
- 1½ cups dry white wine
- 4 pounds mussels, scrubbed and debearded

1. Adjust oven rack 4 inches from broiler element and heat broiler. Combine butter, garlic, 2 tablespoons tarragon, ½ teaspoon salt, and ½ teaspoon pepper in bowl. Spread 5 tablespoons butter mixture on 1 side of baguette slices. Place slices, buttered side up, on rimmed baking sheet.

2. Melt 1 tablespoon butter mixture in Dutch oven over medium heat and cook until garlic is fragrant, about 30 seconds. Add fennel, cover, and cook until softened, about 2 minutes. Stir in wine and ½ teaspoon salt; bring to simmer and cook, uncovered, for 3 minutes. Add mussels to pot, cover, and cook until mussels open, 4 to 6 minutes, stirring twice. Remove pot from heat and transfer mussels to serving bowls using slotted spoon, leaving accumulated mussel broth in pot.

3. Broil baguette slices until lightly browned, about 1 minute per side. Stir remaining 2 tablespoons butter mixture and remaining 2 tablespoons tarragon into broth and season with salt and pepper to taste. Pour broth over mussels and serve with toasted baguette slices.

CHICKEN THIGHS WITH PANCETTA, WHITE BEANS, AND ROSEMARY Serves 4

✔ **WHY THIS RECIPE WORKS:** Cooking the beans with rendered chicken fat and pancetta gives them bold, meaty flavor.

- 8 (5- to 7-ounce) bone-in chicken thighs, trimmed
  Salt and pepper
- 2 teaspoons extra-virgin olive oil, plus extra for drizzling
- 2 ounces pancetta, chopped fine
- 5 garlic cloves, peeled and smashed
- 2 sprigs fresh rosemary
- 2 (15-ounce) cans cannellini beans, rinsed
- 1 cup chicken broth
- 1 tablespoon chopped fresh parsley

1. Adjust oven rack to upper-middle position and heat oven to 450 degrees. Pat chicken dry with paper towels and season with salt and pepper. Heat oil in 12-inch skillet over medium-high heat until just smoking. Add chicken and cook, skin side down, until well browned, about 7 minutes. Transfer to rimmed baking sheet, skin side up, and roast until chicken registers 175 degrees, 15 to 20 minutes.

2. Meanwhile, pour off all but 1 tablespoon fat from skillet and return to medium heat. Add pancetta, garlic, and rosemary and cook until garlic is golden brown, about 3 minutes. Add beans, broth, and ¼ teaspoon pepper. Bring to simmer and cook until slightly thickened, 5 to 7 minutes. Discard rosemary sprigs and season with salt and pepper to taste.

3. Transfer beans to platter and drizzle with extra oil. Top with chicken, sprinkle with parsley, and serve.

TEST KITCHEN NOTE: Don't be shy with the olive oil drizzle. Add at least a tablespoon to boost the creaminess of the bean mixture considerably.

GREEN CURRY CHICKEN WITH GREEN BEANS

**PAN-FRIED MINUTE STEAKS
WITH CAPER-TOMATO SAUCE**

SIRLOIN TIPS WITH STEAKHOUSE CREAMED SPINACH

GARLICKY SKILLET STRATA

PAN-FRIED MINUTE STEAKS WITH CAPER-TOMATO SAUCE

Serves 4

✓ **WHY THIS RECIPE WORKS:** Dredging the steaks in flour promotes faster browning and gives the sauce a textured surface to cling to.

- 4 (6-ounce) beef cubed steaks
  Salt and pepper
- ½ cup all-purpose flour
- ¼ cup vegetable oil
- 3 tablespoons unsalted butter
- ¼ cup capers, drained, plus 2 tablespoons caper brine
- 4 garlic cloves, sliced thin
- ½ teaspoon dried oregano
- 2 ripe large tomatoes (8 ounces each), cored and cut into ½-inch pieces
- 2 tablespoons minced fresh parsley

1. Pat steaks dry with paper towels and season with salt and pepper. Place flour in shallow dish. Dredge steaks in flour, shaking off excess. Heat 2 tablespoons oil in 12-inch nonstick skillet over medium-high heat until just smoking. Add 2 steaks to skillet and cook until well browned on first side, about 4 minutes. Flip and cook until browned on second side, 3 to 4 minutes longer. Transfer steaks to platter and tent with foil. Wipe out skillet with paper towels and repeat with remaining 2 tablespoons oil and 2 steaks.

2. Melt 2 tablespoons butter in now-empty skillet over medium heat. Add capers, garlic, and oregano and cook until fragrant, about 30 seconds. Stir in tomatoes and caper brine and cook until tomatoes are softened and heated through, about 1 minute, scraping up any browned bits. Off heat, stir in parsley and remaining 1 tablespoon butter. Season with salt and pepper to taste. Pour sauce over steaks. Serve.

GREEN CURRY CHICKEN WITH GREEN BEANS   Serves 4

✓ **WHY THIS RECIPE WORKS:** Tossing the chicken in cornstarch promotes a crisp, golden-brown crust.

- 3 tablespoons fish sauce
- 2 teaspoons packed brown sugar
- 1½ pounds boneless, skinless chicken breasts, trimmed and cut crosswise into ¼-inch-thick slices
- 6 tablespoons cornstarch
- 1 tablespoon vegetable oil
- 1 pound green beans, trimmed and cut into 2-inch lengths
- 2 tablespoons green curry paste
- 1 tablespoon grated fresh ginger
- 1 (13.5-ounce) can coconut milk
- ¼ cup cilantro leaves

1. Combine 2 tablespoons fish sauce, 2 tablespoons water, and 1 teaspoon sugar in large bowl. Add chicken, toss to coat, and let sit for 5 minutes. Drain chicken and pat dry with paper towels. Place cornstarch in shallow dish. Heat oil in 12-inch nonstick skillet over medium-high heat until just smoking. Dredge chicken in cornstarch, shake off any excess, and add to skillet. Cook until golden brown, about 6 minutes. Transfer to plate and set aside.

2. Add green beans to now-empty skillet and cook over medium-high heat until bright green and blistered, about 5 minutes. Reduce heat to medium, add curry paste and ginger, and cook until fragrant, about 30 seconds. Stir in coconut milk, remaining 1 tablespoon fish sauce, and remaining 1 teaspoon sugar and bring to simmer. Cook until slightly thickened, about 2 minutes. Return chicken and any accumulated juices to skillet and cook until heated through, about 1 minute. Sprinkle with cilantro before serving.

TEST KITCHEN NOTE: Serve over rice with lime wedges.

GARLICKY SKILLET STRATA   Serves 4

✓ **WHY THIS RECIPE WORKS:** This quick version of a classic cheese strata is cooked on the stovetop until the eggs are set and then finished in a hot oven to melt and brown the cheese.

- 12 large eggs
- ½ cup half-and-half
  Salt and pepper
- 2 tablespoons extra-virgin olive oil
- 4 slices hearty white sandwich bread, cut into 1-inch pieces
- 2 tablespoons unsalted butter
- 6 ounces Canadian bacon, chopped
- 4 scallions, white and green parts separated and sliced thin
- 4 garlic cloves, minced
- 3 ounces Gruyère cheese, shredded (¾ cup)

1. Adjust oven rack to upper-middle position and heat oven to 450 degrees. Whisk eggs, half-and-half, 1 teaspoon salt, and ½ teaspoon pepper in bowl until well combined, about 30 seconds; set aside.

2. Heat oil in 10-inch ovensafe nonstick skillet over medium heat until shimmering. Add bread and cook until lightly browned, about 5 minutes. Push bread to sides of pan and melt butter in center. Add bacon, scallion whites, and garlic to butter and cook until fragrant, about 30 seconds; stir into bread to combine. Add egg mixture and cook, scraping bottom of skillet with rubber spatula, until large curds form, about 2 minutes. Continue to cook, without stirring, for 30 seconds. Sprinkle Gruyère over top.

3. Transfer skillet to oven and bake until surface of strata is slightly puffy and cheese is melted, 5 to 7 minutes. Remove skillet from oven and let stand for 10 minutes. Using spatula, loosen strata from skillet and slide onto platter or cutting board. Sprinkle with scallion greens. Cut into wedges and serve.

SIRLOIN TIPS WITH STEAKHOUSE CREAMED SPINACH   Serves 4

✓ **WHY THIS RECIPE WORKS:** Starting with frozen spinach streamlines the prep for creamed spinach. We skip the heavy cream in favor of a light béchamel flavored with garlic, shallots, and a hint of nutmeg. Sirloin steak tips are often sold as flap meat.

- 1½ pounds sirloin steak tips, trimmed and cut into 2-inch pieces
  Salt and pepper
- 5 teaspoons vegetable oil
- 2 shallots, sliced thin
- 1 tablespoon all-purpose flour
- 2 garlic cloves, minced
- ⅛ teaspoon ground nutmeg
- 1¾ cups whole milk
- 20 ounces frozen spinach, thawed and squeezed dry
- 1 ounce Parmesan cheese, grated (½ cup)

1. Pat steak tips dry with paper towels and season with salt and pepper. Heat 1 tablespoon oil in 12-inch skillet over medium-high heat until just smoking. Add steak tips and cook until well browned all over and meat registers 125 degrees (for medium-rare), 6 to 8 minutes. Transfer to plate and tent with foil.

2. Heat remaining 2 teaspoons oil in now-empty skillet over medium heat until shimmering. Add shallots and cook until softened, about 2 minutes. Add flour, garlic, and nutmeg and cook until flour is golden and garlic is fragrant, about 30 seconds. Whisk in milk and bring to simmer. Cook, stirring constantly, until thickened, about 3 minutes.

3. Stir in spinach, ¼ cup Parmesan, ¼ teaspoon salt, and ¼ teaspoon pepper and cook until heated through, about 2 minutes. Transfer to serving bowl and sprinkle with remaining ¼ cup Parmesan. Serve creamed spinach with steak tips.

Apple-Cinnamon Muffins

It's a simple idea—muffins with bright apple flavor— so why was it so hard to get right? BY REBECCAH MARSTERS

APPLE-CINNAMON MUFFINS, soft and crumbly with vibrant fruit flavor and spicy cinnamon. It's such a simple idea. But, as I learned after testing dozens of existing recipes, the goal is frustratingly elusive. The methods I found were similar (simple batters of oil or melted butter, flour, eggs, and dairy)—until it came to adding in fruit. The recipes I experimented with called for a bewildering array of treatments: grating the apples, cooking them down to a sauce, or just chopping and adding them raw.

All the muffins were failures. Some were wet, others dense, and yet others flavorless. One muffin could only be eaten with a spoon. These disasters only steeled my resolve, though: I was determined to devise a simple recipe for tender apple muffins with plenty of fruit flavor and crunchy sugar tops.

Drawing on the test kitchen's huge reserve of muffin recipes, I started with a basic roster of dry ingredients: flour, salt, cinnamon, and, for maximum rise, both baking powder and baking soda. I mixed in oil and melted butter (for the ideal combination of texture and flavor) along with sugar, beaten eggs, and buttermilk. I folded in chopped Granny Smiths and spooned the batter into muffin tins. After baking, I had beautiful, tender muffins that tasted nothing like apple.

We've found that the best way to amp up the flavor of apples is to drive off moisture with some heat. I grabbed a skillet and sautéed my chopped apples briefly in butter. I then let them cool while I stirred together another batch of batter. These muffins were much improved, with concentrated apple flavor. Another test, in which I incorporated brown sugar and a pinch of salt into the apple sauté, gave me even better muffins: The sugar helped the apples brown and develop a caramel flavor.

I wanted even more apple flavor, so for my next round, I substituted apple juice and apple cider for some of the buttermilk. These modifications created thinner batters, but I baked them off anyway, to great acclaim from my tasters—for the cider version, anyway (the muffins made with apple juice were sickeningly sweet).

The flavor was finally where I wanted it to be, but the muffins weren't doming as well as before—the thin batter was just not rising as reliably. Not willing to give up the added flavor, I instead swapped the buttermilk for equally tangy, but more stable, plain yogurt. I was back to a thick batter that, once baked, rose high and round.

For a finishing touch, I added a sprinkle of cinnamon sugar over each muffin for that crucial crunchy sugar top.

APPLE-CINNAMON MUFFINS
Makes 12 muffins
Do not substitute apple juice for the apple cider. Make sure to spray the muffin tin thoroughly, inside the cups and on top.

TOPPING

- 2   tablespoons granulated sugar
- 2   tablespoons packed brown sugar
- ¼   teaspoon ground cinnamon

MUFFINS

- 2   tablespoons unsalted butter, plus 4 tablespoons melted
- 2   Granny Smith apples (6½ ounces each), peeled, cored, and cut into ¼-inch pieces (3 cups)
- 2   tablespoons packed brown sugar
- ¾   teaspoon ground cinnamon
- 2½ cups (12½ ounces) all-purpose flour
- 2½ teaspoons baking powder
- ¼   teaspoon baking soda
- 1¼ teaspoons salt
- 1   cup (7 ounces) granulated sugar
- 2   large eggs
- ¼   cup vegetable oil
- ½   cup apple cider
- ½   cup plain whole-milk yogurt
- 1   teaspoon vanilla extract

1. FOR THE TOPPING: Using your fingers, combine granulated sugar, brown sugar, and cinnamon in bowl. Cover and set aside.

2. FOR THE MUFFINS: Adjust oven rack to upper-middle position and heat oven to 400 degrees. Spray 12-cup muffin tin generously with vegetable oil spray. Melt 2 tablespoons butter in 12-inch skillet over medium-high heat. Add apples, brown sugar, and ¼ teaspoon cinnamon. Cook, stirring often, until moisture has completely evaporated and apples are well browned, about 9 minutes. Remove pan from heat and let cool for 10 minutes.

3. Meanwhile, whisk flour, baking powder, baking soda, salt, and remaining ½ teaspoon cinnamon together in large bowl. Whisk granulated sugar, eggs, oil, and remaining 4 tablespoons melted butter together in separate bowl until thick and homogeneous, about 30 seconds. Whisk cider, yogurt, and vanilla into sugar mixture until combined.

4. Fold sugar mixture and cooled apples into flour mixture until just combined. Using greased ⅓-cup dry measuring cup, divide batter evenly among prepared muffin cups (cups will be filled to rim); sprinkle muffin tops evenly with topping.

5. Bake until golden brown and toothpick inserted in center comes out with few crumbs attached, 18 to 22 minutes, rotating muffin tin halfway through baking. Let muffins cool in muffin tin on wire rack for 10 minutes. Remove muffins from tin to wire rack and let cool for 5 minutes longer. Serve.

A crunchy cinnamon-sugar topping adds texture and flavor to these moist, tender muffins.

KEY STEP Precook the Apples

Raw apples stirred into muffin batter will weep liquid in the oven, making for soggy muffins. We solved this problem by cooking the apple pieces in butter (with brown sugar and cinnamon) first.

Crab Louis Salad

Once the king of salads, this 20th-century concoction was relegated to the history books.
We aimed to restore the monarchy. BY ASHLEY MOORE

EARLY LAST CENTURY, the question of who invented Crab Louis inspired vigorous debate in western states. Restaurants from Puget Sound to Santa Cruz claimed ownership of this tangy salad of flaky crabmeat, crisp lettuce, and an array of add-ins like tomatoes and hard-cooked eggs, all mixed with a creamy Thousand Island–style dressing. I wanted to bring it back for contemporary tables. But first I wanted to find out its story.

After much digging, our culinary research expert helped clear up the dish's murky origins. The first Crab Louis–style salad listed on a menu was at one of San Francisco's oldest restaurants, the Old Poodle Dog. Founded in 1849, the restaurant (which also maintained upstairs rooms where male clientele would visit with women whose companionship came with an hourly rate) was destroyed in the 1906 earthquake but quickly rebuilt. Just two years later, chef Louis Coutard, working with a bumper crop of crab, developed "Crab Leg à la Louis," the earliest version of Crab Louis. By the time Coutard died just a few years later, the salad had become a favorite.

Recipes for Crab Louis abound in our cookbook library; I assembled several for my tasters to sample. They were uniformly uninspiring, ranging from over-dressed and gloppy to bland and dull. Some called for iceberg lettuce, others for romaine, even one for mixed greens. The team gave all of these the thumbs-down. Instead, they demanded Bibb lettuce, and, after a taste test, I gave them what they wanted. Grape tomatoes won over chopped tomatoes for their consistent sweetness. Adding wedges of hard-cooked egg was a no-brainer.

The dressings I found were equally disappointing; both cloying and boring. My route would be to take the best qualities from each and cobble together something that sang to my tasters. Some dressings had a mayonnaise base, others sour cream. Tasters were divided, so I split the difference and used both. To round out the flavor and texture, I auditioned a wide array of add-ins before settling on chopped green bell pepper, scallions, and, for a bit of brininess, green olives. I also included lemon juice, of course (it's ideal with crab), and—for that signature spicy note—chili sauce.

The elephant in the room, of course, was the crab. Coutard used Dungeness, that inimitable seasonal crab that floods West Coast markets every year, but I needed something widely available at any time of year. Fresh crabmeat—the good stuff at the seafood counter—won the day for its sweet, oceany flavor and soft texture, but in a pinch, canned claw or backfin meat works well, too.

Retro in all the right ways, my Crab Louis Salad was fit for a new century.

With its zesty dressing and wealth of flavorful ingredients, this retro classic is perfectly suited to modern tastes.

CRAB LOUIS SALAD
Serves 4 to 6

Purchase high-quality, fresh crabmeat for this recipe. However, if you can only find canned crab meat, we prefer either claw or backfin meat or a combination thereof (see "Know Your Crab"). Chili sauce, a condiment similar to ketchup, has a sweet flavor and a subtle, spicy kick; do not substitute Asian chili-garlic sauce.

DRESSING
- ½ cup mayonnaise
- ¼ cup sour cream
- ¼ cup finely chopped green bell pepper
- ¼ cup sliced scallions
- 2 tablespoons chopped pitted green olives
- 2 tablespoons chili sauce
- 5 teaspoons lemon juice
- 2 teaspoons chopped fresh tarragon
- ¼ teaspoon salt
- ¼ teaspoon pepper
- ⅛ teaspoon cayenne pepper

SALAD
- 1 pound fresh crabmeat, picked over for shells and pressed dry between paper towels
- 2 heads Bibb lettuce (1 pound), leaves separated and torn into 1½-inch pieces
- 7½ ounces grape tomatoes, halved
- 3 hard-cooked eggs, quartered
- 1 ripe avocado, halved, pitted, quartered, and sliced thin

1. FOR THE DRESSING: Whisk all ingredients together in bowl.

2. FOR THE SALAD: Gently toss crabmeat with ½ cup dressing in bowl. Mound lettuce in center of serving platter. Arrange tomatoes, eggs, and avocado around lettuce. Top lettuce with dressed crab and serve with remaining ¾ cup dressing.

TEST KITCHEN NOTE Know Your Crab
The best meat comes from crabs you've caught yourself, but you'll find acceptable options at the supermarket.

BACKFIN
Small shreds, good in crab cakes.

CLAW MEAT
Higher in fat, deeper in flavor.

JUMBO LUMP
Largest chunks, most expensive.

LUMP
Light in color, delicate flavor.

Pork Saltimbocca

This elegant-looking and fancy-sounding dish is actually easy to make—
if you follow our simple technique. BY ASHLEY MOORE

SALTIMBOCCA, WHICH ROUGHLY translates as "jumps in the mouth" in Italian, is a traditional Roman dish popular in Italian American restaurants. In the classic version, thin veal cutlets are topped with prosciutto and sage, rolled into bundles, seared, and then finished in a bright white wine–and-butter sauce. More common today are deconstructed versions that lay the sage and prosciutto on top of a thin piece of veal (or chicken) before sautéing and saucing.

My goal was to reinvent this dish using pork tenderloin, a cut that, like veal and chicken, is mild and tender. I gathered and prepared a handful of recipes, and my tasters and I found plenty of problems to fix, including tough and chewy meat and out-of-balance flavors.

Different recipes call for various methods for getting the prosciutto to adhere to the pork. Using a toothpick is most common, but I wasn't keen on biting into a forgotten toothpick. Other recipes place the sage between the pork and prosciutto, but I found that this made the sage taste steamed and unpleasantly grassy. Another technique is to pound the prosciutto and sage into the meat, which has the added benefit of flattening the cutlets so they brown more evenly in the skillet. When I tried this approach, the pounding made the prosciutto adhere perfectly, but getting the sage to stay put was a bit of a challenge. Thankfully, a colleague suggested dipping the sage leaf into beaten egg white and lightly pounding it into the prosciutto. It worked.

Store-bought pork cutlets are often cut from the loin, which means they can be very lean and are easy to overcook. In the test kitchen, we prefer to make our own pork cutlets out of buttery-soft pork tenderloin (which has a similar texture to the more expensive veal)— just cut a 1-pound tenderloin into four pieces and then pound each one, cut side up, to a ¼-inch thickness. I was able to nail down the timing through a series of tests: I cooked the pork, prosciutto side down, in a hot skillet for 2 minutes, flipped, and cooked for just another minute. This resulted in tender, juicy pork and perfectly crisp prosciutto.

A quick, traditional saltimbocca pan sauce made of chicken broth, white wine, garlic, and lemon juice highlighted the pork and sage flavors. To bump up the flavor even more, I started the sauce by blooming a bit of extra minced sage with garlic in hot oil.

PORK SALTIMBOCCA Serves 4

Cutlets longer than 5 inches will crowd the skillet; trim large pieces as necessary.

- 2 (1-pound) pork tenderloins, trimmed
  Salt and pepper
- 8 thin slices prosciutto (3 ounces)
- 8 large fresh sage leaves, plus
  1 teaspoon minced
- 1 large egg white, lightly beaten
- 3 tablespoons olive oil
- 2 garlic cloves, sliced thin
- 1 cup chicken broth
- ¼ cup dry white wine
- 4 tablespoons unsalted butter, cut into
  4 pieces and chilled
- 2 teaspoons lemon juice

1. Cut each tenderloin crosswise into 4 equal pieces. Working with 1 piece at a time, place pork, cut side down, between 2 pieces of plastic wrap. Using meat pounder, gently pound to even ¼-inch thickness. (Pieces should be about 5 inches long.) Pat pork dry with paper towels and season with pepper.

2. Place 1 prosciutto slice on top of each cutlet, folding as needed to prevent overhang. Dip 1 side of each sage leaf in egg white and place 1 leaf, egg side down, in center of each prosciutto slice. Cover with plastic and pound lightly until prosciutto and sage adhere to pork.

3. Heat 2 tablespoons oil in 12-inch skillet over medium-high heat until shimmering. Add half of pork to skillet, prosciutto side down, and cook until lightly browned, about 2 minutes. Using tongs, carefully flip pork and cook until second side is light golden brown, about 1 minute. Transfer to platter and tent with aluminum foil. Repeat with remaining pork.

4. Add remaining 1 tablespoon oil to now-empty skillet and heat over medium-high heat until shimmering. Add garlic and minced sage and cook until fragrant, about 30 seconds. Stir in broth and wine and simmer until reduced to ½ cup, 5 to 7 minutes, scraping up any browned bits. Reduce heat to low and whisk in butter, 1 piece at a time. Stir in lemon juice and any accumulated meat juices from platter. Season with salt and pepper to taste. Spoon sauce over pork and serve.

Minced fresh sage in the sauce reinforces the floral, piney pop of the whole sage leaves.

TEST KITCHEN TECHNIQUE The Layered Effect

We divide each tenderloin into four even pieces and then turn each piece on its end between sheets of plastic and pound it thin. We top each cutlet with prosciutto and a sage leaf dipped in egg white, pounding them gently to adhere.

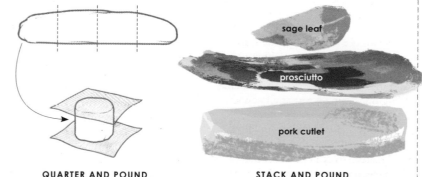

sage leaf

prosciutto

pork cutlet

QUARTER AND POUND

STACK AND POUND

Spicy Cheese Bread

How much cheese could we pack into this Wisconsin favorite without producing a greasy brick of dough? BY KATIE LEAIRD

DON'T BE ANGRY IF you're bumped in the back when wandering through the farmers' market in Madison, Wisconsin. It is likely that the person who walked into you has his or her attention on a giant loaf of steaming, fragrant bread and is pulling off chunks and gobbling them down as he or she strolls. Stella's bakery sells dozens of loaves of their famous spicy cheese bread at the market, where the soft, sweet, chewy, cheesy, spicy snack is legendary.

Since not everyone has easy access to Stella's and the market in Madison, I set out to create a similarly delicious bread back in the test kitchen—one that took minimal active work and yielded a substantial reward. No small task.

I experimented with various breads, including brioche and country-style, but quickly settled on challah as the best. The eggy dough baked up soft, with a thin golden crust, and, as I was thrilled to discover, took just 5 minutes of kneading—in a stand mixer. That's zero minutes by hand.

A much tougher nut to crack was how to add in the cheese. I wanted it to be fully incorporated, but I didn't want to lose the little bits of ooze. I started with the easiest option: simply tossing shredded cheese into the stand mixer while the bread was kneading.

Sadly, when I set the dough aside to rise, not much happened. I placed it on a baking sheet and baked it anyway. What a greasy bust that was. When incorporated this way, the cheese bogged down the dough and prevented it from rising.

I skipped the cheese on my next round and allowed the dough to rise for 2 hours on its own. Then, I rolled the rested, risen dough into an 18 by 12-inch rectangle with the long side facing the counter's edge and sprinkled cheese cubes and pepper flakes evenly over the top. I formed the dough into a tight cylinder and then gently rolled it back and forth on the counter until it measured 30 inches long. I spiraled the dough log and placed it on a baking sheet. After letting it rest and rise a second time, it baked into an even loaf with well-distributed pockets of cheese. (My tasters and I chose a combination of Monterey Jack and provolone for a mild, melty mix.)

But unfortunately the bread was too

A sprinkling of red pepper flakes on top—anchored by beaten egg—reinforces the heat from the pepper flakes in the dough.

dense—nowhere near as soft and airy as the cheeseless challah that I'd baked before. I worried that I'd added too much cheese, so I dialed it back and tried again, to no avail.

On the way to the fridge to gather cheese for yet another experiment, it hit me: Yeast is most active in a warm, moist environment. Perhaps the cheese I was taking straight from the refrigerator was bringing down the temperature of the

dough and inhibiting the yeast. So I let the cheese come to room temperature before adding it to the dough. Sure enough, it rose visibly more this time, and after an egg wash and a generous sprinkle of red pepper flakes (that's the spicy part), the light, chewy, stretchy bread was just right.

Except for one thing: It was losing its shape as it baked. I put together another loaf, this time baking it in a cake pan

rather than on a sheet (see "Shaping Spicy Cheese Bread"). Bingo. My spiral shape was intact, and covering it with foil halfway through its time in the oven protected the top from getting too dark and the sprinkled pepper flakes from burning.

The final step was key: A generous brush of melted butter applied shortly after the loaf came out of the oven helped the crust stay supple and gave it a shine.

SPICY CHEESE BREAD Makes 1 loaf

Take the cheese out of the refrigerator when you start the recipe to ensure that it comes to room temperature by the time you need it. Cold cheese will retard rising. Plan ahead: The dough needs to rise for several hours before baking.

BREAD

- 3¼ cups (16¼ ounces) all-purpose flour
- ¼ cup (1¾ ounces) sugar
- 1 tablespoon instant or rapid-rise yeast
- 1½ teaspoons red pepper flakes
- 1¼ teaspoons salt
- ½ cup warm water (110 degrees)
- 2 large eggs plus 1 large yolk
- 4 tablespoons unsalted butter, melted
- 6 ounces Monterey Jack cheese, cut into ½-inch cubes (1½ cups), room temperature
- 6 ounces provolone cheese, cut into ½-inch cubes (1½ cups), room temperature

TOPPING

- 1 large egg, lightly beaten
- 1 teaspoon red pepper flakes
- 1 tablespoon unsalted butter, softened

1. FOR THE BREAD: Whisk flour, sugar, yeast, pepper flakes, and salt together in bowl of stand mixer. Whisk warm water, eggs and yolk, and melted butter together in liquid measuring cup. Add egg mixture to flour mixture. Fit mixer with dough hook and knead on medium speed until dough clears bottom and sides of bowl, about 8 minutes.

2. Transfer dough to unfloured counter, shape into ball, and transfer to greased bowl. Cover with plastic wrap and let rise in warm place until doubled in size, 1½ to 2 hours.

3. Grease 9-inch round cake pan. Transfer dough to unfloured counter and press to deflate. Roll dough into 18 by 12-inch rectangle with long side parallel to counter's edge. Distribute Monterey Jack and provolone evenly over dough, leaving 1-inch border around edges. Starting with edge closest to you, roll dough into log. Pinch seam and ends to seal, then roll log so seam side is down. Roll log back and forth on counter, applying gentle, even pressure, until log reaches 30 inches in length. If any tears occur, pinch to seal.

4. Starting at one end, wind log into coil; tuck end underneath coil. Place loaf in prepared cake pan and cover loosely with clean dish towel. Let rise in warm place until doubled in size, 1 to 1½ hours. Adjust oven rack to lower-middle position and heat oven to 350 degrees.

5. FOR THE TOPPING: Brush top of loaf with egg, then sprinkle with pepper flakes. Place cake pan on rimmed baking sheet. Bake until loaf is golden brown, about 25 minutes. Rotate loaf, tent with aluminum foil, and continue to bake until loaf registers 190 degrees, 25 to 30 minutes longer.

6. Transfer pan to wire rack and brush bread with butter. Let cool for 10 minutes. Run knife around edge of pan to loosen bread. Slide bread onto wire rack, using spatula as needed for support. Let cool for 30 minutes before slicing. Serve warm.

TEST KITCHEN TECHNIQUE Shaping Spicy Cheese Bread

Achieving an even distribution of spice and cheese takes careful shaping.

SPRINKLE FILLINGS
After rolling the dough into a rectangle, cover the surface with cheese cubes and red pepper flakes.

ROLL INTO LOG
Starting with the longer side, roll the dough into a tight cylinder, trapping the cheese cubes inside.

CREATE SPIRAL
Use gentle pressure to roll the dough log back and forth until it is 30 inches long. Then, create a spiral shape.

PLACE IN PAN
Nestle the spiral into a greased cake pan, cover it with a towel, and let the dough rise for 1 to 1½ hours.

ADD SPICE
Once the dough has doubled in size, brush the top with beaten egg and sprinkle it with red pepper flakes.

Coconut Shrimp

This Miami classic has devolved into bad bar food. We wanted to bring it back to life.

BY LEAH COLINS

COCONUT SHRIMP HAS an image problem. Too many dive bars serve prefab, dried-out, over-cooked shrimp encased in soggy coatings. I wanted sweet, tender shrimp in crispy jackets with vivid coconut flavor.

I did some research into this South Florida favorite and tried a few existing recipes. Some used a simple batter with coconut stirred in, others a bound breading with added coconut. Some were baked, others shallow- or deep-fried. The results were disheartening: sandy breadings, flimsy coatings, rubbery shrimp. My only takeaway was that the deep-fried versions were best. Other than that, I'd have to start from scratch.

Most times, when we want to add a crunchy coating to chicken or fish, we start with a light flour dusting to absorb the meat's moisture, give the meat a quick dunk in beaten egg to create a glue, and press the pieces in bread crumbs. I took this route, adding unsweetened coconut shreds to the bread crumbs. The result? Shrimp with a sandy, not-very-coconutty coating.

For my next round, I kept the initial light flour dusting and then added beer and a bit of baking powder—two ingredients we often turn to for extra-crispy coatings—to the beaten egg. I pressed the shrimp into the bread-crumb mixture and fried them up.

My shrimp were crispy, to be sure, but while I could see the coconut shreds in the coating, I couldn't taste them. I went for broke with a three-pronged attack: One, I added a bit of coconut milk to the beer. Two, I upped the ratio of coconut flakes to bread crumbs to 2:1. And three, I switched from unsweetened coconut flakes to sweetened ones. For zing, I added 2 teaspoons of lime zest.

The flavor was there, but I had inconsistent crispiness and a coating that slid off. Was my oil temperature off? I tried higher temps, which burned the coconut, while low temps kept the coating from sticking. Oil heated to 350 degrees gave me the best results; frying the shrimp in three batches helped ensure that the oil maintained its temperature. For added insurance, I found that chilling the coated shrimp in the fridge for 20 minutes (or up to 2 hours) helped the coating stay on.

My tasters were happy munching on these shrimp as-is, but I wanted a tropical dipping sauce to take them over the top—something bright and balanced. After experimenting with chili sauces and various chopped fruit sauces, I decided that vibrant mango was the way to go. I blended frozen mango chunks (a convenience that saved me the time-consuming step of cutting up fresh mango) with some peach preserves for sweetness and stability. Finally, a squeeze of lime juice and some minced cilantro, shallot, and jalapeño added a pop of freshness and mild heat.

COCONUT SHRIMP WITH MANGO DIPPING SAUCE
Serves 6 to 8

Be sure to gently press the coconut mixture into the shrimp to help it adhere. Frying the shrimp in 3 small batches ensures a consistent oil temperature and even browning. Zest the lime, reserving the zest for the shrimp breading, before juicing it for the sauce.

DIPPING SAUCE
- 6 ounces (¾ cup) frozen mango, thawed
- ¼ cup peach preserves
- 2 tablespoons lime juice
- Salt and pepper
- 2 teaspoons minced fresh cilantro
- 2 teaspoons minced shallot
- 2 teaspoons minced jalapeño chile

SHRIMP
- 1⅓ cups all-purpose flour
- 2 cups sweetened shredded coconut
- 1 cup panko bread crumbs
- 2 teaspoons grated lime zest
- Salt and pepper
- 1½ teaspoons baking powder
- ¼ teaspoon cayenne pepper
- ½ cup mild lager, such as Budweiser
- ¼ cup canned coconut milk
- 1 large egg
- 1½ pounds extra-large shrimp (21 to 25 per pound), peeled and deveined
- 3 quarts peanut or vegetable oil

1. FOR THE DIPPING SAUCE: Process mango, preserves, lime juice, pinch salt, and pinch pepper in blender until completely smooth, about 1 minute, scraping down sides of blender jar as needed. Transfer to bowl and stir in cilantro, shallot, and jalapeño. Season with salt and pepper to taste; set aside.

2. FOR THE SHRIMP: Adjust oven rack to middle position and heat oven to 200 degrees. Line rimmed baking sheet with parchment paper. Set wire rack in second rimmed baking sheet and line with triple layer of paper towels.

3. Spread ⅔ cup flour in shallow dish. Combine coconut, panko, lime zest, 1 teaspoon salt, and 1 teaspoon pepper in second shallow dish. Whisk baking powder, cayenne, and remaining ⅔ cup flour together in medium bowl; then whisk in lager, coconut milk, and egg until fully incorporated and smooth.

4. Pat shrimp dry with paper towels and season with salt and pepper. One at a time, dredge shrimp in flour, shaking off excess; dip into beer batter, letting excess drip back into bowl; then coat with coconut-panko mixture, pressing gently to adhere. Arrange breaded shrimp on parchment-lined sheet. Refrigerate for at least 20 minutes or up to 2 hours.

5. Add oil to large Dutch oven until it measures about 2 inches deep and heat over medium-high heat to 350 degrees. Add one-third of shrimp, 1 at a time, to hot oil. Fry, stirring gently to prevent pieces from sticking together, until shrimp are golden brown, 1½ to 2 minutes. Adjust burner as necessary to maintain oil temperature between 325 and 350 degrees.

6. Transfer shrimp to prepared wire rack and place in oven to keep warm. Return oil to 350 degrees and repeat in 2 more batches with remaining shrimp. Serve with dipping sauce.

Sweetened flakes were one key to amped-up coconut flavor. Coconut milk was another.

Almond Boneless Chicken

You may find this dish in Chinese restaurants, but it was definitely born in the U.S.A.

BY CHRISTIE MORRISON

ALMOND BONELESS CHICKEN consists of boneless chicken breasts pounded thin, dipped in batter, and deep-fried; the chicken is sliced and served on a bed of iceberg lettuce with a mild brown sauce and a sprinkling of almonds and scallions. Also known as ABC, it's a Chinese American staple on restaurant menus in the Detroit region, and almost nowhere else. I wanted to change that.

I recruited a few native Michiganders to act as consultants. They confirmed that the dish, though mild in flavor, is a riot of textures: crunchy iceberg lettuce, crispy battered chicken, velvety sauce.

I found a few existing recipes, all of which used a batter made with egg, water, flour, and cornstarch, plus a leavening agent like baking soda or powder, in varying amounts. One thick batter puffed up like a doughnut as it fried. A thinner batter produced a coating that wasn't crispy enough. I turned to an ingredient we often use in coatings: beer. It added a welcome flavor, and its carbonation lightened the batter. To further enhance the crunch, I battered the chicken first and then dredged it in extra flour; the shaggy bits left by the flour fried up extra-crispy.

With the chicken settled, I turned to the sauce. I was intrigued by recipes that included stir-fry staples like bamboo shoots, water chestnuts, and ginger, but my expert tasters scoffed. "That's not ABC," I was told. They said the sauce

should be a chicken-stock base thickened with cornstarch and scant else. I compromised, enhancing my version with soy sauce, dry sherry, and flavorful hoisin to add sweetness and depth.

One nagging issue was the almonds. Every recipe I found sprinkled chopped almonds over the chicken, but I wanted the nuts incorporated more deeply. I took a decided liberty and added a few toasted and chopped almonds to the batter. The almond flavor was much more pronounced. My tasters, even the purists, called it an improvement.

ALMOND BONELESS CHICKEN
Serves 4 to 6
Use a Dutch oven that holds 6 quarts or more. Choose a mild lager or pilsner for this recipe. In addition to iceberg lettuce, this dish is usually served with rice.

SAUCE
- 1 tablespoon cornstarch
- 1 tablespoon cold water
- 1 cup chicken broth
- 2 teaspoons dry sherry
- 2 teaspoons hoisin sauce
- 2 teaspoons soy sauce
- ⅛ teaspoon salt

CHICKEN
- 4 (6- to 8-ounce) boneless, skinless chicken breasts, trimmed
  Salt and pepper
- ½ cup sliced almonds, toasted
- 2 cups all-purpose flour
- 1 cup cornstarch
- 1 teaspoon garlic powder
- 1 teaspoon baking powder
- ½ teaspoon baking soda
- 1¼ cups lager or pilsner beer
- 1 large egg, lightly beaten
- 2 quarts peanut or vegetable oil
- ½ head iceberg lettuce (4½ ounces), cored and sliced thin crosswise
- 3 scallions, sliced thin on bias

1. FOR THE SAUCE: Dissolve cornstarch in water in small bowl and set aside. Combine broth, sherry, hoisin, soy sauce, and salt in small saucepan and bring to boil over medium-high heat. Whisk in reserved cornstarch mixture, return to boil, and cook until thickened, about 30 seconds. Remove from heat, cover, and keep warm, stirring occasionally.

2. FOR THE CHICKEN: Line rimmed baking sheet with parchment paper. Set

wire rack in second rimmed baking sheet and line rack with triple layer of paper towels. Halve chicken breasts horizontally to form 8 cutlets. Pat cutlets dry with paper towels and season with salt and pepper.

3. Finely chop ¼ cup almonds. Whisk chopped almonds, 1 cup flour, cornstarch, garlic powder, baking powder, baking soda, 1 teaspoon salt, and ¾ teaspoon pepper together in large bowl. Whisk in beer and egg. Combine remaining 1 cup flour and 1 teaspoon salt in shallow dish.

4. Working with 1 at a time, dip cutlets into batter to thoroughly coat, letting excess drip back into bowl. Dredge battered cutlets in flour to coat, shaking off excess, and place on parchment-lined

sheet. Let cutlets sit while oil heats.

5. Add oil to large Dutch oven until it measures about 1½ inches deep and heat over medium-high heat to 350 degrees. Working in batches, add half of cutlets to hot oil. Adjust burner as necessary to maintain oil temperature between 325 and 350 degrees. Fry, stirring gently to prevent pieces from sticking together, until cutlets are golden and register 160 degrees, about 4 minutes, flipping halfway through frying. Transfer to prepared wire rack to cool while frying remaining cutlets.

6. Place lettuce on platter. Cut each cutlet crosswise into ½-inch-thick slices. Arrange slices over lettuce and drizzle with sauce. Sprinkle with scallions and remaining ¼ cup almonds. Serve.

This crunchy fried chicken is served over crisp shredded iceberg lettuce.

TEST KITCHEN TIP
Cool Oil, Uncool Chicken
To achieve the perfect golden exterior, it's essential to have the cooking oil at the correct temperature—350 degrees. Adding too many pieces to the pot will drop the oil's temperature, producing pale, greasy chicken.

PALE FAIL
An overcrowded pot leads to underbrowned, unappetizing chicken.

Cooking Class Herb Roast Chicken

Merely stuffing a chicken with herbs delivers zero herb flavor. Our triple-pronged approach produces perfectly cooked meat, crispy skin, and a savory sauce, all with fresh herb flavor. BY CHRISTIE MORRISON

HERB ROAST CHICKEN Serves 4

The test kitchen's favorite whole chickens are Mary's Free Range Air Chilled Chicken (also sold as Pitman's) and Bell & Evans Air Chilled Premium Fresh Chicken. Note that after the herb paste is applied, the chicken needs to rest for at least 1 hour (and up to 24 hours) before cooking.

- ½ cup chopped fresh parsley
- 1 tablespoon chopped fresh thyme
- 1½ teaspoons chopped fresh rosemary
- 1 garlic clove, minced
  Salt and pepper
- 1 tablespoon olive oil
- 1 (3½- to 4-pound) whole chicken, giblets discarded
- 1 cup chicken broth
- 3 tablespoons white wine
- 1½ teaspoons cornstarch dissolved in 1 tablespoon cold water
- 1 tablespoon unsalted butter, chilled

1. Process parsley, thyme, rosemary, garlic, 1 teaspoon salt, and ½ teaspoon pepper in food processor until paste forms, about 20 seconds, scraping down sides of bowl as needed. Combine 1 tablespoon herb paste with oil in small bowl. Reserve another ½ teaspoon herb paste for sauce in separate bowl. Set aside remaining herb paste for rubbing under skin of chicken.

2. Pat chicken dry with paper towels. Using your fingers, gently loosen skin covering breast and thighs, being careful not to tear skin. Using small spoon, spread remaining herb paste under skin, directly on meat. Rub herb-oil mixture all over exterior of chicken. Tuck wings behind back and tie legs together with kitchen twine. Transfer chicken to plate. Cover with plastic wrap and refrigerate for at least 1 hour or up to 24 hours. Adjust oven rack to middle position and heat oven to 450 degrees.

3. Place V-rack in large roasting pan and spray with vegetable oil spray. Set chicken, breast side down, on V-rack. Roast until thighs register 135 to 140 degrees, 35 to 40 minutes. Remove pan from oven and, using wads of paper towels, flip chicken breast side up. Pour 2 cups water into bottom of roasting pan. Return pan to oven and roast until thighs register 175 degrees, 20 to 25 minutes. Transfer chicken to carving board and let rest for 20 minutes.

4. Carefully pour liquid in roasting pan into fat separator. Transfer ½ cup defatted pan juices to medium sauce-pan. Add broth and wine and bring to boil over medium-high heat. Reduce heat to medium-low and simmer until sauce is slightly thickened and reduced to 1 cup, 8 to 10 minutes. Whisk in cornstarch mixture and simmer until thickened, about 2 minutes. Off heat, whisk in butter and reserved ½ tea-spoon herb paste. Season with salt and pepper to taste. Carve chicken and serve with sauce.

Good to Know

TEST KITCHEN TIPS FOR ANY ROAST CHICKEN

Getting Herbs Under the Skin

Chicken skin is like a raincoat: It's an effective barrier, keeping what's outside out and what's inside in. The best way to maximize seasoning and herb flavor inside the skin and keep it there is to separate the skin from the meat—without creating tears or holes—to create space for the herb paste. Your best tool is your fingers. Carefully slide them under the skin from the cavity side and sweep them back and forth to loosen the skin. Next, do the same from the neck side, creating a pocket that goes all the way through. Once the skin is sepa-rated from the meat, gently spoon in the herb paste, being careful not to tear the skin.

Use Hearty Herbs

Flavorful herbs like rosemary and thyme retain their deep flavor and color better than more delicate herbs like chervil, chives, or basil.

Don't Toss the Carcass

There's a wealth of flavor in those bones. After removing the meat from your chicken, wrap the carcass and bones in plastic and freeze them to use for stock later. We use 2½ pounds of chicken bones for our favorite Slow-Cooker Chicken Stock recipe: **CooksCountry.com/slowcookerstock.**

Our Favorite Roasting Pan

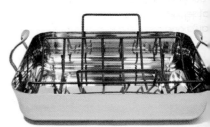

We're fans of the Calphalon Contemporary Stainless Roasting Pan with Rack for its sturdy construc-tion, even heating, and secure handles—which are so roomy that you can carry the heavy pan around comfortably, even while wearing potholders.

1. MAKE HERB PASTE
Process the parsley, thyme, rosemary, garlic, salt, and pepper into a paste that's easy to spread evenly both underneath and over the skin.

2. SEASON UNDER SKIN
Use your fingers to spread the herb paste under the skin, in direct contact with the meat. The salt in the paste will season the meat and keep it juicy.

3. COAT OUTSIDE
Combine the herb paste with the olive oil and rub it evenly over the exterior of the chicken. The oil helps brown the skin and boost herb flavor.

4. TUCK AND TIE
Tuck the wings behind the back to keep them from burning, and tie the legs together with twine to help them cook evenly and make the bird easier to flip.

5. LET IT CHILL
Cover the chicken with plastic wrap and refrigerate it for at least 1 hour or up to 24 hours to allow the salt in the paste to penetrate the meat.

6. ELEVATE CHICKEN
Place the chicken breast side down on a V-rack set inside a large roasting pan to ensure even cooking. Starting breast side down helps retain moisture.

7. TURN IT OVER
After 40 minutes, use paper towels to flip the chicken. This helps keep the white meat from drying out before the dark meat is done and the skin is browned.

8. ADD WATER
After flipping the chicken, pour 2 cups of water into the pan and return it to the oven. The water keeps any drippings from burning and imparting off-flavors.

9. SEPARATE FAT
Pour the liquid from the roasting pan into a fat separator. Reserve ½ cup of defatted liquid and discard the excess fat to keep the sauce from being too greasy.

10. MAKE SAUCE
Combine the broth, wine, and defatted pan juices in a saucepan, and reduce the mixture. Whisk in cornstarch to thicken and finish with butter and seasonings.

11. LET BIRD REST
Let the bird rest for at least 20 minutes before carving. This helps it retain its juices and stay moist. Don't worry: The bird will still be warm.

12. REMOVE LEG QUARTER
After the 20-minute rest, start carving by cutting into the bird where the leg meets the breast.

13. SEPARATE LEG JOINT
Pull the leg quarter away from the chicken to expose the joint. Push the knife down into and through the joint to separate the leg.

14. DIVIDE DRUMSTICK AND THIGH
Cut through the joint that connects the drumstick to the thigh to separate them. Repeat steps 12 through 14 on the second leg.

15. REMOVE BREAST
Cut down along the side of the breast-bone, pulling the meat away as you cut. Repeat on the second side.

16. SLICE BREAST MEAT
Remove the wing by cutting through the joint. Cut the breast crosswise into 1-inch slices. Repeat with the second breast.

One-Pan Dinner Baked Ziti with Sausage and Spinach

Baked ziti usually requires at least three pots and pans. Wouldn't just one pot be better? BY CHRISTIE MORRISON

THERE'S JUST SO much to love about a big, family-size pot of baked ziti: tender pasta, vibrant tomato sauce, oozy pockets of mozzarella, and dollops of creamy, bubbling ricotta.

But it's a project that can quickly spiral out of control: multiple components, numerous pots and pans, a great deal of time and attention, and endless opportunities for things to go south. It's hardly a weeknight kind of meal.

But shouldn't it be? What better way to take the edge off a Monday than this comforting dish? Determined to find out, I armed myself with a single Dutch oven and a big bag of ziti and hit the stove.

A great baked pasta dish lives or dies by its sauce. After creating many iterations over the years in the test kitchen, we know that our favorite baked pasta recipes start with a slow-cooked tomato sauce—we love the fresh, intense flavor that only homemade sauce can provide. Unfortunately, these sauces can take ages to achieve. I wanted the same impact in much less time.

I started with a can of tomato sauce (a convenience product that also includes onion, garlic, salt, and other flavorful ingredients), brightened up with the sharper flavor of canned diced tomatoes (our favorite brand is Hunt's Diced Tomatoes). A few pantry staples—garlic, dried oregano, and red pepper flakes—added complexity and a little heat, while just ½ teaspoon of granulated sugar tempered the tomatoes' acidity. Some fresh basil added a vibrant note, one that stood up even as the sauce simmered and thickened slightly on the stovetop.

Normally, at this point, I'd be waiting for water to boil in a separate pot, in which I'd cook the pasta to al dente before stirring it into the sauce. But I was committed to using just one pot for this entire recipe, so I decided to cook the ziti directly in the sauce I'd just made. I'd need to add a bit of water to make certain that the ziti had enough liquid to stay submerged and cook evenly, but not so much that it left the finished dish too watered down. Two cups straight from the tap proved just the right amount.

But while cooking the pasta directly in the sauce saved me from dirtying another pot (not to mention a colander, since I didn't have to drain it), it also presented me with a problem: cooking time. When I followed the instructions on the pasta box and cooked my pasta in the sauce until "done" before stirring in the cheese and baking it off in the oven, I ended up with mouthfuls of overcooked, mushy, definitely-not-al-dente ziti by the time the dish was finished. So I backed off a bit on the timing, letting the pasta simmer in the bubbling sauce until it had just begun to soften but was still raw in the center, about 7 minutes.

Time for the fun part: cheese. The best baked zitis use a medley of cheeses for maximum meltability, a range of texture, and deep flavor. The most popular combinations include stringy mozzarella, creamy ricotta, and savory Parmesan. It's hard to beat this tried-and-true trifecta, so I decided to stick with it. After a few rounds of stirring and melting various combinations of these

cheeses in various stages of the process, I determined that the best route to ample but not overwhelming cheesiness was to stir ¾ cup of cubed mozzarella and ½ cup of shredded Parmesan directly into the pasta after its initial 7-minute cook time and then top the dish with dollops of ricotta and more mozzarella and Parmesan to melt and brown in the oven.

This quick baked ziti was certainly a one-pot pasta, but without vegetables or meat, it didn't quite qualify as a one-pot meal. Starting the sauce by browning some Italian sausage for a meaty base was easy, and its inclusion added both a hit of protein and some more complex flavors.

Incorporating a vegetable took a little more finesse. We vetoed zucchini

and mushrooms, because they upset the moisture balance and took too long to cook through. Instead, I began experimenting with spinach. I started by taking the easiest route—frozen spinach—but it turned a sad, unappealing shade of green in the pot. Chopped curly spinach stayed firm and vibrantly green, and so did roughly chopped baby spinach. I stuck with the baby leaves for their convenience. Stirring them into the pasta with the cheese worked perfectly and rounded out the meal with a healthful, easy green vegetable.

A final sprinkle of chopped fresh basil over the bubbling brown cheese finished this dinner in a pot. Now came the hard part: waiting for it to cool down enough to safely dig in.

The sausage and spinach make this rich, hearty dish a complete meal.

TEST KITCHEN TECHNIQUE
Saucy Solution

Rather than boil the pasta in a separate pot of salty water, we added dried ziti directly to the simmering tomato sauce to cook. To ensure all the pasta is fully submerged, we also added 2 cups of water to the mix. We took care to remove the pot from the heat before the pasta was completely done, because the pot went back to the oven to broil after the cheese and spinach were stirred in. If the pasta were fully cooked before this final step, it would end up mushy.

ONE-POT BAKED ZITI WITH SAUSAGE AND SPINACH

Serves 4 to 6

You can substitute part-skim versions of ricotta and mozzarella cheese here. Avoid preshredded cheese, as it does not melt well.

- 8 ounces sweet Italian sausage, casings removed
- 3 garlic cloves, minced
- 1 (28-ounce) can tomato sauce
- 1 (14.5-ounce) can diced tomatoes
- ¾ teaspoon salt
- ½ teaspoon dried oregano
- ½ teaspoon sugar
- ⅛ teaspoon red pepper flakes
- 2 cups water
- 12 ounces (3¾ cups) ziti
- 6 tablespoons chopped fresh basil
- 7 ounces (7 cups) baby spinach, chopped coarse
- 6 ounces whole-milk mozzarella cheese, cut into ¼-inch pieces (1½ cups)
- 2 ounces Parmesan cheese, grated (1 cup)
- 8 ounces (1 cup) whole-milk ricotta cheese

1. Cook sausage in Dutch oven over medium-high heat, breaking up pieces with spoon, until lightly browned, about 5 minutes. Add garlic and cook until fragrant, about 30 seconds. Stir in tomato sauce, diced tomatoes and their juice, salt, oregano, sugar, and pepper flakes. Bring mixture to boil, reduce heat to medium-low, and simmer until thickened, about 10 minutes.

2. Stir in water, pasta, and 4 tablespoons basil. Increase heat to high and bring to boil. Reduce heat to medium and simmer vigorously, uncovered, until pasta is still very firm but just starting to soften, 6 to 8 minutes, stirring frequently. Adjust oven rack 8 inches from broiler element and heat broiler.

3. Remove pot from heat and stir in spinach, ¾ cup mozzarella, and ½ cup Parmesan. Dollop surface of pasta evenly with spoonfuls of ricotta. Top with remaining ¾ cup mozzarella and ½ cup Parmesan.

4. Broil ziti until cheese is bubbling and beginning to brown, 5 to 7 minutes. Transfer to wire rack and let cool for 10 minutes. Sprinkle with remaining 2 tablespoons basil and serve.

We were surprised to find that the big problem here was the rice, which either blew apart or stayed chewy—or both—in every batch of soup. BY CECELIA JENKINS

CHICKEN AND RICE soup seems like a natural for the slow cooker: Just brown some chicken and vegetables, dump them into the insert with broth and rice, and walk away. If only life were that easy.

I made several slow-cooker recipes for this classic soup, and all were surprisingly bad. Most featured weak chicken flavor, but the big problem was the rice, which was half disintegrated and yet somehow still too chewy and wholly unpleasant. There was nowhere to go but up.

I decided I'd make a great chicken soup first and then figure out how best to add the rice. I knew that using bone-in chicken pieces would be the way to go, as pieces are easier to manage than a whole bird and the bones add flavor and body to the broth. For ease—and because my tasters asked for dark meat—I chose bone-in thighs. Quickly searing them in a skillet built a nice bit of fond—those little bits of concentrated flavor on the bottom of the skillet. After I softened onions, carrots, and celery in the skillet, I deglazed the pan with white wine to incorporate the fond into the soup and put everything in the cooker with store-bought chicken broth. After 3 hours on low, I removed the chicken pieces, let them cool a bit, shredded the meat, and added it back to the soup. Just a little soy sauce upped the meaty flavor and seasoning, and a bay leaf lent an herbal note. This was good soup.

On to the rice. Having determined that 1½ cups of long-grain white rice was the best amount, I tested various cooking times from 15 minutes to 2½ hours. But every time, the rice was either blown apart, mushy, or too chewy. Sometimes it was all three. I tried toasting the rice in oil and butter before adding it—didn't work. I tried medium- and short-grain rice, wild rice, and even brown rice at different intervals. No luck: The slow cooker never generated enough heat to cook it properly.

I realized there was another category of rice that I hadn't considered: converted rice. Converted rice has two forms: instant (or quick-cooking) rice and "ready" rice. Instant rice is fissured to speed the infiltration of hot water and then dried—it really just needs to be rehydrated. Ready rice is cooked

until almost done and then coated in oil to help preserve its shape. The instant rice was the big winner here, warming through and soaking up the savory chicken broth in about 10 minutes.

SLOW-COOKER CHICKEN AND RICE SOUP Serves 6 to 8

The test kitchen prefers Minute brand instant rice.

- 6 (5- to 7-ounce) bone-in chicken thighs
  Salt and pepper
- 1 teaspoon vegetable oil
- 1 onion, chopped
- 2 carrots, peeled and cut into ¼-inch pieces
- 2 celery ribs, chopped
- 2 teaspoons minced fresh thyme
- ¼ cup dry white wine
- 7 cups chicken broth
- 1 tablespoon soy sauce
- 1 bay leaf
- 1½ cups instant white rice
- 2 tablespoons minced fresh parsley
- 1 tablespoon lemon juice

1. Pat chicken dry with paper towels and season with salt and pepper. Heat oil in 12-inch skillet over medium-high heat until just smoking. Add chicken, skin side down, and cook until well browned, 7 to 9 minutes. Transfer chicken to slow cooker.

2. Add onion, carrots, celery, 1 teaspoon salt, and ½ teaspoon pepper to now-empty skillet and reduce heat to medium. Cook until just softened, about 5 minutes. Add thyme and cook until fragrant, 30 seconds. Stir in wine, scraping up any browned bits, and cook until nearly evaporated, about 1 minute. Transfer mixture to slow cooker. Add broth, soy sauce, and bay leaf.

3. Cover and cook until chicken is tender, about 2 hours on high or 3 hours on low. Transfer chicken to carving board and let cool slightly, then discard skin. Using 2 forks, shred chicken into bite-size pieces. Discard bones and bay leaf.

4. Stir rice into soup. Cover and cook until tender, about 8 minutes on high or 15 minutes on low. Stir in parsley, lemon juice, and shredded chicken. Season with salt and pepper to taste. Serve.

A tablespoon each of soy sauce and fresh lemon juice give the broth backbone and brightness.

Cooking for Two Herb-Crusted Beef Tenderloin

We brought the fancy steakhouse steak home—and left the pricey tab at the restaurant. BY ASHLEY MOORE

WITH A LITTLE KNOW-HOW, most home cooks can purchase and cook a beautiful basic steak that measures up to steakhouse quality—and for a lot less money. But what about a more involved steakhouse preparation, like a tender filet mignon punched up with a crunchy, buttery herb crust? (Filet mignon, for all of its textural virtues, is a mild-tasting cut that benefits from a flavor boost.) I wanted to develop a recipe for this dish that was up to—or even better than—steakhouse standards but would be easy enough for a special weeknight dinner for two at home.

The test kitchen has a fantastic, show-stopping recipe for Herb-Crusted Beef Tenderloin that serves 10 to 12 people, so I figured I'd start there and downsize. That recipe calls for trimming and rubbing a 5-pound beef tenderloin with salt, pepper, and sugar and letting it sit at room temperature for 2 hours so the salt can penetrate and deeply season the hulking mass of meat. The meat roasts for 20 minutes before being coated with a potent herb paste and bread crumbs and returned to the oven to reach a perfect medium-rare.

I decided right away that the most logical cut for my "for-two" version would be two hefty, center-cut filets mignons, which are cut from the tenderloin—same cut, smaller size. And since I wouldn't be slicing the steaks (as you do with a roast), it made the most sense to pile the herb paste and bread crumbs right on

Our potent herb paste and crunchy panko crumbs take tenderloin over the top.

top of them. The herb paste—Parmesan cheese, chopped parsley, olive oil, minced garlic, thyme, salt, and pepper—was easy enough to scale down to the right amount to top two portions. But when I started doing the math to scale down the homemade bread crumbs, I realized I'd only need half a slice of bread. I opted to use panko crumbs instead.

As for the cooking, I knew these gorgeous steaks needed a perfect sear to do them justice. I seasoned the steaks with salt and pepper and browned them in oil in a hot skillet for about 3 minutes on each side; at this stage the outsides of the steaks had a nice sear, but the meat still needed more cooking. I smeared on the herb paste and then the crumbs and popped the skillet into a hot oven for 15 minutes, until the steaks hit 125 degrees for a perfect medium-rare.

Except they weren't perfect—the residual heat in the skillet caused the bottoms of the steaks to overcook. The cooking was much more even when I transferred the seared steaks from the skillet to a wire rack set inside a rimmed baking sheet for their stint in the oven. This move ensured that the oven's heat would circulate evenly around the meat, thereby keeping the steaks from overcooking.

For one final test, I tried salting the steaks and letting them sit for a bit before cooking (a trick we often use for moist, deeply seasoned meat) but procrastinators will be happy to know that this extra step proved unnecessary—my filets were perfect already.

HERB-CRUSTED BEEF TENDERLOIN FOR TWO
Tie butcher's twine around the exterior of the steaks to keep them intact while cooking. Remove the twine before serving.

- 1 ounce Parmesan cheese, grated (½ cup)
- ¼ cup chopped fresh parsley
- ¼ cup olive oil
- 2 garlic cloves, minced
- 1 teaspoon chopped fresh thyme Salt and pepper
- 2 (6- to 8-ounce) center-cut filets mignons, 1½ to 2 inches thick, trimmed
- ¼ cup panko bread crumbs

1. Adjust oven rack to middle position and heat oven to 450 degrees. Set wire rack in rimmed baking sheet. Process Parmesan, parsley, 3 tablespoons oil, garlic, thyme, ¼ teaspoon salt, and ¼ teaspoon pepper in food processor until smooth paste forms, about 10 seconds, scraping down bowl as needed; set aside.

2. Pat steaks dry with paper towels and season with salt and pepper. Tie butcher's twine around middle of steaks Heat remaining 1 tablespoon oil in 10-inch skillet over medium-high heat until just smoking. Cook steaks until well browned on both sides, about 3 minutes per side. Transfer steaks to prepared rack. Spread 2 tablespoons herb paste on top of each steak, then top each with 2 tablespoons panko, pressing gently to adhere.

3. Roast until meat registers 120 to 125 degrees (for medium-rare), 14 to 16 minutes, rotating sheet halfway through cooking. Let steaks cool on wire rack for 5 minutes. Remove twine and serve.

Cooking for a larger group? Our recipe for a full herb-crusted tenderloin serves 12. CooksCountry.com/herbtenderloin.

KEY STEPS To Perfect Tenderloin Steaks
It requires a bit of technique to get the most out of mild beef tenderloin.

1. TIE Use butcher's twine to secure and support both steaks around the middle. Tying the steaks this way helps them cook evenly.

2. SEAR Get the oil nice and hot in a skillet and brown the steaks well on both sides to build flavor. Then, transfer them to a rack in the oven to finish cooking.

No more instant packets. We wanted homemade oatmeal
with fresh stir-ins and minimal morning fuss. BY CECELIA JENKINS

THE CHOICE BETWEEN A bowl of creamy, plump, pleasantly chewy slow-cooked steel-cut oatmeal and the gummy stuff you get from those just-add-water instant packets is a no-brainer—as long as someone else is doing the cooking. But too often, speed trumps quality. I set out to create a recipe for the far superior steel-cut oatmeal with easy flavor variations that was, if not instant, at least quicker.

Convenience varieties of oats are processed in ways that speed cooking; old-fashioned or rolled oats are flattened between rollers to allow them to more quickly absorb hot water, while quick-cooking and instant oats are also steamed, toasted, and cut smaller to hasten cooking time even more. The only processing steel-cut oats go through, on the other hand, is being cut into small pieces.

Cooking steel-cut oats typically requires a long, slow simmer in boiling water, with near-constant stirring, after which they achieve their signature toothsome pop. But I knew that I had to shave off some time—a few minutes at least—if I had any hope of welcoming these into my morning routine. And while we've had great success soaking oatmeal overnight in the past, I frequently forget this step the night before.

Consulting past test kitchen experiments led me to a technique we use for rice pilaf, in which the grains are coated in fat and toasted before hitting the water. I tried it with oats, toasting them with butter, and was rewarded with a toasty, buttery flavor. What's more, it jump-started the cooking process—no small thing for a morning recipe.

I added 4 cups of room-temperature water (experiments with boiling water showed that it didn't cut the cooking time) and let it simmer until thick and creamy, about 20 minutes. A bit of salt seasoned them just enough.

Time for some stir-ins. The classic combination of cinnamon, brown sugar, and raisins was a natural. Other favorites: a bananas Foster–esque mix of dark brown sugar and chopped bananas; a sweet spin on a PB&J profile with almond butter, sliced almonds, and blueberries; a peaches and "cream" version with a bit of milk in the cooking liquid, plus thawed frozen peaches, honey, and vanilla; and a tropical variation with coconut milk and toasted flaked coconut.

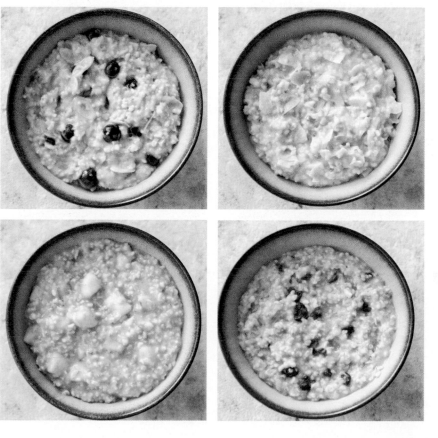

Above, peaches and "cream" oatmeal made with whole milk. Below, clockwise from top left: blueberry and almond, toasted coconut, raisin and brown sugar, and banana and brown sugar.

RAISIN AND BROWN SUGAR OATMEAL
Serves 4

Do not substitute old-fashioned rolled oats in this recipe; the resulting oatmeal will be gummy. The oatmeal will continue to thicken as it cools, so it is best served hot.

- 1 tablespoon unsalted butter
- 1 cup steel-cut oats
- 4 cups water
  Salt
- ½ cup raisins
- 3 tablespoons packed light brown sugar
- ¼ teaspoon ground cinnamon

1. Melt butter in large saucepan over medium heat. Add oats and toast, stirring constantly, until fragrant and golden, about 2 minutes.

2. Add water and bring to boil over high heat. Reduce heat to medium-low and simmer gently, stirring occasionally to avoid scorching, until mixture is creamy and oats are tender but chewy, about 20 minutes.

3. Off heat, stir in ¼ teaspoon salt, cover, and let stand for 5 minutes. Stir in raisins, sugar, and cinnamon. Season with salt to taste. Serve immediately.

BANANA AND BROWN SUGAR OATMEAL

Substitute 2 chopped ripe bananas for raisins, 2 tablespoons packed dark brown sugar for light brown sugar, and 1 tablespoon unsalted butter for cinnamon.

BLUEBERRY AND ALMOND OATMEAL

Substitute blueberries for raisins and 2 tablespoons almond butter for cinnamon. Add ½ cup toasted sliced almonds with blueberries and almond butter.

PEACHES AND "CREAM" OATMEAL

Reduce water to 3 cups and add ½ cup whole milk. Substitute thawed, patted dry, and chopped frozen peaches for raisins; honey for sugar; and ½ teaspoon vanilla extract for cinnamon.

TOASTED COCONUT OATMEAL

Reduce water to 3 cups and add 1 cup canned coconut milk. Substitute toasted unsweetened flaked coconut for raisins and omit cinnamon.

Equipment Review Small Food Processors

We love our winning food processor, but it's big and costs nearly $200. Could we find a cheaper, smaller model that still aces basic tasks? BY HANNAH CROWLEY

OWNING A GOOD food processor is like having a little motorized sous chef living in your cabinet. We use ours regularly to grate cheese, grind bread crumbs, chop nuts, blend soups, prep vegetables, and mix doughs for pizza, bread, cookies, and pie.

While we consider ours indispensable, standard food processors tend to be big and pricey. Smaller processors are a good choice for budget- or space-conscious cooks or for those who want to dip a toe in the processor pond before shelling out nearly $200.

We took a fresh look at the small food processors market to find the most versatile, efficient, and well-designed model. Options ran the gamut from chintzy choppers to miniature versions of full-sized models from major brands. They ranged from 1.5 to 6 cups in capacity (compared to 11 to 16 cups for larger models), but we wanted something that could cut and blend. So we saved the small, basic choppers for later and zeroed in on 3- to 6-cup models, of which we found seven, priced from $27.99 to $99.99. We put the processors through their paces: mincing garlic; dicing celery, onions, and carrots; grating Parmesan cheese; chopping almonds; and making mayonnaise, pesto, and hummus.

Size was an important factor: 3.5- and 4-cup models were ideal. They were compact yet large enough to handle a range of projects.

A few of the machines ran fast, which made it easy to overprocess. Others didn't have enough oomph—their hummus and pesto never got completely smooth and were deemed "rustic" by tasters. Powerful-yet-responsive controls were optimal.

Feeding tubes are essential for making mayonnaise in a food processor: The oil has to be added slowly to properly emulsify with the other ingredients. Four models didn't have feeding tubes; of the three that did, two made smooth, fluffy mayonnaise. The sole model with a feeding tube that still failed to make mayonnaise brings us to our final factor: the blade.

This model's egg yolks fell below its blade, so the ingredients couldn't emulsify; two other processors suffered a similar problem. Whole garlic cloves, almonds, and pine nuts remained stranded under their blades because they spun 5 to 8 millimeters above the bottom of the bowl and couldn't reach the food. Low blades with just 3 to 4 millimeters of clearance made better, more evenly processed food. Sharp, straight blades were also important; serrated blades chewed up food, while straight blades made crisp, clean cuts.

There are downsides to smaller processors. First, they can't handle doughs well; their workbowls are too small and their motors too weak. Second, they're not efficient for large-quantity prep—they don't have grating or slicing blades, and their smaller workbowls maxed out at about 2 cups of vegetables.

But a good small food processor can excel at mayonnaises, dressings, dips, marinades, and sauces—projects that would otherwise require serious muscle or a food mill. They can also handle smaller-quantity mincing, grinding, and dicing. If money or space is limited, you prefer a knife for prep, you only plan to do smaller projects, or you want to try a smaller and cheaper food processor before investing in a large model, the Cuisinart Elite Collection 4-Cup Chopper/Grinder—at half the size and less than a third of the price of our winning full-sized machine (also made by Cuisinart)—is the best small food processor on the market.

KEY FACTOR
Blade Position
A great food processor chops food into morsels of a consistent size. When there's too much space between the bottom blade and the base of the bowl, nuts and garlic cloves get trapped underneath and remain unchopped.

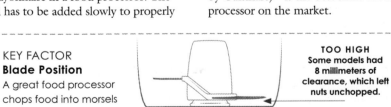

TOO HIGH
Some models had 8 millimeters of clearance, which left nuts unchopped.

JUST RIGHT
Our winner has just 3 millimeters of clearance and left no nuts behind.

HIGHLY RECOMMENDED

	CRITERIA		TESTERS' NOTES
CUISINART Elite Collection 4-Cup Chopper/Grinder **Model:** CH-4DC **Price:** $59.95 **Blade Height** from Bottom: 3 mm **Capacity:** 4 cups	Mincing ★★★ Dicing ★★★ Grating ★★★ Chopping ★★★ Emulsifying ★★★ Blending ★★★ Cleanup ★★★ Durability ★★★		This processor had a sharp blade with great coverage. It turned out crisply cut vegetables and nuts and fluffy parsley. Its strong motor blended hummus and pesto with minimal scraping, and its small feeding tube allowed us to slowly add oil for fantastic mayonnaise.

RECOMMENDED WITH RESERVATIONS

	CRITERIA		TESTERS' NOTES
BLACK+DECKER Glass Bowl Chopper **Model:** EHC3002R **Price:** $34.95 **Blade Height** from Bottom: 18 mm **Capacity:** 4 cups	Mincing ★★ Dicing ★★★ Grating ★★½ Chopping ★★★ Emulsifying 0 Blending ★★ Cleanup ★★★ Durability ★★★		This processor's blade was higher, but a sweeping bar to incorporate food at the bottom of the bowl helped make up for this shortcoming. Its motor was weaker than the winner (pesto and hummus were "rustic" but acceptable), and it had no feeding tube.

NOT RECOMMENDED

	CRITERIA		TESTERS' NOTES
KITCHENAID 3.5 Cup Food Chopper **Model:** KFC3511OB **Price:** $49.99 **Blade Height** from Bottom: 4 mm **Capacity:** 3.5 cups	Mincing ★ Dicing ★½ Grating ★★ Chopping ★★½ Emulsifying ★★★ Blending ★★ Cleanup ★★ Durability ★★★		This machine had nice blade coverage and diced mirepoix and grated Parmesan fairly well. But its motor ran fast, which made it easy to overprocess, and its blade was serrated, so it didn't chop everything cleanly.
HAMILTON BEACH Stack & Press 3 Cup Glass Bowl Chopper **Model:** 72860 **Price:** $29.99 **Blade Height** from Bottom: 4 mm **Capacity:** 3 cups	Mincing ★★ Dicing ★ Grating ★★★ Chopping ★★ Emulsifying 0 Blending ★★ Cleanup ★★★ Durability ★★		This model's smaller bowl inhibited movement—mirepoix was a mess, and almonds were dusty. Because you press down on the lid to activate the motor, we had to unplug it every time we wanted to scrape down the sides, or it turned on with our hand inside.
NUTRI NINJA 2-in-1 **Model:** QB3000 **Price:** $99.99 **Blade Height** from Bottom: 6 mm **Capacity:** 5 cups	Mincing ★★ Dicing ★★ Grating ★★ Chopping ★★ Emulsifying 0 Blending ★★ Cleanup ★½ Durability ★★★		This large processor-cum-personal-smoothie-maker's powerful motor was hard to control and sprayed food up the sides of its carafe, which were lined with plastic ribs that made it tough to clean. It also didn't have a feeding tube.
PROCTOR SILEX 6 Cup Food Processor **Model:** 70452A **Price:** $34.99 **Blade Height** from Bottom: 8 mm **Capacity:** 6 cups	Mincing ★ Dicing ★★★ Grating ★★ Chopping ★★ Emulsifying 0 Blending ★ Cleanup ★★★ Durability ★★★		This processor had poor blade coverage: Garlic and pine nuts sat untouched in its bowl, and mayo never emulsified because half the ingredients fell below the blade. Its pulse button kept spinning far too long, and its rough serrated blade battered parsley.
BRENTWOOD 3-cup Food Processor **Model:** FP-546 (white) **Price:** $27.99 **Blade Height** from Bottom: 8 mm **Capacity:** 3 cups	Mincing ★ Dicing ★ Grating ★ Chopping ★★½ Emulsifying 0 Blending ★ Cleanup ★★ Durability ★★		Because of a weaker motor, a narrow canister, and poor blade coverage, this processor left Parmesan, pesto, and hummus all unacceptably chunky, even with extra processing. It also lacked a feeding tube, so it couldn't make mayonnaise.

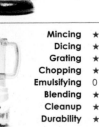

Taste Test Baking Powder

We always assumed all baking powders were created equal. Boy, were we wrong. BY LAUREN SAVOIE

FOR SUCH AN indispensable ingredient, leavening remains an afterthought to most home bakers. But it's undoubtedly essential: Without the transformative powers of leavening, many baked goods would emerge from the oven dense, flat, or hard.

Most leaveners work on the same principle: When added to a batter or dough, they release gas, creating air bubbles that lift the mixture. The most familiar natural leavener is yeast, which consumes the sugars in a dough and produces air bubbles. Resilient doughs, like bread doughs, are elastic and can contain gas bubbles for a relatively long period. Quick bread doughs and runny cake batters can't hold gas bubbles for long, so when making these, we rely on fast-acting chemical leaveners.

There are two commonly available chemical leaveners, baking soda and baking powder. Baking soda is a single-ingredient product, whereas baking powder is a mix, combining baking soda with a powdered acid and a starch (see "What's the Difference?").

But the mix isn't always the same from brand to brand. Since different combinations of ingredients are used in different brands of baking powder, we rounded up six nationally available products and had 21 America's Test Kitchen staff members assess them in white cake, chocolate crinkle cookies, and cream biscuits.

To keep everything consistent, we carefully measured all the ingredients and baked the cakes in the same oven, one after another. When we lined up the cooled cakes side by side, we were astounded at the differences. Some cakes were tall and airy, while others were dense and squat. The thickness of the cakes varied by up to 20 percent—from 0.89 inch to 1.24 inches—and tasters preferred the delicate, tender crumb of taller cakes. (We baked the cakes three more times, always using freshly opened baking powders, and the results were the same.) What was going on?

Modern baking powders are "double acting," meaning they release some of their carbon dioxide when moistened and the rest when heated. (True "single-acting" baking powders, by contrast, release all their gas when mixed with liquid and are rarely manufactured anymore.) Although all the baking powders we tested release approximately the same total amount of carbon dioxide gas, brands vary widely in the ratio released at room temperature versus at higher temperatures in the oven. This is important: If too much gas is released at room temperature, cakes won't bake up tall and airy in the oven.

To get a better idea of the composition of each baking powder, we scrutinized ingredient labels and talked to manufacturers. We learned that the two densest and squattest cakes were made with baking powders that use just one acid, while stronger-performing brands have two forms of acid to bolster lift. Baking powders with just one acid create only 30 percent of their lift in the oven. By contrast, brands with two acids produce 60 to 90 percent of their lift in the oven and create baked goods that are airier, fluffier, and more tender.

But fluffier isn't better in every application: Lower rising baking powders actually made moister and chewier cookies. Brands that performed best in cake made cookies that were just a little too fluffy and cake-like. This wasn't enough to drop these powders from the top of our rankings, but it did push them from the top spot: We were looking for a great all-purpose baking powder, after all. (Don't worry, our winning baking powder still produces a tall, fluffy cake.)

Finally, since tasters didn't notice flavor differences in other applications, we tried the baking powders the plainest way we could think of, in cream biscuits. Texture wasn't an issue in this denser dough, except for one biscuit that took on a speckled, uneven appearance. (Our science editor explained that the baking powder used in that sample includes potassium bicarbonate, which can cause unwanted browning.) Flavor was more contentious, with 30 percent of tasters noting a metallic flavor in two samples. (Ingredient labels showed that the corresponding products contain aluminum compounds.) This wasn't enough to be off-putting, but tasters preferred options with a clean flavor.

While we didn't find any products that would ruin a baking project, we did find brands that make the difference between a decent cake and a great one.

Our favorite was Argo Double Acting Baking Powder, an inexpensive all-purpose powder that produced tender cakes, soft biscuits, and perfectly chewy cookies.

HIGHLY RECOMMENDED

ARGO Double Acting Baking Powder
Price: $1.73 for 12 oz ($0.14 per oz)
Ingredients: Sodium acid pyrophosphate, sodium bicarbonate, cornstarch, and monocalcium phosphate
Average Cake Height: 1.09 in
Gas Released at Room Temperature: 30%
Gas Released in Oven: 70%

TASTERS' NOTES
This brand performed well in every test we threw at it, making "chewy" cookies, "fluffy" biscuits, and "moist" but "airy" cakes. Its easy-to-use plastic tub helped it edge out the competition.

RECOMMENDED

BOB'S RED MILL Baking Powder
Price: $3.29 for 16 oz ($0.21 per oz)
Ingredients: Sodium acid pyrophosphate, sodium bicarbonate, cornstarch, and monocalcium phosphate
Average Cake Height: 1.19 in
Gas Released at Room Temperature: 10%
Gas Released in Oven: 90%

Cakes made with this baking powder were among the tallest and "fluffiest" of the bunch. Biscuits and cookies emerged from the oven "tender" and "airy." Unfortunately, this brand's frustrating plastic-bag packaging got it booted from the top spot.

CALUMET Baking Powder
Price: $2.49 for 7 oz ($0.36 per oz)
Ingredients: Baking soda, cornstarch, sodium aluminum sulfate, calcium sulfate, monocalcium phosphate
Average Cake Height: 1.24 in
Gas Released at Room Temperature: Proprietary
Gas Released in Oven: Proprietary

This brand made "taller," "airier," and "more tender" cakes and biscuits than any other brand, but the extra oomph produced cookies that were a little "too cake-y." Some tasters detected a slight "metallic" taste in biscuits.

CLABBER GIRL Baking Powder
Price: $2.27 for 8.1 oz ($0.28 per oz)
Ingredients: Cornstarch, sodium bicarbonate, sodium aluminum sulfate, monocalcium phosphate
Average Cake Height: 1.1 in
Gas Released at Room Temperature: 40%
Gas Released in Oven: 60%

"Pillowy" cakes and "tender" cookies earned this brand high marks for texture, but 30 percent of tasters picked up on an off, "metallic" flavor in biscuits from the addition of sodium aluminum sulfate.

RECOMMENDED WITH RESERVATIONS

RUMFORD Baking Powder
Price: $3.47 for 8.1 oz ($0.43 per oz)
Ingredients: Monocalcium phosphate, sodium bicarbonate, cornstarch (made from non-genetically modified cornstarch)
Average Cake Height: 1.02 in
Gas Released at Room Temperature: 70%
Gas Released in Oven: 30%

This brand, which releases 70 percent of its carbon dioxide at room temperature, made "shallower," "heavier" cake. While not our preferred baking powder for cakes, this product produced "chewy" crinkle cookies and "fluffy" biscuits.

HAIN PURE FOODS Featherweight Baking Powder
Price: $5.39 for 8 oz ($0.67 per oz)
Ingredients: Monocalcium phosphate, potato starch, potassium bicarbonate
Average Cake Height: 0.89 in
Gas Released at Room Temperature: 70%
Gas Released in Oven: 30%

This brand uses an atypical combination of ingredients to produce a salt-free and corn-free baking powder, but it comes at a price. While cookies were perfectly "fudgy," cakes were "dense" and biscuits had a "speckled" appearance (but tasted fine).

What's the Difference? Baking Powder versus Baking Soda

Baking soda and baking powder both perform the same job (leavening), but each does it in a different way. **Baking soda** is a single-ingredient product that reacts with acidic ingredients to release carbon dioxide and provide lift. In recipes with a high proportion of acidic ingredients like chocolate, fruit juice, yogurt, or buttermilk, baking soda performs well on its own. **Baking powder** is a mix of baking soda (or another carbon-dioxide producing chemical), a powdered acid such as cream of tartar, and a starch to keep the chemicals dry. When moistened, the powdered acid reacts with the soda, releasing carbon dioxide for lift in recipes without a strong acidic component.

Heirloom Recipe

We're looking for recipes that you treasure—the ones that have been handed down in your family for a generation or more; that always come out for the holidays; that have earned a place at your table and in your heart, through many years of meals. Send us the recipes that spell home to you. Visit **CooksCountry.com/magazines/home** (or write to Heirloom Recipes, *Cook's Country*, P.O. Box 470739, Brookline, MA 02447); click on Heirloom Recipes and tell us a little about the recipe. Include your name and mailing address. **If we print your recipe, you'll receive a free one-year subscription to *Cook's Country*.**

HOT GINGER-SPICED MULLED CIDER

Makes about 1 gallon

"The aroma of simmering cider reminds me of the holidays of my youth." —Karen Ward, Bristol, N.H.

You can find cheesecloth in the baking supply aisle of most grocery stores.

- 1 gallon apple cider
- 2 oranges, sliced ½ inch thick
- 1 lemon, sliced ½ inch thick
- 1 (2-inch) piece ginger, sliced ¼ inch thick
- 2 teaspoons allspice berries
- 6 whole cloves
- 1 teaspoon black peppercorns
- 1 cinnamon stick

1. Bring all ingredients to boil in Dutch oven over medium-high heat. Reduce heat to low and steep for 30 minutes.

2. Line fine-mesh strainer with triple layer of cheesecloth and set over large bowl. Pour mulled cider through prepared strainer and discard solids. Return cider to pot and keep warm over low heat. Serve.

U.S. POSTAL SERVICE STATEMENT OF OWNERSHIP, MANAGEMENT, AND CIRCULATION

1. Publication Title: Cook's Country; 2. Publication No. 1552-1990; 3. Filing Date: 9/29/15; 4. Issue Frequency: Dec/Jan, Feb/Mar, Apr/May, Jun/Jul, Aug/ Sep, Oct/Nov; 5. No. of Issues Published Annually: 6; 6. Annual Subscription Price: $35.70; 7. Complete Mailing Address of Known Office of Publication: 17 Station Street, Brookline, MA 02445; 8. Complete Mailing Address of Headquarters or General Business Office of Publisher: 17 Station Street, Brookline, MA 02445; 9. Full Names and Complete Mailing Addresses of Publisher, Editor, and Managing Editor: Publisher: Christopher Kimball, 17 Station Street, Brookline, MA 02445; Editor: Jack Bishop, 17 Station Street, Brookline, MA 02445; Managing Editor: Scott Kathan, 17 Station Street, Brookline, MA 02445; 10. Owner: Boston Common Press Limited Partnership, Christopher Kimball, 17 Station Street, Brookline, MA 02445; 11. Known Bondholders, Mortgagees, and Other Securities: None; 12. Tax Status: Has Not Changed During Preceding 12 Months; 13. Publication Title: Cook's Country; 14. Issue Date for Circulation Data Below: August/September 2015; 15a. Total Number of Copies: 415,142 (Aug/Sep 2015: 417,707); b. Paid Circulation: (1) Mailed Outside-County Paid Subscriptions Stated on PS Form 3541: 333,180 (Aug/Sep 2015: 339,765); (2) Mailed In-County Paid Subscriptions Stated on PS Form 3541: 0 (Aug/Sep 2015: 0); (3) Paid Distribution Outside the Mails Including Sales through Dealers and Carriers, Street Vendors, Counter Sales, and Other Paid Distribution Outside the USPS: 20,664 (Aug/Sep 2015: 20,948); 4) Paid Distribution by Other Classes of Mail through the USPS: 0 (Aug/Sep 2015: 0); c. Total Paid Distribution: 353,843 (Aug/Sep 2015: 360,723); d. Free or Nominal Rate Distribution: (1) Free or Nominal Rate Outside-County Copies Included on PS Form 3541: 1,980 (Aug/Sep 2015: 1,594); (2) Free or Nominal Rate In-County Copies Included on Form PS 3541: 0 (Aug/Sep 2015: 0); (3) Free or Nominal Rate Copies Mailed at Other Classes through the USPS: 0 (Aug/Sep 2015: 0); (4) Free or Nominal Rate Distribution Outside the Mail: 500 (Aug/Sep 2015: 500); e. Total Free or Nominal Rate Distribution: 2,480 (Aug/Sep 2015: 2,094); f. Total Distribution: 356,323 (Aug/Sep 2015: 362,817); g. Copies Not Distributed: 58,819 (Aug/Sep 2015: 54,890); h. Total: 415,142 (Aug/Sep 2015: 417,707); i. Percent Paid: 99.30% (Aug/Sep 2015: 99.42%).

RECIPE INDEX

FIND THE ROOSTER!

A tiny version of this rooster has been hidden in the pages of this issue. Write to us with its location and we'll enter you in a random drawing. The first correct entry drawn will win our winning small food processor, and each of the next five will receive a free one-year subscription to *Cook's Country*. To enter visit **CooksCountry.com/rooster** by January 31, 2016, or write to Rooster DJ16, *Cook's Country*, P.O. Box 470739, Brookline, MA 02447. Include your name and address. Richard Eisenbery of Glendale, Calif., found the rooster in the August/September 2015 issue on page 12 and won our top-rated water bottle.

WEB EXTRAS

Free for 4 months online at
CooksCountry.com

Basic Vinaigrette
Beer-Braised Cabbage
Broccoli with Sesame-Miso Dressing
Cake Stand Testing (full story and chart)
Classic Hummus
Crisp Parmesan Pork Cutlets
Garlicky Croutons
Grill-Braised Short Ribs
Guinness Beef Stew
Herb-Crusted Beef Tenderloin
Honey-Scallion Barbecue Sauce
Natchitoches Meat Pies
Parmesan-Crusted Asparagus
Red Velvet Cake Rounds
Salted Peanut Butter–Pretzel–Chocolate Chip Cookies
Slow-Cooker Chicken Stock
S'mores Blossom Cookies

READ US ON iPAD

Download the Cook's Country app for iPad and start a free trial subscription or purchase a single issue of the magazine. All issues are enhanced with full-color Cooking Mode slide shows that provide step-by-step instructions for completing recipes, plus expanded reviews and ratings. Go to CooksCountry.com/iPad to download our app through iTunes.

Red Velvet Cheesecake

This cake boasts velvety layers encasing easy no-bake white chocolate cheesecake filling. Cream cheese frosting and a garnish of festive red crumbs finish the look.

To make this cake, you will need:

- **2 (9-inch) red velvet cake rounds***
- **2 cups (8 ounces) confectioners' sugar**
- **8 tablespoons unsalted butter, softened**
- **1½ pounds cream cheese, softened**
- **¾ teaspoon vanilla extract**
- **Pinch salt**
- **1½ teaspoons unflavored gelatin**
- **1½ cups heavy cream**
- **6 ounces white chocolate, chopped**
- **½ cup (3½ ounces) granulated sugar**
- **White chocolate curls***

FOR THE CAKE: Using serrated knife, split cakes horizontally 1 inch from bottom. Using your fingers, crumble tops into small crumbs; set crumbs aside in airtight container. Set 1 remaining cake round in 9-inch springform pan; reserve second cake round.

FOR THE FROSTING: Using stand mixer fitted with paddle, beat confectioners' sugar and butter on medium-high speed until fluffy, about 2 minutes. Cut 8 ounces cream cheese into 4 pieces and add 1 piece at a time, continuing to beat until incorporated, about 30 seconds. Beat in vanilla and salt. Refrigerate frosting until ready to use.

FOR THE FILLING: Sprinkle gelatin over ½ cup heavy cream in small saucepan and let sit until gelatin softens, about 5 minutes. Cook mixture over low heat until edges are just bubbling. Add white chocolate and continue to cook, stirring constantly, until just melted and smooth. Set aside to cool slightly, about 15 minutes. Using clean stand mixer fitted with whisk, whip remaining 1 cup heavy cream on medium-high speed to soft peaks, 1 to 2 minutes; transfer to medium bowl and set aside. Using now-empty stand mixer fitted with paddle, beat remaining 1 pound cream cheese and granulated sugar on medium-high speed until light and fluffy, 2 to 3 minutes. Reduce speed to medium-low, add white chocolate mixture, and mix until just combined, scraping down sides of bowl as needed. Using rubber spatula, gently fold in whipped cream until combined.

TO ASSEMBLE: Spread filling over cake in pan and smooth into even layer. Place remaining cake round, cut side down, on top. Cover with plastic wrap and refrigerate until set, about 6 hours. Run thin knife between cake and sides of pan; remove sides of pan. Transfer cake to cake stand or plate. Spread frosting in even layer over top and sides of cake. Gently press reserved cake crumbs onto sides of cake. Place mound of chocolate curls in center of cake. Serve.

▶ *Go to CooksCountry.com for our Red Velvet Cake Rounds recipe and to see how to make chocolate curls.

Inside This Issue